French Costume Drama of the 1950s

This book is in memory of my father William Andrew Hayward (1912–1997) – a tailor and clothes designer whose knowledge of fabric and cut has inspired my writing here.

During the writing of this book, my mother, Kathleen Elizabeth Hayward (née Arnold) died suddenly (1916–2009). It is to her also that I dedicate this scholarship. After all if she had not passed onto me her love of French culture I might never have specialized in French cinema.

French Costume Drama of the 1950s
Fashioning Politics in Film

Susan Hayward

intellect Bristol, UK / Chicago, USA

First published in the UK in 2010 by
Intellect, The Mill, Parnall Road, Fishponds, Bristol, BS16 3JG, UK

First published in the USA in 2010 by
Intellect, The University of Chicago Press, 1427 E. 60th Street,
Chicago, IL 60637, USA

A catalogue record for this book is available from the
British Library.

Cover designer: Holly Rose
Copy-editor: Rebecca Vaughan-Williams
Typesetting: Mac Style, Beverley, E. Yorkshire

ISBN 978-1-84150-318-9

Printed and bound by Gutenberg Press, Malta.

Contents

List of Figures and Illustrations

Unless indicated in the footnotes, all images are sourced courtesy of the Bibliothèque du Film (Bifi), Paris. Many images no longer have copyright, but where they do it is provided next to image.

Acknowledgements

Little did I think, when I began this project four years ago, how huge an undertaking it would become. In the end it was a bit like climbing Everest, as one of the earlier reviewers suggested (without irony) that it might be. Every corner I turned, another aspect presented itself – and I kept going! Certainly, I could not have fulfilled the aims and objectives without the help from numerous individuals and research institutions. I owe a great debt of gratitude to the following for helping me with this work. First, Daniel Brémaud and Fereidoun Mahboubi at the Centre National de la Cinématographie (CNC), Bois d'Arcy, for their genial assistance with screening films. In particular, it is thanks to Daniel Brémaud that I was able to see a copy of *Bel-Ami* (a film I believed lost forever). And thanks to Fereidoun Mahboubi that I came to understand how this particular copy managed against all odds to be still in existence. The patience of the library personnel at the Bibliothèque Nationale de France was invaluable in my trawl for films. The library's video and DVD archives supplied well over half of the films out of the total corpus. I am grateful to the Centre National de la Recherche Scientifique which facilitated my research sojourns in Paris, at the Maison Suger. In particular, a debt of thanks to Madame Françoise Girou and Madame Nadia Cheniour for making my stay in this research centre so agreeable. My thanks, too, to the centre's director Monsieur Jean-Luc Lory for making my stay possible in the first place. Finally, my thanks to the personnel, in particular Véronique Chauvet and Elodie Rivaud, at the Bibliothèque du Film's Iconothèque for their assistance in locating illustrative images.

The British Film Institute Library and the librarians who run it with such knowledge and flair receive my continued gratitude. Simply put, I could not conduct my research and scholarship without the existence of this fabulous resource and equally wonderful staff.

On a more personal note, I would like to thank the following colleagues for their help, either in the form of engaging with the ideas in this book, reading a selection of chapters or letting me borrow from their DVD collection. Jennie Cousins (who has herself written a terrific study of the politics of costume); Sarah Leahy (whose own work on Signoret and Bardot has helped my thinking); Will Higbee and Florence Martin (their feedback on chapters was invaluable); Judith Mayne (for her work on Clouzot and DVD loans); Carrie Tarr (for her work on Audrey and also some DVD loans). Continued dialogues with Ginette Vincendeau, Geneviève Sellier, Raphaelle Moine, Sandra Cook, Phil Powrie and Michèle

Lagny have also fine-tuned some of my arguments. Chrissie Morris and Kathleen Hayward, I count amongst my unique fan-base, along with my cat Ibubese for whom I can do no wrong.

An important thanks and acknowledgement goes to the British Academy. Their Small Grants Award (not so small) funded my extended research trip to the CNC Bois d'Arcy. The University of Exeter University Research Committee funded two initial trips of enquiry to Paris, so my thanks there also.

Thanks, finally, to Intellect Press for encouraging me in this project.

Susan Hayward

Part I

Contexts

Chapter 1

Introduction

Costume drama – a suitable document for study

I would like to begin by quoting from an interview with Rosine Delamare, *the* top designer for costume drama of the 1950s (with some 23 French costume drama titles to her name in that decade alone). She said:

A period costume does not need to be a faithful reproduction. It is not put on screen as a document for study.[1]

Whilst she is certainly correct in the first sentence – costume can only refer to the original: it cannot *be* it – how wrong she turned out to be in her second! Within Anglo-Saxon film studies, as we well know, costume design now constitutes a considerable domain of research.[2] It has become, therefore, a suitable/fashionable document for study. Costume design is integral to the genre – after all, the word 'costume' is embedded in the very typology ('costume drama').

To pause briefly on the definition of costume drama: I am taking it here in its broadest sense as a film set in an historical period that features characters dressed in costumes pertaining to that era. The corpus of films to be investigated in this study will be any French produced film set in the pre-1914 era, the moment when the Belle Epoque came to an end with the declaration of the First World War (the Great War as it was then known). Whilst none of these films are historical films, a handful run close in that they are biopics or fictionalized accounts of real people. But for the most part, the films we are to consider are adaptations (73) and original scenarios (36) grounded in different periods of France's past. As such, as we shall see they inevitably have national resonances. For a full listing of the 109 films in this corpus, see Appendix One.

There are three compelling reasons for the study of 1950s' French costume drama, and, with it, the costume document. The first reason is an historical and statistical one; the second, socio-political; the third, industrial. In statistical terms, the so-called Golden Age of the French costume drama film ran from the Second World War/Occupation period through the 1950s.[3] Here is a breakdown of the figures:

Period	Percentage of costume dramas (CD)	CD/Total number of films
1940–44	13.6%	30/220
1945–49	13.4%	60/447
1950–59	11.2%	109/972

Figure 1.1: Percentages of costume dramas to total film industry production released during the 1940s and 1950s.

Thereafter, from the 1960s onwards, the genre rather rapidly declined and for two major reasons: the shift to location over studio shooting (an effect of the French New Wave) and the actual expensiveness of the product.

The above figures require further comment, however. Whilst costume drama has never been a dominant genre, with an average of 12.2 per cent over its twenty-year Golden Age period, it still remains a significant second order genre – very close in fact to the thriller genre (which averaged 13 per cent of the output in the 1950s). It is also worth remarking that whilst, during the Occupation period (1940–1944), the dominant genre was the melodrama (50 per cent of all production), post-war, through the 1950s, the dominant genre was comedy (some years reaching 50 per cent of production). It is something of a revelation, then, that although 1950s' audiences mostly wanted to laugh (as opposed to feeling caught up in narratives of melodramatic pain), they also liked to be taken back to a past – just as much as they enjoyed indulging in France's own version of the film noir tradition. One final point on this statistical evidence: although, in percentage terms, the costume drama during the Occupation period was greater, in terms of actual volume, its numbers increased nearly fourfold in the 1950s. Alternatively, we could say that, over the twenty-year Golden Age period, the 1940s produced 43 per cent, and the 1950s 57 per cent of all costume dramas. Whichever way you consider the statistics, the genre has a significant enough presence to merit investigation.

If the Golden Age was 1940–59, you might well ask why this study should be restricted to the 1950s. A part answer is that film historians and critics have already extensively researched the 1940s – but this is not the primary consideration. More significant as an answer is the socio-political conjuncture. The 1950s was *the* period of radical modernization in France, whereas the war/Occupation period most patently was not. Indeed, the need for escapism through costume dramas in that context is self-evident. As for the post-war period (1945–1949), this was one of reconstruction. It was not until the 1950s that the economic boom started to take off. So it is particularly interesting to view the costume drama genre within a climate of modernization and economic growth – a trend this retro-seeming genre appears to buck. In other words, the question becomes, rather, why did this Golden Age continue so vigorously during the 1950s? We also need to recall that the 1950s was *the* moment when France (particularly Paris) sought to re-establish a sense of national identity post-war. And one of the major ways that it did so was via fashion (as an export item and as a marker of cultural superiority). What better vehicle for fashion than the costume drama

– even if, especially if, it spoke of a time gone by, thereby confirming the lengthy heritage of France's fashion supremacy, and thus its legitimacy as a nation of taste.

A final reason, industrial this time, explains this focus on the 1950s. This decade was the time of big changes in terms of management and personnel structures within the film studios. In 1948, the decision was taken by studio bosses to no longer keep a permanent team of studio personnel on its books, but to hire as needs be. There were two major reasons for this. The first was linked to the power of the unions. At this time, unions were strong, backed as they were by the Communist Party and their workers' union the Confédération Générale du Travail (CGT, of which much of the film personnel were members). The studio bosses were clear that they did not want to share management with CGT group representatives, nor did they want to risk strike action – so a unilateral decision was taken to rid themselves of permanent staff. The second reason had to do with pension fund contributions. The bosses were unwilling to settle on paying the same level of contribution for personnel as for themselves (by law all contributions had to be the same). These decisions brought about all sorts of knock-on effects. In dismissing the permanent staff, there was no one left to maintain the upkeep of the studios' stock of pre-constructed décors which, in turn, led to its dispersal. In a crucial sense, this dispersal of stock meant the loss of an invaluable resource but also of an intertextual specificity to set design. To explain: because, formerly, sets were reconfigured from one film to another, it could be argued that they represented a sort of intertextualized collective memory (that is, these sets had been seen before even though in a different assemblage and context). Gone, therefore, with this dispersal, was a certain notion of memory – to say nothing of the loss of sets designed by the grand masters of the 1930s, such as Lazare Meerson.

More concretely, there were other areas of precariousness in the industry. Gone were the days when personnel were kept on a payroll – now replaced by another type of practice (hiring at will). Gone, too, was the regular maintenance of the studios. The outcomes were twofold. On the one hand, studios were now much more at risk of being sold on for profit to other concerns. This started to happen in 1956 when, given their prime locations, some were sold off for property development (e.g., Courbevoie), others to the newly expanding industry of television (e.g., Buttes-Chaumont). On the other hand, studios were more streamlined and cost effective. Now, the studios were run by a small management team. Producers hired the studios, selected the top personnel to work on any given film and hired them as needs dictated. The top personnel then, in turn, selected the technicians (and so on) with whom they wanted to work. This represented a massive change in both personnel management and production practices and led, of course, to fierce competition amongst film crew. However, this shift also meant that production values soared in terms of quality. And it is here, arguably, that the term of 'cinema of quality' – so dismissively coined by François Truffaut for 1950s' French cinema[4] – has its greatest validity in a non-derogatory sense. A point to which I shall be returning repeatedly in the course of this book.

Costume drama – a genre in context

The political culture of France during the 1950s, generally speaking, is still an under-researched area, although there is some scholarship of note.[5] In terms of film history, there is very little, let alone any sustained, exploration of specific genres, and this includes the costume drama, which had an important output in production terms (see figure 1.1 above). In audience terms, it was also a very popular genre. Moreover, as we shall come to understand in our journey through this corpus of films, gender identity and sexual relations are often to the fore of these narratives whether it be questions of masculinity, the role of women, or issues of marriage. It is worth bearing in mind that, whilst the costume drama is most readily seen as a women's genre, we know that, in 1950s' France, cinema-going was very much a family affair, weekend audiences making up to 70 per cent of the receipts.[6] Thus it is safe to assume that mainly family audiences consumed this particular product and – since it could be argued that men and women consumed these images in equal parts – this has interesting implications in relation to questions of gender representation in general and that of masculinity in particular. Audiences went to see their favourite stars, suggesting that it was the actors performing in the films that first attracted spectators to a particular film. According to Montebello, the stars with the strongest appeal were either big names or great actors and included amongst others, Jean Gabin, Gérard Philipe, Pierre Fresnay, Sacha Guitry, Pierre Brasseur, Daniel Gélin, Fernandel, Bourvil, Jean Marais, Yves Montand, Danielle Darrieux, Michèle Morgan, Martine Carol, Brigitte Bardot, Simone Signoret and Jeanne Moreau.[7] Montebello also informs us that all spectators were attracted by the likes of Jean Gabin, Fernandel, Danielle Darrieux and Michèle Morgan;[8] the more educated classes' preference was for Pierre Fresnay, Gérard Philipe, Danielle Darrieux and Michèle Morgan; the 'popular classes' preferring Gabin, Gina Lollobrigida and Fernandel.[9] Surely, in this last category, we must add in Martine Carol!

In historical terms, we can see how the costume drama speaks, albeit in a paradoxical even contradictory way, to the socio-economic and political climate of the 1950s. First, France was in denial of its immediate past (German Occupation), yet the themes of treachery and denunciation occur repeatedly in these costume dramas. Second, the socio-economic conditions of the working classes and the gender roles of men and women were in considerable flux at the time, despite attempts to disguise these truths. Third, the representation in these films of France as a nation of culture, with a strong drive as a civilizing force in its colonies, was clearly at odds with its contemporaneous reality as it entered into its first phases of decolonization in the form of wars with Algeria and Indochina. We shall, nonetheless, encounter some interesting exceptions in our corpus whereby a small number of films address these problematic issues, however obliquely. Finally, as with film production after the 1914–18 war, there was a move to exploit the educative potential of these films with the adaptation of the great authors. This strategy was a way by which France used its cinema as a propaganda tool both to educate its citizens in relation to their cultural heritage and to affirm a strong sense of national identity in the aftermath of a devastating war. But,

Author	Adapted Text – film title
Victor Hugo	*Notre Dame de Paris*
	Les Misérables
Emile Zola	*Nana*
	Gervaise
	Pot-Bouille
Alexandre Dumas père	*Les Trois Mousquetaires*
	La Reine Margot
	Le Vicomte de Bragelonne
	Le Comte de Monte Cristo
	La Tour de Nesle
Alexandre Dumas fils	*La Dame aux Camélias*
Guy de Maupassant	*Le Plaisir*
	Trois femmes
	Bel-Ami
	Une vie
	La Rafle est pour ce soir
Colette	*Chéri*
	Minne l'ingénue libertine
Jules Verne	*Michel Strogoff*

Figure 1.2: Most frequently adapted 'great authors' for 1950s costume dramas.

intriguingly, whilst we see this pattern in evidence in the immediate post-war period (1944–1949), by the 1950s these 'great authors' (such as Hugo and Zola) and other less great but still important authors (such as Dumas, Maupassant, Colette, Verne) figure less prominently in costume drama adaptations than one might have at first suspected (see figure 1.2).

The absence of Balzac is striking to say the least. And it is noteworthy that, whilst adaptations dominate the costume drama to the tune of 66 per cent of all the 1950s' films, most of these were the works of popular authors (some contemporary, others of the period) including plays and farces. The overwhelming tendency was towards the popular rather than the so-called 'classical', therefore. Below (figure 1.3) is the actual breakdown of the number of adaptations according to type, including those that were made from 'Great' authors (some of whom were not French: Arthur Miller, Shakespeare, Schnitzler):

Total number of adaptations:	73
Number of novels:	51
Number of plays:	20
Number of operettas:	2
Number made from 'Great' authors:	32

Figure 1.3: Number of adaptations and breakdown into type.

Costume drama – victim of the 'cinéma de qualité' debate

If study of 1950s' cinema as a whole has been negligible so far, a major part of the cause is the legacy of the critics of the *Cahiers du cinéma* (especially Truffaut) who were so dismissive of this period of France's cinema. The effect of their labelling this cinema as 'a cinema of quality' or 'daddy's cinema' has been to cast it into some kind of abyss from which it is only just beginning to emerge, thanks to studies by a few scholars (e.g., Leahy, Sellier, Tarr, Vincendeau and Hayward[10]) who contest this simplified reductionism of a whole generation of cinematic production. But, to date, the focus has been more on auteurs and stars on the one hand and, on the other, the thriller genre and social-realist cinema, rather than on the costume drama. Furthermore, the *Cahiers*' dismissive rhetoric has meant that the relationship between a nation's cultural artefact (cinema) and a very important period of political cultural history (the 1950s) has, by and large, been overlooked. This bleaching out is particularly poignant in relation to the costume drama, given that, although it purports to speak to history, it often speaks less to the past and more to the contemporary moment (albeit through the disguise and displacement of the costumes and settings).

I want to address, here, this accusation of quality cinema that has so floored historians appreciation of 1950s' French cinema. As we know, it began in earnest with Truffaut's vituperative attack on certain scriptwriters in an article published in the January 1954 issue of: 'Une certaine tendance du cinéma français' ('A certain tendency of French cinema'). In it he accuses France's cinema of going down a route of psychological realism that produces an uninventive cinema. The source of this tendency in French cinema can be traced, he claims, to the stranglehold on the industry of a handful of directors, amongst whom he lists Autant-Lara, and scriptwriters, and here he singles out Aurenche and Bost. Under the pretence of giving audiences what they like, Truffaut argues, scriptwriters and directors simplify the literary origins upon which they base their films, meantime hiding behind the label of 'quality cinema', which such literary adaptations afford them, to put on screen their 'usual dose of easy audacity, darkness and non-conformity.'[11] In short, this cinema is formulaic; adaptations, in particular those of Aurenche and Bost, are not true equivalences – they either fall short through 'timidity' or misrepresent the original through downright 'betrayal.'[12]

Truffaut claims that some seven or eight scriptwriters dominate the industry. And he names them: Aurenche and Bost, Jeanson, Sigurd, Scipion, Laudenbach.[13] I have taken the trouble to make a count (figure 1.4 opposite).

A first myth worth putting to rest, then, is the 'stranglehold' of the scriptwriters: the case simply does not hold up – even if Truffaut claims that the Aurenche-Bost influence on other scriptwriters is 'immense.'[14] For it is worth pointing out that this duo are outstripped by Henri Jeanson, the author of quite dark cynical scripts and known for his black humour, but who began his career in the early 1930s, and Roland Laudenbach, whose scripts are a mixture of social-realist texts, often about individuals' crises of conscience, murderers, tales of jealousy and retribution, or costume dramas about swashbucklers. As to the dark

---

Truffaut's first list of 'offenders'

Aurenche & Bost = 15
Aurenche & Prévert = 1
Aurenche = 3 other titles not with Bost
Bost = 2 other titles not with Aurenche
Jeanson = 21
Laudenbach = 22
Scipion = 4
Sigurd = 14
TOTAL = 102 titles out of 982 films made during the 1950s => 11%

Figure 1.4: Truffaut's first list of offenders.

psychological realism that Truffaut so deplores in this cinema of quality, we can see that if indeed it is present in the work of his list of offenders named above then it affects but a small percentage of the total output of the films of that decade.

Truffaut's second salvo targets the directors who exemplify this tendency and who, according to him, dominate the industry of this period: Yves Allégret, Autant-Lara, Clément, Delannoy, Pagliero.[15] Again the figures tell a different story:

Truffaut's second list of 'offenders'

Allégret = 13 films
Autant-Lara = 11
Clément = 5
Delannoy = 13
Pagliero = 6
TOTAL = 42 films out 982 => 4%

Figure 1.5: Truffaut's second list of offenders.

The evidence does not quite stack up. Whilst Allégret, Autant-Lara and Delannoy can certainly be counted amongst the popular directors of the decade, fi gures for *the* most popular tend to have them landing around 20 titles during the 1950s (an average of two per year): André Berthomieu (20), Jean Boyer (20), Gilles Grangier (20), Henri Decoin (19), André Hunebelle (16), Robert Vernay (16) are just a few we can name. Clearly the main target of Truffaut's article is the Aurenche and Bost pairing and, by association, those directors who worked with them. According to Truffaut they are the worst exponents of this cinema of quality.

Truffaut's further reproach is that the scriptwriters claim, in the name of fidelity, to 'invent without betraying'.[16] But this, he argues, means they actually do betray the original text, either by omission or by changing endings. Jeanson's ending for *Nana* is a good example to cite; she is strangled by her lover rather than allowed to die the hideous death of smallpox. The omission, in *Le Rouge et le Noir*, of Mathilde's dramatic attempts to claim Julien's head after his death is another one. Arguably, the scene of Julien's redemption through love was deemed more important to Autant-Lara and the scriptwriters. This seems especially true, given that the censors later saw fit to cut the scene, which suggests it was a powerful moment in the film at the time. As for Jeanson's ending for *Nana*, the decision was actually that of the director Christian-Jaque (and not the scriptwriter). He wanted to dilute Zola's version of this courtesan as bestial in her ability to attract men, as corrupt and deserving of her disfiguring death.[17] Thus, in their invention there is indeed betrayal of the original. But what is served in both examples is a logic of cinema – not always well, it has to be admitted, as is the case for *Nana*. By causing Nana to die of strangulation, Christian-Jaque deprives us of a socio-medical truth (death by small-pox) and spares us the vituperative cruelty of Zola's text. In so doing, he provides the audience with a clean ending. Equally, of course, he preserves Martine Carol's good looks. Arguably, the cinematic logic is not very defensible here. However, in the case of *Le Rouge et le Noir*, Sorel's death is rendered even more tragic in its absurdity – the point is that he dies for no reason, other than to provide a very anti-heroic gesture of defiance. There is power in this ending. In any event, it is far less melodramatically macabre than Stendhal's gruesome Romantic ending whereby Mathilde claims Sorel's head and – as with her great ancestor before her – places his head on a marble table and kisses him.

These endings, to my way of thinking, refute Truffaut's claims that the work of these scriptwriters is not by men of the cinema but men of literature. My argument is that their transpositions of the text are first and foremost cinematic (for reasons explained above, even if we deplore them), and not, as Truffaut claims, literary.[18] Funnily enough, the most literary of the film-maker/authors of this period is surely Sacha Guitry (who made 12 films, many of them adaptations of his own plays). Yet Truffaut sees fit to elevate him to the heady heights of auteur.[19] But this director-scriptwriter is a man who writes and delivers his lines as if they were all from the greatest works of France's literary heritage (see his *Deburau*, *Napoléon*, *Si Versailles m'était conté*, etc). We feel, certainly, that we are watching a great man of the theatre but, arguably, less a genius of the cinema – but that is another story!

Finally, it is worth mentioning that, out of a total corpus of 109 costume drama films, the number made by the acknowledged greats, namely auteurs as acclaimed by the *Cahiers* group, comes to 24 (i.e., 22 per cent). Apart from eight auteurs who made just one costume drama, Yves Allégret, Astruc and Clair each made two; Becker and Renoir three; Ophuls four. Were we, along Truffaut's lines, to add in Guitry with four, we would achieve 26 per cent. With 22 percent of costume dramas being the work of auteurs, we are led to question the assertion that this popular entertainment cinema should be so readily dismissed as 'daddy's cinema' and therefore as uninventive. After all, according to the *Cahiers'* doctrine, to be an auteur meant to have a distinctive style and (if possible) a personalized political cultural message and, as we shall see, neither are missing from the corpus discussed in this study. However, what will also transpire from the analyses to come is evidence to suggest that the other, more popular, film directors were not without invention, technically speaking, nor indeed without a political cultural message of their own. In short, we can often identify the style of a director, popular or auteur. And we can do this, in part, because of the particular director, but, equally, because of the technicians with whom he or she chose to work.

In light of the above comments, it would seem timely to suggest that Truffaut and the *Cahiers* group significantly misrepresented France's 1950s' cinema of quality and that we should endeavour to move away from the virtual self-imposed censorship in French film studies that has been so coloured by Truffaut's sweeping generalizations and largely unfounded attack on quality cinema. Throughout this study the suggestion is that this false, divisive auteurist debate has been with us long enough. Perhaps it is time, at long last, to leave it aside.

In Summary

There are many reasons, therefore, to investigate thoroughly and more globally this area of French film culture, since the 1950s was one of most prolific and popular periods for this genre, with the great majority of the films attracting large audiences. As we shall explain in Chapter 2, a partial reason for this relatively high number of films (given the costs of the genre) comes down to the post-war practice of co-productions. Just over a third of the decade's costume dramas were co-productions, primarily with Italy. This collaboration allowed French cinema to produce costume drama films with high production values during a seven-year period (1953–59) in the form of colour and cinemascope. Intriguingly, costume drama bucked the general downward trend post-1957 for colour and cinemascope films and was the only genre to continue producing at least half of its output in colour until the genre's demise in the 1960s. Colour and cinemascope are, arguably, two vital technological vehicles for the costume drama because they allow for maximum display. Fashion on wide-screen and in full colour was a considerable attraction in a time when the nation was recovering from the bleak after-effects of the war and Occupation, to say nothing of the contemporary political scene in the form of the Cold-War effects, the instability of government and civil unrest over both decolonization and industrialization.

However, this is but part of the picture to be investigated. Whilst just over half of all costume dramas were in colour (58), very few were in a scope format (11), for obvious economic reasons as we shall see. As for the remaining half (51), in black and white, these continued to attract large audiences throughout the decade. Thus, the costume drama becomes something other than just a question of high production values – in fact, in its black and white form it can become, by comparison with colour productions, something of an antithesis to the concept (and thereby codes and conventions) of the costume drama. After all, as a product, the black and white film, when compared to colour, displays its lack of excess. Yet, at the same time, it is still selling excess (in terms of costume, décor and gesture). Already, here, we can start to gauge discrepancies, contradictions within the production of this genre that must in some way speak to the climate and realities of the times. Indeed, several costume designers speak of the ways in which they had to cope with a paucity of means (and disguise the fact). So we have a situation where audiences were avid for this genre since, irrespective of its production values (black and white or in colour); 83 per cent of all costume dramas garnered well above the one-million-spectator threshold, rising even as high as nine million. Certainly, audiences went to see their favourite stars (with the male star often being the greatest attractor of all) but, undoubtedly, this genre responded also to a series of cultural needs – one of which was the felt need for France to display its creative virtuoso irrespective of whether it had a high or low budget to work with (especially in the form of costume and set designs) in defiance of the super-productions coming onto the cinematic market from the US.

The aims and objectives of this book are to open up this genre to a wider frame of analysis and to investigate its relevance within its historical political context. Thus, part of the investigation of this genre will lead us to examine the reasons for its popularity, given that it coincided with one of the heaviest periods of political censorship in France. Furthermore, with 70 per cent of the costume drama narratives being based within the nineteenth century – and more specifically 35 per cent of all costume dramas being located in the Belle Epoque era – another question becomes: how does this cinema, reflecting France's grandeur of a former recent past (as it does), talk to the contemporary 1950s' moment (with its sense of humiliation post-war, and its colonial unrest)? Equally crucially, but far more speculatively: how does it speak to its audiences (speculative, because here we only have audience figures and fanzines to go on)?

We need to understand why, at a time when France was so busily trying to modernize itself (and lose its identity as a rural and under-industrialized society), it should cast its cultural cinematic eye back to the past which, on the surface at least, would appear to contest that desire to modernize. Given that this cinema refers nostalgically back, with a strong penchant for France of the nineteenth century (75 films in all) – more specifically still to the times of Napoleon I (7 films), Louis XVIII (5 films), Louis-Philippe (5 films), Napoleon III (12 films), and especially the Belle Epoque (37) – we might be tempted to speculate about the underlying desire for either strong leadership and governance on the one hand, or, on the other, a cultural gaiety and economic well-being, all of which were presumably perceived as so lacking in the 1950s. However, as we shall see, this is to misread the evidence in the costume-drama films we have before us. The eventual picture to emerge is far more complex. Worth noting also is that the nineteenth century was a period of expanding colonialism, a time when, in the French psyche at least, France was perceived as a more dominant power on the European if not world stage – a fact not lost to 1950s' audiences. Small wonder, then, that cinema audiences sought relief in the form of the costume drama – a place traditionally of visual excess and display, to say nothing of myth construction. In this context the top-grossing films of 1955, Guitry's *Napoléon* (audience of 5.4 million) and Vernay's *Le Comte de Monte Cristo* (7.7 million) stand as exemplars of this trend for heroic and strong types, even if, as we shall discover, they are presented to us as flawed characters. Perhaps it is the ambiguity of the message – be it about personalities or periods – that makes these films resonate so strongly with the 1950s' public.

In order to give a shape to this quite extensive study, I have divided the book into four parts. In Part One, *Contexts*, I explore the various contexts that we need to take into consideration. Chapter 2 looks at the costume-drama genre in relation to history, both the one it purports to portray (the past) and the one from which it emanates (the contemporary) with a view to showing how genre speaks to a nation's psyche. Chapter 3 discusses the more practical issues related to the genre in that it maps out the importance of the contribution of the various practitioners to the genre as well as the impact of new technologies upon it. Part Two, *Fairytales, Foxy Women and Swashbuckling Heroes*, focuses on the films based in medieval times through to the end of the eighteenth century (34 films). Part Three, *Representing History: Epics, Courtesans and Master Narratives*, brings together all films of the nineteenth century that predate the Belle Epoque period (38 films). There are nine chapters to this part – which indicates, as indeed does the title, the degree to which we are dealing with films of significant ambition. In Part Four, *Belle Epoque Mania*, four chapters serve to investigate the diversity of costume dramas (37 films) set in this period. With the exception of four biopics, the focus of these films is primarily on marriage and the problems of domesticity. The contexts vary: Paris, the provinces, or the military.

I have managed to see 94 of this quite substantive corpus of 109 films (86 per cent). In my hunting, I have had some extraordinary adventures with the Centre National de la Cinématographie (primarily described in Chapter 17, which is in some ways dedicated to the CNC). The Bibliothèque Nationale de France was also a wonderful resource for videos and DVDs of the films. I have acquired a considerable number of the titles for my own personal collection, mostly purchased in French outlets, but some of which were given to me by friends. The exploration of 'what was really there' that follows will, I hope, lay to rest certain myths about this cinema. It has a lot more to say, on the one hand, about cinema and the new technologies and, on the other, cinema and political culture than a certain tendency of French cinema critics of the time would have us believe.

Notes

1. Rosine Delamare, quoted in press release by *Unifrance 4*, 19–20 June, 1950, p. 19.
2. See Bruzzi (1997), Cook (1996), Harper (1994) and Street (2001).
3. Delpierre (1988, p. 18).
4. Truffaut (1954).
5. For example, Ory (1989), Cole (1990), Gaffney (1991), Burch & Sellier (1996), Sellier (2001).
6. Montebello (2005, p. 51).
7. Ibid., p. 44.
8. Ibid., p. 51.

9. Ibid., p. 52.
10. Research to date into the 1950s' costume drama has focused in a limited way on stars and their performances with a handful of article-length studies (e.g., Hayward on Signoret (2009), Leahy on Bardot and Signoret (2003 and 2004, respectively), Sellier on Moreau (2001). There has been the welcome recent addition of a book-length study by Leahy (2007) on Jacques Becker's *Casque d'or* and Vincendeau's (2005) invaluable study of French stars.
11. Truffaut (1954, p. 21).
12. Ibid., p. 20.
13. Ibid., p. 16.
14. Ibid., p. 21.
15. Ibid., p. 15.
16. Ibid., p. 16.
17. Chapuy paraphrasing Christian-Jacque (p. 52).
18. Truffaut, op. cit.,p. 20.
19. Truffaut (1975a, pp. 236–40), this is a reprint in his book *Les Films de ma vie* of a 1957 *Cahiers du cinéma* article.

Chapter 2

Setting Out the Terrain: Genre and History

The costume drama genre as a document of a nation's psyche

When discussing the popularity of this genre, it is also necessary to try and understand why, in terms of public taste, it would have a resonance at a particular time in a nation's history. In terms of this specific genre it is equally important to determine which particular periods of the nation's past were the most popular points of reference, because it tells us something about the nation's contemporary psyche. As the cultural historian Pascal Ory and the film historian Geneviève Sellier state, the costume drama – in that it looks at the past – *is* saying something about the needs of the present, contemporary, French psyche.[1] It does so either in the form of a displacement or the expression of a set of anxieties in relation to both its recent past (and for France in this case it would be the Occupation) and/or its present (the Cold War, modernization, colonial wars). In this context, the costume drama fulfils two dominant needs, argues Ory.[2] First, the popular taste for 'history' represents a desire to get away from the present to another time that is not about now. Second, the appeal to audiences of 'historical' figures (from literature) suffering 'great misfortune' represents a classical displacement of fears. If we consider that 31 per cent of all costume drama narratives are in this latter category, we can easily observe how strong a tendency that is in the French psyche.

But let us first consider the particular epochs of history which have prevailed in the 1950s' costume drama. As we can see from the figure below (2.1), the single period that dominates (with 37 films over a 25-year historical period) is the Belle Epoque (1889–1914), itself a period of great modernization and economic boom. Second in importance is the rest of the nineteenth century up until the Belle Epoque era, the time of the two Napoleons and the Restoration and the first twenty years of the Third Republic – five different eras with 38 films over a ninety year time span. Films about Napoleon I and III garnered huge audiences. Guitry's *Napoléon* (1955) had an audience of 5.4 million and Pottier's film about Eugénie's marriage to Napoleon III, *Les Violettes impériales* (1952), 8 million. The top grossing costume drama, however, was Le Chanois' adaptation of Hugo's early-nineteenth-century novel *Les Misérables* (1958) with 10 million, showing that literary adaptations had huge appeal, no matter how tragic the story. Belle Epoque films on the whole averaged audiences of 2 to 3 million. The predilection, clearly, is for the near past of the nineteenth century, either in the form of economic well-being or portraits of great leaders (however flawed) or, again, literary adaptations revealing the misfortune of others. And we need to understand why this might be the case. The significant shift, by the time of the Belle Epoque to issues more readily

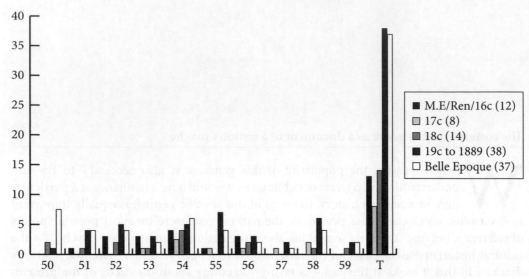

Figure 2.1: Distribution of the costume drama over epochs (box gives specific numbers).

associated with the feminine, such as love and marriage and the greater commodification of femininity (as a marker of man's technological advances as much as an object of display of his wealth) is given pride of place in this cinema of the 1950s, with a third of the film titles falling into that period. This shift has interesting implications where audience consumption is concerned. For we know that, whilst the costume drama is most readily seen as a women's genre, in 1950s' France, cinema-going was very much a family affair, weekend audiences making up to 70 per cent of the receipts.[3] Thus it is safe to assume that men and women consumed these costume drama films in equal parts.

Let us briefly consider the audience figures in relation to these films. For the most part, a costume drama film attracted on average two million spectators – a reasonable figure for the times. Anything over 3 million would be considered a remarkable figure and anything over 5 million a spectacular success. In all, there are 24 films which fall into the big success categories (figure 2.2 opposite).

Of the films with over five million spectators, all ranked in the five top-grossing films of their year, *Si Versailles m'était conté* is the only costume drama to have come first, *Le Comte de Monte Cristo* came second in its year, as did *Les Misérables* – both being pipped to the post by American films. *Fanfan la tulipe* was a remarkable success, given that is not in colour. The huge success of *Les Violettes impériales* can be attributed to the fact that it was a Luis Mariano vehicle, and in colour. In the first half of the 1950s, Mariano was France's most popular male operetta singer. Of the films with three to five million, nine were in colour, the other four in black and white. We can deduce, therefore, that colour was a determining factor in the size of the audiences these films attracted, but we should not forget that the stars would have had their impact value as well – as for example Gérard Philipe for *Fanfan*

Year	Films with audiences 3–5 million		Films with audiences over 5 million	
1951	Caroline chérie (b&w)	3.2 m		
1952	Belles de nuit (b&w)	3.5 m	Fanfan la tulipe (b&w)	6.7 m
	Il est minuit Dr Schweitzer (b&w)	3.3 m	Les Violettes impériales	8.1 m
1953	Lucrèce Borgia	3.6 m	Les Trois Mousquetaires	5.4 m
1954	Ali Baba et les 40 voleurs	4.1 m	Si Versailles m'était conté	7 m
	Cadet Rousselle	4 m		
	Mam'zelle Nitouche	3.8 m		
	Le Rouge et le Noir	4.3 m		
1955	French CanCan	4 m	Le Comte de Monte-Cristo	7.8 m
			Les Grandes manoeuvres	5.3 m
			Napoléon	5.4 m
1956	Don Juan	3.4 m	Michel Strogoff	7 m
	Gervaise (b&w)	4.1 m	Notre-Dame de Paris	5.7 m
1957	Les Aventures d'Arsène Lupin	3 m		
1958	Sans famille	3.3 m	Les Misérables	10 m
			La Jument verte	5.3 m

Figure 2.2: Audience figures for big-success costume dramas (rounded up) – all colour except for those indicated black and white (b&w).

la tulipe. We note also that 1954 stands out as the peak year for major successes with this genre, with five top-grossing titles (averaging out at 4.6m per film). But 1955 also deserves a mention since, out of the four titles, three are high scoring, bringing an average figure of 5.6m for the four. 1954 and 1956 were bumper years for co-productions (mainly with Italy; see Chapter 3). What is also significant is the distribution over historical periods. Five films of this top corpus are set in the Belle Epoque; ten in the period 1800–1885; nine pre-eighteenth century, suggesting that the major attraction, period-wise, is the nineteenth century – a factor substantiated by the preponderance of all costume drama films set in this timeline (69 per cent). Nostalgia for the more recent past prevails, it would appear.

According to Ory, popular film (or, as in this case, costume drama) functions at a symbolic level to alleviate the very real problems experienced by audiences – and, within their own cultural capital, a fit occurs, a match in experience, but one which is displaced and therefore less painful.[4] If we pause for a moment on the nature of these problems, we need to recall that they were far from parochial fears, and were as much global as local. On the global level, when the Cold War was at its height (1947–1955), 41 per cent of the French believed that a Third World War was imminent. For many, the Cold War was just a continuation of World War Two in everything but name. Furthermore, when, in 1954, after eight years of struggle the French handed over their ongoing conflict with their colonies in Indochina to the Americans for them to sort out, the war over there shifted from a colonial war into part of the Cold War – which, as we saw from the above statistic, was considered by nearly half the population as a big threat. This was the period of the '*Grande Peur* /Great Fear' in France, not helped by the outbreak of the Korean War in 1950.[5] Although the Cold War was a war without a *world* war, nonetheless there were many proxy wars, Korea being one of them, Indochina another (later to become infamous as the Vietnam War). The effect of the Cold War was to greatly polarize the world into Eastern and Western blocs of influence. The Marshall Plan (an economic strategy to relaunch Allied and defeated European nations after World War Two, 1947–1949) and NATO (North Atlantic Treaty Organization: a military allied organization of Western nations, lead by the US, 1949) were born out of this drive to consolidate the West against the East (Soviet, communist bloc). France as a nation was, arguably, more deeply affected by this polarization. Where, once, Russia (the Soviet Union) had been a traditional ally, that country was now the enemy.[6] Conversely, Germany, for many years an enemy nation, was now to be an ally.

The impact of the Cold War was considerable. It forced France, for reasons of security, to join NATO, thus making the nation a satellite of the US. France was also obliged, in the light of the Korean War, to accept the rearmament within NATO of its arch enemy, (West) Germany. Even the loss of its colonies was a part consequence of France's relationship with its American allies, who refused to see the Indochina and North-African crises as part of the Cold War and thus gave no aid to secure a French victory. And although the US did finally intercede in France's fight against the Viet Minh in 1952, it was on a financial basis only and it was already too late. Elected prime minister in 1954 on a ticket that he would pull France out of the war with Indochina, Mendès France effectively fulfilled his promise by passing the problem onto the Americans, who proved, disastrously, that they were just as incapable as the French of destroying Ho Chi Minh and the Viet Minh spirit. In the meantime, the Algerian crisis, which had reached violent proportions, was tearing the French nation apart. By 1958, France was at a tipping point in political terms. French army chiefs in Algeria were close to mutiny. Corsica was under siege, and rumours were rampant of an imminent military coup in mainland France. Censorship became increasingly trenchant (in an attempt to bury allegations of torture in Algeria) and demonstrations in the streets were given short shrift by the police. Colonial nationalism had peaked into hysteria. The Fourth Republic had spiralled out of control and the collapse of the régime, so long predicted by General de Gaulle, was now at hand. Given the severity of the crisis, which had brought France to the brink of civil war, the-then government felt it had no alternative but to call on de Gaulle to stabilize the situation. De Gaulle agreed to become the necessary arbiter on the Algerian question and was invested with full power on 1 June 1958. However, he only agreed to this investiture on condition that parliament would grant him the constitutional reforms he deemed necessary to national recovery. The panic caused amongst the general public by the recent stormy events meant that there was a major political swing to the conservative Right in terms of the electoral vote. De Gaulle emerged triumphant with an overall majority for the Right of 416 seats out of 578. This popular support made it possible for de Gaulle to argue the need for a new constitution – from this the Fifth Republic was born. In a nutshell, de Gaulle's new Republic shifted the emphasis of power away from the legislative body (the parliament) and invested it more fully in the executive – namely, the president. Political stability could only come about, argued de Gaulle, if a nation was secure in its self-esteem and if the state made possible a crystallization of social bonds. De Gaulle saw patriotism as the unifying force in French national life. Patriotism and the concept of the nation-state were the two key, closely inter-connected concepts to de Gaulle's thinking.

The trauma of decolonization on France's psyche cannot, therefore, be underestimated, nor indeed the impact of the nation's saviour: de Gaulle. Consider for a moment that in 1949 a very high percentage of the French (80 per cent) still believed that France had a role and a civilizing purpose in the colonies.[7] And, indeed, the colonies were hugely important to France in terms of its export market (wool, cotton, cement, heavy machinery, cars, and so on). Certainly, up until 1955, the North African colonies, especially Algeria, were very significant players in France's economic recovery. However, by 1955, the returns were on the decrease, despite the fact that France was pouring in 400 billion francs into Algeria annually to shore up its infrastructure. Part of the problem was a direct result of France's introduction of better hygiene into the country, which brought about an explosion in the population (up by 25 per cent in 1955). This growth was not matched, however, in economic terms – even Algerian oil was not proving much of a return by the mid-1950s. Couple this with the Algerian fight for independence, which escalated in 1954 once the FLN (the Algerian liberation army, the National Liberation Front) joined in the resistance against France, it is perhaps unsurprising that by 1958 only 27 per cent of the French wished to retain Algeria as a colony.[8]

On a more local level, there were problems in terms of the effects and demands of modernization. Modernization was not an even process, so its effects were far from straightforward. As a symbol of this unevenness, we can point to the reconstruction of cities, which was a very mixed affair – some cities being partially or completely modernized, others pulling on old retrogressive architectural styles.[9] Then again, the 1950s was also an exceptional period in French economic history and marks the beginning of the so-called 'trente glorieuses/ the thirty glorious years'. The economic recovery was miraculous but real, based as it was on an internally-driven market (which included the colonies) that was hugely protectionist. In short, France sold its products to the French (including to its colonies). Household consumption rose exponentially. Th is internally-driven market allowed for solid intervention from the state (what is known in French as the *dirigisme* factor) which invested in modernizing the infrastructures of industries (thanks largely to the way it used the Marshall Aid it received[10]), stimulating production and improving on social inequalities. During the 1950s, France's GNP outstripped both the US and the UK in terms of growth (by 1 percent, and 1.5 percent respectively).[11] The truth of the matter is that these changes would have been impossible had the economy been open to international competition. However, it is also true that protectionism, with growth limited to an internal market, is, in the final analysis, a retrograde economic policy which cannot last. Indeed, this economic practice, which was very reminiscent of practices instituted during the late nineteenth century, meant that, after all, France, with its inward looking policies, was far from modernizing in its thinking. For a protectionist, internal market cannot grow, cannot cope with the demands for expansion, will fail to respond to external pressures and can only survive via inflation. After ten years there was no change in the growth pattern because there was no renewal of the prevailing economic structures or in production output.[12]

France of this period presents a very complex picture to unpick. It benefited from great economic well-being, on the whole. By 1952, the finance minister Antoine Pinay had managed to stabilize the economy by increasing purchasing power through his measures to freeze prices (keeping them artificially low). Credit purchasing also assisted this. By 1955, unemployment was officially non-existent. Yet, this French miracle occurred in the face of some 23 changes of government during the entire period of the Fourth Republic (1947–1959); it occurred, also, despite the fact that the colonial wars were eating up 25 per cent of the budget. It also sustained itself despite the impact on election returns, in 1956, of the populist leader Pierre Poujade who railed against the effects of modernization (largely made possible thanks to American Marshall Aid) on small artisanal businesses and local shop-keepers. His staunch campaigning, via his Union for the Defence of Shopkeepers and Artisans (UCDA), garnered 11 per cent of the electoral vote, which bizarrely caused the brief return of the Left to government in 1956. Bizarre, because the Left's return constituted less of a victory for them than a compromise by the-then French President, René Coty, to block the extreme Right. The traditional Right had failed to win an overall majority at the January 1956 legislative elections, thanks in large part to Poujade's party of the extreme Right, which took seats away from the traditional parties of the Right. Effectively, the Left had some 50 more seats in parliament than either the centre-Right or the more clearly Right-wing Republican Front parties. Even so, the Left – with its social reforms bringing about an inflationary impact on the economy – failed to undermine the Fourth Republic's 'economic miracle'. By 1957 they were out, over a negotiation failure in relation to the Algerian crisis. But they nonetheless managed (despite the conservative economic and political climate) to pass the three-week paid holiday and grant Tunisia and Morocco their independence. By May 1957, however, Pinay was back as minister of finance and once more was spinning his miracle-systems.[13]

The 1950s was a period of enormous social change. At the same time as the reconstruction of the cities and the rationalization of the industries was taking place, there was a huge push to sell the products and in particular, by the mid-1950s, to bring technology into the home – ranging from plastic products (bic biros, vinyl records, etc.) to electronic goods (Hoovers, fridges and so on). This created a new malaise of its own between the haves and the have-nots, to say nothing of the anxieties caused for those entering into the treacherous domain of credit purchasing. All classes were affected, most poignantly, perhaps, the working classes. Change took the form of a fragmentation of their social groupings, particularly for the men, and the effects of modernization both at home and at work radically changed their sense of identity. On the one hand, thanks to product availability and credit purchasing, they were now entering a new class but, on the other, skilled labour was becoming a thing of the past, replaced by the tedium of mechanized (conveyor-belt) labour in the factories.[14] Also adding to this clash between classes, between ancient and modern, comes a major demographic shift. By the mid-1950s, a third of the population was under twenty.

The 1950s also brought a major redefinition of the roles for women. On the one hand, there was a greater commodification of femininity in two dominant domains: fashion and technology. First, the New Look fashion with its hyper-feminine design: the upper body constrained, corset-like with a tight waistline (*taille de guêpe*/wasp waist, as it was known), the lower body englobed in the new, crinoline-look, wide skirts recalling nineteenth-century design. Second, technology entered the domestic sphere in the form of electric goods, with all the hyperbole of advertising constructing the ideal consumer housewife.[15] On the other hand, women had just obtained the right to vote (the law enfranchising women was passed in 1944), suggesting an emancipation of womanhood. I say 'suggesting' because, at the time, the prevailing discourse around women's enfranchisement was that they were not to be trusted to vote 'properly'. The fear was that their votes would be influenced by their religious beliefs. Paradoxically, studies reveal that women's voting practices of that time tended to follow those of their husband or father, which suggests that women had not yet freed themselves of the mental shackles of being considered a minor.[16] In terms of the condition of women, it would be fair to say, then, that enfranchisement (freedom to vote) ran in parallel with, rather than counter to, containment in the form of constructions of femininity. In other words, the design of containment and display, embodied in women's fashion and consumption practices, were part of a process of keeping women in their place, which served to allay male fears of female emancipation.

The costume drama genre speaks to history ' then' and 'now'

A major function of the costume drama is, of course, the re-writing and re-accommodification of history (i.e., making history fit the purpose). But this is not to impugn a flaw in the genre. In our investigation of this genre, the intention is to ensure that the films under consideration are viewed within their historical contexts, both of the period of reference and that of the 1950s. Such frameworking is certain to bring out interesting socio-political conjunctures. For example, the issue of marriage dominates the Belle Epoque films, and we might be inclined to draw an immediate parallel with the 1950s' emphasis on marriage and procreation. Yet, such a parallel does not quite hold. For in all these 37 films, rarely does the issue of marriage bring in its wake the production of children. Indeed, what is striking throughout the entire corpus is the resounding absence of children from the narratives (with very few exceptions). And, as we move further back into history, so the topic of marriage disappears from the film narratives almost entirely. Thus, in this context, the costume drama genre can hardly be said to be towing the line with dominant ideology.

For its part, the issue of masculinity also shifts as we move further back in time. In earlier narratives there appears to be a greater panoply of masculinities: the pre-1789 man is more diverse, less hard-edged than his nineteenth-century counterpart, it would seem. However, this diminution in diversity notwithstanding, this does not mean that the representations of masculinity in the nineteenth-century narratives are any less complex for that. Th is male is not always an appetizing one – even if his sexual appeal is. Indeed, if we consider the nineteenth-century male, the neurotic, self-obsessed, cynical man on the make of the Belle Epoque finds his earlier counterpart in films based in the 1860s. Often he is a roué, a seducer, a ruthless parvenu; only occasionally is he uncertain as to his place in society. As for the nineteenth-century Restoration- and July Monarchy-period films, men seem bent on revenge against society (be it in the form of institutions or displaced onto women). An angry response, doubtless, to the countless wars that left the nation-state weakened. Certainly, this theme of questioning war, however directly or indirectly, re-occurs in many of the swashbuckler films – indicating, at the very least, that a preoccupation with the waste of manhood is present in the nation's collective psyche. Maybe the anger and cynicism in the nineteenth-century-based narratives, in particular, need to be understood in that light. Repeatedly, a sense of the instability of political régimes prevails – part of this being transmitted to the spectator by the clash between the ancient and the modern (be it in the form of conflict between ages, classes, beliefs or questions of technological progress). The role of women in this aura of instability is shown as complex. Men seek to fix them, almost as if believing that in their beauty they could masquerade against the reality of a depleted nation – only to discover that such is not the case, and to punish them for it (arguably here, tropes of film noir come seeping into costume drama).

This does not exclude the fact that the pre-nineteenth-century texts also illuminate the contemporary 1950s. For example, the swashbuckler films come to mind, but so too do the 'fairytales' and 'foxy women' narratives. In the latter case, myth-creation comes under scrutiny, and that will have clear resonances with the myth-making that occurred post-war in relation to France's Resistance. As for the fairytales, these mostly forefront constructions of masculinity and power relations – again crucial issues with regard to the 1950s, with the older generation of men being taken to task by the young coupled with the impact of new technologies on the working-class worker, to say nothing of the usurpation of traditional roles during the war, which saw a considerable increase in the female workforce. Also in amongst these film narratives, we shall see that just a few are mindful of the issue of tolerance (political and religious). For a cinema that purportedly has no grounding in reality (let alone history), we could argue that there is a considerable feast for thought here.

Conclusion

The costume drama's relation to social reality is an ambiguous one, therefore. Authenticity comes in the easier domains of representation, namely the interface between costume and gender, the expansion of the middle classes, the position of women and the crisis of masculinity. Where it struggles is in the arena of sexuality and the body – as if truth under the garments were too much to lay bare. As for history, as we shall see in the other parts that make up this book, there is a social and urban history to be read, even if it is distorted through the prism of personal narratives. We discover anew the objects and concerns of a time that is past, the sentiments that drive people in their ambitions and desires, an occasional glimpse at the grandeur and follies of kings, queens and emperors. It is a feast that invites its audience to delight upon as much as to reflect – a feast this book intends to revel in!

Notes

1. Ory (1989) and Sellier (2001).
2. Ory, op. cit., pp. 112–34.
3. Montebello (2005, p. 51).
4. Ory, op. cit., p. 112.
5. See the *French Cultural Studies* special number on 'France and the Cold War', edited by Ted Freeman, Vol. 8, Part 1, No. 22.
6. Not just in the eighteenth century and France's famous cultural relationship with Catherine the Great, but also during the Belle Epoque period when France made big loans to Russia (Leymarie, 1999: 91).
7. See Marseille (2002, pp. 362–72).
8. Ibid., pp. 362–72.
9. See Ory, op. cit., pp. 129–30.
10. The French used their Marshall Aid ($5bn over the period 1948–52) to implement their First Plan for economic reconstruction – which for the French meant industrial regeneration and funding of other vital economic sectors. The Aid system worked as follows: the US gave dollars to the French; these were then sold for francs and used to import American goods that were deemed necessary for the immediate present – in this context, materials for reconstruction. Thus, the French cleverly worked the money to their own ends, which meant their market was not open to the flooding of American goods that could otherwise have occurred. Instead this circuiting of money allowed for France's mid and long term investment in modernization. (See Eck, 1988, pp. 11–16)
11. Eck (1988, p. 5).
12. See Eck (op. cit., pp. 4–12) for a very clear analysis of France's economic practices during the 1950s.
13. Pinay was member of the Vichy government during the Occupation period. After the war he was briefly suspended from political activity. This proscription did not last long however.
14. See Marseille (2002, pp. 384–5).
15. See Kristin Ross (1995) for a detailed study of the impact of new technologies on the domestic sphere.
16. Gaffney (1991, p. 27) points out that 'studies have shown that it is only recently that this half of the population has begun to "vote for itself", rather than as prescribed by husbands and fathers.'

Chapter 3

Setting Out the Terrain: Technologies, Technicians and Stars

Cinemascope and colour

Two new technologies were introduced in the early 1950s, only one of which, colour, impacted significantly on the costume drama. The other, the wide-screen format cinemascope with four-track stereo-sound had hardly any impact at all (with only eleven costume dramas in this format: a mere 10 per cent of the total output). This might seem quite strange given the properties of cinemascope for spectacle and display on a grand scale – two key elements of costume drama after all. It is also a natural format for epics, arguably a small but not inconsiderable concern of the costume drama genre.

The major reason for this lack of impact of cinemascope upon the French film industry is, of course, economic.[1] Thus, the poor take-up of this expensive format for costume drama is not out of tune with the general trend. The cinemascope format was introduced onto the French screen in the mid-1950s, to much acclaim in the industrial press. However, from 1954 to 1959, only 74 films were made in this and other, less expensive 'scope formats such as dyaloscope and franscope. Film budget constraints were clearly a restricting factor in its use, as were difficulties with exhibition spaces. During the first three years of the 1950s a great deal of investment had already gone into refurbishing cinema theatres. Sumptuous theatres re-opened – the Berlitz in Paris, for example, with seating for well over 1500. Cinemascope, with its different widescreen format and stereo sound, meant all theatres would have to re-invest in yet further changes. The cost of re-equipping a theatre for 'scope was between 3–4 million francs. Unsurprisingly, progress was slow, with only 500 theatres being equipped for 'scope by 1955.

Half a century on from this time, it is hard for us to imagine what an impact this new 'scope technology had. The film trade press (such as *La Cinématographie française*) had weekly, extended articles on this new phenomenon (which seemed to have taken the industry by surprise). Indeed, a completely new kind of spectacle was born with the arrival of cinemascope, not least of which was that it brought more light and more sound to the screen. Edouard Lardillier rightly commented that this was a 'sensational technology that completely overturned contemporary film practice both in terms of filming and projection.'[2] The film-maker Yves Allégret immediately perceived the way the 'vast image gave colour its true value on the big screen'; how it allowed for ambient sound to be more realistic both in terms of its quality and its location (thanks to the stereo effect, of course). He also explained how 'scope gave space for the actors to develop their performance and evolve in front of the camera.[3] The film trade press urged the industry to embrace this technology, claiming that the future was with big-budget prestigious films made in this format.[4] To little avail it would seem. Only major co-productions (primarily with Italy) could manage the financing necessary. Thus, for our part, with so few costume dramas in this format (11 in all), we will need to pay extra attention to when it is in use. For example, an early cinemascope and colour costume drama film was Ophuls' *Lola Montès* (1955) – a very interior type of costume drama based on her love affairs with famous men. Potentially, the epic format of 'scope seems somewhat in ironic counterpoint to the life of this eponymous courtesan and her less-than-grand trajectory.[5]

Colour presents quite a different story from 'scope, especially in relation to costume drama. The first colour films made in France in the early 1950s were all costume dramas. This early period (1951–1953) was known as the 'heroic period' of colour film. Given that each colour system had different sets of imperatives, each one brought with it its own challenges to cinematographers, set and costume designers alike 'heroically' overcame the difficulties. The over-riding preoccupation amongst technical staff at the time was with producing a natural colour effect, even though they were not necessarily enamoured with this principle (but there were directives from the processing companies that had to be respected). However, as the 1950s progressed, this debate widened into considerations of colour's function. The question became: was its function merely technical (serving to reproduce reality) or was it more an aesthetic one, having thereby a dramatic function? Colour as practice or colour as meaning.[6] In the end, as we shall see in this study, it is surely both.

The very first French (sound) colour film, made in Gevacolor, was in fact *Porte d'orient* by Jacques Deroy (production year 1950 and released 26 January 1951) and not, as many film historians have it, *Barbe-bleue* (Christian-Jaque, 1951, co-produced with Germany). The latter film's production year was 1951 and it was released 28 September 1951. What we can say however is that *Barbe-bleue* is the first French costume drama in colour. Christian-Jaque was of the view that film colour was more real than real colour itself. As such, he felt that the use of colour intensified the hyper-real quality of costume drama. Film colour was a way of making dreams become real.[7] We need to recall that colour film at this time was associated (by the industry itself and film theorists) with fantasy, not with realism, which was the province of black and white film. Audiences were not of the same opinion as the purists, however, even though this did not deter producers and directors throughout the 1950s from sticking to their view that social-realist films and thrillers should be in black and white, despite audience taste for colour.[8] Apparently 44 per cent of the audience preferred colour, over the 25 per cent who preferred black and white.[9] Apart from the colour-effect itself, one of the attractions might well have been the stereo sound that colour with cinemascope made possible. But even if stereo had not been possible, colour was bound to attract, especially in costume drama, for it serves to put glamour, extravagance and wealth on display. In its glamour, it takes us outside ourselves. In its effect, it heightens the display of the erotic: flesh made more real – a concept which brings us back to Christian-Jaque's view of colour and the hyperreal, and we need to think, in this study, about the effect of the hyperreal not just upon the genre but also the star body in particular – the image becomes more haptic, more seizable, arguably, thanks to colour.

There are several ways of approaching how we register the number of colour films produced in France during this decade. Either we could count all films produced, but not all of which were released in the 1950s – in which case the figures are somewhat different from the ones proposed below, which refer to films *released* during the decade. In other words, this study focuses on the films that were actually out there on screens for audiences to view. Thus, were we to take on board all colour production that includes releases in 1960 then our global figure becomes 171 colour films, of which 62 are costume dramas (36 per cent). But the purpose of this study is exclusively 1950s' releases, and, as we shall see, the actual percentages do not shift. During the 1950s, 156 colour films were produced and released, of which 58 were costume dramas (37 per cent). Indeed, of the 109 costume drama films made and released, just over half were in colour (53 per cent). The two graphs below illustrate, first (figure 3.1), the yearly output of costume dramas and trace the trajectory of those made in colour; the second graph (figure 3.2) measures the number of costume drama co-productions and the number of colour co-productions. As we can see from figure 3.1, the peak year for colour costume drama (CD) was 1954 with fourteen; thereafter, there was a slow decline: eleven in 1955, ten in 1956, two in 1957, eight in 1958 and a mere three in 1959. The decline has several reasons: costs, a drop, by 1956, in the number of studios (from twelve in Paris to seven) and, by 1959, of sets (from 67 to 46).

As the figure below (3.2) makes clear, although 1953 marks the year when, in percentage terms, there were more costume drama co-productions than at any other time in the 1950s (80 per cent, i.e., eight out of ten), 1954 was, numerically speaking, the peak year for

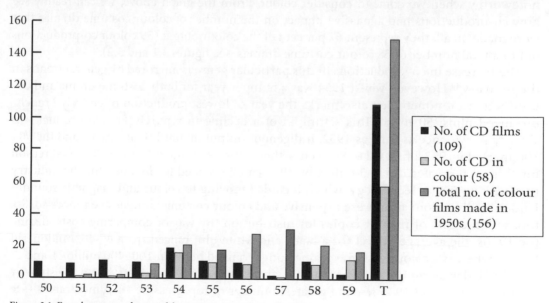

Figure 3.1: French costume drama of the 1950s (output and colour).

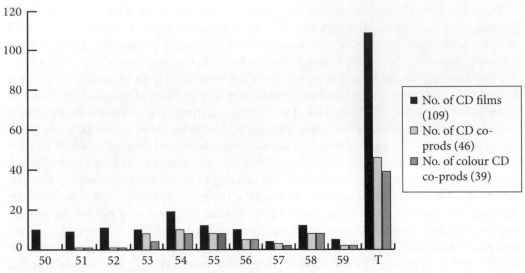

Figure 3.2: Number of co-produced costume dramas compared to total output.

co-produced costume dramas (with ten out of nineteen being co-productions, of which eight were in colour).

Costume drama co-productions represent 42 per cent of overall output for this genre during this decade, which is already a significant fi gure. But it becomes even more noteworthy when we come to consider colour. From the graph above, we can readily see how co-productions had a massive impact on the number of colour costume dramas that were made. In all, they represent 67 per cent of the colour output (39 colour co-productions out of a total number of 58 colour costume dramas, see figures 3.1 and 3.2).

The increase in co-productions in this particular genre is mirrored by general trends in the industry.[10] However, whilst 1954 was a bumper year for both costume drama and co-productions, it nonetheless also marks the year of lowest production of entirely French-produced films: 50 in all. This setting in of a decline in a purely French product was already in evidence as early as 1952. Indigenous output up until then was around the 90–100 mark. By 1952 a first fall to 86 occurs, then a further drop to 61 in 1953. A first reason for this even greater dip to 50 films by 1954 can be related to the need for the industry to renew its ageing technology, which included moving to colour and magnetic sound.[11] Undoubtedly, colour films were expensive and colour costume dramas even more so. So, too, was the cost of making copies for distribution. By way of comparing costs, during the 1950s, the average budget for a black and white film ranged from 47–92 million old francs, whereas a colour costume drama budget ranged between 100–400 million francs.[12] Small wonder co-productions had such a strong appeal to the industry. And the strategy paid off – 1954 and 1955 saw the greatest number of top-grossing costume dramas (see Chapter 2).

However, this dip in indigenous production was not a one-off phenomenon. The following graph (figure 3.3) traces the sorry story of France's production over this decade as compared with the rising force of co-productions. By the end of the decade, French co-productions accounted for a third of all output. And, as we can also see from the graph, by the mid-fifties the average budget for French co-productions was twice that of 100 per cent French films.

Several reasons can be put forward for this decline in purely-French products. The huge increase in colour films for the four-year period 1953–1956 is explained, fi rst, by the increase in co-production practices, post-1952, to facilitate the making of the more expensive products (see fi gure 3.3 below). French co-productions (where France is the biggest investor), whether in black and white or colour, went from 6 per cent of all French production in 1951 (6 out of 104 films) to 31 per cent in 1953 (27 out of 88 films). Thereafter, figures remained between 21–32 per cent until the peak year for French co-productions of 1959, with 35 per cent (36 out of 104 films). The peak years for colour were 1956–1957 with 29 and 32 films, half of which were co-productions. Thereafter, the number of colour films began to decline. And by 1959 only 17 colour films were made (see figure 3.4).

So why the continuing drop in purely-French products, since colour was no longer a major factor, post-1957? Intriguingly, audience decline cannot be blamed. Even if, by 1957–58, a new consumer boom was affecting the way the French spent their leisure money, the late 1950s were, nonetheless, peak years for the industry, with audiences of 400 and 407 million in 1956 and 1957 respectively. And, by the end of the decade, as many people were going to the cinema as had been going at the beginning of the decade (namely, 370 million). Audience predilection for types of film constitutes a part answer to the decline in French

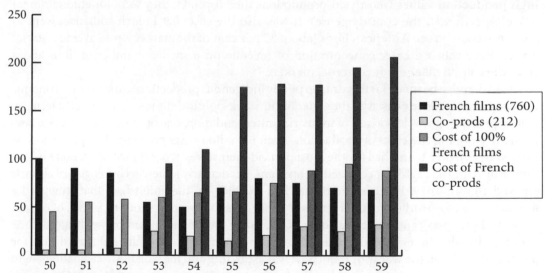

Figure 3.3: France's production in terms of films released during 1950s as compared to French co-productions; plus average budgets of French films compared to French co-productions (in millions of French francs).[13]

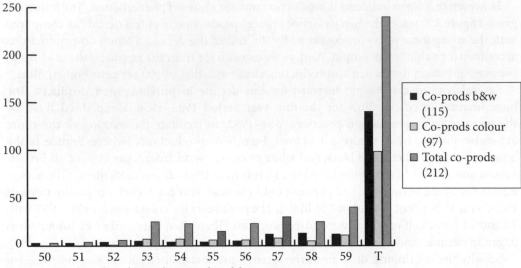

Figure 3.4: Total number of co-productions released during 1950s.

film production, because a shift occurred where consumption practices were concerned. As more products became available, consumers became more selective. A greater sense of wealth, in that it created a more middle-class consumer body, also meant that the cinema-going audiences began to impose their taste and assert choices as to what they would go and see.[14] Audiences now went for the big spectacle (such as *Les Misérables*): films that had high production values (mostly co-productions therefore). Or they went for entertainment value (specifically, the comedy genre). It was also the case that French audiences went in great numbers to see American films (about 37 per cent of the market, on an average year).[15] Thus, there was a greater concentration of revenue on a smaller number of films and a considerable challenge from external markets.[16]

Links can also be made for this drop in purely indigenous production to the overall economic uncertainty in France caused by the generally unstable political climate of the time. In terms of studio practice, it was less a case of industrial unrest and more one of the impact of union laws indirectly upping the costs of production. Even if studio bosses now had the upper hand, as we saw in Chapter 1, and had for the most part rid themselves of permanent staff, nonetheless, they still required highly-specialized technicians, particularly as new technologies of all sorts entered the industry. Further, the bosses had to abide by the union laws that stipulated a five-day week for studio work (as opposed to six days for location shooting). This, of course, impacted on costs (and these are some of the other reasons why studios went into decline over the decade). In terms of the political arena and its impact on the film industry, during the period 1953–1954, the war with Indochina was escalating and the North African nations' fight for independence was becoming bloodier by the week. Wartime or conflict, as we know, has major repercussions for a nation's economy: it may boom the war industry infrastructure, but it makes private funding for the arts less easy to procure. As if to underscore the discomfitures of these times, it is worth noting that during this two-year period, in the costume drama films, there was a greater recourse to earlier epochs in history. Thus, rather than referencing the nineteenth-century Second Empire and, more particularly, the Belle Epoque (periods of great colonialist expansion), films began to show a greater preference for earlier times, such as those of Napoleon Bonaparte, the Three Musketeers, Marguerite de Valois aka *La Reine Margot* (in benign mode), Louis XV and Lucretia Borgia.

Later on in the 1950s, yet another contributing factor to the uncertainty faced by the French film industry was the effect of the radical change in government brought about by General de Gaulle's coming-to-power in 1958. From November 1958 until June 1959, de Gaulle's government in the form of Pinay, the minister of finance, held back on their decision to renew government support for the industry (which until that time had been in the form of the *loi d'aide au développement du cinéma*). Pinay, for his part, was much against the concept of state aid to the film industry. However, in the end, a system of aid was instituted – this time in the form of a *fonds de soutien* (with a much diminished set of funds).[17]

If indigenous production lessened, thankfully co-productions were on the rise for the most part throughout the 1950s, from 1953 onwards as follows:

1953: 27 (up from 10 in 1952)
1954: 23
1955: 19
1956: 25
1957: 33
1958: 27
1959: 36

Figure 3.5: Co-production figures 1953–1959.

So let us now return to 1954, the year of the costume drama genre's greatest output and when five of its film titles were amongst the fifteen top-grossing films of that year.[18] In general terms, this year marks the moment when the number of colour films in France soared. This was due to three factors, all occurring in 1953, thus kick starting something of a boom in colour production. First, the greater availability and improved quality of Gevacolor: in 1953, five films were made in that format. Second, better financing via co-productions led to nearly a tripling of products (see figure 3.5 above). Third, and more significantly still, the introduction into France, in 1953, of the cheaper American colour system, Eastmancolor (a Kodak product) over Technicolor. Significantly, in 1954, 23 colour films were released, of which sixteen were in Eastmancolor. Of that sixteen, eleven were costume dramas (the other three colour costume dramas of that year being in Gevacolor). Indeed, in terms of the French costume drama, Eastmancolor dominates in the 1950s. Here is the breakdown of the 58 colour costume dramas of that decade:

Eastmancolor	=> 32
Technicolor	=> 14
Gevacolor	=> 10
Agfacolor	=> 2

Figure 3.6: Breakdown of costume drama films according to colour process.

Eastmancolor and Technicolor are American systems, Agfacolor, German, and Gevacolor, Belgian (albeit an affiliate of Agfa[19]) – a neat split, mirroring the rivalry between Hollywood and Europe, as it were. Agfacolor and Technicolor were the two main rivals before World War Two (even though Technicolor was the dominant force). In the post-war period and into the 1950s; Gevacolor came to dominate as a European product over Agfa because it was more readily available than the German colour system. Geva and Agfa were of a similar cost (170 francs per metre). But whilst supply and demand was not a problem for Geva, it certainly was for Agfa because of the partition of Germany into East and West. Agfa's reputation for quality was huge, it was known as the mother of all chromogeneous systems. But, by the post-war period, it found itself more or less unable to compete on a grand scale. Agfa had laboratories in both Germanies and, whilst the better product came from the East German laboratories in Leverkusen, it took four months for delivery – as opposed to four weeks from the Wolfen laboratories in the West. In all, Agfa could only supply France with 300,000 metres per year (enough for 10 films or so). Eastmancolor, for its part, came in at a reasonable cost of 190 francs per metre. Where it truly led over all other systems, however, was in its sensitivity to light. Because it was so light-sensitive, it only needed double the lighting necessary for black and white film as opposed to the three other colour systems, all of which required three (Geva and Agfa) to six (Technicolor) times the amount. This cut costs considerably. Whilst on this issue of expense, Eastmancolor certainly enabled an increase in production because, in overall terms, it cost less. We also need to consider that producing copies of colour film to be exhibited was very expensive indeed and because Technicolor was *the* gold-brand system, preferred by export markets over other European systems, it is easy to understand why producers were likely to hesitate before considering colour for their film, especially Technicolor – the most expensive system of all. It becomes clearer, in this light, why France's colour film output for the 1950s remains at a very low 16 per cent compared with the US at 80 per cent. It also explains why producers, primarily guided by cost factors, opted for the Eastmancolor system in the main as soon as it became available.[20]

If Technicolor did not dominate in France, it was because there were several drawbacks to using it, including cost. First, up until 1955, the nearest processing laboratories were in London, causing long delays for viewing rushes.[21] Second, processing costs were far greater than for any other system, not just because it was done outside France but also because it had to be paid for in dollars. Third, Technicolor had artistic control over its product, which meant a colour consultant had to be present at all stages of the film production – a kind of autocratic tyranny that many French film directors did not welcome. A major effect of this control was the great uniformity in look to Technicolor films – equally unwelcome amongst certain directors.[22] Fourth, Technicolor necessitated specialized projection lamps which, until the mid-50s, had to be imported, again slowing down procedures and pushing up costs.[23] It also required twice the amount of lighting power than other colour systems.[24] Finally, even if a production company could afford this system, demand exceeded supply. There was a tremendous demand for Technicolor, which it found hard to meet, even within its own internal market. Lack of availability left space for the rival system, Eastmancolor, to creep in. The other reason why Eastmancolor dominated in the latter half of the 1950s in France was, as we know, expense. Eastmancolor, a tri-pack colour all-in-one system, was a considerably cheaper product than Technicolor. Moreover, as early as 1953, the Kodak factory – which produced and processed the colour film stock – was located at Vincennes (near Paris) and so was close to hand for the studios.[25]

It is important to understand these issues because they affect choices made by the industry when considering which colour system to use: availability, colour rendition, light sensitivity, costs. But what is equally of interest to us in our study is that each colour system produced different effects and that, whatever system was used, colour had to be falsified to come out true. Thus, each system had different requirements for the colours to pass, or render correctly. For example, in terms of the impact on the colour registration of fabrics, Gevacolor was not always stable and had problems with colour saturation, especially under heat. Thus, it made reds turn brown and beiges to become quite dark, even blackish. Sensitivity did improve during the first half of the decade, making Geva almost equal to Eastmancolor, even though the latter had better definition in shadows or darker areas. Interestingly, Gevacolor was better in full sunlight than its American rival, providing great depth in the images and glorious colour in exterior shots.

Technicolor – a three-strip camera colour system (basically a three-film-roll system) and therefore the most expensive – produced deeper, richer, colour textures. Here Technicolor, in overdoing colour (colour saturation), joins in with our earlier comment about the hyperreal. But it does so in a peculiar way. For its colour rendition was often garish, particularly the reds, blues and browns. As Dudley Andrew explains: 'Technicolor had (and promoted) a Hollywood notion of colour: purer than reality, needing a strong artificial light, aggressive, almost whorish.'[26] However, as set designer Max Douy points out, at times the film narrative is well matched by this potential excess of colour, and he refers to Renoir's use of Technicolor in his 1955 film *French Cancan* ('it had to hit you in the eye' he comments).[27] A major advantage of Technicolor over other systems was that it allowed one to rectify mistakes (for example, erasing crowds from a scene) and to do special effects directly on the film.[28] Because Technicolor needed strong lighting to achieve its 'purer than reality' look, it was better suited to studio work than exteriors. Conversely, Agfa and Geva were very suited to outside shooting and provided a sharp natural-documentary look, but they both lacked the consistency that Technicolor could provide. Sadly it is impossible to mix and match the colour systems (picking the best for exteriors and interiors). Because of the colour processing, the outcome would produce a clash.

Thus, any choice of a colour system was inevitably a compromise. But, because Eastmancolor seemed to have the least drawbacks, it became a favourite.

However, as with other colour systems, the Eastmancolor system was not without its own problems. In these early years of its development, it produced quite a pastel effect, which faded with the passing of time. Eastmancolor films of this period notoriously lost depth of colouration. Unless the films have been remastered, it is very difficult to know precisely what was being seen at the time, creating problems for film historians. Crucially, we rely on the interviews with, and recollections of, directors of photography and other technical personnel (in particular costume designers) to understand the effects of this new system. For example, one of the leading costume designers of the time, Rosine Delamare, speaking about the costumes for *Le Rouge et le Noir* (Autant-Lara, 1954) which was shot in Eastmancolor, noted how man-made fabrics, whilst cheap to use (so keeping costs down), 'turned' when filmed. Rayon and nylon changed colour and, worse still, reflected light unless they were very dark. Blue tended to crop up everywhere with these fabrics (even black turned to blue) so Delamare had to use dark brown to get a black effect.[29] The set designer for that film, Max Douy, pointed out that, in the end, a decision was taken to work from a very limited palette of colours and to keep décor to a minimum so as not to distract the spectator from the psychologically-interior nature of the story.[30] In relation to Eastmancolor, set designer Léon Barsacq said that, whilst it was true that you had to limit your palette to fairly neutral colours (because blue cropped up everywhere like a plague), nonetheless it had many merits over Technicolor and the other systems. First, the whole camera operation was far more flexible than for a Technicolor camera (the single Eastmancolor tripack system meant you had a much lighter camera to manipulate). Second, its greater sensitivity to light (over the other systems) gave greater depth of field.[31]

Colour and its rendering once on film was, of course, a major concern for set designers, directors of photography and costume designers alike – particularly in relation to the perceived need, which prevailed at the time, to force the real naturalness of colour. It obliged set designers, for example, to mostly select soft colour tones: greys and beiges and off-whites, reserving the placing of more vibrant colours (in terms of fabrics or other ornamentations) to the higher regions of the set so as to avoid unfortunate clashes with the actors' costumes. In the name of the natural, real effect, colour for sets had to be discreet; the essential thing was to harmonize set colours and costumes so that they rendered realistically on the film's emulsion. But, whilst the dominant tendency was to adopt discreet tones, more vibrant colours could be employed as long as strong contrasts were avoided. Using a whole range of colours was permissible as long as they were of the same intensity. For example, a light-red married well with a yellow of the same intensity. But it would be fatal to mix dark and light colours. Blues and greens must either be pale, or dark, but dull in tone. As Léon Barsacq pointed out so clearly, the worst thing you can do is to think of film colour as an artist's palette; it simply is not the same. Film colour has volumes and densities all its own.[32] Interestingly, the 'scope format made this very evident. For 'scope screening, in terms of colour emulsion, the colour grain had to be smaller than for other formats in order to give good definition. We do not necessarily think of colour as bleeding from its seeming boundaries, but of course it does and the 'scope format made this very evident. Barsacq generously tells us what tended to dominate in terms of his own design palette: the whole range of browns, rust colours, beiges, mauves, blue-greys, pearlized greys. He also found that gold, silver and black rendered well. In short, he did not advocate sticking to pastel colours – far from it. What he did recommend, however, was the need to harmonize, to know the properties of your film stock and to be aware of continuity from one sequence to the next.[33] Since we are now already talking about a set designer's view, it seems timely to move on to the issue of set design.

Set design

What is interesting in this context of man-made materials is that, where set design was concerned, the opposite of the above story was true – new synthetic materials facilitated the task. Products such as polyurethane, vinylite, polystyrene, cellotex and the fast drying paint Astrolex meant that set-building could go much faster and, of course, cost much less. Thus, for example, vinyl-based paint replaced oil-based paint, lightweight polystyrene or plastic mouldings were used instead of wood facsimiles or the real object in cast iron or sandstone (for balconies, paving stones, balustrades, manholes, gaslights, and so on). Cellotex strips were used to muffle sound in sets (e.g., for artificial flooring and platforms). This noise insulation avoided resonance at the same time as it made it possible to use materials lighter than any original would require. This lightness of product meant greater flexibility, but it also, as the great contemporary set designer Max Douy points out, considerably enriched what could be achieved.[34]

Mention has already been made of the dramatic shift in studio practice (from sustaining a permanent staff and equipment to functioning solely on a contract-hiring basis). For the sake of cost effectiveness and productivity, crews became smaller. However, because only the very best were hired, it was also, in some ways, a peak period for consistent quality in studio décor, even though the 1950s marked the decline of the studio. Not all the great technicians got to work, though. Because film production was now run as a capitalist concern, union activity was very unwelcome. Thus, some eminent technicians (such as Henri Alékan) were often overlooked because of their leadership role in the unions. This streamlining of business, however, did lead to some formidable partnerships between film directors and set designers – and of particular interest to us within the context of costume drama were Max Douy with Claude Autant-Lara; Léon Barsacq with René Clair; and Jean d'Eaubonne with Max Ophuls. Less-often mentioned in film history books, but equally significant, were the partnerships between Robert Gys and Christian-Jaque[35] and René Renoux with both Jean Delannoy and Sacha Guitry. If we look at the figure 3.7 below, we can observe just how this attrition of personnel impacted on set design – just over half of all costume dramas were designed by a mere eight set designers, quite remarkable when we consider that it takes two to three months from the initial designs to the completion of building the sets.

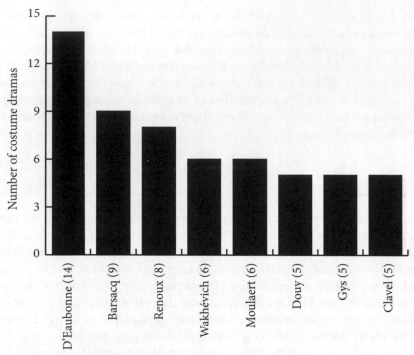

Figure 3.7: Leading costume drama set designers.

Of the eight set designers listed above, apart from Clavel, all were trained up in the late 1920s and 1930s. Clavel began in the early 1940s under the tutelage of Barsacq, Douy and Trauner. Renoux began in the 1920s and was part of the first wave of important set designers of that period which included Gys and d'Eaubonne. The Belgian, Moulaert, came to cinematic set design as early as 1930 after considerable experience in theatre design during the 1920s.[36] He worked from much the same principles as Barsacq, believing that décor must be subsumed to the narrative and shooting needs.[37] Barsacq, d'Eaubonne, Douy, and Wakhévich trained with *the* master of set-design, Lazare Meerson (1900–1938). Meerson's contribution to décor was enormous. He was the first to see décor in terms of framing, lighting and perspective – that is to say, to see set design in architectural terms and then relate his décor to the needs of the camera. He had a brilliant sense of proportion and transferred this skill into his set designs. His sketches took into account camera angles and the different types of optic lenses that would be used. Given the relatively small size of studios, he used reduced scale models in the mid- to back-ground to create the idea of perspectival distance and depth (see, for example, his décor for Clair's *Sous les toits de Paris*, 1930). He believed in using authentic materials for his sets (wood, bricks, etc.). He came to this concept in the 1930s with the introduction of sound. The hollowness of artificial sets resonated. Soundproofing them cost more than using the real thing – in his time cellotex did not yet exist.[38] Meerson's goal was to achieve authenticity, to create a décor that was harmonious with the film, without necessarily striving for realism.[39]

This influence carried forward into the 1950s, particularly in the work of Barsacq and Douy, both of whom conceived their sets in relation to the camera work (framing, angles, and movement). Typically, set designers worked from the scenario and not, like their Hollywood counterparts, from storyboards (a pre-production preparation on paper of shots and sets). Very few set designers went as far as using storyboarding. Douy was one who did with certain directors, in particular Autant-Lara, whom he managed to convince of the efficacy of this system (possibly as a way of containing the director's excesses), and with the film director Clouzot, who always worked from a storyboard.[40] In general, set designers working in the French industry built up ideas around the scenario. They then sketched a series of potential sets to work from, always bearing in mind what lenses were going to be used. This knowledge would be key to their perception. Lenses range from long- to wide-focal lengths – all with different effects. Just to take as an example the more commonly-used lenses: the 100mm and 75mm lenses (long focus length) give a long-shot feel to the frame; they bring a distant subject into focused view but at the expense of diminishing the angle of the view (we cannot see much else); a 50mm is more or less standard to life as we perceive it; 35mm brings things in closer; finally, the 28mm and 24mm wide-angle lenses bring everything in quite close and in focus at the same time. They also give, because of their wide-angle reach and depth of focus, an illusion of depth of field. Clearly, therefore, sets need to be built around the knowledge of how things are going to be framed and what is going to be in the frame. Thus, in constructing any set, a designer has to be aware of the frame size as well as the distance between the camera and the back of the set so that perspective runs true.

Max Douy provides an excellent example of this understanding about the relationship between lenses and set in his description of a bridge shot (done in the studio) for an Autant-Lara film, *La Traversée de Paris* (1956). Overall, the studio space available to recreate the Pont Sully was a mere 33 metres on a diagonal. However, Pont Sully is one of the longest bridges over the Seine and one which straddles diagonally from the left to the right bank of the river across the Ile St Louis. The bridge shot began with a character shouting outside a bistro located on the left-bank Quai des Tournelles. This was held in a 75mm lens to bring the distant character into focus. We see him, but very little of what surrounds him is visible (creating a sense of distance in our own mind's eye). Then, as the camera travelled backwards across the bridge, it shifted to wider and wider lenses to make the bridge seem bigger than it ever could have been in such a small studio space. At the same time, it took in the various landmarks (all constructed in trompe-l'œil) that can be seen as one crosses this diagonal bridge. Lens size went from 75mm to 50mm, followed by 40mm, 35mm, 28mm and, finally, 24mm, by which time the camera had tracked all the way back across the bridge, providing (in an extreme wide-angle shot) the view of Paris from the right-bank end of the bridge in the boulevard Henri IV.[41]

Barsacq reminds us also of the impact of cinemascope on set design. Although not that many costume dramas were shot in this format, it is worth noting the different demands it imposed on set designers. For a start, the set-designer would have to drop the ceilings to accommodate the reduced vertical format. There would also be other impacts on *mise-en-scène*. Given the horizontality of the format, which lessens the sense of depth in the image, objects would need to be more fore-fronted, rather than placed in depth, if they were to be seen. Similarly, instead of going for depth in terms of movement of characters, the director would have to think about moving them in a lateral way; the impact for design is obvious – it, too, would have to function laterally, yield more information to the front and sides than in depth. A major advantage of the 'scope format, according to Barsacq, was that you could have greater fluidity and continuity with your sets. In this same vein of continuity, there was less need to use the technique of shot/reverse angle shot that was so much a convention in dialogue scenes. This, in turn, reduced the complexity and number of the sets to be built – for example the set-designer would not have to construct a reverse-angle fourth wall in the design.[42]

Barsacq believed, like Meerson, that design should be subordinate to the narrative and lend atmospheric support – sets should offer a précis of reality, not reality itself.[43] Thus his designs, particularly of the 1950s, are often light of touch, uncomplex. A good way of seizing the distinctiveness of his style is to compare his décors with those created by Jean d'Eaubonne for Ophuls' films. The ornate, fussy, stylized sets of the latter contrast with the simplicity of Barsacq's designs (see figures 3.8 and 3.9).

Figure 3.8: Gouache by Léon Barsacq for the set in *Bel-Ami* (Louis Daquin, 1954). © Léon Barsacq.

Figure 3.9: Still from *Lola Montès* (Ophuls, 1955), set by Jean d'Eaubonne. © Gamma Films.

The 1950s in general marked a shift from stylization associated with 1930s' and 1940s' décor – itself an effect of both German Expressionism and Poetic Realism – towards a greater, simplified, realism. And this move away from a poetic style to a greater psychological realism also affected costume drama. D'Eaubonne's work in its ornate baroqueness (especially for Ophuls, see 3.9 above) is one major exception, though not the only one. We can count Wakhévich as another ornate designer (even though both he and d'Eaubonne could equally achieve gritty realism) – but overall the trend was one of simplification. This greater realism was something that Douy achieved – even, at times, in extraordinary circumstances, as for example when he worked for Autant-Lara, whose ambitions knew no bounds but whose needs Douy managed, somehow, to rein in and create great sets without huge over-expenditure.[44] He believed that the movement of the characters determined the sets as much as the needs of the camera operator – and indeed, if we look at his sketches, they always take account of the characters in their projected placings.[45] See, for example, his sketch for *Le Rouge et le Noir* (figure 3.10 below).

Douy welcomed the lighter, faster, more flexible materials he had to hand because it meant that he could more readily design his sets in relation to the realism required. As the

Figure 3.10: Max Douy set for *Le Rouge et le Noir* (Claude Autant-Lara, 1954). © Max Douy

1950s progressed, he found the use of enlarged photographs used as backdrops a better, less theatrical, substitute for painted vistas – even though these photographs had to be touched up with colour when shooting in colour.[46] We see instances of this in the garden backdrops for *Le Rouge et le Noir*. Finally, although the loss of the stocks of sets (as a result of the industry's rationalization) was something he deplored, he nonetheless (as with others) turned it to his advantage in his drive for realism. Thus, on the one hand, specialist businesses were used to resource, amongst other things, scaffolding needs for outdoor sets, sculptures, locks – all of which lent to the authentic – and, on the other (more intriguingly), flea-markets and second-hand bric-à-brac shops were used as a source for real objects (because of the poverty, post-war and into the early 1950s, people had to sell their possessions to make ends meet).[47]

We shall return in more detail to our set designers when discussing their work in collaboration with certain directors. We can, however, conclude this section by raising one or two points to consider. The first is a paradox. Both colour and set design – at least in the 1950s – had in common a drive for the natural. In other words, neither sets nor colour were to take our eye away from the narrative, but were there to fill out or complement the content. As Alékan says, it was a case of reproducing the natural rather than striking out.[48] But this is, in and of itself, an odd premise, given that costume dramas are such 'unnatural' products. Even if they appeal in some way to a reality (a period, an historic personage and so on), they are not based in the real. Thus, a tension develops between the drive for natural representation and the unnatural nature of what is being represented. As we shall discover, several film-makers were well aware of this – Ophuls and Renoir immediately come to mind.

We should not, however, read this as meaning that costume dramas are inherently limited or necessarily conservative as a genre – nor of course are they about design alone. But in terms of set design, it is worth reminding ourselves that it conforms to an image we hold of a past, a visual memory. As such, these sets are a composite of real spaces and, in this context, have elements of the hyperreal about them, despite the greater simplicity practised in the 1950s over the 1930s. Sets can be performative and establish a discourse of their own, which may contest the narrative or provide us with a secondary order of reading to the narrative. In this same vein, ambiguity can be encoded into set design. In these various instances, sets can be seen to talk to the political culture of the time. Finally, sets are an action-space once a character starts moving about in it. We need to bear in mind the effects produced by both the body of the actor and the costume they are wearing in this space: does it fit, does it jar? And on that point, it is timely to consider those other significant technicians of the genre: the costume designers.

Costume designers

Costume designers assist the dramatic meaning of the film and create a style based in a number of, not necessarily exclusive, possibilities. The style has four basic starting points. First, the actor – in other words, dressing the body type comes first. Second, design can start from the character; in this instance the designer is addressing the character type (rather than the body type first and foremost). The third starting point can be the narrative. Fourth, and finally, the starting point can be the historical moment. In relation to these last two, it is evident that the designer is seeing the process more globally before homing in onto character and body type. Rosine Delamare is one such designer who takes as her starting point the narrative and historical moment. She begins by making sketches of the ensemble of actors to get the ambience into which her principal actors will fit (see figure 3.11 below as an example of this).

Interestingly, the style can also have as its starting point the costume designer's own favourite penchant for designs and contemporary fashion. Just to cite one example, in the 1950s, this was the case for Escoffier and his fondness for the New Look, with its corseted top and crinolined-skirt effect. In this context, accuracy can very easily go by the board – but, as I explain below, this idea of inaccuracy raises some interesting issues.

In much the same way as we observed the domination of set design by a surprisingly small number of set designers, so we see the same trend with costume designers. A mere six are responsible for over half the decade's output (63 costume dramas out of 109). As we can see from the figure opposite (3.12), in terms of output, the lead designer is Rosine Delamare (with 23 costume dramas to her name). She was an immensely prolific designer of international standing with, during her entire career, some 123 films to her name, of which half are costume dramas.

Figure 3.11: Rosine Delamare's sketches for characters in *Le Rouge et le Noir*. (Claude Autant-Lara, 1954) © Rosine Delamare.

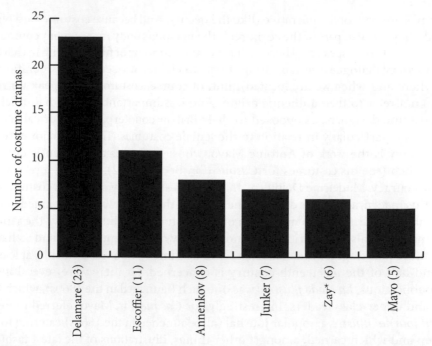

Figure 3.12: Number of costume dramas made by leading costume designers (Jean Zay is asterisked because his record is less easy to assess; most often he was Chief Costumier rather than costume designer per se – as far as I can determine he designed for six costume dramas).

Delamare began her career in the 1930s as a dress designer, working for one of haute-couture's big names of the post-war period (WWI), Jean Patou. Interestingly, Patou's designs went for simplicity of line, whereas, as we shall discover, Delamare's predilection in costume design was for the pretty but slightly over-fussy where women's clothing was concerned.[49] She left Patou's in 1939 and thereafter became a costume designer for cinema for nigh-on forty years. She readily admits her preference for costume dramas above all other genres, and for doing them in studios where she can control the style and get the concept right in close collaboration with the set designer and the director of photography. She is committed to detail (as evidenced by her love of bows and gloves), and also to the authentic within the realms of the possible and the budget. In her view, even though costume dramas do not pretend to be aiming for historical reconstruction, there must be a certain respect for historical accuracy. But even here the designer has to be flexible towards the film-maker's needs and, just as importantly, the actor's body. She cites Martine Carol's somewhat round and petite physique as a case in point – costumes had to bring out her strong features, especially her bosom.[50] In relation to flexibility towards a film-maker's needs, Delamare cites the extremes to which this can go with the instance of working with Autant-Lara on *Le Rouge et le Noir* where he obliged her to get fashion history wrong by lengthening the skirts and tightening the collars on Danielle Darrieux' costumes so she would look more the part of the repressed woman (see figure 3.15).[51]

Costumes are part of the narrative (like the décor). And because costumes are physically inhabited, they are also part of the corporeal (the persona's body makes them come alive). In this context, costumes speak and become part of the economy of film-making in that they cut out unnecessary dialogue or establishing shots (an eighteenth-century aristocratic costume tells us where and when we are located). But, of course, costumes can speak untruthfully if they do not refer to their authentic origin. And it is important to note that in relation to French costume designers, as opposed to their British counterparts, historical accuracy is less rigorous – particularly in relation to the female costumes. The one major exception to this inaccuracy is the work of Antoine Mayo, whose costumes are authentic down to the minutest stitch (see his costumes for *Casque d'or*, Becker, 1952). There is a reason for this greater inaccuracy. Madeleine Delpierre, in her interesting study of French costume dramas, suggests this inaccuracy comes down to the fact that the French were not trained in costume design, unlike the British, who made it an object of study. Nor did they have the same access to the actual originals as the British (i.e., not as many costume museums) and so had to rely on portraiture paintings for their sketches.[52] Yet documentation was available, at least where the second half of the nineteenth century is concerned, for there were several illustrated fashion publications. *La Mode illustrée* was one such (launched in the 1860s), which targeted middle- and upper-class readers. Interestingly, for *Casque d'or*, Mayo referred more readily to *Le Petit journal illustré*, a popular journal (also launched in the 1860s) catering to a broad readership and which carried, amongst other things, illustrations of the latest fashions that would have been worn by the lower and middle classes (rather than the higher echelons of society). These two publications were a wide spectrum apart, since the former was one that would be purchased by women to peruse the colour fashion plates and the second was a supplement to the revolutionarily-conceived paper *Le Petit journal,* which cost very little so that the workers, the poor and other lower classes could purchase it.[53] Thus, images were available to French costume designers – this is not the same of course as having access to real garments – but Delpierre suggests that, temperamentally, they were more inclined to indulge their imagination rather than remaining faithful to documentation.[54] So Mayo stands out as something of an exception – and he is in some ways doubly authentic in that his research took him to the very newspaper that his characters in *Casque d'or* would buy.

However, if we take on board this lack of accuracy, then clearly the document of the costume (to reprise Delamare's words) that we are studying enters into very complex terrains. The impact of the non-authentic, even forgery, or (to play on words) the effect of fabrication surely has to be to falsify the narrative, since costumes are a part of it. What do we make of a costume whose design points more to the contemporary than to the epoch it purports to represent – for example, the cut of an eighteenth-century dress which is more in line with the New Look? Or, again, how do we read a costume which muddles up different fashions of a particular century? Consider the example provided by Delamare, above, where she gave an 1830s' dress a full-lengthed 1890s' skirt, instead of the ankle-length it should have had, and a tight collar as opposed to a more loosely-open one (see figure 3.15 on p. 65 of Danielle Darrieux 'incorrectly' dressed). In the first example, we can see how design is linked to the selling of fashion. In the second, how the body is denied its eroticism (ankle and throat display) and remains repressed. What, finally, do we make of the fact that there is greater imprecision in the female costume than in the male? These are all questions this study will address. But, for now, let us move onto the last section of this contextual chapter: stars.

Stars

It would be impossible to cover all the stars associated with this genre. However, it is interesting to note that there are three female stars and three male stars that recur with greater frequency than any others. These are Martine Carol (9 titles), Danielle Darrieux (8 titles) and Michèle Morgan (7) amongst the women; and Gérard Philipe (8), Jean Marais (5) and Georges Marchal (4) amongst the men. Other female stars with several titles to their name include Danièle Delorme and Dany Robin (5 apiece), Renée Saint-Cyr (4), Françoise Arnoul (3), Jeanne Moreau and Simone Signoret (2 apiece). For male stars: Charles Boyer, Pierre Brasseur, Fernandel and Jean-Claude Pascal (3 apiece), Jean Desailly (2). For our purposes we shall focus on the three leading men and women and offer a brief overview here. As we come to analyse the films, there will be more detailed study of their roles and performances – and, in Part Two, Chapters 6 and 7 will compare their work. Finally, it is worth bearing in mind that these six actors ranked amongst the most popular in France in the 1950s. All had won the French equivalent of the Oscars (the Victoires) at least once. During the 1950s, they figured amongst the top ten grossing stars. And last but not least, they were the six star names that exported best (along with Jean Gabin and, in the late 1950s, Brigitte Bardot).[55]

Let us start with the female stars. Below (figure 3.13) is a chart which allows us to take a comparative overview of them in relation to characterization, representations of desire, and body type:

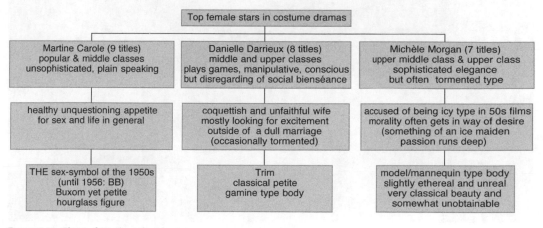

Figure 3.13: Chart of top three female stars.

A first comment that can be made is that, taken together, these three stars cut across the three dominant class groups (popular, middle and upper). Generally speaking, Martine Carol's characters emanate from the popular and the middle classes, although it has to be said that she appears in most films to be almost classless (in the *Caroline* series especially). Alternatively, she is someone who can transcend class, as for example in *Madame Du Barry*. There she moves from her poor beginnings to infiltrate the aristocracy and become the king's mistress. She is depicted as loose and frivolous (superficially at least; a deeper probing reveals other readings). Even when she plays bourgeois roles her demeanour does not change. In her classlessness and sexual ease she obviously pre-figures Brigitte Bardot (a later fifties' icon of sexual liberation). But she is also well ahead of the spirit of the age, which is what makes her such an interesting star to study – as we can see from her nude display in figure below (3.14).[56] France of the 1950s, despite being a Republic, was still a hierarchical and class-conscious nation. Politically and socially, as we have explained in Chapter 1, it was a repressed nation – one that was not yet ready for the sexual freedom of women or, indeed, a blurring of social boundaries, all of which Carol in her roles embodied.

Figure 3.14: Figure of Martine Carol in the nude from *Un Caprice de Caroline Chérie*. (Devaivre, 1952) © 1952 Gaumont.

Danièle Darrieux's roles predominantly lie on the cusp between middle and upper middle classes, between the bourgeoisie and the small aristocracy. She is frequently depicted as having loose morals, sometimes being victim of her circumstances but often quite manipulative. Michèle Morgan is decidedly not loose: she can be quite icy in her demeanour, even if we can sense a desiring being beneath that exterior, and, on the whole, her roles emanate from the upper crust of society, although there are roles where she plays an upper-middle-class woman who has had to take up running a business out of necessity (being a widow for example). With Carol's roles, whatever her class, she is feisty, rapid-firing with her witty responses to the criticisms or rudeness of others. Her verbal verve is matched by her healthy and unquestioning appetite for sex. Hers is a raucous sexuality that often spills out of her costumes, even to the point of nudity (see figure 3.14 above). And we must pause and wonder at this representation, since it is so distinct from the other two female stars. Darrieux's main struggle is trying to overcome a sexuality that she has given away all too easily (see figure 3.15 below). Her characterizations are particularly interesting to investigate, since she occupies several liminal spaces – socially and in relation to desire.

Figure 3.15: Danielle Darrieux (incorrectly dressed) as prim and proper but anticipating adultery! In *Le Rouge et le Noir*. © *1954 Gaumont (France)/ Documenta Film (Italy)*.

Figure 3.16: Michèle Morgan in *Les Grandes manoeuvres* (Clair, 1955). © Filmsonor.

Located somewhere between the prim and the unfaithful, she takes risks and suffers. She embodies a kind of social and sexual *ennui* for which only illicit sexuality can bring any sense of freedom (however short-lived or spurious).

Morgan and Darrieux are two sides of the same coin in terms of bourgeois respectability (one has it; the other is always at risk of losing it). Morgan is never on the cusp. Socially she is always in one clearly-defined class or the other. She is extremely conscious of social boundaries and, for that reason, dominates her sexuality insofar as she refuses to give it away (as opposed to Darrieux) or to negotiate with it (as opposed to Carol). If she loves, it is mostly without sex, without yielding the body (see figure 3.16 below). And how right she is! Her men, on the whole, let her down through their venality or insensitivity, and even to the point of her perishing for their moral betrayal of her pure love. All three women have complex characterizations in one way or another. Either they are caught within numerous tensions that often oppress them, as with Darrieux or Morgan's roles. Or, like Martine Carol, they are emblematic of a free spirit that was not actually consonant with the contemporary times – the 1950s was still full of repression where women were concerned, a truth more readily exemplified, perhaps, by Darrieux and Morgan's characters.

Carol's freer sexuality as a major star creates an interesting anomaly in relation to the other two female stars, Darrieux and Morgan, and merits consideration. In the second half of the 1950s, Brigitte Bardot and, in more secondary roles, Dany Carel would carry this tradition forward. But, where Carol's career is concerned, we are talking of the more conservative era of the first half of the 1950s. A first answer to the anomaly can be found in the fact that, predominantly, Carol's roles are not set in the nineteenth century but in the late eighteenth (see her *Madame Du Barry* or her *Caroline* series). The main exceptions to this are her two 1955 films, *Lola Montès* (Ophuls) and *Nana* (Christian-Jaque), both set in the Second Empire. In her eighteenth-century roles, as Du Barry or Caroline, she quickly loses her virtue and the films' narratives are decidedly comedy capers rather than serious texts grounded in real history. But, be that as it may, there is a greater freedom and sexual insouciance matched by a less-constraining costuming than that represented in the nineteenth-century costume dramas. We could argue that Carol is made to represent the easy morals of a decadent pre-revolutionary period, for which she will get punished (guillotined in *Madame Du Barry*, successively raped in the *Caroline* series), but she has such fun with it all that this seems a bit of an unlikely interpretation, in my view. Her location in a more distant time and her embodiment as an anti-Republican subject do, however, make it easier to represent sex as naughty-fun – especially if we pause to consider her nineteenth-century roles as Lola and Nana, where the stories are far bleaker and embedded in a greater sense of (hypocritical) propriety which, most definitely, cannot tolerate her easy virtue. A second answer lies in the projection of male fantasies onto Carol as the sexually-free and available woman. She was, after all, *the* female sex symbol of the 1950s, losing her place to Brigitte Bardot only in 1956. It is significant that the female body (Carol's) is very much represented in these films as a 'permissived' body. By that, I mean the men 'allow' her free reign to exercise her sexuality, but, in reality, it is never out of their control. Indeed, she is passed or passes from man to man, very much a pawn in their game. Any superficial impression of her characters agencing their own desire is very quickly put to rest by the narrative, which all too readily exploits this so-called free sexuality. That being said, it is important to note its presence in a period when France was far from endorsing loose morality, with its emphasis on the family and increasing the demography through childbirth. We also need to make the point that, in these roles, there is something that anticipates the sexual freedom embodied by Bardot in the latter half of the 1950s.

Let us now consider the three male stars in our cohort (see figure 3.17 below). Of the three, once again only one traverses class: Gérard Philipe. Either he is a man of humble origins who will stop at nothing to get to the top (including using women), or, alternatively, he is of a certain military class who behaves like a cad to get the woman (only occasionally experiencing some remorse). Whilst he may be insubordinate towards authority, he is, nonetheless, a soldier whose courage is never in doubt. And only once is he truly good, as Till in *Les Aventures de Till l'Espiègle* (Philipe, 1956).

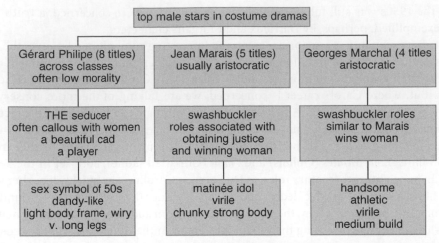

Figure 3.17: Chart of top three male stars.

Of the three, it is Gérard Philipe who most readily embodies a complex characterization. Jean Marais and Georges Marchal are more immediately associated with conventional displays of masculinity – heroic swashbucklers *par excellence* they get their woman in the end by means most honourable, on the whole (see figures 3.18–3.20 below). Marais does occasionally get a more ambiguous role, as with *Le Nez de cuir* (Allégret, 1952) in which he callously deflowers the local wenches and female aristocracy until he meets, too late, the love of his life. Even his physical deformity (hence the nose mask) does not excuse his bad behaviour. For his part, Philipe is often *not* heroic morally, nor does he offer the spectator a typical display of masculinity. His body type is long and languorous, not virile and muscular in the way of both Marais and Marchal. He mostly wins his fights through his intelligence, fencing mastery and sleight of body (he can make himself disappear if things get too hot). His tall, light, body frame plus his exceptionally long legs equip him well to appear more unseizable, less corporeally present than the other two costume drama stars. A seducer, his sexuality is ultimately more free, albeit more scary to observe because of his steely characterization. Whereas Philipe has incontrovertible sex-appeal, and is attractive in his beauty and cruelty to both men and women, Marais is more of a matinée idol: a woman's man, virile yet soft-centred.[57] As for Marchal, he is typified by no-nonsense roles and, as such, very much of a straight man in his swashbuckling endeavours (for example as D'Artagnan, the fourth musketeer in *Les Trois Mousquetaires*, Hunebelle, 1953). In some ways he is more ordinary, easier for men to identify with, and so he comes over very much as a man's man.

Later chapters are going to develop further on these star personas and their roles in the 1950s' costume drama. But we can already observe that, within this genre at least, there are some interesting reversals of note. Given that the real situation for women in 1950s' France was

Figure 3.18: Gérard Philipe as handsome cad in *Les Grandes manoeuvres*. © Filmsonor.

Figure 3.19: Jean Marais as the elegant Comte de Monte-Cristo (*Le Comte de Monte-Cristo*, Vernay, 1955). © Sirius Films.

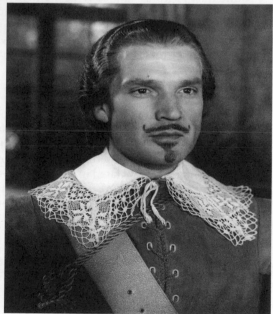

Figure 3.20: The virile Georges Marchal (publicity still). © Pathé Consortium Cinema.

one that struggled to recognize her legitimacy (enfranchisement) and attempted to contain her (through discourses around domesticity and procreation), it is noteworthy that the female roles should be more invested with complexities than those of their male counterparts, an investment which finds echo (as we saw earlier) with the much more complex nature of the costumes themselves. We can speculate that, in terms of audiences, female pleasure in viewing must have been quite considerable. Not only did women spectators get to see beautiful costumes, they also got to observe female stars enacting roles that portrayed women as complex individuals with difficult situations to confront and resolve. Costume dramas, then, offered the possibility of more rounded roles for women than in other, more male-dominated, genres such as the thriller and comedy, and, as such, they stand out as an important exception for us to investigate. This is precisely what the following chapters set out to do.

Notes

1. Other factors contributed to the slow take-up. At first, exhibitors were uncertain as to which of the two new systems – cinemascope or 3-D – would take off (*La Cinématographie française*, No. 1525, 4.7.1953, pp. 11–14).
2. Edouard Lardillier (1953) 'Le Cinémascope dans les salles', *La Cinématographie française*, No. 1525, 4.7.1953, pp. 45–6. Curious film scholars might like to know that during the early 1950s this trade magazine carries article after article on effects of colour and cinemascope. It also devotes numerous pages in each issue to the newly refurbished cinema theatres; by looking at these theatres in all their splendour we can well understand the shock to exhibitors when they learnt they needed to do still more!
3. Yves Allégret (1955) in a series of interviews of film-makers on the qualities and merits of cinemascope conducted by *La Cinématographie française*, No. 1607, 26.2.1955, p. 4 (no given article title).
4. See Gilberte Turquan (1953) 'Films de prestige: prestige d'élégance', *La Cinématographie française*, No. 1530, 22.8.1953, pp. 43–6.
5. The first costume drama in cinemascope and Eastmancolor was in fact *Frou-Frou* also released in 1955 a month before *Lola Montès*. Its production dates also place it before Ophuls' film (the former began shooting three months before the latter).
6. See Léon Barsacq's very useful study on colour in his book (1970, pp. 122–33).
7. Christian-Jaque paraphrased in Arnaud Chapuy (2001, p. 33).
8. See Crisp (1993, p. 143). We need to recall that at this juncture France was not yet hit by the effect of TV, let alone colour TV – this phenomenon would not start to make its impact until the early 1960s, with colour coming in early 1970s.
9. Chapuy (2001, p. 32).
10. Colin Crisp (1993, p. 82) tells us there were 382 co-productions of which 325 were with Italy (85%). Because his figures were so far astray of my own findings, I decided to check his source and am still unsure how he comes to these figures. He quotes *Le Film français* Special Spring Issue of 1961 (884–5). I have referred to this document and find that the listing of co-productions stretches from 1954 to 1961 (not the 1950s as Crisp states). The figure I come up with is 234 co-productions for the period 1954–61. The chart in *Le Film français* refers to actual co-productions which count as French films (because of preponderance of funding). An earlier 1960 special issue

of *Le Film français* (817–818) provides yet other figures. It numbers 212 co-productions out of a total number of French and French co-produced films of 972 (see page 85). This agrees with my own research based on a trawl of *Le Film français* from 1951–1960. Sabria's very comprehensive *Cinéma français: Les Années 50* (Paris, Centre Georges Pompidou, 1988) provides a slightly different picture, namely that, for the 1950s, the number of co-productions that count as French (because the majority financing is French), comes to 238 films of which 174 are with Italy (73%). According to my research, in 1953 there was a threefold increase in French co-productions overall from an average of eleven per year (over the period 1950–2) to 32 films – and 27 in 1954. Thereafter the average remained around 26 co-productions per year (1955–8), after which there was a big upswing again, this time to 42 in 1959 – yielding a percentage figure of 24% of all films made in the 1950s in France. Laurent Creton's (2004, p. 221, n.5) figures tally more closely with my own, with a percentage average of 29% for the period 1953–61. Bonnell (1989, p. 54) yields a figure of 23%. According to Crisp's figures, however, we could be looking as high as a figure of 38% of co-productions in relation to *total* output for the decade. But I am not clear as to how he arrived at this. What we can deduce from all of the above is that it is very difficult to be absolutely precise – and that even the industry's own publications are imprecise or seem to give us more than one set of figures. In each eventuality, however, the actual percentage figures come out fairly consistently the same, whichever sets of figures one works from.

11. See Crisp (op. cit., pp. 121–8) for more details.

12. Chapuy, op. cit., p. 34.

13. All figures come from *Le Film français* (1951–1960). Specifically their Special Winter Issues (usually early February) as follows: Issues number 330–1 (1951, 7); 390–1 (1952, 3); 444–5 (1953, 9); 500–1 (1954, 15: this issue revises figures for 1950–53); 556–7 (1955, 15); 611–2 (1956, 17); 666–7 (1957, 13–6); 708–9 (1958, 69–70); 765–6 (1959, 67–70); 817–8 (1960, 5–6 & 79–86).

14. Maurice Bessy in his series of Editorials 'Qu'est-ce qui ne va pas dans le cinéma?' provides an interesting overview of these shifts in consumerism (*Le Film français* No. 749, 10.10.1958, p. 4; No. 750, 17.10.1958, p. 5).

15. See *Le Film français* No. 487, 6.11.1953, p. 2.

16. Consumption practices included buying vinyl records, listening to pop radio, purchasing scooters. Of less impact was television which, by 1957 and in terms of domestic access, only covered half the territory (from north east to south east France). The whole territory would not have access until 1960. See also Pierre Autré's overview of the French film industry 'Panorama 1959' *Le Film français* (Special Winter Issue 817-8, p. 6).

17. For full details of the *'fonds de soutien'*, see the following issues of *Le Film français*, No. 788, 25.06.1959; No. 789, 3.07.1959; No. 808, 27.11.1959; No. 815, 15.01.1960.

18. See *Le Film français* No. 548, 24.12.1954, p. 3. Titles are: *Si Versailles m'était conté* (7m audience), *Le Rouge et le Noir* (4 m), *Ali Baba et les 40 voleurs* (4 m), *Cadet Rousselle* (4m), *La Reine Margot* (3m).

19. Dudley Andrew (2006, p. 46) speaks of Gevacolor as a subsidiary of Agfa, implying a benign development – whereas Colin Crisp (op. cit., p. 138) speaks in terms of industrial looting post-war of the Agfa system producing derivatives such as 'Gevacolor in Belgium, Fuji in Japan, Ferriania in Italy, and Sovocolor in USSR.'

20. For a series of informative articles in depth on all of these issues see *La Cinématographie française*, No. 1530 (22.8.1953), pp. 43–6; and No. 1538 (17.10.1953), pp. 24–50.

21. As early as January 1950, Dr Herbert T. Kalmus announced he wanted to open processing laboratories in Paris and Rome. But the respective governments clearly blocked this. See *Le Film français*, No. 268, 20.01.1950, p. 4 (no author name or title given).

22. See Barsacq, op. cit., pp. 128–9.
23. By 1953, the French *Compagnie Française des Lampes* had designed the appropriate projectors. The first Technicolor film to use these specialized French lamps was *Lucrèce Borgia* (see Gilberte Turquan's useful article 'Problème d'élégance: les films en couleur', *La Cinématographie française*, No.1501, 17.1.1953, pp. 35–8).
24. Around 5,500 kelvin degrees as opposed to Eastmancolor and Gevacolor which need around 2000–3000 (*La Cinématographie française*, No. 1538, 17.10.1953, p. 34).
25. Full figures for the 156 colour films in the 1950s are as follows:

    Eastmancolor: 96 (60%)
    Technicolor: 20 (13%)
    Agfacolor: 18 (12%)
    Gevacolor: 15 (10%)
    Ferrianacolor: 7 (5%).

    We can see that Agfa actually edges Gevacolor out (albeit only by 2%) where all colour films produced are concerned, reversing the figures for choice of colour for costume dramas where Gevacolor edged out Agfa by 10 to 2. A study of the spread of colour usage during the 1950s shows Agfa taking over from Geva by the mid-1950s. Geva has 15 colour films from 1951 to 1955, thereafter it is dropped; Agfa is sporadic in the early 1950s but by 1956 it replaces Geva in terms of the European colour choice with 13 out of its 18 titles coming in those last three years of the decade.

26 Dudley Andrew, op. cit., p. 44. Andrew writes very interestingly in this chapter about the rivalry between Hollywood and Europe over colour, and the ideological readings we can take from eventual preferences. There are a couple of points he makes that I would nuance, however. On page 47 he remarks that Eastmancolor was not strongly felt in Europe until 1955. My findings are that 1954 was the first peak year for its use, at least in France. He also claims that pre-New Wave directors moved France into colour in the late1950s. Again my findings are different. France had two peak years in the 1950s for colour (1954 with 23 and 1956 with 32) and, thereafter, colour diminished quite significantly (16 in 1959). Crisp also finds that disaffection with colour set in after 1956 and lasted for a decade (op. cit., p. 141).
27 Max Douy interviewed by Berthomé (1981b, pp. 28–9).
28 See *La Cinématographie française*, No. 1538, 17.10.1953, p. 25.
29 Rosine Delamare interviewed by Niogret (1996, pp. 55, 56).
30 Douy quoted in Berthomé (1981b, p. 28).
31 See Barsacq, op. cit., p. 129.
32 Barsacq in *La Cinématographie française*, No. 1538, 17.10.1953, pp. 38–9. His input is part of an extended dossier on colour in this particular issue of *Cinématographie française* which interviews many set designers and some DPs (no given article title).
33 Barsacq in *La Cinématographie française*, No. 1538, 17.10.1953, pp. 38–9.
34 Douy (2003, p. 137).
35 In the 1930s Gys formed an equally important partnership with René Clair.
36 He had some 2000 decors to his credit by the time he turned to film (see Tachela, 'L'Envers du décor: *Patrie*', *L'Ecran français*, No. 23, December 1945, pp. 10–11).
37 Ibid.
38 The set designer Georges Wakhévich interviewed by Cuel and Bezombes (1982, p. 6) supplied this information.
39 Touati (1988, p. 30).

40 See Douy (in Berthomé 1981a, p. 12) and Barsacq (op. cit., pp. 144–5).

41 See Douy (in Berthomé 1981b, p. 24).

42 See Barsacq, op. cit., pp. 135–6.

43 Votolato (2000, p. 66).

44 Berthomé (2003, p. 194).

45 See Douy (2003).

46 This was not the very first time this idea of the photo back-drop was used. Wakhévich found it a good solution to an effect he wanted to create in Renoir's *Mme Bovary* (1934) (see interview with Cuel et Bezombes, op. cit., p. 8).

47 Douy , op.cit., p. 135.

48 See Crisp, op. cit., p. 390.

49 In the 1920s, Patou dressed the tennis star Suzanne Lenglen. In fact, Patou was the pioneer in sportswear for women. The first to design trouser sportswear for women, his designs were adopted by the 'garçonnes' of the 1920s (a term used to refer to independent young women who liked sports and wearing sporty attire).

50 Rosine Delamare interviewed by Niogret, op. cit., p. 54.

51 Ibid., p. 58.

52 Delpierre (1988, pp. 22–3).

53 *Le Petit journal* was subject to intense censorship and scrutiny. Feared by the government for its appeal to the masses, it was not allowed to publish anything on the political front and, if it did so, it was severely fined.

54 Delpierre (op. cit., pp. 22–3).

55 For these details consult *La Cinématographie française* No. 1650, 0701.1956, p.3; *Le Film français* No. 675–676, Special Spring Issue, 71; *Le Film français* No. 725, 18.04.1958, p. 9.

56 I have written at great length about another female star, Simone Signoret, who also broke many of the moulds of the 1950s (see Hayward, 2004). She challenged these representations of femininity as contained far more directly than Martine Carol ever did. Moreover she proposed, through her roles, positions of agency which Carol was never able to (or wanted to) espouse. Yet, given the huge popularity of Carol, it is important for us to recognize her own mould-breaking impact during this stifling decade.

57 Most of us by now are familiar with Marais' gay sexuality, but it certainly does not make his performance style any more or less camp than, say, Philipe's. This is not to say, however, that there might not be times when our understanding of his characterizations might benefit from a queer reading. It should also be borne in mind that Marais was one of the most popular stars of that decade, as attested to by the fan-based mail written about him (see Sellier, 2009, pp. 78–9).

Part II

Fairytales, Foxy Women and Swashbuckling Heroes

Chapter 4

Costume Drama from Late-Medieval to the Eighteenth Century:
An Overview

This part of the book encompasses a broad historical sweep – five centuries to be precise (see figure 4.1 below). For this reason the approach adopted here is primarily generic, although, when it comes to detailed analysis of particular films, they will be considered against the relevant socio-political contexts. The 34 films under review here fall into three convenient generic types (see figure 4.2 below). Intriguingly, the further back we move in history the more male-centred narratives dominate: 23 in all (67 per cent). This contrasts quite noticeably with the nineteenth-century narratives, in particular the Belle Epoque costume dramas, where there is a greater percentage of female-centred narrative (see Parts Three and Four).

In figure 4.1 below, the 23 male-centred narratives are marked with an asterisk. Interestingly, just over half (twelve) are swashbuckler films. Even the fairytales are male – relating the stories of Ali-Baba, Bluebeard, and Quasimodo (see figure 4.2 below). Leaving aside Camilla of *Le Carrosse d'or* (of which more below), a mere eight narratives place women at the centre (these are marked in figure 4.1 with a §). In virtually all circumstances, these women are of dubious morals, scheming harlots and even murderers. The single exception is Marie-Antoinette, who, by contrast, gets reasonable press. All are women of the court, whether noblewomen, mistresses, or queens.

The male to female imbalance where narratives are concerned should not surprise, given the literary sources for most of these films (e.g., five Dumas swashbuckler novels). But the image of early history taught in schools during the nineteenth and the first 60 years of the twentieth century is also a contributing factor. The focus of *that* history has typically been upon Great Men who, arguably, shaped France – in a curious way before what France of the 1950s so lacked until, that is, General de Gaulle came to power in 1958 and launched his own 'politique de grandeur/politics of greatness' for his beloved nation. However, the interesting part of the story revealed by this corpus of films is that Great Men, in the form of kings, astute politicians or military leaders, do not figure – almost as if the film culture was aware that the current period was, itself, lacking leadership. We shall come to see a similar pattern in the nineteenth-century narratives. For all his historical 'greatness', the Napoleon who is portrayed to us is a flawed character by any stretch of the imagination. Napoleon III fares a little better, but is represented as more avuncular than as a man of stature.

The men we have before us in the above corpus are adventurers, ordinary men, occasionally noblemen, who fight for fairness, or to rout a bully; at times to even defend France's honour. The task of representing the 'grandeur' of Royal France falls to the women – and what a shady lot they are; even Marie-Antoinette in her profligacy is not spared the rod. It would, perhaps,

ME/REN

14–15th century: 9	16th century: 3	17th century: 8	18th century: 14
Barbe-bleue*	Les Aventures de Till L'Espiègle*	Les Trois Mousquetaires*	Le Dieu a besoin des hommes*
Buridan héros de la tour de Nesle*	La Reine Margot§	Le Vicomte de Bragelonne*	Fanfan la tulipe*
Lucrèce Borgia§		L'Affaire des poisons§	Le Carrosse d'or§
Ali-Baba et les 40 voleurs*		Don Juan*	Cadet Rousselle*
La Tour de Nesle*		Les Sorcières de Salem*	Madame du Barry§
Notre-Dame de Paris*		La Tour, prends garde!*	Marie-Antoinette Reine de France§
			Caroline chérie§
			La Bigorne, caporal de France*
			L'Aventurier de Séville*

Films not discussed – but set in this period

Le Chemin de Damas* (Glass 1953)	Le Marchand de Venise* (Billon, 1953) **810,582**	Si Versailles m'était conté (Guitry, 1954) **6,986,788**	Véronique§ (Vernay, 1950) **1,927,942**
Les Destinées§ (Delannoy, 1954) **1,181,231**		Le Bourgeois gentilhomme* (Meyer, 1958) **961,947**	Jocelyn* (De Casembroot, 1952) **1,297,239**
Si Paris nous était contée (Guitry, 1956) **2,813,682**			Les Révoltés de Lomanach* (Pottier, 1954) **1,830,168** Les Aventures de Gil Blas de Santillane* (Jolivet, 1956) **1,108,273** Le Mariage de Figaro* (Meyer, 1959)

Figure 4.1: Costume dramas set in late-Medieval times to the eighteenth century (*denotes the male-centred narratives; § female-centred ones). Films of these periods listed under 'not discussed' are included here with directors and dates and audience figures (in bold where available). Figure 4.2 and 4.3 will supply details for the films to be discussed.

be too simple to argue – but it is tempting to do so nonetheless – that the men embody, metaphorically at least, the thrusting Republican ideals of the free individual: beholden to no one, the self-made man who believes in equality and brotherhood. Viewed in this light, it is not difficult to propose that masculinity here stands for the French Republican Triumvirate, *Liberté, Egalité, et Fraternité* newly returned to France in the form of the Fourth Republic.

Conversely, the women represent the anti-Republican values of the sickly, morally-corrupt *Ancien Régime* and all its predecessors.

Let us not forget that the period 1944–1958 saw France endowed with a new Republic and, after nearly two years of deliberation, a new constitution (1946). This long delay says a great deal about the factionalism and power struggles that prevailed in the country between the political parties of the Left and Right. France was not the harmonious nation it so desperately tried to represent itself as being, with its discourses of national unity (mostly centred around the myth of the Resistance). Indeed, political France was hounded, just like the former Third Republic, both by political unrest and political immobilism. But this unease also lies deeply embedded in the French psyche in that part of France's insecurity and political instability stems from the nation's deep ambivalence regarding the legitimacy of its Republicanism. Uncertainty about the legitimacy of the Republican regime (to say nothing of its durability and desirability) finds its roots in the political cultural climate that dates back to the Revolution. Arguably, therefore, many of these films before us reveal a nostalgia for a different type of masculinity, one untrammelled by murky political issues but that goes straight to the heart of the matter: a simple plain-speaking masculinity that makes itself accountable through action rather than words – the perfect swashbuckler in fact. Thus, as cultural historian Pascal Ory reminds us, these films function at a symbolic level to alleviate the very real problems experienced by audiences and, as such, they speak to a perceived need for greater ideological simplicity in the face of the lack of clarity of the 1950s' political climate.[1] As we move through this part of the book, however, we shall discover that, whilst the above holds true, the actual picture to emerge is intriguingly more complex.

But first let us start by setting out the three generic types – Fairytales, Foxy Women and Swashbuckling Heroes (figure 4.2).

If we look at the attendance figures for *Fanfan la tulipe* (nearly 7 million), it is unsurprising that there was an attempt to repeat this successful formula. And with the exception of *Buridan héros de la tour de Nesle*, all swashbuckler films commanded impressive audiences, doubtless aided in part by the presence of a leading star. But we note also that the two other generic types drew audiences of similar sizes. Christian-Jaque comes out as something of a specialist in all three types, with four titles. Hunebelle strikes a chord with his two swashbuckler films having the greatest appeal after Christian-Jaque's *Fanfan*. Finally, Delannoy – who also made *Le Dieu a besoin des hommes* (with a 2.7 million audience) – has two back-to-back 1956 box-office hits to his name: the spectacular *Notre-Dame de Paris* and the consummate heritage film *avant la lettre*, shot in Technicolor, *Marie-Antoinette Reine de France*.

The examination of these three dominant generic types falls into three distinct chapters (along the headings of figure 4.2 below). The primary approach in Chapter 5 is to discuss the fairytales from the point of view of colour and décor. This seems appropriate since, from quite early on in film practice, colour was assimilated with the concept of fantasy (as opposed to monochrome for realism). And as we shall see, décor plays a significant role in the construction of the concept of the 'monstrous' male – be it the devilish wife-killer Bluebeard, the truly ugly Quasimodo (of *Notre-Dame de Paris*), or the various forces of

Fairytales	Foxy Women	Swashbucklers
Barbe-bleue (51) Christian-Jaque/[Pierre Brasseur] **2,662,329**	*Lucrèce Borgia* (53) Christian-Jaque/[Martine Carol] **3,632,139**	*Fanfan la tulipe* (March 52) Christian-Jaque/[Gérard Philipe] **6,712,512**
Ali-Baba et les 40 voleurs (54) Becker/[Fernandel] **4,117,641**	*La Reine Margot* (54) Dréville/[Jeanne Moreau] **2,600,759**	*Buridan héros de la tour de Nesle* (October 52) Couzinet/no major star **637,199**
Notre-Dame de Paris (56) Delannoy/[Anthony Quinn] **5,639,719**	*Madame du Barry* (54) Christian-Jaque/[Martine Carol] **2,378,009**	*Les Trois Mousquetaires* (53) Hunebelle/[Georges Marchal] **5,354,739**
	L'Affaire des poisons (55) Decoin/[Danielle Darrieux] **1,507,420**	*L'Aventurier de Séville* (54) Vadja/[Mariano] **2,487,427**
	Marie-Antoinette Reine de France (56) Delannoy/[Michèle Morgan] **2,280,704**	*Le Vicomte de Bragelonne* (54) Cerchi/[Georges Marchal] **2,399,675**
	Caroline chérie (51) Pottier/[Martine Carol] **3,184,380**	*Cadet Rousselle* (54) Hunebelle/[François Périer] **3,995,468**
		La Tour de Nesle (55) Gance/[Pierre Brasseur] **2,191,984**
		Les Aventures de Gil Blas de Santillane (56) Jolivet/[Georges Marchal] **1,108,273**
		Les Aventures de Till L'Espiègle (56) Philipe/[Gérard Philipe] **2,304,114**
		Don Juan (56) Berry/[Fernandel] **3,442,334**
		La Bigorne, caporal de France (58) Darène/[François Périer] **1,165,131**
		La Tour, prends garde! (58) Lampin/[Jean Marais] **2,311,061**

Figure 4.2: Films by generic type, year of release in parenthesis, director, star vehicle, audience figures in bold.

Oriental skulduggery that Ali-Baba has to overcome. Chapter 5 offers a study of the queens and schemers. Part of the chapter takes the four leading women stars – Darrieux, Moreau, Morgan and Carol – on board in a comparative study of their performance styles. Chapter 6 looks at the swashbucklers. The first film to launch this type in the 1950s was the enormously successful *Fanfan la tulipe*, starring Gérard Philipe. The eleven other titles are all in some way speaking to this prototype, and we shall examine in what way they do this. In so doing, it is fitting to compare the three major stars of this costume drama genre: Gérard Philipe, Georges Marchal and Jean Marais.

Then there is the handful of films that fail to fit any of the three generic types, some of which I will now address in a little detail. One could argue that Renoir's *Le Carrosse d'or*, which has a lead female character (Camilla) within the ensemble of players, is something of a fairytale, with its golden coach. However, it is as much a homage to the Italian *Comedia dell'arte* as a flight of fancy; nor does it fit in the foxy women category, since Camilla is, as I show below, a straight-speaking, golden-hearted woman. Next is Rouleau's *Les Sorcières de Salem*. This adaptation of Arthur Miller's play *The Crucible*, stands out as the most ostensibly political and politicized film of the 34 films under consideration here. I have written about this film elsewhere and shall only rehearse the main arguments, therefore.[2] There are three adaptations of plays that are not about swashbucklers (*Le Marchand de Venise*, *Le Bourgeois gentilhomme* and *Le Mariage de Figaro*); an adaptation of Lamartine's massive epic Romantic poem *Jocelyn*; a peplum, *Le Chemin de Damas*; and an adaptation of an operetta, *Véronique* – none of which I have managed to track down and see, so they remain outside of my discussion. Two other films, by Guitry are sketch films (*Si Versailles m'était conté* and *Si Paris nous était conté*) and do not really fit into any category with ease, so they, too, are left aside. The other film not to fit the generic types above, but which I shall consider, is Delannoy's *Le Dieu a besoin des hommes*. The rest of this chapter, then, will be taken up with a brief discussion of Rouleau, Delannoy and Renoir's films.

Three for the pot: A trio partita for tolerance

Les Sorcières de Salem (1957) Rouleau
1,686,749

Le Dieu a besoin des hommes (1950) Delannoy
2,745,065

Le Carosse d'or (1953) Renoir
780,205

Figure 4.3: Films by Rouleau, Delannoy and Renoir, title, dates and audience figures (in bold).

Les Sorcières de Salem (1957)

Rouleau's film *Les Sorcières de Salem* needs to be read as a plea for political tolerance against the ruthless practices of HUAC (as we shall see again, when discussing John Berry's *Tamango* in Chapter 10, its political value as both an anti-racist and an anti-HUAC film comes to the fore). Although set in the seventeenth century, the story is effectively to be read as a denunciation of the execution of Ethel and Julius Rosenberg (in 1953), who were put to death as spies in the service of the communist USSR. There is another edge to the film however. It was one of the four French co-produced films of the mid-1950s made with communist bloc countries – the others being *Les Aventures de Till l'Espiègle*, *Les Misérables* and *Bel-Ami* (of which, more in later chapters). Whilst French production companies saw this as a chance to diminish their own costs, the communist countries seized upon the cultural exchange as a means of propaganda. And it is significant that all four directors involved were, in fact, either French Communist Party members or sympathizers to the cause.[3] In the case of *Les Sorcières de Salem*, the deal was struck with East Germany and the production company DEFA. It was shot in the East Berlin Babelsberg studios over the period from early August to mid-October 1956, with the production team leaving for the Paris studios to complete the film one week before the brutal crushing of the Hungarian Revolution (23 October–10 November 1956). Thus, whilst its starting point certainly was – as with the original intention of its author Arthur Miller – the intolerance of the United States towards communism, now it could not help but also speak to the political intolerance from the other side of the Iron Curtain. As we shall see in with Philipe's *Les Aventures de Till l'Espiègle* (the first of these four co-productions and shot in early 1956), this unhappy conjuncture with the Hungarian crisis caused both Philipe and Rouleau's films to be pilloried in the critical reviews of the time, even if they were reasonable box-office successes.

The story of *Les Sorcières de Salem* is set in Salem, Massachusetts in 1692: a puritan stronghold in America. The local leaders, driven by greed and a desire to hold onto their power, use any means necessary – especially in the form of witch-hunts – to suppress dissenters, such as the less than compliant John Proctor (Yves Montand). A young woman, Abigail (Mylène Demangeot), is obsessed with John but, once he refuses to continue sleeping with her out of respect for his wife Elizabeth (Simone Signoret), she denounces him to the authorities as indulging in witchcraft. This is all the leaders are waiting for. They seize him, give him a summary trial and find him guilty. They will only spare him if he signs a confession to his non-existent crime of witchcraft. After a painful tussle with his conscience and with the support of his wife, he refuses to collude with those who condemn him and he is executed. The effect is to galvanize the citizens of Salem and to chase the witch-hunters out of town.

Rouleau's film is heavily layered with political meanings and intertexts. The allegorical value of this film – a manifesto against the abuse of human rights, indiscriminate torture and irrational sentencings to death based on hearsay and greed – stands out just as clearly as a political message about the times being endured in France (censorship and torture in the context of the Algerian war), the United States, and the countries of the communist bloc (the show trials and purges of political undesirables). Above all, the film stands, through the mouthpiece of the Proctors, for the exercise of free speech. It is hard to be more universally topical than this.

Le Dieu a besoin des hommes (1950)

Delannoy's *Le Dieu a besoin des hommes*, would appear to veer in precisely the opposite direction. And yet – on this tiny, isolated, desperately-savage Breton island, Ile de Sein, where people can barely survive, there is one man, Thomas (Pierre Fresnay) whose compassion for humankind and understanding of human weakness and brutality makes him stand out as a beacon of tolerance. In order to survive, the islanders pillage shipwrecks (it is possible they cause the ships' demise in the first case). Their last priest could not tolerate their bestial ways and abandoned them. Thomas, the church's sexton, knows all the religious rituals and gradually allows himself to be persuaded by the islanders to take on the role of the priest – even though he protests that he will not go so far as to give communion. This does not prevent him from absolving people from heinous crimes: a son, Joseph (Daniel Gélin), who murders his mother because she is mad and threatens to give all their possessions away (he later commits suicide); a woman who has an illegitimate child; a thief who steals dead sailors' gold coins off their bodies; and so on. Eventually, Thomas' conscience pushes him to travel to the mainland to bring back a priest. But when the priest starts to lay down the law in a way that lacks understanding of the islanders' needs, in particular refusing to allow Joseph a Christian burial, with Thomas in the lead they take things into their own hands. They commandeer all the fishing boats (some 300) and take off with Joseph to give him a religious sea-burial. They then return to the island and go to church to be absolved of their transgression.

Whilst the film looks very much as if it was shot on the actual island, the sets for the village and church of this less than cheery tale were built by René Renoux on the open spaces of the former fort of Romainville (just north of Paris). Interiors and some of the port scenes were done in the studios at Billancourt. Renoux had a reputation for being a stickler about detail and, indeed, the granite houses, made as they are of synthetic materials, are utterly convincing as the islanders' dwellings of the Ile de Sein. Nearly all the houses were mobile: they were built on train chassis and could be easily moved along rails so that Delannoy could set up his shots very quickly.[4] The entire set gives the feel of location shooting and is as dark and gloomy in its lighting and photography as it is in its message. The Bretons come over as close-minded, simplistic brutes – men and women alike. Real hardship makes unpleasant beasts of us all – small wonder Thomas is always yelling at the islanders to be more considerate. Under Thomas' guidance they learn to be more community-spirited. Whilst he acts as their priest, he makes them pay their penitence in useful community service, such as mending the church roof, rather than saying a hundred 'Hail Marys'. It is a very noisy film:

everyone is angry, everyone shouts without listening to their neighbour. To an islander, they are quick to judge. But they are also quick to close ranks against any institutional form of authority, such as the police, seeking to impose its will from outside. In one terrific scene when the police land their steamboat and disembark, ostensibly to prevent the islanders from burying Joseph in the cemetery, the islanders form a wall of human bodies and break out into laughter. That moment of solidarity is both scary and moving and only the newly-arrived priest can put a stop to it.

As the title of the film makes clear, God needs all sorts of men. An interesting twist if we consider the teachings of the Bible which beseech us to look to God. The humanity of the film's message does not save it from being quite a dire piece of work, however, despite the fact that both the Catholic cinema lobby of France and the Venice Film Festival awarded it their annual Grand Prix and that Pierre Fresnay won the French Victoire (Oscar equivalent) for his role as Thomas. But this is 1950; France needs its heroes, no matter how rough and ready. Of the twelve costume dramas released in 1950, this film was the top-grossing one with 2.7 million entries, outstripping all the Belle Epoque films (of which there were nine). It even pipped Fresnay's other film of that year, *La Valse de Paris* (with 2 million), to the post. To see others suffer more than oneself and find redemption doubtless provides quite an uplifting message.

Le Carrosse d'or (1953)

The lines uttered towards the very end of the film, 'peace and reconciliation', are surely at the heart of Renoir's 'fantasy in the Italian style' as he calls his *Le Carrosse d'or* in the rolling credits, in which a troupe of actors of the *Comedia dell'arte* arrive in Peru from Italy and take the small town of Lima by storm. One actor in particular, Camilla (Anna Magnani), steals the heart of three men, but in the end she takes none of them as her lover. In her quest to find what it is that she loves, she discovers that what matters is what she can give to others through her work on the stage – a selfless gesture of love, if ever there was one, for the people. [5]

The golden coach of the title is a 'gift' that Viceroy Ferdinand (Duncan Lamont) has given to himself as a symbol of Spanish prestige in this far-flung land of Peru. Although the coffers are running close to empty, the Viceroy has managed to persuade his Council that this hugely-expensive coach, imported from Italy, is a necessary expense since it will place the local Indians in awe of Spain's might. The only reason the Spaniards are in Peru, as the Viceroy declares, is because of the potential gain to be had from the gold mines – but they have yet to maintain their authority over the territory, hence the important symbolism of the coach. Once Camilla and her troupe of actors arrive in town, everything changes for him, however. He falls in love with her and gives her his coach as a symbol of his undying love. Meantime two other suitors, the young officer Felipe (Paul Campbell) and the brave bullfighter Ramón (Riccardo Rioli), have also fallen for her. Although all three vie for her favours, even to the point of Felipe and Ramón duelling over her, it soon dawns on Camilla that they seek – in differing degrees – to possess her through proof of their love. And yet, as she repeatedly questions, what is this love, what is this man? Ramón is a brute, wanting to take her by force. Ferdinand seeks to buy her with his (ill-gotten) riches. Felipe – the closest to a disinterested love – wants to take her away from everything she loves, the theatre and the troupe of actors, to go live with the Indians whom he declares are not, as the Europeans decree, 'savages', but 'kinder and better than we are'.

In the end, she takes the gift of the coach and hands it over to the church so they can use it to take the sacrament out to the poor and those in need of last rites (such as prisoners on death row). She re-ascribes a new meaning to this symbol of a colonizing power. It becomes now a symbol of charity and compassion. Th is spectacular gesture against the money-grabbing aristocrats surrounding Ferdinand meets with his secret approval. Much as he regrets losing her, for their two worlds can never meet, so, too, he admires her. She also returns all her paramours to where their talents best lie: Ferdinand to be an enlightened Viceroy and stand up to his Council; Ramón to continue to enthral his own audiences in his bullfights; Felipe to go live with the natives away from all that makes men brutal.

Renoir's film is loosely based on Mérimée's novella *Le Carrosse du Saint-Sacrement,* a tale of jealousy and denunciation that is far darker in its message about human vanity than Renoir's film.[6] Indeed, as Renoir tells us, Mérimée's 1829 novella was merely a starting point for his film. He radically altered the original idea because, as he said, he wanted, in his film, to fuse cinema and theatre (his actual words are 'make cinema digest an idea of theatre').[7] This idea that life is theatre has long been a trope of Renoir's cinematic oeuvre – but, this time, it is as if he has reversed the equation to make the point that theatre is life in its most important manifestation: love. Renoir makes clear, through Camilla's decision, that the wonder of artistic creation is the most lasting and important gift of love, serving as it does to strip away the mask of human vanity.

As we shall discover in the following three chapters, this plea for tolerance, in evidence in all three films discussed above, is quite a lone voice. For the most part, the film narratives that dominate the five centuries depicted are ones of revenge, power relations, or heroic gestures for king and country. In this latter category, a number 'end happily ever after' in marriage, but only a handful has the central protagonist standing up against tyranny. These dominant types of discourses within the costume drama genre map quite easily onto other generic types of 1950s' French cinema. Comedy and *polars* (thrillers), the two other main categories of films, produced a similarly-seemingly escapist mode of cinema in that neither genre spoke directly to recent or actual events. Guy Hennebelle argues that the post-Occupation mentality abrogated its political duty not just because of the demoralized spirit of the French but also because of the determination of bourgeois hegemony to impose silence on both the past (collaboration, Vichy, etc.) and the present (colonial troubles).[8] According to Hennebelle and other film historians such as Comes and Marmin, there was no visual sign of the tremendous political upheavals France had just experienced and was still experiencing.[9] With one or two exceptions, they argue, form and content had not changed substantially from pre-war cinema but just evolved into an apoliticism. As this book will endeavour to show, the picture is more complex than that. There are shifts in form and cinematic style; and there is evidence in many of the costume dramas under consideration of a displaced unease and anxiety in relation to the present (the narratives of revenge and power relations are prime examples of this displaced unease). Moreover, even if, as we shall see in Parts Three and Four, bourgeois preoccupations tend to dominate the nineteenth-century narratives, they are far from endorsing a rosy picture of society – films about social climbing, marriage issues, and betrayal abound in that context. It is never safe to assume that just because the films are not self-evidently polemical that nothing is being said. Let us now take a closer look at the first part of our corpus, beginning, why not, with fairytales!

Notes

1. Ory (1989, p. 112).
2. See Hayward (2004, pp. 17–8 & 110–2).
3. The four being: Louis Daquin's *Bel-Ami* (1954) with the Soviet-controlled East Vienna, Austria; and with East Germany, Gérard Philipe's *Les Aventures de Till l'Espiègle* (1956); Raymond Rouleau's *Les Sorcières de Salem* (1957); Jean-Paul Le Chanois' *Les Misérables* (1958). See Marc Silberman for more discussion of these films in the East German context (2006, pp. 21–45).
4. Douy (1993: 182).
5. There are two very good articles on Renoir's film *Le Carrosse d'or* which eloquently speak to most of the issues raised below. Jacques Doniol-Valcroze (1953) 'Camilla et le don', *Cahiers du cinéma*, Vol. 4, No. 21, pp. 44–6. Frank Curot (1999) 'Théâtre, théâtralité et style d'espace filmique dans *Le Carrosse d'or* de Jean Renoir', *CinémAction*, No. 93, pp. 42–50. This film did not do very well at the box-office even if it is now considered a classic. It was Renoir's first film after returning to France from the US. It was made in three versions (French, English and Italian). In each version, Italian is spoken amongst the *Comedia dell'arte* actors when the meaning is not essential to an understanding of the film or when the meaning is so self-evident it needs no translation (as for example Camilla/Magnani getting cross with someone or another.). For some reason, audiences of the 1950s did not take to these multilingual affairs (see the case for *Lola Montès* in Chapter 13).
6. This is the second Mérimée adaptation in our corpus of films (*Tamango* being the other). Indeed, in its tale of a triangulation of lovers hot in pursuit of an independent woman, it is something of a gentle precursor to his *Carmen* (1845) in which passion, death and destruction run rife.
7. Renoir, quoted in Jacques Doniol-Valcroze (op. cit., p. 45).
8. Hennebelle (1974, p. 12).
9. Comes & Marmin (1984, p. 146).

Chapter 5

Mysterious Microcosms: Three 'Fairytales'

The Fairytales

The term 'mysterious microcosms' is borrowed from Victor Hugo, for these are the words he uses to qualify his enormous episodic novel *Notre-Dame de Paris*, first published in 1831. The point about fairytales is that they take us into the darker recesses of our unconscious – into mysterious microcosms, places of enigma and fear. The function of fairytales is both to scare and to provide us with some kind of worthy parable at the end. In the three tales we have before us, these parables could be: greed is not necessarily the source to happiness, love can transcend all (*Ali Baba et les quarante voleurs*, Becker, 1954); beware of making yourself into something you are not, for women can see though masculine masquerade (*Barbe-bleue*, Christian-Jaque, 1951); many a foul deed is done in the name of desire, especially if it is repressed (*Notre-Dame de Paris*, Delannoy, 1956). What is striking, however, in all three films before us, is the degree to which gender relations are fore-fronted: women are not as easily subjugated as patriarchy (and 1950s' hegemonic discourses around women) would have us believe. Let us take a closer look, first, at the tales themselves and consider these introductory remarks before moving on to a consideration of the function of colour and décor in these three films.

In two out of the three fairytales, the original story is either considerably altered: *Ali Baba et les quarante voleurs* (henceforth *Ali Baba*), or the meaning completely reversed: *Barbe-bleue*. In the former film, Ali Baba (Fernandel) is now servant, rather than brother, to Kassim (Henri Vilbert) his rich master. And whereas, in the original, it is the slave-girl Morgiane who foils the various attempts of the thieves and their leader Abdul to regain their loot and kill Ali Baba (and this includes her pouring boiling oil on them when they hide in the urns), in the film she does none of this. Instead, it is Ali Baba who takes action. Morgiane (Samia Gamal) remains a fairly silent and passive object of man's desire until the somewhat ironic closing moments of the film. Clearly, this French-German co-production was primarily intended as a vehicle for Fernandel (with a four-million audience, the producers were backing a hit, for sure), so the original, quite brutal story, had to be made more comedic. This explains why the violence of the fairytale is completely bleached out. Neither of the lead villains, Kassim and Abdul (Dieter Borsche), is killed; the thieves are not burnt alive, even if several perish in a swordfight with Kassim's men.

Becker's film opens with Ali Baba being sent off to the local slave-market to buy Kassim two more women for his harem. There he lights upon Morgiane and, clearly, it is love at first sight. The rest of the story details how Ali will eventually get to win Morgiane for himself.

First, he gets captured by Abdul's band of thieves, ends up in their cave, and steals some of their riches. He then returns to Kassim's house and purchases Morgiane from his master. Having freed her, Ali oddly returns her to her awful exploitative father, who immediately puts her back on the slave-market! Ali buys his own house. Finally, he realizes Morgiane is also in love with him and they marry. Both Abdul and his thieves and Kassim's men turn up on the night of the nuptial feast intent on robbing Ali. To no avail. Kassim and Abdul are captured and pilloried by the locals. Ali then takes all the villagers out to the famous cave and offers the multitude of riches to the thousands gathered. They obligingly proceed to remove the entire contents of the thieves' hoard, thus reducing Ali to the penniless man he was at the beginning of the film. Thankfully for Ali, Morgiane does not care if he is rich or poor; either way she loves him, she declares. Morgiane, Ali's treasured trophy, rides out to the cave to bring him home. In a parodic reversal of a much earlier scene, when Ali brought Morgiane to Kassim's astride his mule, Ali now becomes her trophy. The film ends with Ali astride the mule. Morgiane holds the reins pulling Ali along. In this moment she asserts her own power as much as she becomes emblematic of love transcending all misfortune.

In *Barbe-bleue* we are a long way from any suggestion of the passive female. Bluebeard (Claude Brasseur) is on the hunt for his seventh wife – the other six having mysteriously died. The rumour in the village is that he has brutally murdered them all. However, Aline (Cécile Aubry), daughter to the local village innkeeper and the central female character, is unafraid of the myth surrounding the monstrous Bluebeard. In Christian-Jaque's version of the fairytale, she boldly offers to take his next victim's place as a guest to his ball. Far from terrified by his myth as monster, she is intrigued. She agrees to their marriage, only to discover that the legend surrounding Bluebeard is no more than that. Aline, now his wife, profits by his absence to steal a key she has been forbidden to take and opens a secret cavern where Bluebeard's six former wives are living quite contentedly (albeit in captivity). Thus Aline is instrumental in unmasking the truth about Bluebeard's tyranny: it is all a bluff. Indeed, Bluebeard's macho cruelty is a complete construction created by his Major-domo (Jean Debucourt) – a myth perpetrated so that Bluebeard can safely control his fiefdom. Supposedly, the blue beard is a sign of his cruelty and homicidal nature; instead, it is pure masquerade. Masculinity is exposed here as pure construction. But, the point is also that both men and women are represented as equal. Aline and Bluebeard are fascinated by each other. If they are inappropriate as a couple, it is less because of their age difference and more as a result of his serial bigamy and his weakness in colluding with his spin-doctor Major-domo. As with *Ali Baba*, there is no real violence and, thus, the fairytale is sanitized of that element. But, in so doing, the story becomes more intriguing, more ambiguous, especially in relation to the two lead characters. When, at the end, Bluebeard is banished from his fiefdom and ordered by the Emperor's envoy (Fernand Fabre) to live in harmony with his six existing wives, we possibly feel a tinge of sympathy for him. Particularly since Aline – the one woman he really loves – is now set free to marry her suitor, the village blacksmith Gilles (Jacques Sernas). The hint of regret held in the closing moments is also reminiscent of the end of Cocteau's *La Belle et la Bête* (1946), where Belle is not so sure she is as taken with her beautiful prince as she was with her ugly beast! In any event, order is restored: Aline goes home; Bluebeard is unmasked. In an odd way, his fake monstrosity, whilst it renders him ridiculous, also humanizes him. Equally, it makes the more serious point that if we challenge power we may well find that it is, first and foremost, a question of display. Maybe the parable becomes thus: in exposing power for what it is, a more equitable life is possible.

The oddest thing is that one would suspect, from reading the above, that *Barbe-bleue* had been made not by Christian-Jaque but by Jacques Becker, the great champion of gender equality in virtually all of his films with the apparent major exception, here, of *Ali Baba* – although the ending of the film and my discussion below nuance this take somewhat. Christian-Jaque's representation of women, as I shall again argue in later chapters, is a lot more complex than he has been given credit for. His women are feisty. Empowered to make choices, they battle against being exploited or objectified and resist patriarchal constructs (as we shall see, even the most corrupt of them all, Lucrèce Borgia, bites back). Even if, in the end and to some degree or another, these women are obliged to comply, it will not have been without a fight. In this amusing re-write of the original Perrault story of *Barbe-bleue*, we are reminded of a similar reversal with another fairytale (originally by Jeanne-Marie Leprince de Beaumont) in Cocteau's *La Belle et la Bête,* where Belle was also completely unafraid of the monstrous Bête. Perrault, writing in the late seventeenth century, and Leprince, in the eighteenth, had been intent through their fairytales on providing young maidens with exemplary tales about marriage and obedience. Here, the exact opposite prevails.

Esméralda (Gina Lollobrigida), in *Notre-Dame de Paris*, is the third woman of our fairytales. She lies somewhere between Aline and Morgiane. A free spirit who rejects various suitors' violent advances or declarations of love, she nonetheless falls victim to man's jealous desire. She is true to herself, as is Aline. And there is no mystery surrounding her. She knows what she wants (to dance freely and be loved by Pheobus). However, she eventually falls under the control of, and is killed for, her refusal to conform to the strictures of patriarchy. What is intriguing about this film is that it does not foreground Esméralda as the *femme fatale*, even if the priest/alchemist Frollo (Alain Cuny), the archdeacon of Notre-Dame, pretends it is so. In fact it is Frollo who is responsible for the multiple deaths in this film: Esméralda, whom he allows to be sentenced to death for his own treacherous murder of her lover Phoebus (Jean Danet); and Quasimodo (Anthony Quinn), who dies lying beside his dead beloved Esméralda in the dungeons at Montfaucon. It is Frollo, too, whose treachery sets in motion the beggars' assault on the church of Notre-Dame – in an aborted attempt to save Esméralda – and the soldiers' subsequent attack on the beggars as they seek to drag Esméralda from her sanctuary. Many die as a bewildered Quasimodo endeavours to protect Esméralda from being taken from her place of asylum in the church. Thus, everything that this dark and brooding Frollo touches turns to dust and death – some alchemist! Frollo is the one, therefore, to become a kind of *homme fatale*. His selfish and illicit desire for Esméralda drives the narrative of the film. His function as archdeacon is a source of his suffering because it does not allow him to be a man of flesh and bone – lust for a woman's body is a sin after all. Yet, in the end, this piety is nothing more than a façade, as we see from his determination to control everything. He dominates the dim-witted Quasimodo, spies on people, especially Esméralda, from concealed spaces (windows, darkened corners of streets and so on). He sneakily murders his rival, Phoebus, by stabbing him in the back and lets Esméralda be convicted of the crime. He tries to convert earthly materials into gold. This makes *him* the man of mystery (a ghostly voyeur and a sorcerer), an enigma to be investigated, all of which associates him with the concept of *fatale*. It is surely instructive that, in the opening sequence of the film, we observe him carving the word 'fatality' into the stone walls of Notre-Dame – he knows himself after all.

Constructing fairytales: colour and design

Georges Wakhévitch worked on two of these films: *Ali Baba* and *Barbe-bleue*. He did costumes and décor for both, which makes him quite unusual as the man responsible for the overall look of the film. The director of photography for *Ali Baba* was Robert LeFèbvre, and Christian Matras for *Barbe-bleue*. René Renoux did the sets for *Notre-Dame de Paris* and Georges Benda the costumes; Michel Kelber was the director of photography. *Barbe-bleue*, France's first colour costume drama film, was shot in Gevacolour. The system brings with it some issues which merit consideration, especially since it was also Matras' first colour film. Both *Ali Baba* and *Notre-Dame de Paris* are in Eastmancolor but at very different stages in its viability. *Ali Baba* dates from the early days of Eastmancolor (1954). At this juncture it tended to produce quite a pastel effect, which faded with the passing of time. Eastmancolor films of this period notoriously lost depth of coloration. And we recall from Part One of this book (Chapter 2) what the set designer Léon Barsacq said of Eastmancolor: that you had to limit your palette to fairly neutral colours (because blue cropped up everywhere like a plague). By 1956, when *Notre-Dame de Paris* was shot, Eastmancolor had achieved greater stability.

What interests me first of all is that the *Ali Baba* I saw provided me with the chance to see both the extant version of 1954, which has paled (and indeed is very scratchy), and the remastered version, which has gone through the flash-dupe-mask corrective reproduction system developed by Eastmancolor.[1] This version, therefore, has all the coloration of the original and it is remarkably crisp, with an effervescent, bright palette of yellows, greens and blues set against the sandy browns of the Moroccan landscape. White and gold also stand out in their luminosity – in clothing as much as in décor. The tones are pastel, as we expect of Eastmancolor, but are entirely appropriate for the *mise-en-scène* of this exotic Arab tale. Wakhévitch is unafraid to try also a dark palette range for the black costumes of Kassim's saber-wielding henchmen and the brown of Abdul's thieves when they come to fight at Ali Baba's nuptial feast. So his palette is broad – in contravention of standard wisdom as expounded by Barsacq. As the critic André Bazin says: 'there is one area in which *Ali Baba* must be considered a total success: its colour, aided most remarkably by Wakhévitch's sets. Its transcendent beauty consists in itself a spectacle with the power to make the spirit as well as the eyes rejoice.'[2]

The interior sets of Kassim's and Ali Baba's houses are equally visually exciting. They have depth and light and offer the spectator a wonderful insider view of the various chambers, private and public, that make up the mansions of the wealthy. Indeed, the entire film becomes something of a travelogue for those wishing to visit Morocco, recently granted its independence from France (March 1956). As we shall see below, Becker was intrigued by the culture of this country. The choice of Morocco is not, therefore, an arbitrary one – moreover, as far as the producers were concerned, it was easier and therefore less costly to shoot in a former French territory than in what was then Persia (now Iran) where the Arabian Nights fairytales are purportedly set.

Much of this visual treat can be attributed to Wakhévitch, of course, whose designs, rather than being sourced from the illustrations of the *1001 Nights* by Maxfield Parrish, with perhaps the exception of the thieves' cave, are inspired by his own desire (and LeFèbvre's) to experiment with this new colour system. Given the newness of the Eastmancolor system, another feat of defiance accomplished by LeFèbvre are the exteriors, which abound. The area of Morocco selected for the exteriors was the anti-Atlas region surrounding the town of Taroudannt. As we know, at this juncture, Eastmancolor, whilst it had a great sensitivity to light, was not as good as Gevacolor in relation to full sunlight. However, because it was a faster stock it had greater stability in heat than Geva and, as we can observe from LeFèbvre's skilful use of the system, he was able to control the effects. The definition is good, the depth of focus has clarity and the colours are registered very naturally. Furthermore, LeFèbvre showed consummate skill in the manner in which he made the light and colour palette of these many exteriors match with the interiors shot at the Billancourt studios in Paris.

In this travelogue of local culture, so carefully documented it almost acts as a separate film to the fairytale – or maybe the fairytale is the excuse for the documentary, we get to see the different peoples that make up the eclectic mix of this part of North Africa's Maghreb, wherein Africans live alongside Arabs. The black Africans and Arabs we encounter in the streets mostly wear djellabahs: loose-fitting hooded robes of muted colours. But we are also made aware of the Arabs as distinct tribes with distinct clothing: Berbers in elegant kaftans of gold and silver or green satin who service the domestic needs of Kassim's and later Ali's households; Bedouin men in white robes and kufeya headdress who caravan by camel through the anti-Atlas mountains with their precious wares for sale, which Abdul and his vicious thugs, disguised as Touaregs (in their blue turbans and blue sleeveless tunic tied at the waist), relieve them of. We visit the Arab kitchen as it prepares the nuptial feast and see many of the delicious dishes set out before Ali and his guests: bread ovens baking the pitta breads; tagines full of couscous and roast chicken; large copper trays filled with metzes, or with coconut-based pastries and baklava – a gourmet and gourmand's dream. Amongst the documented are the symbols and sounds of Arab culture, such as the call to prayer from a minaret; authentic instruments, in particular the lute; and indigenous diegetic music accompanying belly-dancing early in the film and, later, the nuptial feast. All extras are indigenous people, some of whom have speaking roles.

It comes as no surprise that this film was dubbed in Arabic for a largely Eastern market. The cachet of Egyptian dancer and actor Samia Gamel would also have helped exhibition practices, even if, by 1954, she was something of a *persona non grata* in Egypt itself. President Nasser had just come to power and Gamel was readily associated with the decadence of the previous regime under Prince Farouk. Gamel had already moved to the United States by 1952, but her home nation, under the new stricter Muslim rule, decreed that Egyptian dance (i.e., belly-dancing) was proscribed. All of which made her an appetizing, if forbidden, star to come and watch.

Her role does, however, raise some of the issues that sit less easily with this film. Of the lead actors, she is the only Arab. Fernandel, Vilbert and Borsche are all 'tanned-up' Europeans. Becker tells us he had long wanted to bring this film to fruition and politely suggests that he had only ever thought of Fernandel for the role of Ali Baba. Such is not the case according to his friend Jacques Rivette, who recalls that Becker had in mind the jazz musician, singer and occasional film actor Henri Salvador.[3] Doubtless he would have been a better choice, if only in terms of his ability to sing and his mixed-race background (his mother was Indian-Caribbean). However, the producers and distributors over-rode Becker's recommendation and insisted on Fernandel – with a 4.1 million audience, they were probably right on that score, even if it meant undermining Becker's desire for greater authenticity, something we very much associate with his work.

The enterprise was, after all, colossal, with a budget of 222 million francs – three times the norm for a colour film at the time.[4] Small wonder the people putting up the money had the final say. Rivette also adds that Becker made this film because he needed the money.[5] What Becker did say in relation to this film was that he wanted to make his own small 'Nanouk of Morocco'.[6] In short he would have preferred to make an ethnographic (fly on the wall) documentary, Flaherty-style, of the local culture, and not a fiction film, nor indeed a travelogue. The wonderment of it all is that he succeeded to a degree in his personal ambition. We sense how the camera lingers over the lives of the indigenous peoples, their actions, rituals and movements. More miraculous still, when we consider Fernandel's tyrannical control over the production: he had insisted, in his contract, on having the final say on everything.[7] The miracle is that Becker managed to work around this all and give audiences a Fernandel they would recognize and enjoy as well as a fabulous documentary on Morocco. Arguably, Becker gets his last laugh over Fernandel in that closing image of Morgiane bringing him home on the mule; and, too, over his other two 'tanned-up' lead actors, by having them pilloried by the indigenous people at the end of the film, because of their murderous intentions towards Ali. There is something very provocative about the image of the two tanned-up white men chained in cages with hundreds of Arabs and Africans throwing rotten vegetables at them. And yet the same board of censors that had found so much fault with Louis Daquin's *Bel-Ami* (also 1954, see Chapter 17), accusing it in its representation of the colonies of 'undermining the French nation'[8], took no issue with these images in Becker's film. Almost as if they failed to see the Empire striking back, as it were.

Wakhévitch teamed up with Matras for Christian-Jaque's *Barbe-bleue* and, once again, the combination of skills works to the advantage of the look of the film. Two versions were made for the French-German co-production: Brasseur was replaced by Hans Alber for the German version; Cécile Aubry did both. But it was the French version that was submitted to the Venice film festival.[9] For his part, Christian-Jaque was known as the Cecil B. de Mille of France because of his extravagant *mise-en-scènes* – we should recall that he began his career as a set designer, turning his hand to the making of film spectaculars as early as 1937 with *Les Perles de la couronne*.[10] Whilst the sets for *Barbe-beue* are as grand as the public had come to expect of its director, interestingly, the choice of colour palette is not. A deliberate decision as it transpires. According to Matras, they used old parabolic projectors of 5 kilowatts for the interiors rather than the powerful arc lights that gave out about 25 kilowatts – five times the power.[11] This low wattage facilitated an exceptional rendering of colour, producing a grey palette in which reds, browns, blacks and whites stood out – thus creating a Brueghelian feel to the images before us. This near-monochromatic, interior coloration continues in the outside winter scenes, shot in Austria, by using arc lights to provide a continuous white light. Below is an example of the tone palette for Christian-Jaque's film (see figure 5.1, sadly reproduced here in black and white only)[12], highly reminiscent of the contrastive tones of Brueghel's paintings. The effect of this near monochrome, as *Cahiers du cinéma* critic Jean Quéval rightly points out, is to create an inner tension within the image in preference to a more straightforward conflict or opposition between images (for example, light colours for outside sequences and dark for those within).[13] When I come to discuss costumes, the importance of this interior tension will become clearer. But it certainly shows us, once again, that some French filmmakers were intent on making something happen with colour other than achieving natural rendition. Colour is made to narrate alongside the story, to act as a metatext, rather than to function merely as a provider of a purer than reality look (à la Nathalie Kalmus school of thought). In this regard, this film exemplifies Christian-Jaque's view that film colour intensifies the hyperreal quality of costume-drama (see Chapter 3).

Of course Brueghel's paintings date some 130 years after the events of Bluebeard, which are set in the 1430s. But we can see how the contrastive tones within the image (in figure 5.1), as with Breughel's work, create a tension – each grouping of the dark bodies cause us to pause on their movement and meaning. In terms of interior décor, we also note the influence of the engraver Gustave Doré, who illustrated the 1867 edition of Perrault's famous fairytale. And, in a similar vein, the costumes are a mixture of fifteenth- and early sixteenth-century styles. But the overall effect of these anachronisms is the creation of an imaginary space, somewhere in Flanders perhaps, with a narrative set sometime in late-Medieval, early-Renaissance times.

In the version I was able to see at the Bibliothèque Nationale de France there is a preface with regard to the quality of the image. Apparently the negative was destroyed and, therefore, the film was reconstituted from existing positives. The effect is a certain degree of pallor, even if the stronger hues still stand out, primarily in form of the costumes. Thus, Bluebeard and Aline's costumes work well in relation to both the décor and their importance within

Figure 5.1: Bluebeard's castle. © Sam Levin.

the narrative. To explain. When we first meet Aline she is in peasant dress of black and greys, playing hide and seek with her erstwhile suitor Gilles. When she goes to the ball she is dressed in red – a strong colour that ensures that she stands out against the greys of the walls. This interior tension within the colour palette underlines Aline's own outspoken ways, and of course Bluebeard immediately notices her. Her attire for both her wedding and nuptial night is white, as befits the virgin that she is. Once she is established in the castle as Bluebeard's wife, however, her costumes lose colour and are predominantly grey, as if to express the boredom she feels being holed up in this lonely place. Her costumes, literally, match the colour of the walls that psychologically, at least, imprison her. This grey forewarns us of her need to be stimulated and, unsurprisingly, as soon as Bluebeard absents himself for a while she immediately disobeys him and steals the key that will unlock the secret of his six other wives – presumed dead but still very much alive! Her disobedience brings the wrath of Bluebeard and his Major-domo upon her head and she is condemned to death. On the day of her sentence being carried out, she appears dressed once more in white, this time to signal her innocence, to await her execution along with the other wives.

Bluebeard's outfits work in interesting ways, with regard to this interior tension I spoke of above. At their first meeting, the ball, he is clothed in white and gold with a black jerkin – a startling contrast to Aline's red dress, suggesting indeed that he is a foil to her (see figure 5.2 below). But there is also the notion that there is a great deal that separates them (as indicated by the extremes of colour palette). After this first meeting, until he leaves her to go hunting towards the end of the film, his outfits more or less match hers, hinting at a relative harmony

Figure 5.2: Bluebeard's ball – Aline (Cécile Aubry) in red and Bluebeard (Claude Brasseur) in white. © Sam Levin.

within the couple. He wears white for the wedding and, thereafter, muted outfits in brown and white. Not all is dull, though. The cut and ornamentation of his doublets are quite spectacular, showing that he is a man of wealth and power. On the day he leaves to go hunting, however, he wears hunting green, thereby breaking the link with his wife – after which all goes awry.

Matras offers us some nice photographic swirls around the castle interiors, so we get a sense of its immensity – it has height and depth and width. The opening sequence is particularly amusing in this light. We are attending the funeral of Bluebeard's latest, sixth wife. He stands in the centre of the church in front of the altar. The camera makes a gradual 360 degree pan, first in front of Bluebeard and across the six tombs of his wives laid out in a semi-circle, briefly pausing on each tomb. It then cuts away into a high angle behind Bluebeard and descends once more, looking from his point of view towards the other semi-circle where the dignitaries are assembled to mourn this latest death. Bluebeard is impatient for it all to be over so he can chase after a new wife. The camerawork functions to keep him imprisoned in a circle of 'gazers-on': those of his dead wives and those of his obsequious courtiers.

The entire film is reasonably paced, with an average shot length of ten seconds (six shots per minute) – so it can hardly be said to drag as some critics have it.[14] It begins very fast with the rout through the village by Bluebeard's men, hunting down young virgins to bring to their master (average shot length 3.75 seconds, 16 shots per minute). This pace does not return until the denouement, when Aline's brothers and Gilles come to rescue her. These are the moments of greatest action. But in between there is a good mixture of slow- and fast-paced sequences: the slower sequences most often being associated with moments of display, such as the ball and the wedding, where ceremony is all; or moments of intimacy such as Aline's wedding night with Bluebeard.

Finally, *Notre-Dame de Paris*. If the *Cahiers* critics were kind to Christian-Jaque's film, *Barbe-bleue*, particularly in regard to the use of colour, such was not their view of Delannoy's film. André Bazin is pretty virulent. Here is what he has to say, first on Delannoy as its director, then on colour:

> I was of the mind that, in 1956, there was only one film director capable of remaining faithful to the spirit of the text and making it visual, I was thinking, obviously, of Abel Gance. Jean Delannoy is in any event the least appropriate for this enterprise…The job of the director is to make us accept the naiveté (of the story) and to give life to all the characters. But it is sadly missing here…The performances are not all bad, even though Delannoy manages for the first time ever to make Gina repellent with frigidity (and also what ghastly costumes they inflicted in her!).
>
> But, realistically, could *Notre-Dame de Paris* be successfully made in colour? Outside of the exterior shots (pertinently absent in this film), the realism of colour stresses the cinematographic falsity. The building materials (staff/plaster) can never be taken for stone. The mock-ups and special effects are glaringly obvious, the medieval filth is no more than a background daubing of greeny paste. Thus, one of the essential ingredients

of the story disappears; I mean the recreation of a social and architectural universe that an abstraction into black and white might just have tolerated.[15]

Harsh indeed. Even if the falsity of the sets is visible and the use of colour is pedestrian, it works, as we shall see, to reasonable effect insofar as this is a 'fairytale'. Moreover, the characterization remains true to Hugo's own. Amongst the men, there are no real heroes; each character is flawed. The knight (Phoebus) is not in shining armour – in fact he is in black, surely a sartorial warning Esméralda should have heeded. As to the archdeacon-cum-alchemist (Frollo), Esméralda correctly registers him as a man who will stoop very low and let others pay the price for his sins. King Louis XI (played by Jean Tissier) is a particular butt of irony for Hugo. He greatly misrepresents this monarch, who was a defender of the little people (*le petit peuple*) again the burghers and managed, through clever diplomacy, to see off the English from most of the territories they had gained through the Hundred Years War. Rather, Hugo, who by the time of writing his novel was discovering his Republican leanings (as we shall discuss in Chapter 11 on *Les Misérables*), focused on the less appetising aspects of this monarch. He was nicknamed by those who disliked him 'the universal spider' (because he was a wily diplomat); he was described as mean-spirited, whereas in truth he was merely a prudent man and certainly not extravagant like the rest of his royal lineage of the Valois dynasty. He hated the court and mostly avoided it. He dressed in a sober manner and wore a hat (*chapeau de médailles*) for which he became famous: a felt hat adorned with medals depicting saints. He was so ordinary in dress and so plain in looks, apparently, he could pass unrecognized amongst the multitude of his subjects. By 1482, the date of Hugo's novel, France was a fairly united country thanks to Louis' devilish genius as a negotiator. However, the country had suffered a year of bad harvests and Louis was greatly in debt (because of all his diplomacy in buying off the English). Thus the Louis that Delannoy serves us up is Hugo's. He is venal and desperate for Frollo's experiments with gold to work. He certainly manages to pass through crowds unnoticed and makes easy pacts with his conscience, as we see when he decides to find a way to annul Esméralda's entitlement to sanctuary in Notre-Dame.

Finally, on Esméralda and Quasimodo, both actors who embody these characters play to their greatest strengths. Quinn's mobile face and expressive eyes (despite the four hour make-up and prosthetics) delivers an anguished and complex hunchback (see figure 5.3 below). Although he could neither speak nor understand French, Quinn gives a wonderful and compelling performance of this deaf, almost mute, monster. Lollobrigida offers an interesting and restrained performance. If we compare her to the role she embodies in Christian-Jaque's *Fanfan la tulipe*, Delannoy obtains a more ethereal rather than earthy performance from her. There is no sultry sexy star, for sure, but there is a spectacular performance to experience, particularly in her singing and dancing routines. Lollobrigida was a soprano of some distinction and had performed *Tosca*, but she could also dance. In this latter context, choreographer Léonide Massine was brought in to work out a routine for her dances in front of Notre-Dame. Lollobrigida gives evidence of a balletic lightness rather than a gyrating vampish routine; her dance tells a story rather than offering her body up

Figure 5.3: Poster for *Notre-Dame de Paris*; Esmeralda (Lollobrigida) dances accompanied by her faithful goat and Quasimodo (Quinn) looks on enchanted. © René Péron.

as an object. She provides a performance about line and bodily grace. Sadly for her, Frollo reads it as the work of Satan.

The sets and use of colour are interesting issues, particularly in light of the discussion above on *Barbe-bleue*, because, here, colour is used in that external way of creating self-evident contrasts. However, this does not necessarily diminish the film's value. First, colour is used to establish the concept of class. Bright pastel colours abound for the rich burghers' clothes and the female nobility. Dark tones of brown, grey and green dominate for the poor (*le petit peuple*) and the band of beggars – known as the *Argotins*. Similarly for the spaces these various classes inhabit: ornate furnishings on the wall, decorated beams, light-coloured interiors for the wealthy; dark for the poor. The beggars' underworld looks like a set from the *Beggars' Opera* – rich in dark browns and dirty ochres, it suggests a more complex system of values than those espoused by the rich and the ordinary people of Paris. Indeed, in this underworld, people (men and women) speak their mind. Justice is meted out pretty rapidly but with humour. Everyone has a place that is met with respect by their leader, Clopin (Philippe Clay), suggesting a less-hierarchical system of power.

Colour also has a narrative function other than these oppositions. Whereas, in the first two-thirds of this 150-minute film, a fairly rich palette of colours dominates, including the dark tones of green of which Bazin is so critical (but which in fact, along with the ochres, make the film feel almost like a Technicolor product), during the last 49 minutes colour gradually disappears from the image as a strong presence as the story moves inexorably to the terrible dénouement. By the time Esméralda is taken before the judges, then tortured into an admission of guilt, colour more or less peters out – all that resonates here, in the predominantly grey tones, is her red headscarf, a sad reminder of her days of freedom. By the time Quasimodo has rescued her and brought her into Notre-Dame for sanctuary, the dominant tones are beige in the daylight and dark greys and browns at night. Again, only Esméralda's red scarf brings any respite to these despairing times.

The sets are by Renoux, who had worked with Delannoy on some twenty films. He also did the giant epic *Napoléon* with Guitry and was responsible for the massive sets of Moscow (see Chapter 9). Renoux began working as a set designer on silent films, so is one of the pioneers of décor. He was particularly noted for his eye for detail, and that is relevant here. His sets for *Notre-Dame de Paris* are, as Bazin says, completely artificial in their materiality. The backdrops to the narrow medieval streets are clearly painted canvas, offering a sense of *trompe l'oeil* rather any realistic attempt at perspectival space. But we are in a fairytale and there is clearly an influence of the illustrations to Hugo's novel for the 1889 edition by Luc-Olivier Merson, in particular the dark, sinister interiors of Frollo's rooms. However, whilst the sets feel false materially, architecturally, they are true to the late fifteenth century to which they refer, including the amazing façade of Notre-Dame. The massiveness of that building as a dominating force is well brought out through the cinemascope format, as indeed is the labyrinthine nature of the streets – the wide-angle reach of 'scope allows us to see several streets as they converge together, their narrowness adding to the sense of entrapment. The effect of the *trompe l'oeil* and sets in general is indeed one of imprisonment:

there seems to be no way out. Certainly, the poet Gringoire (Robert Hirsch) experiences this when he descends from the labyrinthine streets of Paris into the beggars' underworld. This is medieval Paris, after all, a time when the buildings crowded in on people and created a strong sense of claustrophobia – a feeling compounded by the cinemascope format. As the architectural historian Anthony Sutcliffe tells us, in medieval Paris views across the Seine (of which we get a glimpse from Esméralda's rooms) 'were fleeting because banks and bridges were lined by buildings, the only visual release was upwards to the turrets and towers of the churches and onto the heavens.'[16]

The authenticity of Renoux' design merits a further comment in this context because it impacts on the mood created by the sets, and it concerns the house façades. Up until the sixteenth century, timber-framed houses in Paris (as elsewhere in Europe) were jettied outwards from the first floor upwards to create more living space. By the sixteenth century, Royal decree had instituted a design unique to Paris, to create more light within the city. This time, the timber frame rested on the heavy ground-floor masonry that leant outwards whilst the vertical timbers were angled inwards so that the façade leaned backwards.[17] As we note from Renoux's sets, we have the appropriate forward-leaning jetty façades of the fifteenth century (see figure 5.4) which add to this sense of claustrophobia. Only up in the Notre-Dame is there any feeling of life and air to breathe – coming in the form of the flowers

Figure 5.4: Renoux' sets for houses in *Notre-Dame de Paris*. © *René Renoux*.

that grow in the crevices, and the doves that alight. Small wonder that, as soon as Esméralda is down in the nether regions, she is doomed.

To conclude this chapter on fairytales, I turn to François Truffaut's 1955 *Cahiers de cinéma* article on Becker's *Ali Baba*, 'Ali Baba et la politique des auteurs'. According to Vignaux,[18] this is the article that acted as the founding-stone for auteur theory – indeed, she is right, because it is here that Truffaut argues for the case that even if a film is a mainstream, producer-commissioned piece it can still retain enough of the filmmaker's authorial style to make it an auteur film. Here is what Truffaut says:

> Despite the fact that the script has been fiddled about with by over a dozen people, a dozen too many with the exception of Becker, *Ali Baba* is an auteur film, an auteur who has attained an exceptional mastery, a film auteur. Thus the technical success of *Ali Baba* confirms the validity of our theory, auteur theory.[19]

Style, technical mastery: these, then, according to Truffaut, are the hallmarks of the auteur. We certainly do not dispute the term auteur in relation to Becker as a film-maker. What this chapter has, it is hoped, made clear is the central flaw to, or limitations of, the concept of auteur theory as defined by Truffaut and the *Cahiers* group. Namely, that the authorial sign is not singular, as they contend, but plural. Set and costume designers, directors of photography, actors, stars – all are producers of meaning, they too have technical mastery. The overall concept and vision is undoubtedly that of the film-maker. But, as we have demonstrated here, the experimentation, in this case with colour, and the narrative edge brought by set design and costuming, are the province of those other auteurs involved in these three films, be they Wakhévitch, Renoux, Benda, Kelber, LeFèbvre or Matras.

Notes

1. The DVD of *Ali Baba et les quarante voleurs* has a trailer section which is quite lengthy and is taken from the existing print before it was remastered (DVD Studio Canal Plus). The flash-dupe-mask process is a method for creating a 'dupe negative with corrected colour from a print on which colours have faded.' (Konisberg, 1993, p. 129).
2. Bazin (2006, p. 255).
3. See Rivette cited in Vignaux (2000, p. 166).
4. Vignaux, op. cit., p. 165.
5. Ibid,, p. 166.
6. Becker quoted in Vignaux (op. cit., p. 167).
7. Vignaux provides a full transcript of Fernandel's contract (op. cit., pp. 164–5).
8. André Morice cited in Daquin (1960, p. 272).
9. This information comes to us from the production notes to *Barbe-bleue* in *La Cinématographie française*, No. 1429, 11.8.1951, p. 2 (no author name).
10. Profile of Christian-Jaque in *La Cinématographie française*, No. 1404. 17.2.1951, p. 3 (no author name).

11. The information I have from Matras' own description is that arc lights at the time were 225 amps (see *La Cinématographie française* special dossier on colour, No. 1538, 17.10.1953, p. 34). According to electricians, to obtain the kilowatt value you need to multiply the amps by the voltage. In the French studios voltage is at 115 (see Barsacq, 1970, pp. 296–7) so the figure comes out at around 25 kilowatts. The other advantage with using Gevacolor – this time a cost-effective one – as Matras informs us, is that it requires far less heat from the lamps. It operates on 2–3000 degrees Kelvin as compared with Technicolor, which required twice as much heat (see *La Cinématographie française* special dossier on colour, No. 1538, 17.10.1953, p. 34).

12. Information provided in profile of Christian-Jaque in *La Cinématographie française*, No. 1404. 17.2.1951, p. 3 (no author name).

13. Quéval (1951, p. 45).

14. See *Film Monthly Bulletin*'s review '*Barbe-bleue*', Vol. 22, No. 259, 1.8.1955 (no author name).

15. Bazin (1957, p. 55), my translation.

16. Sutcliffe (1993, p. 11).

17. Ibid., p. 17.

18. Vignaux, op. cit., p. 167.

19. Truffaut quoted in Vignaux (op. cit., p. 168), my translation.

Chapter 6

Foxy Women: Queens, Mistresses and Minxes

In Figure 6.1 (below) I have set out our foxy women into two columns, organizing the listings according to star vehicles. It is instructive, but perhaps unsurprising, to note that, out of the six titles, Martine Carol stars in three of them. She was after all associated with audaciously libertine roles and, prior to Brigitte Bardot coming on the scene, she was the sex-symbol of France's popular cinema and the nation's answer to Hollywood's own blond bombshell, Marilyn Monroe. Also worth noting is the fact that, taken together, her three films attracted overall a larger audience than those of the other three stars added together: Darrieux, Moreau or Morgan.

Star vehicles: Foxy Women in <u>historically</u> chronological order

---

Martine Carol vehicles	*Moreau, Darrieux, Morgan vehicles*

Lucrèce Borgia (53)	*La Reine Margot* (54)
Christian-Jaque/[Martine Carol]	Dréville/[Jeanne Moreau]
Technicolor	Eastmancolor
3,632,139	**2,600,759**
Madame du Barry (54)	*L'Affaire des poisons* (55)
Christian-Jaque/[Martine Carol]	Decoin/[Danielle Darrieux]
Eastmancolor	Technicolor
2,378,009	**1,507,420**
Caroline chérie (51)	*Marie-Antoinette Reine de France* (56)
Pottier/[Martine Carol]	Delannoy/[Michèle Morgan]
3,184,380	Technicolor
	2,280,704
Total: 9 million audience	*Total: 6.3 million audience*

Figure 6.1: Star vehicles, audience figures in bold.

Supremely Foxy: Martine Carol – sex, nudity and gender play

It seems appropriate to begin with the three Carol vehicles, since she comes to embody the foxy women triad of queenliness (Lucrèce), mistress (Du Barry) and minx (Caroline). In the first two films, Carol plays a real-live person, even if her own performances are, to a greater or lesser extent, abstract renditions of the original. The real Lucrèce was the daughter of Rodrigo Borgia, future Pope Alexander VI. She was caught up in the machinations of her father's ruthless politics and sexual corruption, much of which was linked to the Papal Court. Her brother César, whose cruelty his father exploited just as he exploited his daughter's beauty for political advantage, was a Cardinal to this court. Rumours ran that César had incestuous relations with his sister. Whilst she may have been victim of her father's abusive ways, Lucrèce was nonetheless a powerful woman. She was given provinces and towns to govern by her father as compensation for her various deeds or setbacks in love.[1] In the Christian-Jaque version of her life we have none of the allusions to the Papal Court, a case of indirect censorship that can be explained by the fact that this film was a Franco-Italian co-production. Nor do we get any sense of Lucrèce as a political animal in her own right. She is represented in the film as a pawn to César's bidding – a much-reduced cipher of powerful femininity, therefore.

As Madame du Barry, Carol is similarly a pawn, a sexual one once more, this time manipulated by Jean du Barry and others. But she also holds her own. She clearly does not mind being trained up to become Louis XV's mistress and she quite obviously enjoys that role once she secures it. She even comes to love the elderly king. The performance in this instance bears a much closer resemblance to the original Madame du Barry than her Lucrèce to its original, with the crucial omission that she was a great patron of the arts. Carol's du Barry remains rather vulgar and 'inculte' in matters of taste and style, which is something of a pity since the real du Barry was, in fact, well-educated and a woman of considerable discernment. She was a great admirer of the Enlightenment philosophers, in particular Voltaire. She was the patron to numerous painters, including Greuze, Fragonard and Vigée-Lebrun, sculptors (Lecomte, Pajou, Allegrain), architects (Ledoux) and artisans (Delanois, Leleu) and introduced the neo-classical style to Versailles.

But let us begin with the film that launched Martine Carol into stardom, *Caroline chérie* (Richard Pottier, 1951). This saucy romantic comedy about a high spirited young woman, Caroline, became the prototype for most of Carol's successful roles. The film opens with Caroline being furious at her birthday being ignored. It has the misfortune to fall on the 14th of July 1789 and word has arrived at her father's chateau that the Revolution has begun in Paris, so all celebrations are cancelled. The rest of the film is taken up with Caroline being pursued by the Revolutionaries, being thrown into prison, escaping danger but very much at the cost of sharing (sometimes willingly, others not) her sexual favours. As the film ends, Caroline has returned to her chateau and gone back up to the attic where she had first met the handsome young count, Gaston de Sallanches (Jacques Dacqmine), with whom she had fallen in love at the very beginning of the film. During her many adventures, their paths had crossed several times and they had snatched brief moments together. Towards the end of the film, but before she returns to the chateau, Caroline tells the count the whole truth about her adventures. At first he rejects her as a 'whore'. She retorts that not all women could be kept safe during the Revolution and she did what she did to survive; thereupon she leaves for her chateau where she says she will wait one month to see if he will come to her. In the end, he forgives her transgressive behaviour and comes to the chateau to find her.

A surface reading of the film offers the fairly trite and conventional outcome of the 'happy ending'. Arguably, however, particularly because Caroline now speaks from a position of strength ('take me as I am or forget it'), a more complex reading could be that, since she has become fully immersed in the knowledge of womanhood (thanks to her sexual adventures and escape strategies), she is a match for the count and that means they *can* live happily ever after (the Revolution having come to an end)! During her adventures, Caroline not only has to fend for herself as best she can, she has to adopt various disguises to remain hidden, the most significant one being to cross-dress as a young man on two separate occasions – first, to make her escape from Paris and, subsequently, from the rebel Chouans. Her sexually-transgressive behaviour, which includes a lesbian moment (with one of the count's mistresses), is matched by her clever strategies for survival, most of which (like the cross-dressing) are equally transgressive (see figure 6.2 below).

Figure 6.2: Caroline (Martine Carol) cross-dressed as young man. © 1951 Gaumont/Studio Canal.

Caroline's disguises serve a dual purpose: they act as survival mechanisms and they alert us to a body that is easily mutable and therefore unstable, unseizable, in its transgressiveness. One of the other interesting threads of *Caroline chérie* is that Caroline is caught between two stools when it comes to her development. On the one hand there is the count telling her (during one of their brief encounters) that she must give up being a child. On the other, there is the elderly aristocrat with the means to save her from the guillotine if only she will remain a little girl. These are two contradictory discourses, both of which Caroline learns to negotiate to survive and become a woman on her own terms. In the end, and this is what makes this film stand out against the times and trends of female subjugation (1790s and 1950s alike), her transgressiveness is one that men, including the count, cannot control.

The author of the original story is Cécil Saint-Laurent, a man of the extreme right (see the discussion of *Un Caprice de Caroline chérie*, Chapter 9). So it comes as no surprise that the Revolutionaries (*les Bleus*) are shown in a pretty unfavourable light: as brutal executioners, erstwhile rapists and so on. However, intriguingly, the aristocrats and other supporters of the royal cause (*les Blancs*) do not necessarily fare any better. The following two sequences, placed back to back in the film, serve as a good example. In the first, Caroline has been taken prisoner, this time by the Revolutionaries, and thrown into the Conciergerie, where she awaits her fate. A roll call for those who are to be guillotined that day is given. We see the aristocrats act with dignity (as 'befits' their class) as they make their way to their execution. This time Caroline is spared. In the next sequence she is taken to a special house, the *maison de santé*, the hospital of Dr Belhomme (Raymond Souplex). He is a man prepared to help save the aristocrats and therefore a sympathizer (*un Blanc*). However, his assistance only lasts for as long as they can pay the extortionate fee of 1000 francs a day. If they run out of money, the younger women and wives can whore themselves to guarantee their survival and that of their husband or lover. The rest get sent back to a certain death (the Conciergerie and the guillotine).

Caroline is a spokesperson for the truth – she rightly accuses Belhomme and the aristocrats of cowardice. She also tells Sallanches that he is a hypocrite with his many mistresses and all. But equally she is seen switching sides (*Blanc/Bleu*) as needs must to survive – even though she claims to have no interest in politics. This ability to switch colours may well reveal a lack of political consciousness but it certainly provides a fairly realistic image of how most people survive dreadful upheavals such as war and revolution. And, as such, it can be read as an apologia for the rather meek and cowardly ways France adopted during the Occupation period. It certainly is a theme that runs through Saint-Laurent's *Carolinades*, as we shall see with *Un Caprice de Caroline chérie*. But that is not all Caroline is. She has strengths too: fortitude and truthfulness. A pattern emerges, therefore, whereby the woman comes to stand, on the one hand, for the murkiness and ambiguities of a nation's psyche during times of political fracture and unease and, on the other, a spirit of defiance and resistance. And in *Lucrèce Borgia*, yet another Saint-Laurent adaptation, these same themes reappear.

This Lucrèce Borgia is odious, but only to a degree. Saint-Laurent's deliberate intention was 'to correct her legend'.[2] In this version of her scandalous life, she is capable of feeling true love – for her husband Alphonso d'Aragon (Massimo Serato) – and this leads her to a kind of redemption, as exemplified by the closing sequence in which, dressed in black, she attends her husband's funeral. Her outfit makes her look more like a nun than the whorish queen or colluder with her brother's murderous ways that she was reputed to be. Indeed, in this film, whatever evils she embodies, such as enjoying the cruel torture of convicts (passed off as mere sporting events), her sins are revealed as being visited upon her by her inhumane brother César (Pedro Amendariz). It is worth noting that this was Carol's most successful film ever. This comes as something of a surprise, given that it is her least palatable role and, arguably, her worst film in acting terms, as I shall now go on to explain.

The main problem lies with the film itself. It is not sure if it is about Lucrèce Borgia – a faction biopic therefore – or a swashbuckler film, with three men, the cruel César, the unfortunate Alphonso and Paolo (another of her lovers to meet his death, played by Christian Marquand), all vying in different ways to possess or control her. My own view is that Christian-Jaque becomes over-interested in the César character, whose embodiment of pure evil is rather fascinating, it has to be said. This dark prince, whose jet-black facial hair (beard and moustache) should warn us of his tyrannical ways, disposes of the lives of others as if they are less than objects. Either, they are impedimenta he must rid himself of – mostly Lucrèce's serial husbands, whom he forces her to marry for political gain and then needs to dispose of by murdering them – or, beings he can toy with in cruel games, such as forcing convicts to joust, balanced on a beam above a huge flaming pyre or making them participate in a deadly game of hunt the human. It is in this latter game that Paolo is put to death by a well-aimed spear thrown by César himself at the behest of Lucrèce, who wishes to silence her former lover from revealing her whorish ways to her new husband Alphonso. As Alphonso says, 'it is ignoble'. And a sign of Lucrèce's collusion with this ignoble torture is marked by the fact that, on this occasion, she wears the same colour as her brother: both are dressed in red. Redemption seems a long way off as yet.

Carol is given the unfortunate task of having to act to her melodramatic worst.[3] Thus, she plays the woman torn between her desire to start her life afresh with Alphonso and being caught as a pawn in César's ruthless game of power: whilst she is represented as a fairly unwilling victim of her brother's cruelty – he beats her, forces her to marry the men he chooses, there is even a hint of incest – she also appears to derive enjoyment from her brother's sadistic games with others. But, in a matter of seconds, she can be in tears telling Alphonso that she is ashamed of her past. Apart from the fact that Carol has not got the acting skills to make these transitions seem properly motivated, it is this swinging from one extreme of temperament to the other that provides us with a characterization that is without definition. Moreover, Christian-Jaque's seeming desire to make a swashbuckler film means that any development of Lucrèce's persona is constantly interrupted by the various chases, swordfights and other scrapes the men get into. She remains shallow, therefore, and the film's narrative is fed to us in scraps, piecemeal – not even episodic.

The other aspect of Carol's appearance in the film that has to be mentioned is the exploitation of her body. That certainly would have been an attraction – explaining perhaps the willingness of some 3.6 million spectators to go and see her in the most explicit nude scenes of all her costume drama performances (see figure 6.3 below).

Beyond the dresses and night attire that she wears, all of which push her breasts up almost to the point of full exposure, there are two crucial scenes in which she is naked and visible, either frontally or from behind, and one scene, when her brother drags her out of bed and throws her to the floor, in which we get a full-shot of her buttocks. In that same scene, after he has violently beaten her, she is left lying prostrate on the floor, her night-dress torn away from her left breast (a breast, incidentally first perceived in *Caroline chérie*). This scene and

Figure 6.3: Lucrèce Borgia-Martine Carol in her nude bath scene. © Sam Levin.

the nude scenes proper all occur at points in the narrative where her brother manifests his abusive power in relation to her and his complete contempt for the man she is currently married to, or her lover. Furthermore, all three occur during her narrated flashback, when she explains to Alphonso how César cruelly controls her. The naked flesh is almost proof of this abuse. The flashback opens with her languishing in the bath-tub as she, meantime in voice-over, explains how she took lovers because her first husband Sforza (Gilles Quéant) left her too much on her own. We see her fully-nude body, her right leg slightly lifted hiding the pubic area only – all else is there to gaze upon: a pretty and well-formed female body (see figure 6.3 above).[4] As if to emphasize the objectifying gaze, we see her negligent husband accompanied by a young boy (his real lover one wonders), nonchalantly peering down over her. She is soon relieved of this importunate husband as César announces he will get rid of him by accusing him of high-treason. In the end, Lucrèce manages to persuade César that a divorce for non-consummation of the marriage is a better ploy. The second nude scene occurs later in this flashback, when Lucrèce is staying at the mansion of the countess of Farnèse (Valérie Tessier). Sforza is determined to restore his reputation by kidnapping Lucrèce and getting her to gainsay her accusation. His henchmen come charging into the bathing rooms, where a group of nude women courtiers are being tended to by masseuses or taking baths. In that group is Lucrèce, of course. We glimpse her entering the bath, naked, from behind. Men burst into this women's space, flailing swords as they attack the home guards. Sforza's men grab hold of Lucrèce, dragging her naked from the bath. She just has time to pull a sheet around her. Meantime, Paolo, who happens to be passing, crashes in through a window and rescues her. He throws a cloak around her and they make off on horseback. This episode more or less concludes the twenty-five minute flashback in which we have seen a fair amount of Martine Carol's naked flesh.

After so much nudity, Carol's next role as Madame du Barry comes as something of a contrast, since there is no nudity whatsoever – at the very best a well-supported bosom and a little cleavage. Mosk suggests in *Variety* that the French producers had their eye on the US market and wanted to avoid the Hayes production code stepping in and preventing a general release (it still saw fit to cut ten minutes from the original two-hour length, however).[5] The British market seems to have missed the fact that there is no nudity and 'X'-rated the film anyway. Moreover, the board of censors cut fourteen minutes. The only shocking element to the film, surely, is the level of corruption to which the Royal Court will stoop to gain favour with the king. We are, of course, still four years away from the British 'Carry on...' film series, with their slapstick, lewd grimaces, innuendoes and double-entendres. In comparison, the tone of *Madame du Barry* is quite mild. There is plenty of innuendo, but also quite subtle parody.

Madame du Barry had the same technical crew as for *Lucrèce Borgia* in terms of set designer, Robert Gys, director of photography, Christian Matras, and costume designer, Marcel Escoffier. But there was a different scriptwriter: the great master of wit and irony Henri Jeanson (who also scripted *Fanfan la tulipe* for Christian-Jaque). He comes in place of the drier and darker Jacques Sigurd who scripted *Lucrèce Borgia*. The story relates Jeanne

Bécu's rise from anonymity as a salesgirl in a drapery store to international renown as Louis XV's mistress, Jeanne du Barry. As the king's favourite, she became a pawn in the struggle for power amongst the courtiers. Thus, on the one side, the cynical libertine Jean du Barry (Daniel Ivernel), who discovered this beauty, more or less pimps her to the king – with a little help from the duc de Richelieu (Denis d'Inès). The former successfully exploits the king's attachment to Jeanne du Barry as a means of sustaining his extravagant lifestyle; the latter to ensure he has the king's ear. On the other side, the Choiseul family endeavour in vain to disgrace her – the comte de Choiseul (Massimo Serato) tries to get her banished in favour of his sister the duchesse de Grammont (Gianna-Maria Canale). Louis XV (André Luguet), alerted to these plottings, banishes the pair instead. The rest of his court is equally antipathetic towards this 'upstart' and, at best, shuns her (as is the case with Marie-Antoinette/Isabelle Pia), at worst, calumniates her. La du Barry (as she is known) takes all of this reasonably well in her cheeky stride, especially once she is introduced to the Royal Court formally as the king's official mistress and he obliges Marie-Antoinette (Isabelle Pia) to recognize her. This official relationship lasts five years (1769–1774), until the king dies. Upon his death, the new king, Louis XVI, under the influence of his wife Marie-Antoinette, re-institutes the Choiseuls. La du Barry is chased out of the palace, sent into exile at her mansion in Louvenciennes, where she more or less remains until arrested as an enemy of the Revolution and condemned to the guillotine in 1793.

Carol's Madame du Barry rejoins her Caroline chérie character in terms of pert insolence and audacity. She also, interestingly, has the same frankness and tells the king the whole truth about her lowly origins, and how Jean du Barry deliberately set about forcing a meeting between the two for his own advantage. The king, at first, is incensed; he calls her a common prostitute. She storms out – clearly, to her mind, that is one label she does not deserve. The king soon regrets his words and is only too delighted to have her back and to oblige the Court to accept her. In her petulance and outspokenness, Carol plays to her strengths as a comic actor. As La du Barry, she is without guile and takes people as she finds them: a double factor for comedic moments in the film. Thus, she is charmed by a young penniless actor of the Comédie française, whom, conversely, the money-grabbing Jean du Barry quickly dispatches. In order to meet the demands of courtly etiquette, which dictate that a king's mistress must be married (to nobility), and since she cannot marry Jean du Barry (he is already wed), she pleasantly accepts that she must marry du Barry's older brother, Guillaume (Jean Debucourt). Upon the king's death, she knows her time is up and, sanguine to the last, it is she who with charming irony greets the comte de Choiseul's arrival with a *lettre de cachet,* ordering her exile. In so doing, she completely deflates his sense of triumph – a clever move on her part, showing that she has as much ability in the chess game of courtly manners as the rest of them. She leaves with dignity.

Madame du Barry opens with the same carnavalesque tour de force of *Lucrèce Borgia.* This time it is the 14th of July celebrations of the Republic, in *Lucrèce Borgia* it was some Roman festival of masks, a religious or pagan moment in the Papal city (it is not made clear). What does stand out is the similarity of camera action in the two films as it swirls or weaves around people, or as people move about in the frame – giving energy to the scene as well as suggesting that unbridled moments are never far away. In *Lucrèce Borgia*, Lucrèce meets a mystery man in this carnivalesque environ and they immediately take off for a romantic and sexual tryst amongst some Roman ruins. Later, it transpires he is Alphonso, her future intended. In *Madame du Barry*, this carnival sets the scene for the flashback into Jeanne du Barry's ascent to king's mistress and subsequent demise. A *sans culotte* (Republican) is the master of ceremonies, commentating a waxwork and slideshow about the fall of the monarchy. He alights on the slide of the draper's store, where, we are informed, the 'putain royale' (royal whore) du Barry worked before becoming the king's mistress. The film concludes on this same slide and same opening comments, suggesting that this story is a main attraction at the fair, endlessly recycled: her story is an object of derision, her person scurrilous and exemplary of the corruption that led to the revolutionary uprising in the first place. Of such practices (repetition and recycling) are myths created.

This, then, is the spectacle that bookends the film. The rest of the narrative, however, goes on to demonstrate just how false these accusations are. In short, the film renegotiates the legend just as the earlier Carol vehicle, *Lucrèce Borgia*, did. Equally, it exposes the venality and corruption of the court, above which Jeanne du Barry rises and which, as we know by the end of the former film, Lucrèce is beginning to withstand. Naturally, neither of these films can be considered radical; they do, however, propose that we cannot necessarily lay history at the feet of an individual woman. The process of post-war France in vilifying women for its own self-determined humiliation under the Occupation, and its subsequent attempts to re-model women according to some icon of French femininity, were probably not uttermost in Christian-Jaque's mind when he made these films. But the point is that, in renegotiating the myth, the door opens to see how and why myths are created in the first place. As the little boy in the 14th of July crowd rightly and repeatedly asserts at the end of the film: 'I want to know all about this du Barry' – 'all' being the operative word. Thus, rather than allowing the French to forget about the recent unattractive part of their history, as Chapuy suggests,[6] perhaps we can argue that Carol functions more as a means of coming to terms, if not with recent history itself, then with its complexities. The public is thus able to do two things: flee from the quotidian concerns (as mentioned in Chapter 1) by watching a reconstructed past on screen, but also take note that history can misrepresent truth and that myths undoubtedly should be questioned.

Classic stars: the dark and the luminous – dissipated queens, poisoners and the myth of the monstrous female

A similar pattern of contesting the myth of the treacherous female and showing the complexities of history emerges in relation to two out of the three other films in this second category of films: *La Reine Margot* and *Marie-Antoinette Reine de France*. Neither of these queens is a schemer. Indeed, in the case of Margot (Jeanne Moreau), the chief schemer is her mother Catherine de Médicis (Françoise Rosay); in Marie-Antoinette's (Michèle Morgan) it is first the Royal Court, then Lafayette, and finally the Republican forces. Sellier[7] and Chapuy[8] are right to insist that the 1950s was a time when patriarchy worked hard to re-assert itself – and one would have thought that the costume drama was a perfect vehicle for putting forward these types of discourses. Male friendship – a form of *fraternité* and certainly a strong emblem of reasserting a masculine dominance – is present in some of these films, as we see in *La Reine Margot*. Here a bond transcending difference is slowly established between the Protestant La Mole (Armando Francioli) and the Catholic Coconnas (Henri Genès). Interestingly, despite the title of the film, which suggests it is about the queen, Margot, Dréville claimed that the 'key roles were above all those of the men, especially Charles IX, played by the remarkable Robert Porte'.[9] And yet, when we watch the film, it is Rosay's Catherine de Médicis that dominates all others, with Moreau's Margot and her mixture of arrogance and compassion acting as an interesting foil to her mother's evil ways. Margot's intelligent sensuality, with almost feline movement, is a good match for the ruthless and scheming Catherine. Thus, these costume dramas reveal that men are perhaps less astute at asserting patriarchal rule than Sellier or Chapuy would have us believe. I am not completely persuaded, therefore, by the argument that there is a 'devalorisation of powerful women figures' as Sellier claims.[10] My view is that the representations are subtler than has so far been argued. We are as much drawn to Margot and Marie-Antoinette by their apparent integrity as by their affairs of the heart. Both tell the truth. Henri de Navarre says to his wife Margot, 'you are unfaithful in love, but you are a faithful friend'. And she proves this on three occasions when she saves his life by warning him of plots to kill him. On two occasions she saves her lover La Mole from death. In the third instance, time is against her and she fails. La Mole is executed. At the end of this harrowing film of treachery and mass murder, it is the Catholic forces of repression and their intolerance of the Protestants that stand out. These forces are embodied by Catherine de Médicis and Charles IX, as well as their courtiers and chief of police, Maurevel (Vittorio Sanipoli). Moreover, still on this idea of a subtler representation of women, after the execution of La Mole, Margot leaves with Henri de Navarre (now Henri IV) and the look on her face is one of resignation and grief at her loss – there is power and dignity in that final shot of the film.

Marie-Antoinette, for her part, shows another kind of integrity. Accused of having the Swedish officer, comte Axel de Fersen (Richard Todd) as her lover, she tells her husband Louis XVI (Jacques Morel), truthfully, that this is not so: 'if my feelings displease you, you have nothing to reproach me for in terms of my actions'. Similarly, she never dissimulates about her attraction to Fersen. However, to spare the king the humiliation of Fersen's presence at court, she accepts her 'lover's' decision to go to America and fight in the War of Independence. Once he returns, she feels constrained yet again to send this man she loves far away (not so far this time but to Valenciennes, some two hundred kilometres from Paris, in north-eastern France).

In the other film under consideration in this trio of women-centred narratives, *L'Affaire des poisons*, we have the truly foxy schemer, Madame de Montespan (Danielle Darrieux) who plots her way through the film to keep Louis XIV to herself by eliminating potential rivals. We could perhaps entertain the view here that women are devalorized (as evil), if it were not for the fact that Darrieux's compelling performance, alongside Viviane Romance's, as the witch-cum-clairvoyant La Voisin, is a magical tour de force. There is much to interest us in their numerous encounters, as we shall see below.

In all three films, it is the woman's love of a man that drives the narrative: Margot for La Mole; La Montespan for Louis XIV; Marie-Antoinette for Fersen. Because in all cases the man is unobtainable (he dies, he has moved on, he is implicitly forbidden), female anguish is another common thread that unites the films – good women's cinema, therefore. History, however inaccurate, functions as a necessary backdrop. But what is interesting in this context is the recurrence of certain themes, even if the periods span some two centuries. *La Reine Margot* is very specifically set around the time of the Saint Bartholomew Massacre (24 August 1572); *L'Affaire des poisons* in the year 1676; *Marie-Antoinette Reine de France* over two decades (1774–1793). The themes are those of denunciation, spying, poisoning (either literally, by liquid, or metaphorically, by pen and song), unnatural desires (incest, black Sabbath, lesbian), finally, more positively this time, female defiance and courage against the odds – all three women stand up, albeit to differing degrees, to those who would control, banish or execute them. Let us now take a closer look, beginning with *La Reine Margot*.

We are right in the middle of the Wars of Religion (1562–1598) between Catholics and Protestants (the Huguenots). This war pitted two royal lineages against each other: the Catholic Valois Royal Family headed by Catherine de Médicis and the Bourbon Royal lineage headed by the Protestant Henri de Navarre. The film opens with news of the Reconciliation decreed by Charles IX bringing an end to hostilities. His mother, Catherine de Médicis, has brought the two families together in marriage – Marguerite de Valois and Henri de Navarre (André Versini) – ostensibly, to consolidate this Reconciliation between the two religions. In fact, she is plotting to assemble all the leaders of the Huguenots and their families into the citadel of the Louvre so that she can systematically eliminate them. This massacre, condoned by her son the king, is set for a few days after the wedding and falls on Saint Bartholomew's day. Some 10,000 Huguenots were killed: a genocide through duplicity if ever there was one. When Margot rescues Henri from this plot to kill him, Catherine sets about to expose him as an adulterer. When Margot saves him from *that* plot, Catherine attempts to poison him, through arsenic. Unfortunately the source of this poisoning, the doused pages of a book on falconry, falls into the hands of the weasely Charles. He licks his way to his premature death (in fact Charles died of tuberculosis two years after the Massacre). On his deathbed, he nominates Henri as his successor (again a distortion of history, Charles' brother the duc d'Anjou became king; it was his lack of a successor that brought Henri de Navarre to the throne in 1589).

This was Dréville's first film in colour. The same is true, incidentally, for Decoin and Delannoy, the directors of the other two films. The latter two worked with Technicolor, Dréville with early Eastmancolor and, as he noted himself, the interiors were more successful in terms of colour rendition than the exteriors.[11] Indeed, there is considerable instability and fuzziness in the exterior chase sequences in particular. The film was shot at the Epinay studios that boasted a fake river (useful for the moat scenes and the chucking of naked women into the river Seine during the Saint Bartholomew Massacre) and a substantial wooded park (10,000 square meters). Unusually, there were the remains of earlier sets by Lazare Meerson for Feyder's *La Kermesse héroique* (1935) which served as the gates of Paris and the drawbridge in Dréville's film. But that did not prevent the cost of the sets, of which there are many, amounting to 50 million francs on their own – suggesting an overall budget in excess of 200 million francs. Indeed, nothing was cheap: Moreau's fee was five million for example – quite a lot, given this was her first major role in cinema.[12]

There is much to suggest that on the production side there were a number of difficulties to be overcome, which may in part explain criticisms levelled at this film about its unevenness.[13] The idea of adapting Dumas' famous historical novel, which itself largely transmutes history by hanging a love story onto the historical event of the Saint Bartholomew Massacre, had first been mooted by Abel Gance. But his project was monstrously long. This was dropped in favour of bringing in Jacques Companeez to write the script. He had recently had a huge success with his script for Becker's *Casque d'or* and had a reputation for quick, sharp and witty repartee, which matched Dumas' mixture of melodrama and swashbuckler humour. As Dréville said, 'in my "Queen", historical truth was very much on the back burner. Like Dumas, we wanted to mix laughter in with serious matters.'[14] Several delays meant that Dréville lost his first choice of director of photography, Henri Alékan, who was there for the beginning of the shoot but had to go onto another film. This is why most credits have his name coming after the man chiefly responsible for the photography, Roger Hubert. A good choice, in the event, since Hubert, who began life as a still photographer before turning his hand to filming in the early 1920s, was just as experimental as Alékan. Illness deprived Dréville of his initial choice of Barbara Laage for Margot.[15] Largely unknown today, Laage was something of a minor blond bombshell, a lesser Martine Carol in essence but with a bit more of a vampish look. Rather wooden in her expression, she has none of the sensual intelligence and nuances of Moreau's acting style. Given that much of Moreau's interpretation of Margot depends on what happens with her eyes, mouth and head movement, we can argue that there is considerable gain in this loss of Laage. Moreau's Margot is a restrained, quiet performance – nothing excessive or melodramatic – until the very closing sequence of the film with La Mole's execution, which is what makes her screams at her lover's beheading so powerful.

Reviews of the time devoted considerable space to Moreau's performance, but especially to the few moments of her purported nudity – which is odd since, first, there was very little of it and, second, it was known that a double stood in for her! This focus, whereby reviewers cried out against the attempt to transform Moreau into a new kind of Martine Carol, seems faintly ridiculous now, given the illustrious career of this extraordinary actor. Mosk says 'she is miscast for nudy roles. She will never give Martine Carol competition in this sphere'.[16] The weekly news magazine *L'Express* states categorically that 'the nudity which made

Martine Carol's fortune is inappropriate given (Moreau's) considerable talent'.[17] *Combat* is equally troubled 'how unlucky Jeanne Moreau is to have inherited a role tailor-made for Martine Carol'.[18] Baroncelli in *Le Monde* talks about the baubles of nudity dangled before the audiences.[19] There are only three such nude scenes. In the first 'nude' scene, Margot has her back to us as she drops her gorgeous deep blue velvet and ermine-trimmed dressing gown. She is rushing her husband into her bed to foil her mother's attempt to expose him as an adulterer. It is a two-second flash. But it is also evident that the rear-view of the body is not Moreau's. The body impersonating hers is much wider at the hips and considerably larger overall. In the second instance, Margot's naked body is hinted at in her one night of love-making with La Mole. Morning breaks; in a tight medium shot we see La Mole asleep and she is leaning over him to awaken him. We see her naked shoulders, no more. The shot is serene and beautifully framed, with La Mole slightly in the shadows, softly lit to enhance his erotic appeal; Margot is in full light giving off the aura of a woman satisfied in love from the night of their sexual encounter. Her face remains masked, so we can only read this from her eyes and her mouth, and they suggest a great deal. The erotics, then, remain in the domain of what is not shown; the lack of the explicit making the image powerful. Finally, and in sharp contrast to the other two 'nude' scenes, Margot comes to the Bastille to endeavour to free her lover and Cocannas. To get to La Mole, she realizes she has to give her body to the prison's governor. It is she who rips her bodice open, exposing a single breast. The importance of the gesture is that she asserts her body-power – she gives, in exchange for access to La Mole. Hardly victim behaviour, a meaning reinforced by the fact that this is, yet again, a flash scene from which Dréville quickly fades the camera.

Moreau plays Margot with a grace of movement that Martine Carol never achieves, even in her best film *Lola Montès* (see Chapter 15). Whereas Carol can neither sing nor dance, Moreau most certainly can. Moreover, Moreau's classical training through the Conservatoire and the Comédie française shines through. She gives evidence of an economy of gesture that Carol is very far from achieving. Carol, for example, uses her hands a great deal to emphasize her meaning. She also grimaces, gives knowing nods and winks to stress a point. Neither of these phatic kinds of gesture are part of Moreau's repertoire. She uses, as I have already indicated, her face and bodily grace to make meaning. I mentioned, above, the dignity and reserve in the final shots of the film. It is worth mentioning that, according to historical accounts, Margot insisted in having La Mole's head – and in Patrice Chéreau's 1994 version of the film, this fairly gruesome, and melodramatic response is included. The omission here by Dréville is significant. Again the idea of victimhood is eschewed, as is any representation of woman as hysterical (something that cannot be said of Isabelle Adjani's performance in Chéreau's version, I fear).

The costumes for the lead roles are truly ravishing – designed by Rosine Delamare. Catherine de Médicis' black dress with its black-veiled headdress makes her look remarkably like the evil black widow spider she is. Her blackness is matched by the outfit of her older son, the king Charles IX – a mixture of venal cowardice and vague incestuous desire for his beautiful sister (exemplified by his pet magpie that he calls Margot and often caresses).

Only upon his deathbed, where he redeems himself by making Henri de Navarre king, is he dressed in white. Margot's dresses are exquisite in their detail: greys with red front panels to the skirt; in other dresses, pinks, lilacs, reds, crimsons abound. The skirts, correctly, are so wide she has to turn to her side to get through doorways. In terms of the colours of Margot's clothes matching and making meaning, the dress she wears the night she sleeps with La Mole, with its crushed raspberry, mirrors perfectly his own crimson attire. All this red, so typically associated with the female and passion, is not without other readings, either. In this scene, there is a significant reversal of what we might expect, since it is La Mole rather than Margot who is languishing on the bed; and it is she who sits above him, asserting her desire as she seduces him (remember, earlier, I pointed out how she awakens him the next day from their slumber in a similar pose). This will not be the only time La Mole adopts the more traditionally feminine role, as we shall see in relation to Cocannas.

As if to stress this idea that gender construction does not necessarily have to be so rigid, the colour range of Margot's sartorial éclat is also matched by her extremely camp younger brother le duc d'Anjou (Daniel Ceccaldi), future Henri III and Catherine's favourite. The pastels of his Renaissance dress, to say nothing of his jewellery, readily mark him out as an unfixed, even queer, body in relation to the certitude of most of the other men's attire, which is either muted grey or based upon a reasonably dark palette. The other exception is the genial and physically robust Coconnas, played by the musical singer and former rugby player Henri Genès. His ability to sit astride the masculine (as exemplified by his excellent swordsmanship) and the feminine (through his tenderness towards La Mole) is reflected in his light satin attire of greys and purples. This places him somewhere in between – unsurprisingly perhaps, since the ultimate message of the film is that brotherly love is stronger, and therefore more important, than the love of a woman. Coconnas decides to stay and die with La Mole rather than escape. As the two are taken to their execution on Place de Grève, Coconnas has to lift and carry the wounded La Mole up the steps to the executioner's block. La Mole's body is limp and feminine held in the arms of his strong burly friend. Dréville offers us a range of masculinities in this film, suggesting that he was interested not just in key male roles but also in the idea of masculinity as a plural concept, of which virility is but one aspect. In so doing, he challenges the notion of gender fixity which, as we shall see with nineteenth-century narratives, stood as an endeavour to assert the rightful place of men and women in terms of a hierarchy of power (see Part Three). Here a greater fluidity is proposed (see figure 6.4 opposite).

Paris' Place de Grève (now Place de l'Hôtel de Ville) merits a pause since it appears in two of these three films. During the Ancien Régime, it was the place of execution where the condemned could be hung, drawn and quartered, or burnt, or simply have their heads cut off with an executioner's sword, such as the one that is wielded so gruesomely at La Mole and Coconnas' beheadings. We actually see their heads flying off into the dust. In *L'Affaire des poisons*, La Voisin is taken there to be burnt – obviously because she is guilty of witchcraft, black Sabbaths that included the sacrificing of infants and young children, and her other more mundane acts of poisoning. During the Revolution, the guillotine was

Figure 6.4: La Mole as a floppy body (and not for the last time!).[20]

introduced and first tried out on a common thief in Place de Grève in 1792. The crowds, by all accounts, were not that enamoured of the speed with which the sentenced man was killed. By 1793, once the executions became political in nature, the venue changed more or less permanently to the Place de la Révolution (now Concorde). It is here that Marie-Antoinette met her death, executed by La Veuve/the widow (as the guillotine was familiarly known). The hatred mounted against her was a media-circus of rumour and innuendo, engineered by pamphleteers, songsters and, later in the 1790s, revolutionary newspapers. Amongst other things, she was labelled Madame Déficit for her spendthrift ways; then, later, Madame Véto for her interference in her husband's affairs; still later, Monstre Femelle – responsible for the bloodbath in Paris as a result of the counter-revolutionary September Massacre in 1792 (when she supposedly had called on Prussia and Austria to come to the rescue via the so-called *Manifeste de Brunswick*). When dragged back to Paris and thrown into prison, she was known as La Boulangère for withholding food from the poor and, finally, La Veuve Capet as she awaited her own execution. Small surprise that, in the end, she was easily found guilty of trumped-up accusations of treason towards the state; even worse, during her trial, she was accused amongst other things of incestuous relations with her son, Louis XVII.

I have spoken of Moreau's measured performance. The same could be said of Michèle Morgan's Marie-Antoinette. Hers is a much longer trajectory to cover – 20 years – starting with the light-hearted and frivolous 18-year-old young woman of 1774 through to the dignified older 38-year-old woman, mother of four children, who defends herself with such elegant verve and stature before the revolutionary tribunal that is determined to find her guilty. Sustaining a characterization over this long period, and maintaining her audiences' interest, represents no mean feat of acting. Since this film covers a 20-year period, it is helpful to break it up into its four distinct epochs which relate to her life.

Part	One	Two	Three	Four
PERIOD	*1774–8*	*1782–4*	*1785–9*	*1790–3*
Sequences	1–6	7–12	13–20	21–33
Length	27'	17'	23'	50'

Figure 6.5: The four periods of the 20 year span of *Marie-Antoinette Reine de Franc*.

We first meet Marie-Antoinette, as does Alex de Fersen, ten minutes into the film. At that moment, she is a mystery woman in disguise at a masked ball held at the Bal de l'Opéra.[21] Her mask is extraordinary – we only see her eyes, but not just any eyes: these are the mythic blue eyes of La Morgan that were consecrated in the famous lines delivered by Gabin in *Quai des brumes* (Carné, 1938), 'you have beautiful eyes you know.' Six minutes later when, having twisted her ankle, her mask falls off, we realize, as does Fersen, who she is. She is wearing a very coquettish dress underneath a turquoise satin cloak. The mask, too, is turquoise, accentuating the eyes, and has a frill on the bottom, almost replicating her attire of a turquoise cloak worn over a pink and white satin dress adorned with bows and satin roses. This is the young Marie-Antoinette of the first part of the film, during which time the Dauphin becomes king and she queen. The six sequences that compose this 27-minute section serve to establish, from her point of view, the very clear difference between the reality of married life with Louis and the experience of true love with Fersen. Compared to Louis' rather sweet bore, more interested in clocks and hunting than consummating his marriage and producing an heir, Fersen stands out as a very glamorous alternative. As she states in relation to her husband, 'I was given to him, not consulted'.

During this part of her dauphine-queenly life Marie-Antoinette sings, smiles and laughs. Thus, the digs at her extravagances (187 dresses in one year – Rose Bertin was famously her designer) do not really register in her consciousness at this stage – and, appropriately enough, we see her arrayed in five different and ravishingly beautiful dresses over these first 26 minutes of the film. Morgan plays Marie-Antoinette with a light touch; she teases her rather dumpy husband and only slightly flirts with Fersen. When she returns from the ball, she glides up to her rooms in Versailles singing to herself. In her rooms she stops to view herself in the mirror, clearly wondering if she has changed as a result of this magic encounter. It is a clever, intelligent and economic piece of acting and one which, of course, consolidates Morgan's star persona as an enigma. Morgan was often compared to Garbo, another enigmatic star, and her unreadability was one that led critics to describe her performance as icy (see Chapter 2).[22] She is no ice-maiden here, however. Her exuberance as a young woman is warm, funny and engaging. This section ends in despair, with Fersen declaring he is to marry Mademoiselle Necker and the announcement that the-now queen of France is pregnant. She is not without malice, however. As a present for her pregnancy, she asks her husband to fire his finance minister Necker – which will inevitably mean the Necker household leaving court.[23]

Part two, which lasts seventeen minutes and is also composed of six sequences, comes in two sections. Both sections are marked by the return and subsequent departure of Fersen: in the first instance to America and the second to Valenciennes. The first section picks up Marie-Antoinette's story some four years later, in 1782. It begins with a reprise of her flirtation with Fersen. She tells him how handsome he is in his uniform when he comes to visit her at her 'country' home, Le Petit Trianon. He elected not to marry – 'a soldier must not', he tells her. It ends some eleven minutes later with his departure once more. Rumours, in the form of scurrilous songs about Marie-Antoinette's attachment to Fersen, are flying around. The only way to put a stop to them is for him to leave. 'We must end it', he tells her, referring as much to the rumours as to their obvious attraction to each other, to which she replies 'how can I live without you?' This time he enlists in the French army and goes to fight in America (on the Franco-American side against the British). The closing sequence to this section of part two sees Marie-Antoinette at her harpsichord, sadly singing a sentimental aria by Niccolo Piccinni as he takes his leave. The power of the performance is in the restraint Morgan exercises. By not allowing the heartbreaking scene to descend into mawkish melodrama, she gains our admiration as much as our pity.

In this first section of part two, the array of dresses is reduced in relation to part one. There are only three. Marie-Antoinette is trying to please her public by being more economic, and by running a small farm on her country estate where, incidentally, she is dressed as a shepherdess – very much as if from a Watteau painting. A second child is born – a son, something she hopes will please her public, her first child being a daughter. However, in the following sequence, her second outfit tells us, the audience, where her heart really lies – or at least the hat on her head does. She is going riding with Fersen, and her outfit, a pale blue dress with a white overcoat, is topped with a hat adorned with blue and yellow feathers, 'à la suédoise'! No wonder a scandal breaks and they have to separate.

The second section of part two (lasting six minutes; two costumes) reprises this pattern. Marie-Antoinette has had yet another child and is posing for her portrait by Elizabeth Vigée-Lebrun. At her request, Fersen returns; the hero of Yorktown. The king complains to his wife that whilst she is faithful to him, she does not love him. She responds with fortitude that she will not see Fersen but, as a reward for his services to France, he must be given command of the army in Valenciennes. We see her strength versus the king's weakness in her making the decision as to what, according to etiquette (certainly not her heart), must be done. The queen, who in the previous section demonstrated her determination to please the public, now seeks, in an act of self-sacrifice, to please her monarch. As Fersen receives the news from her, we read her steely resolve in her eyes and the firm, impassive set of her mouth as she knowingly removes her real love from her side.

Part three opens in 1785 with a scandal – yet another produced by scheming courtiers and the rumour-mongering mill – and ends in 1789 with the humiliation of the Royal family being dragged back to Paris and held under house arrest in the Tuileries. Part four is constructed around the aborted attempt, in 1791, to escape to Brussels, orchestrated by Fersen but undermined by the king's indecision and jealousy. It concludes with Marie-Antoinette's trial and subsequent execution in 1793. From the beginning of part three, the mood of the film has darkened – the tone is one of menace. Fersen hears about the scandal in Valenciennes and goes to confront the queen, who is residing in Le Petit Trianon doing her 'farming'. In this particular campaign to discredit her, she is accused of accepting a fabulous necklace from the Cardinal of Rohan and, thereby, of being his mistress. Marie-Antoinette is completely innocent of the *Affaire du collier*, but mud sticks and, as she tells Fersen, all her efforts to win over the people have crumbled to nothing, thanks to this scandal: 'The people no longer love me'. In this dramatic sequence the queen almost faints when Fersen arrives – 'you still love me', she swoons; and staunchly defends her honour – 'there is no necklace'. At the end she reaffirms her own love for him – 'it cost me so much to distance you'. Intriguingly, she then proceeds to give him mastery over her: 'counsel me, tell me what to do', she says. We observe that she used to ask her husband with these same words to advise her and issue orders. But he was so ineffectual that she eventually had mastery over him, insofar as she made her own decisions and counselled her husband on matters of state. This submission to Fersen initiates a series of crucial turning points. Within the narrative, it marks her loss of force to control events, be they of the heart (Fersen) or of the state (submission to the people's will). Privately, she finally gives up any further attempt to distance Fersen for propriety's sake. Publicly, she complies with the people's menacing bidding: first, that she show herself alone on the balcony of the palace of Versailles and, second, that she go to the Tuileries under their escort. Morgan executes the complexities of these different emotions with a delicacy of trepidation and a force of courage. She flounders before Fersen because of the strength of her feelings for him, so long held in check but clearly never repressed, as her eyes make so evidently clear. Before the people, on the balcony she makes a display of nerves of steel as she stands, impassively, her arms crossed, not in an act of defiance, but to show dignified calm as they continue to bray for her blood.

This same display of private and public emotions continues into part four. In private, these emotions range from care and concern for the safety of her servants and husband, loving tenderness towards her children, and a resigned passion for Fersen – resigned because she knows it has no future. In public, she repeatedly shows her courage before the people and, eventually, the tribunal. Even as they try to humiliate her by insulting her, accusing her of terrible deeds including incest with her son, so she responds with calm and dignity. Her speech to the tribunal, taken verbatim from Marie-Antoinette's trial transcript in which she defies the mothers of France to find her guilty of incest, is a tour de force. During the three-year period of this last part (1790–1793), Marie-Antoinette ages tremendously. In the closing sequences, Fersen attempts a second aborted escape. He comes to the queen to urge her to safety. She now wears glasses, her hair is completely white and her face without make-up. 'Look at me and how I have changed', she says, suggesting there is no point to her rescue – death clearly beckons. Any hope of a love-filled future with him is at an end for her. But there is also a deeper reason for her refusal to escape. Motherhood is the stronger of the two passions. She cannot leave without her son – which is the price she would have to pay for the plan to succeed.

Unsurprisingly, as the mood darkens so too does Marie-Antoinette's attire. Gone are the frivolously-adorned, light-coloured dresses of parts one and two. Her dress code in parts three and four matches the increasing need for greater sobriety: the tones are grey-blue for her evening gown, dark blue for affairs of state – only one spot of colour: her yellow day-coat when she stands on the balcony to confront the people. Once under house-arrest, the tones shift to beige, then grey for the escape (dressed as a citizen) and later, by the time of her trial, to black. This black is her mourning dress for the king, guillotined before her trial – a further example of courageous defiance on her part. This is why she is forced to wear white to her own execution. Black would upset the people at the scaffold, she is told. This could well have been a final stripping of any rights she might have. And yet, even in this last hour, she stands up with courage, refusing last rites from a priest who has turned Republican and to her mind, therefore, is against the Pope (he who consecrates the Royal family). Luckily for her, another priest (Michel Piccoli) hides under the guillotine scaffold and prays for her soul. The gruesome scene ends with her blood dripping down onto his sacristy.

It is worth pausing a moment to consider the pacing of this film. The shape is quite illuminating – see figure below (6.6):

Part	One	Two	Three	Four
PERIOD	*1774–8*	*1782–4*	*1785–9*	*1790–3*
Sequences	1–6	7–12	13–20	21–33
Length	27'	17'	23'	50'
Average sequence length	4' 30"	2' 50"	2' 52"	3' 50"

Figure 6.6: Period time-line and average sequence length for *Marie-Antoinette Reine de France*.

We note that the slowest part of the film is the first – we might have expected it to be the fastest since it represents the light-hearted and frivolous period of the queen's life. However, this part is dominated by the lengthy opening sequence, which serves to establish the relationship between the dauphin and his father Louis XV (8' 54") and the still-lengthier second sequence at the masked ball, which introduces us to Marie-Antoinette and establishes a connection with Fersen (14' 19"). These, then, are the two founding stones upon which the rest of the film is premised: the duties of marriage versus the attraction of true love. But they also set the tone for the quality of the film we are about to experience: fabulous sets, rich costumes, all shot in Technicolor. Indeed, apart from the location exterior shooting at Versailles and Le Petit Trianon, there are 43 sets: an enormous number, executed with realism and precision, which, alone, elevates this production to heritage-film status. Delannoy deployed most of the team that had worked with Sacha Guitry on his epic *Napoléon* (1954). Renoux did the sets; his experience of design on a grand scale was his speciality, as we know. Montazel did the photography; Benda, the costumes. The Technicolor ethos is well in evidence, the colour of the costumes matching the tone of the décors in an appropriate manner. As *Le Film français* can proudly declare: 'In its scope this film places our cinema on a par with grand productions from abroad'.[24] The film opened the 1956 Cannes Film Festival. Arguably, its greatest rival in competition should have been Hitchcock's *The Man who Knew too Much* (a big production suspense thriller). However, big production values did not garner the prizes that year. Cousteau's underwater colour documentary *Le Monde du silence* won the Palme d'Or; Susan Hayward won best actress for her performance as an alcoholic in Daniel Mann's black and white film *I'll Cry Tomorrow* (1955). There was nothing for Michèle Morgan, even if she was France's top-grossing female star at the time.

Montazel was also the director of photography for the other Technicolor film in this trio, *L'Affaire des poisons* – a completely different film in terms of palette since it is primarily made up of tonalities in deep reds and blacks. Luminosity only appears in the gilt interiors of the Chateau de Saint-Germain-en-Laye and the open design of Le Nôtre's gardens. The interiors include Madame de Montespan's apartment rooms, the king's reception rooms, and the theatre where the fatal poisoning of the king's latest mistress, Mademoiselle de Fontanges (Christine Carère), takes place. The rest of the interiors are dark and gloomy and include La Voisin's apartment and her laboratory where her alchemist employee Lesage (Roldano Lupi) creates the poisons; the chapel and cemetery where the black Sabbaths are performed; and the dungeon where she and the Abbé Guibourg (Paul Meurisse) end up before their deaths. Naturally, Jean d'Eaubonne is in his element with the baroque of the light interiors and the neo-gothic of the dark ones – the chapel and cemetery are particularly macabre in their design. 40 percent of the film (40 out of 100 minutes) is given over to the dark places, where the forces of evil reign. This heavy preponderance is matched by the excessively-ponderous musical score by René Cloerec – who scored such other grisly heavyweights as *Le Dieu a besoin des hommes*, *L'Auberge rouge*, *Les Naufrageurs*, and other Gance films such as *Le Rouge et le Noir* and *Le Joueur*. Cloerec's music is, of all the composers for film music of the 1950s, the one that is the most manipulative; the one that most self-evidently stresses the narrative to the point where it becomes very intrusive and overbearing. This is certainly the case here. Just in case we miss the point about the awfulness of the black magic going on, Cloerec's music (40-minutes worth) hits us over the head with his phatic score-mallet! It becomes a fourth character, almost, in the film, after La Montespan, La Voisin and the abbé.

What of the story? It is 1676, in the reign of Louis XIV, the Sun King. As the title of the film suggests, the story is about a particular moment during this reign (1672–1682 to be precise), a time during which a slew of poisonings and other diabolical deeds shocked the Royal Court and Paris. Amongst the culprits, the rumour ran, were some eminent aristocrats. As the film opens, we are privy to the execution of one such, the marquise of Brinvilliers, accused by her former, now dead, lover of murdering her father and then her siblings to get to their share of the inheritance. Found guilty, she is sent to Place de Grève to be burnt. Madame de Montespan and the chief of police responsible for chasing down these poisoners, the comte de la Reynie (Maurice Teynac), watch the proceedings from a balcony with considerable distaste. And yet, Madame de Montespan thinks nothing of having recourse to these methods herself. Once the king's favourite (1667–1678), she is desperate to remove her latest rival, Mademoiselle de Fontanges, from the king's affections and gain him back for herself. She uses a number of ploys: poison in cakes; a voodoo doll; and, lastly, pure poison in a drink – which finally does the trick. All of these La Montespan has sourced from La Voisin. It also transpires that La Voisin and her mentor, the abbé, indulge in sacrificial masses and other mysteries of the occult. Reynie has his eye on these two and eventually rounds them up and forces a confession out of them. The abbé commits suicide in his cell; La Voisin, in a graphic concluding scene to the film, is burnt at the stake in the Place de Grève, watched by La Montespan and Reynie from the same balcony as before. La Montespan escapes capital punishment, but is banished from court.

In the film everything is rather condensed historically to a vague 1676. In fact, Mademoiselle de Fontanges died of pleurisy after complications from childbirth in 1681. La Voisin was burnt alive in 1680. Her daughter accused La Montespan of dabbling in the occult with her mother, and of buying potions from her. However, the king interceded and put an end to these rumours (he also abolished the witch-hunts in 1682). La Montespan was, after all, the mother of seven of his illegitimate children, six of whom he had recognized as legitimately his. To have her banished would have been an admission of her guilt. So she stayed on in his Royal Court (now in Versailles) from 1682 until retiring to Paris in 1691 where she led a devout life. It is this last piece of distortion of La Montespan's story that gives us pause. Why, in the film, should she be banished rather than allowed to redeem herself, as she did in life? Of course, punishment makes for a stronger ending, and given the fact that, in the film at least, we see her participating in the occult and purchasing poisons, she obviously must be made to pay for her transgressive ways. I shall return to this point below.

La Montespan was well-known in court for her acerbic and witty sarcasms; many courtiers feared her biting comments and ridicule. Thus, the choice of Danielle Darrieux for the role – with her ability to play irony, wit and sarcasm with supreme confidence and sophistication – was totally apposite. But, here, she is also ruthless – she sacrifices youth (Fontanges) and her co-conspirator (La Voisin) to preserve her position and save her own neck. Thus, a colder side of Darrieux emerges in playing this role: one we have not seen before, with the exception of her dissatisfied wife- turned-murderer in *La Vérité sur Bébé Donge* (1951), also directed by Decoin. In *L'Affaire des poisons* she accomplishes the task of embodying selfish desire with a consummate nastiness that is compelling to watch. Her cold intellect and ruthless egotism is matched by the earthy nature of La Voisin and her scheming ways. When Romance and Darrieux have their scenes together, it is like fire and ice – the hot-blooded witch versus the cold-hearted vixen. It is not surprising that the longest sequences in the film are between these two, given that there is such a battle of wills going on. It makes for great spectacle. There are four in all and, in duration terms, they occupy 20 per cent of the film time. Thus, they represent half of the film time devoted to the occult sequences (20 minutes out of the 40). In the first, the longest at seven minutes, Romance/La Voisin gradually weaves Darrieux/La Montespan into her web of wicked ways. La Montespan comes to La Voisin's apartments at night to procure a potion that will win her back the favour of her king. But she is tentative. La Voisin persuades her to stay and let her read her fortune in a silver-backed mirror (what else!): her future is secure; the spirits in the mirror assure her that her lover will not leave her. La Voisin's softly-softly approach works; La Montespan is hooked. This is well conveyed through the camera work. First, the two women are held in separate long shots – but there is an eyeline-matching shot from La Voisin's point of view. As they are drawn closer spiritually, this shifts to a series of medium shots in shot-countershot. When La Montespan exchanges her ring for the mirror séance, the two women are held in a two-shot medium shot. A series of single close-ups on the women, in turn, follows, ending with a two-shot medium shot of them as the deal is concluded. This enthralling exchange is full of unspoken menace and collusion as the eyeline-matched shot at the beginning evidences.

A while later, however, La Montespan returns. The spirits were wrong, she declares. This time La Voisin gradually persuades her to give Fontanges poison to disfigure her face, not kill her, by spreading a mixture on a piece of cake. La Montespan is delighted by this proposal since it will allow her rival to witness her own victory – the king is bound to take her back in preference to the ugly Fontanges. This sequence opens and closes with a two-shot medium shot showing the continued collusion of the two women. As the method of spreading the poison is explained, first La Voisin and then La Montespan's hands are shown in close-up executing the dastardly deed. However, what these shots also reveal is La Voisin's increased power and hold over La Montespan. As with the previous sequence, La Montespan is viewed from the back, thus decreasing any sense of power she might be attempting to hold onto. It is clear La Voisin leads the way; she comes and goes in and out of her rooms as she slowly brings together the objects needed for the scheme – much to the impatient annoyance of La Montespan. In the end, this ploy also fails. Fontanges falls sick and the king is beside himself with worry. The third visit produces the voodoo doll, made by La Voisin in the image of Fontanges. Although this does not work directly, it foreshadows her impending demise. La Montespan stabs the face and then the heart with pins, urging her death.

Death comes by a hand of fate. A dress rehearsal is taking place for a musical comedy to entertain the king. Fontanges is starring in it. Someone in the theatre wings puts drops of poison in a drink intended for Fontanges as part of the play; it is supposed to be a sleeping draught. One of La Montespan's ladies-in-waiting, Mademoiselle des Oeillets (Anne Vernon), inadvertently proffers this poisoned glass to Fontanges who finally succumbs and dies. The king is inconsolable. He closes the door on La Montespan forever. In the fourth meeting with La Voisin, La Montespan icily rejects her overtures to help one more time. She attempts, unsuccessfully, to throw her out of her apartment rooms. Eventually La Voisin reels her in again. La Montespan agrees to make a pact with the devil if it will bring her back the king. All is set for the most diabolical of scenes. La Montespan comes to the black Sabbath chapel wearing a black mask and cloak, underneath she is naked; she eventually agrees to submit to the will of La Voisin and the abbé and humiliate herself completely by succumbing to the black mass. As she lies upon the altar, La Voisin and the abbé loom over her; in exchange for her soul they will conjure the spirits to render the king to her. What matters here, first, is the erotic charge of the scene; only secondly the terrible scream, whereby La Montespan refuses this last step into the occult and the abject. The *mise-en-scène* makes clear the sexual nature of this triad formation, including a clear nod to the titillation of lesbianism (see figure 6.7 below). La Voisin has La Montespan in the palm of her hand as she looms over her in a tight close-up; the abbé is poised, ready to come into the action at any moment. But for La Montespan's scream, we sense the perverted sexual triadism would have occurred. Instead, she breaks the spell-binding moment, profanes the ceremony, knocks over the candle, sets fire to the scene and makes her escape.

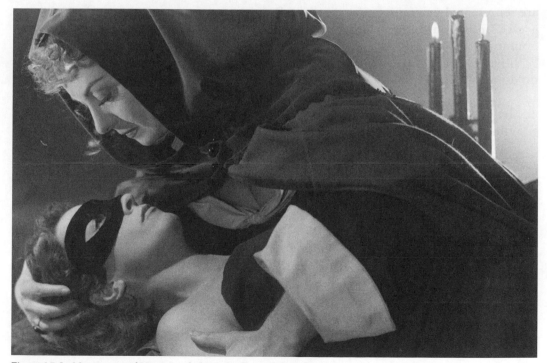

Figure 6.7: La Montespan and Voisin in a lesbian clinch. © 1955 Gaumont.

La Montespan is spared, not so La Voisin. They are two sides of a same ruthless coin, one suspects. This is signified most clearly in the film's ending. There is an eye-line match between La Voisin burning at the stake and La Montespan seated at the balcony, watching her nemesis perish. And when La Montespan says to Reynie in the closing sequences of the film, 'if I had been born a man I would have made an excellent police officer, don't you think?', she could hardly have made the case for her own duplicity better. After all, it is she who sends La Voisin to her death. She buys La Voisin's silence by promising her she will be spared. She brokers a deal only the police could make, but La Voisin believes her – oddly since she had the evidence from the black Sabbath ceremony that La Montespan was quite able to break her word. In the end, the abbé gets wind of the conspiracy and tells the police about it as a way of saving his own soul. He then hangs himself. La Voisin burns. La Montespan did not have to lift a finger!

This quite nasty film does a great disservice to women in general and, of course, a real injustice to La Montespan in particular. History here is quite evidently reworked to service the needs of patriarchy by subjugating women who seek power – banishment for one and burning for the other. Minor female roles show mothers being neglectful of their children so that they are easily stolen and put to the occult practices of the evil abbé (once kidnapped, they have their throats cut as offerings for the black masses). Conversely, men, in particular the forces of law as embodied by Reynie and his deputy Captain Desgrez (Pierre Mondy), are represented in a more favourable light. Reynie is firm but quite tolerant; Desgrez shows great compassion, especially when Mademoiselle des Oeillets is falsely accused of poisoning Fontanges. He cannot bear to see her tortured and eventually engineers her escape.

The spectacle of torture is quite central to this film and the opening preface leaves us in no doubt about Decoin's intentions to show us the truth:

The lack of documentation means that the so-called Case of the Poisonings has long remained a mystery. We would never have known the truth without the discovery and publication of the Bastille archives some two centuries later. These archives contain résumés of the interrogations and notes taken by the Lieutenant General of Police, M. de la Reynie. This film was built upon these archives and notes. Some of the scenes of torture and fanaticism may seem excessive or imaginary. They conform entirely to the truth.

Several of Decoin's films, post-war, disturb in their representation of the darker side of humankind, in particular women. Moreover, *L'Affaire des poisons* was the third post-war film that Decoin made with his ex-wife Danielle Darrieux. He was the first to cast her against type as the calculating murderer in *La Vérité sur Bébé Donge* (1951). As La Montespan she rejoins this dark side once more. This is not necessarily to impute misogyny to Decoin.[25] However, the tone is certainly consistent with the more reactionary devalorized images of powerful women of which Sellier speaks. Patriarchy clearly reasserts itself with the banishing of the troublesome La Montespan. And the source of the truth about the poisonings, the one who could expose all the other eminent personalities involved in these scabrous practices,

La Voisin, is viciously silenced not just in her burning at the stake but also by the diegetic sounds of the braying public and the bells peeling away that drown out her screams and her naming of names. A silencing of the witch and the witch-hunting, if ever there was one.

Such, then, is the small corpus of transgressive females. With most, their sins, imagined or real, are well punished. These women are beheaded, burnt or banished (Du Barry, Marie-Antoinette, La Voisin, La Montespan): in effect, silenced by patriarchal law. On the rare occasion they are not, they either have to re-submit to patriarchal law, however defiantly (Lucrèce, Caroline) or accept their lot (Margot). Only one woman gets her man, Caroline, but at quite a price, despite the ending which suggests the rather doubtful possibility for love on equal terms. But what an interesting array of transgressiveness we have witnessed. These women fascinate in their diversity – poisoners, courtesans, queens and free-spirits. Femininity has not been diminished to wifely duties and reproduction in these films. Even Marie-Antoinette, the only mother amongst the lot, has more to her than making children; with La Montespan there is no hint at any of her seven children by Louis XIV – within the codes of the film narrative, perhaps such a wicked woman could not be associated with motherhood. What remains of these women in our consciousness is their desire – for love, for power, for recognition, for freedom to choose. Where the men are concerned, it is power that dominates as their central concern. With the exception of Dréville's range of masculinities in *La Reine Margot*, there has been little to suggest the same diversity amongst men as we find with our foxy women. What we wonder will our swashbucklers produce?

Notes

1. See Jacques Doniol-Valcroze's learned review of this film 'Caroline Borgia', *Cahiers du cinéma*, Vol. 5, No. 29, 1.12.1953, pp. 54–7. He maps out the difference between the historical Lucrèce and Christian-Jaque's utilitarian model, exploiting, in turn, Martine Carol's reputation as Caroline chérie – hence the ironic title to his review.
2. Saint-Laurent quoted in Chapuy (2001, p. 50).
3. As the review in *Monthly Film Bulletin* put it 'Martine Carol is a peculiarly negative Lucretia' (Vol. 22, No. 256, 1.5.1955, p. 75, no author name given).
4. According to Jean-Luc Douin (1998, p. 106) in his book on film censorship, if Christian-Jaque wanted to get an under-18 visa certification, he had to modify this scene and shoot it with Carol's body covered (in light muslin one supposes). I have not seen the censored version, so cannot comment.
5. See Mosk's review '*Madame du Barry*', *Variety*, 10.11.1954, no page.
6. Chapuy, op. cit., pp.23 & 27. I do not seek to reject Chapuy's reading, merely to suggest that, by a slight reading against the grain, we can find that these films, which have been so pilloried by serious film critics, have more to offer us than pure escapism.
7. Sellier (2001, p. 211).
8. Chapuy, op. cit., p. 55.
9. Dréville quoted in Bernard (1994, p. 82).
10. Sellier, op. cit., p. 211.

11. Dréville quoted in Bernard, op. cit., p. 82.
12. See the press reviews of *La Reine Margot* published in *Avant-Scène du cinéma*, No. 459, p. 87.
13. Ibid., pp. 87–90.
14. Dréville quoted in Bernard, op. cit., p. 82.
15. This information comes from Dréville whose words are quoted in footnote 3 to the press reviews of *La Reine Margot* published in *Avant-Scène du cinéma*, No. 459, p. 87.
16. Mosk, 'Review of *La Reine Margot*', *Variety*, 26.01.1955, no page given.
17. *L'Express* review of *La Reine Margot* abridged and reproduced in *Avant-Scène du cinéma*, No. 459, p. 87 (no author name given).
18. R-M Arlaud review of *La Reine Margot* abridged and reproduced in *Avant-Scène du cinéma*, No. 459, p. 89.
19. Jean de Baroncelli review of *La Reine Margot* abridged and reproduced in *Avant-Scène du cinéma*, No. 459, p. 90.
20. Image accessed from http://images1.vefblog.net/vefblog.net/g/a/galate1/photos_art/2009/07/Galate 1124863033332_art.jpg accessed 13.09.2009.
21. Part of the Carnaval de Paris' celebrations, the Bal de l'Opéra is the most famous. Marie-Antoinette came incognito with her brother-in-law the comte d'Artois.
22. Sallé (1988, p.175).
23. Again history is slightly distorted here. Marie-Antoinette was a formidable enemy of Jacques Necker and only finally managed to persuade Louis XVI to dismiss him in 1781. Mademoiselle Necker went on to become the renowned author Madame de Staël.
24. *Le Film français* production notes for *Marie-Antoinette Reine de France*, No. 623, p. 27 (no author name given).
25. I do not wish to rehearse here the debates around Decoin's 1941 film *Les Inconnus dans la maison* which was misinterpreted after the Occupation as an anti-semetic film. François Garçon (1984) eloquently puts it to rest in his book *De Blum à Pétain*, Paris, Editions du Cerf, 180–2. Both Decoin and Dréville suffered at the hands of the *comité d'épuration* in that they were suspended from work briefly after the war.

Chapter 7

Swashbuckling Heroes

Introduction: The Prototype – Fanfan Philipe, France's answer to Douglas Fairbanks Sr. and Errol Flynn

Hollywood dominated the swashbuckler genre first, in the 1920s, with its major prototype in the form of Douglas Fairbanks Sr., and then, from the mid-1930s through to the early-1950s, with Errol Flynn. France's heyday with the genre was the 1950s, and its first prototype was Gérard Philipe in *Fanfan la tulipe* (1952). French cinema's decision to embark on this genre at this juncture was, in part, a marketing ploy against the post-war American dominance of the film market in general and a challenge, in particular, to its mastery of the spectacular genre. France sought to demonstrate that it could provide an indigenous model to satisfy its home audience, one that was without all the special effects and trick photography of the American model and one that would turn, whenever possible, to location shooting as the dominant practice – thus providing authenticity over the studio feel of the American product, to say nothing of a sense of national heritage; after all France had plenty of ancient castles, villages and woods at its disposal! The nation also had some of the finest literary exponents of the genre. Alexandre Dumas' novels spring immediately to mind – three of his stories are amongst the twelve swashbuckler films that make up our corpus here: *La Tour de Nesle, Les Trois Mousquetaires and Le Vicomte de Bragelonne.* Figures for these films indicate that the industry was singularly successful in this domain (see figure 7.1 below). With a total audience figure of over 34 million for the twelve films, this represents, on average, 2.8 million per film – very good going indeed.

It is noteworthy that it was the very first swashbuckler, *Fanfan la tulipe*, which garnered the largest-ever audience. Christain-Jaque won at Cannes for best direction; the film won the Silver Bear at Berlin. Moreover, both Gérard Philipe and Gina Lollobrigida won the French Victoires that year for their respective roles. The film was also a huge success in the US, with a fourteen-week run in New York. One of the film industry's top 1950s' journalists for *La Cinématographie française*, Gilberte Turquan, explains how this kind of prestige film responds to market needs, particularly when there has been a drop, world-wide, in audiences. To export to the US, she argues, France needs films like *Fanfan la tulipe*: 'big films, original scripts, showing French life and done in a way that is different from their films'.[1] Numerous factors combined to make *Fanfan la tulipe* such a success including Christian-Jaque's growing reputation for spectacle films and Gérard Philipe's increasing popularity both as a young première and an important stage actor. The original script, camera style and location shooting certainly added an edge. But, before entering into a discussion of this film in particular, let us first take a look at the

---

Swashbucklers

Fanfan la tulipe (March 52) Christian-Jaque/[Gérard Philipe]*
6,712,512

Les Trois Mousquetaires (53) Hunebelle/[Georges Marchal]
5,354,739

Cadet Rousselle (54) Hunebelle/[François Périer]*
3,995,468

Don Juan (56) Berry/[Fernandel]
3,442,334

L'Aventurier de Séville (54) Vadja/[Mariano]*
2,487,427

Le Vicomte de Bragelonne (54) Cerchi/[Georges Marchal]
2,399,675

La Tour, prends garde! (58) Lampin/[Jean Marais]*
2,311,061

Les Aventures de Till L'Espiègle (56) Philipe/[Gérard Philipe]
2,304,114

La Tour de Nesle (55) Gance/[Pierre Brasseur]
2,191,984

La Bigorne, caporal de France (58) Darène/[François Périer]
1,165,131

Les Aventures de Gil Blas de Santillane (56) Jolivet/[Georges Marchal]
1,108,273

Buridan héros de la tour de Nesle (October 52) Couzinet/no major star
637,199

TOTAL AUDIENCE FIGURES: 34,109,917

Figure 7.1: Audience figures for the Swashbuckler films; asterisk denotes original script.

French swashbuckler genre in general. The rest of the chapter will then investigate a cross-section of these films in terms of types and in relation to the major exponents of the genre: Gérard Philipe, Georges Marchal and Jean Marais.

The swashbuckler genre is one readily identified with narratives set in the pre-nineteenth century. Certainly, it did not survive long into the new century for the following reasons. The impact of the Industrial Revolution during the early- to mid-nineteenth century meant that society had become increasingly urbanized; the forces of capitalism and its concomitant demands lead to a social construction of masculinity whereby the urban male, at least, was

---

Swashbuckler films

15th century (2)	*16th century (1)*	*17th century (4)*	*18th century (5)*
• *Buridan héros de la tour de Nesle* • *La Tour de Nesle*	• *Les Aventures de Till L'Espiègle*	• *Les Trois Mousquetaires* • *Le Vicomte de Bragelonne* • *Don Juan* • *La Tour, prends garde!*	• *Fanfan la tulipe* • *L'Aventurier de Séville* • *Cadet Rousselle* • *Les Aventures de Gil Blas de Santillane* • *La Bigorne, caporal de France*

Figure 7.2: Swashbuckler films according to depicted century.

increasingly socialized away from displays of violence and muscular prowess much associated with the swashbuckler style. Instead, he entered into a socially-ordered existence. The army was the place for physical prowess; business environs for intellectual acumen; the church for those seeking to avoid the former and lacking the means to enter the latter; hard labour in factories and mines for the deprived working classes; and so on down the chain to utter destitution. In short, within the more financially-secure echelons of society, the male had become a domesticated animal. Not so, to all appearances, in the case of the swashbuckler! Coming from an earlier 'freer' age, he had considerable appeal, therefore, to the imaginary. Thus, we might be led to believe that this genre of film represents a last gasp of free-spirited masculinity. And it probably does, although paradoxically, with the exception of *La Tour de Nesle*, marriage is the outcome of all these narratives.

There are a number of ways to approach the twelve titles listed here. A period approach (see figure 7.2 above), whilst it might be more limiting, provides us with one revealing outcome – the predominance of films set in the seventeenth and eighteenth centuries (four and five respectively). This suggests nostalgia for an action hero who is not so far in the distant past as to be unrecognizable to audiences of the 1950s. We pointed out in Chapter 2 that the costume drama – in that it looks at the past – is saying something about the needs of the present, contemporary, French psyche.[2] Here we could argue that the swashbuckling hero speaks to a society that finds itself in need of models of muscular masculinity after the calamitous epoch of the German Occupation and the ongoing debacles with the colonies. These swashbuckling bodies are men of the Ancien Régime period, or in the case of the eponymous hero of *Cadet Rousselle*, a man who experienced the transition of France from Ancien Régime into Empire. These are moments identified with greatness in the French psyche, Louis XIV's 'Grand Siècle' in particular; a time when France was assured of its place in history, unlike its status in the troubled contemporary decade. As we shall see, however, this muscularity needs some definition; not all of it is a tough as we might think. But what does strike a curious note is the way the Dumas novels, upon which three of these films are based, are re-adapted away from their original nostalgia for the passing of an age and made into far more up-beat stories. In Dumas' musketeer trilogy, we sense the increasing regret at the passing of an age of freedom and adventure under Louis XIII: a *'noblesse d'épée'* as seen in *Les Trois Mousquetaires*, to a *'noblesse de cour'* which Louis XIV gradually imposed in his drive to assert his power as absolute monarch. Dumas' last novel in the trilogy *Le Vicomte de Bragelonne* is particularly melancholic in tone; treachery and intrigue have replaced the former principles of honour. Flattery is more the order of the day than heroic exploits. The hero, Bragelonne, broken-hearted in love, takes off to battle where he dies in a suicidal charge at the enemy. Yet in the film of the same title, Bragelonne overcomes his disappointment at his fiancée's treachery (she has fallen for the charms of Louis XIV), and not only does he foil the plot to usurp the king, he meets a woman who is a perfect match to his own bravura! Swashbuckler narratives, at least of the 1950s, must end happily, it would seem.

Grouped according to type we obtain a somewhat more nuanced political cultural reading. There are three dominant categories involving our swashbuckling individual: he either serves king and country, fights against evil or oppression, or indulges in light-hearted romantic comedy (see figure 7.3 below).

All categories have a heavy dose of action mixed with merriment. Even the darker second category, where individuals are up against some pretty sinister forces, has considerable humour – whether the opponents are murdering queens (*Buridan héros de la tour de Nesle* and *La Tour de Nesle*), or occupying armies (*Les Aventures de Till L'Espiègle*), or the ruthlessness of the mighty who would crush the poor (*La Tour, prends garde!*). *La Tour, prends garde!* could have been included in the first category because, indirectly, the hero does serve his king and, as with three of the other titles in this category, there is direct or implicit criticism of warmongering. But the central thrust of the narrative is the way in which La Tour stands up to tyranny. Of the first category, our hero gets caught up in the political-historical moment inadvertently and yet serves his nation well (*Fanfan la tulipe, Cadet Rousselle*, and *La Bigorne, caporal de France*) – this is a source of comedy, of course,

---

Categories of swashbuckler films

King and country (5)	Against tyranny (4)	Romantic comedy (3)
Fanfan la tulipe	*Buridan héros de la tour de Nesle*	*Don Juan*
Cadet Rousselle	*La Tour de Nesle*	*L' Aventurier de Séville*
Les Trois Mousquetaires	*Les Aventures de Till L'Espiègle*	*Les Aventures de Gil Blas de Santillane*
Le Vicomte de Bragelonne	*La Tour, prends garde!*	
La Bigorne, caporal de France		

Figure 7.3: Categories of swashbuckler films.

but it also allows for a questioning of war by those who have to do the fighting and dying, namely the common soldier. Thus, these films are not without their subversive elements. Alternatively, the swashbuckler hero is committed to his king and trustworthy from the start, as with the two musketeer films *Les Trois Mousquetaires* and *Le Vicomte de Bragelonne*. As to the third category – all intriguingly set in Spain (a place of exotic otherness doubtless) – the three heroes are unwillingly caught up on the other side of the law, as bandits and wanted men – a situation from which, despite their bravura and swordsmanship, only the love of a good woman can finally save them.

As a genre, swashbuckler films are typically made up of a series of peripatetic episodes, including chases, swordfights and other feats of prowess. Because of this bundling together of action-packed elements, there tends to be a rather thin plot-line. These twelve films are no exception. This does not mean to say they do not have a political edge, however. They do. Some are quite conservative in their message – the musketeer narratives with their Royalist leanings, for example. Others are certainly polemical, even potentially racist, as is the case with *La Bigorne, caporal de France* and its thinly disguised (through humour) apologia for colonization. In discussing this film, I shall inevitably be referring to John Berry's *Tamango* (see Chapter 10). Given Berry's political aura, his superficially-silly *Don Juan* has to be read against the grain, despite the buffoonery of Fernandel as the usurping Sganarelle, who accidentally takes the place of his master, Don Juan, as supreme lover. It has all the elements of parody, and, as such, reads in part as an anti-Franco film (the Spanish film-maker and political activist Juan Bardem was one of the scriptwriters). For the most part, women fare well in these swashbuckling narratives, often the match to their male counterpart. Indeed, there is only one film where they are represented as evil: the scheming sirens in *La Tour de Nesle*. Otherwise they have spirit and do rather well as action heroines in their own right. And there is the surprise element of a musketeer heroine in *Le Vicomte de Bragelonne* (to which I shall return). As we shall see, three films stand out as enlightened on most fronts – *Fanfan la tulipe*, *Les Aventures de Till L'Espiègle* and *La Tour, prends garde!*.

More on these issues later. Let me conclude this quick overview by setting out a few more points we need to consider in relation to this genre. Steve Neale offers a useful précis of this genre's ideological function and I shall be referring to it here.[3] The emphasis this genre places on the male body is, of course, the starting point of all the rest. Typically, the camera is focused, almost to the point of excessive fetishization, on a display of masculinity – in terms of what the body can achieve in the form of stunts, but also, of course, on the torso, *the* permitted locus of visible male strength. In this regard, identity – including national identity – is equally at the core of this body and, thereby, the narrative. We spoke earlier of how the genre, in the case of France, was a way of dealing, in a displaced fashion, with the recent effects of World War Two and fascism. France was a nation rebuilding itself from the scars of defeat. The heroic exploits, including masculinity on display, are part of that process. And yet, and here is the rub, who are the swashbuckling hero-types used to embody this rebuilding? Whose bodies figure in the film industry's production of this 'muscular cinema'?[4] None other than the rather sleight, will-o'-the-wisp body of a man of the political

Left (Gérard Philipe); a forceful, powerfully muscular and beautiful body of a gay man (Jean Marais); and, finally, the body of a man desperate to assert his virility over his matinée idol image (Georges Marchal). These three actors dominate the genre with five of the titles. But as we shall go on to see, Marais aside, there is little fetishization of the torso taking place in any of these films. There are, however, many stunning exploits and moments of extreme prowess – all stunts being undertaken by this trio of actors in their respective films. As for our other swashbucklers: François Périer, who has two film titles, is physically not in the same league; no more is Fernandel or Luis Mariano. This leaves only Pierre Brasseur, who has one film to his name (*La Tour de Nesle*, 1955), and, whilst certainly burly and baritone, as a man in his fifties he is a far cry from audience expectation of virile youth. Curiously, Marais, only six years his junior, played a much torsoed La Tour when he was 45 (*La Tour, prends garde!*, 1958). However, he was a natural athlete, endowed with exceptional beauty – a fact that is commented on by both men and women in the film on several occasions – and still, at 45, had managed to hold onto his handsome body and youthful good looks.

As the prototype, what does *Fanfan la tulipe* (henceforth *Fanfan*) and its lead actor bring us? In terms of character, he brings youth, warmth, humanity – as was observed by most critics of the time.[5] Engaging insolence and razor-sharp wit, also (thanks in large part to Jeanson's script in collaboration with René Wheeler). A clever young man outsmarting his elders with humour and cheeky spontaneity, Gérard Philipe's performance as this impulsive youth that nothing can deter was certainly a fresh image on the French cinema screens. Philipe had, until now, provided some quite dark portraits of youth in *Le Diable au corps* (Autant-Lara, 1946), *La Chartreuse de Parme* (Christian-Jaque, 1947), *Une si jolie petite plage* (Yves Allégret, 1948), as a result of which he had become associated with the post-war Black Realist cinema which was tinged with cynicism and a feeling of no-hope. It was a cinema credited with trying to face up to the political realities of the time, including France's less-than-heroic recent past.[6] Interestingly, Philipe had wanted Christian-Jaque to give more gravitas to Fanfan, make him less instinctive and spontaneous, and more responsible for his actions. In short, to politicize the role. Christian-Jaque refused.[7] Philipe would have to await directing his own film *Les Aventures de Till L'Espiègle* to bring political gravity and swashbuckling together. Part of this desire for weight on Philipe's part may have been to do with the very nature of spontaneity. Philipe was never at ease with the idea of improvisation,[8] yet his performance as Fanfan is so lively and spirited that it feels as if he is improvising all the way, such is the lightness and deftness of his repartee, to say nothing of the swift agility of his movements – be it the stunts he executes, the sword-fights he engages in and wins, or the tremendous horsemanship. Before the film, Philipe could neither fence nor ride a horse,[9] yet in the film he performs as if all this was second nature to him. The second aspect of Philipe's performance that stands out – and in fact distinguishes him from most of the other swashbuckler actors under consideration here – is the subtle mobility of his facial features and tremendously expressive eyes, which work to provide an interiority to his acting style. We sense the 'more' of this persona. Marchal and Marais do not hint at this hidden depth in their swashbuckling roles. And Périer, in his roles, is constructed as an ingénu and comedic swashbuckler so that when he does use his face, it is more ticks and grimaces than profundity that is on offer. If we do not see much of Philipe/Fanfan's muscular body – indeed, there is only one torso shot throughout the whole film and that is when he is bathing – then we certainly learn a great deal about his feelings through the quantity of close-ups on him as he jokes his way out of trouble, responds with fearless fortitude to others' hatred of his spirited ways, flirts with Adeline when sober and, later, drunkenly admits to his friend his love for her. In the end, youth vanquishes age; love, cynical covetousness.

In terms of film genre and practice, this film was a first for location shooting on a big scale for a costume drama. It was, moreover, a brand new venture for Christian-Jaque. Shooting began in August 1951, less than two months after he had finished the actual shooting of *Barbe-bleue*, which, as we saw, was predominantly studio work because of the need to stabilize Gevacolor (see Chapter 5). Shooting for *Fanfan* mostly took place in the Grasse area – especially in Saint Christophe, just above Grasse – but exteriors in Nice and Cannes were also used.[10] Certainly, had the film been made in colour, the speed and vivacity of the film would not have been possible at the time (these were very early days for colour, remember, and exterior lighting was cumbersome, as Christian Matras, the director of photography, discovered with *Barbe-bleue*). Here Matras achieves some memorable tracking shots alongside Fanfan and his trusty side-kicks as he chases down the carriage with the kidnapped Adeline. Matras cuts his shots three ways: alternating parallel tracking shots of the riders on horseback and then the carriage; under the carriage with the camera pointed towards the horses hooves as they madly gallop; camera looking back to the riders from within the carriage rear window. This set the tone for many of the chase sequences in French swashbucklers for the decade. We see it repeated in *La Tour, prends garde!* and *Don Juan*. This quick cross-cutting type of shooting is more readily associated with American westerns; and the under-carriage shots bring to mind *Ben Hur*, even if that particular film was not made until 1959, seven years after *Fanfan*. The other aspect of speed and lightness comes, surely, from the conception of the script. Because it is an original script, albeit constructed around the eighteenth-century popular song 'Fanfan la Tulipe', it is not bogged down by the enormity of Dumas' romantic novels (the musketeer trilogy is some 5,000 pages long). Thus, the scenario is one of creation rather than one of cutting down to the bare essentials, as happens with the two musketeer films. This idea of constructing a narrative around popular songs informed both *Cadet Rousselle* and *La Tour, prends garde!*[11] And even if only four of the twelve films are original scripts, it is surely noteworthy that they rank in the top seven of the swashbuckler films (see figure 7.1 above). Audiences liked the swift repartee as much as the more familiar Dumas-type adaptation it seems.

Typically Swashbuckling? War is not the answer

Fanfan also set a tradition whereby the swashbuckler is something of an underdog who wins out against all odds, gains Royal recognition, and wins the woman. Thus, in their desire to emulate that film's successful formula, several films have our hero caught up in events of history that they would quite happily have avoided had circumstances not dictated otherwise. A third of the swashbuckler films, as with *Fanfan*, drop comments about the futility of war. These four films, *Fanfan, Cadet Rousselle, La Tour, prends garde!* and *La Bigorne, caporal de France* are set in the period of Louis XV's reign – also known as Louis le Bien-Aimé (1715–1774). During this period, Louis continued the tradition of his great grandfather's (Louis XIV) warmongering and although he had considerable success within Europe he was singularly inept in relation to France's colonies, many of which he lost to the British (especially in the Americas). This anti-war sentiment in this handful of films should not be overlooked. As we know, violence is at the core of swashbuckling and we do get to see plenty of sword-fighting in these films, and confrontation of the opponent with heroic displays of skilful physical prowess. But when it comes to war, in each instance there is a twist and the concept of war is undermined. The hero finds a way of succeeding in turning things round, either winning the battle by ruse, or accidentally routing the enemy, all without any or too much bloodshed. Of course this twist is a trope of the accidental hero and works to comedic effect. However, what we do not expect in this generic type are words that question, when in battle, why wars should be conducted. Nor do we expect barbs directed at the military. Indeed, in France of the 1950s, a film could be censored if it was perceived as 'injurious to the army',[12] and there was some pressure put on Christian-Jaque to temper the tone of *Fanfan*, but he refused.[13] Here is how *Fanfan* opens. It is in voice-over, uttered by the ever-sardonic Jean Debucourt.

> In the eighteenth century, war was man's favourite past-time; this was the only entertainment of kings where the ordinary people had their role to play. But what is this war we are watching? It hardly matters since all wars resemble one another. A battlefield is a place where we work for posterity by uttering grand statements of historical importance for children to study at school.

During all of this we see infantrymen killing each other and cannons firing away, as Louis XV (Marcel Herrand) observes from afar this latest amusing diversion of war. 'Everything was organized as if in a ballet', says Debucourt, 'it was what we called a war in lace' – referring to the old concept of war in which the nobility from both sides exchanged civilities while their warring sides slogged it out. The images we see here reveal battle-shocked infantry troops with their clothes in rags. Debucourt continues,

> the king's men found this war so pleasant they carried on fighting for seven years. When the number of dead exceeded the living, they worked out that the number of soldiers had diminished and so went on a recruitment campaign to swell the ranks once more.

The irony could not be more explicit. Fanfan is one of those new recruits to this ludicrous Seven Years' War (1756–1763). No sooner is he in training than another anti-military maxim is flippantly tossed in, this time by Captain de la Houlette (a very camp Jean Parédès), commander of the camp, who says 'credulity is the principle strength of the army'. By the end of the film, when Fanfan's chasing after the kidnapped Adeline brings him behind enemy lines, thus causing their rout, the king declares: 'war is too serious to entrust to the military.'

In *Cadet Rousselle*, the opposite view is tendered by a truly pompous general in the king's army (played by Jean Parédès, again in a camp performance): 'war is too complicated to be left to the civilians', he declares. This completely flies in the face of the evidence before us since it is the civilian Cadet Rousselle who successfully routs the enemy – a triumph for which the general, hypocritically, takes complete credit. Cadet Rousselle is, nonetheless, decorated for his valiant endeavours and proudly sports his medal, even if he gets no other recompense. Towards the end of the film, Cadet Rousselle, who has now become a bandit out of economic necessity, encounters Napoleon Bonaparte. He decides to renounce his outlaw life and sign up to serve this charismatic leader, who is returning from his Egyptian campaign to save the Republic. The film then cuts to the closing sequence: we are now in 1804; France is an Empire; Cadet Rousselle is a general in Napoleon's army about to set off to join his Emperor in the battle of Austerlitz – Bonaparte's tactically most dazzling of military campaigns. The message this time is less, perhaps, the futility of war, as at the beginning of the film, than the Republican and Napoleonic notion that even the most ordinary amongst us can rise through the rank and file purely on merit. Questions of rank and power are addressed, therefore, in this film, and the abuses thereof. The way justice is meted out also comes in for criticism – both the courts and the police are subject to ridicule for their ability to twist the judiciary to their own ends. The camp general is matched here by the pompous police commissioner (Noël Roquevert). At one point, Cadet Rousselle is in the dock on trial for counter-revolutionary conduct (unwittingly he carried a note to be delivered to the Royalist camp). The Republican tribunal does not cover itself in glory as it tries to trap Cadet Rousselle into a confession and sentence him to death. He shouts out 'spare me this parody of justice', adding he would rather die on the scaffold an honourable man than denounce innocent people. A little later a similar distrust of the law is evoked, this time in voice-over to explain why our hero has turned to banditry: 'In a period when laws no longer protect those who made them, it is best to seek refuge away from them.' And there he remains until he happens upon Napoleon and forges his career as an army officer, happily married to Violetta (Dany Robin), the gypsy-girl who danced her way into his heart.[14]

'A year without war is like a year without sunshine', we are told in the opening of *La Tour, prends garde!* which shows us Louis XV (Jean Lara) at war with Marie-Thérèse of Austria (Sonia Hlebsova-Klebs) during the Austrian war of succession (1740–1748). We are quickly instructed in the follies of warmongering and warfare, however, since both sides, according to schoolchildren's history books, claim the most recent battle as theirs, be it the French with their Prussian allies or Austria with its Anglo-Turk ones. Swiftly the theatre of war makes way for real theatre with the arrival of the travelling French Comedia dell'arte troupe headed by La Tour (Marais). The two theatres soon rejoin, however, when La Tour performs his song about the stupidity of war, 'C'est la guerre en dentelles/It's a Lace War', to the assembled crowd that just happens to include the king and his courtiers. The song exposes the real cruelty of war as the generals lord it above on the promontory (enjoying the spectacle of war in their lace and flummery, hence the reference to lace) whilst the poor soldiers below are massacred in the battlefield. The song mocks the theatre of war, and also insinuates that the king's current mistress, the duchesse de Chateauroux (Liliane Bert), dragged him into it. Nonetheless, the king applauds La Tour for telling the truth, presumably about the futility of war – but he could also be referring to the lines in the song where those who actively encourage the lace-war, the courtiers, are no better than dogs and rats. In which case, the target of the song is as much the duchesse de Chateauroux as the duc de Saint-Sever (Paul-Emile Deiber). But the king is just as implicated. After all, only a few moments earlier he had ordered the duc de Saint-Sever, as commander of the light brigade, to retrieve the standard that was lost to the Austrians in the most recent skirmish. So, although his comment to La Tour might suggest that he is saying 'down with war', his demand to be served by his officer intimates that, regardless, 'the spectacle of war goes on'!

In *La Bigorne caporal de France*, there is no war per se, it is more a question of defending and acquiring colonies that is at stake. This is a troubling film because, on the one hand, it shows how the lower orders in the armed forces can be forced to take on very dangerous tasks, with insufficient armaments, under orders from their superiors. As such, this continues the problematizing of power relations noted above. Yet, on the other hand, the way in which these hierarchies of power are reproduced within relations between the indigenous black natives of Madagascar and the white 'colonizers' is not without its concomitant problematic, particularly since all the natives are represented as rather gullible and stupid. La Bigorne (François Périer) is an unruly corporal in the French army stationed in one of Madagascar's east coast trading posts. He is a rapacious womanizer; as his superior commander says, 'black or white he has to sleep with them all'. He is ordered to lead an expedition against the British pirates led by Tom Wright (Henri Cogan), and supplied with a wreck of a ship, inappropriately named *L'Indomptable*/The Invincible). His superior commander has sent La Bigorne off to get him away from seducing his wife – not the most honourable of reasons to send a man into action, to be sure, especially since he knows La Bigorne lacks any seafaring knowledge and the ship is a wreck, so there is every likelihood that not only will the expedition fail, chances are that La Bigorne will be killed too. Fortunately for him, the second mate is there to help out. Barely sound to sail, its cannons no longer functioning, the vessel soon falls prey to the pirates and La Bigorne and his men escape onto an island, Île Sainte-Marie (12 kilometres east of Madagascar). After numerous encounters with the pirates – who live the other side of the island – La Bigorne manages to overcome them through craft and guile. His prize is marriage to Bethi (Rossana Podesta), the daughter of the chief. She is of mixed race: her mother was white-skinned, her father the black-skinned chief of the island of Sainte-Marie. At this wedding her father drinks so much alcohol he dies; the island automatically cedes to the eldest child, his daughter, as long as she is married. She then gives it to La Bigorne, who happily cedes it to his king, Louis XV. Needless to say, when he returns to his commander's post in Madagascar, he is greeted as a hero.

Even though this is a comedy, as *Variety* critic Mosk pointed out at the time, there are some problems with this film. Mosk astutely suggests the film 'might not be (considered) so funny here in France with Algeria still touchy'.[15] Clearly he is referring to the representation of the natives as happy in their oppression as colonized beings and to the 'marrying (of) a conveniently half-breed daughter of a native chief'.[16] We are in 1958; the crisis in Algeria is at its hottest. Censorship was tightening all the while. To cite just one example: the police seized Henri Alleg's book denouncing the French army's use of torture in Algeria, *La Question*. On 13 May, the French army made its putsch on the city of Alger in an endeavour to prevent a French government from entering into negotiations with the Algerian National Liberation Force (FLN). The-then President of France, René Coty, issued a decree on 14 May ordering the Army to stay loyal to the government. On 15 May, one of the leaders of the putsch, General Sallan, called on de Gaulle to assume power. De Gaulle declared his readiness and within less than a month he was back in power. Effectively, this putsch was instrumental in causing the Fourth Republic to topple. But if the French army believed they had an ally in de Gaulle for their cause of keeping Algeria French, in the end they were mistaken. On 4 June 1958, the day of this film's release incidentally, de Gaulle was in Algeria, addressing the crowds and delivering his ambiguous speech: 'I have understood you, I have seen what has happened here, I see what you want to accomplish…In the whole of Algeria there is only one category of inhabitant. There are only French people. I, de Gaulle, am opening the door of reconciliation'.[17] Four years later, Algeria was granted its independence. This early summer period of 1958, then, was a very tense time in terms of the colonial issue. Let us consider the opening images of this film – weirdly un-prophetic as it transpires, showing how out of touch with the times this particular film was.

We are told in the opening preface that this film is based on real facts that show how good the Franco-Malagasy relations were. It is worth remembering that in 1750, the year in which this story is located, Madagascar was not a French colony even if in the late seventeenth century the French had established trading posts along the east coast. The indigenous people had also established good relations with pirates in the area. The island of Sainte-Marie was the pirates' base from where they sailed out to attack ships laden with wealthy goods from the Indies. Thus, the idea that France enjoyed good relations with Madagascar relates to their trading practices with the indigenous peoples, not to any concept of the island as a colony, as the opening of the film implies. Calypso music opens the first sequence and we see images of 'happy natives' dancing and singing, but to no evident purpose. This evocation of the easy-going natives enjoying simple pleasures is but a mere smoke-screen for the implicitly-racist representation of the aimlessness of the black community. This myth of 'easy-going-ness' is compounded by another early sequence in which we meet La Bigorne. He is seducing the commander's wife, Madame Rosette (Liliane Brousse); the commander bursts in – but, in that flash second, the black maidservant Titi'Tao (an uncredited role) has taken her place, at which point the commander declares, 'black or white he has to sleep with them all'. If anything, these opening sequences coupled with the closing sequences – when La Bigorne outwits everyone, gains sovereignty over the island of Sainte-Marie and then cedes it to Louis XV – imply that France's eventual colonizing of this territory was a good thing. After all, by defeating the British pirates La Bigorne has made the area safe for trading and thereby, we infer, brought greater security to the Malagaches. We are but a step away from the 'civilizing force' of France's imperialism!

The timing of this film and the fact that the novel upon which it is based was published in 1957 mean we cannot ignore the historical contexts. And, indeed, history tells us that the indigenous peoples of Madagascar were not at all happy with their colonizing French brethren (any more than they had been with the British who intermittingly controlled the island). From 1947 onwards, the country was engaged in a relentless battle to free itself from France. In October 1958 France granted it the status of semi-independence as a Territoire d'Outre Mer; by 1960 it was fully independent. The insensitivity of the film's narrative is striking, to say the least, in that it marks, nay, celebrates the beginnings of Madagascar's colonization. The representation of the indigenous peoples is just as troublesome. The Malagache chief is represented as a hypocrite in much the same light as the African chief of *Tamango* (see Chapter 10). This chief is in cahoots with Tom Wright to begin with; he has even promised his daughter Bethi to him. However, once La Bigorne defeats the pirate, the chief turns coat and allies himself with the newly-powerful French and promises his daughter to La Bigorne. Alcohol intolerance is his downfall, as with the African chief in *Tamango*. But here it is more extreme for, in his stupidity, the chief drinks himself to death (in the novel he is poisoned by Wright). Bethi, the mixed-race daughter, is distinct from all the other women natives on the island of Sainte-Marie in that, whereas they go topless, she wears a rather peculiar bikini (see her in figure 7.4 below). She is, therefore, the same (i.e., a native of the island) but different. Her mother's status as a white woman makes her more white, one suspects, than Aïché in *Tamango,* whose miscegenation is of a less acceptable order: her mother was African and black, her father European and white.

Figure 7.4: Poster for *La Bigorne caporal de France* – note Bethi's 'bikini'[18]

This comedic film must, of course, be read within its time, so the racism inherent in the film has to be understood in the light of events and socio-cultural attitudes to race at the time. This does not, however, prevent the timing of its release as being rather odd. Thus, the political cultural resonances suggest that a pro-colonialist reading is not unfounded. The novelist, Pierre Nord – a pseudonym for André Brouillard – had been a spy, a Resistance hero and a writer of spy fiction, mostly Cold War narratives. During the war he had worked for the Section cinématographique de l'armée (SCA) which was, first, a branch of the Armistice army under Vichy then, later, part of the Free French Forces (Forces françaises libres/FFL). Part of the propaganda during the Occupation period took the SCA to the various French colonies in Africa to show how well the Armistice army was doing in relation to caring for the needs of the indigenous peoples. It is impossible to impugn a political position to Nord/Brouillard; what we do know, though, is that many of his narratives show the little man standing up to the big forces of oppression (be they the Germans, the Soviets or British pirates). François Périer as La Bigorne represents a clear choice for the lead role since it is a characterization similar to Cadet Rousselle (with the exception of his womanizing skills). The little man wins big – an island, a princess – and turns some of his winnings over to his king!

Men or Masks of Iron – Marais-La Tour; Philipe-Fanfan-Till; Marchal-d'Artagnan-Bragelonne

The final section of this chapter focuses on the three dominant star vehicles, although some reference will be made to Fernandel and Mariano because their more asexualized roles act as an interesting foil to the three types of masculinity embodied by Marais, Marchal and Philipe. Below are posters for the various films under consideration (see below, figures 7.5 to 7.8): *Les Trois Mousquetaires, Les Aventures de Till L'Espiègle, Fanfan la tulipe, La Tour, prends garde!* and *Le Vicomte de Bragelonne*. What strikes us immediately is the fact that the only bared torso is that of Jean Marais.

And this is where we need to begin. Because it is not just any bared torso, it is a torso that has been laid bare, flagellated, scarred by whipping and then exposed to all elements as the courageous hero charges off to obtain the king's standard back from Marie-Thérèse of Austria. To explain. As a result of his satirical song, the duc de Saint-Sever, who feels targeted by the words, insists that La Tour be punished. He orders his side-kick Pérouge (Renaud Mary) to see to it. The punishment is to run the gauntlet between two rows of soldiers (15 each side) who beat his bare back with their bayonets (see figure 7.10 below). In fact he is not even permitted to run. After he has been violently stripped of his shirt, his hands are tied in front of him, a rope noosed around his waist so he cannot escape and he is dragged along. Here, he resembles a martyr in a pose that is certainly reminiscent of the iconography of Saint Sebastian.

Beauty is inherent in this image, just as it is in the image of Jean Marais. Moreover, in this scene, everyone looks on: the rest of the theatre troupe who wince with every strike,

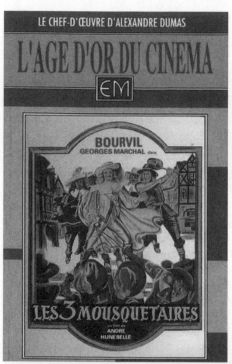

Figure 7.5 (left): Poster for *Les Trois Mousquetaires*. © Pathé Consortium Cinema.

Figure 7.6 (below): Photo still for *Les Aventures de Till l'Espiègle*. © Cinédis.

Figure 7.7 (left): Poster for *Fanfan la tulipe*[19]. © ADAGP, Paris and DACS, London 2009.

Figure 7.8 (below): Photo still for *La Tour, prends garde!* © Véga Films

Figure 7.9: Poster for *Le Vicomte de Bragelonne*[20]

but more significantly, the king who is peering at him through a tiny window in one of the performers' caravans – that of the young Mirabelle (Nadja Tiller), whom he fancies. The object of looking, then, becomes La Tour/Marais, not Mirabelle or any of the other women. Furthermore, this is a different order of spectacle from the two we have just seen in the opening sequences of the film – those of war and comic theatre. Here, we are behind the scenes – quite literally of the theatre's encampment – where nasty things can, and do, happen, supposedly hidden away from public view. However, here we see it all. Thus, this particular torture scene enters a number of queered spaces. First, we witness the public outing of something that is usually concealed: the disgraceful act of torture. Second, the body on display becomes a source not of pleasure but of pain. In a swashbuckler film we long to see the signs of masculinity in heroic action, muscles abounding in physical prowess. But, here, they are kept in check by the tying of the hands and waist, suggesting a constrained if not abject body. What preserves the abject from turning into humiliation is the fact that La Tour returns the gaze upon his oppressor Pérouge and defiantly states that he will avenge this infraction of his human rights. This he does in the very next sequence when he strips himself down to the waist, swims across the river to the Austrian camp and seizes

Figure 7.10: La Tour being stripped ready to run the gauntlet. © Véga Films.

the king's standard. We get all the heroics imaginable: shimmying down the French castle walls; swimming across with great stealth; setting loose the horses and torching the tents to create a distraction; slicing his way into Marie-Thérèse's tent by cutting through the canvas with a sabre; grabbing both the king's standard and the Austrian queen's (it is at this point that we notice the marks of his beating on his back); making his escape by jumping onto a horse and riding back to the French camp. By this time, the Austrians' explosives' tents have also caught fire creating further mayhem. Single-handedly, La Tour returns the standard and a victory over the Austrians to his king. The humiliation is all the duc de Saint-Sever's.

Heroic revenge against the oppressor is also the remit of *Les Aventures de Till L'Espiègle* (henceforth *Till*). Philipe had wanted to adapt the Belgian author Charles de Coster's novel of the same title since first reading it in 1947. Published in1867, Coster's intention behind his own re-writing of the earlier sixteenth-century text was to make of Till a resister to the Spanish occupiers. His Till is, therefore, a far cry from the original scatological mischief-maker who thought nothing of defecating over people's food, crafting his magic to save or damn people, and so on. Coster's Till is very much a clean body. He embodies the spirit of Flanders in the sixteenth century. He comes from modest means – his is a farming family.

The novel mixes historical fact (the invasion of Flanders by the Spanish and their attempts to impose Catholicism on the Calvinist Flemish) and myth (the heroic individual, Till, who stands for freedom); and the story of a family – Till's, whose parents are murdered by the cruel Spanish army – and that of a nation. Philipe's adaptation, written with René Wheeler who scripted *Fanfan* with Jeanson, is a witty, prank-filled version that stays fairly true to the Coster text. As with most swashbuckler films, the narrative is episodic. The film falls into to four fairly even episodes. In part one, Till is still a boy and full of mischief; he has a pretty fiancée Nele (Nicole Berger) but he is not averse to teasing her. His best friend is his cousin Lamme (Jean Carmet), with whom he shares nearly all his escapades. He lives with his parents in the small Flanders town of Damme (just north of Bruges). His father, Claes (Fernand Ledoux), is the leader of the resistance against the Spanish. He is discovered with leaflets and the Spanish promptly condemn him to be burnt as a rebel and a heretic. His last words are to the villagers and Till: 'Flemish people, freedom, freedom, courage, courage! Till my son hear me, flee this place!' Till does so, but only after shouting out, 'long live freedom', thus taking on his father's mantle. And, standing at his father's pyre, he cries out, 'these ashes beat upon my heart, I want to save our country', an indication that he has joined in solidarity with the rest of the community.

In part two, he galvanizes the town's resistance and manages to infiltrate the Spanish court as a buffoon. A blend occurs here, therefore, between Till's two selves: the prankster and the resistance fighter. His disguise and insider knowledge enables him to foil the Spanish plot to kill William of Orange, the leader of the Flemish Resistance. In part three, Till dons another disguise to help the cause. This time he plays the role of a Catholic priest. As books are being burnt by the Spanish in the market square, Till stands up and makes to deliver the anti-Calvinist propaganda of the Spaniards. In so doing, he exposes the ludicrous logic of the Inquisitorial enemy with such lines as: 'The Saint-Inquisition is a mother for you, we think for you, so keep your heads empty, if you were to read you would get the notion of fighting for freedom'. In distracting the Spaniards, Till manages to conceal what the resisters are doing: making weapons. Later on in this part, he persuades, again through his prankster guile, other mercenary armies to join William of Orange's army. In part four, all the rather loose strands are pulled together in a grand denouement. It is winter; Till returns to his home town of Damme. First, there is his showdown with the wicked money-grabbing merchant, Grippesous (Raymond Souplex), who has made a fortune from collaborating with the Spanish (by trading in dispensations, amongst other things) and denouncing Flemish resisters to them. Till, now hardened by all he has experienced, is brutally frank as he tells the merchant (whom he is holding by the throat) exactly what he thinks of him. Terrified, the merchant makes his escape, only to be shot in the back by the Spaniards. Next, Till meets up with Nele, to whom he swears undying love. Till receives news that there is a further plot to assassinate William of Orange. Rallying his men, he takes off in pursuit of the treacherous Spanish. What follows is arguably the most exhilarating sequence of the entire film: Till and his men pursue the enemy in an ice-skating chase along the Flemish canals and, one by one, eliminate their opponents. Once more, Till foils the plot. William of Orange goes on to win the battle; the Spaniards are routed. The film ends with Till back in Damme and reunited with his beloved Nele.

The prankster boy evolves into heroic man. However, Philipe's performance is less beguiling, it has to be said, than his Fanfan, partly because Till remains more boy than man, at least until the last part. The gags become repetitive. He swings a lot from bell ropes and the like, outwits the 'stupid' Spanish by flummoxing them with childish pranks. Furthermore, this childishness is accentuated by his grating nasal laughter, of which there is far too much – almost as if Philipe is unsure how to play this role: seriously for an adult audience or more light-heartedly for a younger one. The message of resistance against the oppressor is certainly overplayed. For example, Till's declamation 'these ashes beat upon my heart, I want to save our country' is iterated far too often – it feels as if a rather heavy mallet has been taken to crack open our political consciousness. Undoubtedly, this film was Philipe's response to his feelings about the recent past and to his own unspoken shame about his father's role as a collaborator during the Occupation.[21] Many of Philipe's generation lost both their youth and innocence thanks to that period during which they were unable, because too young, to do much to prevent France's humiliation. As Serge Reggiani so eloquently puts it, 'he was the only one amongst us to remain solid and honest in spite of his talent and success; for us who are of his generation he was our vindication'[22] – meaning, quite simply, that his integrity stood as marker for this lost generation, one that was disempowered because of its youth. Or again Georges Sadoul, 'Philipe is an explanation of our country and our time'.[23] Of course, Philipe's earlier, late-forties' films, with their dark realism, spoke to those issues – his young men were the cynical victims of that lost generation, angered by their elders' betrayal of their sons' honour (by giving into or collaborating with the German occupier/enemy). There, his youthful personages appeared to have no recourse to action other than cruelty to others or self-destructiveness. Here, however, that balance is redressed. Angry adolescence gives way to intelligent subterfuge and manly courage.

In France, people of all sides of the political spectrum were critical of this film, Gérard Philipe's only one as director – with the assistance of Joris Ivens. For example, Willy Acher of *Cahiers du cinéma* called it a 'painful flop'.[24] Unusually, even the normally up-beat film industry press criticized it for its technical shortcomings – finding fault with the soundtrack and the editing.[25] Finally, the review in *Image et Son* complained that the film accentuated the prankster side of Till and left out the mystical side of his persona altogether (he had healing powers); moreover, the gags, of which there are many, got in the way of the political aspects of Coster's novel. The article also felt that Philipe's interpretation tones down the hatred Till feels against the Spaniards who have murdered his father and ransacked his home town; the concept of religious freedom gets played down in favour of religious intolerance (in the form of the Inquisition) and collusion between the clergy and the occupiers.[26]

I will come to these issues in a moment. But, first, we need to understand the production contexts to see why there was such general critical hostility towards this film. *Till* was one of the four co-productions made during the second half of the 1950s with the East German DEFA studios.[27] This was the first of the four and was to be launched as a flagship of east-west collaboration. However, its timing could not have been more unpropitious. The day of its première in Paris, 7 November 1956, coincided with the brutal repression of the uprising in Hungary. Some critics saw Philipe's *Till* as an allegory against the Soviet Union's oppression, but damned it for being too light-hearted. Others read Philipe's collaboration with East Germany as an indirect endorsement of the Soviet act of intervention. Philipe, a sympathizer of the communist movement, was therefore caught in a cleft stick – either way he reaped the opprobrium of the critics.[28]

Interestingly, Coster's novel met with similar displeasure from the more conformist milieus of the nineteenth-century Belgian establishment, primarily for its expression of liberal views and anti-clerical sentiments. We should recall that the original sixteenth-century tale was as irreverent as any of Rabelais' texts of the same time (for example in the title *Till Ulenspiegel* 'ulen' means wipe and 'spiegel' both mirror and behind). Thus, irreverence was at the very heart of the Till character. Belgium, however, had only recently become an independent Catholic nation with a constitutional monarchy (1830). So the anti-Catholicism vein of the novel was far from welcome, as was the portrait of a successful resistance led by Calvinists. Although Coster's novel was shunned in Belgium, it was widely read elsewhere and is now credited as the first French-language Belgian novel. At the time, French was the official language. However, Belgium was having its own internal crisis in the mid-nineteenth century over its identity as Walloon or Flemish and by the late nineteenth century the Flemish-Dutch language was also officially recognized. This background to the original text therefore allows us to read Philipe's *Till* as an example of nation-building, albeit not the establishmentarian one. Despite the flawed nature of the film, it does seek to redress the malaise felt by a generation that did not get to fight to defend its own name and, thereby, its country's honour during the Second World War. That it does so with a body type more readily described as 'skinny' and 'gaunt', 'cerebral' and 'nervy', as if carrying a '*mal de vivre*/malaise' within him, a 'sense of loss haunting his persona,'[29] marks him out as a rather specialized category of swashbuckler – not seen, before nor since. Philipe offers us an interior, mentally-prowessed and agile swashbuckler, rather than the carved masculinity of Marais or Marchal's swashbuckler type and their ideal image of health, energy, force and power.

To return now to the criticisms levelled at this film. Having watched it several times, I am at a loss to understand the comments in relation to the soundtrack. Philipe used the world-renowned William Sivel; the film process was Technicolor, which, at the time, had the standard two track system for sound (as opposed to the six track available on widescreen formats that permit stereo sound). However, Sivel had a reputation for being able to make mono sound like stereo and this film seems to be no exception.[30] Certain sounds, in particular the bells, do jar, but it is safe to assume this is intentional. As for the editing, it is slow in parts and at times there is a tendency to belabour the point. It seems that Philipe did not know when to cut – when directing he made the classic mistake of most first-time film-makers of trying to edit as he shot; to create a fast pace by cutting sequences short. But the effect, when it comes to editing the film, is, of course, the reverse: the less footage you have to play with, the slower the film appears (at its simplest, inter-cutting cannot happen, there is nothing to cut away to).[31] But no one can fault the fabulous pacing of the fourth and last part of the film. That set of sequences is done with brio, and it leads me to speculate that these are the sequences that were shot under the direction of Joris Ivens. In particular, I would single out the canal ice-skating chase (shot in Sweden in the area surrounding the small medieval town of Tällberg). These were the first shots in the production when Ivens and Philipe were acting as co-directors of the film.[32] Shortly after production got going, however, it became evident that the two could not work together. Ivens' brilliance as a documentary film-maker did not match Philipe's need for someone who could work with actors and, by all accounts, Philipe grew impatient with Ivens' ways of working.[33] In any event, Ivens stood down as co-director and acted merely in an advisory capacity – although to all appearances his advice was not well heeded.

As to the focus and tone, whilst this film can be read as the allegorical story of a lost generation, the value of its message in this context is that, first, it recognizes the courage of the older generation in the form of Till's father and mother and the resisters of Damme – men and women both; second, it promotes the idea that it is not from the heart of darkness (hatred) that we can overcome our enemies any more than we can confront the venality and cruelty of mankind – in a parodic way, humour functions as a powerful tool to undermine the corruption of some, the rigidity of others, the cowardice and brutality of yet others. In this film, humour dominates until Till faces the man who embodies all these traits in his single person: the merchant aptly named Grippesous (literally meaning money grabber). Thus, whilst the local representatives of the Catholic church – from the highest echelons of the cardinal (Jean Debucourt), a master of compromise, down to the priests – are seen as fairly unpleasant examples of collaboration with the enemy, this Grippesous covers himself with ignominy in his denunciating Till and trying to steal his fiancée Nele, making money on all sides of the compass: cosying up to the Spanish oppressors, black-marketeering, and so on and so forth. This is surely the moment when the point is made about the odious taste that collaboration with the enemy leaves in the mouth of a nation. In any event, its strong polemical tone notwithstanding, audiences did enjoy the film: the French version brought in a figure of 2.3 million, the German 3.24 – hardly a flop therefore.[34]

Lastly we come to Georges Marchal and his two musketeer films, *Les Trois Mousquetaires* and *Le Vicomte de Bragelonne* (henceforth *Bragelonne*). I have not managed to trace down and see his third swashbuckler film, *Les Aventures de Gil Blas de Santillane*, so must leave that one aside. In the first musketeer film, Marchal is D'Artagnan, in the latter, Bragelonne, son of Athos – one of the original musketeers. There is a very different feeling, both in terms of tone and hero construction, in these two films. The earlier one (by one year only) was shot in Gevacolor and the colours that resonate the most are reds and blues, the markers of the two camps, essentially: Cardinal Richelieu's being the former; the blue more readily associated with the king, Louis XIII, whom our brave musketeers are engaged and committed to serve. This quite simple palette is matched by the simplicity of Hunebelle's film in that he retains only the first half of Dumas' novel: the musketeers' successful endeavour to foil Richelieu's conspiracy to discredit Louis' wife, the queen of France, Anne of Austria. Swordfights and chases on horseback abound, as does D'Artagnan's serial seduction of women. Action dominates the narrative at the expense of character development, it has to be said. For its part Cerchi's adaptation of *Bragelonne*, shot in Eastmancolor, uses a broader palette of colours suggesting a greater complexity of characterization – as we shall see, this is particularly true of Marchal's Bragelonne. But the role of women takes an interesting twist, also, in that they are not all mere foils to our hero's exploits.

In *Les Trois Mousquetaires,* D'Artagnan comes to Paris to pursue a career as a musketeer. On the way, he is given a drubbing by some of Richelieu's henchmen. Once restored, he continues to Paris where he encounters the three original musketeers, Porthos (Gino Cervi), Athos (Jean Martinelli) and Aramis (Jacques François). They quickly become firm friends. The brotherhood, 'one for all and all for one', is sworn. D'Artagnan, meantime, has taken a fancy to Constance (Danielle Godet), the daughter of his sleazy landlord Bonacieux (Georges Chamarat). She is one of the queen's maids-in-waiting and it is thanks to this tenuous connection that D'Artagnan and his three friends become embroiled in the affair of the diamond pendants. Richelieu (Renaud Mary) discovers that the Duke of Buckingham (Steve Barclay) is in love with the queen (Marie Sabouret) and that she, realizing the impossibility of pursuing the affair, gave her admirer her diamond pendants as a gift of separation. He returns to England with his token of love. These pendants were a gift from the king, however, and Richelieu seeks to expose this infidelity to the king at the most public occasion of the king's ball. The pendants must be retrieved at all costs. After numerous escapades, D'Artagnan – with a little help from his friends – manages to outwit Richelieu and his agents, including the scheming and sultry Milady de Winter (Yvonne Sanson), and save the queen's honour in the nick of time.

We are treated to a considerable display of D'Artagnan's bravery and, thereby, Marchal's muscular masculinity, in this film. There are seven swordfights, four horse chases, much swinging from candelabras and ropes – all the elements of bravura. There is, however, little exposure of the torso – only once, and it occurs right towards the end of the film. As with Fanfan/Philipe before him, D'Artagnan/Marchal strips to the waist to wash outdoors in the courtyard. Our hero is not in action, therefore; merely seeing to his ablutions prior to returning the pendants safely to the queen. The effect is not erotic, but one of humour – as with the scene in *Fanfan*. In a similar way, erotic effects are annulled when we look upon the wounded D'Artagnan at the beginning of the film. He lies supine in bed, his head wrapped in bandages and his shirt slightly undone to reveal the slightest of glimpses of a manly chest (see figure 7.11 below). The erotic charge is removed, however, by the humoristic effect of the bandages swathed around his face as if he has toothache! Intentional or not, this playfulness with display has the ironic effect of countering the muscularity of our hero's courageous feats. Not gainsaying them, merely posing the question around the erotics of masculinity. If male nudity is rendered humorous, does this signal a fear of exposure, a dread of feminization through fetishism? Or, conversely, is it to rarefy the virility of masculinity – keep it all buttoned in and buttoned up (see figure 7.12 below), sheathed away as opposed to the sword which D'Artagnan so readily wields? As we shall see this representation receives almost identical treatment in Cerchi's *Bragelonne* – so something is up!

Figure 7.11: D'Artagnan wounded – less than erotic in bandages. © Pathé Consortium Cinema.

Figure 7.12: D'Artagnan the lover – all buttoned up. © Pathé Consortium Cinema.

Of the two musketeer titles, *Bragelonne* is the more interesting because it breaks quite strongly with the original dark Dumas tale. First, as we explained above, Bragelonne survives his heartbreak. Indeed, he ends up marrying the British noblewoman Hélène de Winter (Dawn Addams), the daughter of the three musketeers' English ally in the earlier novel (and brother-in-law to the devious Milady).[35] The year of the film's release is 1954; we wonder, therefore, if there is a slight nod toward the fiftieth anniversary of the Entente Cordiale since Hélène de Winter is a personage who does not figure in the Dumas novel. Second, there is no apparent nostalgia for a *noblesse d'épée* – our hero is as committed to his sword and horse as before – even if courtly politics and skulduggery are afoot, an effect of the *noblesse de cour*. We are in the 1660s; Louis XIV (André Falcon) is progressively asserting his divine right as absolute monarch, often over-riding the aging Mazarin (Nico Pepe) who is plotting to replace Louis XIV with his identical twin brother, whom he has had under his control since childbirth, by all accounts. Notwithstanding this, the musketeer spirit seems here to be as cheerfully alive as before, as is exemplified in their brave swordsmanship (*noblesse d'épée*). Third, we are completely unaware, in the film, of the musketeers' split over the Fronde of the late 1640s when the nobility rose against the king. Aramis and Athos 'changed sides' joining the rebels, the Frondeurs. D'Artagnan and Porthos remained loyal to Louis XIV and joined Mazarin's ranks – that is until Mazarin declared his support for Cromwell over Charles I. At which point the musketeers reunite and, in alliance with Lord de Winter, swear to avenge the British monarch's execution. Later, it is these two who along with Bragelonne (Athos' son), in defiance of Mazarin, serve their king's desire to support Charles II to the throne. This split, which occurs in the second novel of the trilogy, *Vingt ans après*, is significant within Dumas' narrative since it impacts on the pessimistic tone of the third novel. Thus, there is a toning down in the film of the murky politics, to say nothing of a glossing over of the rift within the brotherhood of musketeers. Furthermore, we are less aware in the film that an age is coming to a close. Rather, manly courage is foregrounded. Those who plot are, for the most part, old and rather seedy men (in particular, Mazarin). And this is not without its interest, especially since the darker elements of the novel appear to have become contained and displaced exclusively onto the love intrigue and Mazarin's plot. Real men's integrity does not get questioned, therefore, and the film maintains our musketeers as heroic. The person responsible for disloyalty in the boudoir is Louise de la Vallières (Florence Arnaud) – the king knew nothing of her betrothal to Bragelonne apparently, and he quickly banishes her when he confronts her with her duplicity. The person responsible for lèse-majesté in the court is the cardinal Mazarin – not quite a man since he is not (supposedly) a sexual being. The real Mazarin was a quite effeminate man and had a strong Italian accent – well caught by Nico Pepe, surrounded as he is by a hoard of kittens!

This displacement causes an intriguing de-responsibilization of masculinity – real men do not plot; only women and feminized men do. This is particularly important to our reading of Marchal as Bragelonne because he is something of a paradox. When we first encounter him, he is under arrest by Mazarin in an effort to intercept a sealed letter to the king. In a dank cell, we see he has been wounded. His shirt is slightly undone partially exposing a handsome, somewhat sweaty chest, but not much more. His is a floppy, weakened and feverish body, therefore: reclining in bed, calling out for his beloved Louise. He fairly swiftly rehabilitates himself in terms of masculinity, however. He makes his escape, gets involved in a swordfight (despite his wounds), and kills four of Mazarin's soldiers. When he reaches safety, he meets up with Hélène, not his beloved Louise. Hélène, who knows of Louise's flirtations with Louis XIV, tries to warn Bragelonne. He will have none of it and moves on to rejoin his king with the message from Charles II. There, Bragelonne discovers the truth about Louise and challenges her lover to a duel (he does not yet realize it is the king). This time he is arrested for breaking the 1630 law forbidding duels. Hélène, cross-dressed as a musketeer in clothing similar to Bragelonne's, facilitates his escape – the two of them fight their way out of a corner with exemplary swordsmanship. Bragelonne complements her on her skills: 'brave little man'. And, thanks to her bravery, he is now able to go on and foil Mazarin's plot. All ends well. He saves the king and marries Hélène.

Throughout the whole film Bragelonne (apart from the prison scene) has remained tightly buttoned up to the neck, whether it be his lacy shirt or his velvet coat and ruffles. In three of the important sequences in terms of his asserting masculine power, he is in the presence of Hélène de Winter and their clothes are a match. The first encounter occurs early in the film, shortly after his escape from Mazarin's men. He and Hélène are in identical red velour outfits – this is the time she warns him not to trust Louise; she offers him friendship but he rejects her. And yet his suspicions are aroused. Once confirmed by one of Mazarin's minions, Bragelonne storms into Louise's secret apartments and challenges her lover to a duel. The defence of personal honour outweighs any of the danger. The second time is when Hélène springs him from captivity as a result of his rash challenge. This time both Bragelonne and Hélène are dressed in identical clothing, black and white cavalier outfits – clearly they are growing closer, as is evidenced also by their working together in the swordfight. Bragelonne is soon under lock and key once more, however, even if this time it is for his own safety. D'Artagnan (Jacques Dumesnil) has locked him upstairs in a country inn outside Paris to keep him away from Mazarin. For a third time Hélène comes to him – still in her cavalier outfit – this is the moment of the first kiss! But before that, this is their exchange:

Hélène: You are always rude to me, yet I got you your freedom, not Louise.
Bragelonne: Why all this?
Hélène: I can't suffer injustice. In England all men are equal.
Bragelonne: Here's what I think of women, the English ones aren't women!

Upon which they kiss, and in the same breath she declares her love for him. 'Not bad for an Englishwoman', declares Bragelonne, who until now has declared that she drinks and behaves like a man. She, meantime, has the last word: 'You have a lot to learn about women'. Indeed he does. By the end of the film – as he, Porthos, Athos and D'Artagnan safely restore order by saving the king from Mazarin's dastardly plan to replace him – Bragelonne, who insisted Hélène stay behind for this escapade, is still referring to her as his 'courageous little man'. Jokingly, she retorts that had he turned her down she would have become a spy – a threat to the nation, therefore. Fortunately for France, Bragelonne accepts her love; the king blesses their alliance; the future of French-British relations is assured, therefore.

Although the comments about Hélène's masculine bravura are made in jest, they come back enough times for us to give pause. It is her intelligence that saves Bragelonne more than once; it is her fortitude that facilitates his rescuing the king; finally, it is her love for him that spares him from the suicide ending that the novel allotted to him. Hélène, in this regard, is therefore more than just a foil to Bragelonne's masculinity. She speaks in terms of equality and justice – she despises cowardice and treachery as embodied by the more simperingly-feminine Louise. She represents a new, strong femininity, I would argue. As a mirror held up to women, Hélène shows how to be man's equal and not enslaved by his construction of her, as is Louise. As a mirror held up to men, she exemplifies the concept that virility and masculinity are not ascribable to men only, and that to see it as such is essentialist. If anything, then, when Bragelonne and she are in the same space, he acts as much as a foil to her as she to him – that is why he has a lot to learn. In this respect, I am also intrigued that he is so often under lock and key. Of course, escaping is part of what a swashbuckler does. But, on two out of the three occasions, he is imprisoned because of his masculine posturing, be it the duel or his hot-headed impulsive rage for revenge over Mazarin (so much so that D'Artagnan fears for his safety). Unlocked, he is unsafe – until his final release, when he groups together and works with others to rescue the king. As he progressively learns, masculinity does not mean having to go it alone and women can be co-travellers rather than meek maidens (as in the case of *Les Trois Mousquetaires*) or scheming vixens.

This point leads me to my concluding remarks on these swashbucklers and the question of marriage. At the end of *Fanfan*, the king blesses the union between Fanfan and Adeline. As they turn to leave the king, Tranche-Montagne's numerous children run to the couple's side. Fanfan lifts up one child; the others grab hold of his or Adeline's hands or skirt. The symbolism of going forth to multiply is self-evident. With the exception of *La Tour de Nesle*, our heroes marry. In most cases, the woman is their match. Even Bethi in *Cadet Rousselle* is not without courage and shows herself capable of heroic rescues. And although La Tour rescues his sweetheart Toinon (Cathia Caro) from deportation to the penal colonies, she has not lacked in showing inner strength and resolve (as for example when she tricks the chief of police into her room and locks him in). In the romantic comedies, set in the more exotic domain of Spain, Gypsies and bandit queens get their men – literally by saving their lives.

What astounds is that these narratives should end in this manner: not quite in the vein of the Romantic ideal of courtly love, but stories where the man finds happiness with the woman he will marry. The whole idea of the swashbuckler-hero swooping in and sorting out problems to then take off to other adventures is repeatedly annulled in these narratives. This man seeks to settle down. As we shall discover, this trend stands in complete opposition to most of the film narratives located in the nineteenth century, where marriages fail, the husband is a cuckold, the woman is destroyed by her lover's perfidy, the wife is dissatisfied, and so on. Here, our heroes are not cynical seducers; the women are not gullible and often work intelligently and with passion to help their loved ones. In this most masculine of all the costume drama types, the hero has space and time to discover other sides to his persona: the strong stunt and action-driven body as much as the weakened limp one; the man of adventure who finds strength in brotherly love as much as in his love for a good woman. Curiously, because masculinity is not in a state of renunciation and is not constrained by a social order of things that seeks to fix gender according to a system of binaries, the message seems to be that there is a third way – one where masculinity need not feel assailed or in crisis. This is not to claim that power relations between the sexes are harmonized or that hierarchies are dissolved in the swashbuckler films. The suggestion is merely that this was a time when a man could be all things to himself, when men were men, strong of purpose yet clean in their ideals and willing to engage with women with respect – even to the point of trying to understand them. A nostalgic ideal image for the man of the 1950s, for sure.

Notes

1. Gilberte Turquan 'Films de Prestige: Prestige de l'élégance', *La Cinématographie française*, No. 1530, 22.8.1953, p. 43.
2. Ory (1989) and Sellier (2001).
3. Neale (2000, pp. 53–60).
4. As Yvonne Tasker so beautifully puts it, quoted in Neale (op. cit., p.57).
5. See Jean-José Richer's review of *Fanfan la tulipe*, 'Les Vacances du Cid' *Cahiers du* cinéma, Vol. 2, No. 12, 1.5.1952, pp. 61–3; Mosk in *Variety*, 10,4.1952 (no page). The synopsis of press reviews in the special issue on *Fanfan la tulipe* in *L'Avant-scène du cinéma*, No. 370, 1,4,1988, p. 83. The only reviewer to criticize Philipe's performance is Penelope Houston in her review '*Fanfan la tulipe*', *Monthly Film Bulletin*, Vol. 20, No. 232, 1.5.1953, pp. 66–7. She argues that Philipe is 'cast drastically against type' (p. 67).
6. I cover this issue of Black Realism in some detail in Hayward (2004, pp. 34–5).
7. Bonal (1994, p.162).
8. Ibid., p, 137.
9. Ibid., p. 161.
10. Production notes for *Fanfan la tulipe*, *La Cinématographie française*, Vol. 1441, 10.11.1951, p. 21 (no author name given).
11. Both 'Cadet Rousselle' and 'La Tour, prends garde!' are children's counting songs; the latter is a bit more energetic since it is a 'I'm the king of the castle' type of song – whoever breaks the circle (representing the tower) gets to be top-dog. So it is a question of determining the weakest link in the circle, something our La Tour is very good at.
12. Douin (1998, p. 196).
13. Ibid., p. 106.
14. Dany Robin trained as a ballet dancer and this is very self-evident in her lovely dance routines in this film. She rather outclasses Gina Lollobrigida in *Notre-Dame de Paris*.
15. Mosk review '*La Bigorne, caporal de France*', *Variety*, 3.10.1958 (no page given).
16. Ibid.
17. See recording of speech on http://www.dailymotion.com/video/x5uzp2_de-gaulle-alger-1958_news accessed 31.08.09.

18. Poster image accessed from http://www.cinema-francais.fr/les_films/films_d/films_darene_robert/la_bigorne_caporal_de_france.htm accessed 01.09.2009.

19. This particular DVD also has a remastered colour version of the film (not for my taste I have to confess).

20. Poster image accessed from http://www.fan-de-cinema.com/films/le-vicomte-de-bragelonne.html accessed 01.09.2009.

21. Bonal refers to Philipe in this context as '*un enfant de la honte*/a child tainted by shame' (Bonal, op. cit., pp. 21–2).

22. Serge Reggiani quoted in '*Les Aventures de Till L'Espiègle*', Dossier compiled by OROLEIS Strasbourg, in *Image et Son*, No. 153/4, 1.7.1962, p. 11 (no author name given).

23. Sadoul quoted in Cadars (1990, p. 8). Numerous are the contemporaries who say this about Philipe, many of whom are cited in Cadars.

24. Wily Archer in his review of *Les Aventures de Till L'Espiègle* 'Philipe perd le nord', *Cahiers du cinéma*, Vol. 7, No. 65, 1.12.1956, pp. 53–4.

25. Review of '*Les Aventures de Till L'Espiègle*', *La Cinématographie française*, No. 1693, 17.11.1956, p. 22 (no author name given).

26. '*Les Aventures de Till L'Espiègle*', Dossier compiled by OROLEIS Strasbourg, in *Image et Son*, No. 153/4, 1.7.1962, pp. 10–2 (no author name given).

27. We should not overlook the fact that *La Tour, prends garde!* was also a co-production with an Eastern bloc communist country, made with funding from UFUS studios in Belgrade, former Yugoslavia, although this was a more open country than some of the other communist satellites, as is well known. Yugoslavia developed co-production links with several European nations from 1955–1976. They were appealing to French producers because costs were lower, location sites more easily accessible and so forth.

28. See Marc Silberman's excellent study of this film's production issues in particular (2006, pp. 28–33) and in more general terms the whole co-production collaboration with East Germany (Silberman 2006).

29. Cadars, op. cit., p. 21.

30. I discuss Sivel's work to in some detail in Hayward (2005, pp. 22–5).

31. Bonal (op. cit., p. 235) supplies us with this information.

32. This information about shooting first in Sweden and difficulties occurring (unspecified) comes from '*Les Aventures de Till L'Espiègle*', Dossier compiled by OROLEIS Strasbourg, in *Image et Son*, No. 153/4, 1.7.1962, p. 11 (no author name given). Silberman (op. cit., pp. 28–31) gives more detail on the tense relationship that brewed up between Ivens and Philipe.

33. Bonal, op. cit., pp. 235–36, and Silberman, op. cit., pp. 28–31.

34. As I point out in Chapter 16, footnote 20, this audience figure did represent a considerable drop for Philipe where his French fan base was concerned.

35. Since Hélène is pure invention by Cerchi, it does not really matter that much that we explain that she is the daughter of Lord de Winter, except that her name could cause us to wonder in what way she is related to the evil scheming Milady de Winter of *Les Trois Mousquetaires*. Hélène's father is Milady's brother-in-law. However, things get a bit more complex when we stop to consider that Bragelonne is Milady's son – his father being Athos!

Part III

Representing History: Epics, Courtesans and Master Narratives, 1796-1888

Chapter 8

Setting the Terrain: France 1796-1888

In political terms, this 92-year period can best be described as an unprecedented struggle for the two halves of France – the Republican on one side, the Monarchist/Royalist on the other (which includes the extreme Ultras[1]) – to resolve their ideological differences and found a constitutional republic based on the principles of the Revolution of 1789. If 1789 split France asunder, then, as its various subsequent régimes show, the split nation still had a long period of political turmoil to confront. This instability manifested itself, on the one hand, in the form of a pursuit for international greatness. In this regard, France waged a series of wars with other European nations – particularly during the Napoleonic years (1796–1814). On the other hand, this instability led to repeated civil unrest and numerous coup d'états on a national level. The nation's internal politics were marked by both indecision and a great disregard for the poorer, disenfranchised classes. The trail of régimes post-Revolution reveals a country floundering for a political identity as it became, first, a Republic, then a Directory, then a Consulate, then an Empire, followed by a series of constitutional monarchies, yet another Republic, another Empire, and, finally a Third Republic, which arguably took 18 years to settle into itself – to then last 79 years. Nowhere is France's political uncertainty better reflected than with regard to the legal make up of its electorate – as is evidenced by the very slow, sometimes contradictory, move towards enfranchisement. Post-Revolution, universal suffrage applied to 'active citizens' (namely, only to those who could contribute a fixed levy) – this represented 4.3 million men (out of a possible total of 7.3). Under the Restoration this system was replaced by a much curtailed enfranchisement based on a 'census vote', which meant that only property owners paying a fixed levy could vote – this reduced the electorate to a mere 100,000. Then during the July Monarchy, it rose first to 175,000 in 1831 and then to 248,000 by 1846. Subsequently, under the Second Republic, universal suffrage was restored to men – this represented 9 million (as we know, women did not obtain the right to vote until 1944).[2]

On the next page (figure 8.1) is the time-line for the period that interests us (1796–1888). We begin in 1796 because of the importance of Napoleon Bonaparte and his impact on early nineteenth-century history. Remember that the Consulate of 1799 was brought about by a coup d'état led by Napoleon and that his return in 1815 was also a coup d'état. Over the period 1799–1888 there were five coups d'état, four of which were led by one Napoleon or the other! Also noteworthy is the impact of popular uprisings over this whole period – particularly by the Parisian populace ('*le peuple parisien*').

The nation's constitutional see-sawing notwithstanding, France secured its position as a great power – primarily, it has to be said, through its colonialist expansion (in Africa and

1796–1804	1804–14	1814–24	1824–30	1830–48	1848–51	1851–70	1870–1940
Directoire	*First Empire*	*Restoration Period*	*Restoration Period*	*July Monarchy*	*Second Republic*	*Second Empire*	*Third Republic*
Bonaparte head of Italian army leads successful campaign against Austrians	Napoleon I Forced to abdicate	Louis XVIII - brief return 1815 of Napoleon I [100 days], battle of Waterloo, he abdicates – in favour of son: Napoleon II; re-restoration of Louis XVIII	Charles X Forced to abdicate because of the people of Paris revolting	Louis-Philippe (1830 and 1832 uprisings of the working classes quashed) Forced to abdicate (effect of popular uprising Feb 1848)	Louis Napoleon President (effect of First Commune June 1848) Republic brought to an end by Louis Napoleon's coup d'état	Napoleon III Abdication brought about by Franco-Prussian War	(effect of Second Paris Commune March-May 1871) Brought to end by World War Two
Directoire brought to an end by coup d'état led by Bonaparte (Le 18 Brumaire)							
Consulate 1799–1804 Napoleon Bonaparte First Consul							

Figure 8.1: Time-line of constitutional systems of governance 1796–1940.

Indochina). Over the century, France gradually freed itself of the papal and clerical grip on its political culture, culminating in the 1904 Act of Separation of Church and State. From the 1830s onwards, thanks to the effects of the Industrial Revolution, the nation embarked on a modernization of its industry and transportation systems and later, post-1850 under Napoleon III, its cities and railways. Again under Napoleon III, free primary education was introduced for both sexes. He saw education as the means of escape from poverty. Later, in 1882 under the Third Republic, this extended to secondary education up to age 13.[3] Significantly, under Napoleon III, a major railway system nationwide, some of which had been initiated in the 1830s, was completed and the electric telegraph system was installed over mainland France, thus offering the nation a 'physical unity unprecedented in history'.[4] Existing ports were expanded or rebuilt, new ones were created to deal with the increased trade with its colonies; the Suez Canal was built (1869) to speed up goods transportation. People, merchandise and information circulated faster than ever before.[5]

Just as France of this period was at the dawn of a new age of modernization, so too (as we have already indicated) was the France of the 1950s. Unprecedented economic growth came as the result of a programme of nationalization and strategic planning (the 1950s saw the introduction of France's famous five-year plans). The technocrats (primarily in the form of senior civil servants known as the *cadres*) took over where bankers had ruled before (banks were now nationalized, so speculation was pretty much proscribed). By the early 1950s, the state employed one-tenth of the working population and, because of its control over banking, it directly influenced 47 per cent of all investment. It is in the context of this buoyant mood that the welfare state was established, ensuring a healthier nation; the cleaning up of insalubrious apartment buildings was launched on an unprecedented scale (not seen since Haussmannization); generous pro-natality programmes paid good dividends with a rise of 5.6 per cent in the population by 1954. But, as with the preceding century's modernization, this new wave of change affected the social structure. Streamlining the agricultural sector, through the concentration of productive units, caused a rural exodus to major cities into the light-industry sector, which had expanded through heavy investment in manufacturing. Thus, France's population went through a renewed wave of urbanization (as it had done in the 1830s and 1860s). Furthermore, better working conditions and pay meant that the working classes now found themselves aspiring to a middle-class quality of life. Women had the vote but still did not have full rights over their person if married. All these shifts brought in their wake questions of social identity – be it in the form of urban versus rural identities, gender relations, class, power relations and answerability to the state as a citizen, to say nothing of the citizen's right to challenge the state. It is hardly surprising, that many of the most successful costume dramas of the 1950s fall into this period that stretches from 1796–1888. For, in them, we see direct reference to social upheaval, to a desire for national greatness, to anxiety around sexual roles and gender identity, to individual ruthlessness and a desire for revenge. It is unsurprising, therefore, that just as in earlier period films (see Part Two) male narratives once more dominate this period (two thirds, see figure 8.3 below). Indeed, as Part Four will make explicit, only the Belle Epoque films favour women-centred narratives, redressing this imbalance – if only to 57 per cent.

1796–1814 Directoire/1st Consulate/1st Empire (7 titles)	Restoration periods 1814–24 Louis XVIII (5 titles) and 1824–30 Charles X (1 title)	1830–48 Louis Philippe (6 titles) July Monarchy	1848–70 2nd Republic-2nd empire (12 titles)	1870–88 3rd Republic (8 titles)
Le Nez de cuir (52) Y. Allégret **1,738,723**	L'Agonie des aigles (52) Alden-Delos **No figures**	L'Auberge rouge (51) Autant-Lara **2,662,329**	La Valse de Paris (50) Achard **2,058,838**	Les Petites Cardinal (51) Grangier **813,990**
Les Crimes de l'amour (1. D'Aurevilly Le Rideau Cramoisi) (53) Astruc **No figures**	Les Crimes de l'amour (2. Stendhal Mina de Vanghel) (53) Clavel & Barry **No figures**	Deburau (51) Guitry **221,638**	Monsieur Fabre (51) Diamant-Berger **1,539,225**	Le Plaisir (52) Ophuls **1,216,723**
Un Caprice de Caroline Chérie (53) Devaivre **2,836,858**	Le Comte de Monte-Cristo (53) Vernay **7,780,642**	Par ordre du Tsar (54) Haguet **1,923,380**	Les Violettes impériales (52) Pottier **8,125,766**	Trois femmes (52) Michel **535,041**
Les Hussards (55) Joffé **2,875,093**	Tamango (58) Berry **2,174,246**	La Dame aux camélias (53) Bernard **2,611,365**	Lettres de mon moulin (54) Pagnol **2,399,645**	Chevalier de la nuit (54) Darène **No figures**
Napoléon (55) Guitry **5,405,252**	Le Fils de Caroline chérie (55) Devaivre **1,667,829**	Le Rouge et le Noir (54) Autant-Lara **4,342,365**	La Castiglione (55) Combret **1,284,292**	Mam'zelle Nitouche (54) Y. Allégret **3,829,398**
		Milord L'Arsouille (56) Haguet **1,632,851**	Lola Montès (55) Ophuls **1,323,062**	Michel Strogoff (56) Gallone **6,920,814**

1796–1814 Directoire/1st Consulate/1st Empire (7 titles)	Restoration periods 1814-24 Louis XVIII (5 titles) and 1824-30 Charles X (1 title)	1830–48 Louis Philippe (6 titles) July Monarchy	1848–70 2nd Republic-2nd empire (12 titles)	1870–88 3rd Republic (8 titles)
Si le roi savait ça (58) Canaille **No figures**	**1824-30 Charles X (1 title)**		*Nana* (55) Christian-Jaque **2,675,373**	*Bel-Ami* (57) Daquin **612,525**
			Gervaise (56) Clément **4,108,173**	*Une vie* (58) Astruc **2,315,098**
	Les Amants de Tolède (53) Decoin **1,158,231**		*Pot-Bouille* (57) Duvivier **2,602,374**	
			Le Joueur (58) Autant-Lara **937,475**	
			La Jument verte (59) Autant-Lara **5,294,328**	
			Les Naufrageurs (59) Brabant **554,664**	

Figure 8.2: Costume dramas allocated according to régime (38 titles [Crimes d'amour is a 2-part sketch film and counts as one]); year film made in parenthesis); audience figures (in bold).

If we look at the distribution of film titles (figure 8.2), we note that there is a fairly even split between those covering the period from Napoleon Bonaparte to the end of the July monarchy (19 films) and those of the Second Empire and the early years of the Third Republic (20 films). But what surprises is the fact that Napoleon I only generates seven titles (more or less on a par with the constitutional monarchies) as opposed to his less-than-spectacular nephew (at least in terms of military expertise and international renown), whose own era produces nearly twice as many. Some of this can be explained by the fact that, in terms of adapted authors, 1950s' costume dramas showed a predilection for Guy de Maupassant (4), Emile Zola (3), Stendhal's Restoration-period novels (2), Alexandre Dumas père (1), Alexandre Dumas fils (1), Victor Hugo (1) and none for contemporaries of Napoleon (although, of course, Stendhal's novel *La Chartreuse de Parme,* which covers the Napoleonic period, was adapted to film in 1948). But let us pause for a moment on this issue of popularity – consider the following audience averages; they tell a slightly nuanced story:

Maupassant: 4 films – 1.2 million audience, on average, per film
Zola: 4 films – 3.1 million audience, on average, per film
Stendhal: 2 films – 2.2 million audience, on average, per film
Hugo: 1 film – 10 million audience for single film
Dumas pére: 1 film – 7.8 million audience
Dumas fils: 1 film – 2.6 million audience

Figure 8.3: Audience averages for great authors and the Dumas adapted to screen.

As we can see, Maupassant ranks the lowest in terms of audience appreciation. Curiously, the great novelist Honoré de Balzac does not figure. This predilection for Second- over First-Empire narratives may also be attributed to different legacies left by the two Napoleons. Napoleon III invested more in social development and modernization compared to his famous uncle, for whom civil law and warmongering seemed to dominate. Civil law is hardly the meat of filmmaking. War epics are expensive to make, so tend to be few and far between – indeed Guitry's monumental *Napoléon* cost 500 million francs. Moreover, Napoleon III's period coincided with unprecedented technological developments which allowed him to see some spectacular projects through, not least of which was his great legacy in the form of a regenerated Paris. Perhaps, therefore, it is unsurprising that, of the eight régimes that straddle our corpus of pre-Belle Epoque nineteenth-century costume dramas, the greatest number is located in Napoleon III's period of rule, with twelve films (see figure 8.2 above). For it was one of *the* moments of exponential growth and cohesion in terms of national infrastructure that France had known until this time.

In the chapters that follow, the films will be studied according to the historical contexts set out in figure 8.2 above. But, before proceeding to that more detailed work, it seems useful to get an overview of the dominant trends. It brings out some interesting considerations for us to bear in mind in the ensuing chapters. Below, I set out the dominant categories of narratives (figure 8.4).

As we can see from these categories, what really strikes is the dearth of 'poverty' narratives and their related typology, that of the courtesans. Given the harsh reality of the times whereby, as a result of the impact of the Industrial Revolution, 70–75 per cent of all city-dwellers were on, or below, the poverty line from the 1830s on, the very least that can be said is that there is little correspondence in these films to the social hardships of the times; only *Les Misérables* and *Gervaise* stand out.[6] Poverty was not just limited to the cities, however – and two narratives, based in real events, tell the gruesome tale of the practice of murder and theft in order to survive. The first, *L'Auberge rouge*, arguably, turns the original treacherous true story into something of a farce. The second, *Les Naufrageurs*, is far bleaker in its austere realism. In its narrative, it is fairly reminiscent of Delannoy's film based in the eighteenth century about a Breton island, *Le Dieu a besoin des hommes* (see Chapter 4). Whereas, in *L'Auberge rouge*, the innkeeper's greed plays its part in the systematic entrapment and throat-slitting of the obnoxious bourgeois travellers, in *Les Naufrageurs*, Breton islanders, driven by famine, deliberately shipwreck a cargo vessel, kill the sailors and sack the provisions. Only one man, the islander's leader Marnez (Charles Vanel), gives himself up to the police for this collective crime. On this island, as with the Delannoy film, superstition reigns, leading to the scapegoating of a 'wild' young woman, Moïra (Renée Cosima), whom the islanders deem a witch. At the end of the film, they kill her as the source that brought the evil-doing upon them in the first place.

Even women who escape the poverty-trap by successfully establishing themselves as courtesans – be it Marguerite (*La Dame aux camélias*), Lola Montès or Nana – fare no better. Momentary riches cannot prevent them from succumbing to illness and dying, either from a disease induced by their life-style or being murdered by a jealous lover, as occurs for Nana (in a rewrite of Zola's novel, where Nana dies of a terrible disfiguring disease, her beauty decomposed by the effects of smallpox). This bleak picture remains the same for the courtesans as for the prostitute and the poor. There is no more salvation for the demi-mondaine who tries to capitalize on her only assets, her beauty, her intelligence and her body, than for those less fortunate. Retribution is swingeing.

What stands out from our categorization below is the dominance of seducer and reality-embedded narratives (i.e., those of real lives or events) – with eleven apiece. In relation to the first category, only two narratives have the female as the would-be seducer – would-be because she either fails to bring her scheme off (*Un Caprice de Caroline chérie*) or she dies in her endeavours (*Le Rideau cramoisi*). Conversely, in the nine other narratives, male seducers are singularly successful, even if, in the end, most are punished for their wicked ways either by dying or losing the real love of their lives because they are not trustworthy (the exception being *Bel-Ami*). Whilst they are vamping the women, they do so with cynicism and élan. Sure of their magnetism, they remain ruthlessly unconcerned for those they damage – a form of brutal narcissism driving them on. In the majority of these seducer films, the men set great store by their physical appearance. It is worth recalling that this is the age of the dandy: a type of masculinity that, in France, grew in response to the Revolution and all but disappeared by the time of the Belle Epoque, if not a bit earlier – in the 1860s (see Chapter 16). In its first iteration,

Seducers (11)	Poverty and prostitution (3)	Courtesans as a way to escape poverty trap (3)	Historical figures and real events (11)	Other (12)
Le Nez de cuir 1814 (hero wounded at French Campaign) ruthless seducer	Les Misérables 1822 through to 1832 poverty narrative	La Dame aux camélias 1840s story of famous courtesan	Napoléon 1762–1821 war and love life	**1. rivalry/revenge** Le Fils de Caroline chérie 1804 (fights first for Spain against Napoleon then for Napoleon against the Spanish) female rivalry
Rideau Cramoisi (in Les Crimes de l'amour) flashback to: 1812–3 (hero fought in Battle of Leipzig) seducer tale	Gervaise 1852 poverty narrative	Lola Montès 1843–59 story of famous courtesan	L'Agonie des aigles 1822 (Demi-soldes seek to restore Napoleon II to the throne – nostalgia for Napoleon I)	Mina de Vanghel (in Les Crimes de l'amour) 1830 love-thwarted woman narrative
Un Caprice de Caroline Chérie set against Italian Campaign 1796 Seduction tales men and women	Le Plaisir 1870s includes prostitution (esp. La Maison Tellier)	Nana 1860s story of famous courtesan	L'Auberge rouge 1833 Based on a real events Somewhat anti-clerical	Le Comte de Monte-Cristo 1815 to 1835 (Napoleon I indirect cause of imprisonment) ruthless rival in love/revenge narrative
Si le roi savait ça 1814 (after the Russian Campaign) evil seducer			Deburau 1839–46 'reminiscences' of famous mime	La Jument verte 1860–80 rape/revenge narrative
Les Amants de Tolède 1825 thwarted lovers and evil seducer			Par ordre du Tsar 1840 'biopic/love story' based around Liszt	
Le Rouge et le Noir 1830s seducer tale			La Valse de Paris 1850s 'biopic/love story' based around Offenbach	**2. racial issues** Tamango 1820 story about slave trading
Milord L'Arsouille 1847 seducer tale (based on a real person)			Monsieur Fabre 1850s to 1914 'biopic' of famous entymologist	Zora (in Trois femmes) 1870s tale of racism

Pot-Bouille
1865
seducer tale (based
on real person)

Bel-Ami
1887
tale of seducer/
political
shenanigans

Le Joueur
1867
seducers, roués and
gamblers

Une vie
1880
seducer tale

Violettes impériales
1848–50
'story' based around
Eugénie's marriage
to Napoleon III

La Castiglione
1853
story of Italian
patriot Olivia
Oldoini who enlists
aide of Napoleon
against Austrians

Les Naufrageurs
1852
based on real events

Michel Strogoff
1880
story of courageous
courier of the Tsar

3. marriage issues
Les Petites Cardinal
1871
political
opportunism/
getting daughters
married off

Chevalier de la nuit
1884
bored
marriage/'sexual'
fantasy

Mam'zelle Nitouche
1880s
operetta/comedy/
marriage

Coralie and Mouche
(in Trois femmes)
1870s
inheritance and
illegitimacy

4. various
Les Hussards
Italian Campaign
1796

Lettres de mon
Moulin
1850s
Various (2 slightly
anti-clerical)

Figure 8.4: Types of narratives.

of the mid-1810s, dandyish dress reflected the influence of the London dandy, brought back in terms of style by the 'exilés' – those aristocrats who had fled at the time of the Revolution but who returned under the Restoration. In this instance, dressing in an aristocratic style represented a protest against the rise of egalitarian values. In its second, the one more readily associated with the 1830s onwards, it took various forms. For the literary and the intellectual aesthetes it became a posture associated with revolt – French dandies modelled themselves on Byron (who was himself inspired by the first dandy of all, Beau Brummell). Barbey d'Aurevilly, the Comte d'Orsay and Baudelaire were some of France's first literary dandies. To an extent, dandyism is a trend linked with the Romantic Movement – correctly or incorrectly – because of the dandy's rejection of the past, his disgust with the mediocrity of society and his constant search for an ideal of beauty. This posture was matched by a desire to live in an exalted state in the present. Fear of the future (in terms of fading beauty) pushed these aesthetic dandies to escape the march of time through their art. Finally, dandyism for these aesthetes was a political act in that this narcissism had 'anti-bourgeois, anti-democratic, anti-work and anti-classical associations.'[7]

Somewhat differently, the dandy effect for the nobility was one of effete self-absorption which included a disdain for the vulgar, most readily associated with the new, emergent middle classes (we see evidence of this in *Milord L'Arsouille*). But the aesthetes and nobility were not alone in this new form of narcissism. The effect of dandyism had its followers, both amongst the bourgeoisie and those aspiring to that class. For the bourgeois or social climber who posed as a dandy, the intention was to imitate an aristocratic or noble bearing, and the purpose was self-aggrandizement (we see examples of this in *Le Comte de Monte-Cristo*, *Le Joueur* and *Bel-Ami*). In all instances, cynicism is the behaviour that prevails. In *Un Caprice de Caroline chérie* we get an interesting reversal of the dandy effect whereby Count Livio (Jean-Claude Pascal) – Caroline's (Martine Carol) would-be lover – gradually undoes his dandy image. We see him, first, dressed as a dandy in a series of complex mirror reflections as he observes the naked Caroline taking a bath. Via these mirror reflections, he successfully attracts Caroline's attention to his glamour and becomes the object of her desire. This mirroring should warn Caroline that Livio might not be all he seems. A bit later, during the 14th of July celebrations, he appears as a ballet dancer in a purple Roman tunic that looks more like a tutu than a piece of masculine attire. This again serves to put his masculinity on display, albeit in an excessive way – since it suggests a sexual bothness (a fine line that a dandy must not cross, of course). Finally, he reveals himself in his true colours: in peasant attire. He was masquerading all the time as an aristocrat in order to find out about the movements of the French army – using his dandyish dress as a means to conceal both his working-class origins and the fact that he was a spy. Whereas Caroline thought she was seducing him, in reality he was cynically playing on her desire to avenge herself of her husband's perceived infidelity to get what he wanted from her – the nation's secrets.

Even though they are based on real women's lives, I have not counted the three courtesan films amongst the biopics. This is partly because, as strongly fictionalized narratives, they depart considerably from historical fact; and partly because, apart from Lola Montès, the courtesans' real names were changed by their authors. Zola's Nana is the fictional portrait of the Parisian star of the operetta stage Blanche d'Antigny. Dumas fils' Marguerite is that of the demi-mondaine Marie Duplessis – his mistress at one point. Thus, if we look at column four of figure 8.4, there are eleven reality-embedded narratives. Eight are biopics and three are based on real events. Of the biopics, or, rather, part-biopics, some tell the story of a specific period in the lives of these famous people – for example *Napoléon,* which stretches from 1796–1815; and *Les Violettes impériales* which narrates Napoléon III's marriage to Eugénie de Montijo. Some of these biopics depict acts of heroism or courage: *La Castiglione, Michel Strogoff*. Others portray cultural personages: *Deburau, Par ordre du Tsar, La Valse de Paris*, or scientific ones: *Monsieur Fabre*. Of the three films based in real events, *L'Auberge rouge* and *Les Naufrageurs*, as mentioned earlier, are tales of thieving and murder. *L'Agonie des aigles* depicts the courage of some of Napoleon I's former officers (hence the epithet 'aigles'). Incensed at the contempt with which they and their great leader are held by Louis XVIII, they attempt, in 1822, to overthrow the monarchy and instate Napoleon's son as France's legitimate ruler. The plot fails, but the courage with which they face their trial and go to their death makes heroes of them all.

In the last category (figure 8.4 column five), we note that marriage issues are present, as indeed they are in the Belle Epoque films. But they are not here to the same degree. Here, there are a mere four titles, as opposed to seventeen in the Belle Epoque period (see Chapter 18). Even if we nuance this statistic to take on board the broader concept of love intrigues, we still come up with a lesser figure than for the Belle Epoque and, most often, their presence is more of a subtext to the main narrative, primarily in the form of the need to safeguard the sanctity of marriage – *La Dame aux camélias* comes to mind. For the Belle Epoque period, where love intrigues are central, we can count some 28 out of 37 titles (yielding a figure of 76 per cent); for the period we are currently investigating, 20 titles out of 38 (53 per cent). Over a similar number of films for these two periods, therefore, more space has been given to a broader span of issues. First, as we noted, there are a greater number of biopics (eight as opposed to four in the Belle Epoque films). Second, albeit to a very small degree, different social questions are being raised: those of poverty and, quite intriguingly, on just two occasions, slavery and racism.

To give a shape to this somewhat unwieldy corpus of films pertaining to this long period of history, what follows is a series of chapters that will deal in turn with the Napoleonic period (Chapter 9); the Restoration period through the July Monarchy (Chapters 10, 11 and 12); the Second Empire (Chapters 13, 14 and 15); the transition period between the Second Empire and the early Third Republic with a particular focus on masculinity (Chapter 16); and, finally, a case study of Louis Daquin's ill-fated and much censored *Bel-Ami* (Chapter 17).

Notes

1. The Ultras were so named because they were the most extreme group clamouring for a return of the Ancien Régime, namely the revival of an absolute monarchy.
2. For details of this complex electoral story see Marseille (2002, pp. 31; 58; 67; 87).
3. Ibid., p. 187.
4. Brogan (1989, p. 128).
5. Ibid., p. 126.
6. Marseille, op. cit., p. 111.
7. Kunzle (2006, p. 82).

Chapter 9

Representing History: 1796–1814 Napoleon Bonaparte/Napoleon I

Before embarking on a discussion of the seven film titles that are set in this particular period of France's history, it is helpful to offer a brief overview of Napoleon's time in office as supreme ruler of the nation. Particularly so when we note how all seven film narratives are linked either directly to his person or to specific campaigns he fought (see below, figure 9.1).

1796–1804	1804–1814
Directoire/1st Consulate/ (3 titles)	*1st Empire (4 titles)*
Napoléon (55)	*Le Fils de Caroline chérie* (55) 1804
1762–1821	Her son fights first for Spain against Napoleon then
Tales of his wars and love life.	for Napoleon against the Spanish.
	Female rivalry.
Un Caprice de Caroline Chérie (53)	*Les Crimes de l'amour* (1. D'Aurevilly *Le Rideau*
Set against Italian Campaign 1796.	*Cramoisi*) (53) Flashback to: 1812–13 Hero fought in
Seduction tales men and women.	Battle of Leipzig.
	Seducer tale.
Les Hussards (53)	*Le Nez de cuir* (52)
Italian Campaign 1796.	1814
Comedy: inadvertent deserters end up as	Hero wounded at French Campaign.
heroes.	Ruthless seducer.
	Si le roi savait ça (58)
	1814
	After the Russian Campaign.
	Evil seducer

Figure 9.1: Seven films set in Napoleonic period allotted according to campaign.

Within our time-line there are two periods of Napoleon Bonaparte's reign of supremacy that we need to bear in mind. The first concerns his successful Italian Campaign through to his nomination and period as First Consul (1796–1804). The real turning point to his career occurred upon his return from the failed Egyptian campaign in 1799 – a failure that was glossed over in France where he was acclaimed as a war hero. As we will see, this is the first of many 're-writings' of truth where Napoleon's arrogation of power is concerned. He found the country in disarray and determined that the Republic must be saved. The revolutionary spirit that still dogged the nation, splitting it into factions, had to be brought to an end and constitutional order restored – by him. To this effect, he plotted a (bloodless) coup d'état, with the support of his brothers (Joseph and Lucien), the conspiratorial collusion of politicians Talleyrand and Sieyès, plus the backing of thousands of bankers. The coup of 9–10 November 1799 (18th and 19th Brumaire) was packaged for the people as a 'saving of the Republic by "a soldier fighting for freedom"', no mention was made of the concept of a 'coup'.[1] Elected as First Consul for life by a huge majority, Napoleon was endowed with strong executive powers. Apparently, half of the three million votes that elected him were 'invented' by his brother Lucien (then Minister of the Interior), including some half a million via so-called army votes that were never cast.[2] Napoleon's greatest period, however, undoubtedly pre-dates this moment of supreme elevation: his four years as First Consul (1800–1804), during which time he managed to calm the various factions of Republican France, appease the clergy (the 1801 Concordat) and institute the Civil Code (1804) which still underpins much of France's institutional functioning.[3]

Hereafter, once elected Emperor (3 May 1804; under similarly dubious voting conditions),[4] the second period begins. Napoleon became increasingly tyrannical. In short, France gradually became a police state. By 1807, freedom of the press was severely curtailed; free-thinkers were spied upon and, to all intents and purposes, the Tribunal (which dealt with legislative matters) was suspended; theatres were closed; the word 'République' was removed from all coinage. In July 1809, Napoleon occupied Rome and placed the Pope under arrest (deported to a fortress in Savone, he was not released until 1814). In that same year, under the guise of the interests of France, Napoleon divorced Josephine (in December) and, four months later, took as his new wife the Austrian princess Marie-Louise of Hapsburg in the hope that it would give legitimacy to his status of Emperor in European court circles and provide him with a son and heir. He certainly achieved the latter (the king of Rome, born 1811); as to the former that is less sure. In spite of the fact that the Hapsburg family and Austria had been his (and therefore France's) arch-enemies until this time, landing the marriage was a considerable coup, but there is no evidence that Napoleon had sealed his status as equal in the minds of the European monarchs.[5]

During these 10 years as Emperor, Napoleon set out to fulfil his ambition to rebuild the Empire of Charlemagne.[6] Thus, he occupied Portugal, annexed Spain, parts of Italy and Poland, the Rhineland.[7] He appointed his brother Joseph as King of Spain in 1808. By 1811, Belgium and Holland were integrated into the Empire. In 1812, he turned against the nation's former allies, the Russians, and attacked them. This, in turn, caused the Austrians and Prussians to align themselves with the Russians and counter-attack France. By 1814, it was all over. Napoleon was humiliated in defeat, forced to abdicate and exiled to Elba, where he was allowed to retain his title as Emperor. He escaped in 1815, returned to France and reclaimed his role as Emperor – but it was a short-lived victory (100 days). The British and the Prussians refused to accept his return and took arms up against him. Napoleon was defeated at Waterloo and exiled to Saint Helena, where he died in 1821.

Napoleon in film: a structuring absence and flawed genius

Let us now consider the seven films. With the exception of Guitry's *Napoléon*, the great man of this period is barely present at all. In *Les Hussards*, he makes a brief off-screen appearance – we only hear his voice as he commends the two Hussards for their courage. The French and Austrians are fighting over Italian territory; inadvertently, two Hussards (played by Bourvil and Blier) lose their horses and are taken for dead by their captain. They hole up in a village, which their captain finally captures. The two Hussards pretend they are holding the villagers hostage, much to the pleasure of their captain. When the French are routed by the Austrians, the two Hussards almost single-handedly see the enemy off. Napoleon Bonaparte arrives and congratulates them for their courage.

Apart from this one voice-off presence, in five of the other films we have the battle and not the man. Napoleon is present only insofar as his various military campaigns serve as a background to the film's actual story – nearly all of which are rather unpleasant love intrigues. In *Si le roi savait ça,* competition for a young woman's hand leads one officer to press-gang his rival into Napoleon's army. At the Russian front, he shoots his rival and yields the secrets of Napoleon's plans to the Russian enemy. On his return to France, he is acclaimed as a hero and forces the young woman to marry him. However, his rival returns and exposes the truth. The treacherous officer is drowned whilst trying to escape his deserved humiliation. Meantime, the young man wins his true love. Once again, Napoleon is merely a structuring absence. This over-riding absence of the 'Great Man' from six out of the seven films is a strange omission by any standards and can be read one of two ways, neither one of which cancels the other out: either Napoleon's epic grandeur is such that his presence is locked into the spectator's imaginary, so he does not need to be present: the mythical value is sufficient to conjure a presence, or, given that most of the films are set against campaigns in which Napoleon was beaten, perhaps his presence would remind the collective psyche of the fallibility and folly of dictators.

Such would seem to be Sacha Guitry's interpretation of Napoleon in his film – he is both grand and fallible, a genius and a monster. Indeed, the Napoleon that Guitry serves up to us, in the two parts of his three-hour epic *Napoléon*, is that of a flawed genius. Part one of the film opens with the announcement of Napoleon's death on the island of Saint Helena. Guitry plays the role of Talleyrand, Napoleon's long-time closest advisor and Minister of External Affairs, whose task it is to relate his version of the great man to an assembled group of guests. It is therefore a selective account. We get a portrait of the young petulant Bonaparte (embodied by Daniel Gélin) who is used to getting his way, followed by that of the increasingly autocratic older Napoleon I (played by Raymond Pellegrin) who ruthlessly asserts his will over siblings, wives, mistresses, politicians, generals, and so on. Both Napoleons (Gélin and Pellegrin's) are moody, irascible, ill-mannered types. There is little depth given to the characterization however – Napoleon seems more of a stereotype than a fleshed-out 'Great Man'. In this one-sided view we have of him, he comes over as a bully, someone who is easily slighted, and who, by the last decade of his reign, is increasingly impulsive, unreasonable and paranoid.

Indeed, in part two of the film, we see him bending his family members to his will. If they refuse, he threatens to exile them. We watch him sign a decree closing all theatres and, in the same breath, establishing a secret police force under the control of one of his allies, Fouché (Jean Debucourt).[8] Upon his return from the disastrous Russian Campaign, in December 1812, Napoleon summons both Fouché and Talleyrand to his offices, where he accuses them both of being traitors. Fouché bows to his inevitable expulsion. However, when Napoleon accuses Talleyrand of conspiring against him, the witty response comes: 'Sire, you are your own worst conspirator.' For reasons of dramatic licence, Guitry conflates a number of historical moments into this single sequence. For, in fact, Napoleon appointed Fouché Minister of Police in 1804, only to sack him six years later, then re-instate him: first as governor of Illyria (1813), then as Minister of Police during the 100 Days. As for Talleyrand, a sort of Svengali of whom he could never fully rid himself, Napoleon accused him on at least two occasions (both in 1808) – and with greater justification – of betrayal: first, over Spain (because Talleyrand refused to support him); then over failing purposively to conclude an alliance with Russia (the so-called 'Trahison d'Erfurt').[9] Nothing is said in the film of Talleyrand's role, in March 1814, in bringing about Napoleon's eventual forced abdication through a sort of '18 Brumaire in reverse' (as he put it)[10], where he effectively sells the Emperor out to the British and the Russians and saves his own political career. But then, to Guitry's mind, this most eminent politician was a great defender of France's interests, no matter the political regime. As if to emphasize his admiration for Talleyrand, it is worth noting that this film marks a reprise by Guitry of this role. In 1947, he had written, staged and acted in a version of Talleyrand's life (Talleyrand). Returning to the role some eight years later was to reunite with one of his heroes, therefore.

If in Guitry's Napoléon we get a flavour of the flawed genius' ill-humoured and despotic struggles as the embodiment of supreme power, it is also true that we get to see very little of the fine military strategist who won spectacular battles, to say nothing of the sharp legal intellect that led him to draft the Code Civil; if anything, in this latter case, we merely see Napoleon strutting around his various gardens, hands behind back, then returning to his desk to scribble some ideas down (it is more of a comic, Chaplinesque routine than a great moment in history that is presented to the spectator). Guitry's Napoleon is blunt and pugnacious – he is, as Josephine (Michèle Morgan) puts it, when she first meets him, 'bull-headed'. We are led to understand that he needs the support of strong men like Talleyrand and Barras (Pierre Brasseur), one of the five members of the Directoire, to find his way to the top. In part, this was true, but Josephine was equally instrumental in furthering his career. As a former mistress of Barras, she managed to get Napoleon his first big break as General of the Italian Army (1796). But, once he was named First Consul, he was very forcibly at the forefront of his own advancement. Indeed, one of Talleyrand's constant complaints was Napoleon's lack of moderation, something he always advised when signing treaties or declaring war (for example Talleyrand had actually tried to dissuade him from going to war with Spain; his views were summarily dismissed and he was accused of treachery for his pains).

In his review in *Variety*, Mosk is not wrong to say that Guitry has diminished Napoleon. I would not go so far as to say that he is reduced to 'a figure in a parlor charade game', but I would agree that Guitry has robbed his figure of its epic stature.[11] Thus, as in a melodrama, we observe a lot of Napoleon's dalliances with women and his attempts to control his rapacious family members. Conversely, we never come to an understanding of what drives Napoleon to war (namely, his ambition to be as great as Charlemagne). Moreover, whilst the film contains a few illustrative scenes from some of the most famous battles (Marengo, Austerlitz, Wagram) and two key reversals (the Russian campaign, including the entry into a burning Moscow, and Waterloo), we never get the measure of his tactical brilliance. Despite the fact that a huge amount of the budget was spent on these scenes (including 8 million francs for the set of burning Moscow)[12], and that a specialist in battle scenes was brought in from Hollywood (Eugène Lourié), they remain disappointing in their execution, particularly since the film was shot in Technicolor, potentially providing the chance to excel in cinematic terms. The direction is sloppy, men drop dead before the cannon fire has reached them; the same locale is used for battlegrounds as distinct from one another as the landscapes of Italy, Egypt and Austria. Napoleon is often to be seen, static, astride his white horse, looking and pointing as if in a silent film, whereas we want to hear him barking his strategies. It is doubtful that this *mise-en-scène* represents a homage to Gance's earlier silent epic of the same title (*Napoléon*, 1927); more probably it is a question of the limitations of a director ill-suited to directing out of a studio-theatre context. It is a shame when one considers that this was a 500-million-franc film with 300 speaking roles and 6,000 extras. More was possible. Indeed the post-synch sound for these battle scenes is nearly always the same and there is no pretence at live dialogue.

There are, however, spectacular moments and aspects to this film, a great number of which must be attributed to set-designer René Renoux and costume-designers Monique Dunan and Paulette Coquatrix. The interior sets of Fontainebleau are delicious in their excessive gilt, and are brought out so well in the Technicolor palette. The *mise-en-scène* for the consecration of Napoleon as Emperor in Notre Dame is as eloquent and massive as the David painting of the same event (and which was clearly used as point of reference). The Directory and Empire costumes, the military outfits for all the warring factions, represent a tour de force. Given that there were some 6,300 people to costume and that, apart from the lead roles for whom costumes were specifically designed, the rest had to be found and borrowed from theatres all around the country, or rented from London, Milan and Rome, there is an extraordinary consistency throughout. The set for Moscow was also a brilliant piece of design and cinematography. Built on a huge turning-plate in the Parc de Sceaux, south of Paris, it was constructed so that, as Napoleon stands in the foreground, the plate behind turns, creating a 180-degree tracking effect. According to *La Cinématographie française*, this sequence represented the first time such a tracking shot was used in a colour film.[13] When we watch the shot we see how totally confused and disorientated Napoleon is by the Russians' strategy of burning their emptied city, just as they did with their farmlands. In his triumphant entry, there is only defeat, since the fire means that there are no supplies, munitions or shelter left for his men.

This epic film, in length alone, lasts 182 minutes. With its star-studded cast (30 in all), it attracted an audience of 5.4 million, ranking second in the 1955 top-grossing French films, outstripped only by *Le Comte de Monte-Cristo* with 7.8 million. It was, therefore, a huge success. However, most of the stars appear extremely briefly. Gabin pops up in part two (for two minutes) as the dying Maréchal Lannes, who, on his death-bed at the battle of Essling (1808), screams out to Napoleon: 'enough of all these wars'. Orson Welles has three lines as Napoleon's captor Hudson-Lowe on the island of Saint Helena. Erich Von Stroheim hams it up amusingly as Beethoven (playing his *Eroica* variations) during Napoleon's pursuit of Marie-Louise of Hapsburg (a rather plump Maria Schell). Luis Mariano, as the effeminate baritone Garat, sings a warning salvo to Napoleon early on in part one about the dangers of love with *Plaisir d'amour*. Later, in part two, singing is reprised on the battlefields of Essling by Yves Montand as Maréchal Lefebvre (again calling for an end to war); Patachou plays his wife (nick-named Madame Sans-Gêne) but, regrettably, does not get to sing. Serge Reggiani has the unrewarding role of Napoleon's scheming brother Lucien. Jean Marais, as the Comte de Montholon, has a brief moment to assert his undying loyalty to Napoleon, whom he will follow to Saint Helena. And, finally (because the list is seemingly endless), Danielle Darrieux is the brainless upstart Eléanore Denuelle, who forces herself on Napoleon. However, she is the one who proves to the Emperor that he can procreate, by bearing him his first son, Léon (1806). The most sustained role, other than Gélin and Pellegrin as Napoleon and Guitry as Talleyrand, is Michèle Morgan's exquisite Josephine. Calculating and seductive all at once, and given Napoleon's tyrannical disposition, she did well to survive so long as his wife (1796–1809). Guitry offers us an amusing scene where Napoleon consults his own Code Civil under 'divorce' to see how he may rid himself of her – for a man who never lived by the rules, his desire to find legal grounds (her supposed infertility) for divorce shows how desperate he was to have a wife ('un ventre' as he puts it) who could bear him a male heir. Always one to repeat a joke, Guitry shows Napoleon, in the very next sequence, again consulting the Code Civil about 'marriage', this time with a view to his pursuit of Marie-Louise.

Josephine de Beauharnais is the single female role in this film developed to any degree of interest – perhaps because she is the only woman to stand up to Napoleon's tyrannical ways. Her back-story and persona are fleshed out enough for the audience to take interest in her. Thus, we learn that she was Barras' mistress. Before that, she was married to Alexandre Vicomte de Beauharnais, who was subsequently guillotined during the Terror period of the Revolution. She was only just spared a similar fate thanks to her 'liaison' with Barras. She was born in Martinique, making her a Creole (a term referring not to a status of mixed-race but to the progeny of a white plantation family). Her woman servant is a black woman called Blanche (uncredited role) who is utterly devoted to her. Perhaps she is inserted to counter certain historians' claims that it was Josephine who persuaded Napoleon to re-institute slavery in 1802, whereas, in fact, it is now widely accepted that he reversed the 1794 abolition of slavery purely for monetary reasons.[14] In the film, we are told she is 'une Créole un peu mûre/a middle-aged Creole' whom Barras wishes to rid himself of and does so by forcing a meeting with Napoleon (when they meet he is 26, she 32). In one look, admirably caught on camera, her devastating beauty seduces Napoleon (Josephine was not called 'La Merveilleuse' for nothing). Some six years her junior, Napoleon, in his marriage proposal to her, both declares his love and decides to take six years off her age and add them to his. He adopts her two children (Hortense, future mother of Napoleon III, and Eugène). The film offers us many scenes of their marriage: a tempestuous affair, marked both by jealousy over each other's infidelities and by her terrible extravagances (especially dresses and gambling). But she was the love of his life – as indeed his dying words (at the end of the film) make clear. True to the real persona, Morgan is radiantly beautiful as the embodiment of Josephine; each time she is on screen she is dressed in yet another rich, Empire-line, dress – be it green velvet, mauve satin, or pure white silk.[15] Her wit shines forth, charming the younger Napoleon. Just as, equally, her ability to show true emotion (crying or being angry) often saves her from Napoleon's wrath or desire to divorce her – that is until 1809.

As is made clear from the beginning of the film, this is Talleyrand's version of Napoleon. One can reasonably surmise that it is also Guitry's – a man not much taken with tyrannical rulers, nor indeed the effects of this tyranny in terms of censorship, unsubstantiated denunciation and imprisonment without trial. For he had been subjected to similar treatment after the Liberation in 1944. Completely without foundation, he was arrested by a group of Resistance fighters (23 August 1944) for being too friendly with the Germans. In fact, during the period of the Occupation, he had kept theatre alive in Paris, precisely as a form of cultural resistance against the German invader and had refused to take his cast and performances to Germany. He had, moreover, managed to save the Jewish author Tristan Bernard and his wife from deportation. Once arrested, Guitry was imprisoned for 60 days without charge, let alone trial. During that time he was denounced by the press on unfounded rumours of 'colluding with the enemy'. The judge assigned to try the case, and lacking any evidence to level at Guitry, rather than dropping the case, and simply releasing him, twice placed an announcement in newspapers asking people to come forward with accusations. Nothing was forthcoming; the case was closed and Guitry was released. However it was not until 1947 that he obtained a *non-lieu* (a dismissal of the case) – hardly a full exoneration and apology. This humiliation and a desire to avenge himself, albeit with great wit and irony, certainly impacted on Guitry's last ten years (he died in 1957) in terms of roles he played, texts and plays he wrote.[16]

Released in 1955, Guitry's film resonates with the personal and the political as much as it does with two historical moments: the rise and fall of two dictators (Napoleon I and Hitler) some two and a half centuries apart. Yet how little is learnt from history! Just ten years after the end of a devastating World War Two, France was yet again embroiled in further warfare, this time over its colonies. Theatres, the press, radio, films and film-makers were all placed under strict censorship. Works in the form of plays or films that made, or were believed to make, reference to these events were banned, so too were actors who signed petitions against the colonial wars. Furthermore, state funding was withheld from film-makers who sought to engage 'undesirable' actors or whose own project and person were deemed to undermine the nation. Indeed, our case-study of Louis Daquin's *Bel-Ami* (1954/7) will reveal the degree to which this repression was exercised (see Chapter 17).

Yet we note that some costume dramas managed to speak back, however subtly. Even the light-hearted Carolinade, *Un Caprice de Caroline chérie*, starring Martine Carol is not without its political resonances with the contemporary. Set against the background of the First Italian Campaign (1796–1797), themes of political intrigue, spying, denunciation and collaboration are all touched upon. Jean Anouilh adapted this supposedly frivolous novel written by Cécil Saint-Laurent – a pseudonym for Jacques Laurent-Cécily. Anouilh had also adapted the earlier *Caroline chérie* (Pottier, 1951) – both times in collaboration with Saint-Laurent. Saint-Laurent was a self-proclaimed extremist of the right with a great interest in history. He was a member of Action française and of the literary right (often referred to as the Hussards). After the Liberation, he was subjected to the Cleansing Committee (*Comité d'épuration*) and was imprisoned for a brief period.[17] He might, therefore, seem an odd collaborator for Anouilh to work with, given that Anouilh was hailed (despite himself) as a hero of the Resistance for his play *Antigone,* which was seen as emblematically anti-Occupation and anti-Vichy, although Anouilh never declared a position on either of these repressive régimes. It is also worth remembering that Anouilh spoke out vehemently against the Cleansing Committee, in general, doubting the efficacy of reprisals against the vanquished and, in particular, took up (along with other liberal luminaries such as Albert Camus) the defence of Robert Brasillach, the editor of the fascist *Je suis partout*.[18]

During the late 1940s and through the 1950s, Saint-Laurent wrote the Carolinade series (namely, *Caroline chérie, Les Caprices de Caroline, Le Fils de Caroline chérie*) to make a living. He was also the author of several of Martine Carol's other great successes of the 1950s, including *Lola Montès* and *Lucrèce Borgia*. His continued interest in strong, witty, even courageous women figures comes, then, as something of a surprise when we consider both his fervently-held political views and the fact that he was an Ultra-Royalist. We might have expected in his women greater submissiveness to the patriarch, certainly less independence of mind. Armand Chapuy in his study of Martine Carol suggests, however, that her 1950s' roles are reactionary – conforming to established stereotypes of the times.[19] He argues that she mostly plays very traditional roles: a woman who is uninterested in politics, who gets into scrapes but who eventually bows to the will of her husband. As such, she reflects, says Chapuy, the dominant patriarchal ideology of the 1950s where women were concerned. He also makes the interesting point that stars such as Carol were not there to represent the domesticated woman at home producing babies for the future of the nation; she was expressly there at the service of re-affirming and keeping masculine virility intact.[20] Her frequent nudity and the emphasis of the cameras on her bosom and cut of costume designs to stress the voluptuousness of her breasts, he claims, serve to signal her availability to men, not to the babies of France.[21]

My answer to the seeming paradox above is that both are true: that she is a stereotype of and for 1950s' femininity, but that there is also more to Carol than meets the eye. In the end, it is not just the man who gets his way; she also has a moral victory over the folly of men (and their wars and revolutions and infidelities). In the first part of this book, I briefly spoke of the types that Carol typically embodied. I suggested that her characterization was of a certain classlessness, or one which cut across class. She also quite frequently cuts across gender, cross-dressing in at least two of the Carolinades (*Caroline chérie* and *Un Caprice de Caroline chérie*) thus presenting an ambiguous sexuality, as indeed she does once more in *Lola Montès* (see Chapter 15). What I would suggest is that she both conforms and contests, as the following discussion will explain.

I will limit my argument to a study of the first Carolinade to refer to this Napoleonic period. I will not dwell on the second (*Le Fils de Caroline chérie*), since Caroline is a mere structuring absence: we never see her except in the form of a miniature painting which eventually helps the foundling son to reclaim his parents (Sallanches and Caroline). I will briefly draw out some interesting threads in *Un Caprice de Caroline chérie* which argue for a less clear representation of women than Chapuy proposes. For, even though his take is substantiated, it is blurred by the muddling effects of Carol's characterizations, which are not straightforward. Indeed, this lack of clarity is produced by the interfacing of her physical presence on screen with some troubling images of political truth. Let me explain. The film is set against the first Italian Campaign: Napoleon is setting up a power base against the Austrians by occupying Italian territory from where he can both repel and attack the enemy. The film opens. Como is an occupied city. The French are garrisoned up on the hill and preparing for the celebrations of the 14th of July (Bastille Day). Caroline, known as *la Générale*, is wife to the commander of this occupying force, General Sallanches (Jacques Dacqmine). None of the Italian dignitaries turn up to the festivities: sensing that their town is about to be liberated, they fear that they would be accused of fraternizing with the enemy. Later, as the insurrection takes hold, Caroline must flee. After several encounters, during which she cross-dresses as a drummer-boy to make her escape and wins the heart of a servant girl, she finally sets off through town (in a servant's dress), whereupon she comes across men meting out 'people's justice' to horizontal collaborators – that is, local women who have slept with the French enemy – by cutting off their hair and tar and feathering their naked bodies before chasing them off down the streets. Direct reference to post-war France's own systems of revenge over women (the *tondues*) and cleansing (*Comité d'épuration*) could not be more evident.[22] But there is more. Throughout the film, people denounce other people. Two types of spies discern themselves: the good, who spy and denounce for patriotic reasons; the bad, who do so for personal gain or revenge. In the former category we can place Livio, the undercover agent for the Italians, who masquerades as a count and a ballet dancer (as a way to infiltrate the garrison on Bastille Day). In the latter category comes Caroline. Believing her husband is being unfaithful to her (she finds him in bed with an Italian princess), she first flirts and then attempts to run away with Livio. Worse, incensed with jealousy and out of a desire for revenge over her husband's purported sexual infidelities, she betrays him by revealing his whereabouts and his military plans to Livio. Fortunately, Livio is an honourable man. Moreover, it transpires that he is not a count but a man of the people, fighting their cause. He is prepared to give his life by surrendering himself to the general in order to save the townsfolk. In the end, Sallanches agrees to an even more decent outcome. Once he discovers that Livio has not taken advantage of his wife, he lets him go free to escape to Austria. Having explained to his wife that he had to sleep with the enemy in order to get access to the townsfolk's secrets, Sallanches and Caroline *la Générale* are reunited in love.

The message of the film, then, is paradoxical. On the one hand, it suggests that women in politics make messes: Caroline misreads what her husband is up to (rather understandably in my view); women in war-time are horizontal collaborators and must be punished. But, on the other hand, Caroline is also quite defiant and self-reliant. She cross-dresses and gets involved in a sword-fight, which she wins; when running through town, dressed as a servant woman, she successfully defends her honour against predatory men. So convincing is her cross-dressing, men and women are taken in – in particular the young woman servant with whom she flirts and eventually kisses in a nice piece of lesbian erotica.

This chapter closes with a discussion of *Nez de cuir*. This film was adapted to screen from the novel of the same title by author Jean de La Varende. Much like Saint-Laurent, he was a monarchist and a man of the extreme right, aligned with Action française. This swashbuckling novel tells the story of young man who is severely wounded in the face during Napoleon's disastrous French Campaign (1814). Embittered by his loss of looks, he vents his anger by cynically seducing women in his local domain in Normandy. Too late, he realizes his love for the one woman who resists his brutal ways; she stands up to him and keeps her virtue intact, even though it is clear she is in love with him. The final straw occurs when she takes pity on his disfigured face, which he insists on showing her. He is unable to accept her love on those terms and takes off to a life of solitude and penance for all his wicked and debauched ways.

Written in 1936, the novel was a huge success, undoubtedly thanks to its short-listing for the Prix Goncourt (France's most prestigious literary prize) which propelled Varende into the Académie Goncourt in 1937. His links with the Germans during the Occupation, however, meant that, in 1944, he had to resign from the Academy (or face being black-balled). This Right-wing positioning of the author is fairly crucial when we consider the filmed version because both the film-maker and his scriptwriter, respectively Yves Allégret and Jacques Sigurd, were well known for their alliance to the Left of the political class. Thus, *Cahiers du cinéma* critic Jacques Doniol-Valcroze is justified when he expresses surprise at Allégret taking on such a film project. Doniol-Valcroze tells us that Allégret stuck out for the project, seeing off such other prestigious film directors as Autant-Lara who also wanted to make the film. How, Doniol-Valcroze asks, could Allégret turn his hand to this over-rated novel when Varende's 'old reactionary's values seem to be at the antipodes of his own beliefs'?[23]

The film's production year of 1951 (it was released in March 1952) coincided with some of the darkest moments in Cold War history. It marked the height of the HUAC witch-hunts in the US, primarily in the form of the sentencing to death of Julius and Ethel Rosenberg – found guilty of spying for the Soviet Union; the Korean War was heating up; the US exploded its first H-Bomb;[24] and France had used napalm for the first time in its war in Indochina. Clearly, films about dashing seducers would appeal to a jaded France, tired of war, and afraid of the renewed threat of war. However, as we shall see, Allégret's film is not so far removed from the cynical and bleak trilogy of films he made from 1948–1950 (*Dédée d'Anvers, Une si jolie petite plage* – both 1948 – and *Manèges*, 1950) all of which have at the core of the narrative some revenge or another, and all of which were scripted by Jacques Sigurd. The darkest and closest to *Nez de cuir* is, perhaps, *Une si jolie petite plage*, where the central protagonist (played by Gérard Philipe) returns to a small seaside resort to avenge himself of the cruel treatment dished out to him as an orphan some years earlier – his victim is an older woman, whom he murders. There are also interesting parallels between *Nez de cuir*'s protagonist, Roger de Tainchebraye (Jean Marais), and the central male character in *Manèges*, Robert (Bernard Blier), who finally manages to take revenge on his deceitful wife by leaving her to her fate, paralysed in a hospital bed after an accident and completely bandaged from head to neck. Both Roger and Robert are feminized by the circumstances that lead them to seek revenge – in short, to reassert a lost virility. In Robert's case, it is the role of cuckold to which his wife reduces him, as she progressively ruins him through her profligacy and diminishes his manhood through her series of affairs. For Roger, it is the terrible disfiguration as a result of his nose being cut off by a Cossack during the campaign on the Eastern front – probably the battle of Fère-Champenoise, where France was crushed by the allies and, in particular, the Cossacks. Thus, Roger asserts his virility by leading a monstrous battle against the female sex – callously seducing then coldly dumping his conquests without a by-your-leave.

What is interesting, however, in the light of the remarks above is the first third of the film (25 minutes in length), during which we see first the carnage of the battle and, later, the effects of Roger's wounds on his mental state. The film opens with sounds of the battle and images of the walking wounded; laid over the screen are the following words:

> Charging the Cossacks, Roger, Count of Tainchebraye, fell in Champagne during the carnage known as the French Campaign…by the end of these battles without hope, during which the Empire, in order to delay its fall, sacrificed in their thousands soldiers no older than twenty.

It was the most desperate of campaigns – the allies (Austria, Britain, Prussia and Russia) outnumbered the French by three to one. And, as we can see from the opening footage, the weather was more than inclement (snow lies on the ground and we can assume heavy frosts abound). The futility of war is underscored in this bleak opening sequence, where men cry out from their wounds, others trudge around completely disorientated while others endeavour to rescue the still-living bodies lying prone in the dark and cold earth. Roger is one such who is rescued by peasant conscripts from his native village in Normandy. They get him back home and, over several months, he is tended to by the local doctor. When he finally comes back to consciousness, his face is completely bandaged and two straws stick through where his nostrils should be to enable him to breathe. It is a fairly uncompromising image. The doctor tells him he will soon be in the saddle again, but all Roger wants to know about is his face. When he learns that it is completely disfigured, his immediate reaction is to want to die. His physical well-being gives him no solace; his lost beauty throws him into despair. Initially, his intact physical virility is of less significance to his sense of a self than his loss of facial beauty. Uppermost in his mind is the fact that his face, which along with his handsome physique did so much to seduce women, is now a lost weapon of attraction. His hysterical response (tearing at his bandages and screaming out) and floppy body (he almost faints back into his bed) work to effect a de-masculinization of this young man of war and noble property, rendering him thus associated with the feminine. His loss of face equates to a loss of virility and, in his weakness, he loses his will to live.

The representation of a de-masculinized France is a consistent theme in Allégret's films in the post-Occupation period (1948–1952), as indeed is the theme of cold calculated revenge as a dysfunctional attempt to re-assert a sense of power in the face of such humiliation. Generally speaking, Allégret's men experience this loss of virility as a physical malaise, which cynical behaviour does little to assuage (except perhaps in the short term). However, it is rare for us to see, as we do in *Nez de cuir*, the man masquerade his own frailty so clearly in the form of the feminine. We have already cited one such example in the film. An even stronger one occurs when Roger finally decides to show himself to the public. It is a complete performance – a coming out of his mutilated, albeit masked face. Roger invites all the local nobility to a ball at his chateau. His mother (and not he) greets the guests as they stand about chattering and gossiping about Roger's deformity (in a skewed reversal of the talk that there might be around a young woman about to be presented at her coming-out ball). Only once all are assembled does he, Roger, make his grand entrance, slowly moving down the wide, central staircase into the ball-room – much as a beautiful woman would do, putting herself on display for all her guests to see and exclaim over (be it her dress, her jewels, or indeed her facial beauty). Even the camera colludes with this *mise-en-scène* of the feminine: first, holding Roger in a long shot and then moving into a tight profile close-up on his white leather mask – fetishizing his nose (as a camera would traditionally the legs, breasts, or face of a woman). Just as the woman's mask remains impenetrable, so too does Roger's. However, the feminine mystique is now completely queered, for we seek not the unknowable behind the mask as we do with the woman. Rather, we seek the unseeable, the unacceptable, that which we know to be ugly, maimed – the image of the defaced beauty that once was France's youth. Allégret's film is as dark as his others about contemporary France, therefore. Indeed, to answer Doniol-Valcroze's question above, through the metaphor of the mask, Allégret creates an allegory that makes visible the effects of war on a defeated nation.

Thus, in this collection of Napoleonic texts, there is nothing very grand that remains. Even the Great Man himself, in the single film to portray him, is diminished. The approach to history in any one of these films, whilst for the most part far-fetched or highly fictionalized, still tells us something about the time in which the films were being made. Not one person stands out as heroic – if anything, quite the opposite. Selfishness abounds, with the slight exception of *Les Hussards,* where self-interest and the simple drive for survival dictate that the two lacklustre Hussards treat their Italian hostages with compassion. The mood for the most part is angry and vengeful – suggesting a psyche that is ill at ease with itself. By the time we get to films representing the 1860s, this anger, as we shall see, will have evolved into a still darker cynicism, reflecting, perhaps, a sense of impotence in the face of great political upheavals and social change of the 1950s. But, before we get there, we have the Restoration and July Monarchy films to consider. So let us move on!

Notes

1. Marseille (2002, p. 65). The parallels with certain presidential elections in the US where a brother helps his sibling into office leap to mind!
2. Ibid., p. 67.
3. With two remarkable exceptions, it has to be said. Under Napoleonic law, women were the property of the men (father or husband); in terms of inheritance, property division in equal lots amongst the offspring meant that widows could be left destitute and farmland parcellated to such an extent that it was no longer viable in agricultural terms.
4. Marseille, op. cit., pp. 67–71.
5. In the end, she was so identified with her aunt, Marie-Antoinette, the French people were far from appeased by this alliance. As for the nobility, they remained unimpressed by this obvious play for respectability (see Marseille, op. cit., p. 76). In the film, it is made clear that she was not his first choice; Napoleon had been quite taken by a Russian princess, but Talleyrand advised him against it on the grounds that it would upset too many nations (Britain, Prussia and Austria). A better solution was Marie-Louise.
6. Ibid., p. 77.
7. Known as the Rhineland Confederation and sanctioned by the Treaty of Pressburg in 1806 after the crushing defeat exacted upon Austria at Austerlitz in December 1805.
8. From 1810–1814, some 2000 suspects were placed under arrest and imprisoned without trial. Madame de Stael was exiled for ten years (1803–1813). (Chappey & Gainot, 2008, p. 71).
9. http://fr.wikipedia.org/wiki/Talleyrand accessed 29.03.09.
10. Ibid.
11. Mosk review of *Napoléon*, *Variety*, 13.04.1955, no page.
12. Gilberte Turquan '*Napoléon*', *Cinématographie française*, No. 1595, 4.12.1954, p. 25.
13. Ibid.
14. http://www.tascher-de-la-pagerie.org/fr/index.php?menu=histoire accessed 29.03.09.
15. Many of her costumes are on display in her residence Château de Malmaison (now a Museum).
16. http://fr.wikipedia.org/wiki/Sacha_Guitry accessed 29.03.09.
17. http://fr.wikipedia.org/wiki/Jacques_Laurent accessed 29.03.09.
18. http://fr.wikipedia.org/wiki/Anouilh accessed 29.03.09.
19. Chapuy (2001, pp. 56–8).
20. Ibid., pp. 56–7.
21. Ibid., p. 41.
22. In the immediate post-war period, such was the frenzy and hatred felt towards any persons who were deemed to have collaborated with the Germans that very summary justice was meted out. Women who had slept with German soldiers were particularly singled out for vicious treatment. They were publicly humiliated by having their hair shaved off – hence the term 'tondues' ('shaven head'). In certain towns they were also stripped naked and forced to run down the main street, there to take the full force of the town-dwellers fury.
23. Jacques Doinol-Valcroze (1952) Review article of *Nez de cuir, Gentil'homme d'amour*, *Cahiers du cinéma*, Vol. 12, March, p. 69.
24. The former USSR exploded its first H-bomb a year later in 1953.

Chapter 10

Representing the Social: Restoration-July Monarchy (1814-1848)

The Restoration through to the end of the July Monarchy represents France's last gasp at monarchic reign. Not quite a series of constutional monarchies, they also fell short of the former pre-Revolution absolutist model. This does not mean to say that the successive kings and their supporters – most notably the Ultras, an extreme royalist party – did not hanker after power. Far from it. But, as I explain below, whilst the successive régimes opposed liberal, republican and democratic ideals, power became a different domain of struggle which threw up, almost by default, a parliamentary system whereby the legislative body sought to hold sway over the executive – arguably a prototype for the contemporary political system in France.

The Restoration period falls into three moments: that of 1814, when Louis XVIII was restored to the throne as the Bourbon king of France; 1815–1824, which marked his re-installation as king after Napleon I's 100 Days; finally, 1824–1830 and the reign of Charles X – the last Bourbon king to reign over France. According to the historian Brogan, the 1815–1824 Restoration is the one that matters, for 'this one marked France for good'.[1] Louis XVIII had the unenviable task of reconciling the Revolutionary heritage with the Napoleonic one and that of the Ancien Régime – something that he achieved, almost by accident, under the Second Restoration. Initially, in 1815, the mood was one of revenge against the Bonapartistes. The first Chamber of Deputies to be elected was almost unanimously composed of the Ultras (350 out of 405). This so-called *Chambre introuvable*/Windfall Chamber[2] was bent on bringing back the Ancien Régime, eradicating the Revolutionary heritage and punishing those who supported Napoleon. The Ultras' control of the Chamber allowed them to pass a slew of repressive laws. Amongst them were laws that led to what was termed the 'White Terror', whereby former Bonapartists were hounded and some summarily executed (Maréchals Brune, Ney and Ramel, to name the most famous of the victims). Such was the mistrust of the Imperial army that former soldiers, loyal to Napoleon, were deprived of their pensions and put on half pay (and became known as *les demi-soldes*). Upon the death of their great leader in 1821, these *demi-soldes* galvanized their forces in a failed attempt to overthrow the monarchy and restore his son, Napoleon II, as Emperor (an event carefully detailed in *L'Agonie des aigles*).[3]

But the lasting irony has to be that because the Ultras deemed Louis XVIII's system of rule too moderate, they became more royalist than the king, insisting on their rights to reinstate the principles of the Ancien Régime through legislation. In fighting for legislative power (the parliamentary assembly) over the executive (embodied by the king), they found themselves (almost unwittingly) transformed into hardy defenders of the rights of Parliament – principles engrained within the very Revolutionary spirit of 1789 which they sought to eradicate![4] The king lacked ultimate power. In many ways he was a convenience king placed there by the conquering allies (British, Russian and Prussian), not by divine right, but as the adjudged lesser of several evils. The allies preferred a monarchy over a Republic or a return of the Bonapartes in the form of Napoleon II.[5] This weakness allowed the Chamber to assert its legislative powers and, thus, parlementarianism was developed for the first time in France's political history, even though it was hardly a representative assembly since the majority of the nation still could not vote – only 100,000 had the right: the so-called 'census vote'. This weakness on the part of the king did not, however, prevent him from striking back. Indeed, the breach between the king and the Ultras reached such proportions that, by 1816, the prime-minister was forced to dissolve the Chamber. Further, by 1817, the law on the electoral vote expanded to include the bourgeois classes which led, in turn, to the emergence of new sources of power, such as that of the bankers Lafitte and Rothschild.[6] The advantage was to the bourgeoisie. This was not the end of the Ultras, however. In 1820, the son of the future king Charles X, the Duc de Berry (himself an Ultra) was assassinated – the Ultras blamed the laxity of the government for this outrage. The outcome was a further change of government; this time, one which favoured the hard-liners. By the last two years of Louis XVIII's reign, the Ultras had regained control – and the Ultra Joseph de Villèle led the government. The Ultras applied pressure on the king to intervene in Spain in 1823 and restore Ferdinand VII to the throne. The campaign, led by the Duc d'Angoulême, the other son of Charles X, was a success – Trocadéro being the French army's most memorable battle. Meantime, the French remained as an occupying army until 1828. Ferdinand VII took power and, profiting from the support of the French troups, very quickly foreswore the Constitution of Cadiz (which ensured the civil rights of the Spanish people) and proceeded to reign with an iron fist. The brutal chief of police in *Les Amants de Tolède*, set in 1825, remains an example of the type of intransigent anti-libertarian rule in force at the time.

Finally, in this snapshot of Louis XVIII's reign, we must refer to the new military organization. Since the 100 Days had made evident the fickleness of the former Imperial army, the old military order had to be abolished. In 1818, the task of rebuilding an army worthy of its name was devolved to the minister of war, Maréchal Gouvion Saint-Cyr, who set up the great military schools (the Polytechnique and Saint-Cyr). Legislation instituted a lottery system, which replaced the now defunct conscription, calling young men to compulsory service. Those with good numbers escaped recruitment, as did those with poor physique. The rich could buy their way out by paying for substitutes to take their place – normally from the peasant class. But while this class supplied most of the annual 40,000 recruits, a third of all commissions were reserved for promotions from the ranks, so a poor man could rise to the top. Clergy students were also exempt from being called up; thus, there was an exponential rise in recruitment to the church of younger men. In particular, the majority of the secular clergy (ie, non-monastic) was recruited from the peasantry. As Brogan puts it: 'the way to power for a poor boy was now to bet on the black, not on the red'.[7] In this context, the film *Le Rouge et le Noir* gives us a ready example of the choices Julien Sorel finds himself confronted with to advance his career.

A more satisfactory king, to the Ultras' mind, was Louis' successor, Charles X (the Comte d'Artois). Essentially, they believed they had a puppet king at their disposal – and his reign was indeed dominated by the Ultras. He made a feeble attempt at the very beginning to introduce a few liberal measures but he soon swung to the Ultras' side. That was until 1827, when the liberal faction of the political class obtained a majority in the Chamber and he appointed a prime-minister politically poised half way between the opposing sides. Displeasure increased on both sides. During the summer break of 1829, without consultation, the king replaced the prime minister with an Ultra candidate, the Prince de Polignac (an embodiment of the Ancien Régime); the interior minister with an even more extreme Ultra, the Comte de la Bourdonnaye (a major instigator of the White Terror).[8] These appointments brought everything to a head. The liberals, unsurprisingly outraged at this un-parliamentarian move, believed this constituted an attempt to re-instate absolute monarchy. The king asserted his right to appoint and dismiss ministers as set out in the Charter of 1814 – which, according to the liberals' view, had been superceded by the new parliamentarianism progressively introduced under Louis XVIII. The strength of reaction grew over the next year, not helped by dire economic conditions and a poor harvest season – a combination which led peasants and the urban poor to various acts of violence (arson attacks amongst them). In March 1830, Charles X announced a military expedition to Algiers to avenge an insult by the Bey of Algiers to the Consul of France. The capital city was successfully taken on 5 July – thus beginning the protracted business of colonizing Algeria (1830–1857).[9] A mere three weeks later, 27–29 July 1830, Paris was up in arms. On 25 July, Charles X and De Polignac attempted to force through a series of anti-constitutional measures (the Ordonnances de Saint-Cloud) dissolving parliament, changing the electoral system (to reduce the number of voters), and suspending freedom of the press.[10] The press was hugely instrumental in whipping up public feeling against these measures, primarily through scaremongering. The *Trois Glorieuses*/three glorious days of the July Revolution forced the king to abdicate. He did so, finally, in favour of the Duc d'Orléans, Louis-Philippe I, *roi des Français*/king of the French, a subtle distinction showing – in nomenclature at least – that he was a constitutional monarch, representative of the French rather than absolute king of France. The French tricolore flag was re-established as the nation's colours, replacing the Royalist white flag. Charles X fled from France; the July Monarchy was born.

By the end of the Restoration periods, it is fair to say that the two monarchs had failed to unite the two Frances (Revolutionary/Royalist). According to historians, 'to the great mass of the French people, of all classes but the nobility, the Revolution seemed, in retrospect, a good thing'.[11] In terms of moving towards a democratic system of governance, this is probably a fair assessment: there was 'the court on one side, the nation on the other'.[12] It did, however, leave a reasonable legacy. It 'liberated' the country from the allied occupiers (in particular the British who were not much liked).[13] It restored public credit; secured the position of France as an independent great power (successful campaign in Spain, colonization); put the army in red trousers (to enable footsoldiers to recognize their own side and not kill them by mistake in battle).[14] Most remarkable of all, however, it had been unable to undo any of the achievements of the Revolution or the First Empire.[15]

Louis-Philippe's eighteen-year reign (known also as the Bourgeois monarchy) was no less fraught with political upheavals than those of his two predecessors. These difficulties were, as with the two former monarchs, just as much a result of his own ambiguous positioning in relation to constitutional monarchy as the vying ambitions of the left and right parties that made up the Chambers of the National Assembly (Deputies and Peers). In truth, Louis-Philippe – who posed as the citizen king in touch with his people with ordinary bourgeois values and tastes – failed or did not elect to understand their wishes. For a start, his attempt at electoral change was fairly pitiful. It was evident that he listened to neither political faction, be it those on the right (known as the constitutionals), including those who wanted to curtail the vote, or those on the left (the republicans) who clamoured for universal suffrage. In the end, the vote was extended by very small margins (from 167,000 in 1831 to 248,000 by 1846) and was still the reserve of the educated property owners: the so-called *hommes éclairs*/enlightened men. This slight increase in the electorate, which now incorporated the property-owning bourgeois vote, meant, interestingly enough, that the outcome of elections was less predictable. It was clear, however, that Louis-Philippe wanted to control these electoral outcomes. To this effect, he put in place a government and prime minister sympathetic to his own cause: to maintain the concept of a monarchy that had the power to govern. Indeed, if he did not like the outcomes of an election, he found ways to dissolve the Assembly and call for new ones. Similarly, if a prime minister was not to his political taste or turned out to be less malleable than he wished, he also found a pretext for getting rid of him. Thus, in the eighteen-year period there were four dissolutions of the Assembly, producing five calls for a precipitated election, seventeen different governments, ten changes of prime-minister, with, finally, François Guizot providing some kind of continuity in the last eight years of the king's reign.[16] It is worth recalling that in the July Revolution there were many calls for a Republic – this was an idea that refused to go away, as the various uprisings made clear, including especially the June revolt of 1832 (graphically illustrated in *Les Misérables*). Indeed, during this period, there were nine major riots, all of which were brutally repressed, often at the hands of Adolphe Thiers – sometime minister of the interior (1832, 1834), at others, prime minister (1836, 1840). Further, there were assassination attempts (1836) and two failed coups by Louis Bonaparte to overthrow the king (1840, 1846). The king once described his mission as 'an unending fight against the forces of anarchy'.[17] Civil liberties were at a low ebb. People were not allowed to gather in groups of more than 20 – this brought about the famous 'false banquets' where radicals got together to plot the revolution. In the end, the king succumbed less to the forces of anarchy than to his own refusal to concede that a constitutional monarch should reign and not govern, as eventually February 1848 made clear when republicans and the people of Paris mounted their revolution to topple him. Despite attempts to suppress the revolt, a majority of the National Guard chose to defend the workers and revolutionaries rather than the king. The Second Republic came into being.

This 34-year period knew moments of economic boom – brought about by the impact of the Industrial Revolution in the form of mechanization of industries, in particular textiles, road-building and railway lines. This created a new wealth and a get-rich-quick mentality, particularly amongst the bourgeoisie. But despite this climate of economic growth, for the most part, the poor fell on extremely harsh times (as is so aptly caught in Hugo's massive novel *Les Misérables,* adapted to screen by Le Chanois in 1958). This period is characterized by a new phenomenon called 'pauperism'. Indeed, during his exile, Louis Napoleon (eventually Napoleon III) wrote a treatise on it, advocating education as the only way out of this trap.[18] The very thing that was bringing prosperity to the few, industrialization, was increasing the poverty of the many. An increased urbanization of the poorer classes (people who had left their rural environs to find work because of a renewed agricultural crisis) plus mechanization through industrial growth (whereby the labour force exceeded demand) meant that France was facing examples of poverty on an unprecedented scale.

The textile industry is a good example to cite. At first, improvement in mechanization created a huge demand for female labour in particular, but supply of labour then outstripped demand and the industry was, thereafter, able to exploit the workforce by reducing wages to below the breadline and firing at will – single mothers being a prime target. Unsurprisingly, prostitution was virtually the only way for the female poor to survive. Such was the concern, the humanely-spirited Doctor Parent-Duchâtelet, a member of the committee for public health, conducted an exhaustive eight-year study (1827–1835) on prostitutes in Paris which was first published in 1836: *La Prostitution à Paris au XIXe siècle.*[19] There we learn that, by the 1830s, figures in Paris had grown to an alarming degree: there were 12,707 registered prostitutes.[20] If we consider that this meant (in official terms) approximately one prostitute for every thirty men (if every male availed himself of one), then, clearly, concerns for public hygiene (especially the scare of syphilis) would become uppermost in the minds of those upholding the public salubrity and family values that had been re-instituted as a major platform by the Restoration. The figures become more interesting still when we consider how integrally-class-bound prostitution was. Nearly all prostitutes came from working-class backgrounds – only 1.2 per cent came from upper-class families.[21] Very few were literate; amongst those that were, a higher number came from the provinces, rather than Paris (which is surprising given that education in Paris was more widespread).[22] Various causes are cited by Parent-Duchâtelet for women turning to prostitution. Utter poverty is the main cause (28 per cent); closely followed by women being abandoned by their partner and left destitute (27 per cent); next is expulsion from the father's house (24 per cent). Thereafter, but with far smaller percentages: abandonment by a lover, thus bringing a woman to Paris (8 per cent); domestics seduced by masters and subsequently thrown out (6 per cent); coming to Paris to hide and find sustenance (5 per cent). This leaves a mere 2 per cent to cover other reasons: to help support their poor family (1.3 per cent); widowers with a family to support (0.7 per cent).[23] Given these figures, we can see how accurate is Hugo's evocation in *Les Misérables* of Fantine's plight as a single mother. Having lost her job working in the factory because she is a single mother, she is reduced to prostitution as the only means to survive. Soon she succumbs to tuberculosis (arguably a euphemism for the taboo illness of syphilis).

The 'hungry forties' were upon the poor. By 1848, bad harvests, the collapse of the railway boom and the effects of international trade regulations took a massive toll on employment.[24] The politics of Louis-Philippe's reign did nothing to assuage this terrible situation. The last two years in particular were marked by a politics of immobilism: do nothing, change nothing – so the outcome, a nation in economic crisis, bankrupt of ideas, was hardly suprising, any more than the remedy sought to resolve it. It came in the form of the February barricades of 1848, which became known as the Second Revolution of the nineteenth century and heralding a new Republic. Louis-Philipe was obliged to abdicate.

During this 34-year period, while Paris remained narrow, dirty and labyrinthine, it grew exponentially – from 650,000 inhabitants in 1815 to 760,000 by 1830 and 1.5 million by 1850.[25] Under Louis-Philippe, for the first time since the seventeenth century, Paris became a fortified city (and remained thus until World War One). Despite measures to improve hygiene, in 1832 a cholera epidemic took hold of Paris in which 20,000 people died (including the Republican General Lamarque, whose funeral procession unleashed the July riots which figure so centrally in *Les Misérables*). By 1828, gas began to light the streets; the first omnibuses made their appearance. Cast-iron impacted on building practices – including, of course, railways and bridges. Despite several rounds of censorship, the press flourished, often making or breaking governments and upping sentiment against the monarchy. Photography was invented: the first print, by Nièpce dates from 1826. Boulevards sprouted grand cafés – like the Cafés de Paris (founded 1798 and first revamped in the early 1800s) and de la Renaissance (1839).[26] During the reign of Louis-Philippe – and as a response to the public nature of the city where light was shed everywhere – bourgeois interiors became the domain where the intimacy of private life went on display, as if they were signatures of the owner's personality. Apartments were over-stuffed with furniture and dominated, in particular, by velvet upholstery and furnishings (even fur trimmings, where possible: on bedspreads for example) – all measures of wealth.[27] Developments in mechanized manufacturing brought in their wake an increase in outlets in the form of fashion houses and shops. Paris became the capital of consumption and the centre for fashion – as is attested by the tremendous growth in fashion magazines in the July Monarchy period (about 30 magazines) and fashion boutiques and luxury shops along the boulevards and streets of the right bank. In becoming the centrepieces for taste and its consumption, the boulevard des Italiens and the rues Vivienne, de Richelieu and Rivoli (the last of which stretches between la Madeleine and the Bastille) effectively redefined urban space – at least for the wealthy.[28] In the 1830s and 1840s, the 1st and 2nd arrondissements were where you shopped if you wanted to be noticed and perceived as part of the elite (whether noble or bourgeois) – this is significant when we consider *Bel-Ami* and the lead character's mobility in these areas. If the manufacturing of textiles was France's premier industry during the July Monarchy, then fashion was amongst its premium exports. It gave national prestige to a country still recovering from its humiliation after the demise of Napoleon I and the international ridicule caused by the weakness of its

Restoration monarchs. There are obvious parallels here with postwar France of the 1950s, when fashion once again was a première flag of national pride, and active consumption of new commodities was seen as patriotic duty of the woman.

In the discussion of the films that follows we will discover an eclectic mix of messages where narratives of bourgeois morality are countered by more polemical ones, reflecting, doubtless, the strangeness of this first half of the nineteenth century as France struggled to assert a fresh identity – one that, despite attempts to disguise the fact, was clearly in conflict with itself. For, as much as France strove to show itself as a modern industrial country, it could not disguise the fact that politically and constitutionally it was still a retrograde nation-state. Parallels with contemporary 1950s' France are clear as it, too, struggled with its identity in the dawn of a new era of modernization. After all, any optimism this new era bred was tarnished by the shadow of the nation's capitulation to the Germans during the war and its renewed 'capitulation' to the enemy, whom it must now embrace for the sake of peace (the Common Market agreements with Germany being the best example of these compromises). Moreover, any sense of greatness to which this nation's damaged psyche could attach itself was, to all intents and purposes, undermined by the fact that France, in its own eyes, was floundering as a country of international importance with the loss of its Empire, to say nothing of the lack of leadership. The Fourth Republic, as with the Third before it, lacked a 'great man' out there leading the country – but apparently dictators (Napoleon I, especially) were not the solution, either. Political uncertainty, social upheaval, shifting class identities wrought by economic necessity, poverty of the many versus the wealth of the few – all these conditions prevailed as much in the new era of the 1950s as they did in the first half of the nineteenth century.

Representing the social: Paris as attraction and selling the sanctity of marriage

Paris from the mid-1820s onwards became a city of attractions to the rich, especially the Russians and the English – most significantly, in terms of our corpus of films, to Lord Henry Seymour (1805–1859), nick-named by the French popular press Milord L'Arsouille. He was a founder-member of the famous Jockey Club (1825) and its first president. It was he who introduced to France, in the 1830s, modern horse-racing along English lines. At first he lived above the Café de Paris (Tortoni's) situated at the angle of the boulevard des Italiens and rue Taitbout in the 2nd arrondissement.[29] He then moved to number 33 Avenue de Friedland, formerly known as the boulevard Beaujon and located in the wealthy 8th arrondissement. In Haguet's 1956 film *Milord L'Arsouille*, set designer Lucien Aguettand offers the viewer a stupendous re-creation, inside and out, of this fabulously ornate house with its three turrets and wooded 'parc' with grottos and fishponds.[30] Aguettand's sets include an artist's studio, lavishly upholstered bedrooms in red silk and velvet, and huge dining and ball rooms. Seymour/Arsouille was a dandy and extremely wealthy, a consummate athlete and fond of boxing. He was, to all accounts, something of a brute, a side we do not get to see in the film.[31]

The mediated persona of Milord L'Arsouille is also, however, something of a re-creation. The term *arsouille* refers to a person of dubious morals and a heavy drinker. Milord L'Arsouille was a nickname given to another personage of the same period as Lord Seymour: a man named Charles de la Battut (1806–1835) who did indeed lead a life of excess, from which he died quite young. It is also true that Seymour was equally an eccentric. He famously had a portrait painted of himself as Saint-Sebastien, pierced not with arrows but with carrots. He was a man with huge appetites, including an extensive wardrobe and an immense collection of cigars, and a quick temper given, for example, to boxing the ears of servants he dismissed. Thus, it is not difficult to see why he became deliberately confounded (by the popular press) with the epithet that belonged to another.[32]

In the film *Milord L'Arsouille*, we are dealing with Lord Seymour – the one created by the media's imaginary and sung about in the lower-class Parisian *quartiers* that he frequents. This Milord (played by Jean-Claude Pascal) is a seducer, well known for two-timing his mistresses, famous for his masked balls and for travelling amongst the poor, where he throws his money about (for less honourable reasons, one suspects, than the film leads us to believe). He, too, has a portrait painted of himself (though not of the carrot-pierced saint), and uses his studio as a pretext to seduce his latest 'conquest' – a young woman from the working-classes, Chantereine (Simone Bach) – who does not yield to his appetites and throws his money back in his face: 'poor people are not play-things', he is warned. The time and year are significant for the setting of the film, March 1847: precisely one year and one month before Louis-Philippe is forced to abdicate. The poor are mustering their people towards insurrection – proudly, they too refuse to be patronized by Lord Seymour ('we need justice, not your charity'). Eventually, redemption befalls our 'hero'. He aligns himself with the poor – with good reason, since it transpires he is illegitimate and of working-class origin. He supports the anti-monarchist cause, which gets him deported to England – in an amusing scene with Louis-Philippe (Jean Debucourt). As the film ends we are in March 1848. We hear the rumblings of the people uprising. The future holds promise for Milord L'Arsouille. His origins and his republican spirit mean that, come the revolution, he will be able to return and claim the woman of his dreams.

The Restoration period saw the rebirth of the concept of the family, and the July Monarchy did much to continue the tradition of family values introduced by Louis XVIII. Restoring the king meant restoring order. The family, primarily in the form of a strong patriarch, was to act as a counter to the chaos of the war-strewn France of the Napoleonic years and the effects of the libertarian Revolutionary period.[33] The right to divorce was abolished in 1816 because it was perceived as giving too much power to the woman, in that it allowed her to challenge the authority of the male.[34] Marriage was also seen as the founding stone of modern society; a 'Good Family' was the foundation of the nation-state.[35] As the bourgeoisie grew, so too did the importance of the nuclear family to protect the patrimony. And, in it, the wife had to submit to conjugal law and patriarchal authority. In short, the family became assimilated to an economic system (as site of production and reproduction) working to protect wealth and the concept of nationhood. The growth of family businesses amongst the bourgeois classes was exponential during this period – a growth made possible initially by the very Revolution and Republican values these classes now rejected in embracing the monarchy anew. The impact of the Industrial Revolution, towards the late 1820s and early 1830s, also had an effect. The family model, whereby the boss assumes the role of patriarch to his workers, is sustained in the newly-established factories as much as within the more traditional family-run businesses.[36] Unsurprisingly, the working classes were perceived as the threat to this new concept of the family, both in terms of health and economics, and so required careful management. In economic terms, this meant paying the father enough to meet the basic needs of his family, but not so much that he would not need to put his children to work as soon as possible (often aged eight) and, intermittently, his wife.[37] In terms of hygiene, the fear was that these working classes were the transmitters or embodiment of the social scourges of the times: tuberculosis, syphilis and alcoholism, and, thus, had to be contained, held apart from the 'good families'. They also had to be counted (as we saw in the case of prostitution) and examined by doctors specializing in social hygiene.[38]

This focus on family as a vital part of nation-building, post-trauma, recurs repeatedly in France's history – each time, after a humiliating defeat. Later on in the nineteenth century, nowhere was this rhetoric more present than in the successive ministries of politicians such as Jules Grévy, Jules Simon and Jules Ferry in their commitment to the process of constructing a strong Third Republic. Indeed, it is from those early years (1876–1877) that dates a family policy proper.[39] This thrust for nation-building re-occurs once more, as we know, in the 1950s during the Fourth Republic, where the emphasis was on respectability, keeping up and saving appearances, as much as it was on reversing the demographic decline. A particular stress was placed on the role of the mother to maintain a clean household – domestic cleanliness was a symbol of a clean nation. Social mobility was equally an important drive. Working classes strove evermore to access the accoutrements of the bourgeoisie. 'Good marriages' were still key to the middle classes (marrying fortunes or increasing one's own).[40]

Thus, what is intriguing is that, on the surface at least, not one of the twelve film titles (listed below in figure 10.1) located in this period under investigation is about marriage, family or child-bearing.

Meanness, cruelty, heartache, ineffectual heroism and cold cynicism abound in most of them. And yet, beneath the surface, the importance of a good marriage is upheld, as are, more poignantly, the sacrifices that must be made on its behalf. Thus, for the most part, these films' narratives do not end joyously. In *La Dame aux caméllias*, Marguerite, the thinly-disguised real-life courtesan Marie Duplessis, is forced by Armand Duval's father to renounce her lover for the sake of his son's good name and marriage prospects. We note, *en passant*, that in *Deburau*, this same Marie Duplessis had already broken the heart of another of her conquests – the famous mime after whom the film is named. A good marriage between the newly rich and the recently enobled is the outcome of *Les Misérables*. Cosette, the illegitimate daughter, made wealthy thanks to her guardian Valjean, marries Marius, Baron de Pontmercy, whose title comes to him thanks to his father's heroic service under

Restoration periods **1814–24 Louis XVIII (5 titles) and** **1824–30 Charles X (1)**	July Monarchy/Bourgeois Monarchy **1830–48 Louis Philippe (6 titles)**
L'Agonie des aigles (52) 1822 – Demi-soldes seek to restore Napoleon II to the throne – nostalgia for Napoleon I	*L'Auberge rouge* (51) 1833 – Based on a real events Somewhat anti-clerical
Les Crimes de l'amour (2. Stendhal *Mina de Vanghel*) (53) 1830 – love-thwarted woman narrative	*Deburau* (51) 1839–46 – 'reminiscences' of famous mime
Le Comte de Monte Cristo (55) 1815–1835 – Napoleon I indirect cause of his emprisonment, ruthless rival in love/revenge narrative	*La Dame aux camélias*(53) 1840s – story of famous courtesan
Tamango (58) 1820 – story about slave trading	*Par ordre du Tsar* (54) 1840 – biopic/love story' based around Liszt
Les Misérables (58) 1822 through to 1832 – poverty narrative	*Le Rouge et le Noir* (54) 1830s – seducer tale
	Milord L'Arsouille (56) 1847 – seducer tale (based on a real person)
1824–30 **Charles X (1 title)**	
Les Amants de Tolède (53) 1825 – thwarted lovers and evil seducer	

Figure 10.1: Themes of films set in Restoration and July Monarchy.

Napoleon I. The desperate, if futile, attempt to keep up appearances in a bourgeois marriage, coupled with extreme jealousy at the prospect of her lover's own advantageous marriage, is what drives Madame de Rênal in *Le Rouge et le Noir* to her death. Thus, the transgressive threat to matrimony – female lust – is eliminated. Death, in the form of Mina's suicide, conveniently staves off threats to the matrimonial home in *Les Crimes de l'amour: Mina de Vanghel*. Mina finally decides that her personal suffering, in the pursuit of her illicit love for Monsieur de Larçay, is too great to bear. To the now-rich and enobled Dantès, Count of Monte-Cristo's entreaties that she run away with him, Mercedes sensibly responds that it is now eighteen years too late. She elects, despite the evidence of her husband's treachery towards Dantès, to remain in her marriage and protect her son's future ('It isn't that easy to leave', she declares, 'I have a son.') – patrimony and a mother's love weigh in more heavily than a lover returned from the dead, it seems.

Thus women will make sacrifices for the stability of marriage. They will even go to the extreme of sacrificing their own happiness to save the life of their true love, as in *Les*

Amants de Tolède. Most of these narratives, then, are about the frustration of not achieving individual goals and happiness. The individual finds him or herself prevented by reasons of politics, class or treachery, or all three combined, from finding fulfillment. We need to remember that this is the period of Romanticism – a movement that came about as a reaction to the former régimes, in particular, the First Empire's penchant for the traditions of Classical Antiquity. Loosely dated from 1820–1850, it is a movement attached to the Royalist years of the Restoration and July monarchy. But, significantly, it is also attached to the new morality of the century – a bourgeois-inspired morality at that, one that is based in emotion, sentiment, and the individual. The language is lyrical, deliberately set to counter the dry materialist philosophy of the Enlightenment. The writer's subject is the desirability of bourgeois domestic life and the obstacles that prevent access to it (poverty, indigence, or immorality); nature becomes the new space of exaltation and terror; the middle-ages and spiritualism also combine in this eclectic mixture that is Romanticism to create a nostalgia for an imaginary past. Equally, architecture and design – including fashion design – look back to the middle-ages, the Renaissance and the past two centuries for retro-nostalgic inspiration. Dumas père's swashbuckling novels (*Les Trois mousquetaires, Le Comte de Monte-Cristo, Le Vicomte de Bragelonne*) and Hugo's *Notre-Dame de Paris* are examples of this love for a nation's imagined past (see the relevant chapters in Part Two). Passionate individualism, a belief that all that is nature is art, and the implicit hugeness of this concept – these are the fundamental tenets of Romanticism. To match this, epic novels (*Les Misérables* is five tomes, Balzac's *Comédie humaine* runs to eight) and epic paintings (by Géricault and Delacroix) give full vent to a dramatic and often tragic perception of the world.

So it is fitting, doubtless, that the three top-grossing films relating to this period are the epic Romantic novels of Hugo (*Les Misérables*), Dumas (*Le Comte de Monte-Cristo*) and Stendhal (*Le Rouge et le Noir*). The following two chapters investigate this trio in more detail. Presently, I want to conclude this chapter with a consideration of another example of exploitation and inhumanity – slave-trading as represented in *Tamango*, a Franco-Italian co-production in Technicolor and cinemascope that stands out through its difference, made as it is by an American film-maker in political exile, John Berry.

Politicising the polemical: John Berry's *Tamango* (1958)

This heavily-modified adaptation of Prosper Mérimée's short story *Tamango* (first published 1829), whilst certainly a treatise against slavery and human exploitation, equally tells the story of the young woman slave Aiché's redemption. In the end she elects to die with her 'own people' in the ship's hold rather than take the offer of safety from her white master, the Captain of the ironically named ship *Esperanza*. It is 1820, Captain Reinker (Curd/ Curt Jurgens), a Dutchman, is on his last mission with the slave-ship. He sets off from the Guinea coast, heading to Cuba, after some hard bargaining with an African chief (Habib Benglia). Amongst the slaves, the proud Tamango (Alex Cressan)[41] tries to rouse the others into revolt. He attempts to enlist the help of Reinker's mistress, Aiché (Dorothy Dandridge). Initially, she refuses. But, when the slaves finally launch their assault and she is taken hostage by Tamango, she decides to remain by their side. By doing so, she chooses death. The slaves are overpowered and take refuge below deck – the Captain orders the cannon to be fired into the hold, thereby wiping out any voice of resistance.

There are several contextual issues that need to be put in place in discussing this film because they reveal a subtle weaving of discourses of interdiction that impacted as much on its making as its reception. John Berry fled from the United States, in 1951, to avoid having to testify at the HUAC hearings (House Committee on Un-American Activities). He was being pursued by the FBI because of the documentary film he made, *The Hollywood Ten* (1950, originally uncredited), about a group of leading screenwriters and film-makers who, in 1947, refused to cooperate with HUAC when asked to name names of possible Communist sympathizers. The idea of the documentary was to raise funds for victims of the hearings. Each of the ten directors made a short speech denouncing McCarthyism and the Hollywood blacklisting by the studio bosses.[42] Of all ironies, it was Edward Dmytryk, one of the Hollywood Ten, who first got Berry the commission for directing the documentary but who then went on to denounce him, in 1951, as a Communist. Berry was blacklisted for this film; he fled to France, where he remained for most of the rest of his life (he returned briefly to the States in the 1970s).

Berry was indeed a member of the American Communist Party. He joined in outrage at both the injustices of the Spanish Civil war and the effects of the Depression on the poor in the States. During the 1940s he worked in theatre under the tutelage of Orson Welles, both on the acting and directing side – this would significantly impact on his subsequent directorial style in that he would work through scenes in rehearsal with his actors before shooting (an unusual practice at the time). Most significantly during this early theatre career, Berry took the production of the African-American author Richard Wright's *Native Son* on national tour (as touring director) in 1940. And in 1946 he directed the national touring production of *Deep are the Roots*. Both plays deal with racial issues as well as inter-racial relationships and Berry's courageous involvement in these productions gained him a loyal following within the American Black community of the time.[43] Berry, then, is identified with a strong belief in the need to fight against oppression, and his film *Tamango*, with regard to the struggle for black liberation and the controversial inter-racial relationship between Aiché and Captain Reinker, stands as a testimony to his desire to fight injustice. Unsurprisingly, the film was banned from the United States until 1962 because of censorship problems – the Hayes Production Code forbad images portraying miscegenation.[44] Furthermore, the timing of *Tamango* – 1958 – brings it smack into the arena of the Black Civil Rights movement in the United States (this was the time of great activities by the NAACP against segregation) and the government's hostility to change via any form of legislation. It is also worth recalling that the FBI and CIA believed the NAACP was a Communist-inspired organization. Thus, images of Black solidarity, so vividly portrayed in the film's ending, to say nothing of the various moments in the film when the Black slaves dance as a marker of resistance to the dominating white man, were certainly going to be read as political. And we can also impute a political intention on Berry's part in his naming of every African cast member in the film during the credit roll at the beginning. Sadly, not a lot had shifted politically by 1962 and, when the film was released in the United States, it was almost immediately buried because of a deliberate policy of poor distribution.[45]

The French were equally sensitive to the subject matter. The film was banned from screenings in France's colonies in Africa for fear it would cause dissent amongst the natives. Furthermore, Mérimée's original text firmly locates the slave-traders as French. That had to be changed to get past the censors – the Captain became a Dutchman and the ship Portuguese. In an outrageous misrepresentation of historical truth, the film opens with the following words, so that France would remain clearly exonerated from any association with slave-running. We have to assume that, for censorship reasons, Berry was obliged to insert this disclaimer:

> It is to France's credit that they were one of the first nations to have pushed for the abolition of slavery. The 4th of February 1794, the National Convention declared that all black slavery in all the colonies was at an end and decreed that all men, irrespective of colour, living in these colonies were French citizens. The 1815 treaty again condemned slavery, but some slave ships, now illegal, continued their trafficking in secret, despite the surveillance of war ships. It is one of these dramatic crossings that *Tamango* relates.

Even if slavery had been abolished in 1794, in truth the French still practiced slave-trading. During the 1820s, the timing of *Tamango*, France was the third-ranking nation in slave-trading.[46] In 1802 Napoleon had re-established and legalized slavery; he then rescinded that law in 1815 (during his 100 Days return) – a decision ratified by Louis XVIII in 1817, although he made no efforts to implement it. Even when the July Monarchy officially abolished slavery in 1848, there were still loopholes. Algeria was exempt from the law, as were any future colonized countries (a prime example being Senegal, where slavery, particularly in the form of enforced labour, lasted until the end of the nineteenth century).[47]

Berry's film greatly changes the nature of Mérimée's polemical story and is clearly a plea for racial equality. It is, however, unclear from the original text what Mérimée's position on slavery was: the French are shown as rapacious and brutal – especially in the person of the ironically named Captain Ledoux; the Africans are revealed as superstitious and rather stupid. In Mérimée's story, Tamango is an African Chief who sells his people into slavery for derisory products (faulty guns and alcohol). He is just as cruel as Ledoux and, in a moment of drunken madness, he banishes his wife Ayché to the slave ship for challenging his authority. When he scrambles aboard in an attempt to reclaim her, he is easily captured and even though he leads the slaves in revolt against their white masters and overcomes them, killing them all, he is foolish enough to spare no-one, so he has no idea how to navigate the ship back to land. In the end, all but Tamango perish and he is later taken to Jamaica where he is enlisted in the army as a cymbalist.

There is no fence-sitting or ambiguity in Berry's film. The slaves all die on the ship as a result of the Captain's cruelty. He blows them to pieces by discharging cannon fire into the hold. The slaves' resistance comes from their voice – just as before it had come from their dancing. They sing their song of solidarity until they are silenced. As Tamango tells his brave fellow slaves: 'In death we win.' As Christopher Miller rightly suggests, Berry's film transforms Mérimée's 'tale that casts Africans in an extremely unfavorable light...into a parable of African liberation on the one side of the Atlantic and an anti-McCarthy, anti-racist fable on the other side'.[48]

Into this complex contextualizing story we must now weave considerations of Dorothy Dandridge, the mixed-race American actor who plays the role of the mixed-race Aiché in the film. Dandridge learnt French to play the role and had considerable say on her characterization as the Captain's slave and mistress. Miller, in his excellent study on this film, tells us that Dandridge was incensed by the shift in tone from the treatment she had agreed to and the final script she read, which she described as a 'sex drama, tawdry and exploitative' and refused to approve.[49] Because Berry was 'contractually obliged to work with Dandridge's approval', changes were made – thus, as Miller points out, presumably the film version 'we see is one that she approved'.[50] These are important points when we consider the negative, even racist, responses from critics of the time who utterly dismissed Dandridge's performance as follows:

From *Monthly Film Bulletin* (UK) – Dramatically everything goes to pieces with the introduction of Dorothy Dandridge as a dusky spitfire charmer.[51]

From *Cahiers du cinéma* (France) – The sole presence of Dorothy Dandridge is enough to sink the film...The cold theatrics of the film are rendered even more grating by the grimaces of the former Carmen Jones.[52]

From the *New York Times* (US) – POLEMICISTS for racial equality on the screen and the simply curious may find something enticing about the prospect of a Teuton-like Curt Jurgens making intense love to Dorothy Dandridge, a Negro, in "Tamango." The prospect of such frankness carries a cultural augury that may attract the unwary of both races to the French-made melodrama that opened at the Capitol Theatre yesterday. However, it is only fair to warn such partisans that "Tamango," despite the fitful embraces of its racially opposite principals, does no great service to the cause of either racial understanding or plain entertainment...The fact that Miss Dandridge's loyalty is torn between her passionate master and her own people down in the hold seems remote from all reality as presented here.[53]

Dandridge had just come from making two films where racial representation had caused some issues with the Hayes Production Code, most significantly *Carmen Jones* (Preminger, 1954), an all-Black version of Bizet's opera based on another Mérimée short story. Dandridge plays a sultry and seductive Carmen. The film was a huge success and Dandridge's performance won her an Academy Award nomination for Best Actress – she did not win, but she was the first African-American actor to be nominated. She then made *Island in the Sun* (1957), which tiptoed around inter-racial love. But with *Tamango*, inter-racial relations are fully on screen, including cinema's first ever inter-racial kiss (between Dandridge and Jurgens).[54] What seemingly bothered the critical reviewers of the time is Dandridge's presence – an embodiment of the very vexed issue of miscegenation which brings in its wake the equally vexed question of where does she, and indeed Aiché, belong? In the 1950s, Dandridge did not sit well in either world. Although totally apolitical, Dandridge had spoken at NAACP meetings. She also always stated that her purpose was to help Black people, especially children, wherever she could.[55] As a result of these commitments, her manager Earl Mills tells us, she 'had to account for many of her activities in Hollywood as she was one of the many artists suspected of being involved in what the House of UnAmerican Activities believed to be "Communist fronts".[56] In a lot of respects, however, she never was allowed to belong. She was shunned by African-Americans because she got involved with white men; equally, she was shunned by the white community, who saw her as Black in a segregated America.[57] In the racially-disharmonious 1950s, Hollywood film-makers could not seem to create a suitable role for the light-skinned Dandridge, and they soon reverted to subtly-prejudiced visions of inter-racial romance.[58]

Thus, *Tamango* became her vehicle for addressing this issue of belonging head on. She, like Aiché, had to confront her 'bi-racialism'.[59] The numerous triangulations, not so readily present in the short story, are crucial to an understanding of this process of awareness. Whilst they are all interlinked, Aiché is at the centre of them all as the following figure illustrates (see figure 10.2):

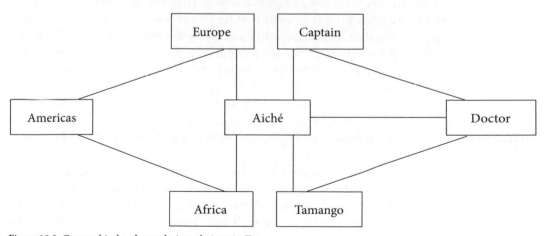

Figure 10.2: Geographical and sexual triangulations in *Tamango*.

The left-hand side clearly defines the Atlantic triangle of slave-trafficking that both Gilroy and Miller discuss in their excellent studies.[60] It also points to the consequences of this triangle via the personages who represent these continents: the Captain and the doctor stand for old Europe and its trading practices; Tamango represents Africa, the exploited continent, whose resources are drained for the profit of others; and Aiché, the new Americas, the continent where slaves were delivered – many of whom fell victim to miscegenation (via rape from their white owners, as is the case for Aiché).

Insofar as all three men are constrained by their desire or, as in the case of Tamango, contempt, to look at Aiché, they are as much in a triangle with each other as they are with the young woman. In some ways they reflect an interesting scopophilic drive that is as much based in race as it is in sex. Driven as they are by visual pleasure or unpleasure, all three seek to fix Aiché in their own fetishizing way, but with differing results. Thus the very white Captain Reinken (which loosely translates as absolute [rein] knowledge [ken]) – who wears white and is very pale skinned with white blond hair – attempts to fix Aiché as his through her body parts: a classic process of fetishization. It is surely instructive that the first we see of her are her hands, then her legs, when she is tending to the Captain's needs in his cabin. She is not fully revealed to us until some thirteen minutes into the film. But this does not occur within the Captain's purview – indeed it is in the presence of the Doctor that she first fully appears. Doctor Corot (Jean Servais) is placed in the triangulations between the very white Captain and very black Tamango. Significantly, he is extremely grey-looking. His clothes are grey; his skin has the grey pallor of a well-used body. Indeed, his is a cynical worldly-wise and world-weary characterization – and whilst he covets Aiché and is jealous of the Captain's hold over her, he cannot hold himself back from confronting her with the truth of her situation: 'You may think you're white inside', he tells her, 'but you're still a slave'. It is in this scene, as if to reinforce the essentializing effect of his words, that we see her framed with a birdcage. The doctor's words perform the fact of fetishism – woman as slave-object – the image does the rest. The doctor is not an original character, so we must ponder why he was written into the film adaptation. It is evident that he acts as some kind of arbiter of racial purity; we see him on the ship measuring and quantifying the physical value of the ethnic other – be it Aiché or the other slaves. He is no contest for the very muscular Captain. But he is cerebral, and endeavours to undermine his boss by playing mind games with Aiché – as if it is all he has left. In essence, he is the collaborator, the man whom circumstances have reduced to selling out. Formerly an officer of distinction under Napoleon, to his eternal shame he finds himself doing lip-service as a doctor and colluding in the most despicable of practices that surely goes against any hyppocratic oath to which he signed up: the trading of human beings.

Finally, Tamango. Our first encounter with him is when the doctor checks him out amongst the other slaves. Fond of labels, it would seem, he also essentializes Tamango by calling him 'a beautiful specimen' – presumably of Black masculinity – thus establishing him as an enslaved object, incorrectly as we shall later learn. When Tamango first meets with Aiché, he is in an even more enslaved position: lying prone on the deck in chains.

Aiché comes to him bearing water – he rejects her offer, calling her 'white man's trash'; she beats him with her fists and explains the inevitability of enslavement (accept or be hanged); he then spits at her and she finally moves away. In short, even from a tied down position, Tamango can both resist the oppression of his chains and assert his own masculinity; simultaneously, he can deliver his verdict in terms of his perception of Aiché. All three men assert Aiché's status as slave. The Captain 'owns' her, as he puts it, and can humiliate her into obedience – possessing her body. The doctor cannot possess her body but he can endeavour to humiliate her by infiltrating her mind. Tamango seeks nothing from her, but challenges her by holding up a mirror she knows to be true – succumb to the white man and you are less than nothing (trash). In the end it is that perception that leads her to her own awareness and consciousness that she too can resist, not through individual acts of aggression (hitting the men), but through a collective refusal to accept the humiliating subjugation of white supremacists.

We now understand better the significance, near the end of the film, of the shot of Dandridge/Aiché standing at the bottom of the ladder that leads from the hold (where all the slaves have congregated in mass defiance) to the deck, where she could rejoin her white master. To do the latter would be to reaffirm the superiority of the white man's power over the Black man and woman. To remain below is to eventually commit and join the struggle for racial equality.[61] Thus the ending is not just about her. Although it is her Rubicon moment, it is also about a willingness to take action, even if all seems lost. For this reason, the way she joins in the singing in the hold, as the slaves en-chant their refusal to submit, testifies to her bodily entry into the collective's corporeal resistance to the white oppressor – the Africans have no weapons other than their bodies, the singing and dancing are their only tools of defiance. If the struggle for racial equality is about creating an environment where race does not matter, perhaps this space of action that Aiché finally occupies is the very one that can be appropriated by a person of so-called mixed-race – a mental and physical space of always already belonging.

Even if the critics were very dismissive of this film, it was nonetheless extremely popular with audiences in France. Some two million spectators went to see it. Certainly, Curd Jurgens was a strong draw. The notoriety surrounding the all-Black cast film *Carmen Jones*, starring Dorothy Dandrige, was another – and this is not just in reference to the daring nature of the film but also due to the fact that, by 1958, because of copyright technicalities, the film had still not been released in France, although it had opened the 1958 Cannes Film Festival.[62] It was also at Cannes that Dandridge's affair with Otto Preminger became public knowledge. Thus Dandridge was both known and not known – known of, but not yet seen on screen. Finally, the remoteness of the story in relation to France – as expressed in the disclaimer at the beginning of the film – made it possible, arguably, to read this film as referring more readily to race relations elsewhere and not to France's current struggles with its own colonial wars.

I close this chapter with two contrasting posters for the film *Tamango* (figures 10.3 and 10.4). The first is for the French release and shows the nature of the race relations quite

Figure 10.3: Poster for French release of *Tamango*. © Rinaldo Gèleng.

Figure 10.4: Polish poster for *Tamango*.[63] © Victor Gorka.

clearly. The second poster is for a Polish release of the film during the Communist era, when anything exposing the brutality of the Americans to the Blacks was a source of propaganda. Here the image speaks to the heroic Black body, suggesting a message of Black solidarity.

Notes

1. Brogan (1989, p. 15).
2. *Chambre introuvable* so-called either because it was not representative of the people (and so cannot be found in this pretence of a constitutional monarchy) or because the king could not have wished for a majority more favourable to his throne than this one.
3. I have only managed to see a 1933 version of this interesting film by Roger Richebé – so I am aware of the narrative but not of the precise version that Alden-Delos created, which so far remains impossible to find.
4. Marseille (2002, p. 90).
5. We must recall that, after Waterloo, the invading armies stayed in France as armies of occupation (Brogan, op. cit., p. 18).
6. Ibid., p. 23.
7. Ibid., p. 28.

8. Marseille, op. cit., p. 94.
9. Followed later by the annexation of Tunisia (1881) and Morocco (1911).
10. Marseille, op. cit., p. 94.
11. Brogan, op. cit., p. 36.
12. Marseille, op. cit., p. 94.
13. Brogan, op. cit., p. 16.
14. These were introduced in 1828, and known as the *pantaloon garance* (because of the bright red). Interestingly garance refers not only to a specific red colour it was also a girl's name that came about during the Revolutionary period.
15. See Brogan, op. cit., p. 51.
16. For a full account of this July Monarchy consult http://fr.wikipedia.or/wiki/Monarchie_de_juillet.
17. Sourced on http://fr.wikipedia.or/wiki/Monarchie_de_juillet accessed 01.03.2009.
18. *L'Extinction du paupérisme*, written by Louis Napoleon in 1844 (Marseille, op. cit., p. 135).
19. Alexandre Parent-Duchâtelet (1981) *La Prostitution à Paris au XIXe siècle* (reprinted by Editions du Seuil, Paris, with a preface by Alain Corbin). All statistics come from this publication (see especially page 75ff).
20. Ibid., p. 75.
21. Ibid., pp. 83–6.
22. Ibid., p. 91.
23. Ibid., p. 102.
24. Brogan, op. cit., pp. 88–9.
25. Griffe (2009, pp. 18-9).
26. Brogan, op. cit., p. 81.
27. Walter Benjamin supplies us with these details in *Paris, Capitale du XIXe siècle*, Paris, Editions Allia, 2004, pp. 25-9.
28. See Hahn's very interesting article on fashion discourses of the July Monarchy (2005, pp. 205–27).
29. Also known after 1804 as the Café Tortoni de Paris (named after its owner Guiseppe Tortoni). It was a rendezvous of the arts world and is often cited in nineteenth-century literature. Balzac in his *Comédie humaine* series; Stendhal mentions the upstairs billiard room in his novel *Le Rouge et le noir*.
30. This house is sadly no longer in existence. Haussmann pulled it down in 1857 to make way for his city plans for Paris.
31. Brogan, op. cit., pp. 79–82.
32. For these titbits of information I consulted the very illuminating website *Savoir-Vivre ou Mourir* on dandyism. There I found some instructive articles on Milord Arsouille *aka* Lord Seymour and Charles de la Battut. http://francois.darbonneau.free.fr/index2.html accessed 11.05.2009.
33. Perrot (1999a: 87).
34. Ibid., p. 86.
35. Perrot (1999b: 93).
36. Ibid., pp. 96-8.
37. Ibid., pp. 93-8.
38. It is noteworthy, for example, that even as most prostitutes had to inhabit the poorer quarters of Paris, nonetheless, in terms of the place of birth of those born in Paris, there is a fairly even distribution across all arrondissements (with slightly higher numbers in the 5th, 6th, 8th and 12th) which gives evidence to this process of pushing the marginal social body to the limits of the city (in particular the 12th arrondissement – the Bastille-Marais area). According to Parent-Duchâtelet's findings, 50% of all prostitutes born in Paris come from the 5th, 6th, 8th and 12th

arrondissements (Parent-Duchâtelet, op. cit., pp. 88–9). The greatest number of illegitimate births, one quarter, can be located in the 12th (the poorest of all the arrondissements). At this time there were only twelve arrondissements – later to be encircled by Louis-Philippe/Thiers' fortifications. A common joke, running until the expansion of the city in 1860 to twenty arrondissements, was 'I got married in the 13th arrondissement' meant the person was co-habiting (unmarried).

39. Perrot (1999a, p. 92).

40. See Pierre Murat (1988, p. 40); Ross (1995).

41. Cressan was a medical student; this was the only film role he played.

42. In 1947, HUAC began investigating the film industry and called various film personnel to their hearings to testify. The ten who took a bold stand and refused were: Alvah Bessie (screenwriter); Herbert J Biberman (screenwriter and director); Lester Cole (screenwriter); Edward Dmytryk (director, who a little later did name names); Ring Lardner (screenwriter); John Howard Lawson (screenwriter); Samuel Ornitz (screenwriter); Adrian Scott (screenwriter and producer); Dalton Trumbo (screenwriter).

43. See the webpage detailing Berry's work with the South African anti-apartheid playwright 'John Berry (Director) and Athol Fugard (Playwright)' http://spot.pcc.edu/~mdembrow/berryfugard. htm accessed 22.06.2009.

44. By the early 1960s the tight hold of the Hayes Code was lessening, finally abolished in 1967.

45. See Christopher L Miller's fascinating account of this film (2008, pp. 179–245). Miller provides details of its US release (p. 224).

46. Ibid., p. 238.

47. http://fr.wikipedia.org/wiki/Abolition_de_l'esclavage accessed 23.06.2009.

48. Miller, op. cit., p. 227.

49. Ibid., p. 226.

50. Ibid.

51. Review '*Tamango*', *Monthly Film Bulletin*, Vol. 27, No. 313, 1960, p. 22 (no name given, just initials P.J.D.).

52. 'Aiche menu', Review of *Tamango*, *Cahiers du cinéma*, Vol. 14, No. 80, 1.2.1958, p. 61 (no name given, just initials E.L.).

53. Richard Nason, Movie review for '*Tamango* (1958)', *New York Times*, September 17, 1959 (no page given).

54. http://www.jeffandcorey.com/ELIG-movies/index.htm accessed 23.06.2009.

55. Mills (1998, p. 117)

56. Ibid., (p. 121) and see also for details of questions she had to answer (pp. 117–20).

57. http://home.hiwaay.net/~oliver/ddstardom.html accessed 23.06.2009.

58. http://www.zimbio.com/Dorothy+Dandridge/articles/2/Dorothy+Dandridge+Biography accessed 23.06.09.

59. Miller op. cit., p. 234.

60. Miller (2008); Gilroy (1993).

61. See Miller, op. cit., p. 236.

62. See http://en.wikipedia.org/wiki/Carmen_Jones accessed 5.08.2009. The film was banned from continental Europe for nearly forty years as a result of a lawsuit brought by the inheritors of the composer Bizet's estate because they had received no copyright fees for the music in the film. In the end it was only in France that it was not screened. This information comes from http://fr.wikipedia.org/wiki/Carmen_Jones accessed 5.08.2009.

Chapter 11

Epic Grandeur: Part One, Philanthropists

The Generosity of humankind: *Les Misérables* (Le Chanois, 1958)

Hugo's monumental oeuvre *Les Misérables* spans just over a decade of the Restoration and July Monarchy periods (1821–1832). In Le Chanois' adaptation to screen, the novel is split into two parts. Part one covers a nine year period, 1821–1830 – most of which is set outside Paris and in which Hugo's broad sketch of the rural poor, the effects of industrialization on the working classes, the brutality of the ruling classes and the judiciary that upholds their value system, gets played out. Part two brings the central protagonists into Paris and is focused around the revolutionary moment of 1832, a period in French history that has been much overlooked but which saw a spontaneous uprising against the July Monarchy for promises not kept, a systematic violation of civil liberties and a lack of consideration for the poor. True to the novel, the film pitches the forces of good and evil against each other; humanity versus greed and ambition; fluidity and openness versus rigidity and conformity; love versus ruthless repression whatever its form, legal or political; instruction versus ignorance. It advocates a new, more equal class system to replace hierarchical powers based in privilege alone. The strength of Hugo's novel and the film is their expression of humanity. Le Chanois' film, as readily as Hugo's novel, shows that morality or goodness is not just the province of the bourgeoisie or the church – the poor and the atheist can also be good. Similarly, venality cuts across all classes. People can have changes of heart: the bad can come good. Once again, this premise cuts across class. In short, class is represented as more complex than a simple equation of the poor versus the rich, the unruly mob versus the morally-upstanding bourgeoisie. As will become clear in the analysis that follows, whilst 1950s' audiences might take solace from viewing this narrative of unrelenting pathos – basking in the knowledge that contemporary France was a cleaner, less poverty-ridden society – they would have also found uncomfortable echoes of their own times, in particular the countless examples of travesties of justice and the images of civil unrest pointing (in their case) to the fragility of the Republican ideal.

Contexts

During the mid-1840s, Hugo, struck by the terrible conditions in which the urban and rural poor found themselves, began writing the novel that was later to become known as *Les Misérables*. By the time he completed and published the five volumes, in 1862, Hugo was already in self-imposed exile in Guernsey. Originally a man with Royalist sympathies, he had upheld the Restoration (and in particular Charles X), only to discover sometime later his Republican leanings, as a result of the July 1832 insurrection described above. Elected to parliament during the Second Republic, he first supported Louis Napoleon's return and rise as President of the people of France (elected as he was by universal suffrage). However, when, in 1851, Louis Napoleon elevated himself to Emperor in a bloodless coup, Hugo was incensed at the immorality of this seizure of power and left France, to return twenty years later – an old man of 69. Thus the text that is adapted to screen in 1958 is one that is embedded in two separate moments of writing, which itself refers further back to the period 1815–1832. The novel is book-ended by two very important historical events: the battle of Waterloo, which marked Hugo for life – both as a tragic bloodbath and an end to Napoleon I whom he admired; and the Paris uprising of July 1832 (*Les Trois Glorieuses*) – which Hugo claimed was at the heart of the novel, partly one suspects because all the central characters are brought together in this moment and show their true colours (good and bad), partly because, in relation to his own professed politics, it was a spontaneous revolt of the people against the forces of repression.

It is important to remember that Hugo was not a radical. Rather he was a middle-of-the-road politician who believed in respecting constitutional law and the legitimate systems of governance it produced, as long as there was no abuse of power. More Republican in his beliefs than Royalist, he nonetheless did not always support popular uprisings, as in the case of the Revolution of 1848 or the Paris Commune of 1871. Almost despite himself, he became a deputy in the Second Republic, where some of his positions mark him out as a reformer (on education and universal suffrage for example). Whilst he deplored social inequality and the plight of the poor, and was a strong advocate of education as a means out of the poverty trap, he remained a politician of a hue more conservative than liberal. He believed in wealth creation but felt the rich should plough their profits back into production to create jobs. A way of measuring his positioning can be explained, perhaps, by these two contrasting standpoints in relation to abolitionism: he was against the death penalty but, where colonialism and slavery were concerned, he believed in France's 'civilizing' mission (we should recall that slavery was abolished in 1848).

Given Hugo's conservative political stance, it is intriguing that the director adapting his novel to screen should be Jean-Paul Le Chanois, a true man of the Left. As we shall see, however, he remains remarkably faithful to the original text. Le Chanois was a member of the French Communist Party, an active trade-unionist in the film industry, and a member of the French Resistance during the war. He was also a Jew who was obliged to change his name (Dreyfus) during the Occupation so as to avoid arrest and deportation. Extraordinarily, he managed to continue working during this period and, moreover, for the Paris-based German film-production company, Continental. His film, *Les Misérables*, is itself something of an intriguing paradox, or anomaly. It is one of only four costume dramas in our corpus to have been co-produced with a communist country. *Les Misérables* and two others were made with East Germany's studios DEFA, Gérard Philipe's *Les Aventures de Till L'Espiègle* (1956) and

Raymond Rouleau's *Les Sorcières de Salem* (1957); the other, Louis Daquin's ill-fated *Bel-Ami* with Projektograph Film in former Soviet-occupied Vienna (1954, see Chapter 17).[1]

Le Chanois had considerable means to make his film. Shooting alone took him seven months (1 April–25 October 1957). East Germany (DEFA) was a major co-financer (putting up 2.9 million marks) along with France (Pathé); Italy (Serena films) was a minor third party. Indeed, this film – as with the other DEFA-French co-productions – was part of a prestige building exercise by the East German cultural authorities.[2] As Marc Silberman tells us, for the French they represented 'first and foremost an economic opportunity…to produce a big-budget look on the cheap'.[3] But this was not the only interesting aspect of the exchange. The film was shot in the super-American system of Technicolor and in Technicolor's own 'scope format Technirama,[4] which is quite remarkable, if we remind ourselves that this represents the top-end of capitalist technology being taken, along with Technicolor supervisors, to the communist-based German DEFA Babelsberg studios in Berlin, where the film was mostly shot. Only the exterior sequences of Toulon, Dignes, the Luxembourg gardens, and the quays of the Seine were shot in France.[5] Daquin's own colour film *Bel-Ami* – admittedly made four years earlier when the Cold War was at an extreme – was made in East German Agfacolor, thus keeping everything within the communist bloc. Here, with Le Chanois, West comes East, and two opposing ideologies endeavour to sink their differences, at least in the realm of film-making!

Thousands of soldiers of the GDR army were used as the extras for the battle of Waterloo and the July 1832 sequences – namely, the street procession followed by the actual insurrection and barricade skirmishes. Authenticity takes on a new meaning, if we consider the stand-up battles between the revolutionaries and the *Garde Nationale* /national guard in the street uprisings, wherein the latter (played by the GDR soldiers) eventually overpowers the insurrectionists. The brutal *fusillade immédiate*/immediate execution of their leader Enjolras without trial does not sit easy if we allow ourselves to consider the show-trials that various communist bloc countries had recently conducted.[6] The film, after all, was shot in 1957, beginning just six months after the quelling of the Hungarian Revolution (October 1956). The repression of this Hungarian uprising led many French communists and sympathisers to question their allegiance (including actors such as Gérard Philipe). Certainly, the lack of justice implicit in the summary executions explains why Enjolras takes such a long time to fall under the hail of bullets and may well be an indirect comment on repressive measures elsewhere. His miserable death, stood up as he is against the filthy wall of the revolutionaries' quarters, is injected with powerful dignity.

The Text: Synopsis of Le Chanois' *Les Misérables*

Three major themes run through the narrative of this film: law, love and class. The first and the last function as a disciplining, institutionalized form of oppression to be overcome by the central theme of love: love for others; for the poor and discriminated against; love of the concept of freedom and democracy. The film reveals how social engineering, implicit in the practice of the judiciary at the service of class, works to discipline the central precept of love – that unmeasured part of the social subject for which several characters are prepared to die (Eponine, Gavroche, Marbeuf, Enjolras in fact and Marius and Valjean in spirit). The only other man to die, Javert, the upholder of the law, commits suicide precisely because he cannot control or understand that central precept of love. As such, because it challenges the oppression of institutions and measures the greatness of individual acts of humanity, we can see what a radical text we have before us – one which needs this rather lengthy synopsis to make these points clear.

The year is 1821; Jean Valjean (Jean Gabin) is set free after 19 years in prison, in the Bagne de Toulon,[7] for the small crime of stealing bread when he was hungry. When in prison, we see how he is brutalized by the system – primarily in the form of the prison governor Javert (Bernard Blier). But we also see how he manages to maintain some vestiges of humanity for others: he runs to the rescue of a fellow inmate trapped under some rocks in the quarry – an act of 'sedition' for which he is given a further three years. This act of solidarity is an invention of Le Chanois (in the novel Valjean's feat of prowess involves shoring up part of Toulon's town hall). Thus we are predisposed from the start of the film to see him as better than his captors, and as a working-class hero. Hugo's intention, somewhat different, was to show us a man defiled by prison and incapable of any altruism. Indeed, as we see, the prison and judicial system is so perverse that even once a free man, he is still effectively a prisoner in all but name. On the day he leaves, a portion of his earned pay is deducted for tax and other concocted purposes: the state cheats him of his fair due. He is given a yellow passport that must be stamped at the gendarmerie in every town he travels through.[8] This visa-control effectively disbars him from getting any work – possible employers take one look at his papers and see an ex-convict, not a man willing to work. He arrives in Dignes, some 200 kilometres north of Toulon. There, he is taken in by a kindly priest, Monseigneur Myriel (Fernand Ledoux), who treats him as a man. Myriel leads an exemplary life of self-abnegation, giving over all his worldly goods to the poor – except for his family silver, which Valjean steals.

Until now Valjean has full evidence that institutional systems and society in general are against him. The priest, however, gives him his first break by refusing to prosecute him. He lets him keep the silver and sends him on his way with these words: 'Give up on evil-ways and turn to the good, it's your soul I am buying'. Valjean commits one further bad deed that he immediately regrets (stealing a young chimney-sweep's money), at which point, we surmise, he has crossed his Rubicon. Henceforth, he leads a life of probity and benevolence. Several years pass. Valjean, now known as M. Madeleine, becomes a wealthy factory owner in Montreuil-sur-mer (in the Pas-de-Calais region). He is the local benefactor, providing free hospitals, schools, pharmacies, and so on, for the poor. For this he is elected mayor. Two major events conspire, however, to turn his quiet, unassuming life on its head. First, Fantine (Danièle Delorme), a single mother forced into prostitution, is arrested under his nose for affray and soliciting by a police inspector whom, it transpires, is Javert's son (also played by Blier). Fantine was, in fact, being tormented by some young upper-class wastrels who pushed snow down her cleavage. As mayor, Valjean has power over Javert and demands Fantine be set free. 'You'd choose a prostitute over a bourgeois' exclaims Javert, 'they are scum, they respect nothing.' Valjean's response is to put Fantine in hospital, not to judge her. He is also horrified to learn that he is indirectly responsible for her destitution – she formerly worked at his factory and when it became known that she was a single mother, the foreman fired her.

In hospital, Fantine is dying of tuberculosis and is desperate to see her daughter (Cosette) whom, five years previously, she had put into foster care with the Thénardier family in Montfermeil (due east outside Paris). Valjean promises to help but, before he can do so, he is jolted into a crisis of conscience by the stiffly-upright man of the law, Javert, who is angered by Valjean's undermining of him over Fantine. As with his father, Javert judges Valjean's acts of humanity as indiscipline. Javert takes his revenge when he realizes Valjean's true identity by denouncing him. He then informs Valjean that another man has been arrested instead, in a case of mistaken identity. Valjean struggles with his conscience (well-represented on screen as a sea-storm in his head), but in the end goes to Arras to give himself up. However, he is also driven by his promise to Fantine and so makes his escape and heads off to Montfermeil to find the 8-year-old Cosette (Martine Havet). She has been cruelly exploited and abused by the grasping Thénardier (Bourvil), whose cupidity is as much responsible for Fantine's fatal illness (bleeding her dry of all she earned) as is Valjean's factory foreman.

Valjean and Cosette take off to Paris. At first they hide away in the Petit-Picpus convent (in the 12th arrondissement), where Valjean becomes their gardener and Cosette obtains an education; later they move to a house on rue Plumet (now rue Oudinot, in the 7th arrondissement). At this point we learn of another gardener, colonel de Pontmercy (Jean Murat). He was badly wounded at Waterloo; enobled for his courage by Napoleon; deprived of his only son (Marius) by his father-in-law, Gillenormand (Lucien Barroux), an Ultra-Royalist recently returned from exile; relieved of his riches by the scavenging Thénardier, who happened to come across him, wounded on the battlefields of Waterloo. Pontmercy is dying; he sends for his son. When Marius (Giani Esposito) realizes what a great and good man his father was, he takes his name and title (as his father wished), rejects his grandfather and goes to live in a hovel in the 13th arrondissement, near the Place d'Italie (on a road now known as rue de l'Hôpital). The first part of this epic draws to a close with adult Cosette (Béatrice Altariba) and Valjean walking in the Luxembourg Gardens. They cross paths with Marius who clearly takes a shine to Cosette. Valjean quickly puts a stop to these walks. Marius returns each day in hope. We are in 1830. Part one ends with young men running into the Gardens waving tricolore flags and calling out: 'A bas Louis-Philippe'. We assume they are part of the revolutionary group seeking the return of the Republic.

Instead, as the opening of part two informs us, the 'Revolution of 1830 did not bring in the Republic but Louis-Philippe'. However, there is unrest afoot and we are now in 1832. The radical ABC group,[9] led by Enjolras (Serge Reggiani) and frequented by Marius, meets up in the café Musain in the Latin Quarter, plotting the revolution. General Lamarque's funeral proves the perfect opportunity to launch an impromptu insurrection. The group assail the horse-drawn hearse, grab it and pull it forwards crying out 'to the Panthéon' (the mausoleum for great men of the nation and, in particular, Republican heroes). This sets Paris alight with Republican fervour; a general call 'to the barricades' is issued. Enjolras and his men take off to their designated headquarters at the cabaret de Corinthe in the Halles, rue St Denis area where they set up barricades across the street. During all of this, the police inspector, Javert, infiltrated the group but was soon denounced and taken prisoner. Meantime, Valjean has been instrumental in saving Eponine (Silvia Montfort), Thénardier's oldest daughter, from arrest for stealing bread (in a similar fashion to the way he saved Fantine in part one). Valjean and Cosette take her home to the Thénardiers, who, once again on their downers, have moved into the room next door to Marius. Unsurprisingly, Thénardier recognizes Valjean and sets about a plan to fleece him of his money. The trap backfires, Valjean escapes.

Valjean prepares to leave with Cosette for England. In the interim, while he waits for passports, he moves them both to apartments on the rue de l'Homme-armé (now part of rue des Archives in the 4th arrondissement). This move means that Cosette, who had managed to meet up with Marius in the gardens of the rue Plumet (where they declared their love for each other), has to leave a message for Marius as to her whereabouts. Eponine, who is secretly in love with Marius (he fails to notice this), intercepts the letter. A despairing Marius, believing Cosette has left for England, throws himself into the insurrection, not caring if he dies. Eponine goes with him and saves his life by taking a bullet fired at him on the rue St-Denis barricades. As she lies dying in his arms, Eponine confesses and hands Marius the note. Alerted of the new address, Marius sends a letter to Cosette, using Eponine's brother, Gavroche (Lucien Urbain), as his messenger. Valjean intercepts the letter and decides to go to the barricades and talk man-to-man with Marius. There, Valjean is entrusted with dealing justice out to Javert. He sets him free. But now Gavroche is shot dead on the barricades and Marius wounded. Valjean helps Marius escape by dragging him through the Paris sewers down to the Seine exit. Before he gets there he bumps into the snake Thénardier who again recognizes Valjean and believes he has murdered Marius. He blackmails Valjean but gives him the key to the sewers' gate. There, Javert stands in readiness to arrest escaping revolutionaries. Instead of taking the two men prisoner, as soon as he learns of Marius' noble parentage, he once again bows to the importance of the upper classes and assists Valjean in taking him home to his grandfather's house on rue des Filles du Calvaire (3rd arrondissement). Valjean gives Javert his new address so he can be arrested. Javert asks why he set him free; 'because I pity you', comes the humiliating reply. In the next scene we see Javert handcuffing himself and throwing himself into the Seine. Indeed, poor fellow, his lack of humanity, his rule-boundedness, his servility to the bourgeoisie, his inability to see true injustice, in the form of oppression of the poor, has meant that he is incapable of understanding Valjean – the man he continually fails to apprehend/seize/arrest. In the end, his lack of compassion for others drives him to suicide. He dies handcuffed to his own law.

Part two draws to a close. Back at the barricades, Enjolras and his men are defeated. Enjolras is executed on the spot alongside his friend Grantaire (Marc Eyraud). Valjean consents to Cosette's marriage to Marius. He fills Marius in on his past and asks if, even though a convict who has broken his parole, he may continue to see Cosette from time to time. Marius, believing he is a bounder and a bad man, says no. In the final sequences we see a lonely old man slowly dying from a broken heart. However, thanks to Thénardier's beastly attempt to screw some money out of Marius by accusing Valjean of being a murderer, Marius finally discovers who his rescuer was and realizes in a flash what a good man Valjean is. He runs with Cosette to Valjean's apartment, they make their peace. Cosette again affirms her love for him as her true father. Valjean dies.

Le Chanois' direction – authentic rendition and mass spectacle

Le Chanois referred to this film 'on human generosity as my life-time career achievement'.[10] The huge public response certainly appears to endorse this view. However, critical reviews were very mixed – and some, especially *Image et Son*, were particularly vehement in their denunciation of the film.[11] The journal's reviewer, writing in April 1958, argues that *Les Misérables* is not a good mass spectacle (some 10 million spectators would disagree) and that it remains condescending to popular audiences to claim, as some critics do, that it is. Popular audiences deserve better, the reviewer continues, even in the name of education.[12] There is no evidence to suggest that Le Chanois ever intended his film to be part of the nation-building education of the masses in which the French government might have been interested. In the article's view, the film is terribly slow; the actors poorly directed; Blier (as Javert) is wooden; we do not get a feel for Valjean; and the décor is disconcertingly inaccurate, especially in relation to the Paris sets; even worse, certain sets are recycled (though barely noticeable, this is true on merely two counts).[13] Given that in the same issue of *Image et Son*, the reviewer was so favourable to Daquin's *Bel-Ami* – a film made under a similar funding aegis[14] to Le Chanois' and with a stronger political thrust, to boot – it is not possible to argue that the dismissive tone of the review is motivated by a mood of anti-communism, nor indeed pro-Republicanism. Moreover, Le Chanois had made it clear to the East German authorities, before shooting began, that his adaptation would remain faithful to the spirit of Hugo's novel – thus there would be no reduction of the narrative to the simple equation of the oppressed masses by the bourgeoisie.[15]

The problem for the reviewer appears to lie with the product itself. So let us consider the validity of these criticisms. What we do know is that the producers insisted on cutting the film down to three hours from its original length (close to four and a half hours),[16] much to Le Chanois' regret – and that the cut footage is permanently lost.[17] Even if occasional voice-overs attempt to fill in the gaps, this severe cutting has made some linkages between sequences feel elliptical, especially in part one, and the film difficult to follow at times – particularly if, as a spectator, you neither know the original text nor the historical context.

But, in general, the episodic nature of the film works to retain the epic stature of the Hugo five-tome novel.

The film's pacing is a mixture of slow and fast. The film is episodic much like the novel, although it follows a more chronological development than the novel, which has episodes running in parallel. Part one falls into three main sections (as in figure 11.1 below):

1. Valjean's period in prison and brief sojourn in Dignes (23 minutes);
2. His life as mayor in Montreuil-sur-mer (32 minutes);
3. His various escapes from arrest by Javert and going to live in Paris (20 minutes).

Figure 11.1: The three sections of part one of *Les Misérables*.

The first and third sections are reasonably paced, including some very fast scenes in section three, when Valjean escapes arrest and takes Cosette with him. The camera follows him as he darts about the warren that is Thénardier's inn, *Le Sergeant de Waterloo*. Editing is extremely fast. The middle section is indeed slow, however: a lot of information has to be inserted. But it is enlivened by Fantine's arrival and the ensuing drama that it causes. This section also includes the first of the film's two flashbacks. This one, seen from Fantine's point of view, shows her delivering Cosette into the care of the greed-driven Thénardier household. The second flashback, set in the aftermath of the battle of Waterloo, is told from the narrator's point of view and occurs in the third section. This time it fills us in on Marius' father (Pontmercy) and gives us further evidence of Thénardier's venality. Part two of the film provides a similar mixture of pace, paralleling as it does the love story (Marius and Cosette) with the July 1832 uprising. Once again, the love narrative between Cosette and Marius and Eponine's infatuation with Marius does slow the film down considerably. But the sequences dealing with the insurrection and fighting at the barricades, predictably, move the film on at a much faster pace.

The more fascinating point to be made about casting and directing, in my view, is Bourvil as Thénardier. He hesitated a long time before accepting the part because he feared the role might damage his image as a genial comedian.[18] Yet, who better to embody the sly, grasping, spineless Thénardier than Bourvil? His crackly vocal chords can emit the pitiful sounds he uses to persuade others he is in more need than they, just as easily as they can imitate the sound of a weasel on the make. His body, spindly and hunched, seems ready to pounce on the slightest chance to make money; his greasy hair adding the final touch to this portrait of utter venality. It was a brave decision to cast against type, braver still to accept it. Yet perhaps a wise one, since it seems to have set him free to take on more interesting, ambiguous roles as a cheapskate (*Miroir à deux faces*, Cayatte, 1958), grasping coward (*Sérénade au Texas*, Pottier, 1958) and spiteful avenger (*La Jument verte*, Autant-Lara, 1959).[19]

The accusation of inaccuracies where the décor is concerned is an interesting one, given Hugo's own concern to get the sense of place right. Whilst writing the novel in exile, he frequently wrote to friends to ensure that his depictions were correct and to modify them if they were not. In truth, by the 1860s, the Paris of the July Monarchy had greatly changed. Several of the locales described by Hugo had made way for Haussmannization. But even under Louis-Philippe changes were wrought, in particular, to the Halles-rue St-Denis area where the stand-off took place between the National Guard and the insurgents led by Enjolras. For example, as a result of the July 1832 uprising, in 1839, the rue Rambuteau was the first major road to be pierced through the medieval centre of the 1st and 4th arrondissements.[20] However, to return to this question of precision, a comparison between Hugo's description of the barricades and Serge Pimenoff's sets reveals a remarkable correspondence. As, indeed, there is for the interior of the cabaret de Corinthe, located at the corner of rue Mondétour and de la Petite-Truanderie where the barricades were elevated and where the insurgents assembled their wounded. The narrowing-down of the road between Petite-Truanderie and Chanvrerie (now replaced by Rambuteau) towards Mondétour, as described by Hugo, is perfectly re-created.[21] This allowed the insurgents to put their barricades in place, thus creating a kind of cul-de-sac which the National Guard would have to go down if they were to launch an attack, making them effectively sitting ducks until the insurgents' ammunition ran out. The dilapidated nature of the buildings (often in such disrepair the beams are exposed) authentically replicates this area of the Halles – then known as the *section des Marchés* – with its long-standing reputation as a place of revolutionary dissidence. Small wonder Louis-Philippe and later Haussmann ran huge boulevards through it.

The cabaret de Corinthe has the two floors mentioned in the novel, linked by a spiral staircase with a billiard table on the first floor. This is where the triumphant National Guard line up Enjolras and execute him. The smart establishments in Paris where Valjean lives (rue Plumet and rue de l'Homme-armé) are also faithfully reproduced. The place he rents on Plumet (now rue Oudinot in the 7th arrondissement) is based on a house from the turn of the seventeenth century, built in the style of the architect Mansart.[22] The interiors are, therefore, not of the Restoration or July Monarchy but the earlier period – hence the wood-panelled dining room and pastel-coloured, Watteau-like wall furnishings of the salon. The house and the garden outside, as described by Hugo, are also faithfully reproduced by Pimenoff. Finally, the funeral procession for General Lamarque, which led to the insurrection, remains visually true both to the real events and to those described by Hugo.[23] We note, dotted along the mourners path, an occasional red flag along with the tricolore: the latter representing the desire for a return of the Republic. The red flag, a sign of the martyrs' blood but also of revolution, is considerably more present in Hugo's novel than would in fact have been the case – its presence in the film is noticeable, but not as extensive (see figure 11.2 below). Hugo uses the red flag in his narrative as the cause and turning point for the mourners to call out for Lamarque to be taken to the Pantheon. A man rides by on horseback, brandishing the red flag – the mood of the crowd changes immediately and chaos breaks out. In less than an hour some 27 barricades are set up over Paris.[24] In the film, Le Chanois curiously omits this brandishing moment, electing rather to have Enjolras grab the hearse and cry out 'To the Pantheon'. Censorship – or the desire to avoid it – could be a reason for this slight shift. The red flag being emblematic in contemporary audiences' psyche of socialist revolution, the board of censors might have insisted on a cut.[25] Spontaneous uprisings are not an unknown aspect of France's political cultural life at any time. However, in early 1958 (the film was released in March) the political climate over Algeria had reached crisis point. Tensions and feelings ran high amongst the electorate, who were split down the middle over the issue of independence. De Gaulle had yet to come to power and 'resolve' the crisis. Government heads were rolling. By May 1958, France was on the verge of civil war. Le Chanois' toning down the *mise-en-scène* of the revolutionary message can be understood in this light. The red flag does, however, reappear towards the end of the film in a highly symbolic way – draped across the dead bodies of the resisting proletariat (Gavroche, Marbeuf and Eponine, see figure 11.2). Thus, Le Chanois slips it in at a moment of great poignancy – emblematically pointing towards working-class solidarity.

The authentic in Pimenoff's sets, of which there are 28 (including 21 interiors), resides, then, in its reconstruction of Hugo's own reconstruction of Paris. Intriguingly, however, the street sets were criticized by some for being anti-national because they had been recreated 'of

Figure 11.2: Lamarque's funeral parade turns into civil unrest – Le Chanois tones down presence of the red flag. © Pathé Consortium Cinema.

all places in studios outside Berlin'.[26] Le Chanois refuted this allegation, stating that shooting in the Berlin studios 'was a purely economic decision' that in no way compromised the film's Frenchness.[27]

The hundreds of costumes, like the sets, were a huge undertaking. Escoffier worked with Frédéric Junker and was assisted by Jacqueline Guyot and Louise Schmidt. These costumes cover the gamut of the rich and the poor over a 20-year period: men and women; uniforms of the soldiers at the battle of Waterloo and those of the National Guard. Here, reference would have been made less to Hugo (who describes clothing in far less detail than the environs) and more to the fashion magazines of the time, and painters, especially Ingres, whose portrait of Monsieur Bertin is a dead ringer for Valjean in his bourgeois outfits. Always true to his class, however, we also note that Valjean happily wears the peasant-worker smock when on the run, gardener's clothes when in hiding at the Petit-Picpus convent, and, as he is dying, he exacts from Marius the promise that he will be given a pauper's funeral (as befits his status). The Romantic vein is readily seen in Cosette's outfits. As a young woman she is mostly dressed in white or light-grey silks, signalling her virginal status. She carries a parasol – essential for maintaining a paleness of skin and the apparent frailty so loved by the Romantics. At this juncture, corsets were back in favour (after the freer times of loose-fitting stays under the Revolution and First Empire) and, with it, the *taille de guêpe* – made possible by new technologies in the iron and steel industries (such as eyelets which allowed corset-lacing to be pulled tighter and an inverted triangular steel or iron breastplate which pushed the bosom up high and the lower abdomen squeezed down to some nether regions). Cosette is no exception to this thin-waisted look, adding to her delicate ethereality. The bouffant mutton sleeves, so popular at the time, further enhance her aura of dematerialized being (see figure 11.3 below). As such, Cosette is emblematic of the Romantic image of the ideal woman – no wonder Marius falls helplessly in love with her, and suffers so from her absence. Skirts are flared thanks to numerous linen petticoats reinforced by horsehair[28] (the wire cage-crinoline did not come in until the late 1840s) and worn just above the ankle, allowing for a little flirtatious display of embroidered silk stockings. Thus, in the Luxembourg Gardens, if Marius can only glance furtively at the lovely Cosette's face, he is able to linger longer on her turn of foot – something that does not escape Valjean's protective and jealous attention.

The distinctiveness between Marius and his grandfather's (Gillenormand) attire represents clearly the generational gap and, ultimately, political poles that separate them. Gillenormand wears Louis XVIII attire (even if the monarch has been dead some five years), more reminiscent of the Ancien Régime than the new century: pale blue satin day-coat over white lacy shirt and satin breeches, white stockings and, on his feet, small black pumps. Small wonder Marius yells at him 'Down with the Bourbons and that pig Louis XVIII!' when he takes his leave in revolt against the grandfather's treatment of his father. This is the moment he rejects his previous soft support of the monarchy and becomes a Republican – embracing his father's democratic values over his grandfather's beliefs in the superiority of the aristocracy (one also thinks of Hugo's change of heart in this context). Marius' attire is associated with the modern man of the time: he wears the contemporary redingote with a velvet collar, waistcoat, and trousers

Figure 11.3: Cosette centre in white virginal mutton sleeved dress; Eponine in foreground; Thénardier and Valjean to the right. © Pathé Consortium Cinema.

rather than breeches. Even when at his poorest and his clothes begin to fray, he fairly quickly manages to borrow a decent outfit from a well-heeled friend so he can continue to pursue Cosette. For their part, the insurgents wear an appropriately motley set of clothes: some with workers' smocks, others woollen coats and trousers (even in the summer month of July) – all are dressed in materials that stand up to wear and tear.

The power of an individual to effect change was something Hugo believed in,[29] and this is best exemplified by Valjean. Indeed, it is represented most clearly in Le Chanois' film by his physical act of carrying the weight of (or for) men on his shoulders, which he does three times in the film. But we also witness the kindness to strangers in Cosette; the solidarity of the insurgents fighting for change – most spectacularly in the two friends, Enjolras and Grantaire, holding hands as the National Guard shoot them; the ability of people of all classes to change their ways, be it Gavroche and Eponine's rejection of their father's upbringing as sneaks and thieves, or the snobby elitism of Marius' grandfather who gracefully accepts the cross-class marriage of Marius and Cosette. Le Chanois faithfully transposes this belief in humanity into the film, as, indeed, he does with the concept of the family – so dear to the Restoration period, and Hugo. But he adds a further dimension to this. In the novel as in the film, the concept of family is varied: the working-class elder Thénardiers, whose grasping nature is resisted by their children; Marius' aristocratic grandfather and aunt who brought him up; the father who longs for reunion with his son (Pontmercy). By the end of the novel, Hugo offers us a *familias intactus* – a model family – in the form of Valjean, the recognized patriarch, and Cosette and Marius as the newly married couple going forth to procreate. In the film, Le Chanois replicates this family, the bourgeois family it has to be said, but mirrors it with another, this time emanating from the proletarian struggle and attached to its working-class roots – that of Eponine, Gavroche and Mabeuf, the three slain martyrs of the July 1832 uprising draped over with the red flag. In the film, these three dead bodies are placed next to each other on the billiard table under a banner which reads 'Equality to man and to woman'(see figure 11.4 below – Gavroche is tucked away, we can just make out his head of hair). No such configuration or banner is present in Hugo's novel; in fact, Eponine had tried to die *with* Marius rather than save him. Thus, only Gavroche and Mabeuf lie in state.[30] In Le Chanois' film, however, the trinity of the mother, father and son are aligned as emblematic of the working class – often the unsung heroes of humanity's struggle for equality.

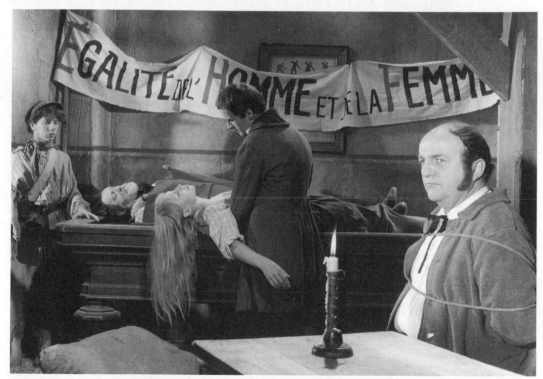

Figure 11.4: 'Equality to man and to woman' – the working-class *familias intactus*: unsung heroes of the struggle for equality. Note Javert (the representative of bourgeois law and order and repression) is tied up in the foreground (right) of this image. © Pathé Consortium Cinema.

Notes

1. Louis Daquin's own contexts as a man of the Left are not dissimilar to Le Chanois (see Chapter 17 for details). For a detailed study of *Les Sorcières de Salem* see Hayward (2004, pp. 110–2). Daquin also went on to make a film with DEFA in 1960, *Les Arrivistes/Muddy Waters*. It is also worth recalling that all four directors were either members of the French Communist Party or sympathetic to the cause (see Marc Silberman, 2006, p. 22).

2. Silberman, op. cit., p. 23. His article on the DEFA-French collaboration of the 1950s provides fascinating insight into the politics of these film co-productions.

3. Ibid., p. 22.

4. The Technirama screen process was first used in 1957, so it is quite possible that this sortie by Technicolor to East Berlin represented an early opportunity to experiment with the new format. The advantage of the Technirama camera was that it created a sharper, less grainy picture than other cinemascope cameras. It achieved this by doubling the normal size of the perforated film frame (from 4 to 8) making a wider image possible – twice the size of normal 'scope cameras.

5. *Film Français*, No. 721, 21.3. 1956, p. 12.

6. Amongst them, Czechoslovakia, Poland, Hungary. It is worth considering that a far more controversial debate at the time of its making and release surrounded Rouleau's *Les Sorcières de Salem* see Hayward (2004, pp. 110–2). In the novel, Enjolras asks to be shot and the national guard soldiers are more kindly towards him.

7. So called because, at the time, prisoners were actually kept on old de-masted galley or slave ships (*bagnes flottantes*/prison ships).

8. It is hard not to see this 'yellow' of the passport as a reference to the 'yellow' of the Jewish star French Jews were obliged to wear during the Occupation. However, because in the original novel the yellow is also commented upon, I leave it for readers to ponder the relevance.

9. The ABC group or 'Amis de l'ABC' was, officially, a group committed to the education of children (hence the ABC). But, in reality, it was a secret society of Republican radicals who met in a backroom of the café Musain in the Latin Quarter.

10. Quoted on http://fr.wikipedia.org/wiki/Les_Misérables_(film,_1958) accessed 21.04.2009. The original quote is sourced on this site as: Extrait de l'essai *Le Temps des cerises*, Editions Institut Lumière/Actes Sud 1996.

11. G. Poix 'Prestige et decadence des *Misérables*', *Image et Son*, No. 111, 1.4.1958, pp. 15–16.

12. Ibid., p.16. And if we review the paucity of great nineteenth-century authors adapted to screen in the 1950s, we recall that they are few and far between (14 titles out of 109 films in total).

13. As far as I can determine, the house façades used for the town of Toulon, through which the prisoners walk at the beginning of the film, are reprised as the town of Dignes (which is odd given that these scenes were shot on location); certainly, the wood-panelled dining room in the apartment on rue Plumet is reprised in the apartment on rue des Filles du Calvaire.

14. It was funded by the Viennese film studios (Projektograph Film) then in the eastern zone occupied by the Soviets. The review is by R. Lefèvre '*Bel Ami*', *Image et Son*, No. 111, 1.4.1958, p. 14.

15. Silberman, op. cit., p. 35.

16. Apparently Le Chanois' original conception was for a 5h 25m film (Silberman,op. cit., p. 36).

17. Details to be found on http://fr.wikipedia.org/wiki/Les_Misérables_(film,_1958) accessed 21.04.2009.

18. Ibid.

19. In *Fil à la patte* (Le Franc, 1955) Bourvil plays a toadying would-be poet. Admittedly though, his role is the trigger for a lot of humour at his expense: a pattern we associate with Bourvil's roles.

20. Thirteen metres in width and 935 metres long, the rue Rambuteau was built in 1839 in reaction to the uprisings but also as a health measure in response to the cholera epidemic of 1832.

21. Very kindly, fr.wikisource.org, have reproduced *Les Misérables* in its entirety. Th is piece of information comes in Tome IV, L12, Chapter I. See: http://fr.wikisource.org/wiki/Les_Misérables_TIV_L12 accessed 19.05.2009.

22. The architect Jules Hardouin-Mansart 1646–1708 was famous for completing the project of Les Invalides.

23. Although, arguably, it is not as dramatically rendered as it is in Raymond Bernard's adaptation of *Les Misérables* (1933).

24. This piece of information about Lamarque's funeral procession and the subsequent insurrection comes in Tome IV, L 10, Chapter III. See: http://fr.wikisource.org/wiki/Les_Misérables_TIV_L10#Chapitre_III._Un_enterrement_:_occasion_de_rena.C3.AEtre accessed 19.05.2009.

25. Not a far-fetched view, if we consider how brutally Daquin's *Bel-Ami* was cut (see Chapter 17). Also, when *Les Misérables* was released in West Germany, the censor cut the revolutionary scenes, electing to highlight instead the sentimental love story (Silberman, op. cit., p. 37).

26. Poix, op. cit., p. 15.

27. Silberman, op. cit., p. 22.

28. These types of petticoats were, of course, deeply unhygienic and probably quite smelly! Some petticoats in the 1830s were given extra rigidity through rings of cord or braid running around the hem. In the 1830s, women started to wear petticoats with hoops of whalebone or willow-cane around the hem. Thus the advent of the cage crinoline – a system of hoops from the waist down – which was a far more hygienic affair.

29. Indeed, Hugo's own life gives several instances of similar acts of humanity – saving his mistress from imprisonment during Napoleon III's coup d'état; giving shelter to Communards in 1871 when he was himself an exile in Belgium (an act for which he was expelled). http://fr.wikisource.org/wiki/Victor_Hugo accessed 24.04.09.

30. See Chapter XVII. http://fr.wikisource.org/wiki/Les_Misérables_TV_L1#Chapitre_XVII_:_Mortuus_pater_filium_moriturum_expectat accessed 26.05.2009.

Chapter 12

Epic Grandeur: Part Two, Avengers

Flawed Heroes and Tales of Vengeance: *Le Rouge et le Noir* (Autant-Lara, 1954) and *Le Comte de Monte-Cristo* (Vernay, 1955)

The novels upon which these two epic films are based, whilst different in tone, nonetheless share a common thread in their attack on the get-rich mentality of the newly-emergent bourgeoisie of the Restoration period and the July Monarchy. *Le Comte de Monte-Cristo* covers the period of Napoleon's 100 Days through to the July Monarchy (1815–1837). *Le Rouge et le Noir* is set around 1830 but in a rather fluid way, since Julien Sorel ages from 18 to 20. As Stendhal puts it, the novel is a 'Chronicle of 1830'. We are in the period of the end months of the brief reign of Charles X, therefore; and, as we learn, the Marquis de la Mole and his friends are plotting the overthrow of the king in favour, one assumes, of the Orleanist Louis-Philippe.

In both these films, as with Valjean in *Les Misérables*, the central hero comes from modest or humble origins. Julien Sorel (Gérard Philipe) in *Le Rouge et le Noir*, whilst educated and able therefore to take up the post of tutor to Monsieur and Madame de Rênal's children, is the son of a carpenter. Dantès (Jean Marais) in *Le Comte de Monte-Cristo* is a merchant seaman who sails the Pharaon alongside two shipmates who become his arch enemies: Danglars, the ship's clerk, and Caderousse, the bosun. Again Dantès is educated and raised through the ranks to captain. But Sorel and Dantès' setbacks in life, as distinct from Valjean's, make them lacking in the humanity that he finds. Bitter about his class origins, Sorel declares war on society. Arguably, his trajectory is one more in his mind than in fact, since he never achieves his goals (unlike Dantès), other perhaps than that of an anti-hero's death on the guillotine. An avid fan of Napoleon, whose memoirs he reads in secret, he reviles the Restoration Monarchy that has reversed the Revolutionary principle that it is merit that counts and not birth (i.e., rank). To his mind, Napoleon embodied this principle. Sorel is determined to use his charm and intellect to rise to the top – he sets about it as if it were a military campaign, but his targets are the women he seduces and the priests whose love for him he manipulates. In his desperation to be of a class superior to his own, he first pursues the idea of finding rank via the army – the '*rouge*/red' of the film's title. When that fails, he turns to the other route for fame and recognition – the clergy, '*le noir* /black'. Finally, when at last ennobled, he returns once more to the red only to be denounced as the cheating seducer he is. For his part, Dantès is cruelly deprived of the woman he loves, thanks to the treachery of a rival for her hand, Fernand Mondego (Roger Pigaut). Dantès is denounced as a Bonapartist by Mondego, who delivers an anonymous letter to the public prosecutor. Dantès is sent to prison for the apparent crime of treason, for which he is never tried – he took a sealed missive from the exiled Napoleon in Elba to deliver into the hands of his supporters in Paris. Eighteen years later he makes his escape from the notorious Château d'If, takes possession of a fabulous fortune that his fellow prisoner, Abbé Faria (Gualtiero Tumiati), told him about, assumes the name of the Comte de Monte-Cristo and embarks on his journey of vengeance over those responsible for his incarceration. Having taken his revenge, he leaves Paris to live in the 'Orient' with Haydée (Maria-Cristina Grado), formerly the daughter of the Pasha of Janina, forced into slavery by Mondego and freed by Dantès.

It is worth considering that the trajectories of both novelists are also those of self-made men, coming as they do from modest or complicated backgrounds. Alexandre Dumas' father was a self-made military man who rose to general under Napoleon. His origins were mixed race – his father was a French military officer living in Haiti, his mother a black slave.[1] Alexandre Dumas had to endure racist taunts from his contemporaries – which is why the ending of the novel, Dantès' marriage to Haydée and departure for the Orient, should probably be read as a slap in their faces. For his part, Stendhal's father subjected him to a strict religious upbringing under the tutelage of a cruel and repressive priest.[2] Stendhal served in the army under Napoleon. He tried to make his fortune as a businessman and by seducing women. As such, he is not a dissimilar figure to the social-climbing Sorel. Napoleon's demise put an end to Stendhal's early ambitions and he became a writer – finding fame and notoriety, particularly for *Le Rouge et le Noir*'s portrayal of Sorel's cynical seduction of Mme de Rênal and Marguerite de la Mole. Stendhal's authorial drive was to expose the hypocrisy of his age and reveal the 'bitter truth'[3] about contemporary society under the Restoration. Dumas also criticizes contemporary bourgeoisie, including those parvenus who get rich by switching political allegiances as easily as swapping hats: one minute being fervent Bonapartists, rapidly converting to staunch supporters of the Restoration Monarchies and Louis-Philippe, as with Mondego and Villefort (Jacques Castelot). He also condemns – in a similar vein to Hugo – the iniquities of the judicial system, the ease and arbitrariness with which a person can be arrested, to say nothing of the corruption of magistrates. Dantès' three arch-enemies – Mondego, Danglars and Villefort, who conspired to put him away – embody the venality of these times. Parvenus, such as the fisherman Mondego (who becomes the Comte de Mortcerf, Peer of France), play the system cleverly and through several acts of treachery become ennobled and gain political status. Others speculate on war and amass a fortune, as with Danglars, formerly the Pharaon's clerk now a wealthy banker. Danglars, jealous of Dantès' promotion to captain over him, was the author of the anonymous letter which Mondego, also consumed by jealousy, delivers to Villefort. The ambitious lawyer Villefort uses the letter of denunciation to protect his name. As it transpires, his father, to whom Dantès delivers Napoleon's missive, is a Bonapartist (a retired demi-solde of the Imperial army). Villefort, by quietening the possible scandal, saves his own skin and rises through the judiciary to become the king's prosecutor.

In the film version of *Le Comte de Monte-Cristo* there are several interesting shifts, not just for narrative economy but also to make Mondego a darker character than he is in the novel. First, Danglars is completely omitted and his story of humiliation – unwittingly marrying his daughter to an escaped convict – is rewritten into Villefort's own disgrace: the convict is now revealed as his bastard son whom he tried to bury alive as a baby. Villefort's wicked attempted murder is exposed in court and he is forced to resign; he goes mad and dies of a heart attack. Second, rather than Danglars writing the letter, it is Mondego himself who dictates the letter to Caderousse (Daniel Ivernel), the Pharaon's bosun. In the novel, Caderousse is the fourth character responsible for Dantès' demise, since it is he who gives the information to Danglars about Napoleon's letter. In the film, Caderousse comes more to the fore. As a character he is much in the vein of *Les Misérables'* Thénardier. Thus, he is unscrupulous in his behaviour at all times, but still fails in his endeavours to get rich. Even in his treachery he fails: when Dantès challenges him, demanding the truth, he confesses to taking dictation from Mondego to disguise the source of the real denunciator. In the end, he is knifed to death by Villefort's bastard son.

The concept of the Romantic individual runs through the narratives of these two novels and is maintained in the film adaptations. More intriguingly, the subjugated condition of women as chattels passed onto their husbands by their fathers receives strong representation in both mediums. In *Le Rouge et le Noir*, we sense the ennui of Mme de Rênal (Danielle Darrieux) and Mathilde de la Mole (Antonella Lualdi), trapped by their domestic circumstances (as wife and mother in the former case and as daughter in the latter).[4] Small wonder they seek stimulation, a sense of aliveness, either through sexual arousal and fulfilment (Mme de Rênal) or a desire to emulate the contexts of medieval chivalry (Mathilde) and be seduced by a real man who dares to transgress. In *Le Comte de Monte-Cristo*, the boredom of Dantès' fiancée Mercedes (Lia Amanda) is well caught as she sits in the window of her house staring port-side, awaiting her lover's safe return on the Pharaon. Once married, almost against her will, to Mondego/de Mortcerf, she is still clearly imprisoned by the moral obligations of being his wife and the mother of his son. So even when handed the chance to renew her relationship with Dantès, once he has told her of her husband's treachery, she ruefully comments: 'It isn't that easy to leave, I have a son'. The good name must be preserved – in vain as it transpires. Dantès later exposes de Mortcerf as the unprincipled opportunist he is by bringing Haydée into the Chambres des Pairs/the House of Peers to expose how he betrayed her father and sold her into slavery. De Mortcerf finally does the right thing and blows his brains out. Mercedes exiles herself with her son to Marseilles where once more she sits in the window, waiting this time for the safe return of her officer son.[5]

Ennui, then, becomes the province of the women: a fairly modern take on the condition of women and one not normally associated with them. The term ennui tends to conjure up the 1950s' existentialist hero (in Camus and Sartre's novels) and within the nineteenth-century Romantic literature context is more readily viewed as a masculine malaise. Thus, it is to Dumas and Stendhal's credit that they perceived it as a female condition and described it as such in their novels, even if for the most part it remains unspoken by the women. Only Mathilde protests outwardly to her father against the inequities of her female condition. Both films remain true to this tone of female ennui. As for the male leads, what dominates in both the original texts and the films is, on the one hand, cynicism and the pursuit of individual glory, in the form of the youthful Sorel; on the other, vengefulness in the form of a disabused Dantès. Both men have the advantage of being driven by moral outrage and an ability to express it and punish others for it. Dantès, whose happiness was destroyed by rumour and denunciation, uses scandal to humiliate his adversaries, thereby causing their downfall. Dantès is coldly aware that scandal is more devastating in its effects than a series of duels, since it will ruin his enemies' reputations (as they did his). Sorel, because he must at all times disguise his true feelings and politics to survive, invokes his own person as an embodiment of hypocrisy put to the purpose of exposing the social hypocrisy of others. Yet, as both these men strive for a sense of their own justice, they do so at the expense of the family. Dantès leaves a trail of destroyed families behind him. Sorel's death sentence signals the end of Mme de Rênal's secure family unit. She leaves her home to be by Sorel's side during the last month of his life. Her husband disowns her. So, in effect, she abandons family life for her lover – she subsequently dies three days later, leaving her children motherless.

Of the three epic novel adaptations under consideration here, all of which were edited into two parts, the only one not to have suffered from compression into a single screening was Vernay's *Le Comte de Monte-Cristo. Le Rouge et le Noir* was cut to three hours from 210 minutes, to avoid a two-part screening. We saw a similar decision taken in relation to *Les Misérables*. Yet *Le Comte de Monte-Cristo* is only a 186-minute film, so this opposite exhibition strategy is of interest. Banking on the popularity of the story and the star appeal of Jean Marais, but also recalling that an earlier version was released in a similar fashion in 1943, the producers of this French-Italian co-production decided to give it a premiere release on two separate dates (Part One on 14 January and Part Two on 27 January, 1955). The producers had good reason to speculate on big returns, given that some 30-odd adaptations of *Le Comte de Monte-Cristo* had already been made.[6] Indeed, this latest version garnered an audience of 7.8 million. There is a further dimension of interest in relation to one of the earlier versions of this film. It was Vernay who also directed the 1943 one. This earlier film had fairly high-production values, considering the times and the austerity of working conditions in Paris under the Occupation. It seems strange, therefore, to remake it so soon afterwards (shooting began in 1953). Arguably, the chance to make it again, but in colour – and Gevacolor at that – was irresistible and doubtless freeing. This colour system, with its reputation for colour fidelity in full sunlight, plus the fact that there were no longer restrictions on his movements, meant that this time Vernay could give greater authenticity to his adaptation through location shooting. Instead of being limited, as he was in the 1943 version, to the Gaumont studios on the Buttes Chaumont,[7] Vernay was able to shoot off the côte d'Azur, including the notorious prison Château d'If on the isle of Ratonneau near Marseilles and the isle of Sainte-Marguerite near Cannes, which posed as the isle of Monte-Cristo.[8] Vernay used the port of Nice (posing as Marseilles) for the boat scenes of the Pharaon; other locations included the Cimiez monastery, Grasse, Antibes and the Esterel coastline.[9] Finally, for his interiors, he had use of the far more expansive and flexible Billancourt studios.

It is intriguing to compare the décors of the two films under discussion, since they are the products, respectively, of Max Douy (*Le Rouge et le Noir*) and Robert Clavel (*Le Comte de Monte-Cristo*). Clavel, we recall, was trained under Louis Barsacq and Max Douy, two of the great realists of set design. Considerable discussion is given to Clavel's designs for *Maxime* (see Chapter 19). In that film, true to the principles of his tutor Douy, Clavel put in merely what was necessary – sets were unadorned for the most part – and only cluttered in the service of psychological realism (as for Maxime's impoverished living quarters). Douy's own style of the 1950s was a pared-down décor wherever possible, allowing for free camera movement and actors to have the space to work their performance – a good example of this can be found in the only Belle Epoque film he designed, Renoir's *French CanCan*. The sets are open and generous as opposed to being cluttered – which would have made camera work tight and intimist, thus giving the spectator closer access to furnishings and bodies but at the expense of space to observe the performance. Thus, the stage setting for the Moulin-Rouge is expansive with plenty of room for the dancers to perform in and to allow the audience surrounding them to be seen standing in depth around them before we get to the actual café tables on the perimeter. The effect is of a broader view.

I thought it necessary to foreground these issues of style because of what happens with the décor in the two epics under discussion. In *Le Rouge et le Noir*, Douy's ability to pare down is at its most extreme – and, as we shall see, was the subject of some controversy. Conversely, in *Le Comte de Monte-Cristo*, Clavel has, for the most part, gone to town on a weighty if not cumbersome design. The homes of the poor – Dantès' and Mercedes' in part one, the hovel in Auteuil (part two) where Villefort buried his infant child – whilst far from ornate are not free of clutter. The various bars, where so much plotting occurs, are sinister in their gloomy low-ceilinged shapes and full of detail. Even more expansive are the sets in part two, in particular the living and working spaces of the wealthy and powerful, which are fully weighed down in Louis-Philippe style. The term weighty is appropriate, especially in terms of the furniture which, for all that it continues in the vein of the Restoration, is of a heavier and darker design, lacking the elegance of the former period. Mahogany replaces the formerly lighter-coloured woods. Ornamentation is limited to the occasional marquetry inlay and bronze for detail. This lack of ornament is due in part to the impact of industrialization on the manufacturing of furniture; although, in truth, the greater simplicity is ultimately motivated by a bourgeois taste for functionality, comfort and endurance. Influences are drawn also from medieval and renaissance sources. In terms of Clavel's designs, we are made very aware of the function of these furnishings. In Villefort's office, for example, the huge mahogany desk central to the *mise-en-scène* is a symbol of his power in decision-making over Dantès' future (and later his own son's life).

Dantès' home on the Champs Elysées in Paris, once he returns as the fabulously rich Comte, is the most outstanding of all the sets because of its incorporation of an Eastern influence, due to his travels to the Orient – particularly Turkey – where he met Haydée, freed her and brought her back to live with him. Haydée's quarters are the most evidently marked by this orientalism – recalling paintings by Delacroix and those even of the earlier eighteenth-century artists such as Boucher and Fragonard.[10] Silks and cashmeres adorn the walls; rich satin cushions and woven fabrics are strewn over Eastern-style divans; thick Turkish rugs lie on the parquet floors; Haydée even smokes a hookah. The entire décor serves to evoke the exoticized harem from which we presume Haydée has fled. However, the point here is that she is free at last to enjoy her own culture, and that Dantès, in his compassion, has set a whole apartment aside for her, to be designed according to her lifestyle and tastes. Furthermore whilst, in terms of *mise-en-scène*, the orientalism is out of synch with the dominant dourness of the Louis-Philippe design and restrained interior wall furnishings, as such, it provides information about Dantès as much as about Haydée. We note his openness to difference and the appeal of the Orient to his sensibilities – remember that at the end of his avenging trajectory he returns with Haydée to the Orient. This *mise-en-scène* refers back to the mid-eighteenth-century's own engouement, and that of the Enlightenment, with Persia and Turkey. Equally, it refers to the impact on fashion and taste of Napoleon's Egyptian campaign at the turn of the eighteenth century and also to the new world about to open up for the French in the Maghreb (in particular Algeria).[11] The implication is that Dantès is more at home in the domain of enlightened thought, which prefers courageous action and spirited adventure over the small-minded and grasping bourgeoisie of his enemies. This does not mean he is without contempt for these people, however. It is instructive, surely, that he turns up at the masked medieval ball, held for 'le tout-Paris' at the Opéra, disguised as an executioner! As we know, he is going to punish all three men who robbed him of his freedom – driving them one by one to their death in an icy and measured fashion (much as the executioner he embodies here). As he says: 'the guiltiest (i.e., de Mortcerf) must see the others die first'.

The sets of *Le Rouge et le Noir* are sparse indeed by comparison. Figure 12.1 (opposite) shows an example of this restraint: Madame de Rênal's room is modestly arraigned and far from excessive.

A partial reason comes down, as we know, to Douy's own design aesthetics. The major contributing factor, however, was economic: the budget for the entire film was set at 250 million francs.[12] At first this seems quite generous, given that the budget for co-produced colour films, at that time, ranged from 117–300 million francs. However, this is a figure for films of 100 minutes or so. Autant-Lara's film was originally 210 minutes (later cut to 180).[13] So, at twice the length, this budget is less than extravagant – particularly if we consider that 47 per cent of the budget goes on studio hire, hiring stars and other related actors, and sets and costume. Indeed, Autant-Lara wanted double the budget plus the right to work the film up to double the length (i.e., a film of six to seven hours) to allow him to be completely faithful to the original, none of which his producers would give him.[14] When he submitted the film at 210 minutes to the press première viewing, he hoped to persuade the producers at least to allow for a two-part release. Again the response was negative. Even at 180 minutes exhibitors would be limited to three screenings per day – barely enough in the producers' view to recoup the investment. We can infer from this how lucky Vernay was to get a two-part release for *Le Comte de Monte-Cristo*. In the end his producers' belief in the product and

Figure 12.1: Douy's décor for Madame de Rênal's bedroom. © Max Douy.

successful marketing paid off. It had a huge audience response – at 7.8 million it was France's top-grossing film of the year. With just over half the audience (4.3 million) for *Le Rouge et le Noir* (third-grossing French film of 1954), Autant-Lara's producers might have shown more faith. As it was, Autant-Lara won the Victoire for best director. [15]

Cuts in *Le Rouge et le Noir* were not just made on the basis of exhibition time alone, however. When the film was submitted for its visa, the censoring board insisted on several cuts, primarily to do with the anti-clerical nature of certain sequences.[16] There were three in all. The first to go was Mme de Rênal's bargaining with God over her son's life. She pleads with him to spare Xavier (as he is known in the film) in exchange for which she will give up Julien Sorel (henceforth Julien). The second is in the seminary (part two) where Julien, in an (hypocritical) effort not to make enemies of his fellow-seminarians by standing out as better educated then they are, degrades himself by 'devoutly' eating a rotten egg that no one else will eat. Finally, the penultimate sequence, in which Mme de Rênal is reunited with Julien in his prison cell, is cut – an odd decision since it allows for Julien to attain some kind of redemption through love. The cut was undoubtedly motivated by a Catholic lobby unwilling to see the sanctity of marriage thrown over for an illicit passion based in sexual pleasure and crime. These cuts have since been restored. But rather than dwell on these excisions, what is more interesting is what was left in. Two examples leap to mind. The first – one which surely ridicules the clergy and exposes its own vanity – is Julien's encounter with the archbishop during the royal visit of Charles X to Verrières. Julien comes upon the archbishop in his quarters practising, in a very camp manner, his act of benediction (the sign of the cross) in front of the mirror and deciding which version is the most alluring. The second is towards the end of part two and concerns Mme de Rênal's letter of denunciation. The power of this scene comes both from what it reveals and dissimulates. It serves as a strong indictment of the power over women of the Church, which manipulates their sense of guilt when in default of 'marital duty'. The priest casts aside the original letter dictated by Mme de Rênal's husband, declaring that it is not strong enough in its denunciation of Julien's conduct. He forces Mme de Rênal to take dictation from him. We never see his face. Instead we see her, sat at the table, tears rolling down her face as the priest roams about the room framed at his midriff issuing his dreadful words of condemnation. The priest's cold lack of compassion for Mme de Rênal's distress, his insistence on duty and compliance to religion, above all else, turn this into a stark scene of moral neglect for the well-being of his flock – small wonder he remains anonymous, faceless. In this scene, Autant-Lara renders without fail and with masterful economy Stendhal's own hatred of religion.[17]

The impact of the restrained budget on the look of the film had the effect of dematerializing the *mise-en-scène* – the spaces are there more as suggestions of a time and place rather than being grounded in realism. The one exception is the court room (see figure 12.2 opposite), set in the round, with its ornate parquet floor, velvet furnishings, wood panelling, crowned by a towering two-tier candelabra – searching no doubt to shed light on this murky tale (was it a crime of passion or premeditated?). The rotunda effect suggests we will never know the truth. The marble figure of Christ on the cross, hanging in the background behind the judge's dais, is a firm reminder that it is not just social prejudice that has brought Julien to justice, as he claims in his tremendous speech, but also religion and its hold on society.

The contrast between the realism of the court and the immateriality of the sets for the two principle places (Rênal and La Mole's houses) enhances the concept of the flashback as a space of memory. The court scene is in the present; it is from here that we segue into the long flashback which serves to explain how Julien ended up accused of murder. However, the flashback is not just Julien's, interestingly, but those of three women: Mme de Rênal, Mathilde, and also the jealous maidservant Elisa. It is her actions that precipitate the first set of anonymous letters denouncing Julien as Mme de Rênal's lover – causing his departure. Although a minor character, Elisa has an important function in the narrative. Not only does she witness Julien's grabbing Mme de Rênal's hand in his campaign of seduction, it is through her rummaging around in Julien's room that his admiration for Bonaparte is exposed. She is searching for proof of another lover to explain why he has rejected the proposal that she and he marry and finds only the portrait of Napoleon. She could, therefore, have denounced him

Figure 12.2: Douy's sketch for the tribunal at Besançon – rich and ornate in textures and meaning. © Jean André and Max Douy.

for his political allegiance, particularly since M. de Rênal had already expressed suspicions about Julien's leanings when he turned up with his trunk – formerly his uncle's – adorned with Napoleon's insignia. Instead, Elisa throws the portrait away, smashing the glass. She realizes that her class of woman is not what Julien wants, which in turn will lead her to denounce him out of sexual jealousy. Her gesture forces Julien's hand. Realizing he might be denounced as a Bonapartist, he decides to speed up his campaign of seduction. He has already successfully accomplished the skirmish of grabbing Mme de Rênal's hand under the very nose of her husband and kissing it; now he is prepared for the full onslaught. 'This is what Napoleon would do', he murmurs to himself, 'attack straightaway'.

To return to the décor: Douy himself provides us with the following information on the sets:

The film was in colour and in two episodes shot in two versions (French and Italian) in less than 10 weeks with a very tight budget.

Moreover, since there were a significant number of sets and that it was a period film, it became necessary to adopt a certain style to which we would adhere for consistency's sake. In agreement with the film director, we decided to simplify the architecture by getting rid of ornamental mouldings and keeping furniture and accessories to a bare minimum.

For the two principle spaces (the Rênal's house and the Duc de la Mole's private mansion) we adopted a unified concept for colour and materials: cardboard felt in dark grey for the former and light vanilla paint for the latter. The only realistic décor is the court.[18]

Nine and a half weeks for a film of this length is roughly half the time necessary (compare *Monte-Cristo*'s 16, and *Les Misérables* 27). There were just over 30 sets to design and build, including 'exteriors' such as the Rênals' ambitiously-designed gardens which, in the film, were in the form of painted backdrops for the sake of economy.[19] Furnishings are minimal: even Mme de Rênal and Mathilde's bedrooms are far from ornate, although they are provided with various gauze curtain hangings, mostly around the bed, to break up the linearity of the interior space. The Marquis' mansion is sparsely furnished showing little accumulation of wealth for a man of such aristocratic descent – the elegant Restoration tables are in view with their well-turned legs. However, there is little else. The spaces of his mansion are suffused with light and the lack of ornamentation allows for the structural lines of the rooms and the superb hallway and staircase to stand out in their eighteenth-century elegance. The less-grand home of the Rênals is suggested by the fact that the house directly faces onto the street – no sumptuous entrance via gates, therefore. The greyness of the walls closes the rooms in on themselves more. They lack the expansiveness and grandeur of the Marquis' home. Similarly, the furniture is unremarkable, although there is slightly more of it in the various rooms than in the Marquis' mansion. In this context of budget restraint, it is small wonder that the costumes (by Rosine Delamare) are also at a minimum: Mme de Rênal has nine, the same number as Julien; Mathilde a mere six. M. de Rênal has three, the rest of the secondary roles have no more than two.

Luckily for Douy and Autant-Lara, the novel itself is a very interior narrative – the action is largely interspersed with various characters' interior monologues – and Stendhal is sparse indeed with his descriptions. Thus, Douy's own sparing design reflects the novel's aesthetics, leaving space for the psychological dimension of the narrative and the characters' performance to evolve. There is a remarkable scene that best exemplifies this aesthetic conjuncture of form and content: the night that Mme de Rênal, unable to contain her desire, goes to Julien's room – a two-part trajectory, narrated in ten shots. Dressed in a luminous lilac satin dress, she leaves her room, glides in stocking-feet along the darkened (grey) corridor past her husband's room, and comes to Julien's door. She leans her face against it, listening, her hand poised above the door knob. She cannot bring herself to turn it but instead holds her face in her hands in anguish. She then returns silently to her room; she leans against the door, the picture of guilty passion and lustful agony. This takes five shots. In the end, however, her desire is stronger than her sense of wifely duty. Once more she leaves her room, glides to her lover's door. This time, Julien hears her movement. He, too, goes to the door and leans his face against it. The two lovers are thus each with their faces pressed into the door that separates them. He opens the door – at last a word is spoken: 'It's you', says Julien; 'I was afraid you would not come', is her reply, taking his hand and leading him back to her room. All done in five shots. Until this moment of exchange not a word is spoken, all is silence bar the very faint rustle of Mme de Rênal's dress. This two-part trajectory of desire is shot with an economy of film style, consonant with Stendhal's own literary expression, and enhanced by the sparse, unyielding, even unsympathetic décor in dour grey speaking to a household which, unlike its mistress, knows nothing of passion.

One of the major criticisms of the film – in its released 1954 form of 180 minutes – was that it focused too much on Julien's seduction campaigns at the expense of the socio-political satire present in the novel. The decision had been taken, by Autant-Lara in collaboration with the scriptwriters Aurenche and Bost, to foreground the love affairs, namely, Julien's seduction, in part one, of the bourgeoise Mme de Rênal and, in part two, of the aristocrat Mathilde de la Mole.[20] However, it is through Julien's behaviour, in relation to the women he seduces, and the social mores he defies in so doing, that the hypocrisy of the bourgeoisie is exposed. Moreover, there are plenty of touches elsewhere that round out this social satire. Exemplary of this is M. de Rênal's persistent concern to protect his social standing as mayor of Verrières and wealthy businessman, and to ensure that others keep to their rank – Julien especially, of whom he says pointedly to his wife: 'Anyone who lives under our roof and is paid a salary is a servant'. A major travesty in the adaptation process was, arguably, to put Julien's trial for attempted murder at the beginning of the film – thus the entire film is one long flashback. The scriptwriters reasoned it needed to come first to ensure that the spectators understood that the underlying focus of the drama was about a man doomed because he sought to advance socially. But this is undoubtedly to underestimate the spectator, especially given that several times in the course of the film Julien's voice-over makes the point that it is only through imitating the bourgeoisie's own skills at hypocrisy that he can hope to climb the social ladder. Unless, of course, the idea was also to set us up as Julien's jury – after all judgment is not passed until the court reconvenes at the end of part two.

What is massively absent is the political jostling and posturing going on in the first part of the novel and, from the second part, the political intrigues, to say nothing of the numerous disquisitions on Republicanism and Bonapartism versus the Restoration monarchy. In part one of the film, M. de Rênal has to act as the political mouthpiece for these issues – but his interjections are mostly about class distinctions. In part two, the Marquis de la Mole has to articulate these political points, albeit in a very diluted form. What comes in place of this absence of political intrigue, however, is greater space for the two lead women roles. Thus, Mme de Rênal comes to us in all her complexities and space is given for a faithful representation of Mathilde. Critics of the time felt that Autant-Lara had misrepresented the Mathilde character and turned her into something of an '*allumeuse*/sexual tease'.[21] Having re-read the novel for the purposes of this study, I find the characterization of Mathilde, as a Romantic ingénue obsessed with the ancestral mythology of her family, quite close to the original. Her whole vision of sexual relations is based in the concept of courtly love, whereby a man must be brave and win his mistress' heart through grand gestures, thus proving his love – as did her ancestor, Boniface de la Mole, Marguerite de Navarre's favourite who was beheaded in 1574 for a treasonable act (Marguerite subsequently kept his head). Julien should be forewarned even if, at first, Mathilde's demands for proof of his love are less drastic. They boil down to him climbing into her bedroom for a midnight tryst, using a ladder which he must then throw away; later, she provokes him into grabbing a sword to attack her when she pretends she is no longer interested in him. In her desire to kill her ennui, Mathilde seeks to feel grand passion; to achieve it, she has to play games with Julien – come close/go away: the same game Julien played with Mme de Rênal. In a sense Julien meets his match in Mathilde in terms of this *fort d'a* game-playing. The only difference lies in rank. She already has high social status, but she does not have a 'real man' (suitors of her rank bore her). Julien, for all sorts of reasons, one of them certainly stemming from class difference (in the novel she refers to him as a spaniel), is the one she aspires to seduce: he comes to her on her terms. Tables turn, however, once Julien knows she is hooked on him – at which point he plays the backing-off game she had earlier played with him. He triumphs. Mathilde demands that her father let her, as his 'dishonoured' daughter, marry Julien. It looks as if Julien's ambitions are fulfilled: the Marquis ennobles him to M. Julien Sorel de la Vernaye and buys him an officer's commission in the hussards. 'My novel is complete', Julien declares 'and it's all of my own doing'. Unfortunately, all this game-playing leads to the final dénouement – Mme de Rênal's letter of denunciation, sought at the request of the Marquis,[22] leads inexorably to Julien's attempted murder of his former mistress causing him to lose his head on the guillotine.

In performance terms, Danielle Darrieux is a convincing Mme de Rênal. Against the immateriality of the décor, her corporeality of a 30-year-old woman who has, until now, repressed – or not known – desire, is compelling to watch. Her costumes suggest this mixture of sensual desire and bourgeois conformity (see figures 12.3 and 12.4 opposite).

The day dresses are consistently buttoned up to the neck, finished with a prim white collar and a bow tie. Even her evening attire is demure – she wears a damson-coloured satin dress with a gauze blouse effect covering what should be the décolletée (done up into a collar as with her day dresses). Neither her day nor evening clothing are as described by Stendhal – which represents an interesting deviation. Once Mme de Rênal meets Julien, Stendhal tells us, she changes dresses three or four times a day, the neckline is décolletée and, for the most part, the dress sleeves are short.[23] Not so in the film. Apart from the sleeves, which are mostly short, she neither changes that often, nor is there any décolletée. The demarcation line for exposure comes only with her night attire in the form of her exquisite frou-frou negligées with their low necklines. This shift in clothing style makes her position in relation to Julien just that more tense in the film, since she does not display her desire quite so clearly as in the novel. Furthermore, it renders the tentativeness of her night-time glide to Julien's room all that more suspenseful because her dress, lilac-coloured and buttoned up to the collar, tells us how socially contained and proper she is, yet her conduct says quite the opposite.

Figure 12.3: Mme de Rênal all buttoned up at the neck. (DVD grabs).

Figure 12.4: Mme de Rênal in décolleté. (DVD grabs).

Gérard Philipe's Julien is less convincing. Primarily, it has to be said, because of his age. When first asked in 1947 by Autant-Lara, who was trying to get a production of the film off the ground, if he would cast for Julien, his reply was unequivocally that he was too old for the part; at that point he was 25. By 1954 he was 32 and, whilst still youthful and extremely beautiful, he certainly could not pass as a naive 18-year-old. His manner as well as his allure was of a man with considerable knowledge of life and, in particular, matters of sexual relations and the art of seduction. The whole point with Julien's character is that he is completely inexperienced when it comes to women, and still a virgin until he beds Mme de Rênal. Thus Philipe's maturity militates against a fully-convincing performance. Two reasons combined to change his mind and take the role, however. The first was a cancellation of another project with Autant-Lara which left him, and the director, with two months on his hands with no work. The second, more significantly, was a desire on Philipe's part to broaden his repertoire and avoid being typecast as the charming young man (as in *Fanfan la tulipe*). In particular he wanted to take on more broody, difficult types.[24]

Gérard Philipe was certainly the popular audience's favourite, even if not of the *Cahiers du cinéma*. He was also the film industry's: for the first half of the decade he was their second most lucrative male star.[25] He won the prestigious Victoire award for best actor four years in succession in the 1950s (1952–1955), during which period he appeared in, amongst others, three of his top-grossing costume drama films (*Fanfan la tulipe*, *Les Belles de nuit*, *Le Rouge et le Noir*). However, the Young Turks (as they were then known) of the *Cahiers du cinéma* continuously railed against him, partly because of the image he projected as a suave charming matinée idol (which jarred against his serious theatre work, in their opinion), partly because of his politics (he was a sympathizer of the communist party and had become, with Yves Montand, one of the principal ambassadors for the French Left), partly because of the directors he chose to work with – most of whom were deemed by the *Cahiers* to be part of the tradition of quality they so inveighed against.[26] Curiously, though, in the case of this particular film, the question of 'tradition of quality' is not what renders *Le Rouge et le Noir* a flawed adaptation. Reducing the text to its sexual adventures and social climbing does indeed make it a lesser piece than the original. But we must recall that Autant-Lara had to make difficult decisions on what to excise, given the time constraints imposed upon him by his producers. If the political side is lost, the attack on the hypocrisy of the bourgeoisie and the church certainly remains. In terms of a flawed adaptation, the real issue, in truth, comes down to a miscasting of Philipe for the lead role – an anxiety Philipe expressed but overcame. The central character loses his naiveté by dint of being interpreted by an older man. The 'betrayal' of the original novel, about which the *Cahiers du cinéma* protests, has some foundation, therefore, if not for the reasons set out.

So much then for the epics: the three major totemic 1950s' costume drama adaptations of literary giants, if not always classics – Dumas is not, after all, considered by those constructors of the French literary canon as a great author. So much, also, for great men of history (well, Napoleon, for none other carves his way into the 1950s' costume dramas covering this period of France's history). As we now move into the second half of this period, 1848–1888, it is curious to note how the concept of grandeur all but disappears. There are narratives of humble individuals who achieve remarkable feats in the fields of the arts and sciences (Offenbach and Fabre). There is only one example of heroic individual courage (*Michel Strogoff*). The lines of social decorum have become grubbier as we move into the Second Empire – courtesans and their suitors, alike, are not the most appetizing of creatures, it has to be said. In this context, therefore, Julien Sorel appeals through his desire to denounce hypocrisy; Edmond Dantès (we feel) is justified in his terrible revenge against his enemies; as for Valjean – here is a man who finds redemption through love. In what is to come, there is no moral high-ground – indeed, what predominates, if anything, is duplicity, greed, self-advancement; in short, an amoral low-ground which indicates a more complex set of critical narratives surrounding this era of the Second Empire. As social change accelerates, so too does the nature of the social beast, be it male or female. Let us now take a look at this overall less-than-flattering representation of an age gone past, and unpick its ambiguities as we do so.

Notes

1. The details are quite shocking. Dumas's father, also called Alexandre, was initially sold by his biological father as a slave. He later bought him back and brought him to France where he began his military career. http://fr.wikipedia.org/wiki/Thomas_Alexandre_Dumas accessed 08.06.2009.
2. This is surely why in the novel and the film Mme de Rênal repeatedly asks Julien to not beat her children.
3. See the citation from Stendhal on http://fr.wikipedia.org/wiki/Stendhal accessed 26.03.2009.
4. A sign of Stendhal's modernity is his awareness of this malaise amongst women. He entitles one of his chapters which deals with Mme de Rênal's state of mind 'L'Ennui' (*Le Rouge et le Noir*, Part One, Chapter 6).
5. Her son Albert de Mortcerf is played by a very young Jean-Pierre Mocky.
6. This is a rate of one new version every 3 years, which attests to the ongoing interest this novel holds.
7. Sadly sold off to television studios in 1954 and since then demolished to be replaced by apartment buildings.
8. Apparently Dumas had sailed around the isle of Montecristo near Elba when thinking about his novel. http://fr.wikipedia.org/wiki/Le_Comte_de_Monte-Cristo accessed 08.06.2009.
9. See *La Cinématographie française* (No. 1541, 7.11.1953, p. 14) for these details.
10. See for example Fragonard's 'Le Pacha' (1732) and Delacroix' 'Femmes d'Alger dans leur appartement' (1834).
11. It is perhaps worth remembering that conflict with Algeria officially began in November 1954.
12. Bernard Bastide, basing his article in the collections held at the Paris Bifi, has provided an interesting overview of the genesis of this film: '*Le Rouge et le Noir*, une genèse tourmentée' http://www.bifi.fr/public/print.php?id=286&obj=article accessed 09.06.2009. The figure of 250 million francs comes from this article.
13. British release was even shorter at 146 minutes; the US: 170 minutes.
14. Cacerès & Chevallier (1964, p. 123).

15. The Victoire is the French equivalent of the Oscar, now known as the Césars. The César replaced the Victoire Awards in 1975.
16. Autant-Lara is no stranger to controversy and cuts to his films are a frequent affair. Interestingly, one feels it is always the 'wrong' cuts that get made – as if the censors miss the truly subtle anti-institutional scenes and select the glaringly obvious ones. A similar situation occurred for *L'Auberge rouge* – a phenomenally funny film in terms of its exposing the fence-sitting of the clergy. The single cut made was the following line because it impugned the dignity of the police: 'What is a policeman in the immense construct that is society? A speck of dust.' (Douin, 1998, p. 36).
17. Stendhal felt tyrannized both by his father and by religion, particularly in the form of the priest his father appointed as his tutor. See http://fr.wikipedia.org/wik/Stendhal accessed 26.03.2009, which quotes from Stendhal's biography to this effect.
18. Douy (2003, p. 197).
19. Douy had commented on the possibility of using photographs that were enlarged and touched up by studio painters (2003, p. 135). Here, though, the backdrops look very theatre-like, leading me to think they are original painted backdrops and not photographs.
20. Bernard Bastide. '*Le Rouge et le Noir*, une genèse tourmentée' http://www.bifi.fr/public/print. php?id=286&obj=article accessed 09.06.2009.
21. André Bazin for example says that Mathilde does not have 'the come-hither look she has been given on screen' (Review of *Le Rouge et le Noir* in *Cahiers de cinéma*, Vol. 7 No. 41, 38-40). Jean de Baroncelli disagrees and senses she is exactly right (Review of *Le Rouge et le Noir* in *Le Monde*, 6.11.1954, no page).
22. In the novel it is Julien who suggests the Marquis write to the Rênals to attest to his good standing: a very curious and arguably masochistic, if not suicidal, gesture on his part!
23. See, Stendhal (1963, p. 52): 'Mme de Rênal, who had a superb skin, wore dresses which left her arms and bosom very exposed'.
24. Bonal (1994: 204).
25. See *Le Film Français*, No. 675/6 Special Spring issue (1957).
26. For more details of this hostility, see Cadars biography of Gérard Philipe (1990, p. 99).

Chapter 13

From the Second to the Third Republic: Innovation, Corruption and New Identities

Historic overview 1848–1888

February 1848 brought in the new Republic. Propelled by terrible conditions of poverty, workers united against the monarchy and overthrew it. This revolution by the people, known as the 'spirit of 1848', brought in its wake the ideals of a Republic based on the principles of freedom and equality embedded in the 1789 Revolution.[1] According to the rhetoric of the time, a Republic of the people, and with a human face, was to be born. Under the Second Republic, the Republican Tricolore flag was re-instituted and universal suffrage decreed (now, nine million voters made up the electorate). The right to work, in the form of *Ateliers nationaux*/national workshops was introduced. These were intended to provide work to the growing numbers of unemployed and brought with them unemployment benefit, doling out social benefit of 2 francs per day (*la sociale*). Freedom of the press was declared. Slavery was once and for all abolished in all colonies and protectorates – although colonization continued to be seen as a duty and a means for France to maintain its status.[2]

This heady state of affairs was short-lived, however. By June 1848, unemployment had again reached such a peak amongst the working and artisanal classes in Paris that the national workshops closed their doors and therefore stopped paying out the dole. Workers took to the streets. Up went the barricades and so erupted an insurrection lasting three days and costing thousands of lives. Earlier in the year, the proletarian classes had revolted against a constitutional monarchy. Now it was the turn of a legally-elected representative government to be rejected by its voters. The electorate turned against those they had voted in by universal suffrage. This people's revolt reinforced the bourgeoisie's fear of 'mob rule'. A fear that lasted throughout the second half of the nineteenth century and which the scheming politician Adolphe Thiers exploited to his own advantage when in cabinet post over these turbulent decades. Largely responsible for the bloody reprisals against the Paris Commune of 1871, Thiers' attitude towards the proletariat was consistently one of contempt. This 'vile multitude'[3] of 1848 became to his mind, by the time of the Paris Commune, symptomatic of a red, that is, socialist, republic that would have to be subjugated.[4]

The 1848 revolt was perceived as a socialist uprising (so-called because the proletariat demanded the restitution of the '*sociale*') and its participants labelled 'Reds'. Fear of the Reds was growing over Europe. Indeed, 1848 was the year of European revolutions (see Chapter 15 on *Lola Montès*). In the wake of these brutal times, and as an attempt to move towards a more democratic system of representation, France voted for a constitutional amendment to elect the President by universal suffrage. Louis Napoleon Bonaparte (who had returned to France and gained a seat as deputy in the Second Republic) won by a landslide (5.5 million votes). He was the people's choice.[5] Three years later he imposed himself as Emperor in a bloodless coup d'état: the Second Empire was born.

There is something quite remarkable about this two-time-failed conspirator finally becoming elected by the people. As Brogan puts it: 'The great mass of the peasant electors knew only one name to set against the Republic: Napoleon. For millions, his name was a programme'.[6] He was in some ways a socialist with Republican ideals and 'genuinely wanted to do something for the workers' and the poor'.[7] But his hands were tied by a government that did not want to let him lead. This included Thiers who called him a 'cretin we can control'.[8] Not everything went their way, however. Thus, for example, Thiers successfully limited the vote to taxpayers (as a way of stifling the 'vile multitude'), thereby eliminating 2.5 million voters and erasing the concept of universal suffrage for men.[9] But Napoleon successfully pushed through some of his social legislation, including the important loi Falloux, which extended free secular education to girls.

Napoleon waited a mere two years before launching his bloodless coup to become Emperor. In December 1851, with the support of the army occupying Paris, he took over the Assemblée Nationale, dissolved government, re-instituted universal suffrage and set a plebiscite before the French electorate to grant him full powers to establish a new constitution. The response was a landslide – over 7 million voters approved the referendum. From there, it was one more step to convince this same electorate to vote for a restoration of the Empire – 7.8 million did so (86 per cent) and in November 1852 the Second Empire came into being.[10] It is worth recalling here that this form of elected dictatorship, for which the Republicans never forgave Napoleon III, would not be revisited again until de Gaulle came to power in 1958. Both the Third and Fourth Republics, burnt by the Napoleon experience, decided that the Senate should nominate and elect the nation's President, not the electorate. De Gaulle reversed this decision when he, too, called for a plebiscite on his constitution for the Fifth Republic (in September 1958) which restored supreme powers to the executive (i.e., the President as guarantor of the nation's independence) – he received 80 per cent of the electorate's support. Four years later, he re-instated the election of the President by universal suffrage.

Napoleon III was convinced that social poverty was a direct cause of political instability and fairly immediately put in place what can be described as a Keynesian model of economics *avant la lettre*. He decided that government investment in public works was a way to counter unemployment and so instituted a massive programme of modernization, much of which was made possible by newly-created stock and investment banks backed by the government, the first of which was the *Crédit Mobilier*. Significantly, in historical terms, nearly all of these were owned by Jewish financiers – a factor that fuelled the growing anti-semitism in the latter half of the nineteenth century.[11] Their funding and speculation made possible the reconstruction of Paris under Baron Haussmann, a re-investment in railways, building new ports and enlarging existing ones, the establishing of the telegraph system, and investment in the Suez Canal.[12] On the education front, we recall both Napoleon's treatise on education and the fact that he appointed a very enlightened man, Victor Duruy, as Minister of State Education. In his early years, the Empire extended its colonies: Senegal in Africa, and Indochina beginning with Cambodia. Napoleon III fought one notable successful campaign: the Crimea war (1854).

But there was also the Napoleon, man of politics and war, who was unsuccessful, most infamously in his campaign against the Prussians in 1870 which, eventually, cost him his 'throne'. Despite his liberal views, for the first six years of his reign he was largely constrained by a right-wing government. An assassination attempt was made in 1858 when he failed to meet his promise to help Italy gain its independence – an historical event reprised in the film *La Castiglione* (Combret, 1955). In 1853, he made an unpopular choice of wife in the form of Eugénie de Montijo – a rather profligate Empress who established a lavish imperial court. She was a consummate horsewoman who loved to hunt. She was, however, somewhat vulgar in her sense of chic and contributed, amongst other things, to the establishing of a rather eclectic Napoleon III style which, in terms of architecture, meant a mixture of the classical, neo-classical and renaissance. In terms of furniture, Eugénie favoured a dark wood design, encrusted with mother of pearl, and over-stuffed chairs and pouffes. Both aspects of this Napoleonic style were, however, much to the taste of the nouveau riche bourgeoisie and continued well into the Belle Epoque. In terms of fashion, she introduced the very large crinoline, with it huge swathes of cloth – possibly because of her admiration and sentimental cult of Marie-Antoinette whose huge panier-skirts were a precursor to the crinoline. In 1858, Eugénie established the first real couturier in the person of Charles Frederick Worth. She was, thereby, the undisputed arbiter of fashion, if not taste. A prime example comes with her passion for passementerie decoration on day dresses, such as the fringe (occasionally with small Spanish-influenced pompoms), braid, gimp, ribbon, tassels, and cord. The fringe effect on the skirt flounces served to accentuate the ripple effects when women moved, doubtless adding to their mystique. But passementerie was also used on furniture and other elements of upholstery – reinforcing the sense of luxury, certainly. Such excess suggests a lack of discernment in terms of taste, just as surely as it implies that women were much like furniture objects, or, again, that they were not to be distinguished from their domestic space. All of the above aspects of Eugénie's persona are readily referred to in *Les Violettes impériales* (Pottier, 1952), a film that relates her meteoric rise as wife to the Emperor. In this film she is represented as a woman for us to admire (see Chapter 14). Indeed, instead of the Emperor, it is she who is the target of an assassination plot (which she escapes). The other side to her persona (which we do not glimpse in Pottier's film) – the devout Catholic disapproving of secular schooling, especially mixed-sex education, and, according to contemporaries,[13] meddler in her husband's politics – is the one we get to see in another film which has a cameo appearance of Napoleon III and his wife: *Monsieur Fabre* (Diamant-Berger, 1951).

I shall discuss much of the Third Republic's pre-1914 history in the Belle Epoque chapters (see Part Four).[14] But these first eighteen years (1870–1888) certainly merit a cursory glance.

First, the ambitious Thiers finally clambered to the top of his political tree and became the first President of the new Republic. This was the man who, by confiscating the National Guard's cannons after the Prussian defeat, triggered the Commune uprising of 1871, which he then went on to brutally repress.[15] He did not last long as President: in just two years, he was forced to resign, and in 1873 the old war-horse Mac-Mahon was duly appointed. The nation's reaction to the 1870 war was one that, intriguingly, matches that of France post-World War Two – one of shame and humiliation. In 1870, the nation turned to the army as a symbol of national unity, something that France could not do in the same way in 1945.[16] Instead, as we know, the myth of the Resistance (a ghost army: *l'armée des ombres* as it was appropriately named) was created as a way of lessening the sense of guilt and humiliation. Whilst the Franco-Prussian war did not deplete France economically, although of course Alsace-Lorraine was lost to them, the nation's international reputation did suffer. France was no longer perceived as a great nation – its defeat by the Prussians made that evident. The Third Republic determined it had to learn from that experience and arm itself so it could stand strong; hence the iconic value placed on the army. France was, in short, preparing to defeat its enemy in any future war – indeed there is plenty of evidence of the army in the Belle Epoque films (see Chapter 20). France also decided to assume a strategy of grandeur by expanding its colonial interests and thereby rival its greatest enemy, Germany.[17] To this effect, Madagascar, Martinique, Reunion, Guadeloupe, Guyana, Tahiti and New Caledonia were all assimilated into the French Empire as overseas territories. Tonkin was brought into French Indochina. Tunis was annexed – a story I detail in my case study on Louis Daquin's *Bel-Ami* (Chapter 17). By 1914, France was the second greatest colonial empire in the world.[18] Intriguingly, once de Gaulle came to power, in 1958, he set about elevating France's national status in his now-famous *Politique de Grandeur,* which included withdrawing France from NATO and launching its own independent nuclear programme. Thus, France of the 1950s, book-ended as it was by the birth of new Republics (the Fourth and the Fifth), strikingly adopted a similar set of strategies as the Third Republic itself at its own inception. One could demur that history teaches us nothing but, instead, let us return to the past and see what was happening on the ground.

During this 18-year period, electricity replaced gas lighting in the capital city (1881), the telephone was introduced (1875), Eugène Poubelle proposed the idea of garbage collection in standardized dustbins (1884). In terms of civil liberties, divorce by mutual consent was made law in 1881, reversing its abolition in 1816. University education was made available to women in 1880. But the 1880s also saw a world economic depression that took its toll on worker employment: the effects of industrialization and the importation of goods from outside the country (from China and Japan via the Suez Canal) impacted heavily, particularly on the silk industry.[19] A bug imported from America, Phylloxera, more or less destroyed the wine industry. Financial scams were also rife (most famously the Panama Canal scandal, 1889). The bourgeoisie, as usual, feared the mob and its strike actions during these difficult times. Zola's novels do much to record the lives of this lower class that the middle-classes so abhorred; not that he spared the grasping bourgeoisie, however, as we shall see in *Pot-*

Bouille (Chapter 16). In the political psyche of this Third Republic, there was a growing anti-semitism on the Right and an increasing anti-clericalism on the Left. The building of the basilica of the Sacré-Coeur needs to be viewed in this light. Its construction was decreed by government in 1873 – the Right-wing elements of the Assemblée saw it as a means of expiating the evils of the Commune uprising and symbolically opposing the anti-clerical Republicans.[20]

Finally, in this rapid sketch, we come to the modern man. He was less of the dandy of the Restoration and July Monarchy period; primarily, it has to be said, through his dress code, which was more sober. But he was still a person displaying considerable nonchalance and cynicism in society;[21] a man with refined appetites, a taste for luxury and pleasure – a man that Maupassant's short stories and novels so readily capture. The collective title given to the film version of three of his short stories, *Le Plaisir* (Ophuls, 1952), aptly sums this up in the word alone; but *Bel-Ami* and *Une vie* (1880) also give us plenty of examples of this new type of masculinity (more of this in Chapters 16 and 17).

Images of the time – Innovation, corruption and new identities

The picture that emanates from the films set in the Second Empire period is a fairly mixed one, but which rather faithfully reproduces the two deeply-intertwined sides of the Napoleonic moment: innovation and corruption; a get rich quick mentality made possible by new technologies and the possibilities of speculation brought about by a system of credits based not in gold but in paper transactions. On the one hand, in this corpus of films, there are the celebrative biopics of Offenbach (one of Napoleon III's favourite composers) and the entomologist Fabre (who also met the Emperor). There is the highly entertaining Eugénie de Montijo's ascendance to Empress in the Luis Mariano vehicle *Les Violettes impériales.* The assassination attempt over Italy, the so-called Orsini affair, is replayed in *La Castiglione,* in which a courageous Virginie de Castiglione entreats the Emperor to help the Italians repel the Austrians. This is more than matched, on the other hand, by the number of narratives dealing with the underbelly of society in the form of courtesans (*Nana* and *Lola Montès*), the poor, (*Gervaise*), and young men with ambitions to get to the top such as Octave Mouret in *Pot-Bouille* and Alexei Ivanovitch, *Le Joueur* – both roles being played by Gérard Philipe, the epitome of the new type of masculinity. By the time we get to the films set in the Third Republic – with the exception of the heroic *Michel Strogoff,* who suffers unspeakable torture, and two comedies about marrying off daughters (*Les Petites Cardinal* and *Mam'zelle Nitouche*) – all we are left with are tales of seduction and sexual exploitation. Here is a reminder of the titles involved:

1848–70 2nd Republic-2nd empire (12 titles)	1870–88 3rd Republic (8 titles)
La Valse de Paris 1850s 'biopic/love story' based around Offenbach	*Les Petites Cardinal* (51) 1871 political opportunism/getting daughters married off
Monsieur Fabre (51) 1850s through to 1914 'biopic' of famous entymologist	*Le Plaisir* (52) 1870s includes prostitution (*La Maison Tellier*)
Les Violettes impériales (52) 1848–50 story based around Eugénie's marriage to Napoleon III	*Trois femmes* (52) 1870s includes tale of racism (*Zora*)
Lettres de mon moulin (54) 1850s Three stories (2 slightly anti-clerical)	*Chevalier de la nuit* (54) 1884 bored marriage/'sexual' fantasy
La Castiglione (55) 1853 story of Italian patriot Olivia Oldoini/La Castiglione who enlists aide of Napoleon against Austrians	*Mam'zelle Nitouche* (54) 1880s operetta/comedy/marriage
Lola Montès (55) 1843–59 story of famous courtesan	*Michel Strogoff* (56) 1880 story of courageous courier of the Tsar
Nana (55) 1860s story of famous courtesan	*Bel-Ami* (57) 1887 tale of seducer/political shenanigins
Gervaise (56) 1852 poverty narrative	*Une vie* (58) 1880 seducer tale
Pot-Bouille (57) 1865 seducer tale (based on real person)	
Le Joueur (58) 1867 seducers, roués and gamblers	
La Jument verte (59) 1860-80 rape/revenge narrative	
Les Naufrageurs (59) 1852 based on real events	

Figure 13.1: Films by period (1848–88) and description of narrative type (1848–88).

In the next two chapters I propose to investigate the films that fall within the period of the Second Empire – focusing primarily on the 'biopics' (Chapter 14) and the films about demi-mondaines (Chapter 15). The subsequent chapter takes a look at the newly emergent masculinity of the 1860s through to the 1880s (Chapter 16). A further chapter, which draws this third part of the book to a close, offers a case study of Louis Daquin's controversial film *Bel-Ami* (Chapter 17).

For reasons of space, certain films will not be focused upon. *Lettres de mon moulin* provides three stories set in Provence which plead for a greater tolerance of human fallibility and argue for an understanding of more traditional methods of production – they are anti-clerical and anti-modernization in flavour. The film, true to Alphonso Daudet's tales, sets tradition against modernity and argues that modernity does not necessarily bring happiness – it can increase production, be it in liqueur production or grinding flour, but it can cost you your self-respect and the regard of others. I leave *Gervaise* aside because it is a well-known film in the canon of French cinema, but I shall be making passing reference to it in my discussion of the demi-mondaine films. *Les Naufrageurs* and *La Castiglione* are films I have not managed to locate, so (sadly) do not feel able to say anything in regard to them. *La Jument verte* is widely available and again has been written about in the context of its star, Bourvil. I cannot, for my part, read it as a comedy. To my mind, it is a very unpleasant apology for female abuse, first in the form of rape and second in the form of patriarchal tyranny over wife and family. Set in rural France, the green mare of the film title is merely a pretext for a rather gruesome story of revenge. *Les Petites Cardinal* and *Mam'zelle Nitouche* are similar in their thematics to many of the marriage-focused films of the Belle Epoque. An interesting anecdote in the former, however, comes down to the fact that the father of the Petites Cardinal, played by Saturnin Fabre, is someone who changes his politics to suit the moment: first shifting his allegiance from the Emperor to the Republic, then to the Commune, then back to the Republic. In this, he reminds us ever so slightly of Adolphe Thiers and his ability, chameleon-like, to adapt to whichever political system was in power, only the better to decry the one that has just fallen. Otherwise, M. Cardinal's hypocrisy is not much different from any other bourgeois.

Michel Strogoff relates the exploits of a Russian hero, and certainly merits a brief discussion. Based on the 1875 novel of Jules Verne, the film touches upon the Tsar of Russia and his endeavours to foil a plot of insurrection by the Tartars against his brother in Siberia. Verne wrote the novel especially to commemorate the visit of Tsar Alexander II to Paris as part of the negotiations for a rapprochement between the two countries (France needed Russia's support against an increasingly aggressive Prussia/Germany under Bismarck).[22] Thus, this text stands as an important political cultural artefact and in celebrating the courage of a Russian hero acknowledges the greatness of the Russian Empire and, of course, its Tsar. The film of 1956 stays close to the novel. Set in the 1870s, Strogoff (Curd Jurgens, who else!) has to travel some 7,000 kilometres across a freezing Siberia to deliver the secret missive to the Tsar's brother about the forthcoming insurgence. In doing so, he is captured by the marauding Tartars, tortured, has his eyes burnt out – yet he still gets his message through! It was an extremely popular film, with audiences of nearly 7 million, so these heroics certainly struck a chord with 1956 France. At the time, Curd Jurgens was a highly-regarded star (as we noted in relation to *Tamango* in Chapter 10). But he was also respected as a man who had shown considerable political courage during World War Two. At the time he was a German actor working in Austria. He was shipped out to a concentration camp in 1944 for his outspoken views against the Nazi regime and imprisoned as a 'political undesirable'.[23] But we can perhaps also gauge that the heroics of this 1956 film speak to a nation at war with Algeria, wherein French soldiers had to deal with the harsh conditions of the desert (the hot equivalent of a freezing Siberia). There were also tales of capture and torture by the FLN (the Algerian Liberation Front) – spread primarily by the French army in Algeria, it has to be said – that were common currency in the nation's popular psyche. The metaphorical value of this film, therefore, has to be borne in mind, even if it does not make direct reference to the contemporary political climate of the times. And it is arguably, apart from *Bel-Ami*, the only film of this historical period to make any allusion to the Algerian question. Chapter 17 explores this in some detail. For now, let us move on, first, to the films of the Second Empire, beginning with the more official image of the period, that of great men and women.

Notes

1. Marseille (2002, p.127).
2. Ibid., p. 192.
3. Thiers quoted in Marseille, op. Cit., p. 137.
4. Brogan (1989, p. 158).
5. Marseille, op. Cit., pp. 127–33.
6. Brogan, op. Cit., p. 97.
7. Ibid., p. 99.
8. Thiers quoted in Marseille, op. Cit., p. 132.
9. Ibid., p. 137.
10. Ibid., pp. 140–1. The story is of course a bit more complex than this. Louis Bonaparte was supported by the 'Parti de l'Ordre', primarily a conservative group of politicians made up of Orleanists and legitimists (claiming a return of the monarchy) and dominated by one Adolphe Thiers. Once elected President, Bonaparte wanted to change the constitution so that he could serve a second term. His party, which held considerable sway in the Assemblée Nationale, refused to support his amendment (July 1851). From then on it was a matter of time till Bonaparte executed his coup.
11. Crédit Industriel et Commercial (1859) Crédit Lyonnais (1863), Société Générale (1864). For more details see Brogan, op. cit., pp. 129–31 and Marseille, op. cit., pp. 142–8.
12. Brogan, op. cit., pp. 125–30.
13. Henri Clouzot (1939) *Le style Louis-Philippe - Napoléon III*, Paris, Larousse, 38-39.
14. The Third Republic was proclaimed on 4 September 1870. However, it was something of an interim Republic since the constitution for the Republic was not voted until 30 January 1875.
15. Marx' account of the Commune offers a fascinating narrative of these bloody days and provides a fierce indictment of Thiers. He followed the events closely and wrote them up in *The Civil War France*, first published in June 1871 by Edward Turnlove in London.

16. The march past of 14th of July dates from this period of glorifying the army.
17. Marseille, op. cit., pp. 193–4.
18. Ibid., p. 199.
19. Ibid., p. 181–3.
20. Mostly paid for by public subscription, it was not completed until 1910 (Griffe, 2009, p. 27).
21. Marseille, op. cit., p. 180.
22. It is worth making the point that Jules Verne was quite embittered against the Germans for France's defeat in the Franco-Prussian war and the loss of Alsace-Lorraine. Alexander II had been affronted during his visit to Paris in 1876 for the Great Exhibition when a Pole made an attempt on his life. Relations between Russia and France cooled and Alexander was apparently not displeased to see Napoleon III fall as a result of the 1870 war with the Germans. It was clear to the French, who were isolated after the Franco-Prussian war, that they needed an ally and they looked to Russia from the mid-1870s onwards. However, it was a very slow process. It took the Russians a number of years to be convinced of their need for France. The triple alliance of Austria-Hungary, Germany and Italy of 1882 was the turning point, as was Russia's increasing need for financial support from outside. In 1888, they looked to France for cheap loans. They were easily forthcoming from the Paris Bourse (stock exchange). Eventually, both nations signed the Franco-Russian alliance in 1889 – an event consecrated by the Alexander III bridge in Paris (1904).
23. See http://en.wikipedia.org/wiki/Curd_Jürgens accessed 05.08.2009.

Chapter 14

The Second Empire in the Pink: Violets, Waltzes, and the Pursuit of Knowledge

This chapter focuses on films that predominantly speak to the greatness of the Second Empire. There are only four titles, hence the title 'in the pink' – intended of course with a little irony since the eight other Second Empire period films are less than flattering to the régime. Leaving aside *La Castiglione*, which I have not managed to see, the other three titles are all loosely-based biopics (some much looser than others). The loosest of all is *Les Violettes impériales*, mostly because this love-musical of sorts, with its star vehicle Luis Mariano, is more about his pursuit of happiness and less about Eugénie de Montijo's rise to fame as Napoleon III's wife, although the imperial reference of the film title clearly refers to her. The other two films, *Monsieur Fabre* and *La Valse de Paris,* run considerably closer to a reflection of two great men's lives (Jean-Henri Fabre and Jacques Offenbach). Let us take a closer look at these three stories.

La Valse de Paris, Les Violettes impériales and Monsieur Fabre

Both Fabre (1823–1915) and Offenbach (1819–1880) are men who found greatness through their own merit – a very Republican and Napoleonic principle. In the films, *Monsieur Fabre* and *La Valse de Paris*, they are played by the same actor: Pierre Fresnay. Indeed, post-war, Fresnay made several biopics, three of which fall into the category of costume dramas; he also plays the lead role in *Il est minuit Dr Schweitzer* (see Chapter 21). There is something intriguing about the precise roles and persons whose biographies he embodied because, without fail, all three of them – Jean-Henri Fabre, Jacques Offenbach, Albert Schweitzer – were in some way outsiders in relation to the nation they came to represent, namely France of the second half of the nineteenth century. Fresnay, too, was something of an outsider. He was a Protestant and Alsatian. I shall develop the significance of this in more detail when analysing his role as Dr Schweitzer so do not intend to address it here. However, we can readily draw some parallels between Fresnay as outsider and the other two personages under discussion in this chapter. Offenbach was a Jew of German origins and a composer famous for his operettas. He came to France in the 1830s to make it his home, suffered many ups and downs in his career, only to be forced to return to Germany during the 1848 revolution and later to seek refuge in Spain during the Franco-Prussian war of 1870 – even though he was by then naturalized as French (in 1860) and had been given the Légion d'Honneur in 1861 by Napoleon III, who admired his ironic, satirical operettas. He also converted to Catholicism in 1844 when he married. But in 1870 neither France nor Germany wanted anything to do with him. He was criticized by the French press as an immigrant agent of Bismark, and reviled in the German press as a traitor to his native Germany. His heydays were those of the Second Empire which he so graciously mocked. And even though he returned to France in 1871, his music had fallen out of fashion and he fell greatly into debt.

Fabre was an outsider because of his non-conformist views. A Frenchman born into poor circumstances in the southern region of France (in the Aveyron), he was a groundbreaking entomologist, but suffered hardship and controversy in his own nation while being fully recognized by other countries for the importance of his work (John Stuart Mill was a personal friend; Fabre influenced Darwin's later thinking). His work on insects, reproduction and natural selection fell in and out of favour, depending on political régimes; only Napoleon III recognized its importance. For the rest, politicians accused his work, in turn, of being either too secular or too spiritual. Mostly self-taught, Fabre worked his way through the various university degrees to get a post in higher education – but essentially he lived a considerable part of his life in relative poverty, achieving financial security and recognition from his own country only in his very late years.

Fresnay built his reputation as an actor with an incisive diction that spoke of a decisive mind. He cultivated a style of acting that could be limpid and yet grand, soft and yet stiff. He was an actor who was able to deliver, unwaveringly, what I term the performance of paradox. Often this takes a physical as much as a moral manifestation. Thus, when his character is under stress or outraged, Fresnay's upper body can literally stiffen before our eyes. When absorbed in something he truly loves it softens, becomes willowy, limpid. Fresnay could portray the dedication and single-mindedness it takes to achieve greatness; his ability to mix comedic delivery with censorious lines about the world, to combine noble virtues with human flaws – all of these attributes singled him out as a natural choice for these edifying roles of Fabre and Offenbach. But so, too, did his status as a major French star. Hugely acclaimed on stage as much as on screen, Fresnay was box-office gold.[1] Nor can we overlook the fact that these biopics delivered strong nationalistic messages, on at least two counts. First, the very Republican and Napoleonic idea that a man could forge his own destiny against all odds if he is motivated by his talents and not by greed, the pursuit of truth and beauty being more important than the pursuit of renown and wealth. Second, with little to celebrate, post-war, national pride could be restored by these refreshing examples of greatness in the face of adversity, allowing the nation to reflect on the role France played in these men's achievements.

As for the third of these tales of real lives: Eugénie de Montijo – she was bent on fulfilling a dream, or her mother's dream, which was to marry a prince. In the film, *Les Violettes impériales*, we get the impression that the first meeting between this beauty and the Prince-President (soon to be Emperor) was a *coup de foudre*. The truth is less flattering. Napoleon was by now 44 and Montijo 27 years old – quite old in the marriage stakes at the time. Napoleon, just before his wedding, is quoted as saying: 'I would have preferred to marry a woman I knew and respected to a woman I don't know and with whom an alliance will bring advantages mixed with sacrifices.' Hardly a big endorsement. She was certainly a beauty, passionate but at the same time restrained, even though not all contemporaries were so convinced as to her virginal status. Victor Hugo bluntly stated: 'the Eagle is marrying a cocotte'.[2]

All three films are, to one degree or another, love stories: love of music, love of science, love of power. Let us begin with *La Valse de Paris,* which tells the story of Offenbach and Hortense Schneider (played by Yvonne Printemps, Fresnay's wife) 'in the years when his operettas were the rage of Paris and she one of their most dazzling interpreters'.[3] Whilst, at one point in the story, they both believe they are in love with each other, in the end they discover that it is the artistry in each other that they truly appreciate. In Hortense Schneider, Offenbach not only finds his muse, he also discovers his love for her voice. In Offenbach, Hortense comes to love his music. If the professional admiration they had for each other was true to life, their actual love affair was not. Offenbach did have a discreet liaison with Zulma Bouffar whom he met at the height of his fame in 1864 and who starred in his 1866 operetta *La Vie parisienne.* However, for the most part he was a shy man and a devoted father to his five children (of whom we see nothing in the film). He met Hortense in 1855 just as he was setting up his own Théâtre des Bouffes-Parisiens (in the 2nd arrondissement).

As the film begins, Offenbach receives yet another visit from the bailiffs at his theatre – his fortunes are on a downturn. He loses what little furniture he has, including his piano, upon which he had been playing the first bars of *La Valse de Paris* – a waltz, he informs us, his parents used to dance to and his mother sang to him as a child. He can only remember the first few bars, however. With no instrument to play, Offenbach strolls out into the Parisian night, more or less blind as a bat. As he walks along the garden railings of the Palais Royal (in the 1st arrondissement), he makes out the form of a woman in white. When he first 'meets' this woman, he has a moment of misrecognition. He hears, the other side of the railings, a lovely voice intoning the opening bars of *La Valse de Paris.* Enchanted, he takes the figure in a white dress, that he can but dimly make out, to be his mother – a strange Oedipal moment, since he will eventually fall in love with this simulacrum, who is, of course, Hortense. They chat a while and she then gives him the slip. A few days later, the same day as the bailiffs return his belongings to his theatre, Hortense turns up for an impromptu audition; he recognizes her voice and hires her on the spot.

In the film, this initial meeting is highly stylized and brings together several elements of theatre history. The composer from the Bouffes-Parisiens meets the singer from the Palais-Royal. The Palais-Royal was a gracious seventeenth-century building that housed cafés, boutiques and the famous Théâtre du Palais-Royal where first Molière and, a little later, Lully performed. The Palais-Royal was the place that Le Tout Paris went. But it was also a place of dissidence and debauchery. During the Revolution, it was from here that all the major marches began and where heads of the guillotined were first paraded. During the 1871 Commune it was destroyed. The point here, of course, is that Offenbach represents the new musical theatre of light-hearted and witty operettas with a satirical edge, whereas the Palais-Royal theatre stands for the more classical opera. Hortense began her career in the Palais-Royal theatre. Thus, her presence *inside* the Palais-Royal gardens and Offenbach's

Figure 14.1: Fresnay as Offenbach with his trade-mark pince-nez and Hortense (Yvonne Printemps) – note the way Fresnay tilts his head. © Lux Films.

standing *outside* operate metaphorically for what needs to merge if he is to succeed: a singer with operatic qualities to her voice, but one who is knowledgeable about the slightly looser side of life.

Hortense Schneider was, as in the film, extremely flirtatious and had numerous lovers, including the Khedive of Egypt, Ismaïl Pasha. But Offenbach was never one of them as far as we know. Doubtless, the love element was added to give spectators the frisson of watching husband and wife, Fresnay and Printemps, exchanging witty and flirtatious barbs. Given the solidity of their personal relationship, audiences must have enjoyed her delivering such lines as: 'I am a liar and I can't be faithful'; and singing the song 'Que les hommes sont bêtes/ Aren't Men Stupid'. Marcel Achard, who scripted and directed the film, tells us that 'apart from Offenbach's myopia and cigar and Hortense's beautiful voice' none of the rest bore any resemblance to the historical personages. He then adds an interesting codicil to the effect that 'virtue is not always rewarded',[4] presumably referring to the fact that Offenbach often struggled to make ends meet, except for the heydays of the 1860s.

Fresnay plays a convincing Offenbach whose myopia makes him almost blind, but whose ability to observe the truth of human relations permits him to transcribe it into his songs. Fresnay lets us feel this blindness by tilting his head to one side and slightly upwards as if the pince-nez is more of a handicap than of use (see figure 14.1 above). We sense in these gestures his ability to scrutinize closely the way we live our lives – and the titles of the many songs that Hortense sings serve only to endorse this talent for closely observed social foibles. As Brogan puts it, Offenbach caught 'the spirit of the city in music'.[5] Certainly, the film captures the brilliance of this high period of the Second Empire and its facile, somewhat frivolous mood. The film, with its fifteen songs (a rate of one every six minutes), has that same 'light touch and insouciance'[6] associated with the epoch.

Achard also makes the point that in his film, beyond the interest value of these two major entertainers of the Second Empire and the other historical personages such as Napoleon III (Lucien Nat) and Eugénie (Raymonde Allain), there is considerable realism to be found both in the décor by Clavel and the dresses designed by Christian Dior. We recall that this film was in production during the year 1949, two years after Dior had launched the New Look, which brought back the flared skirt, nipped in waist and fitted upper-bodice style associated with the Second Empire look so favoured by Empress Eugénie (in particular, the enormous crinolines). Dior's design was originally called the Corolle line because of the huge skirt. This New Look caused considerable controversy, primarily because, in a time of great austerity and rationing, enormous swathes of cloth were used to create the effect. It was accused of extravagance and artificiality.[7] Simone de Beauvoir described this 'elegance as a form of enslavement', and fashion of the time as 'nostalgic and physically constraining'.[8] Coco Chanel was also incensed at male designers' control of the female form, accusing them of 'making outfits in which women could not move'.[9] Even Jean-Paul Sartre had his view, seeing the New Look as a reactionary design, putting women back into constructions of femininity from which the war had allowed them to escape.[10] The furore made Dior into an international name – a name that certainly added huge value to Achard's film and enticed audiences to see Yvonne Printemps/Hortense Schneider's parading in his magnificent designs, executed by the chief costumer Jean Zay. Indeed, the dresses for her stage performances – including her command appearance before the Emperor and Empress – could hardly have managed any more crinoline. The skirts of the dresses are massive: swathes of satin taffeta for the operettas; for the command performance, a white satin dress with a triple-tiered skirt of flounces full of mousseline effects. The dresses themselves become, in these moments, the spectacle (see figure 14.2 below).

Though not quite a catwalk, this film certainly endorsed the fact that Dior had reasserted Paris' reputation as the capital of fashion.[11] Thus the contemporary harks back to the 1858 period when Worth became the first Haute-Couturier and Paris the centre of fashion. A time when excess was its hallmark – as in the 1950s' New Look. A time, remarkably, where a similar construction of a feminine mystique occurs. After the 1920s and 1930s, when women designers dominated female fashion, male designers are, in the 1950s, once again in control of the look – the concept of the total woman is back, with rounded hips and elevated bust. Moreover, during the 1950s, this fashion of excess (and implicit conservatism) spread to most classes through the democratization principle of mass consumption. In real terms, this meant original copies (of Dior say) for the reasonably well-heeled, middle-class women and prêt-à-porter fashion imitations for those of lesser means. Women bought into the image of their

Figure 14.2: Hortense in a Dior-inspired dress – at the Emperor's Ball in *La Valse de Paris*. © Lux Films.

own repression, as it were, during a period in French political-cultural history that we know was one of conformity; a time dominated by a desire amongst a newly-emergent middle class for respectability, to be seen to have taste. Just as in the Second Empire (thanks to Eugénie's enormous stranglehold on style), there is in the 1950s an invention of a bourgeois model that is based in the feminine (and an excessive sense of what was considered taste). How different from the Restoration period, where a bourgeois style was a masculine conceptualization, producing, as we saw, amongst other styles, that of the dandy.

Clavel's décor is typical of the Napoleon III style – very strikingly so at the reception held after the command performance with tall marble pillars, wide marble dance-floor, plenty of crystal and silver and gold on the tables. Clavel very cleverly suggests through his décor, however, that whilst it looks expensive, much of it is factitious. In this, he remains true to the so-called splendour of the Second Empire. Little that glistened was gold; most of it tended to be electro-plated, even if the glitter was dazzling enough.[12] We sense that all is on borrowed time, a bit of a house of cards. Pastiche culture – as indeed it was. Eugénie, with her penchant for Marie-Antoinette, stripped the Louvre museum of its finest Louis XVI furniture and had copies made of other famous furniture designers' pieces.[13] In the film, Hortense's *pavillon* (small mansion) is another remarkable example of this pastiche culture.

Whilst it has restrained classical lines outside, inside is a highly decorated space, full of rich fabric ornamentation and over-stuffed with an eclectic collection of weighty furniture.

In Chapter 12, we discussed Clavel's heavy décor for *Le Comte de Monte-Cristo*. Here it is again. However, in both instances, Clavel is being completely realistic in his set design. But the interesting effect is the suggestion that these non-Republican epochs in France's history appear, if not vulgar and ostentatious then, at the very least, in need of grounding their ideological selves through sheer mass (bulk of furniture and female attire) and certainly through a reference to the past, despite the effects of industrial modernization. How interesting, therefore, that fashion in the form of Dior's 1950s' New Look also sourced its inspiration from nineteenth-century glamour, and thereby must be considered retro. Indeed, it certainly goes against the grain of other design domains of the 1950s, in particular the contemporary design of architecture and furniture, which was ultra-modern, light and with clean lines drawn from the work of Le Corbusier and Alvar Aalto (amongst others).

In both periods (Second Empire and 1950s' France) we sense, then, this tension between the draw of the past and a desire to transcend it – as if new technologies had both to be tamed and allowed to break boundaries; to be both feared and admired. As always, it is worth reminding ourselves of the unease felt during the early 1950s in terms of the clash of political ideologies and the new age of nuclear technology. Recall that the Western Allies founded NATO (1949) in the light of what they perceived as the communist threat as exemplified by Mao Zedung's defeat of Chiang Kai-shek and establishing the Peoples Republic of China (1949); the former USSR's creating its first Atom Bomb (1949); and the war in Korea (1950–1953). NATO's purpose was, ostensibly, to prevent the spread of communism, which everyone believed would unleash a Third World War – this time an Atomic one. In effect, the Korean War was the first proxy war in the global Soviet-American Cold War (1945–1989) which was all about spheres of ideological influence and which, in its 44-year time span would produce countless conflicts (Vietnam, Afghanistan), many of which remain unresolved even today.

But let us return to our film and its technicians. Christian Matras was the director of photography for this film, as indeed he was for *Les Violettes impériales*. Whilst much has been made of the influence of film director Max Ophuls on his cinematography (see Chapter 19), we have evidence here of Matras' own inventiveness with other film directors, especially with Marcel Achard, which suggests that Matras is not necessarily quite so conservative as certain critics make out.[14] Achard was primarily a dramatist who wrote for cinema (most significantly, in the corpus of our films, he wrote the script for Ophuls' *Madame de...*). He directed only three films; doubtless, therefore, he was reliant on his director of photography to achieve the overall look of the film. There are some remarkable sets of shots, in particular those in the operetta sequences that take place in Offenbach's Théâtre des Bouffes-Parisiens. For example, in the first presentation of Offenbach's new operetta *La Vie parisienne,* there are five camera positions during Hortense's delivery of her song 'Il est content mon colonel/My colonel is happy'.[15] The following figure makes this complexity of camera positioning clear:

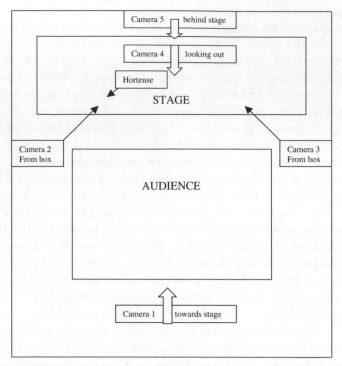

Figure 14.3: Camera positions for operetta *La Vie parisienne* – in *La Valse de Paris*.

The first comment to make about the camera positioning is the blurring of boundaries between operetta and real life. The suggestion is that there is not such a clear demarcation line – in particular camera 5 makes this point, located as it is behind the stage backdrop but able nonetheless to see through the stage out to the audience. Audience involvement from three positions – box and the stalls (cameras 1, 2 and 3) – completes the criss-crossing of boundaries offered by the multi-positions of the camera. Finally, Hortense directly returns the gaze to the box, thereby implying complicity between what she is singing and the person she is looking back at. This criss-crossing of camera point of view acts metaphorically for the crossover between real life and operatic fantasy. As we continue through the film, from this sequence on, every time Hortense sings a song, the crossover between life and operetta is complete: at times Offenbach's songs resonate in real life, at others, Hortense's life become the source for yet a new song. Unsurprising, therefore, that, when they are presented to Napoleon III, he says: 'You are inseparable in my admiration'. And, as we know from the end of the film, at Hortense's suggestion, Offenbach turns her life into his famous operetta: *La Belle Hélène*.

If we now turn to *Les Violettes impériales*, Matras, as the director of photography, had different issues to deal with this time, beyond those of space, because this film was made in colour, using the Gevacolor system. This was Matras' first film in colour and it was a co-production with Spain, which meant handling two sets of locations and crew.[16] The most significant issue for Matras was getting the light right for the colour system in order to achieve the desired realism. Pre-production took several months so as to carry out the trials necessary to check out the colour in terms of its reaction to light, the actors' skin, the material of their costumes, and so on.[17] As we saw in the discussion about colour systems, even if Gevacolor gives good resolution in full light, it nonetheless presents difficulties since it is not always stable and has problems with colour saturation, especially under heat, turning red to brown and beige to black. Shooting for this film was in the summer months, June through September: hot months in Spain. According to Gilberte Turquan, to avoid the dangers of saturation, Matras went for a muted colour for Spain's landscape; this, in turn, had the effect of allowing the white of Eugénie's costume to contrast effectively with the dark one of her mother's.[18]

Sadly for me, the version I saw of this film had lost all colour definition and so felt like a black and white film. However, Matras' camera work here has all the fluidity that we associate with his work in partnership with Ophuls. The musicality of the film, with its several numbers sung by Luis Mariano, naturally lends itself to tracking and circular shots as he moves around the set. The film's director, Richard Pottier, was primarily associated with films about music-hall stars, be they dancers (e.g., *La Belle Otéro*) or singers. He had an established record of making films with two of France's top popular singers, Tino Rossi and Luis Mariano (he made four films with Mariano in the 1950s). Yet, oddly, given the song and dance routines that he needed to film, he rarely used the same camera operator twice in his 1950s' products. And this was true of Matras, arguably one of the most adept at fluid camera work, but with whom he made only this one film. In this film, Matras excels himself in camera fluidity and movement. Apart from five song routines with Mariano, he tracks three different types of dances: the Spanish flamenco, the waltz and the quadrille. Matras' virtuosity is particularly tested in the waltz sequence, which takes place in the fairly restricting dining-room (5 by 3 metres or so) of a country inn. There is one long table down the centre around which Mariano waltzes, in turn, with six different seamstresses and their supervisor-designer. At the same time, he sings 'Le Miracle de Paris/The Miracle of Paris' (a song about the skills of dressmaking). In this sequence, Mariano easily persuades these young women to forego their birthday celebrations and make a beautiful dress for Eugénie de Montijo so that she can go to the Emperor's ball (see figure 14.4 below). After the waltzing they all willingly settle down to create their chef-d'oeuvre – they have four hours to do so, a miracle indeed! The dress is, of course, beautiful: pure white silk-satin, tightly bodiced, with a huge crinoline. The base of the skirt is decorated with mousseline, sparkling with mother of pearl. We see it for the first time when Eugénie (Simone Valère) enters the ballroom. Her crinoline is so wide, the widest of all, she literally brushes aside those smaller than hers – including her rival for Napoleon's attention, Madame de Pierrefeu (Marie Sabouret).

The love story in this film is in fact double and, as becomes clear, the title refers to this: '*impériales*' designates Eugénie; '*violettes*' the young gypsy woman Violetta. We begin in

Figure 14.4: Eugénie in a massive crinoline for the Emperor's Ball – *Les Violettes impériales*. © Les Films Modernes.

Spain, 1851. Eugénie and her mother (Colette Régis) arrive in Granada – in the gypsy quarter, apparently Eugénie's favourite part of town. There, Eugénie dispenses gifts to the bedraggled children. A beautiful gypsy, Violetta (Carmen Sevilla), touched by Eugénie's kindness to the poor, reads Eugénie's future and confirms she is soon to wear a crown. Eugénie's mother entertains high hopes of her daughter marrying a prince and mentions this to her friend Prosper Mérimée (Raymond Girard), who happens to be in town writing his play *Carmen*. He foresees that Louis Napoleon will soon accede to power, whereupon Eugénie and her mother head for Paris accompanied by her cousin Juan de Ayala (Luis Mariano) as their male chaperone. Juan – a bit of a playboy – professes love for Eugénie, but she kindly rejects him. In the meantime, before leaving Granada, he has also met Violetta at a taverna where she performs an exquisite flamenco. Very taken by her, Juan now covers her with blandishments about love. She refuses to fall for his charms, although she is clearly smitten.

Once in Paris, mother and daughter learn that their trunks with all their clothes and ball gowns have got lost in transit. Eugénie is in despair: how can she go to the Emperor's first imperial ball? The enterprising Juan dashes off, buys a trunk load of silks and mousselines, tracks down the seamstresses working for the top dress designers 'Caroline et Sophie', enchants them with his song and dancing ('Miracle de Paris') and they fabricate the most beautiful of dresses (see figure 14.4 above).

At the ball, during the quadrille dance, the Emperor is immediately swept off his feet by Eugénie, to the fury of one of his mistresses, Madame de Pierrefeu, who plots Eugénie's downfall. Her first move is during a hunt, when she endeavours to set a trap whereby the Emperor will find Eugénie alone in Juan's company in a hunting lodge. It fails because Juan gets wind of it and warns Eugénie, who hides behind a screen whilst he takes Violetta, now Eugénie's lady-in-waiting, into his arms. Once Empress, Eugénie banishes Madame de Pierrefeu from court. Meantime, Violetta, embarrassed at having to pretend to be Juan's lover and unconvinced by his declarations of love, wants to return home to Spain. Eugénie, whose own life is now settled, tries to persuade Juan to stop philandering and marry Violetta. He refuses, saying he could never marry a gypsy. Violetta overhears this humiliating conversation and runs out into the night; a thunderstorm crashes overhead. She ends up in a park where she overhears Madame de Pierrefeu telling an anti-Bonapartist about a plot she has hatched to assassinate Eugénie – by throwing a bomb under her carriage that very night. A drenched and feverish Violetta tries to warn Eugénie, but she refuses to listen. Whilst Eugénie is distracted, Violetta grabs her mistress' cloak, dashes into the carriage and takes off. Juan and the cavalry take pursuit to try and save her, but the carriage is blown up. Thankfully, the injuries are not fatal. Convinced now of the depth of feelings he has for Violetta, Juan asks for her hand in marriage (see figure 14.5 below).

Although Mariano is the lead star in this film, what dominates, both in terms of fashion and décor, is the feminine. The costume designer for the women was Marcel Escoffier; the chief costumier, Jean Zay. In other words Zay implemented Escoffier's designs in much the same way as he executed Dior's fashion designs for *La Valse de Paris*. André Bardot was responsible for dressing Mariano.[19] The dresses worn by the women – in particular Eugénie, but also Violetta – are given centre stage and, intriguingly, are occasionally mirrored in Juan's outfits in terms of colour-tone, cut of jacket and fabric. Thus, he sports light-coloured satin waistcoats that match the light colours of Eugénie's attire. Some of his jackets are inspired by the Spanish bolero cut, and complement Eugénie's white satin bolero jacket with dark brocade trimmings that she wears at the beginning of the film. One of Juan's waistcoats is made of tartan fabric – a fabric much in vogue during the Second Empire and also worn in the film by Eugénie. Until this point, therefore, his clothes align him more with Eugénie than Violetta. Only at the very end, when he returns to Granada to marry Violetta, does he sport a matador-style outfit which readily pairs him with her Spanish-cut dress and big mantilla hanging from her shoulders to her ankles.

Juan may be the charmer, but it is actually the women who make the decisions in this film, thus reinforcing this sense of feminine space. Violetta refuses to be seduced; eventually Juan comes to her on her terms. After the bomb attack, she returns to Granada to make up her mind about Juan and call him when she is ready. Eugénie is the one to guide Juan in

Figure 14.5: *Les Violettes impériales* bent on selling marriage – Juan finally does the decent thing by Violetta. © Les Films Modernes.

matters of the heart; she also sets her own sights on Napoleon and more or less manages the campaign of seduction single-handedly, especially once she gets to the ball, where she effectively sidelines Madame de Pierrefeu. She exposes her rival's pettiness over seat-ranking – a crucial matter in Court circles – and provokes Napoleon into action on her behalf. Madame de Pierrefeu endeavours to control where she, Eugénie, should be allowed to sit. Napoleon intercedes and places Eugénie on the first rank of seating, much to Pierrefeu's fury. He then proceeds to dance the quadrille with Eugénie, only to apologize to her for his clumsy dancing, confessing 'One can be Emperor and gauche when one is full of emotion'. Eugénie has him eating out of her hand!

In relation to this dominance of the feminine, and indeed historically, this was the first time since the Revolution that a woman held sway where style was concerned. This did not mean that gender and role divisions were not fully in evidence at this time, however; far from it. They were signalled by style and effectuated in social behaviour. Thus, in keeping with his status as Emperor, the main Tuileries apartments were rich in décor, with a great deal of red velvet and gold on the walls, and huge crystal chandeliers. Conversely, Eugénie's apartments, which were private and not part of the display of political power, were not ornate at all, even if they were rather over-stuffed with furniture. Her three salons were each in a single distemper colour: pink, blue and green respectively. Set designer Barsacq faithfully reproduces her rooms – the walls are plain with plaster relief, although I cannot determine the colour since the Gevacolor has faded away. These rooms are filled with eighteenth-century furniture and contemporary over-stuffed chairs. In her dressing room, the walls again are light and her dressing-table is covered with white lace and blue ribbons.[20] The overall effect is, once again, very feminine. It is instructive that in the film, apart from the ballroom, we never penetrate into the Emperor's apartment rooms – the film, after all, is ultimately far more focused on Eugénie's triumph and Mariano's love affair with Violetta.[21]

Colour, the star Mariano, the musical element, all doubtless contributed to the enormous success of this film – if we compare audience figures for these three biopic films (see figure 14.6 below) it is clear the French public were far from the opinion of the British review *Monthly Film Bulletin,* which stated that 'Mariano sings an occasional song, but something rather more substantial in the way of musical accompaniment seems needed to prop up a plot which still looks like the skeleton for an operetta'[22] and went in their droves to see the story of the adventuress Eugénie and hear Mariano sing (indeed this film was the second top-grossing of the year, out-stripped by Duvivier's *Le Petit monde de Don Camillo,* starring Fernandel).

Les Violettes impériales	8 million
La Valse de Paris	2 million
Monsieur Fabre	1.5 million

Figure 14.6: Audience figures for the Napoleonic-period biopics.

Lastly we come to *Monsieur Fabre*. Fabre came from peasant stock. He was born in St-Léons in the Plateau Lévézou area of Aveyron, halfway between Milau and Rodez. This southern area of France was the perfect territory for the observation of insect life. The poverty of means of his childhood home meant that he struggled to get an education, despite his father's best attempts. Thus, Fabre's education was severely interrupted. At times he was in school, at others he was self-taught. This helps to explain why some of his positions in relation to education were so radical for the time. He supported the concept of free, secular education for all and for mixed-sex schools. This liberal, open-minded view brought him frequently into conflict with the directors of schools he eventually taught in, and with the dignitaries of the various small southern towns in which he lived. It did, however, gain him the admiration of Napoleon III and the support of the Emperor's enlightened Minister of State Education, Victor Duruy. Fabre's work as an entomologist also made him the scourge of the small-minded provincial bourgeoisie, who saw his evening-school classes on insect behaviour as no less than instruction in sex education. Needless to say, Fabre's run-ins with the authorities meant that his financial means were often very reduced. John Stuart Mill, a fervent admirer of his work, occasionally stepped in to help him out.

Fabre was the first to really investigate the life of insects and, as such, he was much in advance of his time. Where he remained a traditionalist, however, was in relation to family life. And it is this man of paradox that Diamant-Berger serves up for us in his film: Fabre the scientist with his absolute love of insects and Fabre the patriarch, the embodiment of strict family values. At home he rules the roost with a commanding presence. To get his way, he bellows at his wife and numerous children. He issues *dictats* as to how his household shall behave: basically, obey him! Whilst he actively encourages his daughters' education, he precludes his daughters from marriage: 'the Fabre girls do not get married' – in the end, mercifully, they are defiant and choose their own paths. There is no doubt, from the performance Fresnay gives us as Fabre, that this extraordinary man, whilst a loving husband and father, was so microscopically obsessed with his insects that he overlooked the smaller details where his family was concerned. This comes out most poignantly in relation to his son Jules (played by a very young 5-year-old Patrick Dewaere). Fragile in health, he is nonetheless inspired with the same love of entomology. Father and son regularly go out on a Sunday to observe insects (see figure 14.7 below). On this particular day, they are watching

Figure 14.7: Fabre (Fresnay) with his son Jules (Patrick Dewaere) in *Monsieur Fabre.* © Le Film d'Art.

ants at work. Fabre tells his son: 'Nature is not interested in moral issues; it's the strongest that wins. Ants sacrifice themselves to save the nest; that is their heroism even if they don't know it'. Fabre then turns his attention to something else and his son falls into the water. He runs home with him, puts him in a hot bath to counter the chill. But he then goes to his study to write up his experiments and forgets all about his son, thus compounding the chill, causing pulmonary problems that eventually lead, eleven years later, to his untimely death.

What Fresnay brings out most poignantly in his embodiment of Fabre is his inability to be attentive to the emotions of others because of his own repressed feelings. Each time he is confronted with difficult family situations he withdraws into his study. Fresnay's performance – whereby he stiffens in the presence of emotion and visibly loosens up when examining his insects – suggests this is because it is easier to identify with his insects, whom he credits with an instinctual drive, where no sides can be taken in relation to their behaviour. When it comes to human beings, he is awkward around his wife when he sees she is upset. Instead of consoling her by hugging her tight, he mumbles a few words of apology and rushes off to his study. The only strong reaction comes after his son has died. Yet it is thanks to his own driven nature that he had failed to notice that his son was constantly trying to keep up with him and that by working too hard, staying up all hours to observe insects, his health deteriorated to the point of collapse. Even in his grief, just as in his discomfiture, Fabre still turns to his work for consolation and escape.

Early in the film, when observing the kindness of caterpillars to one another, he remarks, 'if only we could learn from nature' – and that is essentially the thrust of the eleven documentary inserts of insect behaviour that punctuate this film. According to Diamant-Berger's son, who added an interesting post-script to the DVD release of *Monsieur Fabre*, the various insect documentary inserts came from found footage in the US.[23] This footage, in the film, is given French authenticity by the voice-over of Fabre/Fresnay, who explains the relevance of what we are seeing. The eleven inserts amount to fifteen minutes in all and it is through Fabre/Fresnay's commentaries that we get a sense of his own scientific understanding of this world, and its relevance to ours. Thus, from the endeavours of the wasp building its nest, we take the lesson that we should never give up: a principle Fabre embodies through his own scientific study. Of the spider and its web, in which it catches and eats everything it destroys, Fabre has to say: 'That is the appropriate war. The winner eats the vanquished. Our wars between people I do not understand. Man has not got the right to kill man'. We can learn, he tells us, from the industry of insects who turn solid earth into mud to build their nest; from the wasps who knew, long before man, how to make paper from wood by pulping it and making it into their hexagonal hives. What we also learn is that it is the law of the species that we must come to understand, but without letting our emotions get in the way. To bring moral values to the observation of insects is to anthropomorphize, which leads to a clouding of judgment.

This is the precise lesson he brings to the Emperor's court when he is presented to Napoleon III and Empress Eugénie to receive his Légion d'Honneur (1869). This sequence occurs halfway through the film. The scene opens with Fabre explaining to the Emperor how La

Fontaine's fable about the 'Cigale et la fourmi/The Cricket and the Ant' is a misrepresentation of the insects' real behaviour. The ant is far more astute than La Fontaine suggests, for it not only works hard to store its own food, it steals from the cricket who, by burrowing into the sap of the tree, makes a whole new store of nutrition available to its so-called rival. The Emperor is amused by the insects' lack of morals. To which Fabre replies 'Insects don't have morals, only instinct. Morality comes with intelligence, the sole province of humanity'. Napoleon chuckles and suggests that Fabre has too high an opinion of mankind: 'Few are worth more than your insects'. To which Fabre retorts, 'But man has the choice to be good'. During this encounter, Fabre stands before the seated Emperor and Empress. Fabre is clumsily dressed in a suit that is a bit too large for him. His hair is sleeked back but straggly at the ends. Most unfitting of all, he is not wearing his gloves as he addresses the Emperor. Instead he has them squashed up into a ball in his right hand as, with his left, he points and emphasizes parts of his argument – not quite in the face of the Emperor but close. All those around him are wearing white gloves. Fabre's are not even white but a dark colour and, eventually, he stuffs them into his inside breast pocket. Clearly Fabre is breaking protocol – however, the Emperor does not seem to mind.

The person who does mind is Eugénie. As soon as Fabre has taken his leave she lets her displeasure be known, on several counts. First, she indignantly asks if he is religious. Napoleon answers, with humour, 'Sovereigns who are too religious often end up on the guillotine'. She then turns her attention to Duruy, who is standing by, and queries Fabre's giving coeducational classes, which she understands are quite risqué. Duruy explains that he encouraged Fabre to set them up and they have been a huge success, and then takes his leave. Eugénie sneers that 'he smells of the proletariat'. Napoleon now reacts, telling her not to interfere in his politics. She accuses him of being a revolutionary. He laughs at her: 'Don't speak ill of revolutions, we owe them a lot in our family', implying that none of the Napoleons would have been in power without them.

The Eugénie we see in this film is closer to the one we know of historically. Rosine Delamare costumed this film and her dress for Eugénie, consistent with the Empress' style, is fully crinolined, tight-bodiced, in white satin overlaid with bejewelled mousseline trim. To remind us of her Spanish origins, she has a black mantilla shawl. We are quickly made aware that she is a devout Catholic, against secularism and something of a snob. She is uncertain whether she wants either Duruy, as minister of education, to have a say in who shall act as tutor to her son, or Fabre, whom he is proposing, as his actual tutor. It is not just their possible anti-clericalism that bothers her, however. They are too radical in their educational thinking and, as she tells her husband, from the wrong class. Napoleon asserts his own liking of the common man. Duruy, he assures her, is very popular with the people and he will keep him in post. Fabre is the son of a peasant. As such, he concludes, 'both are excellent for the regime' – showing his desire (still, in 1869) for social reform. In fact, in 1867, Duruy passed the law on the democratization of secular education which included opening secondary education to girls. This law caused such a furore it would cost Duruy his ministerial post (in 1869) and Fabre his teaching post (in 1870). Reactionary beliefs, especially in the provinces, forced Fabre's hand to resign. Napoleon had no choice but to let his minister go, once the more conservative elements of the Assemblée Nationale gained the upper hand in the June 1869 elections and were able to put pressure on him to change his government completely.

Intolerance and censorship of ideas based in scientific evidence are what dogs Fabre's life – and they are well brought out in the film. On several occasions, we see Fabre being disciplined by the town dignitaries but, thanks to the Emperor and Duruy's support, they cannot fire him. Once the Emperor is gone, however, it is a different story. Here the film narrative tweaks history a little to make the points more forcefully. As we know from the above, Fabre had already resigned in 1870. In the film, the resignation he tenders is in 1871 – the Franco-Prussian war is lost, the Commune of Paris has been quelled, but instead of a change for the better, according to Fabre, things have merely got worse. Here is what he says, as he trudges off to town to meet with the Conseil de Discipline/Disciplinary Board:

> After the brief hope for an enlightened Republic that corresponded to my heart, the defeat (of the Commune) brought out all sorts of hatred and underhandedness. Men sunk to their lowest and my own enemies were unrelenting, affording me no respite.

The board is after him because he has been teaching about sex between plants in his evening classes. Fabre warns them: 'Because the Empire is over you think you are the strongest and can take away the evening classes, but it will come back some day. The poor will not be held in ignorance forever'. In these words he very much echoes Napoleon III's own sentiments set out in his 1844 treatise, *L'Extinction du paupérisme*.

The film does not end here. In a brief concluding sequence we meet up with the elderly Fabre, now 90 years old. It is 1913; he has remarried (and had a further three children). Président Poincaré comes to visit him to pay homage on behalf of the French nation. The film ends at this point with a rousing performance of the Marseillaise. At last Fabre is consecrated as a great French national hero.

Notes

1. Fresnay drew a 2m audience for *La Valse de Paris*; 1.5m for *Monsieur Fabre*.
2. Both these quotes come from http://fr.wikipedia.org/wiki/Eugénie_de_Montijo accessed 27.06.2009.
3. Review of *La Valse de* Paris, *Monthly Film Bulletin*, Vol. 17, No. 203, December 1950, p. 191 (no author name given).
4. Achard quoted in Jean Houssaye 'Yvonne Printemps et Pierre Fresnay tournent dans *La Valse de Paris*, sous la direction de Marcel Achard', *La Cinématographie française*, No. 1330, 24.9.1949, p. 15.
5. Brogan (1989, p. 112).
6. Jean Houssaye, op. cit., p. 15.

7. See Cawthorne (1997, pp. 108–9; 121).
8. Steele paraphrasing De Beauvoir (1998, p. 40).
9. Coco Chanel quoted in Steele, op. cit., p. 38.
10. See Chapsal (1986, p. 11).
11. Cawthorne, op. cit., p. 150.
12. Brogan, op. cit., p. 109.
13. http://fr.wikipedia.org/wiki/Eugénie_de_Montijo accessed 27.06.2009.
14. See Alain Jessua's commentary 'Working with Max Opuls' on DVD of *Madame de...*, where he asserts that Ophuls enabled Matras to break the mould of his traditional conservative style (Second Sight DVD).
15. We can see here how Achard had very little interest in reality with respect to the true chronology of things. *La Vie Parisienne* was first performed in 1866, two years after *La Belle Hélène* which is supposed to be based on the story we have just seen unfold in the film, namely Hortense's fickleness in love.
16. 1952 was the second year of France making any productions in colour – two were made in this year.
17. Turquan (1953, p. 35).
18. Ibid., p. 35.
19. He also did Marais' costumes for *Le Comte de Monte-Cristo*.
20. Details of Eugénie's rooms can be found in the informative essay by Olivier Courteaux, 'Charles Frederick Worth, The Empress Eugénie and the Invention of Haute-Couture' published online http://195.154.144.20/en/reading_room/articles/files/471885.asp accessed 30.06.2009.
21. Barsacq did have a big set to design for the ball sequence so he turned to trick photography to create the effect. Here he used the true scale for the lower half of the ball-room and for the upper half – balcony and roof – he used a plastic model. The camera is set at about 1.5 metres from the plastic model as it shoots through the model and into the set in which the action is taking place (See Barsacq, 1970, p. 163).
22. Review of '*Les Violettes impériales*', *Monthly Film Bulletin*, No. 260, 1.10.1955, p. 141 (no author name given).
23. 'A propos de *Monsieur Fabre*', in DVD extras of *Monsieur Fabre*, Pathé Distribution, 2006.

Chapter 15

The Second Empire in the Raw: Martine Carol's Celebrity Courtesans

The Demi-mondaine – a new species of womanhood

The courtesan, or demi-mondaine as she was also known, was a phenomenon of the nineteenth century. What distinguishes her, in particular, say, from famous mistresses of the kings of France in the previous century, was her lack of a place in society. The courtesans occupied a world in between, a demi-monde, as Dumas *fils* so astutely coined it.[1] Dumas was well-placed to do so – we recall that he turned his own famous liaison with Marie Duplessis into a bestselling novel, *La Dame aux camélias*, one year after her death. A different class from the earlier mistresses, the courtesan emerged as society became more mobile, both commercially speaking (in relation to the increased flow of money across the middle classes) and physically through transportation (for example a number of these demi-mondaines were foreign in origin: Cora Pearl, Lola Montès). Whilst these demi-mondaines were inadmissible into Court (Royal or Imperial), many held great sway in all of top society's circles and were pursued by men of the aristocracy as much as by the rich bourgeois – which is an amazing feat of self-promotion when one considers that almost all courtesans came from poor backgrounds (despite what Dumas *fils* claimed).[2] The point is, however, that they obtained celebrity status through sheer hard work. They educated themselves, learnt the appropriate social skills, turned themselves into stage artistes, became highly cultured – all as a means of capitalizing on their allure to capture the attention of the extremely wealthy. As a result, not only were they fabulously rich, they were also much admired by intellectual and artistic circles. Several of France's finest courtesans of the period were the centre of attraction for writers, artists, politicians and the like. Some even founded their own salons, such was their wit, intelligence and style. There was also a fine line between women of the theatre and the courtesan: Hortense Schneider, Caroline Otéro, Mery Laurent and Sarah Bernhardt come to mind. Whilst they were hugely successful in their art, they were, nonetheless, supported in their extravagant lifestyles by very rich lovers. There were other courtesans, of poorer talent it, has to be said, who commanded equally dizzying sums of money – amongst them, Lola Montès (1820–1861),[3] and Blanche d'Antigny (1840–1874), who was, first, Manet's model for the painting of *Nana* (1877) and later, in 1879, the source of inspiration for Zola's novel of the same name. It is these demi-mondaines who are the focus of our study here.

Box-office fodder: Christian-Jaque's *Nana*

The critic who accused Christian-Jaque of turning Zola's bleak novel *Nana* into a Feydeau farce is not far off the mark.[4] The film bears very little relation to the original story about the dark passions released by the heroine, even if it might bear some resemblance to the life of a courtesan who progressively ruins her lovers: the corrupt banker Steiner (Noël Roquevert), who embezzles and sells false shares to sustain Nana (Martine Carol) in a lifestyle she expects; the aristocratic Vandoeuvres (Jacques Castelot), who loses everything and commits suicide; the parvenu Comte Muffat (Charles Boyer), Napoleon III's right hand man, who ruins himself for her, loses his reputation and becomes so addicted to her that he strangles her at the end of the film, simply because he cannot live without her. Of Nana's degradation in life, as in death, we see nothing. Just a high-spirited, ruthless and rather vulgar opportunist portrayed by a Martine Carol, whose body is on constant display – especially her bosom, which is pushed up high in the various bodices or corsets she wears, and her elegant, sensuous legs. The film omits the many interesting facets to Nana's sexuality, including a lesbian relationship with one of her friends, Satin, in favour of a simplified version of this demi-mondaine where she plays one lover off against another. There is none of the courtesan as skilled entertainer or intelligent interlocutor, but plenty of playful innuendo, which severely reduces Carol's role to box-office fodder. The 2.7 million-strong audience would get their pound of flesh, but nothing resembling the portrait Zola served up in an attempt to expose the bestiality of mankind whose lust is fuelled by the carnal amorality of women such as Nana. In short, Nana is toned down (in terms of unbridled sexuality), softened up (rendered pleasurably sensual), and deprived of her thrust for independence which made her a free spirit, despite Zola's cruel ending for her in the form of a terrible disfiguring smallpox. In Christian-Jaque's *Nana* we are presented with a tease who gets her just deserts; in Zola's we get a full-blooded '*insoumise*' – a woman who refuses to be registered as a prostitute with the police and thereby placed under their control; a woman who fights, no matter how unsuccessfully, to overcome a patriarchal model that oppresses her and others like her. Even if Zola despises prostitution and demi-mondaines, we nonetheless understand the circumstances that drive these women to sell their bodies. We also receive a vivid portrait of the men who brutalize them. Zola intended his *Nana* to expose the connection between prostitution, fraud, dishonesty, greed, stupidity and the empty frivolity of the Second Empire. Christian-Jaque's *Nana* offers, instead, a safe portrayal of loose morality that is suitably punished, and which stands as a warning to women who transgress: become a woman of easy virtue, exploit and belittle a man, take his money and reputation at your peril, which is the essential message of Nana's death by strangulation. Napoleon III (Jean Debucourt) comes over as a kindly, avuncular figure, particularly when giving advice to his disgraced minister Muffat, and not as the embodiment of a corrupt power system that Zola abhorred.

In both instances (novel and film) socio-political discourses – be they of the end of an Empire (time of the novel) or the beginning of a heavily-censored, new Fourth Republic (time of the film) – get played out upon the body of the female. We find a similar pattern in the other film to be considered, also starring Martine Carol: *Lola Montès*. Lola, the daughter of a music-hall performer, is unlike her predecessor Nana, who was born into dire poverty – the daughter of a washerwoman (her mother is Gervaise whose own story appears in Zola's *L'Assommoir* and which Clément adapted to film, *Gervaise,* in 1955). Yet Lola's trajectory is not dissimilar: her meteoric rise, due more to her allure than to her skills as a dancer, is matched by her equally resounding crash into poverty and illness. Neither her story nor that of Nana has the edifying apotheosis of Marguerite in Dumas *fils'* Romantic novel *La Dame aux camélias,* where she sacrifices herself for her lover. The story of the courtesan of the July Monarchy as portrayed in Dumas' novel and the film is a tragic, rather idealized one. Compared to Lola and Nana, whose lives as courtesans lasted 16 years, Marguerite's was a mere seven. In Bernard's film adaptation of Dumas' novel, we see Marguerite (Micheline Presle) reduced to utter poverty, dying of tuberculosis as she hallucinates her marriage to Armand (Roland Alexandre), her beloved. A more poignant, Romantic image could not be composed. With *Nana,* the tone is far more cynical in the get-rich-quick environment of the Second Empire where men have to speculate to accumulate. Nana behaves no differently from the men, except that she speculates with her body, her exhibitionism and scandalous renown. Lola is something of an in-between – like Marguerite, she moves in auspicious and cultured circles, yet, like Nana, she promotes herself as a performer. The beginning of her career as a courtesan (1843) more or less coincides with Marguerite's (1840). It ends around 1859 (two years before her death), a year after Nana's begins. Lola straddles two periods, therefore – the July Monarchy and the heyday of the Second Empire. This distinction between Nana and Lola is perpetuated in the lovers they attracted. Lola's were writers, composers, princes and kings, whereas Nana's were types: the Jewish Banker Steiner, the good for nothing speculator Fauchery (Dario Michaelis), the parvenu Comte Muffat, and so on. Furthermore, Lola was an international performer and courtesan – her nationality an ever-changing one (born in Ireland, British father, naturalized German, bigamously married to an American). Nana is resoundingly French. What they both share, however, is a fine sense of style, and they are often ahead of the time in their attire. For example, Lola wears crinoline before it properly came onto the market – we see this clearly in her visit to King Ludgwig I of Bavaria (Anton Walbrook). The date is no later than 1848 – when the crinoline was first designed, but it was not fully commercialized until the 1850s. Similarly, Nana is ahead if her time with her dress shape. She favours the new trim Princess line with, at the back, a bustle and tournure (a small rear-shaped crinoline) that replaced, in 1870, the huge crinolines.

Caught in a Cage: Max Ophuls' *Lola Montès*

The film *Lola Montès*, as with *Nana*, is loosely based on the life of a real courtesan – Marie Dolores Eliza Rosanna Gilbert, who adopted the stage name of Lola Montès. In real life Lola was a far more spirited person than the tamed, caged 'animal' we have in Ophuls' version of her story. She ran away from her brutal husband – Captain James (her mother's former lover) – and set herself up, aged 22, as a Spanish dancer. From this moment on until her death, she more or less managed and mis-managed her own career as dancer and courtesan. Amongst the many lovers with whom she spent *her* time and *their* fortune, we can count Franz Liszt, Dumas *fils*, the Prince of Orange, and King Ludwig I of Bavaria. She travelled far and wide, living and performing in Europe, Australia and America. Eventually, her notoriety became her *raison d'être* – celebrity culture at its most extravagant. Thus, by 1851, when Lola was once more in dire straits, she began to stage shows about her life (for example, 'Lola Montès in Bavaria'); a few years later, when she could no longer dance or perform, she gave lectures on her own memorabilia.[5] She suffered a stroke in 1860; a year later she succumbed to pneumonia. The essential point being made here is that *this* Lola had agency, even if her fortunes fluctuated wildly.

Whereas the real-life Lola exploited her own sexual attraction, made a spectacle of herself, in Ophuls' film she becomes a spectator of her own objectification. Ophuls presents us with a woman as 'seen in a world designed by men'.[6] Ophuls clearly perceives Lola as someone who has been caged all her life and who only 'gained acceptance as a body, as an object of desire'.[7] Indeed, the swirl that Ophuls women get caught up in – be it *La Ronde*, *Mme de...*, or *Lola Montès* – is graphically represented in Christian Matras' cinematography. It is as if Ophuls' women are victims of their own illusions, always moving on but getting nowhere – a true place of disempowerment if ever there was one, and one that certainly has contemporary resonances with 1950s' France. As Peter Harcourt puts it: 'In spite of his period settings and melodramatic plots, his world is paradoxically modern'.[8] Just as Ophuls' women live in a world where the 'fluctuations of emotions' clash with 'the rigidity of social codes',[9] so, too, the 1950s was a period when conservatism vied with modernism; when a new post-war social order feared the emancipation of its women. This Fourth Republic, which had finally achieved universal suffrage for all, much like the troubled nineteenth century before it (which first gave the vote to all men, then took it away, only to give it back again), was uncertain as to whether it could trust its newly-based electorate.

The Lola that Ophuls serves up to us, then, is quite a different one from the real one. This Lola is now in her last years and performing her life in a circus under the control of the ringmaster, Monsieur Loyal (Peter Ustinov). It is instructive that the real Lola had actually turned down an offer by the great American circus impresario P. T. Barnum to put on such a show. No matter. We are in the realm of fiction. This Lola – with her life on display – is emblematic of the grotesque consequences of celebrity culture. She is ill; each performance is a terrible strain on her already weakened heart. People come to see the performance of her past lives as much as to witness, maybe, her death in the ring. At the end of each performance, Lola climbs to the circus top where she dives from the trapeze platform, held by the thinnest of threads, and hurtles herself down. There is no safety net – how much longer can she survive?

A great deal has been written about Ophuls' misunderstood 'masterpiece' *Lola Montès*, and the dreadful mutilation it received before the producers agreed to release it. I intend, therefore, to sketch in these issues only insofar as they concern the concept of *Lola Montès* as a costume drama. According to film historian David Thomson, the package for the film had been pre-ordained before it ever got to Ophuls.[10] It had been conceived of as a super-production involving the successful husband and wife team, Christian-Jaque and Martine Carol, with a script by Cécil Saint-Laurent (of the Carolinades fame). The original Swiss producers pulled out and Ralph Baum of Gamma films picked up the project in co-production with Unionfilms/Munich. Baum had produced other Ophuls' films and, together with Unionfilms, he brought the project to Ophuls. The producers were looking for a blockbuster and invested a massive $2 million.[11] The Franco-German producers insisted on the film being in Eastmancolor, in stereo-sound and cinemascope, none of which appealed to Ophuls – but which he used in interesting ways, as I shall explain below. They also insisted on keeping Saint-Laurent's scenario (there is no evidence of a script[12]) and Martine Carol for the lead. With her successful track record of roles as courtesans and women of easy virtue (averaging an audience of 3 million) she seemed a surefire investment. She had won the French Victoire two years in a row (1952 and 1953) and was also the top-ranked French woman star in the US.[13] None of this appealed to Ophuls, either. He completely re-wrote the story, keeping only Saint-Laurent's idea of the circus, which comes at the end of his script but which Ophuls makes the centrepiece to his film[14] – using the circus to show 'depth hiding behind banality', as he put it.[15]

This was the brilliance of the undertaking. Because Ophuls was convinced Carol could not act, he decided to pull on her failings and her strengths and make a film that was less about the light ribaldry of a courtesan (à la Nana) and more a disquisition on fame and cinema's role, amongst other mediations, in feeding into and off that fame. As he said:

> When it was proposed that I do 'Lola' it seemed to me that the subject was completely foreign to me. I don't like lives in which a great many things happen. At the same time, I was struck by a series of news items which, directly or indirectly, took me back to 'Lola': Judy Garland's nervous breakdown, the sentimental adventures of Zsa Zsa Gabor. I meditated on the tragic brevity of careers today.[16]

Since Carol's acting abilities were limited, Ophuls sat her upon a performing platform in a circus – people paid their fee and were invited by the ringmaster to ask her a question about her life; this then led to a tableau being enacted in the form of a flashback. Carol sits impassive – she becomes object (see figure 15.1 below). The humiliation of her present status, petrified like a mummy – a wax doll is Ophuls' term[17] – is enhanced by the replicas of her head, impaled on spikes, being carried about the circus ring by cavorting, faceless figures in red uniforms (all of whom bear a number, reinforcing this idea of her insignificance and ultimate replaceability). The flashbacks flesh out her love affairs and her early childhood, but without depth: we see Lola constantly on the move (her own mantra is 'life for me is moving on'), so there is no time for psychological exploration. Thanks to Carol's wooden performance, Lola remains an empty surface (Truffaut called her a 'plaster statue'),[18] not even a mirror upon which we can project our own desires. The erotic value of her blonde

Figure 15.1: Lola sits wooden-like as M. Loyal the ringmaster takes command. © Gamma Films.

mane is undone by Ophuls' obliging her to sport black hair. Even her sexuality – or, at least, gender – is playfully questioned. In the first flashback, she is in quite mannish attire. She lies back, resplendent in a fancy waistcoat and smokes a cigar, as Liszt (Will Quadflieg) tinkles away at the piano. Indeed, gender roles appear reversed here as well: Liszt plays to entertain, much as a wife would for her husband.

Any titillation based on expectations from Carol's previous film roles – such as exposing her bosom, flashing her legs, or even offering a nude profile – are all removed from this film. There is the one exception, when she has to escape from Bavaria. She is in bed wearing a nightgown, her bosom rising and falling as she cries. She then leaps out of bed but, before we can see much else, she pulls a mantle cloak around her and runs away. Other than this, Lola is in long-sleeved dresses that are buttoned up to the collar. And even if she begins to tear open her dress, as she does in front of Ludwig I of Bavaria, the camera immediately cuts away! Moreover, Lola is often semi-obscured from view, which further serves to frustrate spectator expectancy. Either she is behind grilles (as in the country inn with Liszt) or she is behind lace or muslin curtains. When she performs her acts in the circus, she is, for the most part, held in a very long shot; and when she dances the fandango she is wedged between two real female Spanish dancers so we cannot note how poor her dancing skills are, although a rather crude wiggle is maintained. It is here that Ophuls manages to turn the tables on the producers who tried to get him to make a film without art – by dissimulating the very star body they wish to consume. In fact, he serves her up nude only in a painting commissioned by Ludwig, but which no gallery in Bavaria will accept.[19] As Tom Milne so perceptively puts it: 'Lola Montès might be defined as a film about the humiliation of film-making within an industry demanding one's life blood be turned into spectacle.'[20] In this regard, M. Loyal (Peter Ustinov) comes to represent these producer-entrepreneurs. For while he may believe he is in love with his star, he exploits her scandalous life shamelessly.[21]

Let us return to the mutilation of the film. When it was premiered in December 1955, it met with a hugely hostile response from critics and audience alike. No one could understand the intention behind the film; audiences found it boring and disliked the presence of three different languages, which meant the use of subtitles. The producers immediately pulled the film and recut it for exhibition in several different lengths and guises from 1956 to 1957. But still it flopped.

What was there to misunderstand? Ophuls shot his film in three languages, producing three separate versions (French, English and German) so that the producers could have maximum impact on the international market with their blockbuster (although the English version appears to be lost). But all three original versions were, to a greater or lesser degree, multilingual to acknowledge the presence of the international cast of French, German and English-speaking actors. This multi-nationalism also reflects Lola's own wanderings across continents and her trilingualism. In the French version, whilst the French language dominated, certain scenes (the sequence with Liszt and most of the scenes in Bavaria) were kept in German with French subtitles. The German version was, however, truly multilingual – the circus sequences were in German; elsewhere French and German were mixed in together (in the long Bavaria episode for example). The producers, claiming audiences could not cope with the multilingualism, reduced each version to a single language. In reaction against the episodic nature of Ophuls' film – with its mixture of circus scenes and flashbacks – they re-cut it so that the narrative ran chronologically.

Nor did the producers like Ophuls' use of the soundtrack – they wanted stereo and he had not given it to them. Although there was a four-track recording system, Ophuls mistrusted this new technology and, for the most part, eschewed the use of stereophonic sound.[22] The dominant effect is similar to a single monophonic-track (as was standard practice in black and white film at the time, with the optic soundtrack to the side).[23] He did, however, use stereo in remarkable ways within the circus scenes – for example, we hear the voices of the spectators asking questions off to both sides of the screen, where they sit in darkness, and the ringmaster's more booming voice coming from the centre, creating a marvellous sense of width and off-screen space. To create the sense of depth in some of the more complex stagings – such as Lola's mother (Lise Delamare) negotiating her daughter's marriage – we hear, vaguely, what she is saying in the background as Lola and her mother's current lover (Captain James/Yvan Desny) sit and chat uncomfortably in the foreground. Just prior to that moment, Lola and her mother had ascended to the Paris Opéra box of her future intended. As the camera gradually tilts, panning left to right and right to left, following the two women, so, too, the sound of their voices go from left to right and vice versa. Ophuls also uses ambient, or what we now term Foley sound, to daring effect, considering the newness of this stereo technology – this is particularly the case for the opening chaotic sequence of the circus and elsewhere – for example, the background murmurs of voices in different languages.[24] The producers liked none of this and reproduced stereo sound overall, flattening these special achievements.

Finally, they were completely baffled by the choice of different colour palettes used for the various episodes. So they neutralized the effects by bringing everything back to a naturalistic colour. The original film length of 140 minutes was cut by 30 and, in some instances, 40 minutes.[25] Sadly, Ophuls died in March 1957 before he could protect this, his last film, from these terrible mutilations. Thankfully, however, since then there have been several remasterings, including two of the French version, both of which I have seen. The first was in 1968, thanks to the producer Pierre Braunberger. This came close to the Ophuls' version – including keeping the monophonic sound central to the image, but the length is around 110 minutes. More recently, there is the restored version of 2008 by the Cinémathèque française – also 110 minutes. This is the one deemed closest (and is now available on DVD). The German dialogue is back in the scenes in Bavaria, albeit in short doses. Stereophonic sound has been reinstalled as Ophuls intended it.

Let us now turn to the film itself. Before we get to meet Lola for the first time, we are drawn into the circus by a shot panning down that follows the lowering of the chandeliers. The camera rests briefly upon a white theatre curtain with twelve black and white tableaux etched upon it – these are the twelve tableaux of Lola's life the ringmaster, M. Loyal, promises we are to see. The curtains are pulled aside for M. Loyal to stride through and begin his ceremony – cracking his whip, he orchestrates the *mise-en-scène* of the seemingly-randomly-chosen tableaux. Two things are of interest to us here. First, the even numeric but not temporal division between the number of tableaux presented within the circus ring and those presented in flashback (see figure 15.2 opposite). The former are of course the ringmaster's staging, the latter are Lola's. Second the use of colour. This was Ophuls' first (and only) film in colour and he made precise use of it, almost as if implementing Alékan's belief that colour brought with it the possibility of striking out rather than reproducing the natural.[26]

Each tableau in flashback has a different colour palette attached to it. As we can see (from figure 15.2 opposite), the dominant colour for the circus is blue – although the colours of the other episodes are there to a minor degree, signalling that all stages of Lola's life are co-present in this circus ring.[27] But it is the dominant cold, scrutinizing metallic blue colour that exposes Lola. As Ophuls puts it: 'Thus, grotesquely deformed in this giant circus, in an over-accelerated rhythm so dear to the Americans, under the crude light of the arc-lamps, the "vertiginous ascension of this concubine" is played and danced out'.[28]

Tableau number	Place Circus – Present	Duration	Colour	Tableau number	Place of Flashback	Duration	Colour
1	The ring: M. Loyal intones: 'Parade of her lovers' – (segues into **2**)	7' 16"	Blue dominates; Jugglers and grooms in red; Lola in gold	2	On the country roads and in auberge with Liszt. Fading passion	10' 52"	Dull crimson red and ochre (autumn)
3	The ring: M. Loyal. 'Change of time to her brilliant adolescence' (segues into **4**)	2' 37"	Blue	4	On boat returning to France from India. At L'Opéra theatre in Paris	11' 35"	Mixture of metallic greys, dark blues, rusty brown
5	The ring: M. Loyal 'Marriage of love' – Lola in white and her new husband on roundabout	1' 58"	White	6	Into her real marriage – in Scotland with brutal husband; Lola escapes	1' 58"	Predominantly brown
7	The ring: M. Loyal 'Lola builds her career' – 'Rumour, scandal, passion, this is what she has chosen' Backstage: Doctor visits circus manager concerned about Lola's health	9' 11"	Blue for circus ring arena; red for circus sets. Brown and beige for backstage	8	Nice, exteriors: Showdown with her married lover, the orchestra conductor.	1' 05"	Red and white
9	The ring: M. Loyal 'Lola smokes Cuban cigars'	1' 03"	Red	10	Nice, interior, Lola's apartment: M. Loyal comes to try and sign Lola up	4'	Mixture of browns; Lola stark white dress
11	The ring: M. Loyal Lola's ascendancy as a trapeze act – 'Lola climbs, up, up, up' She climbs up to circus top	2' 15"	Blue	12	Bavaria: Lola's affair with King Ludwig I brought to a rapid end in 1848 by revolution	43' 55"	White (winter)
Total times		**23' 04"**				**73' 55"**	Brief flash of summer colours.

CODA TO FILM:
Lola up on circus top platform prepares to dive and survives.
Film draws to close, men come by Lola in cage to kiss her hands

DURATION 8'

COLOUR
Circus ring: Blue
Backstage: Brown

Figure 15.2: Lola's twelve tableaux; duration of episodes; colour palette.

Vertiginous is also an appropriate term for Christian Matras' cinematography. In the circus, the Paris Opéra theatre and King Ludwig's palace in Munich, the camera tilts up and down, pans left to right and back again. In the circus ring, it swirls round with the performing acrobats and roundabouts that dominate the arena. It travels back and forth, left and right into rooms and apartments where Lola lives. On two occasions only in the entire film, it holds M. Loyal, then Lola, in oblique and distorting low-angle shots – suggesting that both collude in this exploitation of fame. The first occurs in Lola's Nice apartment, when Loyal tries to persuade her to sign the contract and join the circus (tableau 10). The second comes right at the end, in the Coda, as Lola prepares to take her fall.

In relation to the tableaux, what interests us further is the greater length of time, three times as much, given to Lola's flashbacks over M. Loyal's presentations. This suggests that Lola's flashbacks are meant to defy M. Loyal's hyperbolic or salacious interpretations. For example, Liszt (tableau 2) is not made representative of the 'parade of lovers' – rather it is the ending of their affair, where, without drama, they take mutual leave of each other. We also note in particular the extreme length of Lola's final flashback (Bavaria, tableau 12) which amounts to 40 percent of the film's duration. This length indicates, doubtless, the simple story that Ophuls might have preferred to film, plus his fondness for his own favourite theatre actor, Anton Walbrook.

The precious details of the desired colour palette, which come from Ophuls' typed script for *Lola Montès*, are logged on the Cinémathèque française website about the restoration of the film.[29] Ophuls indicated on the script his intention to present Lola's life in four seasons – each with their dominant colour. Yet these are hardly temporal seasons as we know them – at least, as far as Lola's flashbacks are concerned. We note the arbitrary beginning in autumn (tableau 2) and the conclusion in winter (tableau 12). Very little of Lola's flashbacks brings us into touch with any idea of spring or summer – there is a brief moment of summer on the Côte d'Azur (tableau 8 in Nice) and, again, a flash of summertime in tableau 12 when she rushes off on horseback to force a meeting with Ludwig. With the exception of her white-time with him – seemingly the man she really loved – and her autumnal ending with Liszt, the remaining three flashbacks are dark, gloomy and very brown (tableaux 4, 6, 10). These memories are Lola's and they certainly do not correspond to M. Loyal's disloyal representation of her past as 'a brilliant adolescence' (tableau 4) or 'a marriage of love' (tableau 6). For example, in the circus version of her marriage to Captain James (tableau 5), Lola is all in white. Indeed, the whole tableau is in white – in stark contrast to the dominating blue associated with the circus (see figure 15.3 below, the white stands out even if this is a black and white print).

The hyper-reality of this false representation (like a white lie) clashes with Lola's own brown-coloured memory of that marriage (tableau 6). This suggests to us how much M. Loyal falsifies truth to make the audience happy (and probably represents a dig by Ophuls at his producers). Yet, peculiarly, this white foreshadows a later truth: Lola's true moment of happiness with Ludwig and its ensuing tragic ending (tableau 12). Here, finally, when she meets the love of her life, all is white around her. However, a fashion note of warning tells us

Figure 15.3: Lola's white wedding as staged in the circus; note the excessive *mise-en-scène*.[30]

to beware. Lola wears satin dresses in metallic purple (for her first audience with the King), and then either metallic pale blue or grey. Her clothing, in its metallic hues (reminiscent of the circus) jars with the hope and 'tenderness' of the white environment.[31] As she says, on her escape from Bavaria: 'It's too late'.

All is too late, and this is what the palette of colours tells us, as indeed do the various sets – all designed by the master of the ornate baroque, Jean d'Eaubonne. Whichever tableau she is in, the spaces in which Lola moves are restricting – so much for her belief that she can keep on moving. Time is indeed running out. There is a particular scene, just before she becomes Ludwig's mistress, that makes this so clear. Ludwig has come to visit Lola in the theatre. Everyone has left. The two of them are alone on stage. As Ludwig begins his wooing of Lola, a rope swings gently back and forth across the screen in the foreground: as much like a pendulum swinging as a foreshadowing of the rope tied every night around Lola's ankle as she leaps from the circus top.

What a grizzly reality is the life of a courtesan once she either fades (Lola), falls ill (Marguerite), or betrays once too often (Nana). However, the narrative is driven in such a way that what is not questioned is the economic necessity that pushes these women to 'prostitute' themselves, nor indeed are the men exposed for their selfish, even ruthless, exploitation of this situation: using these women to their own vain advantage, only to drop, abandon, murder them when they have gone too far. As we have noted in the study so far, female-centred narratives are far from dominant; we shall have to wait and see what the Belle Epoque produces in terms of a more rounded and extended set of narratives concerning women. For now, let us turn to the more dominant issue of masculinity. As we saw with the swashbuckler films, the male was able to put on display a varying set of masculinities without fear of his virility being put into question. Such, however, is not the case for our post-1860 male, as we shall now go on to discuss.

Notes

1. The word demi-mondaine came out of the title of Dumas *fils'* play, *Demi-monde*, which he first published in 1855.
2. He said, perhaps a little defensively: 'Let us establish, for dictionaries of the future, that the *Demi-Monde* does not, as people believe and say in print, represent the mob of courtesans, but the group of society people who have come down in the world'. (Dumas quoted in Denis Arnold (2004, p. 31) But in fact most women, including his Marie Duplessis, did emerge from the poorer classes; alternatively they might be the illegitimate daughter of some well-heeled person who refused to recognize her (but this was pretty rare).
3. There is considerable uncertainty as to her birth date: it varies from 1818 to 1821.
4. Jacques Siclier, in his review of Clément's *Gervaise*, mentions, by way of comparison with other adaptations of Zola, how Christian-Jaque's *Nana* has reduced Zola to the scale of Feydeau. ('Un film experimental: *Gervaise*', *Cahiers du cinéma*, Vol. 11, No. 63, October 1956, pp. 42–4).
5. Joanne Roberston provides a lively synopsis of Lola Montès' life in 'Lola Montez – Her Life', *Monthly Film Bulletin*, Vol. 45, No. 537, 1.10.1978, p. 210.

6. Harcourt (2002, p. 7).
7. Ibid., p.12.
8. Ibid.
9. Ibid.
10. David Thomson 'Fame and Misfortune: *Lola Montès*', *Sight and Sound*, Vol. 19, No. 7, July 2009, p. 92.
11. This figure comes from Mosk in *Variety* (25.1.1956, no page). *Cahiers du cinéma* (Vol. 10, No. 55, 1.1.1956, p. 55) set costs between 600–700 million francs. In either case, it was the most expensive film ever made in France up to that date.
12. A treatment of sorts was in existence apparently, but the novel by Saint-Laurent *La Vie Extraordinaire de Lola Montès* on which the film was supposedly based did not exist at the time and was not published until 1972.
13. See Gilberte Turquan 'Nos vedettes, valeur d'exportation' in *Cinématographie française*, No. 1666, May 1956 special Festival issue. On page 41 she lists French stars according to their export value.
14. Yann Tobin supplies this interesting titbit (1980, p. 58).
15. Ophuls quoted in Rivette & Truffaut (1978, p. 27).
16. Ophuls quoted in Burns (1996, p. 39).
17. As the script indicates: 'Her face is a mask. Completely detached, like a shadow of her life, in this circus review she wears the strange expression of a wax doll'. The script in its entirety can be viewed on http://lolamontes.cinematheque.fr/choix_max_ophuls.html accessed 17.07.2009.
18. Truffaut (1956, p. 29).
19. The painting is very reminiscent of Manet's own nudes, especially his 1863 *Dejeuner sur l'herbe* which was refused a showing in the official Salon of that year. Napoleon III, in his wisdom, opened a separate Salon des Refusés in a room annexed to the main exhibition where more daring paintings could be exposed. There is something very amusing about this piece of anachronistic art history!
20. Tom Milne 'Retrospective: *Lola Montès*', *Monthly Film Bulletin*, Vol. 45, No. 537, 1.10.1978, p. 209. I am sure that readers familiar with Godard's 1963 *Le Mépris* will draw many parallels between Ophuls' film and his in relation to the pressure he was under from producers to expose Brigitte Bardot and, too, of the inventive uses he made of colour.
21. Truffaut (1975b, pp. 255–6) confirms this view that Ophuls wanted to attack the indecency of spectacles based on scandal.
22. See Berthomé's very useful article on Ophuls' use of sound and language (Berthomé, 2002, pp. 130–3).
23. Ophuls was not keen on the new magnetic sound-track (as opposed to the mono-optical track). He used only the front four channels instead of the wide channels and decided to overlap soundtracks so that people in both the fore and background were heard. See also Stefan Dressler's interesting lecture online: http://theeveningclass.blogspot.com/2008/11/lola-monts-stefan-drssler-pfa-lecture. html accessed13.07.2009; and http://lolamontes.cinematheque.fr/son_stereophonique.html accessed 23.04.2009.
24. See Berthomé (2002, p. 133). Here it is made clear that Ophuls wanted the mono-optical effect. Details about the sound track can be found on http://lolamontes.cinematheque.fr/son_stereophonique.html accessed 23.04.2009.
25. See Romano Tozzi 'The Sins of Lola Montès', *Films in Review*, Vol. 10, No. 9, 1.11.1959, pp. 562–3. I have read elsewhere that it was released as a 90 minute film and again as a 75 minute film – see Stefan Dressler's lecture online http://theeveningclass.blogspot.com/2008/11/lola-monts-stefan-drssler-pfa-lecture.html accessed 13.07.2009.

26. Re: Alékan, see Crisp (1993, p. 390). Ophuls enounces an interesting disclaimer in relation to a self-conscious use of colour in an interview with Jacques Rivette and François Truffaut (originally recorded in 1957) in which he states the following: 'I was surprised to be taken for a revolutionary, or a renovator, because I thought that all I'd done was the most normal thing in the world. I assure you that there isn't a single element of research in *Lola Montès* – I was really involved in the subject and still am today. I can assure you that when I was watching the rushes and the projection people said to me "That blue! That red! It's too daring!", I didn't understand. Everything good in *Lola* happened because of my inexperience with colour and cinemascope – when I looked through the camera's viewfinder, it was as if I'd just been born: I did everything as it presented itself to me.' (Rivette & Truffaut, 1978, pp. 23–4) This somewhat disingenuous statement runs counter to Ophuls' actual script, which has precise indications of the colours he wanted to achieve for the various parts of his film. Perhaps he was being playful in this interview. Especially when he says elsewhere: 'Although I may insist on a dominant colour for a particular episode, I want all colours to collide with each other in the arena of the circus, because my circus runs through an entire life, encompassing all its stages' (Ophuls quoted in Yamaguchi, 1978, p. 65).

27. This reading is affirmed by Ophuls comments in the above footnote (Ophuls quoted in Yamaguchi, op. cit., p. 65).

28. http://lolamontes.cinematheque.fr/choix_max_ophuls_scenario2.html accessed 17.07.2009.

29. http://lolamontes.cinematheque.fr/restaurer_version_orginiale_lola.html accessed 23.04.2009. Browse through this lengthy website, it is full of golden nuggets: information on how the film was restored, how the stereo sound was remixed from the four tracks, colour re-instated correctly (etc).

30. Still image accessed from http://witneyman.files.wordpress.com/2008/11/lola_montes_21.jpg 11.09.2009.

31. The term 'tender' is Ophuls. His choice of colour for this episode is 'White, matt silver and gold, tender wintery blue'. See http://lolamontes.cinematheque.fr/couleurs_origine.html accessed 23.04.2009. So precise was Ophuls that, for tableau 2, he had a road painted ochre and the country inn hung with red muslin because the owner refused to let him repaint it red.

Chapter 16

From Empire to Republic: A Modernized France Emerging

A New type of masculinity 1860s–1880s

Before coming to the last chapter in this third part of the book, the case study of Daquin's *Bel-Ami* (Chapter 17), I want to offer a consideration of the new type of masculinity mentioned in Chapter 12. As we shall see, the films relating to this new masculinity provide an interesting and ambiguous set of representations. Several combining factors contributed to the emergence of this new type from the 1860s onwards. First, the greater mobility afforded by locomotive transport brought young men into the cities, especially Paris, to seek work in the new industries. Second, the growing financial world, thanks, in particular, to the redevelopment plans for Paris under Baron Haussmann, expanded the speculative markets and created a new wealth, based in stocks and bonds. Paper rather than gold came to have value. This brought in its wake a nouveau-riche category of man. And, finally, there was a new kind of businessman born out of the exponential growth of the retail business, from 1850 onwards, thanks to the development of department stores – the first of which was Le Bon Marché, 1852, and which inspired two of Zola's novels set in the early to mid-1860s, *Pot-Bouille* and *Au Bonheur des Dames*.[1]

By the early 1860s there is a marked change in masculine identity, which has been noted by historians and, of course, writers of the time. The form it takes is physical, sartorial and moral – producing a new type of virility; a shift induced by a number of factors beginning with the new kind of bourgeoisie that emerged as an effect of the Haussmannization of Paris. Whereas in the Restoration period it was bankers such as Rothschild who founded a new wealth and created a new type of bourgeois, now it was the speculator who formed the basis of this newest breed, be it in the form of trading bonds and shares or supplying products and services for mass consumption. The growth was swift. For example, in the1860s, the stock market tripled its share holdings (from 118 stocks to 307).[2] Furthermore, the new businesses and practices mentioned above brought in their wake a growth in staff in the form of clerks, shop assistants, journalists. In both instances, men of these bourgeois classes went to work, travelling to their offices, and so on. This, in turn, brought about a change in sartorial attire – what has been referred to by Flügel as the great masculine renunciation.[3] Clothing became more utilitarian as a result of having to move about in the world of work. Whereas, before, black was *de rigueur* for evening dress only, now it was also worn during the day to ease the effects of wear and tear. The evolution in male clothing was towards greater austerity and rigidity. Men wore dark suits, stiff collars and starched shirt-fronts.[4] Waistcoats were worn under jackets that buttoned high and had smaller lapels. The dandy gave way to sartorial conformity.

Flügel, writing in the 1930s, has read this masculine renunciation as emblematic of a new morality. But it is fairer to read it as a necessary adaptation to the demands of a new social order of work. Where he is correct is in the implicit repression that this conformity brings about and, thereby, its knock-on effects. In the first instance, as Wilson and de la Haye put it, such 'masculine dress produces an erotic masculinity precisely by means of disavowal'.[5] This suggests a far-from-straightforward adherence to the social code in that what is repressed, the erotic, will find its expression – create its effects. These effects are at least twofold. In this transition from display to renunciation, Flügel argues that the man 'does not renounce his exhibitionism at all but experiences the pleasures of "vicarious display" through the desired woman'.[6] In essence, the male displaces his own repressed eroticism onto the female – she becomes the arena for the display and exhibitionism that he has foresworn but which he can now contain and control (through the woman). As Flügel explains, 'The desire to be seen' is 'transformed into the desire to see'.[7] In this regard the dark suit becomes a site of power, and the male within it the subject of the gaze.

But there is also a flip side to this shift. The effect, in terms of the male body politic, as Foucault points out, is a move from 'a society of spectacle to one of surveillance'.[8] As Foucault notes, there is a gradual shift from the pre-nineteenth century pageantry of power that was the province of kings and tyrants. This included not just the display of courtly wealth but also the power of the court to exact fearful punishment such as public executions (see, for example, representations of this in *L'Affaire des poisons* and *Marie-Antoinette Reine de France*, discussed in Chapter 6). What has gradually replaced this, in nineteenth-century France, as a result of increased urbanization and a greater dispersal of wealth, is a need to control its populace through a disciplining mechanism. This becomes the province of 'a complex series of systems of surveillance in which being observed or being conscious of the possibility of being observed produces conformity to the demands of power'.[9] We are all, to some degree, caught up in this mechanism, watching as we are being watched, and of course, dress is a key to this conformity. It is surely significant, in relation to this concept of surveillance, that the rebuilding of Paris around a series of '*grandes percées*' – long and broad boulevards to prevent mob insurgence, or at least to permit the surveillance of mass movement around the city – should coincide with this shift in the dress-code of the male body politic. The sartorial combines with city planning in a grand scheme of social engineering, the outcome of which is to create a homogenous sense of conformity (rather than community).

A concomitant effect of this shift, as historian Anne-Marie Sohn has noted, beginning in the 1860s, is a marked withdrawal from violence as an expression of virility to a quieter masculinity that asserts itself through impertinence rather than anger, reasoned dialogue instead of fists, control of emotion rather than hot-blooded response.[10] Interestingly, although a few duels still continued after 1860 (as we shall see in the Belle Epoque chapters), they are very much on the wane by this period. For example, in *Pot-Bouille* and *Bel-Ami*, the central characters, the arriviste Mouret and Duroy (respectively), find neat ways to avoid fighting a duel (see below and Chapter 17). We shall also note that, in the main, this new man, with his sartorial attire and social climbing, renounces his more showy lighter clothing for sober outfits in keeping with his status as a bourgeois who has arrived and who has plans to go further.

What is not suggested by these historians is that this shift constitutes a crisis in masculinity. The newer male appears to have supplanted his forebrothers, even to the point of taking over the army officer's side-burns and moustache. However, in the seven films before us that foreground this new masculinity, this is not the only image to prevail, which suggests that not all was as straightforward for the new man as might be believed – as we shall see, a man could fail, or already have failed, to make the mark. This representation of failure suggests an anxiety on the male's part in relation to these shifts. Society's changes make demands on the individual, but the individual also reacts, not always positively, to these demands – sometimes with disastrous outcomes, as we shall see. A further indication of this unease seeps through in some of these films insofar as it is not always the male who does the watching (in *Pot-Bouille* and *Une vie*, in particular, it is the women). It is not difficult to read these changing times for men in relation to the contemporary 1950s. Social change, as we know, was also huge: modernization, freer flow of capital through credit, loss of working-class identity within a newly emergent lower middle-class, enfranchisement of the women. These represented a huge challenge to traditional masculinity and thereby to man's position in society. Indeed, one of the directors, Astruc, actually makes the point about the contemporary value of his film, *Une vie*, which he describes as a portrait of individual solitude in the face of a couple's failure to communicate.[11]

Representing New Masculinity

Even though this is the period that saw the birth of a new kind of masculinity, it is surely noteworthy that, in four out of the seven films, the male either struggles to find a place in this new world-order of the sleek and slick new male, or he is prevented from asserting his dominance in sexual relations because the woman 'gets in the way' (see figure 16.1 below, column three, under exceptions). This is not to say, though, that patriarchy and misogyny do not remain intact. They do, as we shall see. But the slight predominance of 'failures' is intriguing, especially if we consider the crisis of masculinity in 1950s' France – and audience figures below suggest that, with the exception of *Pot-Bouille* and *Une vie*, spectators were not too keen on this kind of representation. And one suspects that it was the star personas that drew audiences to these two films (Gérard Philipe with a super strong supportive cast for the former; Maria Schell for the latter). Even the three narratives where the men do advance their careers (see columns one and two) do not appear to have a great deal to commend them to viewers (*Bel-Ami* is an extraordinary case which I address in the next chapter). Clearly, the swashbuckler was more attractive precisely because not only was he more honourable, he was more ambiguous than this new male, self-serving upstart (see Chapter 7).

Of the four films in this category, three of the titles are adaptations of Maupassant, *Le Plaisir*, *Trois femmes* and *Une vie*. The fourth is the rather peculiar *Chevalier de la nuit* –

Post-1860s 2nd Empire	Post-1870 3rd Republic	Post-1870 3rd Republic The exceptions
Pot-Bouille (57) 1865 seducer tale (based on real person) (2.6m)		Le Plaisir (52) 1870s includes prostitution (esp. La Maison Tellier) (1.2m)
Le Joueur (58) 1867 seducers, roués and gamblers (0.9 m)		Trois femmes (52) 1870s includes tale of racism (Zora) (0.5m)
		Chevalier de la nuit (54) 1884 bored marriage/'sexual' fantasy (no figures)
	Bel-Ami (57) 1887 tale of seducer/political shenanigans (0.6m)	
		Une vie (58) 1880 seducer tale (2.3m)

Figure 16.1: Films representing post-1860s' new masculinity (audience figures in bold).

a story that comes from and was scripted by Jean Anouilh. I shall begin with these four and conclude with a brief analysis of two of the more representative portraits of the new masculinity in *Pot-Bouille* and *Le Joueur*. The next chapter will focus in greater depth on the interesting case of *Bel-Ami*.

New Masculinities: Four Failures

It is instructive that three out of the four exceptions to the rule are adaptations of Maupassant – a dry and ironic observer of the human foibles of mankind. A great deal has been written already about *Le Plaisir*, a trilogy of short film sketches, so I want to make the shortest of comments to the effect that in all three sketches it is the male who, in some way or another, loses out – either against himself or the women who surround him. In the first sketch, *Le Masque*, an elderly man cannot bear that he has lost his youth and vigour. Each night he dons a mask as a handsome young man and goes off dancing in a Paris nightclub. One night he collapses and has to be taken home. His wife explains to the doctor that her husband refuses to give up his pursuit of pleasure. Decrepit masculinity at its worst, it could be argued, manifesting a pitiful desire to be part of the vanguard of the new masculinity. In the second sketch, the best known of the three stories, *La Maison Tellier*, Madame Tellier (Madeleine Renaud) has a change of heart about the house of pleasure she runs in Paris – as do her girls, after they have all gone out to the country to a family celebration of a first communion, where they observe how nice and pure normal life is. Their city clients, meantime, have to come to terms with the new order of things: clean fun replaces the less-than-pure act of prostitution. The women decide that the female body is to become less accessible as a source of carnal pleasure. Finally, in *Le Modèle*, an artist who has made his fortune through painting his model, who is also his lover, gets fed up with their constant bickering and takes off. The model, seeking him out, learns that he is to marry another. She confronts him and, when he refuses to listen to her pleas, throws herself out of the window. She is not dead, but consigned to a wheelchair, and we see the unfortunate couple, now married, moving slowly along the seafront. In all three tales, men are made to pay for their desires – hardly the image of the new thrusting masculinity as described above, but perhaps closer to the truth of the times, thereby exposing, in interesting and diverse ways, how much of a social construction this new man in fact is. An ideal image more readily sought after than necessarily attained: dressing and performing it is one thing, being it quite another.

Trois femmes is another mixed bag where representations of masculinity are concerned. In the first story, *Zora*, a young and very timid foot soldier, Antoine Boitelle (Jacques Dubuy), falls in love with a fairground performer from the Ivory Coast, Zora (Moune de Rivel). His whole courtship of her is tentative – physically he is small up against Zora's ample body. To marry they must obtain his father's consent. So they travel by train to Meudon in Normandy to the family farm. If the fairground with all its exotic animals (parrots, lions, etc.) was a great attraction, Zora's arrival in this small provincial part of France makes that pale into insignificance. Villagers stare open-mouthed as she walks down the main street, adorned in a satin taffeta dress, a tartan hat-piece of African design full of ribbons and bows on her head, an African necklace for jewellery. She looks sumptuous – but not to the Boitelle family, all collected together in the barn to celebrate the engagement. One by one they take their leave. Heartbroken, Zora cries at the hurt. Eventually the parents also get up to go. The father tells his son, 'she is too black' and he must choose between them (and implicitly his inheritance) and her. By the time Antoine has turned around to claim Zora, she has left and caught the three o'clock train back. Antoine runs across the fields but it is too late. She has gone from his life. Modern and open as he is in his thinking, Antoine is unable to fulfil his dream. His love remains crushed by the prejudice of others; and he, physically penned in by the patriarchal order – literally, he runs along the perimeter fence of his father's property as he tries to reach the train flying out of reach.

The second tale, *Coralie*, is one of inheritance. A young woman, Coralie (Agnès Delahaye),[12] cannot expect to touch her aunt's bequest unless she produces a child within two years of marriage. Time is running out and Coralie is getting agitated at the idea of losing this fabulous fortune. Sadly, her husband Eugène (René Lefèvre) is rather weak and irresolute. He takes to his bed. He fails to respond to aphrodisiac food. Physically he remains floppy. With such a lack of appetite for sexual consummation, the possibility is raised that he is infertile. In a horrible showdown with him, Coralie screams:

Me, infertile? Infertile with you, yes, because you are not a man! But had I married someone, anyone do you hear me, I would have had children! This is costing me dear, to have married a drip like you!

In the end the husband is forced to accept that a surrogate father impregnates Coralie. All is well; she becomes pregnant and gets the inheritance. The emasculation of her husband, however, is total.

The third tale, *Mouche*, is set in idyllic countryside where five young men have congregated to do some rowing. There they meet up with a young woman, Mouche (Catherine Erard), who takes each one on, some timid some bold, as a lover. She loves whom she wants, she claims. When she falls pregnant, the five men initially try and dodge their responsibility; but finally they all agree to look after her kid. However, Mouche loses her baby in a boating accident – 'Never mind' say the five men 'we'll make you another one.'

Maupassant, the master of irony, is comically unsparing in his reflections of masculinity in this trilogy of stories – but the point remains that, to differing degrees, all are weak and unassertive males and women can pretty much get on with their lives by themselves. Such is not the case, however, with his next, most unattractive of males, the severely brutal Julien de Lamare (Christian Marquand) in *Une vie*. Maria Schell (of *Gervaise* fame) stars opposite Marquand as his hapless wife Jeanne. What intrigues in this representation is just how much spying and surveillance goes on. Yet, the holder of the gaze is not Julien but Jeanne. She spies on his various infidelities from a first floor bedroom window. It is she who is in the know and who, in the possession of this knowledge, inadvertently reveals to the husband of one of Julien's conquests the precise location of the unfaithful couple (an old gypsy caravan on top of a sea-cliff). Jeanne runs to warn them, but she is followed by the husband who, in a rage of jealousy, tips the caravan over the cliff and kills both his wife and Julien. So much for the masterful, disciplining masculine power – all it can wreak is havoc and death.

The camera work, in its restlessness, also feels like a supreme voyeur in this tale of a mismatched couple. It is always on the go, following the comings and goings of these unhappy prisoners of a marriage that is doomed from the start, because they get married for entirely distinct reasons. When, earlier on, Jeanne is saved from drowning by an unknown fisherman (Julien), she falls in love with an idea of masculinity: that of a handsome saviour, which is far from what Julien eventually offers her once they marry. Indeed, if only she had been attentive to the ways he treated her in their courtship – grabbing hold of her rather than attempting seductive moves, moodily disappearing for days on end only to return and threaten to leave forever unless she marries him – she would have been warned against this brute. Instead, they marry – in a scene very reminiscent of the wedding in Vigo's *L'Atalante*. From then on, he torments her, not just with his infidelities, or with his ruthless manner (he is quite given to lashing out at her), but also in his desire for solitude in the form of long walks in the countryside and hunting and shooting wild animals. One of them, we suspect, might just as well be Jeanne, especially when we consider that he takes a flick-knife to cut through her corset lacing to consummate the marriage in a cornfield on their wedding-day.

As it transpires, Julien has had to return from Paris because he is financially ruined. His trajectory is the exact opposite, therefore, of the new young man who goes to the city. The huge debts he has incurred have to be paid off – and Jeanne is his obvious source. Thus, his marriage is cynical as it is utilitarian. Moreover, he shows incredible bad faith when Jeanne later reproaches him for his unkindness towards her. He turns on her and tells her, 'because of you my life has been ruined'. Astruc claims that he was faithful to Maupassant's portrait of life's difficulties as a couple.[13] Yet, in Astruc's interpretation, Jeanne is clinging and calculating. Conversely, he reads Julien as someone who is not calculating but who reacts. Astruc tells us, 'I wanted people to understand him'.[14] Why not Jeanne as well? This more misogynistic take must give us pause since, in the original text, it is Jeanne who is the oppressed victim. Astruc claims he sought to appeal to contemporary audiences and modernize the story into a couple's failure to communicate, and expose the concomitant solitude felt by the individual.[15] But the portrait we receive is of a man who is taciturn by nature, ill-suited to marriage in the first place and who – for those very reasons – feels trapped in a relationship. His way out is to embrace his solitude when it suits him, seduce other women – including Jeanne's servant Rosalie (Pascale Petit), whom she has treated more like a sister than a person in her employ. If we are to understand this film as a contemporary allegory for coupledom, then it bodes ill for women: broody existential hero can beat up wife when he pleases, she must not ask questions about his movements and affairs, and, above all, she must not show her passion for him. It is hard not to read this film as a treatise against marriage, putting the blame squarely at the feet of the women. Astruc's film seems a long way away from Maupassant's originally-compassionate tale where women were concerned. And, given Astruc's intellectual entourage (a man of the Left who knew the contemporary debates around gender relations) his interpretation reads as a backlash against such feminist texts as Simone de Beauvoir's 1949 polemic *Le Deuxième sexe*. There, she argues against the oppression of women forced into a secondary position by the male sex; here, Astruc appears to suggest that it is inevitable that women will be dominated – especially if they trap men into marriage!

Astruc is famous for his 'Caméra-stylo' essay that did more perhaps than Truffaut's 'Certain Tendency of French Cinema' essay to launch the concept of *auteur* cinema that became such a trend in film studies from the1960s onwards.[16] We can see in this film evidence of Astruc's endeavours to forge an authorial style via a fluidity of camera movement that is not unlike a flowing pen as it tracks after its characters. But there is also full evidence of the other authorial signatures. The masterly cinematography of Claude Renoir is matched by Paul

Bertrand's brilliant creation of space in his sets: the interiors resonate with emptiness; the corridors let us feel the separation between the married couple as Julien insists on his own bedroom. All is sparse, there is little to suggest a happy and fulfilled life. A life (*Une vie*), but what a bleak and unhappy one.

Shot in Eastmancolor, this film straddles four seasons but spread over a chronological span of six to eight years. The story opens in summer and ends in spring. Claude Renoir keeps a tight rein on his palette: yellows and reds for summer, light greens for spring. These impressionistic tones book-end the poignant dominance of burnt yellows and browns for the autumn and deep blues for the winter.[17] Autumn feels close to death in its darkness; winter is cold and cruel. In the bleak, snowy mid-winter Rosalie gives birth to her baby daughter – literally, she is sprawled out in the snow until she is dragged into the stable to give birth! Spring comes, but it is six years later – during which time Julien has apparently behaved, grown a beard (so he looks even more menacing) and given Jeanne a son, Paul (Michel de Slubicki), who is now nearly the same age as Rosalie's daughter. This spring is full of menace, however. Julien meets up with an old friend and his wife, Gilberte (Antonella Lualdi), whom he promptly seduces. He abandons Jeanne, whose solitude is now compensated for by her son with whom she has a quasi-incestuous relationship – he clearly has become the substitute for Julien (he shares her bed, defends her against his father when he gets violent, etc.). A few weeks later, when guests are attending a rural wedding reception, a thunderstorm breaks. Everyone scatters. Julien takes off with Gilberte for a tryst in the caravan atop of the cliff. A move that, as already mentioned, seals their death.

Compared to *Une vie*, we could almost read the last of the four exceptions, *Chevalier de la nuit*, as a parody of masculinity. A couple (played by Renée Saint-Cyr and Jean-Claude Pascal), now together for five years, are bored with each other and squabble all the time. She wishes she could have the man she loved back again. Instead, thanks to a chance encounter with a magician (or is he the devil?), her husband is given a potion which unleashes both his good and his evil side. The evil one, the dark knight, becomes obsessed with his good side – especially in bed where he seeks to surpass his rival. After several criminal acts of arson and unpleasant, even brutal, interactions with his wife, the dark knight is killed off by the good one. Unsurprisingly, the wife is happy to have her husband back again. This Jekyll and Hyde story merits this brief mention primarily because Jean Anouilh scripted it – perhaps he wanted to explore the theme that all human beings have a good and bad side. But the deeply-misogynistic message remains: the woman should be content with her lot, or who knows what her dissatisfaction will unleash in her man.[18] The 1950s' woman does not have a lot to hope for in marriage, it would appear.

New Masculinities: The Triumphant Ones

Lastly, we come to the films that represent more closely the new masculinity spoken of above. I shall deal here with the two Gérard Philipe vehicles, *Pot-Bouille* and *Le Joueur*, leaving *Bel-*

Ami aside for a more developed case-study in the next chapter. Here, in these two films, the cynical male both survives and does extremely well for himself – the former on a fast ascending curve in the world of commerce, the latter, intermittently, depending on how his gambling goes. Claude Autant-Lara's *Le Joueur* is based on a Dostoevsky novel of the same title which, in turn, relates quite closely to Dostoevsky's own experiences as a compulsive gambler. Set in 1865, in the German spa-town of Baden-Baden (which Dostoevsky had humorously renamed Roulettenburg in the novel), Alexei Ivanovich (Gérard Philipe) is a young tutor in love with Pauline (Liselotte Pulver) – stepdaughter of General Zagorianski (Bernard Blier). The General is also his master. As the story unfolds, we come to realize that Pauline is ambivalent toward Ivanovich. For the most part, she treats him with utter disdain. Yet she admires his rude, cocky ways. But she rightly perceives that he lacks backbone, nor does she much approve of his gambling. In this latter respect, it is when he endeavours to win a lot of money to spare her the humiliation of her fiancé's rejection that she, incensed at the idea that a poor man could buy her (or, more ambiguously, because she wishes that patriarchy as embodied by the General would allow her to love a poor man), decides to take her life – and shoots herself. Before all this occurs, however, we witness the General's discomfiture as he grows increasingly in debt to the Marquis De Grieux (Jean Danet), a beastly Parisian arriviste and financier of dubious credentials who has forced the General's hand into 'selling' Pauline to him by way of insurance against his gambling debts. The General is awaiting the imminent death of his aunt to inherit her fortune, clear his debts, and marry Blanche de Cominges (another Parisian parvenue, played by Nadine Alari). However, far from dying, aunt Antonina (Françoise Rosay) turns up at Baden-Baden and gets hooked on gambling herself – losing all her money. At the end of the film, everyone from the General's entourage leaves – dead or alive – except Ivanovich who stays on, happy to continue with his gambling practices. After all, as he says: 'how is gambling any more stupid than other ways of making money?' – implying that all business ventures are forms of gambling and not, therefore, that respectable.

Philipe, now thirty-six, has to embody the 20-year-old Ivanovich with all the immaturity of inexperience and, with it, the tendency to be dismissive towards others. There are echoes here of his role as Julien in *Le Rouge et le Noir* – where he had to play the part of someone fourteen years his junior. Curiously, in *Le Joueur*, Philipe brings it off very convincingly because he looks scrawny and physically quite weak, which perfectly conveys the persona of Dostoevsky's hero, who is cynically world-weary before his time. Part of the reason for Philipe's countenance has to be that he was suffering from exhaustion due to the amount of film work he had taken on because he was constantly in need of funding for his various projects, personal and professional.[19] Further reasons for this exhaustion were his theatre commitments, on stage and as leader of the newly-formed actors union (Comité National des Acteurs, later Syndicat Français des Acteurs).[20] But this exhaustion was also due to his as-yet-undiagnosed cancer (which would kill him in a year's time).[21] In *Le Joueur*, Philipe has a terrible pallor, he looks gaunt and a bit feverish – this suits him admirably for the role of the impetuous, abrasive, slightly neurotic, certainly angry young man and adrenalin

Figure 16.2: Still of Philipe as Ivanovich in *Le Joueur* (with Pauline/Liselotte Pulver). The image captures Philipe's gaunt appearance. © 1958 Gaumont (France) / Medusa Cinematografica (Italy).

junkie that is Ivanovich. His skin visibly sweats, and not just when he is at the roulette table. He wears a round pill-box hat which squashes his already close-cropped hair, adding to his gaunt appearance. His facial hair, a scruffy downy ginger-coloured beard, compounds his look of an ill-nourished youth. Finally, his clothing, which seemingly never changes from a sombre charcoal grey suit, merely accentuates his pallor. Philipe is far from the iconic beauty we associate with him in all his other films. Thus, he embodies rather well the desperate, bitter and somewhat nasty gambler of the film's title (see figure 16.2 above).

Philipe had made 18 million francs out of his role for Autant-Lara's film *Le Rouge et le Noir*, so perhaps it seemed he could gamble again on a winner with this same director (and script-writers Aurenche and Bost) for *Le Joueur*. If so, he was well off the mark. *Le Joueur* garnered just under a million spectators, a mere twentieth of his audience for *Le Rouge et le Noir*. At the time, the film was dismissed as a mediocre adaptation of Dostoevsky's novel – again, in much the same way as Autant-Lara's earlier adaptation of Stendhal's famous novel in 1954. Cadars argues that 'rather than concentrating on the original emphasis of moral degeneration, Autant-Lara and his scriptwriters concentrated on the vices of the bourgeoisie and the social climbing of an individual'.[22] Baroncelli wonders if Philipe is tired of cinema:

'The film is mediocre…Gérard Philipe seems to me inappropriate in the role of Alexei. Did he not 'feel' the character?' Monod complains: 'Gérard Philipe does not help the film. Does he believe in it?'[23] According to Bernard Blier, who plays the role of the Russian General, everyone in the cast found the film faintly ridiculous.[24]

Having watched the film several times and read the novel, I find myself disinclined to be so critical. It seems that a number of factors combined against a positive reception of the film. The first is Autant-Lara himself – now on the *Cahiers du cinéma* critics' 'hate list', along with Aurenche and Bost (for example Eric Rohmer detested the film)[25] – and most press reviews were very unsympathetic to his adaptation. The second is Philipe, who appears to be playing against himself – that is, he is not the suave arriviste or swashbuckling hero of so many of his other films. Rather, he is a somewhat unpleasant, unattractive one-dimensional human being endowed with an inane laugh. Th ird, and last, is the novel itself which militates against spectator pleasure. The point of view is entirely that of Alexei Ivanovich, an embittered young man who wants to take his revenge on the bourgeoisie by making his fortune and throwing it back in their faces. He has much of an existential anti-hero about him since, ultimately, he can profess to no real convictions, be it his supposed love for Pauline, his apparent addiction to gambling, or his desire to offend his superiors. He is, in short, an empty vessel. Ivanovich's narrative is deeply caricatural of the rich – including aunt Antonina who (deliberately or not is left unclear) loses her fortune so as not to bequeath it to her lacklustre nephew, the General. In the novel, Ivanovich's position is also uncomfortably chauvinistic (especially against the French and the Germans) and disturbingly anti-semitic (including several side-swipes at the Rothschild family). As one would expect from Autant-Lara, he keeps the dark side of Ivanovich and the digs at the bourgeoisie, but leaves aside the more scurrilous elements of ethnic and national chauvinism. As Autant-Lara puts it, Dostoevsky's novel was flawed. He endeavoured to improve upon it, including, strangely, having Pauline commit suicide at the end of the film.[26] In the novel, she withdraws to a life of unhappiness in Switzerland. Is her suicide a case of the Pauline character taking a strong stance against the corruption that surrounds her? If so, it is pretty extreme and counters the idea, in the novel, that she is punished for being part of a class that oppresses – no matter that it oppresses her too. The suicide removes the ambiguity.

What humour there is in Autant-Lara's film is caustic and at the expense of others; not one character is likeable. In this regard, the director does not stray from the original text, it has to be said. In both instances we are left with a fairly nasty taste in our mouth as to the cupidity and stupidity of people. If the film is mediocre, as some critics claim, then it is surely because the middle-classes are represented as such: greedy and obsessed with keeping up appearances. After all, when we consider the great success of Autant-Lara's other film about human greed and venality, *L'Auberge rouge*, and that spectators went in their droves to see it (2.6 million of them), obviously something in audience taste has shifted in the seven years that separate the two films. One suspects it comes down to class – after all Fernandel (of *L'Auberge rouge*) and Philipe were equally popular stars, even if the former was cruder and more caricatural in his performances when measured against Philipe's typically assured and interior style of acting. In the earlier film, the crassness of the bourgeoisie is exposed and punished by the lower-class felons (who fleece and then murder them) – it is all highly amusing. Arguably, a middle-class audience, especially the newly emergent one of the late 1950s, is less at ease when watching its own behave quite so preposterously and, moreover, seeing the perpetrator of so much mayhem amongst their class (the impecunious upstart Alexei Ivanovich) succeed in their place. After all, he remains in Baden-Baden to conquer another day at the roulette tables. By the end of the film, he is wealthy and elegantly dressed: a state that we know cannot last (in gambling, who wins eventually loses). As for the others, all else is ruin and death: quite a trail of destruction, even if Ivanovich is merely the catalyst of other people's folly. What pleasure for the audience is to be derived from his lack of any moral code, to say nothing of his anarchic tendencies with money and people? In all, his performance amounts to an uncomfortable indictment of capitalism and an exposure of its very precariousness. Not for nothing are the two longest sequences in the film given over to, first, the aunt's roulette game: 16 minutes, and, later, Ivanovich's: 22 minutes.

What Autant-Lara does accentuate from the novel, successfully in my view, is the individual's greed – nothing counts more than money to all except the nihilistic Ivanovich. He can happily win or lose; what attracts him is the erroneous belief that there is a formula for winning and the vertiginous thrill of playing roulette. If he has any compulsion, it is to win – but only with a view to humiliate those of the upper classes who have humiliated him in his servitude. The film, equally, brings out a constant theme of the novel: that of surveillance. We see Ivanovich spying on Pauline. In the Casino, private policemen are on guard to ensure that no one steals another's money on the roulette tables; above, in the manager's office, windows look down onto the gambling tables so that disruptive behaviour (such as the aunt's) can be curtailed and tables closed if, as happens for Ivanovich, someone is winning too much money. From the very beginning of the film (and novel), the idea of spying and denunciation is brought into play. Ivanovich is travelling on a train to Baden-Baden. People overhear him speaking in his sleep. He is dreaming about killing a woman – Pauline, as it transpires. When he arrives in the spa-town, he is immediately arrested on charges of murder, having been denounced by fellow-travellers.

Finally, on this idea of surveillance, the set for the Hôtel de Paris, where all the main characters are holed up, and the Casino merits a mention. Max Douy, Autant-Lara's mainstay set-designer, condensed the two separate places into one circular space. Thus, the Casino is opposite the hotel on a grand circle – both semi-circular buildings are in neo-classical style. Douy has taken the design of the real Baden-Baden Casino, recreated it and matched it with an imaginary hotel the other side of the circle. The point made by the design and the flow of people from one side of the circle to the other is to show how, ineluctably, they are caught up in the madness of the roulette game, spinning as it does in a circle. This spinning is accentuated by the incessant presence of waltz music (be it diegetic or not). But, moreover, this very circularity allows for surveillance at all times. Many shots are taken from hotel windows looking into the rotunda of the circle – in particular, privileging Ivanovich's point of view as he watches the comings and goings of the General and his entourage of parvenus and other hangers-on. New capitalism, as we noted from Foucault above, produces a society of surveillance – an uncomfortable message to digest for 1950s' France, currently in the throes of a new kind of capitalism of their own (credit-based), modernization, and intrusive censorship.

If Ivanovich presents us with an unappetizing, if not slightly mad, version of the Gérard Philipe we find difficult to admire, then his role as the social climbing Octave Mouret in *Pot-Bouille* delivers to us the handsome cynical rogue we have come to expect. This film was released just a year before *Le Joueur* when Philipe was at the height of his cinematic fame and stardom.

This third 1950s' adaptation of a Zola novel is once again criticized for its lack of faithfulness to the author. I do not intend to enlarge on that debate, merely to develop on Duvivier's intention when he made the film. He said:

> I have betrayed Zola in the respect that *Pot-Bouille* with its cruel, sordid world of bourgeois vices, frequently described in excessive naturalistic depth, leaves the reader with feelings of despair. I have treated *Pot-Bouille* as a comedy, as an amusing satire.[27]

The shift, then, is one of tone – but it is also, as Russell Cousins points out in his useful study of the adaptation, a film intent on capitalizing on a known star, which meant fitting the film narrative to his cachet as a romantic lead.[28] Philipe's recent, relatively rather disappointing, audience figures with *Les Aventures de Till l'Espiègle* (see Chapter 7) gave evidence that roles where he defaulted from the screen lover did not please his fan base so much. Indeed, up until this film, Philipe's audience had been in the range of 5.3 million to 6.7. The audience of 2.3 million for *Les Aventures de Till l'Espiègle* represented a significant drop in popularity, therefore. Strange, then, that he should have reprised this character type in *Le Joueur* a year later. *Pot-Bouille*, relative to Philipe's earlier successes, was not a massive hit, either, with a 2.6 audience; not that far above the figures for *Les Aventures de Till l'Espiègle*.

However, to return to *Pot-Bouille*. In this version of Zola's novel, Philipe plays Octave Mouret as a charming seducer, whereas, in the novel proper, he is a brute and takes women as he pleases and with force. He is not the object of desire he so ostensibly becomes in Duvivier's rendition of the original. As Cousins says, whereas in Zola's text Mouret was used as a type to expose the hypocrisy of the bourgeoisie, here his dark satire is turned into a romantic comedy.[29] Bourgeois hypocrisy remains, but we are led to laugh at it rather than be repelled by it, as Zola's harsh narrative required. It is also the case, as with two other Zola adaptations, René Clément's *Gervaise* and Christian-Jaque's *Nana*, that the star body replaces the Zola-esque type. We delight in the spectacle Martine Carol/Nana offers us of her body. We identify and sympathize far too much with Gervaise as victim in the film because the focus of the narrative is entirely on Maria Schell who embodies that character. In *Pot-Bouille*, we are seduced by Mouret/Philipe's ease with women and titillated to know if he will manage to defrost Madame Hédouin (Danielle Darrieux), the owner of the drapery shop, Au Bonheur des Dames.

'*Pot-bouille*' is, first, a culinary term referring to the idea of habitual family fare, normally a stew of rather meagre proportions; it is also used in an expression '*faire pot-bouille ensemble*' to mean shacking up together. And it is both these meanings that Zola has in mind. The *Pot-Bouille* he presents us with is that of the bourgeoisie – showing us what goes on amongst the various bourgeois families living within the confines of a newly-built Haussmannian apartment building on the rue de Choiseul (in the 2nd arrondissement in Paris). Under the veneer of respectability, their behaviour is as disgusting as an unappetizing stew. A harridan of a mother, Madame Josserand (Jane Marken), basically pimps for her girls in her endeavours to marry them off. The owner of the building, the elderly Monsieur Vabre (Gaston Jaquet), seduces the maidservants, speculates fraudulently and dies whilst copulating with one of the servants. His son-in-law, a high court judge, Maître Duveyrier (Jean Brochard), neglects his wife and has an artist's model for a mistress but disapproves of her posing nude (in a reference, doubtless, to Edouard Manet's *Olympia*, 1863). Even the architect of the building, Achille Compardon (Georges Cusin), has a live-in lover (Gasparine/Pascale de Boysson), right under the nose of his hypochondriac wife in the guise of a house-servant.

Duvivier in his film serves up the same household, but the taste is less bitter. The story is as follows. Octave Mouret comes up from the provinces (Aix-en-Provence, a fourteen-hour train ride, we are informed). He has come to stay at the 'Maison de la rue de Choiseul' as it is known since it is the first new building on the street. He is a relative of Rose (Jenny Orléans), wife of the architect, Achille Compardon. Achille has arranged for Octave to rent a room on the fourth floor, just below the maidservants' quarters, and has sorted him out with a job as salesperson in Mme Hédouin's drapery store across the road. Conveniently, in narrative terms, most of the various inhabitants turn up at the same time as does Octave. First to arrive, on foot and drenched by the rain, is Mme Josserand with her two daughters, Berthe (Dany Carel) and Hortense (Danielle Dumont). They are just returning from an unsuccessful '*chasse aux maris*/husband hunt'. Berthe takes an instant shine to Octave – a flirtation that Octave will later pursue. The Josserands live on the fourth floor in rather cramped rooms. Aspiring bourgeois, they have little money. Next to arrive, by carriage, the Vabre household: old M. Vabre looks decidedly dodgy on his legs; the son-in-law, Maître Duveyrier, is accompanied by the rather haughty Mme Duveyrier – née Vabre (Claude Nollier). They live in the elegant apartment rooms on the first floor. Théophile Vabre (Jacques Grello), also lives on the first floor, in an apartment opposite his father. He and his wife Valérie (Micheline Luccioni) have a loveless and sexless marriage that drives Valérie into paroxysms of hysteria – a condition Octave is only too pleased to alleviate from time to time. Achille, his neurotic wife and live-in servant, Gasparine live on the third in fairly comfortable rooms.

Barsacq has elegantly captured the dignified if ponderous décor of the Haussmannesque interiors. The staircase leading up to the various apartments is quite resplendent in its marble and wrought-iron detail. Achille informs the eager Octave that the entire house has gaslighting on all floors and that even the staircase is heated. There is, of course, a social hierarchy in that those with greater status live on the first floor, the lesser rank and file being housed higher above in decreasing order of financial means. The second-floor apartment, a slightly smaller replica of the first floor apartments, elegantly furnished, is where the newly-weds Berthe and old Vabre's other son, Auguste Vabre (Jacques Dubuy), eventually end up. Auguste runs the rival drapery store ('Vabre') on the ground floor of this imposing building. Finally, to the top floors of the house. Although Octave is lodged on the fourth floor, his room is off on a tucked-away corridor towards the back of the building. On this same corridor resides the neglected housewife Marie Pichon (Anouk Aimée), whom Octave will also help to alleviate of her boredom. Above all this are the fifth-floor maidservants' rooms – a space Octave does not, interestingly, infringe (having, perhaps, bigger fish to fry). The women who live up here serve, however, as a Greek chorus on the goings-on in the household. We get to hear their take on Octave's sexual exploits for example – which so annoys him that he decides to put an end to his more-than-convenient affair with the married Berthe.

This, then, is the household into which Octave arrives and behaves like a cocky rooster. Whilst attracted to Berthe, he quickly declares that 'men from the south don't marry', thus forcing her mother's hand to marry Berthe off to the less-than-appetising Auguste – played by Jacques Dubuy in a wonderful cameo role as the useless shopkeeper and ineffectual husband, struck by nerves and migraines, more adolescent 'girl' than man when it comes to matters of sex. All the men serve as foils to the gracious Octave. The Vabre brothers, Théophile and Auguste, are impotent; Maître Duveyrier, a possessive and imbecilic lover; Achille, a conniving hypocrite. No wonder all the women in the building want a dose of Octave! All, that is, except Gasparine, who, ashamed at being found out, denounces Octave's philandering ways with the married Berthe to the frosty (but interested) Mme Hédouin. Earlier in the film, Octave had miscalculated his moves on Mme Hédouin. He declared undying love after a particularly successful day in the shop. In telling her of his plans for a more successful business in partnership with her, he gets carried away by his irrepressible enthusiasm and arrogant self-confidence and naturally assumes she will yield to his entreaties to become his mistress. She rejects all sides of the proposal and Octave resigns from his job to go and work for the opposition at Vabre. He manages to turn the ailing business around. In a scheme to get Octave back to work for her, Mme Hédouin plants a grain of suspicion in Auguste's ear (shamefully, when attending her husband's funeral). Auguste is incensed. He discovers his wife in bed with Octave and foolishly challenges him to a duel. Both Auguste and Octave manage to wriggle out of the duel: the former out of fear for his life; the latter because it would inconvenience his plans to get to the top. Octave leaves the Vabre shop. Mme Hédouin calls him over. They seal their business arrangement with a kiss. They will marry and make a huge success of Au Bonheur des Dames. On this high note, the film ends.

The story begins in 1861, although the women's fashion on screen – designed by Escoffier – suggests we are at least in 1865, the year that the bustle firmly replaced the crinoline. The haute-couturier Charles Frederick Worth abolished the huge crinoline in 1864 and replaced it with a skirt shape that was flattened at the font, with a bustle at the back and half-crinoline producing a fullness – a cone shape in effect. Skirts were pulled up and back into a train. However, in Escoffier's designs the cone effect is not there at all. Indeed, dresses are more along the lines of the 1870s' princess style. Flat skirts at the front with bustle rear are the norm for day dresses in this film, but there is no sign of any crinoline at all (even the half-one), again suggesting a post-1870 design. The more formal evening dresses are, for the most part ruched, with polonaise effects front and back (see figure 16.3 below).

This interesting anachronism in dress fashion may explain why some reviews, at the time of the film's release, mistakenly place this narrative in the 1880s. But that would have gone entirely counter to Zola's intention, which was to expose the newly-emergent middle classes as grasping speculators and self-promoting businessmen under Napoleon III's Second Empire. The men's fashion, however, shows us the effect of urbanization on their attire. Indeed, when at work and in the evening, they wear black. The central protagonist, Octave Mouret (Gérard Philipe), is a bit more stylish in that he wears a dark three-quarter-length jacket, unbuttoned to show off his white satin waistcoat, and pin-striped trousers rather than the standard hip-length jacket and all-black day suit. When not at work or not in evening dress, he wears a light-coloured suit: one appears to be a grey flannel with silk-ribbon trim

Figure 16.3: Example of evening dress design (1870s). In this image Berthe (Dany Carel) is being prepared by her mother (Jane Marken) for the 'chasse aux maris/husband hunting'. © Marc-André Limot.

(much as on a regatta blazer), the other of light-coloured tweed. He also sports a bowler hat on these occasions – again a modern touch to his attire: the bowler hat was first introduced in 1849 but did not peak in popularity until towards the end of the nineteenth century. Symbolically, the bowler hat is seen as a middle-ground between the top hat associated with the upper classes and the cloth cap of the working classes. In essence, it stands for a new class – that of the entrepreneur, the clever businessman, the one that Octave is determined to spearhead. Octave, therefore, bucks trends and remains extremely modern in his thinking. As a businessman, he has a diploma in economics and is full of new ideas as to how the retail market can be expanded. It is his concept of buying in bulk and selling cheap that will revolutionize commerce and eventually lead him (once he has married Mme Hédouin) to launch the prototype of the department store.

The follow-up to Zola's novel *Pot-Bouille* is *Au Bonheur des Dames*. By now Mouret has married Mme Hédouin and the new big store is about to be opened. Zola based his idea for the store Au Bonheur des Dames on the very first *grand magasin* established by Aristide and Marguerite Boucicault in 1869, Le Bon Marché, which is, in fact, in the 7th arrondissement of Paris and not the 2nd where rue de Choiseul, with its rival shops (Vabre's and Mme Hédouin's), is located. Yet Zola sets it in the 2nd for specific political reasons – the most abiding one being his complete distaste for the Emperor. By placing Octave Mouret's department store on the corner of the rues de Choiseul and Quatre Septembre, Zola, writing in 1882, makes direct reference to the date of the collapse of the Second Empire.[30] Nothing could please him more. Throughout Zola's twenty-volume *Rougon-Macquart*, he attacks the Emperor's corrupt regime from all sides. This massive opus details, moreover, the transformation of Paris under Haussmann. There are constant side-swipes at this undertaking, which he both admired and detested. For 20 years, the whole city was under construction. The colossal noise and disruption is well recorded in Zola's work, as is his belief that Haussmann, whilst a genius in his rethinking Paris, was a crook who speculated with other cronies on the tripartite plan to rebuild the capital city. Haussmann's project ran into financial difficulties by the end of the 1860s. The whole decade of expropriating property and land had proved very expensive (because of the get-rich-quick speculators, who, thanks to insider knowledge, bought up property before the government was able to obtain it for a reasonable price). Once there was no more money, Haussmann took the blame, eventually being obliged to stand down in 1870 (a few months before the end of the Empire).[31] This again places the real timing of the novel and film towards the end of the 1860s, since old Monsieur Vabre, the owner of the building in which he and most of the protagonists live, dies both intestate and ruined, thanks to his speculating on the expropriation market.

Octave Mouret is the embodiment of the new 1860s' masculinity (see figure 16.4 below). He is an ambitious and ruthless young man. A man who has travelled from the provinces to make his fortune, he has the know-how and the belief to succeed. He has some training (his diploma). In social terms, he is both insolent and charming – two aspects of his personality he puts to good use to expose the hypocrisy of others and to seduce women into bed. He has no attachment to either the women or men by whom he is surrounded, calculating only how

Figure 16.4: Octave (Gérard Philipe) as the perfect example of the 1860s' new masculinity. Berthe and Mme Hédouin (Danielle Darrieux) cling to his every limb! © Marc-André Limot.

useful they will be to his career path and personal pleasure. So articulate is he, he manages to wriggle out of a duel by pretending that avoiding it is the very last thing he wants to do. In doing so, he provides the impetus for one of the seconds of his opponent (Auguste) to find an argument not to fight by claiming that, if he does fight, he will compromise his career and that, for the sake of business, the slate should be wiped clean! Essentially, Octave's strategy is always to pretend to play straight, thereby allowing others to manufacture arguments to get what they want, which, in the final analysis, is what he also wants – whether it is seducing Berthe, winning Mme Hédouin as his wife or avoiding fighting in duels. He is a man of words and poise, even of silence, where needs be, so others can fill in the space with their revealing chatter. As we shall see, in the next chapter, he is an exemplary forerunner of the equally supercilious Georges Duroy of *Bel-Ami*.

Notes

1. Other big stores of the period were Les Grands Magazins du Louvre (1855); Le Printemps (1865); La Samaritaine (1869).
2. Marseille (2002, p. 144).
3. Flügel (1930, p. 111).

4. Ruppert et al. (1996, p. 268).
5. Wilson & de la Haye (1999, p. 4).
6. Bruzzi paraphrasing Flügel (Bruzzi, 1997, p. 57).
7. Flügel, op. cit., p. 118.
8. Warwick and Cavallaro paraphrasing Foucault (Warwick & Cavallaro, 1998, p. 73).
9. Ibid., p. 74.
10. See her very interesting study: Anne-Marie Sohn (2009) 'Sois un homme'. La Construction de la masculinité au XIXe siècle, Paris, Seuil.
11. Astruc paraphrased by Hadiquet (1965, p. 108).
12. Interestingly, Agnès Delahaye's production company produced Astruc's Une vie.
13. Astruc paraphrased by Hadiquet, op. cit., p. 108).
14. Ibid.
15. Ibid.
16. Alexandre Astruc (1948) 'Naissance d'une nouvelle avant-garde: la caméra-stylo', first published in L'Ecran français (No. 144), reproduced in Olivier Barrot (ed) L'Ecran français 1943–1953: Histoire d'un journal et d'une époque, Paris, Les Editeurs Français Réunis, pp. 236–40.
17. Astruc wanted the use of colour to function as a counterpoint to the narrative, not act as an auxiliary. See Allombert (1958, p. 11).
18. It is also rather difficult watching Renée Saint-Cyr, now 50 years old, attempting to pass off as a successful prima ballerina with a fragile temperament. Saint-Cyr produced this film and it can be seen as her attempt to counter roles she was getting as 'the older mature woman'. Her son, Georges Lautner, is the assistant director of this film. A little later, he became a film-maker in his own right and cast his mother in some ten films, thus giving her career a second or even third wind.
19. I can find no evidence that Les Aventures de Till l'Espiègle contributed to Philipe's financial worries, as several film historians claim (see, for example, R. Cousins, 1989, p. 144). Whilst a critical failure, it was a quite reasonable box-office success, both in France (with an audience of 2.3 million) and in the former German Democratic Republic (with 3.2 million). What we can say is that it was the first time Philipe's home audience figures took a significant drop. Furthermore, emotionally and professionally, it was a chastening experience for Philipe – he realized that film directing was not his forte (See Silberman, 2006, pp. 33 & 43).
20. See Bonal (1994, p. 255).
21. In January 1958, Jean Rouvet, the administrator of the Théâtre National de Paris was shocked by Philipe's sudden loss of weight and extreme pallor (Bonal, op. cit., p. 256).
22. Cadars (1990, p. 124).
23. Both Jean de Baroncelli and Martine Monod are quoted in Cadars, op. cit., p. 194.
24. Bonal, op. cit., p. 255.
25. Cadars, op. cit., p. 194.
26. Claude Autant-Lara quoted in 'Dostoievski revu et corrigé', Image et Son, Vol. 15, No. 95, July 1958, p. 42.
27. Duvivier quoted in R. Cousins (1989, p. 144). In this article Cousins provides a very clear argument for the shifts between novel and film.
28. Cousins, op. cit.
29. Ibid., p. 143.
30. This was when the rue du Dix Septembre (date of Napoleon's election as President) became the Quatre Septembre.
31. See Jean Des Cars and Pierre Pinon (1990, pp. 169–73). They give a resume of Zola's views on Haussmann's Paris.

Chapter 17

Censoring the Classics: *Bel-Ami*, Louis Daquin (1954; released in France 1957)

Perhaps the most protracted censorship story, where the film industry is concerned, was the case of Louis Daquin's *Bel-Ami* based on Maupassant's novel of the same name. As we can already note from the chapter's title, there was a three-year delay in its release in France for reasons which will be made clear below. It is, however, helpful to remind ourselves straightaway of the following political contexts as a way of understanding why this film became such a target for the Commission de Contrôle des Visas. The year 1954 was the real beginning of France's protracted decolonization process. Morocco and Tunisia were in discussion and would gain independence in 1956. The situation in Indochina, which had been at war since 1946, had deteriorated to the extent that France's armed forces suffered an ignominious defeat at the hands of the Viet-Minh at Diên Biên Phu. By July of that year, the Geneva agreements were signed and Vietnam was split in two. By November 1954, the Algerian crisis had hit a new high and, to all intents and purposes, France was at war with its colony. Censorship in mainland France was therefore at its peak during this mid-fifties' period, particularly in relation to Algeria, for reasons of national security. This, then, is the context within which we need to first examine Daquin's ill-fated film. But first a synopsis of the film.

Synopsis

Recently returned from Algeria, where he served for two years as a hussar in the French army, Georges Duroy (Jean Danet) – known as Bel-Ami because of his good looks – has great ambitions to enter into Parisian society of the mid-1880s. He is penniless, however. Armed with his charms and persuasive ways of seduction, this parvenu sets out on a campaign to climb the social ladder. His first piece of luck occurs when he bumps into an old army friend, Forestier (Jean-Roger Caussimon), who gets him a job as runner for the right-wing newspaper *La Vie française*, owned by the Jewish banker-magnate Monsieur Walter (René Lefèvre), who uses the paper to make and break governments (and thereby increase his personal fortune and sphere of influence, of course). Georges quickly gets rid of his first mistress, Rachel (Jacqueline Duc), a working-class woman of easy virtue but generous spirit, who hangs out at the Folies-Bergère on the make for a louis or two. She is replaced by a demi-mondaine, Clothilde de Marelle (Anne Vernon), who helps Georges on his way. She is not the only woman to foster his ambitions, however. Madeleine Forestier (Renée Faure), a wealthy bourgeoise of independent means (thanks to a former lover bestowing his wealth on her), also takes a shine to him, even though she warns him she will never be his mistress. She helps Georges write his first article – a piece on Algeria – that launches his career as a journalist. He very soon becomes the expert on North African affairs for the newspaper, which his boss, Monsieur Walter, uses to his advantage to speculate, first with, and then against, the government. After some persuading, and using his newspaper, he ropes Duroy into a financial scam by playing the card of speculation on the stock exchange, about whether France will invade and thereby annex Morocco in retaliation for its purported acts of hostility on French Algerian soil.

Meantime, fortunately for Duroy, Forestier dies of tuberculosis and he is able to marry Madeleine, who suggests that he enoble himself to Du Roy Du Cantel. He needs no persuading. She also continues to foster his career by dictating articles to him (much as she did with her former husband). But, very soon, Georges – a trifle tired by his wife's modern views of marriage (she describes marriage as an equal partnership)[1] and irrationally jealous of her deceased husband – begins to set his ambitions higher still. His next target is his boss's wife, the virtuous and very catholic Madame Walter (Christel Mardayn) whom he easily manages to seduce. She is prone to revealing secrets to her lover, including the fact that his own wife, Madeleine, is having an affair with the rather odious and arrogant journalist-turned-politician, the minister for foreign affairs Laroche-Mathieu (Lucas Amann), whose job Duroy is determined to obtain. Georges catches them in *flagrant délit* and immediately sues for divorce. On the back of the scandal, Laroche-Mathieu resigns his ministerial post. Duroy attempts to persuade Walter to give him the backing of the newspaper to get into politics. However, Walter is getting tired of the upstart Georges Duroy (as indeed are his fellow colleagues at the newspaper) and so fires him. Furious, Georges vows his revenge. He unceremoniously dumps Madame Walter and actively pursues the Walters' virginal daughter Suzanne (Maria Emo). He manages to get her to elope with him, thus forcing the Walters' hand into consenting to the marriage. All is well for Georges Du Roy Du Cantel. He is at the top – or almost, for he still harbours the ambition to enter the Assemblée nationale (his father-in-law can hardly refuse now to help him). As he stares over to the Assemblée from the steps of the church of la Madeleine, where he has just got married, it is obvious, as the on-looking Rachel remarks, that 'he will soon be minister'.

Censorship stories

Daquin had been trying to get the project of *Bel-Ami* off the ground since 1950.[2] As André Bazin, in a courageous article published in the *Observateur* in 1955, points out, given the political climate of the time in France (war with Algeria), which led to strict censorship, and given the nature of the film's subject matter (with its references to Algeria and Morocco and corrupt speculation), it was highly unlikely that he would have got the scenario through the pre-censorship board.[3] In any event, he could not find a French producer to back him. Eventually, Austria came to his rescue – more precisely, the-then Eastern (communist) bloc of Vienna and Projektograph Film, as part of the attempted thaw which saw several studio collaborations between East and West bloc countries.[4] They supplied the money and the film stock, Agfacolor, which came from Eastern Germany. However, in exchange, Projektograph contracted Daquin to make a German version of the same film but with Austrian actors and technicians. He agreed and duly shot both versions in a short turnaround time of 10–12 weeks. The French version, for its part, was made almost exclusively with French personnel and was edited in Paris. Two small French production and distribution companies (Malherbes and Marceau) were also involved (but at what juncture remains unclear, except it would seem at the distribution end of things). However, this was but the start of a series of difficulties the French version of the film was to encounter, beginning with its 'nationality'. In November 1954 (at its first submission to the Commission of Visa Control), it suited the minister responsible for signing off the exhibition visa – the minister of industry and commerce, André Morice[5] – to deem the film foreign. He argued that, since it was made with foreign money and foreign film stock, it was not a French film, so he refused to ratify the visa. This was despite the fact that the film had already been accorded French nationality by the CNC in September – a position the (cowardly) CNC reversed in December of 1954.[6] The Commission ordered that all references to Algeria and Morocco be cut. Daquin complied. However, in 1955 (during its second submission for a visa), Morice this time deemed it to be French and banned it in the interests of the nation because 'it gave evidence of a systematic denigration of the nation and placed the accent at a particularly sensitive time on the colonial issue' and represented a threat to public order.[7]

In April 1955, several major film directors and scriptwriters signed a petition demanding that the film be released. Morice again refused.[8] The film was the subject of debate at the Assemblée nationale (17 May 1955), with deputies arguing, on the one hand, that Maupassant's novel, set in 1880–1881, was indeed inspired by the Third Republic's first great period of financial speculation, and that it was a true reflection of the moral climate of the late nineteenth century, marked as it was by the collusion of three great powers: money, politics and the press. On the other hand, others, in particular Morice – possibly seeing too many uncomfortable parallels with the contemporary Fourth Republic and the burgeoning crisis in Algeria – argued that Maupassant's oeuvre had been misrepresented by the film and used to 'undermine the French nation'.[9] Apparently the film had been screened no less than eighteen times at the Ministry of Information. Yet, for all of that, Morice was no further enlightened and he clearly had not read the novel (as deputies at the Assemblée were quick to point out).[10] Morice insisted on a further cut of two sequences. Finally, in 1957 a much mutilated *Bel-Ami* – reduced from 106 to 86 minutes – was granted general release in France.

As indicated above, two versions of this film were made (with distinct casts and technicians): one in French, one in German, with completely separate exhibition trajectories. The German version came out in Austria and Germany and had a normal shelf-life. As for the French version, although banned in France, thanks to the prevarication about its 'nationality', it was possible to distribute the original in its integrity outside of France as an Austrian-produced film. The French version was first released in London, in 1954, to considerable acclaim – albeit with an 'X' certificate.[11] It was then later re-distributed on general release in the UK in 1956 with the first set of cuts imposed by the Commission (and ran at 100 minutes). This time, curiously, it obtained less-favourable reviews, doubtless because, by now, it was tarnished with the story of censorship. As *Monthly Film Bulletin* put it: 'Louis Daquin and his collaborators have here transformed Guy de Maupassant's story into a fairly thorough Left-wing tract, and it is presumably the numerous references to colonialism and wicked politicians and financiers (modern parallels hinted at) which caused the film to be banned in France'.[12] Clearly the reviewer (J. G.) had not read the original novel. Maupassant had been to Algeria, in 1881, as a special correspondent for the newspaper *Le Gaulois* when much of the North African troubles were brewing. So he had first-hand experience of the effects of colonialism and, in his articles, as much as in his novel, felt compelled to expose the lack of justice towards the Arabs. He sought to challenge prejudice and awaken people's consciousness.[13] His articles clearly show that he had adopted an anti-colonialist stance and his novel makes no bones about exposing the shenanigans between high-finance, the press and politicians, all poised to make money out of the colonies. The *Monthly Film Bulletin* reviewer goes on to criticize the pacing of the film – again an unfair reproach since, by French standards, this is a fairly fast-moving film. With an average shot length of 9 seconds (7 shots per minute, therefore) and sequences of no more than three minutes on average, it is reasonably fast-paced (see figure 17.2, pages 336–7 for the timing of sequences).[14] And the ensemble casting of Renée Faure, Anne Vernon, Jean Danet and René Lefèvre is far from lacking in verve and wit as they claim.

The importance of *Bel-Ami*, both as a film and as a marking political moment in France's 1950s' history, should not, therefore, be underestimated. Let us consider the contexts of this film further. Its director, Louis Daquin, was a member of the Resistance during the war; he was also a member of the French Communist Party – as indeed were his two co-dialoguists Roger Vailland and Vladimir Pozner. Daquin was the General Secretary to the film industry's technicians' trade union (the very institution the 1950s' studio bosses railed against). During the 1930s, he had worked with some of the great directors of the time (most directly with Jean Grémillon, whom he greatly admired and from whom he learnt his craft, but also Renoir and Clément). Yet, talented though he was, reaction to his political pedigree by producers and politicians alike was to thwart his ambitions as a film-maker and he made only nine films in France.[15] As Daquin puts it himself, the system of censorship in place during the 1950s was unrelenting towards him, and the 'Affaire *Bel-Ami*' was the last nail in the coffin as far as his film career was concerned.[16] The film was banned for three years and he was never able to work on a film in France again. He went to Romania and East Germany but to all intents and purpose his career was at an end.

When I embarked on my research into this film, it seemed that no copy of *Bel-Ami* remained in existence. I searched all film-library and archive catalogues possible. Imagine my excitement, then, when I finally managed to locate a copy at the Centre National de la Cinématographie's (CNC) archives out in Bois d'Arcy – thanks, it has to be said, to the assiduous search made on my behalf by Daniel Brémaud of the CNC. It then transpired that the only copy they had was the '*version russe*'. At first I was dismayed, but upon seeing it I realized I had a jewel before my eyes. For indeed that is exactly what it was – Louis Daquin's much-censored film available in its original version, albeit dubbed in Russian. Finally, posthumously, Daquin had his revenge on the censoriousness of the 1950s, thanks to the French Communist Party restoring the film in 1985 for presentation in the former USSR. Somehow it had ended up in the CNC's film archives. Thankfully, Daquin had logged all the cuts and amendments insisted upon by the board of censors so I could hear and see that they had been returned to this version of the film.[17]

In all, twenty minutes of cuts were imposed by the French board of censors before its visa was finally signed off in 1957.[18] The original film was 106 minutes long, the greatly-reduced French version, a mere 86. The Russian version I saw was 109 minutes long because of some extra inter-titles.[19] Apart from the cut of the opening 14 shots, showing Georges Duroy as a hussard in Algeria, all the excisions are restored and the dialogue re-writes replaced with the original lines. In the original film, the opening 14-shot sequence illustrates the brutal treatment meted out by Duroy and his fellow soldiers to the Arabs, including holding them to ransom and murdering them for their livestock. We also see Duroy stealing a necklace off the neck of an indigenous woman (see figure 17.1 below).[20] The board of censors demanded it be cut in its entirety. Daquin replaced it with a written text: 'Paris 1885, Georges Duroy, recently returned from Algeria, where he served two years in the *Chasseurs d'Afrique*, reminisces about his exotic conquests with his new Parisian conquest'.[21] The new conquest is Rachel, the young woman who hangs out at the Folies-Bergère. However, the board of censors were not satisfied and demanded a further cut as follows: 'Georges Duroy recently returned to France, after serving two years in the regiment, reminisces about his exotic conquests with his new Parisian conquest'. In the Russian version of the film it is the first text that is retained. So, although the written text replaces the brutality of the 14-shot sequence, at least it refers to the country 'Algeria' and the idea of conquest. As such, the opening retains more of the film's original intent than the one finally approved by the French board of censors. Furthermore, in this Russian

Figure 17.1: A censored image from *Bel-Ami*: Georges (aka Bel-Ami, Jean Danet) stealing an Arab woman's necklace. © Les Films Malherbes/Projektograph Film.

version, during this opening sequence set in the café area of the Folies-Bergère, Duroy talks away to his mistress about the appeal of North Africa in general, and ends by saying: 'You see there is a lot to be had in Morocco' – whereas for the French version this was yet a further line that the censors demanded be diluted (to 'there's a lot to be had in those countries').

Most significantly in relation to this Russian version, two sequences that were entirely cut are reinserted, giving a much greater sense to the film.[22] The first occurs between Duroy and Monsieur Walter and his senior political correspondent and deputy at the Assemblée, Laroche-Mathieu, whom Walter is trying to get into government as minister of foreign affairs (to grease his own palm, of course, by fostering his commercial interests in North Africa). In this sequence, Laroche-Mathieu endeavours to get Duroy to confirm (by showing him on the map of North Africa) that the Moroccans have illegally invaded Algeria at Azilal. This incursion is tantamount to an invasion of French territory, argues Laroche-Mathieu, who can now accuse the present minister of foreign affairs of ineptitude or concealment – thus getting him sacked and himself appointed foreign minister. Duroy, who still has some sense of integrity, insists that the Moroccans are nowhere near the border. As he points out, Azilal is in fact 300 kilometres inside Morocco, far away, therefore, from the Algerian border. Laroche-Mathieu refuses to be swayed and the story is published with the following headlines: 'Laroche-Mathieu challenges the government over the Azilal scandal'. In the paper he argues that France must take action against Morocco and annex it. The coup works, the government falls. Laroche-Mathieu is appointed minister. In the belief that Morocco will be annexed, parliament votes in favour of credits (basically, incurring debt) to finance the counter-attack. Walter becomes a major investor, so, too, Duroy, who also invests, his brief experience with integrity being rapidly overcome by his cupidity.

The second restored sequence takes this story further and occurs some months later. Duroy (now Du Roy du Cantel) has married the recently-widowed Madeleine Forestier and is spending his honeymoon in an hotel at the spa town of Bagnoles-de-l'Orne in Normandy.[23] He is visited by Walter and Laroche-Mathieu. In this sequence Duroy is more or less told to publish a story to the effect that the annexation of Morocco will now *not* take place. The impact of this news on the Bourse (French stock exchange) will be to cause a huge crash. However, unbeknown to Duroy, the play is double. First, to publish that the annexation *will not* take place, thus causing a crash, allowing Walter to buy back government debt very cheaply. Second, to confirm that the annexation *will* take place and see stocks soar again, at which point Walter can sell at top price (an insider-dealing scam, in short).

Neither of these two sequences are inventions on Daquin's part. They are clearly to be read in Maupassant's novel.[24] Indeed, Maupassant had transposed over into Morocco events actually taking place in Tunisia.[25] In 1881, the-then prime minister, Jules Ferry, broadcast the story (very similar to the one proposed by Laroche-Mathieu) that tribes of Tunisian brigands (the Khoumirs) had illegally invaded Algeria. This allowed Ferry to get funding from the government to counter-attack the invasion – send an army of 30,000 men into Tunisia and annex the country as a French Protectorate. This, in turn, created tensions with Italy over railway development rights in that country, which the French now controlled –

Tunisia was rife with financial speculation.[26] And, as we know, from Maupassant's novel, Walter had all sorts of business interests in 'Morocco'.[27] We can also see that Daquin, in his endeavours to placate the censors, had set his film four years later than the original text (1885 instead of 1881), but, as we know, this was still not enough: to pacify Morice, the date and the word Morocco had to be excised from the film – hence the cutting of these two crucial sequences and, thereby, any notion of a financial scam.

As Bazin asserts, to accuse Daquin of misrepresenting the novel is quite false: 'Daquin is guilty only of fidelity to himself and to Maupassant'.[28] Elsewhere, the reviewer in *Image et Son* argues eloquently that 'nothing is more relevant to today than Maupassant's text. Motives for wars of colonization haven't changed, it is the same classes who get rich and in the same way'.[29] There is a strong political edge to Maupassant's novel; therefore, to condemn Daquin for systematically opting for the political story over the social or psychological aspects of the story is erroneous.[30] We sense the desperate *arrivisme* of Duroy who uses women to get to the top; the ironic observation of the world of journalism (particularly through the wonderful performance of Renée Faure as Madeleine Forestier); the political sleaze embodied by Walter and Laroche-Mathieu; and a complacent bourgeoisie happy to display its wealth with its richly decorated apartments. In truth, Daquin took very few liberties with the original. He cut one important character, Norbert de Varenne, who early on in the novel gives Duroy a treatise on his philosophy: that we live more for material well-being than for thought; that, in the world of the blind, the near-sighted are kings; that the folk he, Duroy, mixes with are stuck between Scylla and Chybaris (money and politics). Varenne's final warning that, having once made it to the top the only way is down, is only too well exemplified by Laroche-Mathieu's eventual disgrace.[31] As Varenne tells Duroy, all is greed and vanity, and the newspaper he works for 'sails in the wake of state money and the nether-regions of politics' – murky waters indeed.[32] Although Varenne is elided, Daquin felt he kept his philosophy there in the film[33] – a point *Image et Son* concurs with: 'Daquin takes us backstage into the workings of a right-wing newspaper of the period, *La Vie française*, a racist and ultra-nationalist rag that unhesitatingly makes or breaks governments'.[34] On this point let us leave the final word to Daquin:

> I do not feel that I violated Maupassant. I feel if he had been writing now, he would probably have emphasized the influence of society more. All the same, Vailland, Pozner and myself studied the book thoroughly and I don't think we added anything. When you read it carefully, you realise that it is, in fact, the first anti-colonialist novel.[35]

Bel-Ami – a film in four parts

A film in four parts, the narrative of *Bel-Ami* unravels much like the quadrille that is danced at the Walter's ball towards the end of the third section. Each of the four parts is clearly demarcated by Duroy's next ascension on the social ladder he climbs, thanks to his exploitation of women – as the following figure makes clear:

Part One	Part Two	Part Three	Part Four
=> *from Rachel to Clothilde de Marelle*	=> *from Clothilde to Madeleine Forestier*	=> *from Madeleine Forestier to Mme Walter*	=> *from Mme Walter to Suzanne Walter*
a) Folies-Bergère • Duroy is penniless • Meets Rachel his first mistress	**a) 127 Rue de Constantinople (Clothilde and Duroy's little hideaway)** • Duroy begins affair with Clothilde	**a) Spa hotel Bagnoles-de-l'Orne** • Duroy's hand is forced by Walter and Laroche-Mathieu; to write that Morocco will not be invaded • Mme Walter and Suzanne also at Spa hotel – brief exchange with Duroy (both clearly rather smitten by him)	**a) Hotel particulier** • Duroy bursts in on his wife and Laroche-Mathieu; instigates divorce
b) Bois de Boulogne • Meets Forestier who invites him to dinner • Is introduced to Mme Clothilde de Marelle (on horse-back)	**b) Newspaper offices** • Duroy's hand is forced by Walter and Laroche-Mathieu over invasion of Algeria by Morocco • Duroy is furious at humiliation; Forestier laughs at him	**b) Walter's mansion: reception/ball** • Mme Walter shows interest in Duroy; sets rendez-vous at La Madeleine • Quadrille dance	**b) Newspaper offices** • Walter symbolically washes hands of Duroy; tells him Morocco will be invaded • Duroy humiliated, plans revenge (Suzanne as his trophy)
c) Forestier's apartment • Meets Walter who offers him a chance • Meets Clothilde (again), Madeleine, Mme Walter, Suzanne	**c) Folies-Bergère** • Takes Clothilde to Folies-Bergère • Rachel sees them both as they go through the *promenoir* to their loge • Humiliating showdown between Rachel and Clothilde	**c) Church of la Trinité** • Mme Walter hints that Madeleine is having affair with Laroche-Mathieu; & exposes Moroccan scam • Duroy puts move on Mme Walter; she 'resists'; he takes her off in carriage	**c) 127 Rue de Constantinople** • Dumps Mme Walter • Clothilde comes by for assignation
d) Newspaper offices • Publishes his first article thanks to Madeleine Forestier's dictation	**d) Newspaper offices** • Newspaper article on Azilal scandal printed • Duroy prepares to makes his move on Madeleine	**d) 127 Rue de Constantinople** • Seduction of Mme Walter completed	**d) Newspaper offices** • Walter fires Duroy
			e) Quai de la Seine • Rendez-vous with Suzanne; they take off in a carriage
			f) Church of la Madeleine • Duroy marries Suzanne • Duroy is rich; world at his feet; even Clothilde serves him a knowing wink

a: brown fur-trimmed coat
b: brown fur-trimmed coat
c: turquoise quilted smoking jacket
d: brown fur-trimmed coat
e: fur-trimmed evening coat
f: wedding jacket and trousers

30 minutes/12 sequences

e) Forestier's apt
• Duroy visits Madeleine

f) Newspaper offices
• Article produces results; government resigns; Laroche-Mathieu made minister; champagne celebrations

a: charcoal grey jacket, light-grey trousers
b: elegant dinner suit
c: brown fur-trimmed coat
d: white shirt; pale blue waistcoat and trousers

21 minutes/8 sequences

g) Forestier's apt
• Forestier dies
• Duroy marries Madeleine

a: red quilted smoking jacket
b: grey-blue tweed suit, red waistcoat
c: fur-trimmed evening coat
d: brown fur-trimmed coat
e: light-blue silk worsted suit
f: as in b
g: black pin-striped suit

32 minutes/9 sequences

=> **Duroy: sartorial changes**
In a, b and d wears same worn out clothes
In c wears a hired dinner suit

26 minutes/9 sequences

Figure 17.2: *Bel-Ami* structure.

We can see from the timing of the sequences that the film speeds up in the second half of the film. Parts one (3 minutes per sequence) and two (3.5 minutes per sequence) mark the complex ascendancy of Duroy to middle-class respectability in the form of marriage to Madeleine. Parts three and four (both at 2.5 minutes per sequence) indicate the rapidity with which Duroy has gained mastery of the game of social climbing. Indeed, the word 'game' is a key word to unravelling this film, beginning with the quadrille (in part three). Just prior to this dance, Duroy had been perched on a balcony overlooking people waltzing. Madame Walter approaches him, lays her hand on his, makes a rendez-vous with him – for she has important bits of information for him (as we later discover, when he meets her at the Trinité church, these are about his wife's infidelity and the fact that Monsieur Walter has used him over the Moroccan incident). As we adopt his point of view over the dancers, we observe, as does Duroy, his previous conquests: Clothilde and Madeleine dancing (the latter with Laroche-Mathieu). His sly smirk hints he has other conquests to make, at which point the camera cuts and we rejoin Duroy downstairs participating in the quadrille. This dance becomes an excellent metaphor for the game he is playing. All along, Duroy has thought of nothing but conquest – his whole ambitious purpose has been conducted like a campaign.

The quadrille itself is a term of military origin and refers to an equestrian performance: a military parade within which horses make square-shaped formations, criss-crossing through the centre. As a dance, the quadrille became extremely popular during the nineteenth century. It is an intricate dance, usually with four couples lined up in columns and dancing in vis-à-vis – that is, either opposite each other or at a diagonal (see figure 17.3 below). The couples meet up moving forward or across, the man enlaces the woman, they twirl around in the middle, either return together on the same line or separate and cross over to the other side. The interesting thing for us, in this film, is that the quadrille is executed by a crossing over on the diagonal to join the partner, rather than dancing forward to the person directly opposite. Duroy first engages with Clothilde. They talk, she is quite cross with him and he puts on the charm. The next crossing brings him to Madame Walter, who smiles radiantly as he enlaces her (no need for talk here!). Back to their lines and a third crossing brings Duroy back to Clothilde. She teasingly reproaches him for abandoning her (it is clear from this interaction that he will soon resume his liaison with her). The fourth engagement brings Duroy to Madame Walter once more and, at this point, they affirm their assignation at the Trinité (Madame Walter remains radiant). Now back on their lines, Duroy moves forward and this time it is Madeleine he encounters – almost as if she is there as an afterthought. They pull back to the lines and Duroy's final encounter is with Madame Walter once more. The sequence fades out on the couple as they twirl in the middle.

The dance and the crossing over are key to our understanding of Duroy's duplicity, as indeed Daquin himself asserted.[36] The military connection and the idea of performance are also key. In his campaign, Duroy performs the exquisite lover. He plays and toys with his women, twirls them around, uses them and double-crosses them. Furthermore, in this dance, only three couplings have been engaged. So the question becomes: where is the fourth (victim/conquest)? She is yet to come and, immediately upon the fade-out on this dance,

Figure 17.3: Dancing the Quadrille in *Bel-Ami*. © Les Films Malherbes/Projektograph Film.

Duroy is seen with Suzanne (the Walters' daughter) in the conservatory – full of tropical plants and therefore quite humid. Small wonder the valet comes looking for her and, casting a filthy look at Duroy, takes her back to her fiancé!

Of course, Duroy is not the only one to play at double-crossing: both Walter and Laroche-Mathieu do it – arguably at a more lethal level, since their practice takes place in the domain of finance and politics. However, Duroy is not far behind, representing as he does the press, and we know of his political ambitions. Just as he replaced one man, Forestier, so we can see that soon he will replace Laroche-Mathieu. Dead man's shoes indeed. Walter will not be able to wash his hands of Duroy as easily as he believes – his fortune will be next in line. There is a capital scene in part four which makes this clear. The sequence opens with a close-up on Walter's hands playing cards: a game of patience, in French known as '*une réussite*', literally 'a success'. As Walter and Duroy talk, Walter moves over to a wash-stand cabinet; he opens the lid in which there is a mirror; as he washes his hands, we see Duroy's smug reflection in the mirror – he is asking Walter to back him, now Laroche-Mathieu is out of the political frame (thanks to the divorce scandal). Walter dries his hands and closes up the cabinet, clearly angry at having lost a valuable asset in government, thanks to Duroy. He cuts the conversation short by refusing to help; Duroy storms out, furious. Walter leaves an unsealed letter on Duroy's desk in the adjoining offices, sacking him. One of Duroy's colleagues reads it before he comes back to his desk, adding to Duroy's sense of humiliation. Walter believes he has sealed Duroy's fate. No such thing. Duroy sits at his desk, immediately plotting his revenge, the next move on his campaign: Walter's own humiliation through eloping with Suzanne.

Ruthless as he is, not all the women are entirely his 'victims'; more his 'game' – in the sense of the hunt – and not all succumb or fully submit. It is only Madame Walter who really suffers (and later, we assume, her daughter Suzanne). Rachel stands up to Duroy and Clothilde at the Folies-Bergère (see figure 17.2, part two, section 'c'). Madeleine is no mean challenge either. It is she who dictates to him the first article he writes for *La Vie française* (and continues to do so once they are married). It is she who refuses to be his mistress and marries on her terms (of equality and non-possessiveness). It is she who first suggested that Duroy 'entertain' Clothilde, and that he make a friend of Madame Walter so he can get close to her husband and advance his career prospects (as we know, Georges takes this further than she intended). In essence, she has shown him the way forward (even to the point of suggesting he ennoble his name to Du Roy). When Madeleine is exposed as an adulteress, she says nothing during the entire scene; merely, the most delicate smile of irony adorns her lips. We sense her distaste for Duroy's jealousy, coupled with an indifference to his vulgarity by bringing the police and the notary into the adulterer's bedroom to immediately write out the divorce writ – he is not classy enough to challenge Laroche-Mathieu to a duel. She is as much in charge of her game as he is of his. Clothilde never fully disappears from his amorous life, either. She is willing to accept the ups and downs of her relationship with the elegant young man. As if to signal Duroy's moments of entente with these two women, we see how their costumes reflect his (see figure 17.2 for details of Duroy's outfits). Thus, when all is going well with Clothilde, who is herself very much associated with the colour red, Duroy is seen sporting red (either a smoking jacket or a waistcoat). When all is going well with Madeleine, in the various stages of their relationship, his costume directly matches hers: pale turquoise-blue; white.

The one whose dress code rarely matches his – with the exception of the ball (where both are in black and white) and the meeting at the Trinité church (when both are in brown) – is Madame Walter. These moments of entente aside, and excluding one other noteworthy exception where everything jars, she wears black. We sense she has adopted the clothing suited to a middle-aged matriarch, and one that professes a devout Catholicism (as a counter to her husband's Jewishness, perhaps, as is suggested in Maupassant's novel).[37] Thus, apart from the initial stages of the campaign of seduction, she is out of step with Duroy's sartorial persona. There is a little hint of a coquette in the form of the small pink hat that she wears just the once, along with her black dress, at the champagne celebrations for Laroche-Mathieu's elevation to minister (in part two). However, there is one moment within her sartorial display that startles. It occurs (in part three) at the Spa hotel at Bagnoles-de-l'Orne where she is dressed in a red and white striped dress such as Clothilde or a demi-mondaine might wear, certainly not a matriarch of forty or so. Her daughter is in pink, but Madame Walter is hardly a match, even as she aspires to a youth long past. This is the moment that Duroy really notices her – for it is the one time that Mme Walter 'derails' in terms of her attire. No matter how unconscious her choice, it represents in its inappropriateness a sign of availability – one that Duroy cannot fail to read and log into his campaign of seduction.[38]

Class and political ambition drive Duroy. The dance is one metaphor, but so too is his free movement over the various geographical locations in Paris. One, incidentally, that is matched by Clothilde, whose main ambition appears to be to hold onto Duroy as a lover. Both Duroy and Clothilde are, in a sense, the outsiders trying to penetrate into the domains of the well-heeled Parisian inhabited by the Walters and the Forestiers, who occupy sumptuous apartments in the 8th and 9th arrondissements (rue du Faubourg Saint-Honoré and rue Fontaine respectively). Duroy lives in the rather insalubrious 17th, just above the boulevard des Batignolles in a crummy attic room. Clothilde has rooms in the 7th, on the fourth floor (a small apartment therefore) on the other side of the Seine in a narrow street off the rue des Saints Pères (rue Verneuil). However, despite their lesser means, both have the greatest mobility – suggesting, amongst other things, their mutual ambition and suitability in terms of each other. In their movements around the city they mirror each other. They visit all the points on the map, as it were, criss-crossing Paris: the 17th, 7th, 8th and 9th arrondissements, the Folies-Bergère in the 9th, the newspaper offices just off boulevard Haussmann (near the Bourse in the 2nd), very much as if in a quadrille of social mobility. Moreover, it is not long before Duroy takes up residence on rue Constantinople, within the prestigious domain of the 8th, albeit in a small two-room suite more reminiscent of a lovers' nest than an exclusive bachelor's pad. It is instructive that it is Clothilde who first set him up there when he was penniless, rather than go to his scrubby rooms in the 17th. As soon as he has the means, however, he takes it on as his own place, to tryst with more than just Clothilde. Madame Walter's movements take her to churches, her husband's newspaper offices, the Forestier's and, fatally, to Duroy's place on rue Constantinople. Intriguingly, the woman who moves around the least is Madeleine. Consistent with her standing as a woman of political culture, people mostly come to visit her – as if her place were a *salon*. This suggests she is at the centre, a bit like a spider in its web. Her centrality also suggests that she may well be another kind of *meneur du jeu/mistress of ceremonies* to Duroy and that he has, in the ultimate analysis, profoundly misunderstood her significance. If we return to the metaphor of the quadrille, we recall that she appeared to figure as an afterthought – in Duroy's mind, certainly. But this criss-crossing of the city, in which both he and Clothilde participate, suggests an instability and therefore insecurity of position, as opposed to the established certainty of Madeleine Forestier/Du Roy. Perhaps his future is less assured than he believes.

This stability on Madeleine's part is compounded by her sense of taste. In relation to the other central characters, she is clearly a woman of greater refinement. Compared to the two other main apartments we visit in the film (Duroy's batchelor pad and the Walters'), in terms of décor, hers is the most tasteful. The walls of her rooms are lined with silk cloth – pale blue to turquoise – the various doorways hung with grey-blue velvet curtains. In contrast, the

Walters' mansion exudes pretentiousness, as is most evidenced (in the ball sequence in part three) by the excessive décors of marble and gilt in the ballroom and the dark mahogany panelling and rich tapestries in the reception area. Rue Constantinople, Duroy's place, is more of a cocotte's space with its swathed wall furnishings in turquoise and beige – hinting at a vulgarity and spatial inappropriateness that are both consonant with Duroy's character and impulsive *arrivisme*.

Décors, then, speak of the individuals who inhabit them and Barsacq, the set designer, had an excellent lead in Maupassant's novel for most of them. As we know, the film was shot in the Eastern bloc of Vienna, in the Rosenhügel studios. These studios are the largest in Austria. The interior is 25 metres by 90 (at least the size of the Studios de Boulogne, France's biggest studios); the exteriors, a massive 25,000 square metres with sets of 8,000 square metres, one of which contains a revolving floor so that exteriors obtain best sunlight. Pre-war, they were the cutting-edge studios in terms of technology and still, in the 1950s, they represented a wonderful luxurious working environment. The year of *Bel-Ami*'s production was 1954 – the final year of the occupation of Austria by the allies – so obtaining materials was less arduous than in the first years. During the ten-year occupation, Rosenhügel, in a similar vein to the Austrian sister studios in the western bloc, tended to produce costume dramas that did not challenge current ideological positions (for example the *Sissi* series, starring Romy Schneider). Thus, in large part, the method and means for Daquin's own costume drama were already in place for his technical team, brought from France. Even so, there were 29 sets in all to construct, including the major exteriors of les Halles, the Madeleine and la Trinité, rue Constantinople and the Quai de la Seine. Furthermore, at least three interiors demanded great staging in depth: those of the two churches and the Walters' ballroom at their mansion. The result is a remarkable feat by any standards. Barsacq speaks of the freedom these huge studios afforded over the smaller French ones. First, the exteriors were facilitated by the fact that the vast terrains already had established trees and parks – greatly assisting the Bois de Boulogne shots. Second, because they had so much space, pre-existing constructions stayed in place, greatly facilitating his task for some of the massive façade structures.[39]

We know, from our discussion in Part One of this book, that Barsacq believed that design should be subordinate to the narrative and lend atmospheric support: sets should offer a précis of reality, not reality itself.[40] His goal was to achieve authenticity; to create a décor that was harmonious with the film, without necessarily striving for realism.[41] Thus, his designs, particularly of the 1950s, are often light of touch, uncomplex. The décor of *Bel-Ami* was criticized by some reviewers for its over-sumptuousness. And the use of Agfacolor, with its washed tints, failed to convince others.[42] The Agfacolor stock came from East Germany, from the Leverkusen laboratories, and was acknowledged as a superior product to the West German version (see Chapter 2 and the discussion of the different colour systems) and whilst it was the only stock available, it clearly matched Daquin and Barsacq's needs. But this rather misses the point of Maupassant's own descriptions. The spaces he evokes are quite detailed. The Forestiers' apartment is a pale blue affair; the Walters' is described as an un-ending extravaganza of luxurious staircases, carpets, salons hung with stupendous silken tapestries leading to a huge conservatory full of exotic plants, a dining-room with enormous marble columns and Gobelins tapestries, and so on – browns, whites and gold, green dominate here.[43] Such an ostentatious display of wealth was clearly repugnant to Maupassant. As for Duroy, it makes him even more jealously determined to accede to the Walters' wealth.[44] In terms of Maupassant's detailed descriptions, apartments are blue or turquoise (the Forestiers' apartment and Duroy's place on rue Constantinople); the newspaper offices are predominantly brown; red dominates the Folies-Bergère, with blue-tinted woodwork. All this Barsacq faithfully reproduces. We should recall that, in general, what tended to dominate in terms of his own design palette was the whole range of browns, rust colours, beiges, mauves, blue-greys, pearlized greys. He also found that gold, silver and black rendered well. In short, he understood the need to harmonize, to know the properties of the film stock and to be aware of continuity from one sequence to the next.[45] What dominates in *Bel-Ami* is certainly a harmonization of blue, blue-greys, pearlized greys and browns – with red reserved for the Folies-Bergère (a place of illicit encounter – as indeed, by extension, is Clothilde in her red outfits).

On this issue of choice of palette, it is worth pointing out that Barsacq's interior of the Trinité is very brown and dark, and not at all like the church itself, with its great white columns and wide, expansive white marble steps up to the gilt altar. Interestingly, Maupassant offers no detailed description himself, mentioning only the huge altar, without any reference to colour.[46] Clearly, Barsacq made an aesthetic choice, here, to deviate from the authentic and create a set that remains in keeping with the characters. Thus, the set has the columns that Duroy hides behind – albeit they are brown wood, not white marble. The brown confessionals are there, lined up along the wall near where Madame Walter and Duroy kneel, and to which she runs in her desperation to confess. The decision to move away from the ostentation that the Trinité displays undoubtedly emanates from a conviction that it would not have worked visually in relation to Mme Walter's character and her devotion to good works. Nor would it have worked in relation to the sin she feels at this illicit rendez-vous with Duroy, which can only lead to further sin. Thus, for the sake of the narrative logic, the interior is altered; it becomes dark and lugubrious, sinister even. In fact, the interior resembles far more that of the Madeleine church, which is very brown within, and where, at the end of the film, the wedding takes place. The Madeleine's dark interior, matched as it is by the minor key of the music played on the organ, does not bode well for Suzanne's happiness in marriage, it has to be said – particularly when, as the couple emerge outside, onto the huge steps of the church, a triumphant (extra-diegetic) fanfare of trumpets greets them as Duroy stares greedily at the Assemblée nationale over the river.

Conclusion

In an interview in 1979, Daquin makes an interesting comment in relation to the 1950s' supposedly uninventive cinema of quality. It is worth referring to it by way of conclusion to the discussion of this film. He talks about how, during the 1930s, in terms of a film aesthetic, he, Grémillon, Becker and Renoir were quite taken with the Hollywood filming technique. He explains how the Occupation period contributed to a detoxification from the American system. Thus, for many, the '*qualité française*' that came into being in the 1950s was a manifestation of that rejection – an affirmation that there was a French film aesthetic (not, as Truffaut would have us believe, a sterile cinema). Daquin gives as a couple of examples in relation to *Bel-Ami*: first, the fact that he stopped using the shot/counter-shot (although there is one incidence of it in the film – crucially, when Madeleine becomes complicit with Duroy in helping to write his first article); second, that he very rarely used music, which, to his mind, is mostly unmotivated yet hugely manipulative.[47] As we note from *Bel-Ami*, on the few occasions it is used, it is primarily diegetic (Folies-Bergère; the ball at the Walters', the wedding organ). The one non-diegetic moment of music occurs right at the end, in the trumpet fanfare – surely an ironic comment on Duroy's ambitions?

Daquin's film remains, therefore, an important one on a number of fronts – all of them political in some way. It is a film made by a Frenchman who wanted to celebrate, in his work, the oeuvre of a great narrative master: Maupassant. In his endeavour to adapt to screen a French classic, he was thwarted at all stages of the process. Yet he made a film which he readily labels as French and qualifies as an exemplar of the much maligned '*cinéma de qualité française*'. He showed great fidelity to the original text and was heavily censored for it. Crucially, and sadly, because of the political furore caused by this most French of texts and because the film itself was confounded with the politics of the man behind the film, *Bel-Ami* – a very good film and fine costume drama, in my view – has, to all intents and purposes, disappeared from the French film heritage, remaining only in the form of a 16mm '*version russe*'.

Notes

1. In Maupassant's novel, *Bel Ami*, Madeleine spells it out very clearly: 'I mean to be free…I will not tolerate being controlled, any jealousy or any discussion of my behaviour.' (Maupassant 1999, pp. 208–9, my translation).
2. Daquin (1960, p. 268).
3. See Bazin quoted in Daquin, op. cit., p. 268.
4. See Silberman (2006).
5. Something of a paradox, Morice came from a stalwart left-wing background. In 1940, he was taken prisoner of war (released 1943). However, during the Occupation his company (l'Entreprise nantaise des travaux publics et paysagers) continued to supply equipment to the Germans, making him a tidy profit. Post-war, Morice was exonerated of any wrong-doing and went on to have a very successful political career adhering to a Right-wing political culture (http://www.assemblee-nationale.fr/histoire/biographies/IVRepublique/Morice-Andre-11101900.asp accessed 14.02.2009). He was a fierce proponent of French Algeria (hence doubtless his ferocity with Daquin's film). He even designed the so-named *Ligne Morice*, a barrage that was both mined and electrified, to separate French Algeria from its neighbours and prevent the infiltration of the National Liberation Army. (http://fr.wikipedia.org/wiki/André_Morice accessed 14.02.2009).

6. See Daquin, op. cit., p. 270.
7. Morice in Daquin, op. cit., pp. 272–3.
8. Ibid., p. 286. The signatories include: Autant-Lara, Billon, Bost, Ciampi, Clair, Carné, Clouzot, Cocteau, Dréville, Gance, Grémillon, Jeanson, Le Chanois, Ophuls, Painlevé, Prévert.
9. Morice in Daquin, op. cit., p. 272.
10. Daquin, op. cit., pp. 272–3.
11. Ibid., p. 270.
12. *Monthly Film Bulletin* review of *Bel-Ami*, Vol. 23, No. 266, 1.3.1956, p. 27 (J. G. given as author).
13. See Adeline Wrona's *Dossier 2* in Maupassant (pp. 386–400).
14. In the 1950s, Hollywood ASL average varied between 6 to 8 seconds. So Daquin's film is not that far off their median.
15. The nine films are: *Nous les gosses* (1941); *Madame et le mort* (1942); *Le Voyage de la Toussaint* (1943); *Le Premier de la cordée* (1944); *Patrie* (1946); *Les Frères Bouqinquant* (1947); *Le Point du jour* (1948); *Le Parfum de la dame en noir* (1949); *Maître après dieu* (1951).
16. Daquin in interview conducted by Robert Grelier (1970, p. 19).
17. See Daquin (1960, pp. 274–85). Since going to press, I have discovered the University of Paris III have a copy. I have yet to see it.
18. Daquin (1970, p. 68).
19. In their 1957 production and review notices on the film, both *Le Film français* and *La Cinématographie française* give its 'nationality' as Austrian and its length as 85 minutes.
20. See Daquin (1960, pp. 155 & 274) where he supplies these details. *Monthly Film Bulletin* has it at 100 minutes (so, clearly, the original uncut version was the one screened – minus the 14 opening shots). The Austrian production company, Projektograph films, lists it at 106 minutes. The version I saw was 109 minutes – the three minutes or so being due to the inserts of explanatory shots of various letters and printed articles in Russian script. These extra shots would have been made in 1985. It is noticeable that, when no cut-away to a close-up on the written word alone can be made, the newspaper remains in French. Thus, these inserts add a few minutes to the running length.
21. This text corresponds fully to Maupassant's own words (see p. 48). Further reading around this interesting case of censorship took me to Daquin's book *Le Cinéma, notre metier,* wherein he acknowledges that the cut was a good thing because to have kept it would have 'skewed the film and taken the spectator down a different path' (1960, p.155, my translation).
22. When this latest request was made in 1956, Daquin agreed to them but did not have the heart to do them himself (Daquin, 1960, p. 273).
23. The 19th century witnessed a growth in leisure retreats outside Paris, including spas. Bagnoles-sur-l'Orne was well-known for its thermal sources and curative waters. And the Grand Hotel is exemplary of late 19th century architectural elegance (doubtless the model for the Duroys' honeymoon).
24. See Maupassant, op. cit., pp. 237–9; 264; 284–7; 294–6; 299–300; 315; 366. In particular, on page 284 he makes almost direct reference to Jules Ferry.
25. See Daquin (1960, pp. 268–9).
26. See Maupassant, op. cit., p. 148, footnote 1.
27. In particular copper mines (Ibid., p. 285).
28. Bazin quoted in Daquin (1960, p. 269).
29. Lefèvre (1958, p.14).
30. See the reviews in *Today's Cinema* (Vol. 8, No. 7441, p. 7, no author name given [M. M. W.]) and *Image et Son* (Lefèvre, op. cit., p. 14)
31. Maupassant (161-5).

32. Maupassant, op. cit., p.151.
33. Daquin (1960, p.164).
34. Lefèvre, op. cit., p. 14.
35. Daquin interviewed by Jean-Pierre Berthomé (1976, p. 8).
36. 'We can regret that, in certain scenes, Bel-Ami's duplicity as lover and ambitious gets lost in favour of the lover. However, the scene of the quadrille, completely invented, serves precisely to redress this and to show this side of Bel-Ami' (Daquin 1960, p. 164, my translation).
37. Maupassant writes: 'her marriage to an Israelite obliged her, she believed, to a certain religious reserve' (p. 256, my translation). Daquin makes no direct allusion to Monsieur Walter's ethnic origin; we surmise it or know it from the novel).
38. There is a similar moment in the novel when Duroy encounters Mme Walter on the way to a party: '(Duroy) was surprised to see her in a light coloured dress…He thought her most desirable…Her daughter, Suzanne, was in pink as if in a Watteau painting'. (Maupassant, op. cit., p. 255).
39. Barsacq (1970, p. 156).
40. Votolato (2000, p. 66).
41. Touati (1988, p. 30).
42. *To-day's Cinema* finds fault with the over-sumptuousness of the décor (Vol. 86, No. 7441, p. 7, no author's name); *Image et Son* with the washed out colours of Agfacolor (Lefèvre, op. cit., p.14).
43. Maupasant, op. cit., pp. 319–24.
44. Ibid., pp. 316–22.
45. Barsacq in *La Cinématographie française*, No. 1538, 17.10.1953, pp. 38–9.
46. See Maupassant, op. cit., pp. 270–8.
47. Daquin interview with Frantz Gévaudan (1979, p. 34).

Part IV

Belle Epoque Mania: Paris, the Provinces and Biopics

Chapter 18

Belle Epoque Films: An Overview

The Belle Epoque 1889–1914

Even naming and finding an agreed set of dates for the Belle Epoque period is something of a task. As a name for a period, the term is a retrospective one that emanates from a post-war mentality that was nostalgic, after the horrors of the Great War, for a 'lost' and in some ways imaginary golden epoch. The term was also, as one of the characters in Renoir's film *Eléna et les hommes* (1956) repeatedly reminds us, an expression in common usage in the nineteenth century: 'Ah la belle époque', this elderly woman keeps intoning whenever something in the contemporary moment (1889) distresses her; presumably she is referring to when Napoleon III was in power.[1] As we shall see, for some, this period of prosperity and expansion was a golden age; for others, far less so. It was an epoch of great changes, class mobility (especially in the form of a new, emergent middle class), technical innovation, mass culture and colonial expansion. But it was also an age of deep socio-economic inequalities, demographic decline, social disease in the physical form of tuberculosis, venereal disease, cholera and typhoid, all of which manifested itself, in a more abstract form, through discourses that were anti-republican, anti-parliamentarian, anti-feminist, anti-clerical and anti-semitic, amongst others.

In terms of the epoch's duration, some historians speak of a start date of 1896, the year France emerged from a long period of economic crisis (beginning in 1885 and affecting the West in general).[2] Others set it in 1893,[3] yet another 1884.[4] What they are all agreed upon is its end-date: 1914, in the form of the beginning of the Great War (as World War One was then known). For our own purposes we are dating the Belle Epoque era from 1889 to 1914. We choose 1889 because this year marked a turnaround in the Republic's fortunes on two counts. First, the implementation in heavy industry of the Gilchrist-Thomas process greatly increased the potential of steel-making in the iron-ore district of Lorraine.[5] France truly entered the steel age (as exemplified by its 1889 *Exposition Universelle*/World Fair – *La Tour Eiffel*), thus enriching its coffers. Lorraine, a formerly-poor province, became the heart of France's steel industry. Second, this was the year of the failed attempt by General Boulanger to overthrow the Republic. He was principally backed by Royalists, the army, and clergy – all enemies of republicanism (although some Radicals who were impatient for change, Clemenceau in particular, also supported him). In surviving the poorly-managed putsch, the Third Republic demonstrated, however shakily, that republicanism had come of age and that it was not, ultimately, vulnerable to the *coups d'états* which had so marked this revolutionary century (those of Napoleon I and III being the most significant ones).[6] Unlike its predecessors, this Republic would have a very long life – seven decades, as opposed to little more than a decade for the first Republic and a mere three years for the second.

This is not to say that the Belle Epoque, nor indeed the Third Republic, was a period of uniform tranquillity. Far from it. It is also worth remembering that Republican France was quite isolated in what was predominantly a monarchical Europe. France further isolated itself in Europe on a religious front: first, by voting a law forbidding unsanctioned professional bodies, namely clerics, from teaching (loi du 1er juillet 1901 sur les associations); second, by waging a systematic campaign of confiscating property from religious orders (1902–1904); third, by breaking off relations with the Vatican in 1904; and, finally, by instituting the separation of church from state in 1905. Although, as this slew of legislation makes clear, the political body of the nation was deeply anti-clerical, this by no means meant that anti-clericalism was a widespread phenomenon amongst the citizenry. Furthermore, such radical positioning did not mean that the anti-republican mood in France itself had evaporated. Indeed, these were turbulent years. In the 25-year span of the Belle Epoque, there was at least one more attempt at a *coup d'état* (1899); there were two major scandals (the Panama Canal, 1892, and the Dreyfus Affair, 1894); the assassination of two major political figures (Sadi Carnot, President of France 1887–1894, and, in 1914, Jean Jaurès the founder of *L'Humanité*); and five general strikes, all brutally repressed by the army.

On an international level, Germany continued in its attempts to deflect France's attention from the Rhineland. Indeed, Bismark set out on a deliberate plan to both distract and isolate France by encouraging the latter's intervention in Tunisia (1881). This caused such bad feelings with Italy (who believed it had historical rights there) that it refused to participate in the Paris World Fair of 1889. Tensions increased between immigrant Italian workers and the French and in 1893 there was a big show-down in the Provence area of Aigues-Mortes, where seven people were killed. A year later, an Italian anarchist murdered President Carnot.[7] The outcome of this meddling by Germany was that, at last, the recalcitrant Italy joined Germany and Austria in the Triple Alliance. In 1882, France's relations with Great Britain foundered over Egypt. Both France and Britain were chief creditors to Egypt's debt and Britain was the second biggest shareholder of the (French-built) Suez Canal. Britain wanted to force Egypt to pay back its debts which, in turn, caused a nationalist uprising. France refused to send troops; Britain was left to restore order, thereby taking over control of the territory. France felt betrayed.[8] Crucially, on all three sides of its borders (north, east and south) France found itself isolated. Yet it managed to transcend this on two counts: first, by expanding and subsequently consolidating its empire (from 1 million square kilometres in 1880, to 9.5 million by 1895[9]), thereby creating a new export market, to say nothing of appropriating a new set of terrains to exploit raw materials (especially oil),[10] and, second, by finding itself a new ally, Russia. Beginning in 1888, France agreed to underwrite several big loans, which Germany had refused to bankroll, to the nearly-bankrupt Russia. In so doing, France forged an alliance that lasted well into the mid-twentieth century. But even more significantly, it was able to display an economic might to its enemy Germany and offer a rebuttal to its own isolation by having its former enemy pincered on two sides: to the east and the west.[11] Furthermore, with a birth rate that was only one sixth that of Germany's, perhaps France could relax somewhat in the knowledge that both its expanded colonies and its alliance with Russia should make up for its own demographic shortfall in soldier manpower in the event of further confrontation with Germany.[12]

The Belle Epoque as a concept is very much aligned in the imaginary with Paris; unsurprising really, given the consecutive World Fairs (1878, 1889, 1900) and the great transformation undergone by the city. After all, the 1890s also marked the near-completion of the modernization of Paris, first undertaken by Baron Haussmann in the mid-1850s. Thus, by the time of the Belle Epoque, Paris was a brand new city (at least in the central areas), with new, elegant boulevards and buildings. But for paintings by the likes of Pissarro, which give us some idea, it is difficult to imagine today just how pretty the new Paris looked.[13] The buildings' stonework was somewhat washed-pink in its glow with red chimneys and the street lamps brown-bronze in colour.

Even the railway stations – most of which were built in the 1840s (Gare de Lyon and d'Orsay being the exceptions as early-1900s' constructions) – were refurbished in the second half of the century if not completely made-over, as was the case with the Gare du Nord.[14] Paris became the world's playground. Indeed, with three World Fairs in fairly rapid succession to promote its importance, Paris established itself as the world's leading host for these international venues up until the Great War.[15] Paris became a cultural centre – a mecca of 'the arts, music, medicine, science, scholarship'.[16] Streets that had formerly been lit by gaslight were now, in the late 1880s, afforded a 'blinding brightness' with the introduction of electricity.[17] The dazzling Moulin Rouge opened its doors in 1889 (the year of the World Fair) at the same time as the Eiffel Tower shone 'as bright as day'.[18] A tantalizing city of light – at least for the wealthy, namely the bourgeoisie, the upper classes, and a newly emergent middle class.

The Belle Epoque period was a time of great prosperity for France on a global scale, with huge financial holdings in Russia, Italy, Austria-Hungary, Turkey, and Britain.[19] Economic growth was estimated at 250 per cent over the Second Empire period.[20] France was rich, but its increased wealth created a wider gap between the rich and the poor. With 1 percent of its inhabitants holding 30 per cent of all wealth,[21] it comes as no surprise to learn that two thirds of the population lived in varying degrees of poverty.[22] If we just consider the following figures of the active population at the turn of the century (20 million) we can see that a mere one third of those in work were earning a decent wage. Professional classes accounted for 0.5 per cent of the working population; the military, 4 per cent; civil servants, 2 per cent; a newly emergent middle class, a further 25 per cent; the industrial urban working classes represented 17 per cent; the predominantly female domestic working class 5 per cent; the remaining 47 per cent of the active population were primarily the rural classes.[23]

In terms of class hierarchies and demographic shifts, there were two important developments that occurred at the turn of the century: on the one hand, a new middle class, basing its wealth in small businesses, and, on the other, an expanded urban working class, drawing its numbers from the rural exodus (attracted by the higher wages offered by industry). To put things into perspective, this was only a modest improvement in earning power: since 60 per cent of these wages went to feeding the family; very little was left for lodgings or for leisure activities that had to be paid for.[24] By 1906–1910, the industrial working classes had grown a further 7 per cent and now accounted for 24 per cent of the active population; the domestic working class nearly doubled to 8 per cent. Industrial expansion explains this rise in great part, new industries such as electricity, automobile, aeronautics, cinema and aluminium especially. For example, in the ten-year period 1900–1910, Renault went from employing 110 workers to 4,000.[25] But the other significant impact on employment statistics was the one caused by the new middle class that began to emerge at the turn of the century. This class, which aspired to the bourgeoisie, was made up of shopkeepers, small industrialists, small landlords and small businesses in the domain of food, hairdressing and construction.[26] The development in construction businesses and small industry, in particular, created further jobs, primarily for male workers. But so, too, did the aspirations of this new middle class to 'better themselves' and display their wealth: it led them to take on domestic staff (hence the swelling of those ranks), which showed that they had both money and knowledge of social expectations. Chéri, the eponymous protagonist of Pierre Billon's adaptation of Colette's novel (Chéri, 1950), emanates from this class, as, of course, does his preposterously vulgar mother.

There is no doubt that the exponential growth in urban working classes was a cause of great concern for the bourgeoisie. Indeed, as early as 1889, they were frightened by the impact on class hierarchies of the growth in steel production, preferring 'dumb' peasants to the swelling ranks of skilled workers.[27] Such was the bourgeoisie's fear of the mob (and memories of the Paris 1871 Commune) that brutal repression of strikers was a common resort. A major incident in the annals of history took place on the first of May 1891, when the army was brought in to suppress a strike at the Fourmies foundry and ended up shooting at the strikers, killing nine (including four young women).[28] Moreover, despite the great transformations the nation was undergoing, there is little doubt that France (or rather, moneyed France, the well-heeled France mentioned above) was still a country based in a mentality of small properties, small business – one which distrusted, even hated, big factories for fear of a strongly unionized working class.[29] A distrust that was significantly shared by bankers, who, whilst wealthy, were disinclined to invest in industry in the way that Germany was, showing more interest in proffering loans –as we saw, to Russia, amongst other nations.[30] This France (bourgeois and middle class) was one that, by and large, felt a great resistance to state intervention (including laws on employment) and preferred stability to movement and growth; individual freedom to collective organisation.[31] Fortunately, not all industrialists operated in this way, especially those in the new industries (e.g., Michelin, Renault, Peugeot, Blériot, Pathé, Gaumont). Nor did this resistance to change prevent France from being a leading industrial nation, even if it lagged behind Germany in terms of investment.[32] For example, until the Great War, France outstripped Germany in terms of aeronautic and automobile production.[33] France was, however, hampered in its growth because of its massive reliance on the importation of raw materials (58 per cent) and could only compensate by exporting manufactured goods to the same percentage level. Luckily, it had its newly-consolidated empire as an export market (to the tune of 15 per cent, the remainder being exported primarily to European markets).[34]

Echoes in history – Costume Dramas, the Belle Epoque and the 1950s

If we now return to Pascal Ory's concept of displacement, discussed in Chapter 2, it is significant that the dominant epoch for costume drama is the Belle Epoque period. With 37 films, it represents 35 per cent of all costume dramas. This suggests a cultural recognition between the two periods in that they speak to each other. As it transpires, the political culture briefly sketched above is, interestingly, not without its echoes with the 1950s period. We know that within the genre of the costume drama there occurs a nostalgic harking back to former times. But, when we see the enormity of the parallels between these two periods, it is fascinating to note how, despite the aura of difference between the two, there is far greater similitude in preoccupations and fears than at first might be apparent. We could, therefore, speculate that the idea of costume drama as a cinema of escapism is not quite such an easy equation to make after all. Let us investigate this further.

The Belle Epoque was, like the 1950s, a time of modernization and renewal. In terms of the nation's psyche, both periods emerged from nearly twenty years of economic depression, wars lost with Germany and a profound sense of national humiliation. Chapter 2 set out much of the circumstances of the 1950s, so let us consider now the Belle Epoque. The economic resurgence in the late 1880s brought an expansion of wealth – primarily, it has to be said, in the cities. It was also one that benefited the middle- and upper classes. For, despite this resurgence, we need to recall that two thirds of the country (rural or urban) was still poor. Nor can we gloss over the impact of the two major scandals of the period: the Panama Canal fraud (exposed in 1892 and which brought down the government, many of whose parliamentarians were implicated in the fraud) and the Dreyfus Affair, which ran for twelve years (it began in 1894 when he was found guilty of treason, then pardoned in 1900, and finally rehabilitated in1906). Despite these scandals that rocked the nation, France was on a resurgence, economically speaking at least. Banks were wealthy. This was a period of major reconstruction of cities. New industries flourished: Michelin, Peugeot and Renault in the rubber and automotive industry; Pathé and Gaumont in the film industry; and Azaria in electricity.[35] Transport systems grew: trams and omnibuses for the general public; private automobiles for the more wealthy; bicycles designed for the sporty men and women as much as for the workers in need of a functional mode of transport. The Belle Epoque period was the time of the second wave of industrialization, where production was more focused on consumer goods than on production systems themselves, as occurred in the first wave of industrialization (1830s). This, in turn, produced new modes of consumption. Advertising on hoardings, selling via catalogues and, most significantly, the exponential growth of Department Stores first seen in the 1860s, all meant that there was a wider public awareness of and greater access to products.[36]

This was a time of modernization, when gas and electricity not only came into the streets but into the home. Technology entered the female sphere in other forms, as well. Sewing machines and the telephone (in the 1950s, we recall, there was a similar re-salubration of housing, with bathrooms and water closets being brought into the homes; electrical goods – new technologies – also entered the domestic sphere). For the well-heeled, clothing, particularly for women, became a different type of display of wealth. Now that time had become divided between town and country, social events and outdoor sports, the wardrobe had to match all eventualities. Thus, an endless change of costume became a sign of one's wealth as much as all the other symbols (cars, city apartments, country houses, etc.). In terms of design, the new expansion in clothing was driven by industry and particularly affected women as the bearers of the signs of wealth. Technology entered design more fully than ever before. Sewing machines, blind-stitching machines, pressing machines and steam irons led to the mass-production of clothing, targeted at the nouveau riche and newly emerging bourgeoisie. New systems of corseting – brought about thanks to advances in technology – created a hyper-femininity where the woman's body was forced into the exaggerated artificial form of the 'S' silhouette (tiny waist, elevated bust pushed forward and posterior pushed out at the rear). Dress codes, then, insofar as they fixed the female form, became specifically about sexuality, about trying to stabilize gender positions and, thereby, the social order of things. As fashion historians Buckley and Fawcett explain, there was a crisis around gender during the Belle Epoque and especially anxieties around female sexuality, brought about by the increase in venereal disease.[37] The need was felt to clarify boundaries between men and women. Interesting that a crisis in masculinity should bring about a hyper-feminization of clothing design – and we note how, in the 1950s, this same pattern reproduces itself with the hyper-feminine New Look. An earlier shift in men's clothing had already begun in the 1860s, primarily due to a change in working patterns (see Chapter 16). As the world of work greatly expanded for the bourgeoisie and the lower middle classes, so men wore more utilitarian clothing to work, primarily in the form of the black suit. It was a sartorial evolution provoked by economic reasons, therefore, rather than a crisis in masculinity. But it was one which began the process of this more marked distinction in gender– what Flügel referred to as the 'Great Masculine Renunciation'.[38]

This pattern of gender distinction also finds echoes in terms of women fighting for emancipation. In the Belle Epoque, the suffragist movement was at the stage that became known as the first wave of feminism – the second wave being that of the 1950s. Belle Epoque women were kept in a position of subjugation, with no civil or political rights. Those in power deemed that giving women the vote was tantamount to giving a vote to the priests (even the Pope, in 1906, condemned the woman's vote).[39] We recall the same fears being raised in the 1950s around women and the vote. In short, a commodification of femininity occurs in the Belle Epoque and a constructing of the ideal female consumer (especially in the light of the new consumerist palaces: the department stores) that is very similar to systems of containment that were in practice in the 1950s. There is also the important fact that in both epochs, technology and the female body were concepts that were tightly entwined – be it in the form of either clothing or technological objects entering into the home. As Buckley and Fawcett correctly point out 'the commodification of femininity was a key element in the emergence of modernity.'[40] But, by making woman the bearer of the sign of modernity, its icon even, it is evident that there will be a desire to control. The very act of externalizing male technology is to exert control. By making it exterior to his self, man can both adore and abhor the object-technics of his imaginings. In our corpus of Belle Epoque films, therefore, we can expect this neurosis to be reflected in narratives of adulation and backlash.

Let us develop further this issue of commodification of femininity in these two temporal contexts (Belle Epoque and 1950s) and engage it with the generic form of the costume drama. Given that the commodification of femininity is so central to costume drama, it is perhaps not surprising, based on what I have delineated above in terms of the containment of women, to discover that the Belle Epoque has such appeal as an epoch for this genre during the 1950s. Clearly, an ideological function has to be read into this preponderance of films set in this period – as well as the fact that it is in this epoch that female-centred narratives come to dominate (see figure 18.2 below). And concern about the status of women – increase in their civil rights during the 1950s – is one of the issues that finds its displacement in the Belle Epoque costume drama. If we consider the ideology of the feminine costume of the Belle Epoque and then weave it into considerations of the 1890s and 1950s, we can see that it was one of constraint and over-investment in the female body (the breast, waist and the bottom) which worked to three effects. First, it stabilized gendered positions. Second, it constructed an ideal of femininity, but one that was literally controlled by men who designed the constraining objects and put their technology to this use. Third, it placed bourgeois respectability and wealth on display. We need to recall that the 1890s represented yet another big expansion of the middle classes (the others occurring in the 1830s and 1860s). The function of women here, therefore, was to secure this emergent bourgeoisie. They stood symbolically for the legitimacy (and propriety) of this new, entrepreneurial class. In a similar vein, we note that the function of women in the 1950s was to secure masculinity post-war and, too, the ideology of the new Fourth Republic in the form of a reassertion of family values and nationhood – childbirth and domesticity being the key roles ascribed to women.[41] But of course it is here, in that term 'display', that the ideological function starts to crack because display is not just about putting on a show of respectability (and wealth), it also links up with the erotic (putting the body on show) – and costume analysis is one way to investigate this crack, as is the investigation of the star-body vehicle. Also, as we shall see, many of our encorseted women are far from obliging patriarchy and resist, in a number of ways (but primarily through the erotic), the demands bourgeois ideology places upon them. If the lead female is married and bourgeois, the tendency is for her to seek out a lover (or lovers). In general she gets punished for this or, more demeaning still, she is ridiculed for her endeavours.

Thus, in our analysis, questions arise: What do our female leads in the costume drama get up to in this context of a filmic reconstruction of the Belle Epoque? Do they conform to the ideological function of securing masculinity of the 'then (1890s)' or the 'now (1950s)', or both? It will come as no surprise to say that they both do and do not. And here is the paradox already pointed to in relation to the Belle Epoque itself and the notion of 'display'. Given that one of the major functions of the costume drama is the commodification of femininity, it is hardly surprising that sexuality dominates as a thematic. However, much as femininity may be commodified, there is far from a predominantly happy ending in these films – of the 37 Belle Epoque narratives, only twelve end well for the woman – less than a third, therefore. This represents a fairly low outcome, suggesting that marriage is a difficult relationship to sustain and it is a rather surprising statistic, particularly if we take account of the impact-value of this kind of message on women audiences. In these films, what becomes evident for the bourgeois female, in either instance (wife or mistress), is their need for economic security – which, for the most part, only men can supply. But the other clear message is that 'promiscuity' or sexual liaisons outside marriage do not pay. The costume drama points, then, to the paradox of her condition. On the one hand, the genre makes evident the reality (value) of the female erotic body: she is obliged to be on display either as a marker of bourgeois wealth (if a wife), or as body that is worth investing in (if a mistress). On the other, it shows how dangerous and destabilizing female eroticism is once it is no longer contained within marriage. The result is that the female suffers retribution in the form of loneliness or loss of status – not, we note, the male in the form of husband or lover (the one exception being the ageing Maxime in the film of the same title). Retribution against the woman, it seems, secures the ideological imperatives of bourgeois capitalism.

Intriguingly, however, as we shall see in the chapters that follow, the Belle Epoque woman gets off more lightly in terms of retribution than the women of the earlier part of the nineteenth century (from the Restoration through the Second Empire). In these pre-Belle Epoque films, as we saw, if the central character is a courtesan (a kind of upper-crust prostitute), or an adulterous wife, in general she meets an extreme end. In the pre-Belle Epoque films, there are nine instances of female deaths. Four are by illness, three by murder, two by suicide. Given that, during the first major urban expansion of the nineteenth century of the 1830s, venereal disease and other health issues such as cholera were on the increase, and were the concern of city-employed physicians, these deaths hardly reflect medical trends of the time. But they do suggest a fearsome desire for retribution. In the Belle Epoque films, retribution is less extreme. In the main, the transgressive woman loses her lover and finds herself doomed to a life of loneliness. Only occasionally does she die, but less often from illness than we might suspect. In fact there are merely four deaths in the corpus – one which cannot be counted as retribution since it concerns the saintly Thérèse de Lisieux, who died of tuberculosis (in *Le Procès du Vatican*). Of the other three, two are suicides (Marie-Louise in *Les Grandes Manoeuvres* and the eponymous heroine of *Christine*) and one a heart attack (the eponymous heroine of *Madame de…*).

This bleaching out of medical fact continues even more forcibly into the Belle Epoque costume dramas. There is a complete lack of any reference to sexually-transmitted diseases. This comes as something of a surprise, especially since during the Belle Epoque, as we already mentioned, the great obsession was with venereal disease. However, as we saw in Chapter 15, even the sickness affecting the courtesans of the pre-Belle Epoque films is a sanitized illness. It is not the dreaded venereal disease to which they succumb, but tuberculosis (known at the time as 'phtisie'). Moreover, this illness strikes but a tiny handful of women in the entire corpus – three to be precise: *Fantine in Les Misérables, Marguerite in La Dame aux camélias* (Bernard, 1953) and *Lola in Lola Montès* (Ophuls, 1955). This complete erasure of sexual disease, whilst running counter to the reality of nineteenth-century society, could be seen to reflect, in an abstract manner of course, the 1950s' drive to cleanse itself in relation to its recent past (the German Occupation and collaboration): a desire for a clean nation that was exemplified in fact by the closure of brothels under the loi Marthe Richard (1946).

There is another curious twist with regard to Belle Epoque films. Given the dominance of love intrigues (over three-quarters of the films), there is a considerable exposure of flesh and 'easy' morals on the part of middle-class women. Men may have mistresses but so, too, do women have lovers. However, they are made to pay the price for their indiscretions or infidelities. In a more subversive way, reading somewhat against the grain, we can see how this order of costume drama points to a common dilemma for middle-class women of both the 1890s and 1950s – the fact that, boredom aside, they often had to resort to prostitution in order to survive or to have independent means from their husbands. Interestingly, in films portraying prostitutes of the working classes, the women tended to fare less awful fates than their middle-class sisters, as death and dishonour seem not to apply! This is, of course, a complete misrepresentation of history – especially when we consider that most working-class women who turned to prostitution did so primarily because they had nowhere to live.[42] Thus, in a way, filmic representation in these costume dramas serves to reverse the truth in that female representatives of the bourgeoisie (wife, mistress or courtesan) get a worse deal than their lower-class sisters – suggesting that, as a cultural artefact, speaking to 1950s' sensibilities, costume dramas were more preoccupied with middle-class female propriety and containment than with accurate representation.

So this is the France to which our Belle Epoque films supposedly speak. A France of new technologies in the form of cars, aeroplanes, and cinemas; telecommunications were much improved by being nationalized in 1889; the first public screening of a film was in 1895 and radio entered its early years post-1895 as small atelier enterprises.[43] France became a nation of new or modernized transportation systems: the first métro was inaugurated in Paris in 1900, by 1914 there were six lines; the motorized omnibus first appears in 1907 gradually replacing horse-drawn systems; the network railway system was completed by 1914; roads to accommodate cars received heavy investment; bicycles were much improved upon with pneumatic tyres (the first Tour de France was launched in 1903).[44] This was an economically strong France, despite its unwillingness to consolidate into large industrial blocks and invest massively in manufacturing, preferring to be a big player amongst the money markets. This was a France where wealth was in the hands of the few, where the working class was, in general, shabbily treated with the exception of a few philanthropists such as Baron Rothschild, who endeavoured to improve their quality of life by establishing total-concept housing projects such as the Fondation Rothschild (1908) in the 19th arrondissement of

Belleville.[45] A France divided by the Republic's drive for a lay society. A France divided also by the Dreyfus Affair. Finally, a France which struggled with the idea of the emancipation of women – a long-standing paradox when we consider that women represented 37 per cent of the workforce throughout the epoch; that they received the right to free secondary state education in 1880, entered the Sorbonne in the same year, had the law bar opened to them in 1900, could practice medicine (e.g., the doctor Madeleine Pelletier), be scientists (e.g., Marie Curie), be teachers but could not vote; that they were entitled only to a pay that was half that of men; and that they had no civil rights. Small wonder that the first wave of feminism was born from this climate which placed women very much at the margins of the Third Republic.[46]

Filming the imaginary Belle Epoque

Listed below are the 37 titles of the Belle Epoque films made during the 1950s, 64 per cent of which are literary adaptations (23 titles).

Early 1889–1899 (9 films)	Middle 1900–1909 (19 films)	Late 1910–1914 (9 films)
Maria Chapdelaine (1950)* Marc Allégret	*La Dame de chez Maxim's* (1950)* **1900** Marcel Aboulker	*Chéri* (1950)* **1913** Pierre Billon
Le Mariage de mlle Beulemans (51)* **1890** André Cerf	*Minne l'ingénue libertine* (50)* **1900** Jacqueline Audrey	*La Maison Bonnadieu* (51) **1910** Carlo Rim
Casque d'or (52) **1898** Jacques Becker	*Miquette et sa mère* (50)* **1900** Henri-Georges Clouzot	*Il est minuit Dr Schweitzer* (52)* **1912–1914** André Haguet
Procès du Vatican (52) **1888–1897** André Haguet	*Une Nuit de noces* (50)* René Jayet	*Koenigsmark* (53)* **1914** Solange Terac [supervised by Christian-Jaque]
La Belle Otéro (54) **1895 ff** Richard Pottier	*La Ronde* (50)* **1900** Max Ophuls	*Frou-Frou* (55) **1912 ff** Augosto Genina
C'est arrivé à Aden (56)* **1897** Michel Boisrond	*Tire au flanc* (50)* **1900** Fernand Rivers	*Les Grandes manoeuvres* (55) **1913** René Clair
Eléna et les hommes (56) **1890** Jean Renoir	*Olivia* (51)* **1900** Jacqueline Audrey	*Les Aventures d'Arsène Lupin* (57)* **1910** Jacques Becker
Sans famille (58)* **1890s** André Michel	*Le Dindon* (51)* **1900** Claude Barma	*L'École des cocottes* (58)* **1910** Jacqueline Audrey

Sérénade au Texas (58)
1898-ish
Richard Pottier

Les Belles de nuit (52) 1 sketch in
1900
René Clair

Madame de… (53)* **1900**
Max Ophuls

Raspoutine (54) **1904–1916**
Georges Combret

Scènes de ménage (54)* **1900**
André Berthomieu

Secrets d'alcove (54) 1 sketch **1900**
Le Lit Jean Delannoy

C'est la Vie Parisienne (54) **1906 ff**
Alfred Rode

Le Fil à la patte (55)* **1900**
Guy Le Franc

French CanCan (55) **1900**
Jean Renoir

Christine (58)* **1907**
Pierre Gaspard-Huit

La Belle et le tzigane (59) **1900**
Jean Dréville

Messieurs les ronds de cuir (59)*
1900
Henri Diamant-Berger

Maxime (58)* **1914**
Henri Verneuil

Political time line
1887–1894 Sadi Carnot
President (assassinated)
1889 Boulanger affair
1892 Panama scandal
1894 Dreyfus affair
1894 Indochina consolidated
as a colony
1894–1895 Casimir-Perier
President
1895–1899 Felix Faure
President (died)
1896 Madagascar becomes
a colony

Political time line
1899–1906 Emile Louret President
1904 Separation of state and
church and Entente Cordiale
signed with the English
1906–1913 Armand Fallières
President
1906 Dreyfus rehabilitated

Political time line
1913–1920 Raymond Poincaré
President
1912 Morocco becomes a French
protectorate
1914 Archduke Ferdinand
assassinated (June); Jean Jaurès
assassinated (July);
War with Germany (August)

Figure 18.1: Belle Epoque films 1889–1914 (37 titles, release date in parenthesis), date they refer to in bold (if known precisely). Where I have put 'ff' to a date this indicates it may stretch beyond the Belle Epoque era. The asterisk (*) indicates that it is an adaptation. Below each column: the corresponding 25-year political time-line.

Of first note is the predominance of films referring to the turn of the century period (1900–1909) arguably the peak decade of the Belle Epoque. Second, that what abounds are women-centred narratives. This represents a significant departure from the other two periods we have been examining (pre-nineteenth and post-Revolution to 1889) where male-centred narratives dominated. Of the Belle Epoque films, 21 out of the 37 films (57 per cent) are female-centred (see figure 18.2 below). Moreover, the dominant trend is for love intrigues, 28 out of 37 (76 per cent), indicating a strong desire on the part of producers to attract female audiences, even if 13 have unhappy endings. As we come closer to the contemporary 1950s, it is curious, therefore, to note the reduction in the number of male-driven narratives. Why, in an age of increasing modernity, should such a shift occur? We could be forgiven for expecting the opposite. However, all but two of the adaptations were written by authors contemporary to the Belle Epoque; thus, in that they reflect the woman newly emergent into urban society, they are clearly echoes of their times. As we shall note in the films we are to investigate, the greater visibility and mobility of women came about as a result of the modernizing changes brought to the cities, such as street lighting, cleaner boulevards, department stores (and so on), where propriety and safety were assured. The growth of the female workforce also added to this sense of a woman's presence in society.

Love intrigues – Paris as background	Love intrigues - outside Paris	Love – military as background (also set outside Paris)	Biopics
La Belle et le tzigane* 767,376	Les Belles de nuit 3,499,199	Christine* 2,848,858	La Belle Otéro* 1,885,468
C'est la Vie Parisienne* 1,473,244	C'est arrivé à Aden* 1,956,334	Les Grandes manoeuvres* 5,301,504	Il est minuit Dr Schweitzer 3,300,484
Chéri 964,572	Koenigsmark 2,119,107	La Ronde 1,509,923	Procès du Vatican* 1,326,384
Casque d'or* 1,917,248	La Maison Bonnadieu* 1,000,071		Raspoutine 2,216,785
La Dame de chez Maxim's* 1,780,356	Maria Chapdelaine* 2,170,533		
Le Dindon 570,628	Le Mariage de mlle Beulemans* 1,010,104		
L'école des cocottes* 1,072,620	Miquette et sa mere* 2,159,275		**Adolescence/childhood**
Elena et les hommes* 2,116,337	Sérénade au Texas 2,555,768		Olivia* 1,043,732

Le Fil à la patte
1,797,375

French CanCan
3,963,928

Frou-Frou*
2,300,666

Madame de...*
1,619,154

Maxime
1,978,792

Minne l'ingénue
libertine*
1,776,482

Scènes de ménage*
1,244,329

Les Secrets d'alcove*
1,560,469

Une Nuit de noces*
1,012,157

Sans famille
3,331,928

Other

Les Aventures d'Arsène
Lupin (set in Paris and
Alsace) **2,970,265**

Messieurs les ronds
de cuir (set in Paris)
1,141,278

Tire au flanc
1,882,484

Figure 18.2: Spread of narratives of Belle Epoque films listed alphabetically and according to category; audience figures in bold (the asterisk* denotes a female-centred narrative).

If we break this spread of narratives down further: 17 films are set within the very specific context of Belle Epoque Paris – whether it be high or low society – with clear references to café society, the high-life cabarets of the *Moulin Rouge* or the low-life environs of Belleville and Montmartre. These attractions are widely represented in the films in this category, although what is singularly lacking is any reference to cinema! It is almost as if there is a nostalgia within these films' narratives for a time, preceding the advent in 1895 of cinema, when the music-hall dominated in terms of popular entertainment. Transportation systems such as the métro and an occasional motor-car are also in evidence. All films under the love categories have betrothal issues or love intrigues at their core, or marital conflicts – be they infidelities, suspected or real. The films in the second column, set outside Paris, are all are comedies – except *Koenigsmark,* which stands out with its desperate narrative of murder, jealousy and impossible love. Out of the total of 29 love stories/intrigues, only three are set against a military background (none of which end well). Of the films remaining in the final column, as we see, there are four biopics, of which only one has Paris as a partial background, *La Belle Otéro.* From Otéro's various performances we learn a considerable amount about café concert and music-hall life: the difficulty in securing employment as an artiste and the demanding nature of the audiences (who are all too ready to throw insults and missiles at the poor entertainer). Needless to say, Otéro tames her audiences and is a huge success. Two films deal with adolescence (although one, *Olivia*, could also be counted in with the unhappy love narratives since it deals with a young schoolgirl's crush on her schoolmistress). Of the remaining three films, one deals with the misdemeanours of French civil servants (*Messieurs les ronds de cuir*); another is an all-male military comedy (*Tire au flanc*); the third focuses on the mythical gentleman thief Arsène Lupin. Strikingly, not one single narrative in the films manages to produce a new-born child, which is, in and of itself, quite remarkable given the emphasis in both epochs (1890s and 1950s) on natality. Indeed, children and mothers are very little in evidence in these costume dramas. Rémi in *Sans famille* is the only child we get to see, and his is a quest to find his long-lost mother who abandoned him at birth. In both *Miquette et sa mère* and *Minne l'ingénue* the daughters are of marriageable age – Minne's mother dies soon after her daughter marries; Miquette's mother joins her daughter in a double marriage to a Count and his nephew (respectively) who have traipsed around after them in their theatrical endeavours.

This lacuna aside, 79 per cent of all Belle Epoque narratives are based in the least tangible aspect of an historical moment – namely, affairs of the heart (as opposed to affairs of state). Affairs of the heart are often dismissed as appertaining to the province of women's films and yet they concern, ultimately, questions of utmost importance, bound as they are to the well-being of capitalism – be this in the form of securing a good marriage, protecting property, ensuring there is an heir (even if none of these films do so), and so on. But this panoply of films also demonstrates how the Belle Epoque is both perceived and portrayed. After all, many of these films are adaptations of contemporary writers – people who lived through that period. Of the 25 adaptations, only two of the original texts were written by authors living outside that era (the novelist Louise de Vilmorin who wrote *Madame de…*in 1951; and the dramatist Gilbert Cesbron who wrote *Il est minuit Dr Schweitzer* in 1950). We note that very little political-historical moment prevails in these films. Not a glimpse of the Dreyfus Affair. The Boulanger Affair is referenced in *Eléna et les homes*, albeit indirectly (Jean Marais plays General Rollan, a fictitious character loosely based on Boulanger). In *Maxime*, the narrative is book-ended in its opening sequence by documentary film of the Franco-British relationships at the turn of the century (including mention of the signing of the 1904 *Entente Cordiale*) and, in its closing sequence, by newspaper headlines announcing the declaration of war. Of the biopics, two stand out for their basis in fact: *Procès du Vatican*, which portrays the saintly life of Thérèse de Lisieux when she was a Carmelite nun (1888–1897) and *Il est minuit Dr Schweitzer*, which details the efforts of this famous medical missionary in the French colony of the Gabon before being arrested at the outbreak of World War One (as an Alsatian, he was deemed a German). Of the other two, *La Belle Otéro* is only lightly linked to her real life (for example, it completely glosses over her addiction to gambling as a compensation for her unhappy love-life) and *Raspoutine* offers us a very hammy version of this spiritually flawed priest.

Significantly, even if we include *La Belle Otéro* and *Messieurs les ronds de cuir* which do have Paris as its backdrop, only 53 per cent of all Belle Epoque films are set in Paris (20 out of 37), which is a lower figure than we might have expected, given that this period is so associated – historically at least –with that city. Less surprising as an oversight, perhaps, given the aura of censorship surrounding the 1950s, is the complete lack of reference to the two major scandals of the Belle Epoque period: the Panama Canal debacle and the Dreyfus Affair, which are both, in a way, linked. The former scandal revealed the fraudulent complicity between the world of politics, the money market and the financial press which kept secret the very real state of near-collapse of the project. Small investors lost their shirts, whilst politicians and the press were kept silent by the payment of sweeteners. That is, until three years after the project's virtual collapse when a right-wing journalist (Edouard Drumont) finally blew the whistle – he denounced the fat cats getting rich on keeping the bankruptcy secret as a Jewish conspiracy. Drumont wrote a lengthy tract, *La France Juive*, accusing Jewish investors of making money out of the huge debts incurred by the canal project. As Brogan says, this tract 'may claim the dubious honour of being the first great explosion of modern anti-semitism.'[47] The second explosion was the Dreyfus Affair. But then, given France's more recent role in the 'Jewish question' during the Second World War/Occupation and its active participation in the deportation of some 75,000 Jews to concentration camps, it is hard to see how any mention *could* be made.

What we are left with in this cinema of the Belle Epoque, however, is a great sense of the social environment of the time. We learn predominantly about middle- and upper-middle-class mores and taste (the latter mostly revealed to us via the décor and the costumes), whether in Paris or outside. In relation to Paris, all 18 film titles listed in the first column (see figure 18.2 above) deal with love, marriage and issues of class, as detailed in what follows. We see the impact of the new middle class on the economic lives of others in four films (*Chéri, Eléna et les hommes, Minne l'ingénue* and *Maxime*). We learn about Parisian bourgeois life in *Le Fil à la patte, Dindon, Madame de…*and *Scènes de ménage*. In all of the above there are snapshots of the more upper-crust edge of café, music-hall and cabaret life. *La Dame de Chez Maxim's* and *L'Ecole des cocottes* reveal this life to us from the other side – that of the performers. We are also treated to the more liminal space (Pigalle-Montmartre) on the periphery of Paris between the poor and the rich. There are seven films in this latter domain: *La Belle et le tzigane, C'est la Vie Parisienne, French CanCan, Frou-Frou, Une Nuit de noces* – to which we add *La Belle Otéro*. As for the Parisian underbelly, in the form of the criminal classes (gangsters or *apaches* as they are known), apart from one or two flashes in some of these films, there is only one title completely given over to that representation, *Casque d'or*. As we move out of Paris, still in the vein of films about love and marriage, there are films offering insight into both the bourgeoisie and the life of the less well-heeled in the form of musicians or travelling artists. In the former category (some of which are even set outside France), we can list *Koenigsmark, La Maison Bonnadieu, Maria Chapdelaine,* and *Le Mariage de mlle Beulemans*. In the latter category: *Les Belles de nuit, C'est arrivé à Aden* and *Miquette et sa mère*. Finally on the subject of love, the military are portrayed as cynical lovers, albeit beautiful specimens of masculinity on display – particularly in the case of Alain Delon in *Christine* and Gérard Philipe, who is cast in *Les Grandes manoeuvres* and *La Ronde*.

So much for this snapshot overview. In the chapters that follow I will take a look in more depth at a representative corpus of the different categories. Chapter 19 investigates the representation of Paris life and includes three case studies (*Maxime, Madame de…* and *Eléna et les hommes*). Chapter 20 provides a brief discussion of the second category of love films (set outside Paris) followed by a more detailed analysis of two of the military love stories (*Les Grandes manoeuvres* and *Christine*). Chapter 21 takes on board the biopics.

I have managed to see all of these films except three that I could not find (*La Belle et le tzigane, Dindon* and *Koenigsmark*). But, obviously, choices have to be made; not all films can be covered. Thus, I am deliberately setting aside *Casque d'or* from my analysis since Sarah Leahy has just completed an excellent single study of this film;[48] similarly *La Ronde* is left aside since I give consideration to several other Ophuls' films in this book; the *films à sketches* covering various epochs (*Les Belles de nuit* and *Secrets d'alcove*) are also left out except for brief mention where relevant; finally, of Renoir's costume dramas, I have chosen to focus on *Eléna et les hommes* in preference to *French CanCan* because it has had considerably less critical attention paid to it than Renoir's very popular homage to the Moulin Rouge.

Recently *Positif* produced a rather fine dossier on Belle Epoque films, under the direction of Alain Masson.[49] I concur with many of his findings but feel the tone of the Belle Epoque films is more cutting, less the utopia of frivolity he argues for.[50] He also finds the tenor of the films to be largely ahistoric, a world without a sense of the times. Whilst I agree there are big absences, I do not find these films to be without history – if by history we also mean a sense of the social and economic moment. The focus on marriage is part of history, after all, as is masculinity's response to social evolution – all of which the following chapters explore. Finally, Masson claims that this cinema is largely based on adaptations that are lightweight and whose provenance is primarily the theatre. He is right on the first point; however, adaptations from novels roughly equal the number of plays (twelve and eleven respectively).[51]

Notes

1. See also the excellent study of this period compiled by Diana Holmes and Carrie Tarr (2006).
2. See Marseille (2002, p. 224).
3. See Leymarie (1999, p. 8).
4. See Rearick (1985, p. xi).
5. Brogan (1989, p. 183).
6. Ibid., p. 182.
7. Marseille, op. cit., p. 203.
8. Brogan, op. cit., p.177.
9. Holmes & Tarr, op. cit., p. 11.
10. Leymarie, op. cit., p. 254.
11. Marseille, op. cit., p. 203. Russia's borrowing from France thereafter allowed the Tsarists to crush the 1905 revolution (Brogan, op. cit., p. 210).
12. Leymarie, op. cit., p. 11.

13. See for example Pissarro's *Avenue de l'Opéra* (1898).
14. Given the tensions with Germany during this whole second half of the century, it is curious that of all things this station was redesigned by the German architect J. I. Hittorff.
15. Sutcliffe (1993, p. 108).
16. Brogan, op. cit., p. 184.
17. Schlör (1998, p. 66).
18. Ibid., p. 63.
19. Leymarie, op. cit., p. 31.
20. Ibid., p. 29.
21. Marseille, op. cit., p. 225.
22. Leymarie, op. cit., p. 30.
23. Ibid., pp. 59–85.
24. And a mere 10% went on alcohol! See Leymarie, op. cit., p. 61–2.
25. Ibid., p. 45.
26. Ibid., p. 84.
27. Marseille, op. cit., p. 189.
28. Ibid., p. 189.
29. Ibid., p. 190.
30. Leymarie, op. cit., p. 33.
31. Marseille, op. cit., pp. 191 & 224.
32. Ibid., p. 224.
33. Leymarie, op. cit., p. 45–6.
34. Ibid., p. 35.
35. See Marseille , op. cit., p 224 and Leymarie, op. cit., pp. 28–33.
36. See Buckley & Fawcett (2002, p. 17).
37. Ibid., p.26.
38. Flügel (1930, p. 111).
39. See Leymarie, op. cit., pp. 16–19.
40. Buckley & Fawcett, op. cit., p. 9.
41. Ross (1995) develops this argument.
42. See Leymarie, (op. cit., pp. 58–62) for more detail and for what follows. Accommodation for the working class was notoriously sparse and insalubrious (less than 3% of households had bathrooms and less than 18% had lavatories). It is also worth considering that, as a work force, the urban working-class woman represented 38% of the workers; that nearly half of that female force worked in the textile industry (either in factories as weavers or at home as seamstresses), over a third worked as domestics in service. Also noteworthy is that, in terms of budgetary expenditure for working-class families, 62% of their meagre pay went on nutrition, 16% on renting their living quarters, clothing 8%, light and heating 6%. Thus, as these meagre living conditions and terrible conditions of work took their toll on certain of the menfolk and they turned to alcohol (taking 10% of the household revenue out for this habit and eventually becoming alcoholics), the family budget became progressively dissipated. How else was a woman to feed her children but to turn to that quickest commodity of exchange value, her body? But more commonly, because lodgings were so difficult to find, the working class woman found she had to turn to prostitution because she had nowhere to live.
43. Ibid., p. 51.
44. Ibid., p. 49. By way of an interesting anecdote, the bicycle has been credited with increasing the average height of the French population by reducing the number of marriages between blood relations.

45. Lucan (1992, p. 53).
46. Leymarie, op. cit., pp. 19. See also Holmes and Tarr (2006) for a good overview of the condition of women in the Belle Epoque era.
47. Brogan, op. cit., pp.: 187.
48. Leahy (2007). I also give it considerable space in my book on Simone Signoret (see Hayward, 2004).
49. Masson (2006).
50. Ibid., p.88.
51. Ibid., p. 89.

Chapter 19

Parisian Society of the Belle Epoque through Film

Parisian display – the modernity of technology and the archaism of marriage

If we consider the 17 Belle Epoque films specifically located in Paris (see figure 19.1 below), it is instructive that six titles have at their core (or at least as a strong reference) cabaret, theatre or café life. Whilst there are song and dance routines that afford a certain gaiety to these films – thus nodding to the concept of a gay and carefree Belle Epoque – most of the narratives have a far-from-happy outcome especially for the women. In this instance, fiction is close to truth, as we shall see with *La Belle Otéro* – a film about the renowned eponymous Spanish dancer (played by Maria Félix) that I shall discuss in the biopics chapter (Chapter 21). Despite her brilliant career, she has no success in love. *C'est la Vie Parisienne* does not bring much joy either. A young Viscount, Paul de Barfleur (Philippe Lemaire), falls in love with Cricri (Claudine Dupuis), a café concert singer who works at La Vie Parisienne. But the Viscount's father, on the grounds that such a marriage could never work, persuades Cricri to renounce his son. In *Frou-Frou*, an innocent flower seller (Dany Robin) is beset by a bunch of older men who launch her career as a *chanteuse*. Although she repulses their attempts to seduce her, she does succumb to an artist. He offers her marriage when she discovers she is pregnant. She rejects the offer, fearing a life of poverty, thereby causing her unstable lover to engineer his own death before her very eyes. Having chosen financial security, her closing words to her daughter are that, nonetheless, she feels she has wasted her life. In *La Belle et le tzigane,* two sisters vie over a gypsy performing artist. Georgia Wells (Nicole Courcel), a rich American, married to the Duc de Vintheuil (Jacques Dacqmine) comes to Paris to dissuade her sister Gladys (Colette Déréal) of her infatuation with the gypsy, Janci Rigos (Gyula Buss). Georgia falls for Rigos' charms and they run away to Hungary, even though she is stripped of all her wealth. But both miss Paris too much, and return. Georgia accepts a job in the Folies Parisiennes cabaret. The showdown comes when, on the night of her première performance, her sister tries to sabotage the performance. Georgia realizes the error of her ways, leaves the now-jealous Rigos and her avenging sister to return to her husband.

French CanCan offers a not dissimilar narrative of female rivalry, this time over Danglard (Jean Gabin), the man who launches the successful Moulin Rouge. Finally in this quick overview we come to two farces where, for once, everything ends happily. In *Une nuit de noces* a newly-wed couple attempt to consummate their marriage in peace, but a jilted mistress in the form of a cabaret star, Sidonie (Martine Carol), puts a spanner in the works until all is resolved. In *Le Fil à la patte* the aristocratic Fernand de Bois d'Enghien (Noël-Noël) leads a double life and ends up engaged to be married to both a cabaret star, Lucette (Suzy

---

Love intrigues – Paris as background

La Belle et le tzigane*	*Elena et les hommes**	*Scènes de ménage**
767,376	**2,116,337**	**1,244,329**
C'est la Vie Parisienne*	*Le Fil à la patte*	*Les Secrets d'alcove**
1,473,244	**1,797,375**	**1,560,469**
Chéri	*French CanCan*	*Une Nuit de noces**
964,572	**3,963,928**	**1,012,157**
Casque d'or*	*Frou-Frou**	
1,917,248	**2,300,666**	
La Dame de chez Maxim's*	*Madame de…**	
1,780,356	**1,619,154**	
Le Dindon	*Maxime*	
570,628	**1,978,792**	
L'école des cocottes*	*Minne l'ingénue libertine**	
1,072,620	**1,776,482**	

Figure 19.1: Love intrigues – Paris as Background (Asterisk* denotes female-centred films).

Delair) and an ingénue from the bourgeoisie, Viviane (Geneviève Kirvine). His duplicity is eventually uncovered, bedlam breaks out, but all ends well (enough): Viviane forgives him and he marries into the appropriate class; Lucette gives up her exciting career and marries a rich Mexican.

If this is a portrayal of the frivolous Belle Epoque, then, as far as women and sexual relations are concerned, it seems they either have to choose between love or a career, renounce a man because of class issues, or fight each other for a man's love. And marriage, if achieved, is not by any means touted as a happy solution for either party. If anything, in these films, it is the folly and constraining nature of marriage that is foregrounded.

Casque d'or takes us to Paris' gangster-life (the famous *apaches* and their molls) located in the (ironically named) Belleville district. Again, the ending is a tragic one, with the main protagonist Marie (Simone Signoret) losing her loved one to the scaffold. As for the remaining eight films, each one reveals different aspects of bourgeois and middle-class Parisian life. One film, *La Dame de Chez Maxim's*, humorously exposes the values of the bourgeoisie through the point of view of a cabaret singer. Three women friends gather in a Parisian tea house to exchange stories on the shortcomings of their husbands in *Scènes de ménage,* only to conclude that they are 'tous des chameaux/all scoundrels'. Three of these eight films portray the newly-emergent middle class. *Minne l'ingénue libertine* and *L'École des cocottes* expose different aspects of female sexuality – although in both instances the pill is bitter-sweet. Minne (Danièle Delorme) finds love and sexual fulfilment at last with her husband, but after some painful lessons. Ginette (Dany Robin), the cocotte, makes it to the top of Parisian society, but at the expense of her true love. Persuaded by an aristocrat, who has nothing left to sell except his breeding, that it is her patriotic duty to help perpetuate the capitalist ideology of commodity exchange, she agrees to give up her working-class roots as a milliner's assistant and her local pastimes at the *Chat qui miaule* cabaret to be trained up as a top-of-the-range cocotte at the Institute of Good Manners.[1] Her decision costs her her independence: she is now the Count's pupil to do with as he wishes. She also loses her man, who, a bit unfairly, accuses her of betraying her class. Indeed, she never abandons her friends; she keeps them close and helps improve their position as she makes her own 'lift' in society. She also obtains salary rises for the local workers from her businessman lover. But she understands the heavy price she has paid for all the luxuries she obtains in exchange. As her wry smile at the end of the film makes clear, even as she has left (abandoned) her class origins, so, too, is she caught in a system she knows she can no longer disentangle herself from – a world driven by the belief that social status is all. *Chéri* offers not just a tale of masculine ennui, embodied by the eponymous 'hero' (Jean Desailly), but also a dark cynical portrayal of a grasping new social type in the form of his *nouveau riche* mother (Jane Marken) and his own mercenary values: marrying to further financial and social status. Intriguingly, however, Chéri's ennui and despair at what is lost in the form of his former mistress, Léa (Marcelle Chantal), leads him to commit suicide at the end (suggesting he is capable of deep feelings despite his caddish ways). Léa ends tragically, old and alone. At first, Chéri is almost relieved their affair is at an end as he enters into bourgeois marriage, but his attachment to Léa is too strong and it is he who dies. The other three titles, *Eléna et les hommes*, *Maxime*, and *Madame de...*, all have as their central character a person whose financial circumstances place them in difficulty. In Maxime's and Eléna's case they find themselves much reduced from their former bourgeois or upper-class standing. Both Maxime and Madame de...are to some degree or another destroyed or dishonoured as a result of their imprudence in money matters. As with the cabaret films, whilst there may be giddy moments of waltzing to a tune of amorous dalliance, here the outcome is bitter-sweet, if not tragic. Only *Eléna* provides us with a happy ending.

Of the modern Paris, we get to see the new technologies, albeit not in huge abundance. Thus, trains figure in several films, notably to take lovers, mistresses or wives away from the object of their desire (rather than *to* or *with,* as might be expected). Chéri leaves for and returns from his honeymoon with his wife, whom he has married more to secure money than love. He leaves behind him in Paris his beloved – but by now aging – mistress Léa and cannot wait to get back to her, even though this arrangement cannot last, as Léa is only too aware. In *Madame de...*, Madame's husband, the General (Charles Boyer), first puts his mistress (whom he has now discarded) on a train to Constantinople, and, later in the film, does the same with his wife, Louise (Danielle Darrieux), who has fallen in love with a Baron (Vittorio de Sica). She takes flight to prevent herself pursuing her desire. In all three cases, the lover, the mistress and the wife climb aboard a train, leaving their loved one behind – quite the opposite of the contemporary mystique surrounding the train as a metaphor for sexual encounters. In *Maxime*, the train first takes away and then returns a rival, thereby endangering Maxime's pursuit of the woman he loves: Jacqueline (Michèle Morgan).

Cars are infrequently in evidence and cause more problems than not. In *La Dame de chez Maxim's*, it brings the interfering wife from Paris to the country estate, an arrival which sets in train a multitude of misunderstandings. In *Maxime*, it once again helps the rival's cause since he gets to offer a lift to Jacqueline, whose own car has broken down. In *Eléna et les hommes*, Eléna (Ingrid Bergman) and her very new (if elderly) fiancé are on a mission to help General Rollan escape from house arrest. However, they arrive in a car that clearly dates from the early 1900s – it is a four-wheeled covered motor-car. Thus, the car enters as an anachronism, for no such car was available in 1890, the year in which the film is set. The first cars were the four-wheel steam dog-cars (1885), followed a bit later (1898) by the three-wheel, twin-cylinder petrol engine of the open horseless carriage (as it was known). Anachronism notwithstanding, the car still causes problems since, in the end, it is abandoned because the fiancé is not confident it will make it back to Paris. As a result, the car is the inadvertent instrument that (by its very failure to transport) brings together, once more, Eléna and the man she really loves (but had foresworn for the older man) – a catastrophe for the aspirant fiancé. Other technologies cause catastrophes of an even-greater kind in this film. The French army is testing a new hot-air observational balloon; unfortunately the cable snaps and the two commanders aboard drift off and land in German enemy territory. Their arrest and subsequent internment as spies is what sets in motion the whole saga surrounding General Rollan: as minister of war he manages to broker their release, thus causing a huge rise in his popularity amongst the masses, who call for him to run for president in the forthcoming elections. Fears that he might, as an army man, subject the Republic to a dictatorship bring about his house arrest.

Aeronautics, which were in their infancy at this time, get a brief airing in *C'est la Vie Parisienne* when Paul de Barfleur agrees to test-pilot his friend Le Garrec's (Noël Roquevert), invention. The machine hops a bare three and a quarter metres (ten feet) above the ground, but Barfleur and Le Garrec are heralded as heroes of French aviation, as the *Marseillaise* is proudly played upon his safe 'landing'.[2] However, given that this film is set in the early 1900s, it is hardly a great achievement since, by 1905, the Wright brothers has already flown 39 kilometres (24.2 miles) over the Huffman Prairie in Ohio. Lastly, on this issue of modern transport systems, the opening sequence of *Scènes de ménage*, which is set in the 1910s, offers us real documentary footage of the traffic circulating through the city and the chaos it caused: cars, motorized omnibuses charging hither and thither; we are also treated to Louis Blériot's bi-plane flying 80 metres high over the Channel. The chaos of the traffic, we are told in voice-over, is matched by the Parisians' constant state of rushing everywhere: men to their business, women to their *'toilette'* (!) – at which point we cut to the tea-rooms where the three woman meet up and dissect their marriages in front of each other; all three are in different but certainly striking outfits (each hat out-doing the other's in excess of flowers or feathers), as are the rest of the women in the tea-rooms.

Electricity, which first made its appearance in Paris in 1881, has its presence flagged up in both *French CanCan* and *La Dame de chez Maxim's,* albeit in different ways. In the former this is the new technology of the moment which, in the same year as the launch of the Moulin Rouge (1889), saw the lighting of the Tour Eiffel. Electricity in this film is about Paris as the city of light and spectacle. In the latter film, electricity has by now entered the domestic sphere (1900s) – although it is still a sign of wealth to have this form of lighting rather than gas. Indeed, this household belongs to the well-heeled bourgeoisie, as we can determine by the fact that the master, a doctor, also owns a car. The mysteries and magical qualities of electricity as a new technology are, however, alluded to in this film in the form of the doctor's newly-acquired electric chair. This is an electric treatment chair which puts the patient in a trance – it is known as *un fauteuil ecstatique/*an ecstatic armchair, but it is never clear what it can achieve, other than knock out the person sitting in it – in particular the doctor's meddlesome wife.

All of these films provide us with an immensely rich resource of the Belle Epoque's *habitus* of domestic and social life. We see cabarets, café-concerts and music-halls from front of house and backstage. But we also enter numerous types of domestic spaces, and it is here that particularly revealing things occur – more interestingly, arguably, than the shenanigans on or off-stage. To begin with, we are made aware through the various décors that there is no one blueprint for bourgeois interiors. Indeed, what remains gratifying are the differentiations made – to the effect that, in terms of taste and means, there is not a single homogenous middle-class, anymore than there is a single working-class taste, or economic means for that matter. Thus, for example, in *Scènes de ménage* – set-designed by Jean d'Eaubonne, whose reputation for ornate style finds space in this film – we are taken into three different types of middle-class households. First up is that of Aglaé (Sophie Desmarets) and her husband, Arthur (Bernard Blier), a wealthy businessman. Their apartment gives every evidence of modern taste: the furniture is contemporary Art Nouveau with highly-stylized, fl owing curvilinear lines; the ornaments include René Lalique vases; their rooms are lit by electricity. In the background to the bedroom we can see a full-sized bathtub with taps – again pointing to the well-being of this couple who, sadly, only seem to know how to squabble in amongst all these trappings of wealth. As Aglaé explains to her women friends in the tea-rooms, her marriage is stuck in a rut. Arthur is consumed by jealousy. Thus, each time they return from a ball, he accuses his wife of flirting and infidelity, gets into a rage and starts breaking furniture and smashing vases; a witty shouting match ensues, but there is no doubting who comes out on top; Arthur is made to look rather foolish. The second apartment is Valentine's (Marie Daems), a very different affair. Her husband, Edouard (François Périer), a would-be great author, makes a living writing serialized stories for a Parisian daily newspaper. Their fifth-floor apartment is modest, if pleasantly appointed with wood parquet flooring, papered and wood-panelled walls. Furniture is sparse and far from modern. They clearly struggle to make the month's end and he keeps a tight rein on the purse strings. So, when Valentine accidentally breaks a Falguière lamp (an Art Nouveau style lamp in cast iron and stained glass), she has to replace it with a fake one. Domestic harmony does not reign here, either. Edouard has decided to punish Valentine for her wayward ways by fining her: 'I have done everything to make you happy', he claims, 'but like all women you don't realize this.' Spanking her did no good; breaking things was too costly; so now he has decided upon financial punishment to discipline her. There is very little she can do, entirely dependent as she is on him for support and, in this instance, housekeeping money. Her choice is to stay and accept his terms or go home to her parents. Eventually she stays, but it is a tense moment and fairly revealing of the socio-economic condition of women, who, for the most part, once married, were trapped in it. Finally, in this film, Ernestine's (Marthe Mercadier) apartment. This is a grande-bourgeoisie affair, over-stuffed with an eclectic array of furniture ranging from the late eighteenth- to mid-nineteenth century. This mixture was characteristic of upper-class apartments of the time – as a sign of wealth through heritage, doubtless. The walls are lined with silks; heavy velvet curtains adorn the windows and doorways to keep in the warmth. Blazing fires abound, as does electric light. In this marriage, the husband (Louis de Funès) accepts his wife's affairs and they live in tolerant harmony to the point where they join ranks in a wonderful series of pranks to see off a bounder who has tried to infiltrate their household as some kind of distant cousin up from the provinces.

Domestic space and socio-sexual relations probably get one of their best airings in *Le Fil à la patte*, a Feydeau farce adapted to film by Guy Lefranc, set-designed by Georges Dumesnil. There are three distinct apartments: that of the wealthy Baronne du Verger (Gabrielle Dorzat) and Viviane, her daughter (betrothed to Fernand); Lucette's apartment; and Fernand's. Each apartment has a specific shape to it. The du Vergers' is elegantly decorated, furnished with heavy, verneered wardrobes and tables and dotted with silk screens. It is spaciously set out along an extensive corridor, with the main reception room one end and the 'master' bedroom the other. In between, all sorts of rooms lead off, into which servants come and go – as indeed does Fernand as he tries to avoid confrontation between his two 'fiancées' at the engagement party held in his and Viviane's honour, and to which Lucette has been invited to sing. But even all this space does not spare him – eventually he is exposed, in the bedroom of course. Lucette's apartment is the least spacious and most contained of the three. She has three main rooms running off a central reception-hall area: a salon with a bedroom off to one side and, on the other side of the hall, a dining room. As opposed to the long, almost rectangular proportions of the du Verger home, this space feels more like a rotunda, encircling its occupants – and indeed, but for the reception hall splitting the space in two, there would be no means of hiding from exposure, let alone escaping (as Fernand does by the most meagre of margins). What Lucette lacks in space she makes up for with décor. Apart from the hall, all the rooms are over-blown with their frou-frou fabrics tumbling down from the walls and windows, the bedroom most of all. Money has also been frittered away on porcelain figurines and other knick-knacks. Lucette herself matches the excesses of her interior design in her over-the-top day dress, trimmed at the shoulders with fur, as she receives her guests for lunch. She embodies a lack of decorum and rebelliousness wherever she goes: bed, cabaret, carriages, etc. And her staff displays a similar lack of decorum towards visitors. Finally, Fernand's apartment. If ever there were a bachelor's getaway pad, this is it. Designed in a horseshoe shape around the staircase, it has two exits – one either side of the landing. The interiors are decidedly masculine: solid mahogany furniture, no frills, everything in its place (thanks, perhaps, more to Fernand's butler than his own assiduity). But the trick is that people can come and go without crossing each other's path. Thus, if one woman comes in one door, another can leave by the other. Until, that is, both women decide to remain on the landing and demand an explanation. At last Fernand is caught in his own web of deception – a *fil à la patte* indeed!

Three case studies – the superficially superficial Parisian bourgeoisie *Maxime, Madame de...*and *Eléna et les hommes*

So much for the overview. Let us now take a closer look, taking as our sample *Maxime* (1.9m audience) and *Madame de...*(1.6m), followed by *Eléna et les hommes* (2.1m). These work as a corpus in that the trigger to the three films is the financial difficulties experienced by the three lead characters, all of whom are part of the Parisian bourgeoisie. The three films were costumed by Rosine Delamare, which gives us a further useful point of comparison (although Annenkov was also involved in the costumes for *Madame de...*). Intriguingly, the first two films make a good pair. Charles Boyer stars in both of them (respectively as Maxime and the General).[3] Both had the same director of photography (Christian Matras), although he produced substantially different styles of shooting. And, despite their seemingly-disparate narratives, they actually have a significant amount in common – beginning with the clash of the old with the modern, as exemplified by the characters that Boyer embodies. In their values and beliefs, both of his characters smack more of the 'vieille époque' than the new 'belle époque' in which they find themselves. Both are in their mid-fifties – products, therefore, of the Emperor Napoleon III's age rather than the Third Republic. As Maxime, Boyer is the eponymous 'hero' who has fallen on hard times because of his love of both women and horse-races. In *Madame de...*he is a General in the artillery, very wealthy and married to the capricious and flirtatious Louise, who is a good twenty years younger. Boyer's two characters seem to abide more by rules embedded in an older order of reserved civility, where menaces are laid down with icy-cold good manners clothed in a velvet voice, and disputes settled behind closed doors or by duels. Both, it appears, hold similar views of women: whilst they are to be adored and revered, they are also objects of adornment, accessories to male pride, even if they are frivolous, inconstant creatures who must be kept in line. On two occasions, Maxime pontificates on the nature of women. First, when he accuses all women of being 'garces/bitches' under the veneer of breeding and, second, when he dismisses his former lover Jacqueline as being too loose in her morals for his taste – despite, a few hours earlier, having challenged his rival to a duel over her. On several occasions, the General pronounces on how his wife must behave, or chastises her for her behaviour. He also pontificates on what is the truth of a matter – including their marriage ('our marriage is in our image. It is only superficially superficial'). Yet, wealthy though he is, he allows her (unknowingly, it is true) to indebt herself to the point that she has to sell her diamond earrings, a wedding present from him – an action which in the end causes the entire edifice of their marriage to crumble.

Maxime lives in a single, rather dismal though not squalid, attic-floor room. He is befriended by a *nouveau riche* stockbroker, Hubert Treffujean (Félix Marten), who asks him to instruct him in good manners. This includes setting him up with classy women whom he cannot hope to obtain by himself. With Maxime's exquisite good manners acting as the bait, he reels them in and then passes them onto Treffujean. Not quite pimping, not quite grooming, but close. As if this was not sign enough of how low Maxime has fallen, Treffujean's new assignment – 'landing' the elegant Jacqueline Monneron – will send him into the depths of despair. Treffujean embodies new money and he expects to get everything he wants, including this latest woman to whom he has taken a fancy. He crudely importunes her in the most public of places: Chez Maxim's for example, where *le tout Paris* turns out. He has her followed by a private detective to find out her every move so he can cross her path at any time to suit him. To no avail. Jacqueline rebuffs him at each occasion. Treffujean implores (financially bullies) Maxime into helping him. Unfortunately, whilst executing Treffujean's orders, Maxime falls in love with Jacqueline instead and she appears to reciprocate the feeling. At first, Treffujean's ostentatious vulgarity is no contest; Jacqueline is charmed by Maxime, her 'man of mystery' as she calls him. Gradually, however, his enigma unravels, despite himself. Interestingly, it is not his dire straits that bring her to reject him. At one point she turns up unannounced at his pitiful abode, having failed to trace him in the telephone directory. He had claimed to live by the Parc Monceau, whereas, as she discovers, the truth is far less salubrious. Nor does he have a telephone – he has to use the concierge's downstairs in the very public arena of her kitchen. But this is not the lie that alienates Jacqueline. If anything, it brings them into closer intimacy – his reduced circumstances neither shock nor put her off and, in that regard she shows true class: recognizing the man for his personal value rather than fiscal worth. What does eventually cause the scales to fall from her eyes is an encounter with a former lover of his, Coco Naval (Jane Marken), an extremely vulgar cocotte, now in her mid-sixties, who comes crashing into their dinner party at Chez Maxim's (celebrating a centenary performance of the Théâtre des Capucines). Coco totally exposes his past with her, some 33 years ago when he was a mere 20-year-old. Worse still, she treats Jacqueline as if she is exactly the same as herself: a cocotte and one of Maxime's 'mascots' or trophies (as she puts it). The humiliation runs deep and Jacqueline ends the relationship. The man of mystery is no more. He is old, a man with an unsavoury past. Over the ensuing weeks, all attempts on Maxime's part to bring about a reconciliation fail (which leads him to make the misogynistic pronouncements mentioned above). Moreover, he no longer represents a challenge to Treffujean, who gradually wins Jacqueline over – even to the extent that, when he confesses how he used Maxime to try and ensnare her, she forgives him (something she refuses to forgive Maxime for, incidentally).

Treffujean (his protestations of love for Jacqueline notwithstanding) nonetheless feels compelled to cheat in order to close in on his prey. He manipulates Maxime, pulls fast ones behind his back (such as switching seating plans at the Capucines' soirée at Chez Maxim's to ensure Maxime's eventual discomfiture). New money (as embodied by Treffujean) behaves badly; tramples over others in its determination to get what it wants. It does not like bending to old codes of valour. Thus, when Maxime 'nobly' challenges Treffujean to a duel, he is dismissed as old school and ridiculed for demanding his card so he can call on his seconds. As Treffujean says later to Jacqueline, 'in 1914 people don't duel, we aren't living in the Middle Ages'. There is a sense of pathos in Maxime's desperate attempt to provoke a duel with his former ally – even if, in the end, Treffujean has to accept to fight. However, this challenge is not all it seems. It is Maxime's cunning trump card to get Jacqueline to come to him so he can put a final proposition to her: 'sleep with me tonight and I will spare you Treffujean'. She is shocked at his blackmail and the impossibility of the price to pay – for, despite it all, she now loves Treffujean (however distasteful or unbelievable to us her choice may seem). Maxime, realizing the futility of his demands, having trapped her, then goes on to dismiss her with scorn and, in the same breath, reneges on the duel. As for the security of her liaison with her new lover, war with Germany is announced; Treffujean's youth is unlikely to spare him the battlefronts. At this point the film ends.

If this ending is bitter-sweet, then how much more cruel is that of *Madame de...*. Here there is a familiar triangle with husband, lover and the object of their pursuit: the wife. By the end, lover and wife are dead. The former is challenged to a duel (with pistols) and dies at the hand of the master-marksman, the General. As for the wife – who has come in a vain attempt to prevent the duel – she swoons, faints and finally succumbs to a cardiac arrest. At the centre of the story are the diamond earrings in the shape of hearts that the General gave to his much younger wife, Louise, on their wedding night. The opening sequence of the film, in which we observe only her hand, shows her hesitantly sifting over her belongings to see what she can sell to relieve her of her debts. She selects the earrings, thereby showing how little they mean to her as a love token from her husband (as she says: 'I like these the least'). The jeweller to whom she sells them alerts the husband, who buys them back. Initially, we suspect he is going to confront his wife. However, he has the pressing matter of ridding himself of his mistress, whom he dispatches on a train to Constantinople. As a sweetener, he gives her the earrings. These are then pawned in a Turkish casino so she can carry on gambling. The Baron later purchases them and takes them with him on his diplomatic mission to Paris. At the Swiss customs he is held up briefly – a pause which allows him to encounter Louise for the first time as she, too, sails through customs to her train. Only the briefest of eye contact, in a wonderfully economic four-shot scene, tells us they have registered each other and been attracted.

These three protagonists move in the same Parisian social circles and soon meet up at a dinner party. The Baron is an old friend of the General and finds himself sat next to Louise. The flirtation begins. The General is sent off on manoeuvres and Louise and the Baron are next seen dancing waltzes together in a succession of balls as their love affair advances. Upon his return, the General realizes that this is not just a normal flighty flirtation. His wife is in love with another man. To fight this feeling, Louise insists she must leave Paris for a while. However, seven weeks later she returns, her love undiminished. The Baron and she resume their meetings.

Before her self-imposed exile, the Baron had bestowed upon her the earrings as a token of his own feelings for her. Those earrings, which formerly meant so little, now become emblematic for her of a passionate love. Upon her return to Paris, instead of hiding them away, she is desperate to wear them at a forthcoming ball. First, she lies to her husband, claiming she has found them in an old pair of gloves she has not worn for some time. Second, she lies to the Baron, who is amazed she can wear them in public, by stating that she told her husband they were part of an inheritance from a family cousin he profoundly disliked. The General, who rumbles Louise's scheme, then tells the Baron that the earrings were originally a wedding gift from him to his wife. From this moment, the debacle ensues. The Baron rejects Louise. The General buys the earrings back off the Baron via the jeweller and then obliges Louise to take them to one of the family cousins who, being on hard times, then sells them back to the jewellers. Louise's fragile health now begins to falter: she becomes grey and gone are the fineries of her attire; she dresses dowdily; shuns her husband. Finally, she sells all her possessions just to have the earrings – the symbol of her passionate relationship with the Baron – once more in her hands. Furious, the General takes his revenge. He insults the Baron, challenges him to a duel, kills him and, in so doing, kills his wife.

Whereas, in *Maxime*, honour only seemed to be the province of one man, thereby making him something of an anachronism in the new world order of the late Belle Epoque, here honour drives both men. But then, both are members of a social class that lives by a code whose rules are not to be questioned (unlike Treffujean in *Maxime*). The General abides by this set of encrusted rules – so much so that we often see him standing stiffly in his various army costumes, as if starched into them. Thus, as befits a man of his status, he has a wife and a mistress. He behaves impeccably with both, according to the *Code Napoléon*, which 'institutionalises male adultery on condition that the husband's mistress does not enter the conjugal home.'[4] His terse, icy *froideur* when speaking reveals his inability to be flexible. At one point, when trying to impress upon Louise the extent of his love, he walks around the apartment crisply closing windows and curtains whilst uttering the most declamatory (Racinian) of lines. He says: 'I admire you, I esteem you, I love you.' A three-point delivery line more reminiscent of a politician's speech or a general giving orders to attack than the tender words of a lover. As a general and a count he may well live by a code of honour, however, strangely enough, it only seems to come into play when his own dignity is at risk. His wife's lying about the earrings certainly triggered the whole debacle, but he does not seem to be concerned that he too lies to his wife, nor indeed that he concocts a reason for fighting the Baron; at the best this constitutes a false premise and is close to cheating.

The Baron, an Italian diplomat, is as much stuck in his status as the General. He too lives by a code of honour which dictates that he will fight a man over a trumped-up reason rather than admit to the truth that there is nothing to fight over. After all, he has rejected Louise, a woman he professed to love, because she lied to him. Both he and the General place honour above all else, and what a hollow elevation this turns out to be, the poignancy and futility of which is underscored, in the closing duel sequence, by the exclusive use of natural sound – bleak after so much waltz music that has now, finally, been silenced. The Baron is shot dead, a bullet through the heart; the General's wife, watching nearby, succumbs to a heart attack.

Ironically, the only one who is not the embodiment of what she is supposed to be is Louise. According to the General, she is a coquette, a frivolous flirt who makes men suffer – he announces this to his long-standing friend, the Baron, upon their first encounter at the dinner. Yet she it is who demonstrates her great capacity for love. When she is unable to renounce it, she accepts it as her fate. Of the three, it is she who recognizes the futility of their social class and standing. Until meeting the Baron and having these passionate feelings, she was deeply aware of her own pointlessness – as exemplified by the long-drawn-out opening sequence when she trails her hand through her possessions, trying to determine what to sell. Ophuls famously said to Darrieux that he wanted her to 'embody the void', yet to do so in such a way that the audience would take to her.[5] Darrieux achieves this in a number of ways, one of which is a gentle pout; but the most consistent marker of her detachment is signified through her slightly-lowered eyes which we often see glancing off to the left or the right into a non-space. The anonymity of her name, Madame de…, points to her inexistence – she stands as a symbol of that class and its emptiness (see figure 19.2 below). That is until

Figure 19.2: Louise embodying the void – Danielle Darrieux's sideways glance. © 1953 Gaumont (France) / Rizzoli Films (Italy).

she discovers true feelings, so evocatively expressed as she closes the door on the Baron the night she decides to leave and declares softly, full of love, 'je ne vous aime pas/I don't love you', which is so patently not true. At that moment her passion leads her, by placing love above honour, to transcend that class. A transcendence that is understood – by the rules of the society in which she lives – as a transgression, and for which she will ultimately perish. Though she lies over 'small things', she tells the truth over the most substantial one – or rather her gestures reveal the truth (her running away, her grasping the returned earrings with such passion in her eyes). In so doing, she disrupts the patriarchal social order which states that, in marriage, she is the property of her husband.

As Andrew Britton so astutely points out, Ophuls' film offers 'the most lucid and suggestive analysis of sexual relations under capitalism'.[6] Louise is entrapped – as, indeed, her all-too-real malady of the heart exemplifies. She faints several times in the film when under stress, seemingly in a manipulative way. Yet we later learn (when she dies) that her heart was weak and so these collapses are, in fact, genuine – something the General fails to grasp and of which he is entirely dismissive. The falsity of their relations begins here in his inability to perceive more than Louise's surface construction, to which he has largely contributed and, indeed, with which she has colluded – although her coming from a family that has fallen on hard times might well have something to do with this. What the General refers to as the 'superficiality' of their marriage is all too well known to her – only the General persists in denial (as exemplified by his over-zealous attempts, early in the film, to locate the lost earrings at the Opera). The earrings and Louise's relationship to them are key to Ophuls' delicate exposure of the fraudulence of bourgeois (capitalist) social relations. Thus, Louise challenges the concept of ownership twice and on both occasions it has to do with the sale or purchase of the earrings. This she does, in the first instance, by selling the earrings. As she herself asserts, 'after all I can do what I like with them'. Second, she asserts herself once more, right at the end of the film, when she buys them back for herself and then bequeaths them to her church. It is in these moments of capital exchange that she adopts a role not ascribed to married women of that time. In marriage, the woman and her property becomes her husband's; she is, therefore, without capital. Here, Louise transgresses in that she sells her husband's property – they are his gift to her for marrying him, a commodity exchange as much as a love token. We can read the act of selling them as her expressing the view that her marriage is no longer of any value to her. However, more significantly, it is through this gesture that she rejects the concept of being a capital asset to her husband. When she buys them back, she again asserts her power over her husband to value them as she wishes (her passion for the Baron) and to dispose of them as she wishes (leaving them to the church). On both occasions, she disrupts the patriarchal code, so she is very unlikely to get away with her transgression – indeed she perishes for it. But what also intrigues us in this portrayal of an empty marriage is the way in which she shoulders responsibility for her role in it all: 'The woman I was made the misery I am today', she declares; whereas the General utters: 'I don't particularly like the personage you have turned me into' – thus laying responsibility for his own failings and the subsequent debacle of their marriage at her feet.

How different is the representation of bourgeois upper-class social relations shown in this film – based as they are in capitalist exchange – as compared with those in *Maxime*. Jacqueline is the modern woman of the late Belle Epoque, whereas Louise is the product of the mid-Belle Epoque era (1900) and economically dependent. For Jacqueline's part, she is free to manoeuvre her feelings as she sees fit because she has the capital means to do so. She owns her car, her apartment, her clothes. If she wishes, she can take trips on trains on her own, without being accompanied to the station; go to Chez Maxim's unescorted; and so on. Her codes are rooted in a sense of personal dignity, not in ideas of property, honour and strict adherence to bourgeois moral codes. Thus, she feels free to take whom she pleases as a lover and to discard him not because of his indigence but because he causes her humiliation, as is the case with Maxime. Interestingly, in *Madame de...*, when the invalided Louise tells her husband that she is suffering from humiliation, as she lies prostrate in her bed after the Baron's rejection, he retorts 'take care, misery is its own invention!' What possible escape, other than death, can there be for her?

The third of our female protagonists, Eléna in *Eléna et les hommes*, is also one who displays a great sense of freedom far in excess of the reality of the times: the early Belle Epoque of 1890. In this narrative, a destitute princess foregoes a marriage of convenience to marry the man who wins her heart. Women making free choices in the late nineteenth century is undoubtedly more myth than fact and its representation in film says more about the contemporary perception of the 1950s' woman as free. Yet, in truth, whilst enfranchised in the strictest sense of the term by having the vote, she was nonetheless, in law, far from free. To cite but the instance of marriage: once married, she was still owned by her husband (for example, she had to have his permission to work) and the extent of his legal rights over her, again, came down to property. In marriage, all her wealth devolved to him and, in the event of a divorce, only he could sue. Thus Eléna of the late 1880s, as with Jacqueline, seems a great deal freer than her 1950s' sisters.

In *Eléna et les hommes*, new money pursues old titles; thus, the rather elderly Monsieur Martin-Michaud (Pierre Bertin), a new type of industrialist whose business is in shoes, seeks to 'land' as wife the impoverished Polish princess Eléna (a widow) and, thereby, buy into titled respectability. However, he is also perfectly canny when it comes to his own money in that he seeks also to wed his rather wayward son, Eugène (Jacques Jouanneau), to his fellow industrialist's daughter, Denise Gaudin (Michèle Nadal). M. Gaudin (Frédéric Duvallès) is in rubber, manufacturing elastic braces and sock suspenders as well as pneumatic tyres. As he proudly announces, the tyres on M. Martin-Michaud's car are his! Clearly, the marriage of rubber with leather will secure an even greater industrial platform. Not without reason do we see the betrothed, Denise and Eugène, cycling around M. Martin-Michaud's estate as Eléna, for her part, canters alongside them on a horse, sitting side-saddle. Eléna by this stage is Martin-Michaud's fiancée, and she appears to embrace her role with gracious equanimity, as here. Respectably dressed in the customary riding costume, she represents the more seemly order of woman at leisure. Denise, however, represents the young go-ahead girl (even if she is not very convincing as a cyclist). Dressed in the modern woman's cycling bloomers, she has doubtless been given this new mode of transport by her father, who in many ways seems to embrace without difficulty the idea that young women should have the freedom to cycle, just as men. Further, despite the considerable disquiet at the time about the risk to young women's health, to say nothing of the concern as to their liberated dress-code, her father is obviously not worried that his daughter would lose her virginity on this mechanical beast.[7] As social historian Sian Reynolds tells us, there 'was much head-wagging over the possibility of masturbation, defloration, or damage to women's internal organs' by this machine, which was described as a 'sterility-machine'.[8] So there is some daring in this freedom that Denise enjoys.

M. Martin-Michaud is canny in yet other ways. Politicians surrounding him try and get him (through the intermediary of his fiancée Eléna, to whom General Rollan has taken a fancy) to persuade Rollan to stand in the presidential elections. Martin-Michaud agrees, provided they will ensure that there are tariffs imposed on the importation of shoes. Astutely protecting his own interests at all times, later on in the film it seems he has changed his mind. Apparently he has signed a deal with some Austrian shoe manufacturers so, now, he asks these same politicians to lift all tariffs on imported goods. Comic though the moment is, it shows how fist in glove industrialists are with politicians and how business deals are ultimately brokered largely assisted by government policy. Of the two industrialists in this film, M. Gaudin is undoubtedly the most modern, trading as he does in manufactured rubber goods. One side of his manufacturing business produces pneumatic tyres; these were first introduced in 1889 (by Dunlop and a little later Michelin), which just goes to show how much M. Gaudin is at the cutting edge of the new technologies. Smart, certainly, but a little vulgar, it has to be said. He cockily demonstrates the elasticity of his braces to Eléna, who obliges by snapping them at his request; he is halted just in time from getting her to repeat the exercise with his sock suspenders!

The narrative of the film is a sprawling affair, with many comings and goings, various love triangulations, lovers separated then reunited, standard farce situations, and so on. But then, as the credits themselves announce, the film is a 'fantaisie musicale' and nothing is to be taken as fact. Yet the background story of General Rollan's rapid rise to power and his popular acclaim align him quite closely with General Boulanger's own story (see Chapter 18). It is true that in order to avoid any inference that this film was a direct reference to General Boulanger, Renoir located it a year later: 1890 (hardly a massive shift, so the nod to the Boulanger affair remains). And even Renoir's enigmatic disclaimer, 'people say I am making a film on General Boulanger. But we thought it best to stay in the realm of fiction,'[9] does not exactly dispel the idea that there are definite parallels. The backstory of Rollan is both the simplest to sum up and is the backbone of the film, so let us start there. Rollan, a charismatic general, is promoted by the President of the Republic to war minister. When two army commanders are imprisoned as spies by the Germans, it seems Rollan alone can vouchsafe their release. His success in this matter only serves to increase his popularity with the French. A coterie of politicians surrounding him is keen to see him elected as President. The actual President gets wind of this scheme and places him under house arrest. However, such is his popularity, his coterie believes he could gain power through a coup d'état. It seems that only Eléna can persuade him to do so – he mistakes her faith in his power to succeed as love and so accepts, if she will marry him. This is not in Eléna's plans. Eventually, Rollan makes his escape, is reunited with his mistress, and renounces any idea of a coup d'état.[10]

Running in parallel to this story is Eléna's own. She, it transpires, is only interested in men (*les hommes* of the title) for what *she* can do to help them fulfil their potential – and to that effect gives each of them one of her daisies, not as a token of love, but as a talisman of belief in their power to achieve. First, we see her with a young talented composer to whom she has given such a flower. Now that his opera has been accepted by La Scala (Milan), she can abandon him to his secured future. But, because she is penniless, she also needs to ensure the well-being of her entourage, so agrees to marry M. Martin-Michaud (to whom, incidentally, she never gives one of her magical daisies). This opening of the film coincides with the celebrations of the 14th of July – the Republic's birthday. General Rollan is going to review the troops. Martin-Michaud and Eléna set out in his carriage to join the festivities, but the carriage gets stuck in the throng of people. Eléna gets whisked away in the crowd on her own (not a good omen for her new status as fiancée) and eventually bumps into the very lovely aristocrat Henri de Chevincourt (Mel Ferrer). There is clear electricity between the two. She insists on going to see the main attraction, Rollan. It transpires he is a personal friend of Henri's. When introduced, Rollan falls for her undoubted charms but Eléna insists on giving him her daisy to bring him the success he so deserves. Almost immediately he is promoted to war minister, proving the infallibility of her talisman.[11] She supplies him with her special talisman on two further occasions (his mistress keeps coming across them and tossing them away). The first brings him success in releasing the army commanders. The next is intended to spur him on to the greatest of things, namely the presidency of France; but in the end he chooses his mistress over a coup d'état. Eléna, meantime, now that her work is done, is finally free to love Henri, the only one who neither needs nor wants anything from her (not even a daisy) – a man without ambition who, as he confesses to Eléna, wants to do nothing.

Renoir did say of his film that 'I built a satire, I amused myself with these stories about generals. I wanted to show the futility of human ambition, including the one they call patriotism.'[12] The film is, in its own way, quite an indictment of small-time dictators (which Rollan/Boulanger could so easily have become if he had agreed to the coup d'état) and grubby politics, including state-industrial deals. But it does not pronounce itself as profoundly Republican, either, since the hurrahs for the Republic ('*vive la République!*') are shouted by Eugène, the less-than-charismatic son, who only a few moments beforehand had denounced the secret whereabouts of Rollan to the police. A snitchy Republican sounds just as opportunist as the coterie of politicians attempting to push Rollan into an act of treason. As Martin-Michaud rightly asserts at the end of the film (even though he has lost Eléna) 'This was quite a crazy enterprise, but dictatorships don't stand much chance in a country where love is so important.' A very Renoir-like sentiment!

To complete the discussion of these three films, let us now consider the technicians, beginning with Ophuls' film *Madame de…*. Much has been made of the Ophuls' style of filmmaking, particularly his love of the waltz and the way in which he manages to construct his films as if they are whirling around an axis, in the same way that dancers twirl around in a waltz. To achieve this look, he has presented his directors of photography with quite a task, and Christian Matras' role in *Madame de…* is no exception. The camera work is nervy, hardly ever at rest. The long-held, single continuous panning and tracking shots which pervade this film – averaging out, with deep regularity throughout the film, at one every two minutes – tell us a great deal about the characters and the narrative. The shot is used to allow us, in real time, to observe the movements of the three main protagonists as they gradually become more and more enmeshed in the cage that encircles them. A cage of their own making, it has to be said, based as it is in honour, love and betrayal. These movements of body and camera are revealing of each character. For the most part, the General is panned/tracked as he strides left and right in sharp zigzags – a man of military precision in action. The Baron's movements more closely resemble the softer flow of a dancer, first going to the right then gently turning to move to the left – as doubtless befits a diplomat. With Louise, it is more as if she floats, whether accompanied by either of the two men or not, suggesting not just her frivolity or lightness but also, ultimately, her fragility. As to the camera's relation to the narrative, the famous ball series sequence (34 minutes into the film), where Louise dances with the Baron, is the most revealing of all. The panning and tracking shots tell the story; words are barely necessary. In this five-minute sequence, there are four separate panning/tracking shots, one for each ball, but all joined up by dissolves from one to the next, so it feels as if it is one long panning/tracking sequence. Over the duration of these four movements, we witness the growing love between the two dancers – the final one, which lasts two minutes (twice the length of the others which last only a minute each) being the most poignant of all. We read the lovers' desire, even though they are mostly held in long shot, just as we read their despair. The ball has long ended and they are the last two slowly twirling on the floor, with their coat and furs on, but still they will not leave – there is nowhere to go. We see the weary musicians depart one by one as the camera pans round 360 degrees following them; then, in a similar movement, the maître d'hôte goes round and snuffs out the candles, one by one, until, at last, a dark cloth is placed over an instrument and the sequence ends in a black screen. We know this love affair is fated to end badly, but we do not yet know how.

To return to Louise, however. It is instructive, surely, that on the only two occasions when there is a one-take panning/tracking shot sequence, both are associated with her. The first, lasting two minutes and thirty seconds, occurs at the very beginning of the film when Louise is going through her belongings. This one-take single shot sequence tells us about her frivolity and spendthrift nature – we see her hand in relation to the objects of consumption she is looking to sell. The second one-take sequence, lasting one minute and thirty seconds, is at the point where she has decided to go away, having recognized the danger of her feelings for the Baron. Here she is assured, if contemplative, in her movements as she glides around the room. She is packing her bags, as her beloved nurse is reading the cards forecasting her future. There is, then, a marked difference between the two sequences, as if to show how she has moved away from her frivolous ways. Whereas, before, she had shown only cupidity to save her own face and, ultimately, indifference to her marriage, this time she shows courage in her moral choice to leave – to preserve her husband (and thereby perhaps their marriage) from the humiliation of this love she bears for another. As she says to her husband, her absence will give their circle of acquaintances time to forget her indiscretion.

If camera work tells a large part of the story in this film, in *Maxime*, Matras' contribution to the narrative, as director of photography is far less obtrusive (pointing in some ways to his earlier training in the 1920s as a newsreel photographer). The triangulation of relationships is well composed through three-shots and shot reverse-angle shots. Panning and tracking, however, are very little in evidence – although, when they are, we are reminded of his work for Ophuls. These shots occur in a noticeable fashion in the few sequences set in Chez Maxim's and the Café de Paris; but, for the most part, the camera moves about very little. Cuts are used in preference to panning shots for the movement of characters. Alain Jessua, commenting on Matras, tells us how on the whole he was a fairly conservative cinematographer and not a risk-taker except when working with Ophuls, who pushed him.[13] An earlier discussion of his camera work for Pottier on *Les Violettes impériales* disputes that view (see Chapter 14). Certainly here, however, *Maxime*'s narrative devolves to us more through the classical style of full shot, cut to medium close-up, cutaway to next shot and so on. Conventional, but effective nonetheless; colder in style and considerably less ornate when measured against the work done for Ophuls.

Jean d'Eaubonne designed Ophuls' sets; Robert Clavel those for Henri Verneuil's *Maxime*. The former reveal d'Eaubonne and Ophuls' love for the baroque and rococo, and I shall return to d'Eaubonne's sets when discussing the costumes. Clavel's work on *Maxime* speaks to his former training under Louis Barsacq and Max Douy, two of the great realists of set design. Whilst Verneuil mostly worked in the comedy genre, especially with Fernandel, he was also known for a handful of films that displayed a gritty realism.[14] Thus *Maxime* has this realist edge, both in terms of décor and grounding in an historical moment, even if our three main protagonists seem to remain blissfully ignorant of the political turmoil that surrounds them. The flashes of newspaper headlines take us from April to June 1914 – a period of great political unrest for France, with several changes of government (Doumergue, Viviani, Ribot, and Viviani again) culminating in headlines announcing the assassination of Archduke Ferdinand. Just as the headlines of the newspapers in the film capture the rapid succession of governments, so too the strikes are alluded to (especially the taxi strikes). These flashes of historical accuracy are dotted throughout the film, which opens with a series of documentary clips about Franco-British relations leading us back in time to the *Entente cordiale,* as if to ground us in the Belle Epoque era. Finally, on this topic of historical truth, in terms of the stock market, this was a time for getting rich quick (à la Treffujean) on the back of the re-armament of France – particularly by investing or selling shares in Creusot, the biggest manufacturers of cannons.[15]

The sets, by Clavel, oppose two worlds: the wealth of Treffujean and Jacqueline versus the indigence of Maxime. Curiously, it is Maxime's small habitat that is cluttered, whereas the Ritz apartment where Treffujean lives and Jacqueline's house on rue Eugène-Flachat in the 17th arrondissement are fairly unadorned, full of light, including interior electric light, elegant, yet unostentatious in taste. It was perhaps a bit foolish of Maxime to claim he lived in the Parc Monceau area, since it lies a mere 800 metres from Jacqueline's home! In any event, his real abode is lacking in light, with its small attic window. Interior lighting is gas; the room is cramped with furniture. There is a small gas stove and, more particularly, pictures and photographs that refer to his more heady days of wealth and importance – a painful abundance pointing to what is lost. However, he does (somewhat oddly) own a rather gorgeous Siamese cat. The third space created by Clavel is that of the cafés and theatres. Of Les Capucines, however, we only get to see backstage – the place where the likes of Maxime can go (carrying out others' dirty work for them). We are treated to several visits to Chez Maxim's and just the one to Café de Paris (where Jacqueline takes her English friends). The latter is clearly more sophisticated in clientele – just as it is more ornate in décor and grander in style than Maxim's. Yet dancing is more modern here. The tango has arrived at the Café de Paris and, with it, the suggestion not just of a desire to be abreast of the new but also pleasure in the risqué, visible aura of sexuality on display. It is also the less predictable when it comes to matters of seduction, as we see with old school Maxime, who, to his embarrassment, cannot perform the tango and Jacqueline, modern as always, has to lead him.

Both d'Eaubonne and Clavel's sets show us a world that is, sooner or later, about to be lost because of the Great War. Yet it seems as if our central characters, in their hedonism and greed on the one hand and their upholding of principles of the *vieille époque* on the other, are completely unaware how short-lived this era will be – much like the politicians and diplomats who surround them. The general in *Maxime* is constantly iterating that there will not be a war with Germany, a view echoed by Viviani's government in the headlines of the newspapers we catch a glimpse of. And in *Madame de…*, the President of the Council reads a speech declaiming peace amongst nations.

Eléna et les hommes, the only one of the three films to be shot in colour, is located historically at the very beginning of the Belle Epoque – an exciting time of renewal, thanks, as we saw in the previous chapter, to breakthroughs in the steel industry and the birth of new industries, all of which brought France new-found wealth. It was also a time of considerable civil unrest, which this film acknowledges through General Rollan's story. What stands out in this film is the energy of Renoir's ensemble of actors breathing life into his fantasy-narrative. Renoir's set designers were Jean André and Jacques Saulnier, and his director of photography was his nephew Claude Renoir, with whom he had worked previously, most noticeably on *Une partie de campagne,* where the obvious influence of Pierre-Auguste Renoir and the Impressionist movement can be felt. The same is true of *Eléna.* Many of the street scenes, dancing scenes and the scene in Montmartre (place du Tertre) are strongly derivative in colour, lighting and composition of Jean Renoir's father's oil paintings, which find a perfect resonance in Claude Renoir's skilful use of Technicolor: a system that allows for a rich arrangement of colours and tones, very much like oil-paint itself.[16] In terms of composition, Claude Renoir often manages to achieve the same decentring effect that was a hallmark of the Impressionists. Framing is often asymmetric, the central protagonist not necessarily holding a prime position. There are several ready examples of this in the interior scenes – think for example of the opening sequence where the piano dominates the frame rather than the two players; or again how the window becomes the centre of the frame, with Eléna one side and her pianist paramour the other. Gentle high-angle shots on dancers or milling crowds also recall the trend of Impressionism to catch people and objects from new spatial perspectives. In the street scenes, people are fleeting impressions as much as objects – in this way, the figure loses its importance, space becomes democratized rather than individualized. Narratives are no longer grand and about heroic moments or men. All people have their value, hence the presence of the street-singer (Léo Marjane) in Renoir's film telling us of the merits and dangers of Paris – indeed, all that makes up Paris matters. This is the world of the collective – 'Eléna and the men', rather than just 'Eléna' – sentiments very close to Jean Renoir's thinking and which are so clearly embodied by the ensemble playing which dominates this film.[17]

Finally, let us turn to the female leads and their costumes – all designed by Delamare. Bows and frills adorn all three lead women's attires, although the least adorned is Jacqueline, the modern, late-Belle Epoque woman. Indeed, each woman is representative to a greater or lesser degree of her time in the Belle Epoque era. Eléna's dresses repose upon the corseted and bustled silhouette of the 1890s, providing an ample bosom, tightly fitted and boned waistline curving into full hips. Her dresses are heavily trimmed with lace and ribbons, with trains at the back as befitted the era. However, the first dress we see her in, a day dress, is more daring than it should be with its low neckline across the bosom; in reality the dress would have sported a high neckline collar or a *jabot* (a decorative lace frill). This fashion anachronism is, of course, in keeping with the persona Renoir wanted Eléna to project: a free-spirited woman – very quickly in evidence, from the beginning of the film, especially during her bucolic revelry on Bastille Day. In terms of accessories, she wears large hats adorned with feathers. But we soon gather that she is not one for the fussiness or even the fetishistic value of accessories, as exemplified by what happens during the Bastille Day celebrations. As she sets out in her cream-coloured low neckline dress (mentioned above), she is carrying the traditional parasol, a small handbag, black gloves, and a straw hat adorned with feathers and a veil – all very much in keeping with the fashion accoutrements of the day. She manages to lose the first, have the second stolen, leave one glove behind in a bistro, and toss her hat away at a man in the orchestra. She also manages to spend the whole day and evening with Henri, with whom she dances and enjoys numerous intimate hugs and caresses that she eventually puts a stop to (realizing she is fiancéed elsewhere!).

Altogether, Eléna wears eight different outfits; not a great many, one could surmise, for a princess (but then she is no longer wealthy). Interestingly, with the exception of the first day dress described above, all her day outfits are appropriately high-necked. After Bastille Day, it would appear that she enters the realm of seriousness. Thus, her riding outfit worn at her fiancé's country estate is the height of decorum, and it is she who attempts to establish order over the unruly Eugène. She even wears one outfit twice – a red velvet *tailleur* (tailored suit) with a high-necked white blouse underneath. On both occasions when it is worn there

Figure 19.3: Eléna in her mauve evening dress, note the frills and roses! © 1956 Gaumont/ Studio Canal.

is serious business afoot in terms of advancing General Rollan's career (once, when she is cheering him on for his success in releasing the captured army commanders and, again, a bit later when she plots Rollan's escape from house arrest). There is no doubt that Eléna is in charge of the situation. Whereas in the Bastille Day celebrations she was unruly, now she commandeers the unruly with authority and engineers both Rollan's good fortune and his escape (thanks also to her lucky talisman, the daisy).

Two of her evening gowns are fancy affairs with off-the-shoulder straps adorned with gauze frills or feathers: the first is a sumptuous mauve that she wears to her (interrupted) engagement party (see figure 19.3 above); the second, in pure white silk, she wears out to dinner with Henri. Her last dress in the film, also an evening gown, is a curious mixture of an off-the-shoulders dress in deep red satin completely covered by black brocaded gauze (or tulle); her accessory, which she quickly dispenses with, is a plain black gauze shawl. Whilst the colouring of her gown indeed matches the black and red of the army officer's outfit, worn first by Rollan and then by Henri (to facilitate Rollan's escape, he and Henri swap clothes), her costume in its sobriety also suggests a rather muted Eléna, one who fits in rather than stands out – who accepts rather than commandeers. After all, this is the moment when Rollan relinquishes his ambitions, despite her insistence that he be heroic and fight for the presidency. It is also the moment when, finally, she accepts Henri as her suitor. The right man in the right uniform matched (in all ways) to the woman he loves.

Louise's seventeen outfits in *Madame de...* are as revealing of her personal trajectory as they are emblematic of late-1890s', turn-of-the-century fashion. Both Delamare and Annenkov worked on the costumes for Danielle Darrieux and in fact were nominated for a joint Oscar for their work. Delamare is very modest about her input (to the point of saying very little); Annenkov, quite the opposite. It is as if he has forgotten that this was a joint effort.[18] There are a few sketches published by Annenkov, which at least indicate which costumes he did design for Darrieux, and these are of her travel coat when she leaves Paris and the dark fur-trimmed *tailleur* she wears throughout the end section of the film.[19] The ball gowns and the more decorated day outfits, however, bear the hallmarks of Delamare – frills and bows – and are taken as hers.

The costumes Louise wears to the balls carry echoes of Charles Frederick Worth's ball gowns of 1894–1895, particularly because of the presence of the trains that Worth introduced when he abolished the crinoline. The day outfits in the early part of the film, with their frills and bows, and the riding outfit also recall Delamare's style. The less ornate and more straight-lined jackets and skirts of Louise's day outfits worn after the hunting sequence, later in the film, bear the hallmark of Annenkov's costume design with its restricting corseting, which further suggests where his contributions lay.[20] This design speaks more of the turn of the century fashion – particularly because of the presence of the S-bend silhouette (however gently suggested in Louise's demeanour) which was so popular between 1895 and 1904 and which was created by tight corseting.

Madame de... falls into three parts. Part one, lasting 39 minutes, is the build-up to Louise acknowledging her love for the Baron and ends with the famous ball sequence. Part two, lasting 36 minutes, begins with the hunting sequence, lasts through the lovers' separation until Louise returns and is rejected by the Baron, at the ball, for her lies. Part three, the shortest at 20 minutes, follows Louise's gradual disintegration and ends with the fatal duel. In part one, Louise wears ten different outfits: three day outfits, one fancy night attire and six ball-gowns. There are no repeats. In part two, she wears six new and different outfits: the hunting outfit, travelling coat, a plain nightdress, a dark cloak, a sombre *tailleur* adorned at the sleeves with white gauze frills and sporting a lacey *jabot*, and finally a stunning ball-gown. There are two repeats in this part from part one: the fancy night attire (as she discusses, with her husband, her leaving Paris), the travelling coat when she is on the train (this time with a shawl, since it is deep winter), presumably returning to Paris for the New Year celebrations. In part three, she wears only one new outfit: a very dark *tailleur* trimmed with fur. There are two repeats from part two: the *tailleur* trimmed with frills (which she wears to her cousin's) and the plain nightdress with a bed-jacket. The narrative could not be more simply told:

Figure 19.4: An example of d'Eaubonne's décor 'obscuring' the costume[21]

from frivolity to despair via a passionate romance; from ornament to unadornment; from husband's showpiece to dowdy misery.

Although costumes abound in part one, what is remarkable is how little we get to see of them because of the intense nature of d'Eaubonne's décor. For example, we only catch glimpses of Louise in her ball gowns in the long five-minute series of waltzes. She wears four separate gowns, one for each ball – the first and last are black, the middle two, white. The camera tracks and pans alongside the couple's dancing like an observer walking by in the wings, so to speak. Thus, the camera is always separated from the dancers by pillars, large leafy vegetation, paintings on easels, and so on. Rarely do we get a full view. This truncated view is not just limited to this sequence; it occurs whenever she is with the Baron or in his presence. When he first glimpses her in the customs office at Basle, she tears through the office and we only briefly catch sight of her outfit (as, indeed, the Baron barely catches sight of her). A little later, when their two carriages collide, we only have a limited view of her hat and jacket. When with her husband, similarly, we rarely get a full view. At the opera, she is sitting in the box and we merely see her shoulders (as indeed does her husband); later, as she takes her leave down the ornate (Garnier-like) Opéra staircase, we catch a brief view of the front of the gown under her furs and the camera then cuts to place behind her where we see only the lower half of the gown with its train and velvet bows. Just as the camera only half sees her, we sense that the two men but marginally grasp the real woman beneath these fineries.

Above (figure 19.4) is an example of this obscuring effect of d'Eaubonne's décor. Louise has just learnt the Baron is breaking their liaison – all is lost, therefore. Note also the blank look on the face of Darrieux (as per Ophuls' instructions).

Only when she is on her own do we have longer to peruse her attire. Thus, on her visits to the jewellers, at the beginning and at the end of the film, we get to see her costumes.

And what a difference there is between these two moments. In the early sequence there is the gaiety of her first outfit, with its frills and adornments (velvet ties at the neck and bows tied around the waist dropping down the back of the skirt, frilly sleeves) and voluminous petticoats, of which we espy a great deal as she goes up and down the narrow spiral staircase in the jewellers. Conversely in the later sequence, there is the dowdiness of her last outfit as she sits, round-shouldered, cast down in her gaze, grey in her complexion and completely wrought with genuine despair as she pleads with the jeweller to take all her fineries (that were so on display in the opening sequence) in exchange for the now-much-desired earrings. In part two, clothing and set design function once more in a contrastive way to create meaning. As Louise prepares to leave, we see her in her demurely-cut travelling coat as she moves around the room – an all female space (she and her nurse and a servant) in which she organizes herself to go. Thereupon the Baron arrives. She descends to greet him. During their exchange, as she tells the Baron of her imminent departure, standing in her husband's gloomy (and very militaristic) study, she and he are mostly kept separate (aided by the various heavy furnishings of the room) in single medium shots. That is until they come close together in a two-shot. For the Baron has come to bestow a gift upon her. At which point the demure nature of her costume begins to shift. We now see her outfit in a completely different light from its former appearance of restraint. As she rushes upstairs to her room to find the earrings (hidden in the bouquet of flowers he has brought her), her excitement is palpable, her petticoats are again in full view from the low-angle camera position. Until the next ball-gown at the end of this part, we do not see this flighty or flirtatious person again. In between these two moments she is dressed almost as if in mourning: the dark cloak, as she walks along a wintry sea-shore, offers one of the most poignant insights into her state of mind. One of the only two location shots in the film (the other being that of the duel), we are struck by the barrenness of this space as opposed to all the baroque of the interiors seen so far. She is stripped bare in this moment, restless in her impossible conflict between passion and duty. The shot is almost Bergmanesque.

By the end, all is lost. No attempts on her husband's part, to rally her spirits and bring her back to the lively companion she once was, have any impact – least of all his foolish belief that by killing the Baron in a duel he will win her wifely devotion. Whilst he has certainly observed her physical decline, he clearly has not realized the full meaning of her sartorial message: that she is doomed, her heart broken, and there is no coming back. Bleak indeed.

Finally, we come to Delamare's designs for Michèle Morgan's costumes for *Maxime*, of which there are ten. Delamare was responsible for Morgan's outfits only. The rest were designed by Blanche Van Parys. This sets up an interesting clash of styles where the women's costume are concerned – undoubtedly a deliberate one, for Van Parys' designs act as a foil to show just how modern are those of Jacqueline Monneron. Whereas Van Parys' designs are based in the traditional corseted silhouette and are often over-festooned and excessive, not to say rather lacking in taste, Delamare's are free-flowing in their understated elegance. There can be little doubt – even if her frills and bows are still in evidence on some of the outfits – that the inspiration for Delamare here was Paul Poiret, the pioneering designer of the 1900s. Indeed, at one point in the film we enter his fashion house, where a cat-walk is underway. Maxime has come to meet Jacqueline, who is upstairs trying on an evening gown designed for her by Poiret. His modern vision of the female silhouette, freed from the constraints of the corset, and his new conception of women's fashion, with softly fitting garments, fit perfectly with Jacqueline's own characterization as a modern society woman (see figure 19.5 below).

Poiret's looser-fitting designs were also influenced by the costumes of Diaghelev's *Ballets Russes* when the ballet series came to Paris in the early 1900s. Inspired as they were by the Orient, they had an enormous impact on Parisian fashion: for example, in 1911, Poiret created the *style persane* with turbans and harem pantaloons. Earlier, in 1905, he had promoted the kimono shape – which we see in a number of Jacqueline's coats (evening and day). He also designed the hobble skirt, where the material was cut and draped to narrow and split at the mid-calf. It freed the hips, but it did not allow for a great deal of ankle movement, hence the term hobble – women could only take short steps. We see a less stringent version of this style in two of Jacqueline's outfits – once in the park when walking her dog and, later, at the train station.

Figure 19.5: Jacqueline in modern society clothes. © Les Films Raoul Ploquin.

In terms of design and technology, there is no doubting that Jacqueline has firmly moved into the new, twentieth century. In a sense, her affair with Maxime and its termination is indicative of this desire to break with the past and embrace the present, if not the future. The Belle Epoque is, when all is said and done, at an end. No one more clearly epitomizes this death knell than the forward-looking even impulsive Jacqueline and her equally impulsive, if somewhat overly self-confident, lover Treffujean. The fact that both are wrong to be so assured about their own glittering future in no way diminishes their arrogant belief that an old world is at an end. We do not, I suspect, as an audience, particularly take to any of these characters, whichever era they embody: the Belle Epoque that was, or the modernist era to come. The author of this story, Henri Duvernois, was well poised to record with a certain dark cynicism the climate of the times, even if he wrote the novel in 1929. Before the Great War, he was a journalist for *Le Journal* and *Le Matin,* amongst others, (hence the presence of newspaper headlines in this film). He published his first novel in 1908 and, having survived the war (albeit wounded), he went on to become a novelist of considerable repute – particularly noted for his astute observations of the so-called Roaring Twenties (known in France as 'Les Années Folles'). In *Maxime* we have a fairly candid portrait of a slice of society (bourgeois and middle class) that brashly refuses to see the evidence that confronts it – the inevitability of war with Germany – at the same time as it desires nothing more than to move into the fast lane of motor cars, quick money and profit. Some dawn of some new age! As we shall see in the next chapter, this dark edge of cynicism is equally present in the third category of Belle Epoque films we identified: love set against a military background.

Notes

1. Included in the 'etiquette' lessons to which these aspiring cocottes are subjected comes a lesson on 'how to strip-tease for your lover'. A model seductively strips down naked before the assembled young women, leaving her hat until last – 'as etiquette [read 'good taste'] demands', pronounces the count!
2. Le Garrec may be a reference to Clément Ader, a French electrical engineer who, in 1890 created a steam-powered heavier-than-air machine that managed a brief uncontrolled hop. The actual sequence is an exciting moment as we see pilot and machine strain to get off the ground. The French had not managed to get much further than a few feet off the ground when, in 1905, they heard of the Wright brothers' exploits which considerably outshone their own.
3. *Madame de...*marked Boyer's return from Hollywood. It was his first film in France since he left for the US in 1934 and became a naturalized American (in 1936).
4. Andrew Britton (1982, p. 101). This very interesting article offers an impeccable Marxist reading of Ophuls' film.
5. Max Ophuls, quoted by Pierre Besanger (1963, p. 116).
6. Britton, op. cit., p. 92.
7. Reynolds (2006, p. 85). Leaving the anachronism of the car aside, it is worth noting two things about the supposed date of this film 1890. First, a very small percentage (1%) of women owned bicycles – they were expensive (three times a teacher's monthly salary) (Ibid., p. 85).

8. Ibid., p. 85.
9. Renoir cited in Beylie (1962, p. 26).
10. The proximity to General Boulanger's own story is self-evident. The only difference being that, in reality, these same events occurred over a three-year period and were not all condensed (as Renoir has it) into one year. In 1886 Boulanger was made War Minister; in 1887 he was removed from office; in 1889 he ran for and won a Paris by-election; he then fled under rumours (leaked by the government) of his imminent arrest.
11. It is worth remarking that in this film all of Rollan's supporters end up sporting the daisy as their badge of allegiance in much the same was as Boulanger's supporters sported a red carnation.
12. Renoir cited in Beylie, op. cit., p. 26.
13. Alain Jessua's commentary on DVD of *Madame de...* issued by Second Sight Films Limited. There is also a very interesting discussion of some of the key scenes by Tag Gallagher.
14. An earlier film, *Des Gens sans importance* (1955), set in the 1950s, tells the graphic story of a young, working-class woman who dies from an abortion (her visit to the abortionist is spine-chilling in its realism). His crime thriller, *Une Manche et la belle* (1957), a tale of greed and concupiscence, is an adaptation of the novel by the British crime writer James Hadley Chase (known for his harsh, realistic narratives).
15. Marseille (2002, p. 230).
16. Claude Renoir is clearly making references to his illustrious Impressionist grand-father's work. Obvious references to Pierre-Auguste Renoir's work are *Le Moulin de la Galette* (1876), *The Arbor* (1876), *The Luncheon of the Boating Party* (1881), and *Dance at Bougival* (1883). Also worth noting is that Claude Renoir trained under Christian Matras and Boris Kaufman – two great cinematographers of their time.
17. It is perhaps worth recalling that, by the 1890s, the Impressionist movement had peaked after nearly thirty years in the limelight. Considered scandalous in the late 1860s when it was launched, by the late-1880s it no longer shocked and had become well accepted into the art establishment. It was about to make way for the turn-of-the-century, post-impressionist and modern abstract art of the likes of Cézanne, Gauguin, Matisse and Picasso. Thus, Renoir's film is not just a musical fantasy, it is also a nostalgic homage to an art movement already on the wane – making this film an odd mixture of the anachronistic modern (e.g., the motor-car) and the retro.
18. See Annenkov (1962, pp. 63ff).
19. Ibid., p. 66.
20. See Jennie Cousins (2008, pp. 84–5). Her discussion of Annenkov goes into considerable detail on his work in all of Ophuls' films (see her Chapters 3–5). Annenkov in his book on Max Ophuls claims that he designed the earrings (they are credited to Gaucheraud) and the hats (Annenkov 1962, p. 66).
21. Still image accessed from http://cinegotier.blogspot.com/2008/12/ophuls-ou-le-reflet-fministe.html 09.09.2009.

Chapter 20

Truth and Lies and the Pursuit of Marriage: Love Intrigues outside Paris

T here are ten films in this category of films (see figure 20.1 below). Four of these love intrigues are located in some unspecified provincial town of France. The other six, however, are set outside of the country (*C'est arrivé à Aden, Christine, Koenigsmark, Maria Chapdelaine, Le Mariage de mlle Beulemans, Sérénade au Texas*): an internationalization of the difficulties of human relationships that can be explained in part by the fact that, all but *Sérénade au Texas*, are adaptations of works by authors whose novels or plays' (set in foreign lands) continued popularity into the 1950s made them attractive to the film industry. Pierre Benoît's novels were the basis for *C'est arrivé à Aden* and *Koenigsmark*. The latter title had already been made into a film twice so it had, by now, acquired considerable pedigree. Benoît was the son of a military officer and had done his own military service in North Africa in the early years of the twentieth century – his understanding of foreign parts, as reflected in

Love intrigues – outside Paris	Love – military as background (also set outside Paris)
Les Belles de nuit+ 3,499,199	*Christine** 2,848,858
*C'est arrivé à Aden**+ 1,956,334	*Les Grandes manoeuvres** 5,301,504
Koenigsmark 2,119,107	*La Ronde* 1,509,923
*La Maison Bonnadieu**+ 1,000,071	
*Maria Chapdelaine** 2,170.533	
*Le Mariage de mlle Beulemans**+ 1,010,104	
*Miquette et sa mere**+ 2,159,275	
Sérénade au Texas+ 2,555,768	

Figure 20.1: Love intrigues set outside Paris (* denotes female-centred narrative; + a comedy) audience figures in bold.

his novels, also made him a strong candidate for adaptation, offering something new. The same applies for Louis Hémon, who emigrated to Canada where he wrote his famous novel *Maria Chapdelaine*, also adapted to film during the 1930s.[1] *Le Mariage de mlle Beulemans*, written in 1910 by two Belgian playwrights (Franz Fonson and Fernand Wicheler), was a huge success. When first performed, it went on to enjoy a 16-year run (home and abroad) and was often staged thereafter. This success revealed that a play mixing French with the Belgian dialect could be an international hit. Indeed, the director of the film, André Cerf, had previously acted in the earlier adaptation by Julien Duvivier (1926) – small wonder he wanted to turn his hand to directing this witty piece.

Of these ten films, we can say that the pursuit of marriage is not always a happy one. Even if six of them can be considered comedies, some films end in compromise, unhappiness, or worst of all, suicide. This chapter falls into two parts. The first part examines briefly a cross-section of these films, focusing on representations of marriage or gender relations. The second part takes two of the military love-intrigues, *Les Grandes manoeuvres* and *Christine*, as case studies for a broader investigation of this type of costume drama.

Love and marriage

The message of *Les Belles de nuit* may well be: 'be content with when you were born and with your lot'; it has several elements that set it aside from the majority of the love narratives located in the Belle Epoque. First, unusually, its central protagonist is a young man: Claude (Gérard Philipe). Typically, the central protagonist of these types of films is female (out of a total of 28 'love films' set in the Belle Epoque era, only five have the male as central: *Les Belles de nuit*, *Chéri*, *Koenigsmark*, *Maxime*, *Sérénade au Texas*). Second, although Claude is poor, he has a profession (a music teacher) and a talent (a composer of operas). Mostly, male characters are defined by their rank or class – here he is designated as a talented artist. Finally, the film is composed of 'dreambacks' rather than a flashback – suggesting a working of the subconscious that is quite rare in these films, and particularly in relation to men. As the narrative goes, Claude lives in contemporary 1950s' France, but he is unhappy with his lot: it is too noisy; people do not appreciate his talents, including his best mates (all of whom are working class); and he is so busy being miserable he fails to see how loved he is by Suzanne (Magali Vendeuil), the garage owner's daughter above whose workshop he lives. However, he is magically endowed with the ability to time-travel in his dreams back to 'better epochs', amongst them the Belle Epoque, the 1830s and the conquest of Algeria, the Revolution, and the time of the three musketeers. As he does this, he gradually learns that those times were as perilous, if not more so, than now (he nearly loses his life in a duel in the Belle Epoque, his manhood in Algeria, his head in the Revolution). The contrast that set designer Léon Barsacq and director of photography Armand Thirard create between the two worlds (dream and reality) equally serve to make clear where our protagonist hero's allegiances should lie. In this black and white film, to distinguish the imaginary scenes of the past and so as to differentiate them from the present, Matras used white tulle over the lenses to filter and soften the white.[2] The gritty realism of the contemporary décor has a tangibility, a haptic quality to it over the flimsy faux-semblant of the dream sequences with their painted backdrops and over-exposed lighting effects. Eventually all ends well: Claude's composition is accepted by the Paris Opéra – he is a success; Suzanne and he fall in love and are to marry. Who needs costume dramas! Except to instruct us in how much better the present is where, apparently, class boundaries no longer operate and success is achievable on merit alone for those with talent. For such could be a way of reading this René Clair film.

As we have seen in the previous chapters, costume dramas teach us that it is primarily through exploiting others and establishing useful connections that men advance. Whereas horizontality, aligned with wit and cunning, are about the only ways women of little means can make any social progress. Clair's gentle dreamer-misfit is not consonant, therefore, with the masculine types we have already met and will meet again through the narratives below (including Clair's own *Les Grandes manoeuvres*). In other respects, however, this film conforms to type: women are mere ciphers in *Les Belles de nuit*, acting as no more than triggers to Claude's various sexual dalliances. Gina Lollobrigida as Leila, the Algerian 'Salomé-type', who seduces him into her compound, and whom he later spies on taking a bath in goat's milk, best exemplifies this.

As we shall go on to see, several of our Belle Epoque women in this small group of films set outside Paris or the French nation break with this mould and are strong and feisty. Such is not the case however for the eponymous heroine of Marc Allégret's film *Maria Chapdelaine*, who is over-burdened by a sense of national duty. This film has an odd status in and of itself: the original novel is that of a Frenchman (Louis Hémon); the story is set in the bleakest snowy French Canadian Québec State; it is French directed, adapted by Allégret; its lead technician (Armand Thirard as director of photography), the scriptwriter (Roger Vadim), and its stars (Morgan and Rosay) are all French. Yet the production company is British (Everest Pictures), as are its distributors (British Lion). Nelson Scott produced the film (seemingly his only film) independently, on a tiny budget.[3] It was shot in the Shepperton Studios (except for the wild exteriors, which were filmed in Austria). It was made in English (under the title of *Naked Heart*) and subsequently dubbed into French (for French release). However, despite its intrinsic British 'nationality' in terms of financing alone, the film is listed as a Franco-British co-production.[4] It garnered a 2.2 million audience in France, so for all that it was 'pilloried' by reviewers both sides of the Channel, it did remarkably well. [5]

Maria (Michèle Morgan) returns to her rural home after five years at a convent school. Her religious background has provided her with little knowledge of the ways of the world – so, when it comes to men, she is prone to ally her romantic beliefs with what she sees before her eyes. There are three suitors: the exciting and intrepid trapper François Paradis (Philippe Lemaire); the dark and dangerous bank robber Lorenzo Surprenant (played by the Irish actor Kieron Moore); and the dull but dutifully sincere stay-at-home Robert Gagnon (the British Jack Watling). She is caught between three types of men: the brave, the bad and the ordinary. Doubtless, as she first falls for the charm of François – whose courage and manliness she surely believes could bring her close to paradise – she forgets that trappers are on the run all the time, snaring their animals and skinning their pelts. So, when he inadvertently humiliates her by dancing with, and joyfully kissing, another women at the local spring dance, in her world according to love, he has betrayed her and she rejects him. Eventually, he will perish in the snow as he tries to make his way back to her through a blizzard. Lorenzo represents a far more complex image of masculinity. Whereas François had boyish charm and a flirtatious manner, Lorenzo exudes sexuality. His lust for Maria is tangible – the strong highlighting of his handsome features in close-up does all the talking. In one scene, Maria is hanging out the washing and he stares longingly at her exposed unshaven armpits – it is quite shockingly erotic as a shot and Maria quickly drops her arms, forbidding him to look at her 'in that way'. Towards the end of the film, Lorenzo (who is now on the run for a bank robbery and murder) comes to her to repent for his past criminal life and ask her forgiveness and that she accepts his love for her. As he tries to convince her that his love is true, he knows he is about to be tracked down and shot by the posse after him, so time is short. Finally, she succumbs to his entreaties and it is her turn to speak and act in lustful terms: she declares her love for him, adding: 'I want to bite your lips, make them bleed'. They kiss. The posse arrives. He charges towards them, a glint in his eye as he imagines the death she will witness as his ultimate token of love (very '*surprenant*'). They shoot him. He collapses into the snow. As Maria rightly asserts, she is 'mad'. Only Robert is left now. Thanks to her mother's sensible advice that 'you don't find love, you have to earn it bit by bit, day by day', she realizes that he is the one she must marry. She foregoes all the excitement her other suitors represented and finds the right path.

Set in 1912, all three men represent different aspects of turn of the (last) century Canada: the pioneering frontiersman François, who loves the silence of the snow-driven mountains and does not want to settle down; the reckless gangster Lorenzo, who loves the city and the noisy bustle of modernity, and chooses death over life; the grounded Robert, whose steadying ways will guarantee the survival of traditional values of rural French Canada. Her choice (or rather, compromise, since Robert is the only man left standing) resonates with the nationalist discourses of the opening sequence which tell us that this film brings us 'the story of one of Canada's own women, Maria Chapdelaine'. The narrative ultimately stresses the importance of transmitting the heritage of the pioneering ancestors and guaranteeing the nation's future. Love of the sort she has experienced earlier has no place. The temptation of the wild and the passionate only drove her mad, as we saw. Land, family and religion are the values to which she must commit. This slightly Pétainist discourse is rather out of place, one feels, in 1950s' France, particularly coming from Marc Allégret, a man of the left and a disciple of André Gide [6] – unless we consider that in the film Maria has, in a Gidean sense, taken the 'narrow path': that of the commonplace and common sense. Perhaps, most crucially, Allégret sought to re-unite with his fetish actor of the 1930s: Michèle Morgan – the star he brought to light in *Gribouille* (1937) and *Orage* (1938) before she went to Hollywood during the Occupation.[7]

Conformity is the exact opposite of the eponymous heroine's behaviour in *Le Mariage de mlle Beulemans*. This Franco-Belgian co-production offers a comedic treatise on marriage, to say nothing of a dig at Belgium's least favourite francophone neighbours, the French. As such, this film did remarkably well at the box office in France, with an audience of 1.1 million. Set in Brussels in 1890 (although some of the exteriors are shot in Bruges), it shows us a determined young woman, Suzanne Beulemans (Francine Vendel), far in advance of her years, not to say those of the Belle Epoque! She makes her own choices and casts aside her intended, whom she discovers has another secret life with a mistress and a child. She challenges his cowardice, obliges him to make an honest woman of his mistress by overcoming his class prejudices ('she is a mere laundry-worker' he protests) and recognize the paternity of his child. Having once sorted out her ex-fiancé, she then feels free to pursue her own interests, which include running her father's election campaign for President of the Belgian Breweries Association and blowing hot and cold over the young Parisian, Albert (Christian Alers), who has come to work in her father's brewery. There are two major reasons for her intemperate relations with Albert. The first is the example in marriage offered by her bickering parents (played by Elise Bernard and Hubert Daix); the second is a linguistic one – 'we do not speak the same language' she keeps saying to the poor confused Albert. Both are sources for her misgivings about the matrimonial state – her parents' arguing makes her unhappy; she sees how their love has been transformed into pettiness and meanness. Language barriers do not just come down to the Belgian thick, guttural French accent or dialect, or to the fact that the Belgian workers at the brewery ostracize Albert for his fancy Parisian ways of expressing himself. The issue is also one of integrity and honesty. As Suzanne says: 'here everyone speaks their mind' (implying that the French do not). Thus she admonishes her parents to be nicer to each other. And in the end, Albert proves himself an eloquent match for her: he gives a stirring speech in support of her father's candidacy, persuading the assembled voters to elect him President, then sways Suzanne with his marriage proposal.

The Belgian-born set designer, René Moulaert, captures the ponderous weight of the Belgian bourgeoisie's Flemish interiors that seek, unsuccessfully, to oppress Suzanne.[8] Her parent's home is overstuffed with furniture and plants (aspidistras to all appearances) which serve to display their status and wealth – even if they are penny-pinching and reluctantly replace the broken gas incandescent mantles and recycle dirty, fly-stained sugar cubes for their guests by wiping them clean. Suffocation beckons, morally and physically, and Suzanne is right to resist becoming stifled by them in turn, for we suspect these trappings of wealth have not helped the rather overweight Monsieur and Madame Beulemans find harmony in their married life.

Moulaert also did the décors for *C'est arrivé à Aden*, a film with a similarly spirited demoiselle in the form of Albine Ordioni (Dany Robin). Again very popular (2 million audience) it tells the tale of a troupe of actors who are obliged to dock in the British-owned port of Aden, located in the South Yemen. As they await the next passenger boat, the women actors are courted by the British soldiers stationed at the garrison and Albine falls for Captain Burton (Jacques Dacqmine). Because they are short of funds, the director of the troupe, Zafarana[9] (Robert Manuel) agrees to put on a performance of three plays over three days; *Othello*, *La Surprise de l'amour* (a Marivaux master-servant comedy), and *Ernestine découche* (a bedroom farce). We can observe – as indeed does the local British prelate (Michel Etcheverry) and the Governor Sir Richard Wilkinson (André Luguet) – that there is a progressive decline in 'taste' and morals in this choice of texts. As if to point to the British hypocrisy (not just in their desire to censor the more risqué sections of these plays), these three performances punctuate the unfolding saga of relations between the British and the local Arab Prince Khamarkhar (the blacked-up Jean Bretonnière). In short, as the Governor becomes more and more desperate to persuade the Prince to sign a treaty of alliance, so he stoops lower and lower in his means to an end. Noting the Prince's attraction to Albine, he invites him to the first performance. Unfortunately, the Othello character, Lusignan (André Versini) another of Albine's suitors, when blacked up for his role, looks and is dressed in an identical manner to the Prince. The insult is felt deeply until the Governor offers the Prince some theatre glasses to better examine Albine's beauty. With each performance, he offers increasingly more powerful telescopic instruments (binoculars, telescope) to the Prince, who is determined that she is his and refuses to sign unless he gets her. The Governor fervently hopes, for the sake of the treaty-signing, that Albine can be bought by the Prince's many gifts. But Albine refuses to be made into an object of exchange. Moreover, she rejects Captain Burton when she realizes that, whilst not a cad, he will always put duty above love to the point of acting as a pimp for the British government. When the Governor orders Burton to persuade her that she must befriend the Prince in order to get the treaty signed, she asks, 'Do you realize the job you are doing?' Meantime, the Prince, tired of waiting for people to do his bidding, kidnaps Albine at the end of the third play (the bedroom farce, appropriately). The French Ambassador complains to the Governor. A major diplomatic incident threatens to explode: 'You have already stolen our Joan of Arc,' thunders the Ambassador, 'we will declare war if Albine is not returned to us.' The Governor sends Burton and his troops to reclaim her. To no avail; Albine is happily installed with her Prince, whom she has tamed into more seemly (western) ways. The Prince signs the treaty regardless, whereupon Albine takes the Prince home with her to Paris, where, we assume, he will learn still more civilized ways with his French wife.

The political cultural resonances of this film are rather interesting to unpick since they straddle the two moments (1897 and 1956). By 1897, Aden was a long-established British crown colony (75 square miles) and the port was an important *entrepôt* or way-station for the British cargo steamers en route to India via the Suez Canal. Pierre Benoît, the author of the novel, *Les Environs d'Aden*, from which this film is adapted, served as a soldier in North Africa at the turn of the last century (1900s) before becoming a civil servant and subsequently an author.[10] He knew this world of military intrigue, therefore. His second novel, whilst a far more light-hearted affair than his first, *Koenigsmark*, is not, as with the film, without its side-swipes at the British. We should remember that, as far as the French were concerned, the Suez Canal was 'theirs'; designed by the French engineer Lesseps, it was a French creation and the Canal Company was a French corporation until the British took it over in 1882. Benoît undoubtedly had British perfidy in mind in his novel, set in 1897, inasmuch as they try to use Albine as a pawn to secure the signing of a treaty of alliance with the Prince of Khamarkhar (possibly a thinly disguised renaming of the Sultan of Kamaran). The film's timing, 1956 (shot in the spring and released in August of that same year), could hardly be more apposite since it coincides with the Suez crisis – when President Nasser of Egypt, having first obtained the departure of British troops in June 1956, then went onto nationalize the canal in July. It was equally a crisis for the French, however, since it was as much a main route of goods transportation for them as for the British. The French, British and Israelis attempted to mount a coup to regain control of the canal only to find their plan scuppered by the Americans and the Canadians, who insisted they forego their attack on Egypt.

In terms of gender politics, Albine is a strong character. She decides how she will be treated and determines what she wants from life. She refuses to be manhandled by any of her suitors – even the Prince, after he absconds with her, since she soon puts him straight on how to treat her. She is not disaffected with the idea of love, however, and clearly hopes to find a suitable lover. Wearied by all the shenanigans between the British and the Prince, she briefly retreats into the idea of proposing marriage to one of her actor-colleagues, Grémilly (Jacques Dubuy), whom she knows is in love with her. But, bravely, he refuses her proposal and she readily recognizes that he is too pure and kind for someone as capricious as she. In this rather moving scene, honesty prevails, thus putting paid to the Governor's rather snooty remark about the French (and Albine in particular) that they 'have no moral values'. In fact, they are the only two characters who do – for neither can be bought. Interestingly, Grémilly plays Iago in their performance of *Othello*, yet he would never betray Albine; if anything he helps her be true to her heart.

With half a century's distance from this film and epoch, it is not helpful to be critical of the 'blacking-up' process that occurs in this film. It is worth noting its presence, however, because this film has elements of the authentic which show an understanding of Arab culture (emanating from Benoît, doubtless) and, moreover, because what levels of racism are present are somewhat counter-intuitive (there are some parallels to be drawn also with the way Becker, in his *Ali Baba et les quarante voleurs*, challenges racist stereotyping – see Chapter 5). On several occasions, the westerners are reminded that they are not following Arab protocol when in the presence of the Prince. The Prince's outrage at the duplication of his person in the flesh in the form of Othello makes complete sense. It is an accidental offence, but it crosses a line (producing graven images of or masquerading as royalty is a taboo). His violent reaction at the Governor's ball, when he is introduced to Albine and she touches him on the arm, is also the result of a misunderstanding – Albine is unaware of the socio-sexual rules of conduct which, in Arab law, dictate that women should not touch men in public. Yet, once the Prince has absconded with Albine, this is where shifts occur which smack of western superiority – to say nothing of the neutralization of the exotic. First, she forbids him from taking her by force; if he is to win her heart then he has to woo her to gain her favours. Second, she refuses to wear the veil (in order to conform to Arab law). Finally, and most significantly, she has so 'tamed' her man that he agrees to return to

Paris with her (as man and wife) to make a new life. In short, the counter-intuitive nature of this racism ends up by stating that a white French woman can marry a black Arab man and bring him home to live in France. Given the climate of hostility in France towards the homogenized concept of the Arab as the 'Algerian terrorist', such a happy outcome in reality is very unlikely.

These 'out of Paris' love intrigues offer a mixed picture, then, in terms of marriage. On the one hand there are some happy beginnings – *Les Belles de nuit, Le Mariage de mlle Beulemans* – to which we can add *Le Sérénade au Texas* and *Miquette et sa mère* (where again it is the strong women who get their man). But, on the other, there are the marriages of compromise such as Maria Chapdelaine's, or ones where the women feel trapped, as in *La Maison Bonnadieu*, which will serve as my last brief example. Madame Bonnadieu (Danielle Darrieux) may be bored by her bourgeois life in a provincial French town but she manages to counter her boredom by leading a secret liaison with an attractive young man, Pascal (Michel François). Her husband's attempts to prevent this only lead her to set her sights higher for her next lover. Bernard Blier plays the hapless husband who runs a corset-making factory (hence the title of the film). Yet, for all that he constructs these edifices of containment of the female body, he cannot contain his wife. In one remarkable scene, as he sits in his office in despair of ever controlling his wife, he hallucinates his dummy corsets twirling and dancing around in his show-room – an ironic waltz to his ineffectual husbandry. We are hard pressed to know who to sympathize with in this dysfunctional marriage: the emasculated husband or the unfulfilled wife.

In terms of gender politics we have commented quite fully on the strength of women in these films but said little about the men, who, for the most part, are reduced to a very second order. Some are stripped of their masculinity and made to look ridiculous, as with poor Monsieur Bonnadieu, who resorts to his sick-bed when all other plans to contain his wife are without effect. Furthermore, he completely fails to woo her back into his bed via his new jaunty attire – in tweed plus-fours and hunting jacket he looks quite a fright, it has to be said, and certainly does not give off the aura of a seductive gentleman. In this range of films, older men are portrayed as lecherous types (mostly embodied by Saturnin Fabre) who, for the longest time, outwit their less able but much younger rivals (as in *Miquette et sa mère*). If they display strong athletic and sexual masculinity, as with two of Maria's suitors (François and Lorenzo) in *Maria Chapdelaine*, they fall weak-bodied into the snow and die – and it is her least virile of suitors, Robert, who (more like a brother than a sexual partner) finally gets her hand in marriage. His one concession to modernity is that he learns to read and write so he can be at the same level as his erstwhile childhood friend Maria and be a match for her. Yet it is this newly-acquired skill that unwittingly brings about the death of one of his rivals, François. He sends this vagabonding trapper a letter telling him how much Maria loves him, warning him that he must come home and claim her before he makes his own move to capture her heart. It is in his attempt to get home that François falls foul of the mighty Canadian blizzard. In *Sérénade au Texas*, Jacques Gardel (Luis Mariano) is a gentle provincial *ingénu* most remarkable for his love of singing and soft gentlemanly manners.

When he has to traipse over to Texas to claim his inheritance of the town of Big Bend, it is not he who takes action against lawless corruption of the macho bullies, embodied by the Black Horsemen (*Cavaliers Noirs*) and their unpleasant ruthless leader Dawson (Jean Paqui) who want to steal Jacques' land from him. Rather, it is the gun-carrying, trouser-wearing Sylvia (Sonia Ziemann) who steps into the breach and galvanizes men and women to outwit the baddies. Jacques had first encountered Sylvia on his way to Big Bend. She took pity on him and his useless laywer, Quilleboeuf (Bourvil), and offered them a ride in exchange for signing up with her small troupe of travelling performers (consisting of her father, her sister, and herself). Sylvia's bravery inspires Jacques (by now very much in love with her) to fight the bullies, and his reward, finally, is her hand in marriage. There is little doubt whose ambition will drive that relationship, however. Newly enriched by the oil discovered on his land, Jacques sells it all back to the townsfolk at a reasonable price and uses the money to set up his wife's dream cabaret theatre. The closing sequence gives us a fabulous dance routine set against fantastic stage designs of an imaginary American city – and, of course, Jacques/ Mariano singing *Ma Sérénade au Texas*.

Men in these films, then, are bossed about or dominated by the women. They are less than virile in many of the narratives; become tamed by their woman in others – an odd kind of submission to the domestic sphere, if we consider the truth of those times (as much as with the 1950s) where women had so little power. These costume dramas serve, therefore, as a displacement of the male's imaginary fears when confronted by women, namely, that his is not the stronger sex after all, that men are more acted upon than are agents and, therefore, less in charge of their destiny than they might at first believe. As we shall now go on to see, even when men – military this time – believe they do have agency, in the end it is a false truth. They lie to themselves in their assuredness that they can control the love situation they find themselves in – ultimately at a terrible price.

Beware the military – love and suicide

Three years separate the release of *Les Grandes manoeuvres* (1955) and *Christine* (1958). Both films were very popular with audiences (if not with the critical film press). *Les Grandes manoeuvres* won the Prix Louis Delluc. Clair, Philipe and Morgan took the Victoires awards for 1955. Indeed, with a 5 million audience, *Les Grandes manoeuvres* is the strongest draw of all the Belle Epoque films (with *French CanCan* a close second on 4 million). Strong star vehicles in the former film, Gérard Philipe and Michèle Morgan, undoubtedly drew spectators to Clair's film, whilst curiosity about the new star, 17-year-old Romy Schneider, drew those to *Christine* (2.8 million). She had recently starred in a series of Austrian-produced films, *Sissi*, about the young princess of the Austro-Hungarian Empire. These had been huge hits with French audiences; doubtless they were keen to see her in a French film. She was partnered by a then relatively unknown Alain Delon; this film effectively launched his career.

Both films are French-Italian co-productions and are shot in Eastmancolor, so we expect quite light pastel shades to dominate – as indeed they do. Thus, when colours stand out through their strength (as with the officers' uniforms) or their garishness (as with some of the women's costumes) then we need to pause and consider what is going on. Both films were costumed by Rosine Delamare, so we can anticipate a consistency in style, since both films are set around the same late period of the Belle Epoque: 1910s for *Les Grandes manoeuvres*; 1907 for *Christine*. Both films, although produced and released some three years apart and shot by different directors of photography (Le Febvre and Matras respectively), nonetheless have similarities in terms of fairly static camera work, thus allowing character movement within the frame to create meaning. As we shall also see, the same is true for the similarity in set design (by Barsacq and d'Eaubonne respectively), which again brings these two films into closer resemblance.

The two films tell a not-dissimilar tale of love and betrayal, although *Les Grandes manoeuvres* is undoubtedly the more cynical of the two. It does, after all, engage with the lives of a more mature couple. Marie-Louise (Morgan) is a Parisian divorcée and Armand (Philipe) a well-established lieutenant in the dragoons and a committed seducer. Both, therefore, know about the game of love and one can suspect that Marie-Louise is going to be particularly careful, given her divorced status and her move from Paris to a small provincial town, where she is well aware that tongues will wag. Although Clair calls his film a *comédie dramatique* it is an intensely bitter-sweet dramatic comedy. It may well begin in a comic vein, with Armand and his friends boasting about his easy conquests, but when he agrees to a bet that he can seduce any woman chosen by chance before he has to leave in a month's time on manoeuvres, little does he suspect that he will fall genuinely in love with Marie-Louise, or, indeed, that his hideous bet will be revealed to her by his rival, thus causing her to reject him forever. This outcome, arguably tragically, punishes him for his former cruelty to all his other lovers who, ironically, have a role in uncovering the truth about Armand to Marie-Louise when she overhears them singing a song about him in the local café-concert.

Until he finally recognizes the truth of his sentiments, Armand behaves like the flirt and supercilious joker he has become as a result of years in the army where the predominant mood is one of ennui. On two occasions he gets involved in a duel: in both instances because of a devil-may-care arrogance and flippancy. The first time is with Victor Duverger (Jean Desailly), his rival for Marie-Louise's favours. They get into an argument over her. Armand insults Duverger, who contemplates a duel – but, given his *nouveau-riche* background, he is completely unskilled in the art of duelling (be it swords or pistols), thus he manages to wriggle out of it. Duverger's family put pressure on the dragoons' colonel and Armand is posted on manoeuvres for a fortnight. Towards the end of the film, Armand again gets involved in a duel, this time with his friend, Félix (Yves Robert). Armand insults Félix over his girlfriend, Lucie (Brigitte Bardot); and Félix retorts with a rude comment about Marie-Louise. They argue, Armand goes too far and will not apologize, so a duel is fixed. Knowing his friend is a poor shot, Armand does not take aim but shoots into the ground – a decent thing to do, some might say, but one that does not show respect for the rules of engagement and, therefore, the opponent (as Félix himself states).

Armand's fortnight's banishment of course places his chances of winning the seduction bet under severe pressure. Not that he is any longer concerned because, by the time he has to take his leave, his interests lie only with his love for Marie-Louise. During their separation, an intense exchange of love-letters ensues. That is, until Marie-Louise overhears the women in the café-concert talking and singing about his seducer tricks. Realizing what a dupe she has been, she refuses any further contact. Armand returns and pleads with her, saying he is a changed man. But she tells him she is afraid of him, even though, eventually, she gives him a second chance (thanks to his duel with Félix, where she fears for his safety). However, he has omitted to tell her about the bet. Thus, when Duverger presents her with the signed evidence – which includes her name as the randomly-selected victim – all is lost. With this final proof that she is right to be afraid of him, she banishes him. How, she asks him, can she ever trust a man who thinks nothing of a woman's honour and can cheapen her in such a way; when would she ever know if he was telling the truth (see figure 20.2 below)?

Figure 20.2: Marie-Louise (Michèle Morgan) still looking unconvinced as to Armand's (Gérard Philipe) integrity. © Filmsonor

The young couple in *Christine* are far less worldly-wise. Frantz (Alain Delon) is trapped in a relationship with an older married woman, Baronness Léna (Micheline Presle). He got involved with her under the advice of his more experienced friend, Théo (Jean-Claude Brialy), who sold him on the benefits of such an alliance, arguing it freed him from being pursued in marriage. Sadly, he omitted to tell his friend that it did not spare him the danger of being challenged to a duel by the affronted husband, as happens here. Paradoxically, whilst it is clear that Christine (Romy Schneider) is the young ingénue when it comes to matters of love, nonetheless, she is quite clued up on the soldiers' reputation as seducers and she is not an easy conquest. She also has the ability to see through lies and deception. Her own decency is not quite matched by Frantz, for, even though he very early abandons any idea of attempting to seduce her, he cannot quite bring himself always to tell the truth, and therein lies the fatal flaw. He realizes quite quickly that he is in love with Christine, but, when given the opportunity to make a clean breast of things about his mistress, he fails to do so. On an outing together, Christine suspects that the woman she sees him with briefly in the tea-garden (Léna) is more than a mere acquaintance and she even offers him the chance to explain, but he brushes it aside. In affairs of the heart, it is he who is the ingénue – or even quite child-like, since when confronted by Christine's openness he cannot always respond with honesty. Moreover, he is far too readily influenced by Théo and yet lacks the lightheartedness with which his friend deals with women. Thus, he gets embroiled and is unable to behave in a cavalier fashion towards women, including his mistress. In a very touching scene that shows his own lack of experience as a hardliner soldier-seducer, he tries to release himself from his obligations to his mistress. He begins in the way advised by Théo, brutally matter-of-fact. But he very quickly reverts to his own type and makes the break in a far more amicable way (he and Léna tenderly burn their love letters together). The saddest moment comes when he is unable to tell Christine that he has been challenged to a duel by Léna's husband, even more so when it is evident, from the conditions set by the affronted Baron (Jean Galland), that he, Frantz, will succumb to the first bullet.

Clair's film, *Les Grandes manoeuvres*, is set in a very clean 'somewhere' in the French provinces in the early 1910s – the sets, designed by Barsacq, are of an elegant eighteenth-century garrison town, with façades in greys and pastel yellows, that could as easily be an imaginary Fontainebleau as it could the old city-centre of Nancy. The interiors of these buildings are equally tasteful, if bland, in their grey and white embossed wallpaper and colourings of a similar ilk (see Marie-Louise's shop in figure 20.3 below).

The officers' garrison apartments are equally sober. The one exception is the art-nouveau décor of the café-concert; the place where slightly saucy songs are sung and young women singers parade themselves in risqué, brightly-coloured outfits. The sets tell us that this is a provincial town of bourgeois respectability, with a tiny corner of naughtiness. Yet it is one where everyone whispers behind each other's backs. The gossip factor is high. Men and women fear scandal and are concerned to keep up appearances. Marie-Louise's suitor, the manipulative and cowardly Duverger, is continuously anxious about rules of decorum and social propriety. His two very nasty meddlesome sisters, Juliette (Lise Delamare, Rosine

Delamare's sister) and Jeanne (Jacqueline Maillan), do their utmost to thwart their brother's plans to marry Marie-Louise because she is a divorcée. This loss of social status as divorcée also makes Marie-Louise afraid of scandal, even though she is tempted by the handsome but dangerous Armand.

The costumes, by Rosine Delamare, tell us a great deal about the characters. For the most part, Marie-Louise wears very demure outfits, doubtless in her efforts to fit in. Her day outfits are invariably composed of a grey satin pleated skirt, slightly ruched at the back, high-neck blouses in light colours (white or pastel green), some with lace, others buttoned up to a collar, and (if she is going out) a smart jacket in grey with a velvet collar (see figure 20.3 below).

Only occasionally does she stand out in her attire (see figure 20.2 above). There are four occasions where her outfits are spectacular, either for their consummate delicate taste or for the strength of their difference from her normal day attire. In the former category, she wears a couple of ball gowns, one in light lilac satin the second in cream. In the latter category, the most striking is her Sunday-best dress in polka-dot muslin (black dots on white) which she wears when she calls in on the Duverger sisters for tea. There she is snubbed and goes on to the tea-dance in the park. Finally, the rich blue *tailleur* ensemble she wears to the wedding of the *préfet*'s daughter stands out in its boldness from her normal palette of fabric colours.

Figure 20.3: Marie-Louise in demure outfit in her shop – and Lucie (Brigitte Bardot) for that matter! © Filmsonor

In all instances, however, the elegance and good taste of her outfits mark her out against the range of vulgarity and poor taste of the provincial womenfolk, who think nothing of wearing strident yellow bows in their hats and bright saffron-yellow dresses to the local café-concert. Even Brigitte Bardot's Lucie is a bit too pink and showy with her bows (see figure 20.3 above); and the two Duverger sisters look like wedding cakes in their evening gowns and hardly fare much better in their predominantly rust-brown day dresses. None are a match for the sophisticated Parisienne, except when it comes to their tongues – Lucie's included. They are as responsible for wreaking havoc in Marie-Louise's life as is Armand and his feckless band of bored army mates.

As for the men, apart from Duverger in civilian clothes, we note very little about the costumes other than those of the soldiers. Duverger is clad, for the most part, in suits of either slate-grey, bland beige or metallic-blue. The fabric is a satinated light worsted, so the effect is quite shiny – nothing sticks (exactly as Duverger would want it in his business affairs, which he hopes his attachment to Marie-Louise will not compromise). The soldiers in their dark-blue tunics and red trousers certainly add a dash of strong colour to the predominantly pastel shades of the other costumes (and sets) – but their uniformity also gives us pause for thought. Apart from pips or decorations on the shoulders, it is hard to distinguish one rank from another – and even then, the outsider (such as Lucie) would need to be told what they signify. Thus, the ranking signifiers speak to those already in the know, namely the military, suggesting an institutionalized order of meaning. This ranking also attests to the fact that everyone who is part of it knows their place, accepts the hierarchy of authority and succumbs to it – even Armand. The uniform in this mode bespeaks conformity, a willingness to be disciplined and, indeed, punished if rules are contravened. Yet, once the uniform is on display, outside of the military confines of institutionalized conduct and discipline, it takes on another meaning. This time it is about show and performance, about being a peacock. It acts as a disguise, almost, giving the wearer free licence to become the unruly male on the hunt for female trophies, and other acts of transgression. Whether in its institutionalized or counter-institutionalized mode, the uniform clearly has fetishistic value. Masculinity asserts itself in both: in the former it takes the form of male-bonding camaraderie, but one where the leader is adulated (in this case Armand); in the latter, all parts of the uniform are on display, either lovingly polished (belts, boots, silver buttons, képis or helmets) or startlingly clean (jackets, trousers and smart brown gloves). The effect is dazzling, so much so that the effect is for the person within them to become that uniform.

Clair, who wrote the script, declared that the film was a portrait of provincial town morality;[11] which of course gets disrupted when an outsider (Marie-Louise in this context) moves in. Marc de Launey, in his analysis of the film, is right when he points out that Clair is fairly unsympathetic to most of the characters.[12] Of the town-dwellers, the men are mostly spineless and the women back-biting. The military are noisy, proud, brash and aggressive. Male camaraderie prevails only in the ranks of the soldiers. Elsewhere, amongst the provincial bourgeoisie, it is everyone for themselves.

Several critics of the time dismissed Clair's film as bearing no relation to contemporary 1950s' France and labelled it as sentimental nostalgia.[13] But this is rather to miss the point. Within Clair's sketch of bourgeois provincial life lies, embedded, a portrayal of the boredom experienced by the soldiers who, in their ennui, as they wait for war, think nothing of playing cruel games of seduction on the young women, or drinking and daring each other into dangerous escapades, and so on. This black sense of ennui is but one of this film's several resonances with 1950s' France, where ennui was *the* philosophical angst of the decade (Sartre wrote about it nowhere more elegantly so than in *La Nausée*). The fear of war was still amongst the French citizenry of the 1950s – not just a Third World War, but colonial wars – particularly in the mid-1950s (1954 saw the end of 97 years of colonial rule in Indochina; and the beginning of the war with Algeria). The female social condition, where women still did their husband's bidding, was also a truth of those times. The anonymous critic in *Le film français* gets it right when they talk about the newness of the film, not just in relation to its expert use of Eastmancolor technology and new décor materials but also in terms of its bitter-sweet assertion of male friendship against the cynicism and melancholic irony of the love narrative.[14] The mirror the film holds up, therefore, is to the paradox of the times: fraternal love (*fraternité,* a core element of the French Republican triumvirate) did not save France in the last world war, nor is it working now in the light of the divided nation over the colonial wars.

A similar message comes through in *Christine*. Fraternal love does not help spare Frantz from the Baron's deadly bullet, even if his close friend Théo resigns his commission in protest at the army's refusal to intercede and put a stop to the duel. We also see soldiers, driven by boredom, at play in the game of love and seduction. Théo, for his part, has a whole repertoire of rules and maxims as to how the game should be played. He even repeats a well-known saying from Napoleon, namely, that 'in love, the sole possible route is escape.'[15] Given the refusal to engage with emotions seriously, love on these terms is a ritual used to fill time. Yet it is a trajectory Frantz does not follow in relation to Christine; and in relation to Léna, it has to be said he was fairly constant, since the affair had been going on for a year. Even Théo, once he has left the army, seems happy enough to settle down with Christine's best friend Mizzie (Sophie Grimaldi).

The film is set in 1907 Vienna. The play from which it is adapted, *Libelei*, is by Arthur Schnitzler. Pierre Gaspard-Huit's *Christine* is a remake (of sorts) of an earlier version made by Max Ophuls (*Libelei*, 1933) which starred Romy Schneider's mother Magda in the lead role. There are other curious mirrorings of circumstances. Gaspard-Huit used Christian Matras as his director of photography, Jean d'Eaubonne as his set designer, and Rosine Delamare for costumes – all collaborators with Ophuls on *Madame de...*; and, as we know, Matras and d'Eaubonne worked on Ophuls' other 1950s' films. And yet, the film has nothing of the elaborate baroque of d'Eaubonne's sets for Ophuls. Indeed, with the exception of the ornate ball-room, the Vienna Opera house and the rather lugubrious apartment rooms of the Baron and his wife Léna, the sets in *Christine* bear remarkable similarities to those of Barsacq for *Les Grandes manoeuvres* in their over-riding sobriety and simplicity (see figure

20.4 below). Whilst location shooting took place in Vienna, the studios used were Boulogne Studios, the same as for *Les Grandes manoeuvres*. These studios were remarkably effective for Eastmancolor production since, of all the French studios, they possessed the highest electrical energy output – and thus were able to give the film process of Eastmancolor the maximum light-effect it needed.[16] This could explain why both films look so alike in their brightness. Matras had a reputation as one of the most respected and admired lighting cameramen in the business and it certainly is in evidence in *Christine*.[17] Yet the camera, as with his work on *Maxime*, is overall quite lacking in movement, with three notable exceptions – all of which mark turning points in the narrative. The first is a tracking and panning shot of young people waltzing at an outdoor tea-dance. This takes place early on in the film, just before Frantz meets Christine. The second is, again, a pan and tracking of a dance sequence, this time a ball at which Frantz and Léna are present and are twirling around and talking at cross-purposes. Frantz is desperate to tell her he needs to end the relationship; Léna is equally desperate to break the good news that her husband is about to leave for a fortnight, which will free them to be together. However, another of Léna's admirers sneakily suggests to the Baron that there is more to Léna and Frantz than meets the eye, which, in turn, sets in motion the beginnings of the terrible dénouement. On the very evening that Frantz has summoned the courage to break with Léna, everything falls apart. This falling apart is heralded by the third example of the most mobile of shots: the series of crane pan and tilt shots in the Vienna Opera House (performing *Don Juan* of all things)

Figure 20.4: Example of d'Eaubonne's simplicity of set design – Christine (Romy Schneider) in foreground (*Christine*).[18]

where the Baron begins to have his suspicions confirmed. Noting the absence of Frantz in the audience, he leaves the opera mid-way to return home, glimpses Frantz as he leaves by the back door, finds the key to Frantz' apartment in his wife's secret drawer (which once had housed the burnt letters), confronts both her and Frantz in turn with their adulterous relationship and sues for the duel.

In terms of costumes for *Christine,* we find a similar play with contrasts as we did in *Les Grandes manoeuvres,* although this time more complexly so. Marie-Louise's outfits spoke of her restraint, her desire to fit in, at the same time as they pointed to her sophistication as a Parisienne when measured against the outfits of the provincial townswomen. This time, Delamare has three distinct types of women to costume. First, the two women who have the greatest impact on Christine's well-being, Mizzie and Léna, are dressed in such a way that they clearly act as foils for Christine's innocence and virginality. Léna is always in very dark or black attire; sophisticated, yet already in mourning for her lost youth, her empty marriage, and her doomed affair with Frantz. But also, of course, the black widow who casts a deathly shadow on Frantz and Christine's burgeoning love for each other – as Christine had first feared when seeing Léna with Frantz in the tea-garden and as, later on, when all is lost and Frantz is dead, she so aptly acknowledges just before committing suicide by throwing herself off the balcony.

In complete contrast to Léna, and indeed Christine, is Mizzie with her bright, even garish, costumes. The first time we see her she is in a vivid purple day-dress at the tea-dance. Christine for her part is in a white satin *tailleur* with pink polka dots. She wears a three-quarter sleeved bolero-style jacket, a skirt slightly flared at the mid-calf adorned with a pink belt, and a high-collared white blouse with pink buttons. Even her straw hat continues the pink theme with the ribbon. In a slightly later sequence when Mizzie, Théo, Christine and Frantz go out for a foursome picnic, Mizzie sports a light-yellow square-necked dress adorned with light-blue trim and decorated in places with fake cherries. Christine wears a simple white cotton dress with a pink belt, a high-neck with a little pink velvet bow-tie, a white ribbon in her hair. It is easy to see who is ready to be eaten by the seducer-wolf-soldier and who is not. In this sequence, Mizzie is only too happy to dive off behind the bushes with Théo for some serious dalliance. Christine is left with Frantz with only very rudimentary training on how to flirt – supplied by her rather forward friend Mizzie. Of course her tactics fail to work and she and Frantz agree to be friends and not to lie to each other (something Frantz will never fully be able to do).

What one can say about Christine's attire is that it is redolent with a tonal range, appropriately demure for a young twenty-year old virgin; thus, she wears light-grey or light-turquoise skirts in satin or taffeta, white, pale-pink or cream high-collared blouses, and *tailleurs* with smart little bolero jackets (see figure 20.5 below). Whilst most of this points to a well brought-up young miss (not to say schoolgirl) rather than a sophisticate, nonetheless, the presence of the bolero jacket is instructive since it was part of the new fashion look of the early 1900s. It reveals that Christine is keen to be up to date (in the same way as she is keen to be instructed in matters of flirtation by Mizzie). She is, then, fashion conscious,

Figure 20.5: Christine all buttoned up in demure attire with Josef. © Speva Films.

albeit modest with it. Only once, when out on her third date with Frantz, does she veer from the high-necked blouse to wear something vaguely daring. She and Frantz are in an open carriage, she is attired in a black and white chequered skirt, with a red belt (a significant change from the pink or yellow ones worn before), supported by other red accessories hinting at a wilder spirit and sexuality (red handbag, red ribbon around the hat). But, most significantly, she is wearing a V-neck white blouse with bobbin lace edging the décolleté V-neck. The outfit suggests a more coquette Christine (see figure 20.6 below). Especially since in the previous sequence with her ex-boyfriend Josef (Jacques Duby) she had been tightly buttoned up in a white blouse. At the cleavage she is wearing a small brooch which serves to draw our eyes, and Frantz's, to this part of her body.

Thus, this third date marks a turning point for her, a willingness to trust Frantz's sentiments. However, earlier in the film, Christine had mockingly told Frantz how she was well aware of the game of seduction the soldiers play: by the third date they are looking to extricate themselves. This particular third date she is on with Frantz draws to an end when they stop at the tea garden and, whilst Christine is off purchasing cakes, who should turn up but Léna, whom Frantz is obliged to greet. Christine slightly misreads the greeting – half-guessing that Léna might be Frantz's mistress. In a similar vein, Léna also misreads it, believing she still *is* Frantz's mistress. Neither readings are true, in one sense; but they are true insofar as Christine very obviously feels threatened by the encounter. Rightly so, since this moment

Figure 20.6: Christine in décolletée with Frantz. © Speva Films.

marks a new turning point in the film and their relationship (Frantz lies to her about Léna) which will shortly be brought to a tragic end. These readings bear a grain of truth, therefore. And, indeed, in the very next sequence there is yet another slight misreading. This time on the part of Léna's other admirer. Léna has come to Frantz's apartment but he stands her up. This proves to have been an impulsive move on her part because her admirer (who just happens to be in the neighbourhood) observes her leaving Frantz's building and puts two and two together. He then tells the Baron, with the results that we know.

Up until the moment when, towards the end of the film, Christine goes to her audition with the conservatory – to sing, of all things, *Ave Maria* – she has worn predominantly light-coloured outfits, often white, always demure blouses (with the slight exception of the V-neck mentioned above, and a décolletée evening-gown she wears to the opera). Here, she wears a dark grey satin daytime *tailleur*, consisting of a bolero-style jacket trimmed black bobbin lace on the bodice and black velvet on the lapels, a dark-grey skirt with a black belt, and a cream chiffon blouse with a jabot frill at the neck. The only other light touches, in terms of colour, are her straw hat (adorned with a black ribbon and cream silk roses), white kid gloves and white and black boots. At the very peak of her own personal success, it is as if her dark costume is foreshadowing the misery she is about to encounter. Yet she is blissfully unaware as she runs to share her success with Frantz who, once again, cannot bring himself to tell her the truth about his own plight in the form of the forthcoming duel with the Baron.

Poor Christine, who at the beginning of the film had rejected her stuffy boyfriend Josef by declaring 'I am only twenty, I want to live', then told Frantz, a few moments later, 'operas are not like life, I don't like stories that end badly', only to find herself caught in a very operatic-style melodrama of her own and then to toss herself over the balcony, just as the heroine of Puccini's *Tosca* (1900) had done before her.

Conclusion

Class issues run through these various love-intrigue films, as does their associated concern for respectability, which, in turn, brings in its wake malicious gossip and hypocrisy. And it is not just within the bourgeoisie that this behaviour is apparent. The military also lives by a code that merely reproduces class hierarchies. Thus, Franz's senior commander, the Colonel (Jean Davy), lets him go to his death rather than suffer the dishonour of asking his opponent, the crack-shot Baron, for twenty more paces in the pistol duel, which would give the inexperienced Franz a chance. Implicit also in this refusal to intervene is that the Colonel would rather lose his young lieutenant than have him marry the penniless Christine, an alliance that would demean the officer class. Bourgeois respectability and the price one has to pay are well embodied by Danielle Darrieux in her various vehicles and by Michèle Morgan in *Les Grandes manoeuvres*. I leave the last word on bourgeois respectability to Alain Ferrari, who sums up Darrieux' contribution to the Belle Epoque costume drama in the following terms:

> In the provinces as much as in Paris, people told each other pretty much everything, that is men did to each other; and amongst the women the same; but between husband and wife nothing much got said other than chit-chat and platitudes…Danielle Darrieux knew how to embody the cruel dilemma into which the woman of the 1900s had been forced: either keep forever the mask of respectability stuck to her face, or accept total exclusion from 'good society' and float in the cold winds of freedom.[19]

As we have seen in the Belle Epoque films under consideration, rare is the woman who gets her man, keeps her independence and her social standing. As with the other periods, this trope of oppression is a fairly constant one. All of this offers a pretty bleak image of joy in love or marriage, it has to be said. It is not possible, therefore, to attribute to the costume drama the idea that it sells an image that colludes with the overt thrust of 1950s' ideology where the role of women is concerned, namely, women happy in domestic life with many children. Rather it serves up, time after time, a warning to women on what awaits them if they behave transgressively. Thus in that respect it certainly serves patriarchal hegemony, albeit from a dramatically-negative discursive line: behave or else! But let us now move onto the last chapter and consider the four biopics set in this Belle Epoque era and see what occurs there.

Notes

1. Hémon was also the author of *Monsieur Ripois et la Némésis*, famously adapted by René Clément in 1954 with Gérard Philipe in the lead role. This novel was based on Hémon's sojourn in London prior to his departure for Canada. Tragically he was killed, in 1913 when struck by a train and never knew of the huge success of *Maria Chapdeleine* and very successful adaptation of *Monsieur Ripois*. For more details of this enigmatic personage see http://fr.wikipedia.org/wiki/Louis_Hémon accessed 09.09.2009.

2. Touati (1988, p. 32).

3. $500,000 according to Myro in *Variety* (13.12.1950, no page).

4. Myro in *Variety* claims it is a Franco-British quota-quickie (13.12.1950, no page). But these drew to an end in 1938. More likely it was part of the lively exchanges between the UK and continental Europe, post-war. Allégret had made another film in the UK a couple of years earlier, *Blanche Fury* (1948); he went on to make *Blackmailed/Mrs Christopher* (1951). Indeed, this period of late forties to early fifties is seen as Allégret's British period ('*période britannique*') http://www.cineartistes.com/fiche-Marc+All%E9gret.html, accessed 02.03.2009).

5. André Fortier (1981), in an overview article of the two existing versions made of *Maria Chapdelaine*, asks why Allégret agreed to make such a poor film. Fortier even goes as far to doubt whether Allégret had complete control over the scenario, particularly since he transforms one of the central characters, Lorenzo, into a hoodlum. *Variety* (cited above in footnote 4) is rude about it, as indeed is the anonymous reviewer in *Monthly Film Bulletin* (Vol. 18, No. 204, January 1951, p. 206). A wholly-French version had been made in 1934 by Julien Duvivier, this time in Canada. It was far more faithful to the original – for example: Lorenzo is kept as an entrepreneur and not turned into a gangster; he fails to persuade Maria to come with him to America (seen by him as the land of opportunity); the sobering event that pushes Maria to choose the traditional ways (remain on the land and marry her childhood chum) is her mother's death. Interestingly, Armand Thirard was originally Duvivier's DP for the film and indeed went to Canada for the first set of film rushes of the winter scenes. In the end, however, he was replaced by Jules Kruger for the exterior spring/summer shots and Georges Périnal for the studio shooting. It seems that Duvivier and Thirard had a falling out – since Duvivier was quoted as saying he would never separate from him (Ibid., p. 29). Thus, Thirard's return to shoot the entire story some sixteen years later has a bitter-sweet edge.

6. As Fortier (op. cit., p.29) points out. Allégret was also at one point Gide's lover (the liaison lasted from 1915 to 1927: http://en.wikipedia.org/wiki/Marc_Allégret, accessed 02.03.2009).

7. Morgan went to Hollywood in 1940. There she married Bill Marshall and had a son by him (Michael). She made four films, none of which she seems to be that proud: 'I'd rather they weren't seen over here' she declared upon her return to Paris in November 1945 (these titbits are to be found in 'Michèle Morgan perdue et retrouvée', *L'Ecran français*, No. 23, December 1945, pp. 6–9, no author name).

8. Much as he did for Cocteau's *La Belle et la Bête* (1946). In fact Moulaert is quite associated with seventeen-century Flemish interiors: *La Kermesse héroïque* (Feyder, 1935), Louis Daquin's *Patrie* (1945).

9. An odd name for a French troupe and its owner, particularly since it seems to refer to the ancient Yemeni walled-city of Zafar, some 300 miles north of Aden.

10. He first wrote *Koenigsmark* (1918) – a tragic love-story which was adapted to screen no less than three times (1923, 1935, 1953).

11. René Clair quoted in De Launey (1973, p. 65).

12. Ibid., p. 66.

13. De Launey quoting Bazin, op. cit., p. 64; Richer (1955: 39).

14. Review of *Les Grandes manoeuvres* in *Le film français*, No. 594, 4.11.1955, p. 13 (no author given).

15. A maxim which we first heard, interestingly, in the mouth of the General in *Madame de...*

16. See Barsacq (1970, pp. 295–98) for details on studio capacity.

17. See: http://movies.nytimes.com/person/101723/Christian-Matras/biography accessed 14.10.08.

18. Still image accessed from http://merveilleuseromy.typepad.fr/inoubliableromy/film1958christine/ 09.09.2009.

19. Ferrari (2006, p. 95).

Chapter 21

Making Li(v)es: Belle Epoque Biopics

There are four biopics (see figure 21.1 below) which fall into the Belle Epoque period, all relating to lives at the turn of the nineteenth century: *Le Procès du Vatican* and *Il est minuit Dr Schweitzer* (both by André Haguet, 1952), *La Belle Otéro* (Richard Pottier, 1954) and *Raspoutine* (Georges Combret, 1954).

Biopics

Procès du Vatican
1,326,384
Il est minuit Dr Schweitzer
3,300,484
La Belle Otéro
1,885,468
Raspoutine
2,216,785

Figure 21.1: Belle Epoque biopics (audience figures in bold).

The four films were made and released during the first half of the decade, during a turbulent post-war political phase for France on both a national and international scale (the legacy of the Occupation, the struggles to assert a Fourth Republic, economic and social modernization, the Cold War, colonial wars) and it will be interesting to observe what interfaces might occur between film artefact and 1950s' political culture. At first there seems to be little to suggest any immediate parallels; however, merely to consider the types of biopics will reveal that this is not so. The biopics fall into two very distinct categories that could not be more extreme in the difference between the two. On the one hand, we are presented with the excesses of two cultural icons that are not in fact French: the Spanish dancer Caroline Otéro and the Russian monk Rasputin. Both these personages led life to the full, even as they paid a heavy price for their excesses. Otéro capitalized as a performer on her talent and sex appeal, but gambled away her vast wealth. Rapsutin's mysticism and sexual appetites, when mixed with political meddling, proved too potent a cocktail and precipitated his assassination. On the other hand, spiritual goodness drives the lives of Thérèse de Lisieux (*Le Procès du Vatican*) and Dr Schweitzer. Audiences were, it seems, eager to see both sides of human nature, as the figures above make clear (figure 21.1). In Rasputin's case, moral turpitude and political shenanigans made for safe viewing precisely because they are embodied by the foreign other. It enables the nation's psyche to point a finger at the corruption of other nations. In Otéro's case, audience fascination with her story is less to do with her easy virtue and far more with her meteoric rise to stardom, tempered though it is by her disastrous love-life. Interestingly, nothing is made of her gambling addiction in the film. Undoubtedly, the female audience will draw its own conclusions about this woman who wants it all. All is not possible, the film tells us. Compromise has to hold sway over excess. As we know, Otéro fails to learn this lesson. Thus the film biopics of these larger-than-life people serve a triple purpose: first, a displacement onto the foreign other of a nation's unsavoury traits; second, a sense that retribution is the fate that befalls the mighty when they abuse their positions of power; third, professional success for women comes at a personal cost. Conversely, the two other biopics tell a very simple uplifting story: moral probity and restraint reap their reward in heaven and on earth. Thérèse and Dr Schweitzer's biopics serve well to remind the nation they can take pride in their national heroes and saints. In the early 1950s' political culture, given the uncertain climate of the times, such clear lines of demarcation when it comes to personal conduct would have reassured the several million spectators who were still facing the sometimes impenetrable complexities of their own age. The nomination of Auguste Pinay as prime minister in 1952 is a good example of this murky, somewhat sordid, political world. During the Occupation, he had voted in favour of Marshall Pétain and served on Vichy's national council. He also remained mayor of his town in the Loire. In 1945 he was declared ineligible for elected office. Yet, by claiming some tenuous link to the Resistance, he was soon able to re-enter political life and become premier. In fact, where the administration of the country was concerned, many ex-collaborators were returned as deputies and to political office. The Fourth Republic, therefore, was not as clearly separated from Vichy as myth would have it.[1]

Thus, some parallels can be drawn with the contemporary. But what is very clear is that these biopics make less reference still to the turn-of-the-nineteenth-century political arena than the pure fiction films. No mention of the various affairs and scandals that rocked the nation (especially not Dreyfus). No reference to the expanding empire, merely that Dr Schweitzer goes to Lambaréné in the French Gabon. Not a whiff of the shifting political scene, even though Aristide Briand (a major figure within the Socialist Left) was Caroline Otéro's long-time lover. The only exception to this silence is the inevitable mention of the outbreak of the Great War with Germany in *Raspoutine* and *Il est minuit Dr Schweitzer*. Inevitable, because Rasputin was a partisan for peace with Germany – a position that cost him his life (Russian officers suspected him of treason and spying for Germany). Inevitable, also, because as a German-Alsatian, Schweitzer was arrested at the outbreak of war (at midnight, hence the title of the film).

Pure in body and mind: reconstructing the real

In 1952, two biopics made by André Haguet were released – both based upon spiritually-minded persons. The one, Dr Albert Schweitzer, did get to fulfil his ambitions to serve humanity as a doctor in Africa. The other, Thérèse de Lisieux, who, despite her strong desire to be a missionary and go to Tonkin in China to save souls, could not – because of ill health. Nonetheless, she led a life of great deprivation and humility as a Carmelite nun and was eventually canonized (1925).

Thérèse was the last surviving daughter of quite elderly parents – she was born in 1873 (in Alençon) when Louis was 50, his wife, Zélie-Marie, 42. Both parents were extremely pious. When they married (in 1858) they had decided to live in abstinence as brother and sister. However, once dispensed of this austere devotion, they went on to have nine children, of whom only five, all daughters, survived. Zélie-Marie had determined that she would give up all her children to the church – and that is exactly what happened, although she died of breast cancer before she saw her wishes fulfilled. The family moved to Lisieux and, over the years, the five daughters entered orders, with four entering the most arduous of all orders: the Carmelites (in Lisieux).[2]

Haguet's film reproduces Thérèse's road to sainthood as faithfully as possible. His version of her life is based in her autobiography *L'Histoire d'une âme*, which, as we learn during the film, she was writing as she was dying of tuberculosis. As Haguet puts it: 'I cannot stress enough my desire to remain faithful to her story.'[3] Thus, in the film, we see her emerging from a childhood in which she loses her mother as a 4- year-old, is subsequently brought up, first, by one sister then another, only to see them both enter orders, leaving her abandoned yet again. It is small wonder, one feels, that she found solace for her lost 'mothers' in fervent religious practice and should want, in turn, to become a devout Carmelite. At nine, when left by her sister Pauline (her second mother), Thérèse became seriously ill. The illness lasted seven months until she implores the Virgin Mary to heal her. The sequence in the film reflects the severity of her physical distress; we see her hallucinate and have visions of the Virgin. This leads her to command that the statue of the Virgin be brought into her room. We witness the ardour of her appeal with her rapturous face bathed in white light emanating from the statue. Miraculously she recovers.

The film is composed of three parts: her early childhood, through until she gets her way and is allowed to join the Carmelite order at fifteen; her arduous novitiate; her final vows into the order and her subsequent death in 1897 (France Descaut plays the adult Thérèse, Marie-France the young child). Throughout the three parts we bear witness to her suffering and spirituality. Her suffering includes the numerous ordeals she is made to undergo (which are either confirmed to us by a male voice-over or graphic illustration) and the several bouts of illness, culminating in her long drawn-out death which lasts some 26 minutes (23 per cent of the film's length). As to her spirituality, we bear witness to it in a number of ways but most significantly through her ability to hear voices and have visions (of the Virgin Mary, Jesus and Saint Paul). She is able to intercede on behalf of others in life and in death. In life, we see a sequence in which, through prayer, she manages to save the soul of a condemned murderer. Her prayers reach him, in the nick of time and from afar as he ascends the scaffold to the guillotine, where he recants from his denial of his crime and confesses to God. On several occasions Thérèse miraculously recovers from her illnesses (thanks to her visions of the Virgin Mary) – even on her death-bed, she rises from the dead for a brief moment – fuelling the discourses around her saintliness. In death, we see how she protects the lives of soldiers on the front in World War One and saves the Carmelite convent in Lisieux from fire during a bombing raid in World War Two.

Clearly the main audience for a film biopic of this nature would be a Catholic one. But it is worth recalling that in 1952, the date of the film's release, the huge basilica of Sainte Thérèse of Lisieux, built in commemoration of this local saint and her miracles, was still in its final stages of construction (1929–1954) and religious fervour was far from dormant in lay Republican France of the 1950s. Audience figures for this film, at 1.3 million, would indicate that the timing of this film did much to help the cause of the basilica as a place of pilgrimage. What would especially attract the devout to the film is its cachet of authenticity. The spectator gets to see the interior life of the convent, including the various ceremonies from novitiate to final bride of Christ. The director Haguet managed to obtain special permission from Pope Pius XII to enter the convent where Thérèse had lived and died, accompanied by his set director, Jean Quignon, so that they could document it properly for its recreation in studio.[4] Indeed, Quignon recreates the stony-cold austerity of the convent where abstinence is all. Warmth emanates not from the spaces – which do seem (to an outsider) very harsh and incarcerating – but from the good hearts of a few of the sisters in the convent, most markedly Sister Geneviève (Catherine Fonteney), Thérèse's ailing mentor who dies shortly after Thérèse takes her final vows.

As part of the authentic, we get a sense of the divisions within the convent upon ideological and personal lines, and it is a vital force of the narrative. Thus, the Mother Superior (Valentine Tessier) is continually questioning Thérèse's motives in her quest for perfection in God's eyes. Does she not run the risk of the sin of pride?, she asks. Whilst she prevents Thérèse from undertaking the dangerous mission to China because of her ill-health, she thinks nothing of inflicting the hardest of chores on her in an effort to tame her so-called pride. The Mother Superior is also a believer in the more stringent practices of the Carmelites: the strictest observance of silence (thus Thérèse only finds out through her sister's eye movement that her father has died), and mortification of the flesh. A defiant Thérèse in the third part of the film suggests this practice of flagellation is wrong and she warns the indignant Mother Superior that 'after my death I can challenge your ways'. Even as Thérèse is dying, the Mother Superior still firmly believes that her humiliation of Thérèse over the past seven years is the only thing that has preserved her from 'becoming a little saint', adding 'God will judge me'. Perhaps it is for this reason that the ever-generous-spirited Thérèse, full of beatic love, forces some kind of reconciliation prior to her death by asking her to hear her confession.

Nothing, however, can stop a saint on a mission, as this film proves. Sister Geneviève assists Thérèse on her journey to perfection through suffering. After her crisis of doubt (a state known as dereliction) brought on by her physical suffering through tuberculosis, she has a series of visions (which occur during a raging storm) where she finally finds the path ('the little path' as she calls it) and can declare: 'At last I have found my vocation, it is love'. Later, on her death-bed, she declares: 'In death my mission will begin; I want to spend my heaven doing good on earth.' She will be, as she says, 'a missionary of love'. Just as her icon before her, Joan of Arc (with whom she solidly identifies), made a martyr of herself to what she perceived as a just cause, so too does Thérèse to her love of God.

Haguet's preoccupation with authenticity, already so much in evidence in *Le Procès au Vatican*, is equally present in *Il est minuit Dr Schweitzer*. Once again Jean Quignon is responsible for the set design, and his recreation of the village compound Schweitzer built in Lambaréné replicates the original exactly. The film also respectfully reconstructs a period in the life of a hero of France's colonial history. Schweitzer, an Alsatian protestant pastor in Strasbourg and an accomplished musicologist and musician, was horrified to read, in 1904, about the sufferings of the natives in the French Congo and decided to train as a doctor specializing in tropical medicine. By 1913 he was set to go to Lambaréné to establish a hospital to help contain malaria, leprosy, sleeping sickness and yellow fever. He travelled there with his wife, Hélène Bresslau, who was also medically trained. Between them they set up a compound which included a school, a surgery, a dispensary as well as a hospital with operating facilities, and isolation rooms for the infectious. However, once war with Germany was declared, Alsace, their homeland, became part of enemy territory, with the Germans ordering the mobilization of its men. As such, and according to the rules of war, the Schweitzers' situation in French Gabon was no longer tenable – they had become the enemy. As Germans, they were placed under house arrest by the French army but, sensibly, allowed to continue with their good work. In 1917, after four years, exhausted and unwell, the couple were officially arrested, deported and imprisoned in a garrison, first in the Hautes-Pyrénées, later in Saint-Rémy de Provence until July 1918. Upon their return to Alsace, now French territory, they were accorded French citizenship. Schweitzer returned to Lambaréné in 1924, equipped his hospital to receive thousands of suffering natives, and established a leper village for 200 victims of the disease. He described his service to the Africans as an act of atonement and, apart from visits to Europe to give fundraising organ recitals for his hospital, he remained in Lambaréné for the rest of his life.[5] In 1952 he was awarded the Nobel Peace Prize. He died in 1965.

The Schweitzer we see on screen, embodied by Pierre Fresnay, reflects this humanitarian reverence for life. Fresnay is in many ways the perfect fit. He, too, was something of an outsider. Born in Paris of Alsatian parents, he had an understanding of the strange dislocations suffered by that small region repeatedly torn by wars between France and Germany. He was also, like Schweitzer, a Protestant – another source of his outsider status in France, a predominantly Catholic country. During the Occupation he worked on a number of films (including the controversial *Le Corbeau*) produced by the German production company based in Paris – Continental. This work led to him to being imprisoned for six weeks after the Liberation (on charges of working with the enemy) even if, in the end, the charges were dropped and he was exonerated. Before the war, he established himself as both a film and theatre star, playing fictional roles in cinema as varied as those of a Marseillais sailor in Pagnol's *Marius* (1931, the film that launched his career), an anarchist (*Sous les yeux de l'Occident*, Marc Allégret, 1936), and a proud aristocratic soldier (*La Grande illusion*, Renoir, 1937). After the war, he took on a series of edifying roles of important historical persons – including the one under discussion here (see Chapter 14 for a discussion of his other costume drama roles).

Fresnay, then, could characterize precisely the deterritorialization felt by inhabitants of an occupied territory that is seemingly never quite French and never quite German. He knew how to mimic Schweitzer's thick Alsatian accent in a persuasively authentic manner – an accent that reveals the effects of a land so frequently re-territorialized that it can never achieve full native fluency in either domain. Fresnay's demeanour is such that we never, for one moment, doubt the goodness of this man. Indeed, the film itself opens with a line spoken from the Ten Commandments: 'Thou shall not kill'. And, as the voice of Jeanne Moreau tells us, over images of men at war seemingly dedicated to the perfectioning of death, 'one man stands out through his lifetime commitment to relieving suffering: this man, this Frenchman, is called Dr Albert Schweitzer.'

Yet this statement and the opening credits give us pause for thought on this reconstruction of a life, because there is a persistence with which the idea of Frenchness is asserted again and again. In the opening credits there is a curious juxtaposition both in terms of image and sound. The still image is of a black man's head, doubtless a native of French Gabon; an image that is confirmed by the sound track of the indigenous tam-tams. However, these tam-tams are quickly superseded by the swelling organ symphony music of French composer Charles-Marie Widor (played by the world renowned Marcel Dupré, one of his most gifted pupils – as indeed was Schweitzer). The credits proudly announce that all images from the Gabon were taken thanks to the support of Air France transport. The pianist (who dubs for Fresnay) is Raymond Trouard and the piano, we are told, is a Gaveau (from Paris). All of this grounds the Gabon we are about to see within an idea of Frenchness – and a civilized, cultured Frenchness at that. An idea that is confirmed by Moreau's voice-over mentioned above.

In 1952, Gabon was still part of France's equatorial territories (only gaining independence in 1960). It was, therefore, at the time of this film's release and in the national psyche at least, still part of the colonial might of France – Gabon was one of the richest African nations for timber, minerals (iron ore, manganese and uranium) and oil. The timing of the film could not have been more propitious since this was also the year that Schweitzer received the Nobel Peace Prize.[6] Thus, almost before the film begins, it bears heroic proportions: the greatness of the Frenchman Dr Schweitzer and the greatness of France as a civilizing force – all of this embodied in the star persona of Pierre Fresnay, one of the all-time great French actors. With such comforting images of France as an educative and caring empire-state, no wonder it attracted a huge audience (3.3 million spectators).

But the narrative has a couple of curious twists that are worthy of mention because they falsify the real story. The first is the deliberate omission of Mme Schweitzer, to whom the film is dedicated. In a voice-over, by Pierre Fresnay this time, we are told that 'we respectfully dedicate this film to Mme Albert Schweitzer, whose irreplaceable role next to Dr Schweitzer will not be evoked here.' No further reason is supplied (at the time she was still alive). Instead, this nurturing female presence is replaced by Marie, a young student nurse (played by Jeanne Moreau), who asks to go with Schweitzer because her heart has been broken by her fickle fiancé. This, in turn, brings Schweitzer to enunciate the first of many of his home-spun maxims, as if he had never left his pastoral pulpit. In his ponderous punditry he asserts that she is 'leaving against rather than for'. 'Nothing worthwhile ever comes from "against"', he warns – adding, with fervently closed eyes, that 'we must go through life with our soul unblemished'. Considering that Marie is often the recipient of his spiritual wisdom (although the natives are not spared either), it is as well, perhaps, that she does replace the wife as the woman who supports the doctor in his humanitarian endeavours! For in terms of power relations, she remains forever his pupil and dutiful member of his congregation – far more so than the natives, it has to be said, whose tribal ways (which he several times terms 'savage') he never fully overcomes or 'civilizes'. Thus, Marie's presence affirms a relative patriarchal power. As a woman trained in medicine, imbued with principled ethics and educated in the spiritual ways of the Lord, she becomes the perfect image of the heroic, orderly and obedient, self-sacrificing Marianne. A perfect model of restraint and fortitude for France's womanhood of the 1950s, even though, as the American film critic Mosk rightly noted at the time, 'Jeanne Moreau lends a piquant, tired face to the crusading Marie',[7] suggesting perhaps something of a subversive touch of irony introduced by Moreau's performance.

The second twist comes at the end when Dr Schweitzer is arrested and deported (at midnight) on the eve of the outbreak of war. This is November 1914, therefore, and not 1917, the real moment of the Schweitzers' arrest and deportation. Further, his moving final farewell suggests that, despite the fact that his nurse Marie decides to stay on behind to keep things running, the hospital will have to await the end of the war for him to rebuild everything – as if Marie's work were of no matter. His comments offer little regard for Marie's nursing and administrative skills (of which we have seen many examples in the film) and, by pointing to her lesser importance, his words serve to undermine the role of women in positions of command. This patriarchal, dismissive rhetoric aside, this scene points to the insanity of war and the stupidity of petty bureaucratic regulations. The arresting officer, Leblanc (André Valmy), is a 'jobsworth' (as he himself declares, he lives by and obeys rules) and is made to look very foolish for carrying out orders that can help no one, least of all the vulnerable natives. However, the concept of house arrest (which is what really happened to the Schweitzers) probably would not have sat well with France of the 1950s – too close to the realities of post-war *épuration*/purge when numerous collaborators in the public eye were placed under house arrest (the film actor Arletty being one of them to say nothing of Fresnay's own imprisonment). But there is also the more secret agenda concerning Alsace itself – surely the third personage in this film. As a structuring absence, 'she/Alsace' almost stands within the film for the missing wife; she is the longed-for territory – not France, not Germany. Three times we hear from Schweitzer and Marie how much 'she' is missed, how far away 'she' is, how 'her' odours now escape their memory. Even before he leaves, Schweitzer says mournfully, 'yes I am leaving Alsace' – as if it is forever. Alsace, in every French imaginary, is the land it owned but which was forever being occupied by France's worst enemy – the German. Alsace: a region under French control since 1648; torn asunder by the Prussians in the Franco-Prussian war of 1870; regained by the French in 1919; taken by the Germans again in World War Two; restored to France in 1945. Each moment of loss is evoked as 'the saddest of misfortunes and the most poignant of sufferings'.[8] It was a bloodbath during the First World War that was returned to a 'mutilated' France in 1919.[9] When occupied in the next world war, Alsace again became a site of death and had the ignominious dishonour to house a mini-Auschwitz in the town of Natzweiler-Struthof.[10] Thus, Alsace is a territory redolent with memories of the barbaric German invader, the land's violator. It is also a metonymy for France's recent suffering and, indeed, shame during the Occupation. A place, within the film, of nostalgic *heimlich* – but also, ultimately, a place of mourning.

These two twists (Marie's substitution for Madame Schweitzer and the change of deportation date), permit, then, a reading that speaks to contemporary 1950s' France – namely, the nation's desire to assert its greatness as a civilizing force, to reaffirm the social order of things post-war, including the place of women in a dominant patriarchal society and, finally, to gloss over the guilt of the Occupation. What, however, of the relations between white Europeans and the indigenous peoples of Gabon? Predictably, western logic and know-how is pitted against the superstitious ignorance of the natives. Schweitzer's playing Bach on his Gaveau piano inspires silent awe amongst the indigenous people gathered in his compound; even his pet pelican stops to listen. This spiritual, cultural and civilizing effect compares favourably with the violence later released by the tam-tams we hear calling the tribesmen to action: they sack and pillage the compound, they go after the local priest, Père Charles (Jean Debucourt), and brutally murder him. White medicine is little understood by these African people, who believe that when a patient is under anaesthetic they are dead, and miraculously brought back to life by the white doctor when the drug wears off. In other words, the performance and accoutrements of the white doctor (the white witch-doctor as they call him) are interpreted via the same discourses as those used to understand the practices of their own witch-doctor. For them, there is no difference between killing a patient and bringing him back to life – such as the white doctor causes to happen when he anaesthetizes a patient who later comes back to consciousness – and sacrificing a child as commanded by the witch-doctor to save the life of his ailing father. According to western logic, however, there is a difference. And Schweitzer's response is that there is still so much more to be done to educate the natives away from such barbaric practices, including cannibalism of the dead – which constitutes, along with taking life, a mortal sin. Even though he later acknowledges a flaw in this logic, since the white man is guilty of taking life ('cannibalizing their own' as he puts it) in times of war.

The message is clear. Good men and women of France are prepared to go to huge lengths, make enormous sacrifices (including their own life in the case of the priest, and marriage in the case of Marie) to help the natives who, when they are not being portrayed as menacing barbarians, are represented as lazy and indolent (sitting around rather than getting on with chopping down trees or cooking, or whatever other task they have been given). In their lack of understanding of western ways they are made to look foolish, even stupid. For instance, since they are illiterate, it is small surprise that they do not understand how to take the medicine dispensed to them. Until, that is, Marie explains clearly how to do so. In a similar way, Schweitzer comes to understand the needs of the natives in that he sets up the compound in such a way that it remains familiar to the native population. Rather than build big brick buildings that would alienate them, his surgery and other buildings are simple hut structures; the sick can bring with them their families, who can supply the wherewithal to feed them.

In the end, the film does carry the message of France as a civilizing force. And we need to recall that in 1914, the time of the film's location, France still perceived Africans as inferior, even if politicians very much doubted the right of the colonizers to reduce the natives to slavery.[11] Nonetheless, the film offers an ambiguous message that prevents it from being reduced to a simple apology for colonialism or racism. Indeed, the big white man does *not* know best. As Schweitzer points out, the white man conducts civil war in Europe (white against white), irresponsibly neglects the well-being of the countries it has colonized, is absurd in his confidence that he is always right, has God on his side and is always superior to other races. Schweitzer acknowledges this failure of the white man and attempts to transcend it. And yet it is perhaps fitting that even he cannot enjoy an egalitarian relationship with the black man. As we see in the case of his relationship with Joseph (Candy Well), the young black man he saves. He attempts to be fraternal – 'I am the doctor's slave' says Joseph; 'no', retorts Schweitzer, 'you are my friend.' But despite these declarations the relationship is still an unequal one – Joseph is under the doctor's instructions always; lectured on the difference between good and evil and subjected to his knowing punditry. Schweitzer's ways are paternalistic and Joseph, like Marie before him, is just another pupil. This paternalism, whilst not overtly colonialist, shows how thin the line is between patronizing superiority and racial oppression.[12] Given the imbalance of power-relations, it is clear the two cultures have a long way to go to find a common ground. As the military jobsworth Leblanc asserts, despite the white man's mission to civilize the indigenous peoples, the witch-doctors are still the rulers of the forest (as exemplified by the brutal slaying of the priest). There is an awful lot to be done, or undone.

Biopic amnesia: sanitizing difficult women

La Belle Otéro is based on the memoirs of the singer-dancer Caroline Otéro (published in 1926), who was still alive at the time of the release of the film. It offers a much-sanitized version of her rather picaresque, even scandalous life, during which, amongst other things, princes and kings fell at her feet[13], men ruined themselves for her, fought duels over her and others, including her American impresario Ernest Andréas-Jurgens, even committed suicide.[14] To win her favours, the American millionaire William Vanderbilt bought her the fabulous pearl necklace of the former Empress Eugénie (Napoleon III's wife and herself a Spaniard, an irony one imagines Otéro savoured).[15] Another American millionaire placed priceless pure white pearls in oysters specially ordered for her when they dined at Chez

Ledoyen in Paris. She was fêted everywhere she went (Paris, New York, St. Petersburg, and so on), even if she was labelled 'une horizontale' – a scurrilous term used to refer to her ascendancy to riches through her sexual affairs.[16] At the turn of the nineteenth century, she formed a friendship with Colette and became known as an *Amazone* – a term used to refer to strong-minded (sometimes lesbian) women.[17] She remained attached to no one – her love of wealth, especially in the form of jewels, extravagant hats and rich furs being matched only by her addiction to gambling.[18]

By the time the film was mooted by the director Richard Pottier, Otéro was living in Nice in dire circumstances – virtually a tramp – as a result of having gambled away her fortune (several times, it has to be said), primarily in Monte Carlo. The revenues she received from the film (considerable, one must guess, given the popularity of the film with 1.9 million spectators) allowed her to return to her addiction. It did not, however, prevent her from disliking the film. She thought the Mexican star who embodied her role, Maria Félix, was not pretty enough, nor did she dance well enough or with the élan of her own performances; but worst of all, in her view, was the fact that her representation on screen as a romantic, faithful and lovesick woman was the complete opposite of her own persona and a far cry from the independent woman that she was.[19] Arguably, all that remains of her persona in Félix's characterization is her outspokenness.[20]

Otéro's early years were far from promising: born in Spain (1868), she was raped at twelve, ran away from home, became a prostitute and was rendered sterile as a result of an abortion. Her two successive pimps were also her lovers, both called Paco. She taught herself to dance the flamenco and worked in cabarets to make ends meet. In the late 1880s, her then lover, a wealthy Spaniard called Stevez, brought her to Paris with a view to promoting her as an exotic dancer, but instead he ruined himself for her.[21] The couple took off to Marseilles, where Stevez left her and returned to Spain to raise more money for his mistress. Stevez brought Otéro to Paris a second time (1889) and introduced her to the impresario José Oller (a Catalan) who helped launch her career. Stevez was soon abandoned. This pattern becomes a familiar one: Otéro toys with the men driven wild by her sexy eroticism, happily divesting them of their fortunes in order to pursue her love of gambling. Over a career spanning more than 20 years, Otéro performed in all the top Paris venues, including the Folies-Bergère, the Moulin Rouge and Olympia. Her performances were the height of daring for the time: amongst her stage costumes she wore fur coats with a skin-tight flesh-coloured bathing costume underneath and would open them up to perform her dance of wanton sexuality.[22]

The Otéro we see in the screen version is a considerably watered-down one, even if elements of the real Otéro and her story remain, especially towards the beginning of the film. In the very first sequence she is already in Paris; however she is represented to us as a poor gypsy girl (a narrative conceit since we know she arrived richly endowed by Stevez in real life). She is also represented as honest. As she strolls in the park with her lover Pablo, she comes across a gold watch, which she returns to its owner – the wealthy playboy Jean Chastaing (Jacques Berthier). She always speaks the truth. She has a clear sense of her career trajectory. It is she who insists that the impresario Martel (Louis Seigner) must engage her, and she dances a magnificent flamenco on his staircase to prove it. But, from here on, the fiery Otéro gives way to a more muted version of the original. Unlike the real Otéro, Félix' performances are demure, certainly not libidinous. In her first stage appearance, at the café-concert Kursaal, her dances are wholesome rather than mesmerizing and she remains fully clothed in a Spanish-influenced costume of a red and white latticed skirt overlaying full petticoats. Given the blandness of her performance, the way she turns the disgruntlement of the crowd in the stalls into cheering applauding encores is far from convincing. As for her lovers, they are the exploiters who constantly disappoint her, rather than she them. Either, they use her: Pablo (José Torres), with whom she arrives impoverished from Spain, steals her last remaining jewellery and abandons her to her fate; the rich playboy, Jean, seduces her with a view to using her as a pawn in his game of revenge against a former mistress. Or, they try to control her: Mountfeller (Maurice Teynac), the rich American impresario (far less interesting than the original Ernest Andréas-Jurgens), takes her to New York only to subject her to the hypocrisy of 'proper' society conduct. He pretends not to be her lover and sends her repeated telegrams reprimanding her for her bad behaviour – a part of the narrative that has all the overtones of an Edith Wharton or Henry James novel. Small wonder she dumps him and returns to Paris. Throughout, Jean remains the true love of her life, even though he repeatedly hurts her. When, finally, he realizes that he loves her, it is too late. He gets himself embroiled in a duel with a journalist who wrote scurrilous things about Otéro and is killed.

The authentic in this film remains far more readily in the *mise-en-scène* and costumes. Using a palette of colours in slate-greys, light yellows and soft greens, very reminiscent of Edouard Manet's paintings, Robert Gys' recreation of the turn of the century café concerts and music halls, of the open-air restaurant, Au Vert Galant (in the Bois de Boulogne), gives the modern viewer a clear sense of Parisian society's leisure time during the Belle Epoque. For such a flamboyant character as Otéro, there is a modest number of costumes: eighteen in all – and not, as *Le Film français* claims, thirty.[23] Marcel Escoffier, whose background training was in historical costumes, was the designer. He was also, formerly, design assistant to the Haute Couture House of Paquin. Jeanne Paquin had a penchant for historical garments and in particular liked to trim evening dresses with fur, net and lace.[24] Excess and adornment, entirely appropriate for a star performer such as Otéro, coupled with historical accuracy, at least in terms of line, are what Escoffier provides us with. His costumes detail Otéro's rags-to-riches narrative and, at a second-order narrative, her unfulfilled love affair with Jean Chastaing. In relation to the first-order narrative, Otéro arrives in Paris dressed in gypsy-like attire: a white blouse, a black shawl, a dull-brown ankle-length skirt but with ample white petticoats beneath. By the time of her last performance, at the Café de Paris in Monte Carlo, she is wearing a white satin gown with a bodice dripping with diamonds. Undoubtedly, this costume hints at a more famous one of the real Otéro which featured her breasts covered with glued-on precious gems and which is said to have inspired the design of the twin cupolas of the Hotel Carlton in Cannes, which were modelled after her breasts.

In between these two moments, and in terms of costume styles, Otéro experiences two journeys. The one, physical, which takes her to New York and back; the other, more internal,

Figure 21.2: La Belle Otéro at the Palladium. © Les Films Modernes.

and which puts on display her increasing despair at Jean's rejection. In the former, once she arrives in New York (in a demure but classy white travelling outfit), we mostly see her clothed in costumes of excess. Her mauve dress for her first night at the Palladium, with the matching boa and enormous wide-brimmed ostrich-feather hat in white with black plumes arising from the centre (see figure 21.2 above), is such an eye-catching outfit we almost forget to watch the actual, rather tame, song and dance routine she performs (indeed, if anything, it is the male dancers around her who put in the most effort). The excess of this dress and hat is matched, offstage, by the yellow silk taffeta evening gown she wears to the reception afterwards: a huge crinoline skirt (more reminiscent of the 1860s than the 1890s[25]), tight bodice with a high collar of netting, topped off with a white plumed hat. She is thereafter perceived in a series of low-cleavaged black evening gowns, each one lower-cut than the former and one of which is adorned with yellow roses (in real life Otéro's favourite flowers[26]).

All these outfits speak not only of a woman showing off her wealth, they also display an unruly body, since in each and every one of them she 'misbehaves' according to Mountfeller's set of rules concerning appropriate behaviour. In the first, she slaps then kisses the Palladium's master of ceremonies; in her yellow gown, she gets drunk on American whiskey, dances on tables and gambles her jewellery away; in her black dresses, she is seen living the high-life in New York. Each incident provokes a telegram from her outraged Pygmallion (Mountfeller). Small wonder the independent and fiery Otéro wants to return to Paris. Interestingly, their separation takes place in a set of circumstances that defy all of American society's rules: Otéro receives Mountfeller in her hotel bedroom alone, wearing a very pretty and revealing negligee.

In relation to this issue of propriety, given her huge passion for Jean, it is surely significant that she is never in a state of undress before him. Instead, the two men who do see her in this state are her impresarios, Martel and Mountfeller. Martel (surely the most interesting of her relationships with men on screen) first sets his eyes upon her wearing a gorgeous blue-mauve corset as she changes out of her flamenco dress back-stage at the Kursaal. Later, in New York, he brings breakfast to her in bed where she is wearing a very low-cut white nightie. They even exchange comments on how inappropriately they are behaving, according to American decorum. This idea that the wrong men are looking at her in a state of semi-nudity (and therefore accessibility) does not bode well for the course of her true love.

Let us now turn to the internal journey where this idea of seeing is quite relevant to the narrative. When Otéro first sets eyes on Jean in the open-air gardens, he is in a beautifully-tailored suit and accompanied by an equally elegantly-attired woman. Otéro is in her downbeat gypsy clothes, thus it is rather a case of her seeing him than he her. Indeed, she

Figure 21.3: Otéro in black confronts Jean. © Les Films Modernes.

observes him as he absent-mindedly drops his gold watch; she picks it up and runs after him in an attempt to return it. This attempt fails because, as she rightly tells him later, he never noticed her. Jean does, however, notice her when she first performs at the Kursaal – this time *she* is centre stage and wearing her flamenco outfit. And that very night he sets about his seduction strategy, which is totally successful. The next time we see the couple, it is two weeks later. Otéro turns up to meet him for lunch in a white polka-dotted muslin dress, parasol and a large hat with an upturned black brim filled with white gauze embossed with flowers and sporting a single trademark yellow rose in the front. It is a stunning outfit and the whole restaurant is silenced by her entrance, except for Jean, who is alone in not really seeing her. Thus, all her effort is for naught. This is confirmed by the fact that Jean wants to separate. He uses the same strategy he always uses (a sick uncle in the country he must rush and attend to). Totally crushed, Otéro understands the coded message and takes off with Mountfeller to New York. Twice, in his blindness to her, Jean has rebuffed her.

The excess in her dress when in New York represents the grieving love-lost Otéro putting herself on display, even though the man it is intended for, Jean, is absent, unseeing. Thus, it represents a displacement of her yearning in the only modality she knows: performing desire through an excess of costume. It is surely instructive that when she returns to Paris and goes to Jean's house, she wears a small black hat with a widow's veil and that, underneath her fur trimmed winter coat, she sports a black day tailleur with a Spanish brocaded bolero jacket (see figure 21.3 above). It is showdown time at its most serious (unlike with Mountfeller) – and one senses from her outfit that she fears the worst and is already in mourning. Indeed, Jean is unable to make a commitment and again rejects her, even though he admits he loves her. She leaves, throwing his gold watch back at him. Both are doomed – he to a life of loneliness and she to go from pearl necklace to pearl necklace, because, as she warns him, he remains blind to the value of their love. Her black widow's dress signals the death of their relationship, but also foreshadows the death of her lover.

It is fitting that the real Caroline Otéro did not like this film. It is a backlash film, much like other costume dramas of the Belle Epoque that focus on women artistes or cocottes. We see a similar narrative in *Frou-Frou* (1955), where the eponymous heroine finds fame and fortune but at the expense of true love and marriage. In *Chéri*, Léa's life as a cocotte means she has left it too late to marry. At least none of these independent minded women perish, as with the cocottes of the earlier nineteenth-century costume dramas. Here, the women are doomed merely to a life of loneliness if they do not marry and settle down (unless the woman self-sacrifices for a worthy cause as in the case of Dr Schweitzer's nurse Marie)! The message is simple: marry – if you are lucky, for love, as in *Eléna et les hommes* and *Miquette et sa mère*; or as a compromise as for Lucette in *Le Fil à la patte*. Otherwise, you will end up unfulfilled. Be strong-minded and independent at your peril. Otéro's fierce determination to be self-sufficient and a free spirit was not a message the political culture of the 1950s could easily tolerate it would seem, which is undoubtedly why the narrative was romanticized and her own biography reduced to the purely fictional story of her unhappy relationship with Jean.

Biopic excess: filth as attraction

Combret's *Raspoutine* relies on a very sketchy series of historical facts to create its image of the lusty monk in the form of Pierre Brasseur. As much a bon-viveur as his prototype (drugs, alcohol, womanizing), Brasseur describes his career in a way that is remarkably consonant with that of the monstrous monk Rasputin: 'It is made of the best and the worst, but I am proud of it because this perpetual chaos is proof of the vitality and the unexpected that never lets me rest on my laurels nor indeed completely despise myself'.[27] Indeed, the Rasputin we see on screen suffers from a similar mixture of extremes which he refuses to resolve. Combret wanted Brasseur to play Rasputin as a man torn between good and evil.[28] Yet one senses in his characterization a man who is not particularly ill at ease with his two selves – there appears to be no 'torn self'. At one point towards the end of the film, as the plotting to get rid of him begins, he is confronted by his two most loyal allies: Anna (the Tsarina's lady in waiting, played by Micheline Francey) and the priest, father Alexander (Claude Laydu), the former urging him to show no pity towards his enemies, the latter proposing that he must renounce his dissolute behaviour and change his ways if he is to survive. Heeding neither and rudely ejecting them from his quarters, he declares: 'I am God and the devil all rolled into one.'

The film covers the last eleven years of Rasputin's life, from when he came to St Petersburg in 1905 and was introduced to the Tsarina Alexandra and her entourage until his assassination in December 1916. Rasputin was a mystic and self-styled religious elder (*starets*) whose reputation as a healer brought him to the attention of the Tsarina, in need of help for her haemophiliac son Alexei. He was a peasant from the village of Pokrovskoye in the southern area of the Russian Empire – some 1,562 miles due south from St-Petersburg. He was used to travelling these enormous distances, beginning in 1894, when his life as an errant monk began. Over the eleven-year period he gained increasing influence over the Romanovs – both the Tsar and the Tsarina. The Tsarina because, as a profound mystic herself, she believed in Rasputin's power to heal; the Tsar because he was both weak and easily dominated by his wife. A prime example lies in his contradictory political behaviour. As a response to the 1905 revolution, the Tsar sanctioned the democratic principle of the legislative assembly (the State Duma) only to flout it by dismissing and appointing ministers upon Rasputin's recommendations. We see examples of this in the film on two occasions: first, to usurp a powerful minister in favour of a young aspirant to politics; second, more comically, in a drunken moment when Rasputin appoints a minister of peace (I will return to these moments later). Rasputin was a pacifist and, on several occasions, tried to dissuade the Tsar from entering into war (the Balkans conflict of 1909; later, World War One). The Tsar – believing in his self-appointed status as head of the military – did not heed him, however. Most crucially, when Germany declared war on Russia, the Tsar elected to go to the front, leaving the Tsarina and Rasputin in charge of administering the nation. A fatal decision. Rasputin accumulated enemies on all fronts: politicians, the army and the clergy. And by 1916, people began turning against the Tsarina because of her German origins. Both she and

Rasputin were perceived as enemies of the state and, indeed, rumours ran that Rasputin was an agent for the Germans. From there it was a short step to plot his disappearance.

If the film compresses the historical facts, it nonetheless provides a reasonably accurate physical portrait of the anarchic and rebellious monk. Brasseur oozes the sensuality of the man in all his grubbiness. His hair is long, greasy and straggly, as is his beard (see figure 21.4 below). He has an enormous appetite for food, drink and women. He literally bursts onto the scene, dominating the entire screen with his larger-than-life personality. Significantly, as a marker of his overpowering persona, Rasputin/Brasseur is present in virtually every sequence – his huge body crashing into the frame, exuding excess and causing chaos. Even when he is absent, his is a structuring absence. For example, at the Tsarina's grand ball (again an anachronism for it occurred in 1903, not 1905), men and women talk about him – the women approvingly of his healing powers, the men negatively about his control over the Romanovs. In the end, of course, these two elements (his debauched life and his power over the Tsar and Tsarina) are precisely the ones that will cause his downfall.

The film falls into two main parts, focused around Rasputin's two periods in St Petersburg. It is significant that the turning point in both parts is triggered by his meddling in politics. The first part (corresponding to the period 1905–1911) loosely refers to his initial introduction to the Romanovs and his growing influence over them. In the opening sequence we see him driving his sleigh across the snow-bound Russian Steppes towards the royal city. At one point on this journey he picks up father Alexander (the priest who, as we saw above, endeavours always to be Rasputin's good conscience). This encounter allows the narrative to sketch in details about Rasputin, including his self-styled religion and his

Figure 21.4: Rasputin dominating the dance scene. © Radius Productions.

powers of hypnotism. During this six-year period we see his introduction to the Tsarina Alexandra (Isa Miranda) and several miracle cures effected by him upon the Tsarevitch Alexei. We also see his gradual accumulation of enemies, including the powerful Premier of the Duma, Stolypine (Michel Etcheverry). The turning point transpires when Rasputin is outmanoeuvred by another minister, Stumerof (Raphaël Patorni). Stumerof attempts to persuade the Tsar (Robert Burnier) to banish the unruly monk with photographic proof of his debauchery (cavorting with nude women in their bathing rooms). As an act of revenge, Rasputin succeeds in removing Stumerof from office. His chance occurs when the Grande Duchesse Militza (referred to as Vera in film and played by Renée Faure) brings along one of her protégées, Laura (Milly Vitale), who wants Rasputin to work his powers of persuasion on behalf of her fiancé Gouliev (Robert Lombard) to finagle a ministerial post. Incensed at being sacked by the Tsar and replaced by an ingénue, Stumerof challenges Gouliev to a duel and kills him. Such is the scandal, the Tsar has to warn Rasputin that if there is any more outrage, public opinion will turn against the Romanov family. Rasputin, refusing to be made a scapegoat (as he puts it), announces to the Tsar that he is returning home to Pokrovskoye. In real life he was exiled to Kiev as a result of a report on his licentious behaviour compiled by secret police surveillance and ordered by Stolypine.[29]

The second part of the film corresponds to Rasputin's 1912–1916 stay in St Petersburg. An assassination attempt on his life brings him back to court and not, as in real life, his mystical intervention (in 1912), via a telegram, which again saves the young Tsarevitch's life. In the film, Laura, incensed by her fiancé's 'murder' (he was a terrible shot) and by the fact that she had let herself be seduced by Rasputin in order to secure Gouliev a ministerial post, comes to his village on a mission of revenge. The stabbing is not fatal and Rasputin refuses to take any action against her. The Tsarina's distress at the near loss of her son's saviour does the rest and he is back in favour with the Romanovs. However, here once again history is falsified for narrative expediency and for the sake, perhaps, of keeping clear the demarcation lines between the rich and the poor – whom Rasputin is purported to represent in this film. In reality, the assault took place in June 1914, the day after Archduke Ferdinand was assassinated, and it was a beggar woman and former prostitute (Khionia Gousseva) rather than an aristocrat who attacked Rasputin. This was a religiously-motivated attempt – the woman was under orders from the local village priest, who disapproved of Rasputin's mystical beliefs.[30] This shift in motivation (Laura's is a sexual vendetta rather than a religious one) and class (from poor to rich) is significant for the simple reason that it brings the focus to bear onto Rasputin's sexual appetites. In short, his mythical power becomes overshadowed by his libidinous excesses (Laura, the nude women bathers, and so on). The effect is to render him more grotesque and monstrous, even quite risible, rather than threatening and dangerous. Even if he does have a commanding physical presence on screen, and clearly dominates the Romanovs, his political scheming always backfires and it is his ineptitude that is foregrounded. We are also repeatedly reminded of his poverty and peasant stock. He tells the Tsarevitch that he is 'one of his peasants who only wishes him well'; he only takes alms for the poor, not for himself. Indeed the only gift he keeps is the silk shirt the Tsarina gave him.[31] Yet we also see him cavorting around a fire with peasants, singing and dancing and advocating 'purification through sin' – a permanent mantra for this licentious priest, it would appear, which makes him faintly ridiculous rather than menacing.

And it is one of his absurd political shenanigans that constitutes the turning point in this second part of the film. It arises when, one evening in a very upper class St-Petersburg café-concert, drunk on power as much as alcohol and considering himself 'the boss (*le maître*)', Rasputin makes a mockery of political and military power by appointing a baritone chorister as minister of peace. The army officers in attendance are furious and vow to rid themselves of this troublesome monk – especially since this appointment, as with the earlier one, backfires (a little later this same minister of peace is seen profiteering through arms sales). Félix Yusupov (Jacques Berthier), a former friend of Rasputin's, and several other officers, in collusion with Stolypine, plot his assassination. Rasputin, invited to Yusupov's home for a meal, turns up wearing the Tsarina's gift of the silk shirt (the one time we see him in it). First, he is served drinks laced with cyanide; when this fails, Stolypine and the rest of the group burst into the room and shoot him down like a dog, bundle him up in a sheet and toss him into the river Neva. In real life, Yusupov did indeed lead the assassination plot. However, Stolypine by this time had already been assassinated in Kiev in 1911 in front of Rasputin's very eyes (Rasputin had warned him, when he was exiled from the court, that this would happen). The cyanide was administered in cooked cakes, which is why it did not have immediate effect (the cooking slowing down the process of poisoning).

This compression of history and its consequent inaccuracies serve to skew the story and somewhat distort the complexity of Rasputin's life. And they are worth pointing out, given the film's claim to authenticity. A claim that begins with the décors, of which there are 31 (22 interiors and 9 exteriors). Pierre Robin, writing in the film industry press magazine, *La Cinématographie française*, tells us that set designer Jean Douarinou drew on first-hand experience for his design of the Winter Palace in St Petersburg since he had visited it, aged ten, in 1914 when his mother was presented to the Tsar's court. By the1950s, under communist rule, the Imperial palace was clearly put to completely different purposes (mainly administrative offices for the Russian Soviet), so in its current state it could not really act as a reference point (even if access had been permitted). Douarinou therefore consulted documents held in the French Bibliothèque Nationale to supplement his knowledge of the palace's interiors.[32] Thus, where the Winter Palace is concerned, the sets, of which there are eight, come from memory and black and white photography or lithographs. Before pointing to the differences between reality and reconstructed reality, it is worth quoting Douarinou on this:

> Décor must not draw attention to itself, but must act as a foil to the actors, which is why colour is dangerous. So the set will not have too much furniture and must use neutral colours.[33]

Let us begin with Douarinou's first point. *Raspoutine* was filmed in Eastmancolor, and, at times, it did pose problems, actually drawing attention to itself more by accident than design. When viewing the film at the time of its release, the film critic Mosk notes that 'color has a tendency to be uneven with Brasseur's face running from red to blue in ensuing scenes.[34] This is particularly true of the exterior scenes (especially the opening sequence) and in these instances, clearly, it is a failure to contend with the weaknesses in the properties of the colour process. We recall from Chapter 2 that Eastmancolor (at least in its early years) did not perform very well in full sunlight. Unlike Gevacolor, it could not provide the depth in the images or the glorious colour in exterior shots of its German rival. Thus, those faults remain in the film. But where this desire to guard against colour drawing attention to itself is most sharply in evidence is in the interior sets. Obviously, it was uppermost in Douarinou's mind when planning the set for the Tsarina's ball. If we compare the set of the main staircase that the Romanovs descend with the flashiness of the palace's original, we see how, here, it is held to a minimum. Whilst the shape of the staircase and the stunning whiteness of the marble are correct, what is massively absent is the gilt around the windows and various marble statues of the famous Winter Palace's baroque Jordan staircase.[35] Other rooms in the Palace, such as the Tsar's office, the day or music room where the children play, are sparsely furnished – again to limit the danger of décor drawing attention to itself – although the beautiful marquetry on the parquet floors provides an interesting warmth to the otherwise rather cold interiors of the palace. These empty spaces make room for Rasputin's irruptions into the rooms. However, in the main, their *mise-en-scène* allows for a series of composed tableaux: the Tsar at work, the children at play, the Russian aristocracy entertaining. Oddly, the only room that does not match up with Douarinou's proscription is the Tsarevitch's bedroom, with its mauve walls ornately decorated with plaster garlands of flowers, with a chapel for praying to one side (also in mauve) and, in general, an excess of furniture. The room is more like that of a cocotte's than a sickly boy's – the over-stuffedness and colour perhaps reflecting the Tsarina's obsessive protection of her son (we do catch her praying in the chapel quite often).

What is also interesting is that, with the exception of the churches, the rest of the interior sets – be it the café-concert, the village taverna, or Rasputin's quarters in town – are all fairly cluttered. Douarinou explains that he crowded Rasputin's apartment with furniture so that the messiness told us about him.[36] The places of entertainment bespeak his excessiveness as he sings, drinks, dances and womanizes in them. In contrast, the church interiors are – by Russian standards – modest, perhaps reflecting the asceticism Rasputin should be aspiring to achieve. It is significant that the two moments when he is inside a religious space we witness the two extremes of his behaviour. The first time (towards the beginning of the film), he interrupts a prayer time and defies his religious superiors, who have ordered him there to denounce his mysticism. The second time – towards the end of the film, when everybody is turning against him – he kneels and cries for God's mercy. But too late, the church has already symbolically closed its doors upon him, as exemplified, a little earlier on, by the chief prelate's refusal to give Rasputin sanctuary when being pursued by angry army officers who beat him up.

Annenkov's costumes lay their own claim to authenticity.[37] Apparently he knew Rasputin – indeed he lived in St Petersburg at the same time as the monk, studying fine art at the university. Thus Rasputin's look is based on first-hand knowledge. Annenkov's Russian background and previous work with Max Ophuls made him an obvious choice as costume designer for this film, especially given his love of military costume, which he shared with Ophuls.[38] Annenkov's costumes do indeed reflect fairly faithfully the contemporary preoccupation of the Tsar with all things Russian. In Russia, the correlation of dress with status and power was central to Tsarist ideology. Opulence equalled sanctity of rule and was a symbol of Imperial might. In the film, this is signified through the tapestry of the double-headed eagle and the extreme luxury of the Tsarina's ceremonial attire at the ball (her ermine cloak) and those of her guests. As part of his attempts to assert a national identity and in keeping with previous Tsars of the nineteenth century, Nicolas II saw being head of the army as integral to that drive. Thus, he designed the army's and his own military attire. Most crucially, he adopted the Russian peasant tunic style for his army (which we see Yusopov wearing) as a style statement for Russia. The tunic becomes emblematic of the Russian nation, therefore. However, being a vain dresser, this did not prevent him from excess at times. For the famous 1903 grand ball, he wore an ornate, richly-bejewelled, traditional Russian seventeenth-century style coat and tunic woven in gold thread with red velvet embossed sleeves and pearl cuffs. Crucially, in both instances – modest or excessive – the style is nationalistic: pure Russian.

In the film, true to the Tsarist ideology, we see Nicolas in uniform always – but, as we shall see, to ironic effect. With the exception of the ball, where he wears a red military jacket, he is mostly in a blue military jacket, the one exception being the white jacket when he sacks the minister Stumerof. Given Annenkov's own revolutionary involvement, post-1917, and his association with the Soviet avant-garde, before exiling himself to Paris upon the death of Lenin in 1924, it is hard not to attempt an ironic reading of the Tsar's costumes. The deliberate lack of any magnificent robing for Nicolas at the ball, especially in contrast to his wife's stunning ermine cloak, reduces the man in terms of stately hauteur. He is merely clothed in a conventional military jacket – albeit red. Further, the dusty, French-blue of the military jacket (which he mostly wears) acts to understate the concept of Imperial power. Only the white jacket stands out as startling. First, because we associate it with the navy – yet the Tsar insisted on his role as head of the army so he would surely be more inclined to dress in the appropriate colour (and indeed what evidence of his attire exists, mostly sees him dressed in either sombre green or dark blue[39]). Second, it is in this white outfit that he sacks Stumerof. Not only is he unable to dismiss his minister in his regular uniform, he has to masquerade in a colour and outfit not associated with his person at any other time. The white acts ironically for his complete submission to both Rasputin's whims and his wife's domination. He is, after all, anything but whiter than white. In truth, all the costumes serve to show us a different Tsar from the image he sought to create of himself. He emerges as a man who is diffident in relation to his wife, easily swayed by irresponsible favourites, distrusting of his ministers, yet lacking in the strength of will to assert his (self-anointed) autocratic rights.[40]

This period in Russian history witnessed a strong drive in nationalist ideology, coming on the back of its defeat in the war against Japan (1905) and a humiliating climb-down over the Balkans affair (1908–1909). Russia, in the form of the Tsar, sought to block the annexation of Bosnia-Herzegovina by the Austro-Hungarian Empire. However, he was forced to agree to the annexation or risk exposure through the leaking of documents which would prove that, over the course of the past 30 years, Russia had agreed that Austria-Hungary had a free hand to do as it liked with Bosnia-Herzegovina.[41] Russia's legacy, on the one hand, of defeat, poor diplomacy, double-dealing, and, on the other, a renewed practice of nationalism, finds ready echoes with France's own nationalistic drive of the early 1950s and its attempts to reassert its global importance. This was something that was particularly difficult to achieve, given that France, humiliated in war, was made to feel a second-class citizen in the NATO camp. Even more humiliating was the fact that it had to accept West Germany into the NATO fold if it was to become a member itself.[42]

In terms of France's socio-political context, by 1954 the Fourth Republic was into its thirteenth government – suggesting a great deal of political unease. The best illustration of this political uncertainty is evidenced by the strength in positions of extremes where electoral choice was concerned. The extreme right-wing of politics had found a new populist champion in the form of Pierre Poujade, whose own rhetoric around nation-building (based in anti-government fiscal policies and anti-Marshall aid from the US as much as in anti-semitism and racism) brought him to form a party in defence of small businesses and artisans – garnering (in the 1956 general election) about thirteen percent of the national suffrage. As for the left-wing, the French Communist Party (PCF), also against Marshall aid, still held huge sway with voters. The PCF represented just over a quarter of the electorate. Yet, even though it was the biggest single party in terms of votes and had the most seats in the Assembly, it never held power nor, indeed, a ministerial position post-1947.[43] The anarchic and unruly Rasputin we see in the film, his bodily filth matched only by the moral filth of the rich, points to a nation that France certainly did not want to emulate – but with which in some uncomfortable ways it might identify. The populism of Poujade finds ready parallels with Rasputin. The lack of proper representation (mentioned above) is another example. Finally, a further example is the indecent speed with which ex-Vichy ministers came back into the political fold, as we saw, most notoriously, with Antoine Pinay in 1952.[44]

With an audience of 2.2 million, *Raspoutine* had strong appeal – primarily thanks to its star vehicle Pierre Brasseur. Given the reality of tensions with the USSR, this imaginary Russia the French spectator sees on screen is, however, also a comforting one. It is one where the nation is clearly not a strong Empire. Its country is backward, its leader is weak, the military and politicians are self-serving rather than hungry for change and modernization.[45] The Soviet Union of 1954 was a far harder reality to countenance. In 1953, Stalin died and Nikita Khrushchev became first secretary. With him came the potential for a thaw, yet this was seemingly undermined when the USSR announced, in 1953, that it had the H bomb – particularly sinister when, in the United States in this same year, the Rosenbergs had been found guilty and summarily executed for trading atomic secrets with the Soviets. But then America was not exactly a panacea, either. In accepting Marshall aid (in 1947), France had to forego its political, economic and military independence. The Americans and the Soviets were fighting an ideological battle in Europe. And France, more so than any other European nation, was caught between the two. Rather like Rasputin – a mystic and a pacifist, an anarchist and a self-promoter, a bon-viveur and man of God – caught between his own extremes!

Notes

1. Hayward (1993, p. 133).
2. The fifth sister, Léonie went to Caen and joined orders as a 'visitandine'. http://fr.wikipedia.org/wiki/Thérèse_de_Lisieux accessed 06.02.2009.
3. Haguet, quoted in production notes for *Procès au Vatican* (*La Cinématographie française*, No. 1444, 1.12.1951, p. 17, no author name given).
4. Ibid., p.17).
5. http://fr.wikipedia.org/wiki/Albert_Schweitzer accessed 04.12.2008.
6. The film was not distributed to UK market until 1958 although it was in the US in 1952.
7. Review of *Il est minuit Dr Schweitzer*, by Mosk, *Variety*, 10.12.1952, no page.
8. Marseille (2002, p. 194).
9. Ibid., p. 260.
10. Ibid., pp. 348–9).
11. Marseille (ibid., pp. 198–9) provides an illuminating summary of politicians and philanthropists views on the African native.
12. Several journalists and sociologists went out to Lambaréné to visit Schweitzer and evaluate his work. Some found him to be patronizing, paternalistic or colonialist in his attitude towards the Africans. Chinua Achebe has quoted Schweitzer as saying 'the African is indeed my brother but my junior brother.' http://en.wikipedia.org/wiki/Albert_Schweitzer accessed 12.12.2008. It is in this flawed thinking that the fraternal can be maintained alongside with the hierarchical that Schweitzer shows, as Fanon might put it, that he still has colonialism in his psyche.
13. These include the Prince of Wales (the future Edward VII of England), Alphonso XIII of Spain, Leopold II of Belgium. Schiffer (2008, pp. 274–5).
14. Ibid., p. 266.
15. Ibid., p. 257.
16. Ibid., p. 240.
17. Liesel Schiffer in a radio interview on France-Inter (15.07.2008) mentions Otéro's liaison with Colette (even though Otéro was apparently quite homophobic) and the labelling of Otéro as 'une Amazone'. It was not unusual for cocottes or music-hall stars to turn to women for their greater intimacy – as Schiffer points out in her intriguing study of Otéro, her friend Emilienne d'Alençon and her stage rival Liane de Pougy both turned to women as a resistance to their exploitation by men (2008, pp. 265–6 & 272).
18. Ibid., pp. 248–9. Otéro's estimated fortune in jewels alone at the turn of the nineteenth century was around 5 million francs. To give a sense of both her wealth and her profligacy, in 1910 she had to sell a bolero jacket dripping with diamonds and emeralds to pay off casino debts of 8 million francs (ibid., p. 270).
19. Ibid., pp. 287–8.
20. Ibid., p. 240.
21. Ibid., pp. 240–50.
22. Ibid., p. 286. It is also worth mentioning the comment by the reviewer for *Le Figaro* who describes her as having 'the whole of the Orient in her hips' – a sure sign of her exotism (quoted in Schiffer, op. cit., p. 253).
23. Review of *La Belle Otéro* in *Le Film Français* (No. 54319.11.1954, p. 18, no author name given).
24. Cousins (2008, pp. 125–6).
25. This example of anachronism in dress design could be read as Escoffier's nod to the house of Paquin's take-over of the house of Worth in 1953. Charles Frederick Worth was the man who

launched the huge crinolines during Empress Eugénie's patronage. The other reason for this anachronism could be the nod to the Empress herself (as with the necklace).

26. Schiffer , op. cit., p. 258.

27. Brasseur cited in Andrée Sallé (1988, p. 91).

28. Film review 'Raspoutine' in *La Cinématographie française*, No. 1576, 10.07.1954, p. 10 (no name given).

29. The Tsar's secret police were known as the Okhrana. In a most amusing scene in the film, Rasputin makes fun of the two policemen assigned to snoop on him by locking them up in his own quarters and giving them the slip. The odd thing is that they are dressed in black suits and wearing bowler hats and look alarmingly like the Dupont brothers, the private detectives of *Tintin* fame.

30. http://fr.wikipedia.org/wiki/Raspoutine accessed 27.11.2008.

31. Apparently, in real life, she also gave him an enormous cross (http://fr.wikipedia.org/wiki/Raspoutine accessed 27.11.2008). We do not see this on his person, however.

32. Pierre Robin 'Raspoutine' in *La Cinématographie française*, No. 1543, 21.11.1953, p. 16.

33. Douarinou, cited in Pierre Robin, op. cit., p. 16.

34. Review of *Raspoutine*, by Mosk, *Variety*, 06.10.1954, no page.

35. Apparently, the real ballroom measured 70m by 30m. Joinville studios only had 36m by 34m. So hangar doors were taken off and a huge marquee erected outside to create the real length (Pierre Robin, op. cit., p. 16).

36. Ibid., p. 16.

37. This nugget of information comes in the film industry paper *La Cinématographie française* production notes on *Raspoutine*. In the same article we read that the film used Russian exiles in Paris as extras which gives an added realism to the song and dance routines and the chanting in the churches (*La Cinématographie française*, No. 1547, 19.12.1953, p. 15).

38. Cousins (2008, pp. 72–3).

39. The Victoria and Albert Museum recently had a display *Magnificence of the Tsars (Ceremonial Dress of the Russian Imperial Court, 1791-1917)* where much of Nicolas II ceremonial dress was on display including his magnificent 1903 ball outfit (Exhibition dates: 10.12.2008-29.03.2009).

40. See Ann Pasternak Slater's interesting article on the *Magnificence of the Tsars*' exhibition: 'Tsar turns', *Saturday Guardian*, Review Section, 22.11.2008, pp. 16–17.

41. This very complicated betrayal of the spirit of and subsequent amendment of the Berlin Treaty is what set in motion the events leading up to the assassination of Archduke Franz Ferdinand (in 1914) by a Serbian nationalist (Gavrilo Princip), which, in turn, brought about the outbreak of World War One.

42. Goetschel and Toucheboeuf (2004, pp. 241–5).

43. Becker (1998, pp. 49 & 64). Cartels of the centre-left kept the communists at arm's reach from political power. Clearly the PCF's anti-Americanism risked alienating the US and put the reception of Marshall aid at risk – this is doubtless one of the hidden reasons why Prime Minister Paul Ramadier banished the PCF from its ministerial posts, although the ostensible reason was the PCF's urging strike action for better workers' pay and conditions (through its union the CGT). See also Bezbakh (1990, pp. 166–7).

44. McMillan (1985, p. 153).

45. Yet a further misrepresentation, since Stolypine was a fierce modernizer.

Conclusion

This study has taken us across a huge corpus of films. Numerous trends have highlighted themselves – some surprising, others not. Whilst the conservative nature of this particular genre has been uppermost in my considerations, nonetheless, whether reading against the grain or not, what has emerged is that despite the predominant conformism in the narratives, other discourses have revealed themselves, suggesting that there are, embedded within the film texts, resistances or deviances in relation to dominant ideology. I have sought to bring these out in an effort to demonstrate that it would serve us well to consider this popular French cinema genre with greater respect than hitherto. Throughout these chapters, I have endeavoured to redress the rather biased view, initially put in place by the *Cahiers* group, and since then fostered by film historians, that this cinema is of little value, cinematically or in content. This is not a cinema that should be dismissed as 'daddy's cinema', for that is precisely what it is not. In taking on new technologies, as explained in Chapter 2, and dealing with new studio systems (see Chapter 1) it is evident that production practices had to be reinvented. Moreover, in terms of the criticism that this cinema was one of adaptation, certainly two thirds of all costume dramas fall into that category. However, only a third of them were adaptations of 'Great' authors, the other third being a mixture of popular novels, plays and operettas. The idea, then, was to entertain, and if only a handful of films were outwardly challenging – so much so that they were subjected to different levels of censorship – then all this tells us is that, as with all other periods or epochs of cinema, it is but a small percentage that strikes out as different. The Poetic Realist films of the 1930s were not that numerous any more than the radical New Wave films of the 1960s.

There are two reasons for taking this genre on board more profoundly. The first comes down to its very materiality; the second, to its engagement with history. By materiality, I mean its décors, costume and cinematography. It is in this domain, in particular, that French cinema showed itself to be an outstanding master of the new technologies available, managing, on budgets well below those commanded by Hollywood, to produce a range of great spectacles. As if the technicians carefully judged, rather than flaunted, the potentialities and values of the new materials at their disposal. Let us begin here.

In this study, special attention, wherever possible, was given to directors of photography in relation to their work in monochrome and colour and, on the rare occasions, with 'scope formats. Analyses highlighted the importance of their understanding of the various properties of the different colour systems. Studies showed how colour contributed to the narratives, sometimes in a straightforward way (through matching colour to the mood), other times in a more complex, interior way (where colours within the frame, in dialogue with each other, produced interesting readings). Camera work and style (including lens choices) also became a focus of attention – revealing how directors of photography worked differently with respective film-makers, even if, in these pairings, a certain number of these directors of photography still maintained a distinctive personal style of their own.

We have seen how deeply costume and décor are not just part of the concept of spectacle, a crucial aspect of costume drama, but are also part of this genre's narrative. In particular, analysis has shown how costume does not merely dress the star body, it also addresses the interior persona. We glean considerable information about the psyche of our characters, thanks to their dress. Similarly, décor functions to allow us to perceive more than we actually see. There is an interiority to set and costume design, therefore, that has added to our understanding of the costume drama as both a generic type and an historical document, its occasional inauthenticity notwithstanding. Reducing history to a story does not necessarily deprive it of political value, as we have seen on numerous occasions throughout this study. There has been a politics to consider. No matter how veiled in costume fabric and framed by synthetic materials it might be, it is impossible to polyurethane over the cracks, it would seem. Questions of sexuality, the female condition, masculinity (both in certainty and in crisis) have abounded throughout the corpus of films we have considered. But so too have other more real-politik questions such as war and its consequences: its barbarity, its folly, the conflicting types of behaviour it produces – cowardice and courage, denunciation and fortitude, betrayal and a desire for justice, to name but a few.

The somewhat comprehensive nature of this book has not allowed us to dwell that much on a star-study approach, although the focus on the six main costume drama stars has lead to some interesting readings around class, where the three female stars are concerned, and masculinity in relation to the male trio. Virility, as embodied by Marais, Marchal and Philipe, has been a double-edged thing – ambiguous even. Nor, with the exception of the Marchal roles, have their characterizations followed along clean lines. Rather, Philipe and Marais, in differing ways, have epitomized a masculinity that is capable of bitterness and resentment, leading them to behave badly in social and sexual terms. The world in which they find themselves is one that almost crushes them – think of Sorel (*Le Rouge et le Noir*) and Dantès (*Le Comte de Monte-Cristo*) in particular – which suggests a world that fails to value the individual. Both Sorel and Dantès are victims of institutional injustice: the former of social institutions that classify him as a nobody, the latter of a legal and political hierarchy that seeks to protect its status at any price. The echoes of this world with the contemporary one are glaringly self-evident. As we know, the 1950s was an age of accelerated modernization in which new technologies and new systems of governance (corporate bureaucracy, five-year plans, etc.) did have a dehumanizing effect on the individual, who became just one element of a set of socio-economic practices, a cog caught up in the logic of a new form of capitalism.

It becomes easy, therefore, to draw parallels between the angry distress felt by our male stars and contemporary man's sense of anxiety in the face of 'the destructive potentiality at work beneath the shiny surfaces of modernity', as Beugnet and Ezra so eloquently put it (a point to which I return below).[1]

Let us now turn to this issue of costume drama and history. A major function of the costume drama is, of course, the re-writing, re-accommodification of history (i.e., making history fit the purpose). But this is not to impugn a flaw in the genre. After all, this process already takes place in the historical novels that, in turn, get adapted. For example, Dumas wrote *La Reine Margot* in 1844, four years before the end of the July Monarchy – when France was, as we saw, in a state of immobilism. In that novel, Dumas makes Margot and Catherine de Médicis into negative stereotypes of femininity: the younger, a sexually-voracious, predatory female (Margot) and the older, a vengeful and scheming crone (Catherine). In short, they become travesties of their real historical original. This is not just because of Dumas' own antipathy towards women having a role in politics, it also has to do with the containment and displacement onto the female other of what ails the nation-state at the time, namely, a country that is unable to take action. That is, in the author's perception at least, a nation that is de-masculinized. In Dréville's adaptation, Catherine certainly remains the malignant string-puller. But as we saw, the director chose to focus more on the men, as a result of which the three lead male characters (Coconnas, La Mole, Charles IX) came to display an interesting array of masculinities and, in Charles' case, neuroses. But by shifting the focus, we also noted how the Margot character was able to emerge as a personage of greater complexity than that ascribed to her by Dumas.

While we might have thought female narratives would dominate this corpus of 109 films, such was not the case. With the one notable historical period of the Belle Epoque, it is a masculine world that prevails – to the tune of 63 per cent of the narratives as opposed to 37 per cent for the women. A rather startling statistic, it has to be said. Even more noteworthy, the penchant towards male-dominated narratives becomes a fait accompli by 1954. Up until then (except for 1952) the distribution was fairly even. Here are the figures:

Year	1950	1951	1952	1953	1954	1955	1956	1957	1958	1959
Male	5	5	9	5	11	8	7	4	11	4
Female	6	5	3	6	8	5	4	0	2	1

69 stories to 40 is an impressive quota – showing how overriding the masculine remains in terms of representation. But it also suggests a concern with the status of masculinity – namely, that its dominance needs to be asserted in the face of evidence which implies the opposite. We know that 1954 was critical in terms of France's colonial wars. This was the year when the Empire truly began to crumble – Indochina first, Algeria close on its heels. If, from this year onwards, the masculine supersedes the feminine in costume drama narratives, it

is difficult not to draw parallels with the contemporary moment in which France's sense of nationhood was under threat.

What of the female? As we noted in the various discussions, up until the Belle Epoque there was very little foregrounding of the female condition. And even when she is present, the woman's tools of resistance to dominant patriarchy are located almost exclusively in the domain of the erotic. In other words, she fights oppression (social and economic) through her body – small wonder she so often fails. Within this context of representations of femininity there is very little evolution, it has to be said. Four major exceptions stand out: Aline in *Barbe-bleue*, Suzanne in *Le Mariage de mlle Beulemans*, Jacqueline in *Maxime* and Eléna in *Eléna et les hommes*. Here, the women command via their intelligence; they transcend the moment in which they are located and, as such, they present themselves as very modern women. But that is about it. The woman's lot is not a very appetizing one, in truth. In most of the other narratives, she is contained, commodified, unfulfilled, a victim of ennui. There is little, therefore, for the woman of the 1950s to enjoy in these images of submission other than the costumes themselves and the occasional spirited attempts to outsmart patriarchy. And yet compliance, in the form of a domesticated female, is precisely what 1950s' ideology expected of her. The mirror held up to the female of the species was, then, a disconcertingly conservative one, even if the costume drama returns an oddly ambiguous message: as a woman you must conform to what patriarchy demands of you, but do not expect to enjoy it!

That being said, this does not mean that these women-centred narratives are without political resonances. Ambiguity allows for cracks to appear, as we well know. Indeed, we have seen how female bodies or actions are marked by history. Even the Martine Carol vehicles offer challenging readings to the spectator – she resists, certainly via her body, but nonetheless in multifarious ways which include cross-dressing, masquerading as a lesbian, pistol-toting and sword-flailing. Danielle Darrieux' numerous attempts to outfox her controlling husbands or to outwit her enemies may end in failure, even death, but her spirit and its subsequent crushing, whilst it does not give us much space for hope, at the very least points to the reason why feminism had to be invented! We saw, too, how a number of female roles spoke to the recent murky past of France in terms, primarily, of the Occupation. Certainly, the female body remained a scapegoat for those discourses of treachery and denunciation, however unfair that representation remains. In terms of displacement, it is clear that the female body was made to stand for the numerous ambiguities of France's recent history.

This study has endeavoured to ensure that the films under consideration were viewed within their historical contexts, both of the period of reference and that of the 1950s. Such frameworking has often brought out interesting socio-political conjunctures, especially in relation to Belle Epoque films. But the pre-nineteenth-century texts have also illuminated the contemporary 1950s. The swashbuckler films come to mind, but so, too, do the 'fairytales' and 'foxy women' narratives. In the latter case, myth-creation comes under scrutiny; in the former, constructions of masculinity and power relations. Also in amongst those earlier narratives we saw that a handful were mindful of the issue of tolerance (political and religious). For a cinema that purportedly has no grounding in reality (let alone history), we could argue that there is a considerable feast for thought here.

This is not to argue that the 1950s' costume drama is a political cinema, for clearly it is not. Besides which, the greatest majority of all films give back to audiences what they already know about the social world – be it human relationships, power relations, dysfunctional marriages, personal ambition or political greed. Redemption or retribution is often the punctum of these fictions, but they are unlikely to radically alter human comportment as the spectators take their leave of the cinema theatres. However, the 1950s – of all the twentieth-century decades – was, arguably, the greatest decade of transition. World wars as they were understood had come to an end but were replaced by the terror of nuclear war. Capitalism had reached a peak, as signalled by the impact of Marshall aid on western markets, the growth of big corporations, even multi-national corporatism. State socialism was burgeoning to the east. The 1950s marked the beginning of decolonization. It was also a time when France realized it had to renounce its former Malthusianism and embrace internationalism, as it did in founding, with West Germany, the Common Market. For France, the 1950s marked, then, the beginning of the process whereby the material (be it in production, money markets, institutional frameworks), in short, the instances of modernity, started to be prioritized over the individual. It was not just a case of greater wealth dissolving class, nor of better managerial systems in the form of the famous *cadres* (technocrats), rendering the nation more efficient with its various five-year plans; the point was also to engineer consensuality; to bring France to forget its recent trauma. The aesthetics of cleanliness, which Ross so cleverly exposes in her brilliant study of 1950s' French culture of consumption, was part of this consensuality, effectively slamming the door on the dirty past, even the far-from-clean present.[2]

France's ideological machine practised a culture of amnesia and selective memory, and critics have been quick to judge the costume drama film as part of that strategy of oblivion. But this is to simplify. The 'history' these costume dramas serve up to us is not, in the main (as we have seen), that of great historical personages. Indeed, the stories we have witnessed are those of ordinary human beings, be they from the bourgeoisie, the middle- or working classes. If anything, what dominates is the 'small', not the 'epic'. And this 'small' portrays the individual, for the most part in a crisis of some sort – be it in masculinity, the domestic sphere, or sexual relations. What these costume dramas send back to us, in the end, is more than familiarity (the already known). In their own unease – be it through the cynicism of their heroes, the dark endings for many of the women, the repeated message that ambition and crude materialism are rarely rewarded – these films stand almost as a silent seething (most evident perhaps in the sense of anxiety displaced onto the male stars), as if sensing the coming of a systemic violence attached to capitalism. It is as if a menace is running underground – a coming of a profit-driven economy that will railroad the individual. As we know, the 1950s witnessed the beginnings of the 'trente glorieuses', the thirty-year boom which came to an almighty crash in the mid-1970s with the petrol crisis and from which, arguably, the nation has not yet recovered. In this regard alone, our mighty corpus of 109 costume drama films has not been without leaving its message.

Notes

1. Beugnet and Ezra (2010, p. 27). This intriguing essay on French cinema gives considerable space to the effects of modernity on the nation's psyche of the 1950s.
2. Ross (1995).

Bibliography

Allombert, Guy (1958) 'Variations cinématographiques sur des thèmes de Maupassant', *Image et Son*, No. 112, pp. 11–13.

Andrew, Dudley (2006) 'The Post-War Struggle for Colour', in A. Dalle Vache & Brian Price (eds.) *Color, The Film Reader*, New York & London, Routledge, pp. 40–9.

Annenkov, Georges (1962) *Max Ophuls*, Paris: Eric Losfeld, Le Terrain Vague.

Arnold, Denis (2004) '*La Traviata*: From Real Life to Opera', in Nicholas John (ed.), *La Traviata*, English National Opera Series 5, London: John Calder, pp. 17–34.

Bazin, André (2006) 'The Cinema of Jacques Becker: Four Original Reviews, *Rue de l'Estrapade, Ali Baba et le quarante voleurs, Les Aventures d'Arsène Lupin* and *Montparnasse*', (transl. Bert Cardullo), *Literature/Film Quarterly*, Vol. 34, No. 4, pp. 252–6.

Bazin, André (1957) 'Hélas! "Notre-Dame de Paris"', "Cahiers du Cinéma' Vol. 12, No. 67, p. 55.

Barsacq, Léon (1970) *Le Décor de film*, Paris: Seghers, 1970.

Becker, Jean-Jacques (1998) *Histoire politique de la France depuis 1945*, (sixth edition), Paris: Armand Colin.

Bernard, Jean-Jacques (1994) 'La Reine Moreau', *Première*, No, 206, pp. 80–3.

Berthomé, Jean-Pierre (1976) 'Interview with Louis Daquin', recorded at Louis Daquin's home, Paris, January 1976. Introduction and interview by Jean-Pierre Berthomé. Translation from the French by Jacqueline Berthomé. *Film Dope*, No. 9, pp. 1–9.

Berthomé, Jean-Pierre (1981a) 'Entretien avec Max Douy (2)', *Positif*, No. 244/245, pp. 2–12.

Berthomé, Jean-Pierre (1981b) 'Entretien avec Max Douy (2)', *Positif*, No. 246, pp. 22–35.

Berthomé, Jean-Pierre (2002) 'Lola inconnue – Une version ignorée de *Lola Montès*', *Positif*, No. 495, pp. 130–3.

Berthomé, Jean-Pierre (2003) *Le Décor au cinéma*, Paris: Cahiers du Cinéma.

Besanger, Pierre (1963) '*Madame de…*', *Image et Son*, No 165/166,pp. 113–22.

Beugnet, Martine & Ezra, Elizabeth (2010) 'Traces of the modern: an alternative history of French cinema', *Studies in French Cinema*, Vol. 10, No. 1, pp. 11–38.

Beylie, Claude (1962) '*Eléna et les hommes*, Fiche établie par Claude Beylie', *Image et Son*, No. 153/154, pp. 22–7.

Bezbakh, Pierre (1990) *Histoire de la France contemporaine de 1914 à nos jours*, Paris: Bordas.

Bonal, Gérard (1994) *Gérard Philipe*, Paris: Editions du Seuil.

Bonnell, René (1989) *La Vingt-cinquième image: Une économie de l'audiovisuel,*, Paris: Gallimard.

Britton, Andrew (1982) 'Metaphor and Mimesis: *Madame de…*', *Movie*, No 29/30, pp. 90–107.

Brogan, Denis W. (1989) *The French Nation from Napoleon to Pétain 1814–1940*, London: Cassell.

Bruzzi, Stella (1997) *Undressing Cinema: Clothing and Identity in the Movies*, London & New York: Routledge.

Buckley, Cheryl & Fawcett, Hilary (2002) *Fashioning the Feminine: Representation and Women's Fashion from the Fin de Siècle to the Present*, London: IB Tauris.

Burch, Noel & Sellier, Geneviève (1996) *La Drôle de guerre des sexes du cinéma français 1930–1956*, Paris: Editions Nathan.

Burch, Noel & Sellier, Geneviève (2009) *Le Cinéma au prisme des rapports de sexe*, Paris: Vrin.

Burns, Mickey (1996) 'Lola Montès', *CinéAction*, No. 40, pp. 38–43.

Cacérès, Benigno & Chevallier, Denis (1964) 'Dossier: *Le Rouge et le Noir*', *Image et Son*, No. 176/7, pp. 113–23.

Cadars, Pierre (1990) *Gérard Philipe*, Paris: Editions Ramsay.

Cawthorne Nigel (1997) *Le New Look: La Révolution Dior*, Paris: Celiv.

Chapsal, Madeleine (1986) *L'Elégance des années 50*, Paris: Herscher.

Chappey, Jean-Luc & Gainot, Bernard (200) *Atlas de l'empire napoléonien 1799–1815*, Paris: Editions Autrement.

Chapuy, Arnaud (2001) *Martine Carol filmée par Christian-Jaque*, Paris: L'Harmattan.

Cole, Alastair (ed.) (1990) *French Political Parties in Transition*, Aldershot: Dartmouth.

Comes, Philippe de. & Marmin, Michel (1984) *Le Cinéma français 1930–1960*, Paris: Editions Atlas.

Cook, Pam (1996) *Fashioning the Nation: Costume and Identity in British Cinema*, London: British Film Institute Publishing.

Cousins, Jennie (2008) *Unstitching the 1950s Films à costumes: Hidden Designers, Hidden Meanings*, unpublished PhD Thesis, University of Exeter.

Cousins, Russell, F. (1989) 'Recasting Zola: Gérard Philipe's Influences on Duvivier's Adaptation of *Pot-Bouille*', *Literary Film Quarterly*, Vol. 17, No. 3, pp. 142–8.

Creton, Laurent (2004) *Histoire économique du cinéma français: Production et financement 1940–1959*, Paris: CNRS Editions.

Crisp, Colin (1993) *The Classic French Cinema, 1930–1960*, Bloomington and Indianapolis: Indiana University Press.

Cuel, François & Bezombes, Renaud (1982) 'Les Décorateurs: Georges Wakhévich', Interview with Georges Wakhévich, *Cinématographe*, No. 76, March 1982, pp. 6–11.

Curot, Frank (1999) 'Théâtre, théâtralité et style d'espace filmique dans *Le Carrosse d'or* de Jean Renoir', *CinémAction*, No. 93, pp. 42–50.

Daquin, Louis (1960) *Le Cinéma, notre métier*, (preface by René Clair), Paris: Les Editeurs Français.

Daquin, Louis (1970) 'Louis Daquin' Interview with Daquin, *Cinéma*, No. 151, pp. 68–9 (interviewer M. M.).

De Launey, Marc (1973) '*Les Grandes Manoeuvres*', *Image et Son*, No. 274, pp. 63–7.

Delpierre, Madeleine (1988) 'Les Films à costumes. La mode de l'antiquité à 1919 vue par le cinéma français', in M. Delpierre, M. de Fleury, & D. Lebrun (eds.) *L'Élégance française au cinéma*, Paris Galliera, Musée de la Mode et du Costume, 13–35.

Des Cars, Jean & Pinon, Pierre (1991) *Paris–Haussmann*, Paris: Edition de Pavillon de l'Arsenal.

Douin, Jean-Luc (1998) *Dictionnaire de la censure au cinéma*, Paris: Presses Universitaires Françaises.

Douy, Max & Jacques (2003) *Décors de cinéma: Un siècle de studios français*, Paris: Editions du Collectionneur.

Eck, Jean-François (1988) *Histoire de l'économie française depuis 1945*, Paris: Armand Colin.

Ferrari, Alain (2006) 'La Belle Epoque du vaudeville et de la chanson', in Alain Masson (ed.) 'Dossier Spécial: La Belle Epoque à l'écran', *Positif*, No. 548, pp. 93–6.

Flügel, J-C (1930) *The Psychology of Clothes*, London, Hogarth Press.

Freeman, Ted (1997) France and the 'First' Cold War: Introduction French Cultural Studies 8: pp. 2001–2.

Gaffney, John (1991) 'French Political Culture and Republicanism', in John Gaffney & Eva Kolinsky (eds.) *Political Culture in France and Germany*, London & New York, Routledge, pp. 13–33.

Garçon, François (1984) *De Blum à Pétain*, Paris: Editions du Cerf

Gévaudan, Frantz (1979) 'Evocation I: Louis Daquin', interview, *Cinéma*, No. 241, pp. 29–40.

Gilroy, Paul (1993) *The Black Atlantic: Modernity and Modern Consciousness*, London & New York: Verso.

Goestchel, Pascale & Toucheboeuf, Bénédicte (2004) *La IVe République: La France de la Libération à 1958*, Paris: Librairie Générale Française.

Grelier, Robert (1970) 'Louis Daquin', Interview, *Image et Son*, No. 239, pp. 18–21.

Griffe, Maurice (2009) *Chronologie de Paris: 20 siècles d'histoire*, Le Cannet: Editions Tableaux Synoptiques de l'Histoire.

Hadiquet, Philippe (1965) '*Une vie*: Fiche établie par Philippe Hadiquet', *Image et Son*, No. 187, pp. 107–10

Hahn, Hazel (2005) 'Fashion Discourses in fashion Magazines and Madame de Girardin's *Lettres Parisiennes*', *Fashion Theory*, Vol. 9, No. 2, pp. 205–27.

Harcourt, Peter (2002) 'Circles of Delight and Despair: The Cinema of Max Ophuls'. *CinéAction*, No. 59, pp. 4–13.

Harper, Sue (1994) *Picturing the Past: The Rise and Fall of the British Costume Film*, London: British Film Institute Publishing.

Hayward, Susan (1993) *French National Cinema*, London & New York: Routledge.

Hayward, Susan (2004) *Simone Signoret: The Star as Cultural Sign*, New York: Continuum.

Hayward, Susan (2005) *Les Diaboliques*, London & New York; I. B. Tauris.

Hayward, Susan (2009) 'Simone Signoret: Costume drama and the star text (a case study: *Casque d'Or*, Jacques Becker, 1952)', in Tutty Solya (ed.) *Stellar Encounters: Stardom in Popular European Cinema*, London & New York: Routledge, pp. 121–31.

Hennebelle, Guy (1974) 'La Grande trahison du cinéma français de 1945 à nos jours', *Ecran*, No. 21, pp. 4–16.

Holmes, Diana & Tarr, Carrie (2006) *A Belle Epoque? Women in French Society and Culture 1890–1914*, New York & Oxford: Bergahn Books.

Konisberg, Ira (1993) *The Complete Film Dictionary*, London: Bloomsbury Publishing Limited.

Kunzle, David (2006) *Fashion and Fetishism: Corsets, Tight-lacing and other Forms of Body Sculpture*, Stroud; Sutton Publishing (first published 2004).

Lardillier, Edouard (1953) 'Le Cinémascope dans les salles', *La Cinématographie française*, No. 1525, 4.7.1953, pp. 45–6.

Leahy, Sarah (2003) 'The Matter of Myth: Bardot, Stardom and Sex', *Studies in French Cinema* 2003, Vol. 3, No. 2, pp. 71–81.

Leahy, Sarah (2004) '"Neither charm nor sex appeal." Just what is the appeal of Simone Signoret?'. *Studies in French Cinema*, Vol. 4, No. 1, pp. 29–40.

Leahy, Sarah (2007) *Casque d'or*, London: I.B. Tauris.

Lefèvre, Raymond (1958) '*Bel Ami*', *Image et Son*, No. 111, p. 14.

Leymarie, Michel (1999) *De la Belle Epoque à la Grande Guerre: Le triomphe de la République (1893–1918)*, Paris: Livre de Poche, Librairie Générale Française.

Lucan, Jacques 1992) *Eau et gaz à tous les étages: Paris 100 ans de logement*, Paris: Edition du Pavillon de l'Arsenal.

McMillan, James F. (1985) *Dreyfus to De Gaulle: politics and society in France 1898–1969*, London: Edward Arnold.

Masson, Alain (2006) 'Une autre histoire', in Alain Masson (ed.) 'Dossier Spécial: La Belle Epoque à l'écran', *Positif*, No. 548, pp. 86–111.

Marseille, Jacques (2002) *Nouvelle histoire de la France: De la Révolution à nos jours*, Paris: Perrin.

Maupassant, Guy de (1999) *Bel-Ami*, annotated and commented by Adeline Wrona, Paris: Flammarion.

Miller, Christopher L. (2008) *The French Atlantic*, North Carolina: Duke University Press.

Mills, Earl (1998) *Dorothy Dandridge: An Intimate Biography*, Los Angeles; Holloway Publishing Co.

Montebello, Fabrice (2005) *Le Cinéma en France*, Paris: Armand Colin.

Murat, Pierre (1988) 'Les unes l'autre: les acteurs et la naissance de BB', in Jean-Loup Passek (ed.) *D'un cinéma l'autre: notes sur le cinéma français des années cinquante*, , Paris: Centre Georges Pompidou, pp. 40–55.

Neale, Steve (2000) *Genre and Hollywood*, London & New York; Routledge.

Niogret, Hubert (1996) '"Je n'ai que de bons souvenirs", Entretien avec Rosine Delamare', *Positif*, No. 425/6, 53–8.

Ory, Pascal (1989) *L'Aventure culturelle française: 1945–1989*, Paris: Flammarion.

Perrot, Michelle (1999a) 'La Famille triomphante', in Philippe Ariès & Georges Duby (eds.), *Histoire de la vie privée*, Paris: Editions du Seuil, pp. 81–92.

Perrot, Michelle (1999b) 'Fonctions de la famille', in Philippe Ariès & Georges Duby (eds.), *Histoire de la vie privée*, Paris: Editions du Seuil, pp. 93–107.

Poix, G. (1958) 'Prestige et decadence des *Misérables*', *Image et Son*, No. 111, 1.4., pp. 15–16.

Quéval, Jean (1951) 'Le Tartuffe terroriste', *Cahiers du cinéma*, Vol. 1, No. 6, pp. 44–6.

Rearick, C. (1985) *Pleasures of the Belle Epoque: Entertainment and Festivity in Turn-of-the-Century France*, New Haven & London: Yale University Press.

Reynolds, Siân (2006) '*Vélo-Métro-Auto*: Women's Mobility in Belle Epoque Paris', in D. Holmes & C. Tarr (eds.) *A Belle Epoque? Women in French Society and Culture 1890–1914*, New York & Oxford: Berghan Books, pp. 81–94.

Richer, Jean-José (1955) 'Il faut qu'une fenêtre…' (review of *Les Grandes manoeuvres*), *Cahiers du cinéma*, Vol. 9, No. 53, pp. 39–40.

Rivette, Jacques & Truffaut, François (1978) 'Interview with Max Ophuls', in Paul Willemen (ed.) *Ophuls*, London; BFI, pp. 15–30.

Ross, Kristin (1995) *Fast Cars, Clean Bodies: Decolonisation and the Re-ordering of French Culture*, Cambridge Mass & London; MIT Press.

Ruppert, Jacques, Delpierre, Madeleine, Davray-Piékolek, Renée & Gorguet-Ballasteros, Pascale (1996) *Le Costume français*, Paris: Flammarion.

Sabria, Jean-Charles (1988) *Cinéma français: Les Années 50*, Paris: Centre Georges Pompidou.

Sallé, Andrée (1988) *Les Acteurs français*, Paris: Bordas.

Schiffer. Liesel (2008) *Femmes remarquables au XIXe siècle*, Paris: Vuibert.

Schlör, Joachim (1998) *Nights in the Big City*, London: Reaktion Books.

Sellier, Geneviève (2001) '*La Reine Margot* au cinéma: Jean Dréville (1954) et Patrice Chéreau (1994)', in O. Krakovitch, G. Sellier & E. Viennot (eds.) *Femmes de pouvoir: myths et fantasmes*, Paris: L'Harmattan, pp. 205–18.

Sellier, Geneviève (2009) 'Le Courrier des lecteurs de *Cinémonde* dans les années 50: la naissance d'une cinéphilie au féminin', in Noel Burch & Geneviève Sellier, *Le Cinéma au prisme des rapports de sexe*, Paris: Vrin, pp. 67–90.

Silberman, Marc (2006) 'Learning from the Enemy: DEFA-French Co-productions of the 1950s', *Film History*, Vol. 18, No. 1, pp. 21–45.

Simsi, Simon (2000) *Cine-Passions: 7e art et industrie de 1945 à 2000*, Paris: Editions Dixit.

Steele, Valerie (1998) "Se vêtir au XX siècle: De 1945 à nos jours", Paris: Adam Biro.

Stendhal (1963) *Le Rouge et le Noir*, Verviers: Collections Marabout.

Street, Sarah (2001) *Costume and Cinema: Dress Codes in Popular Film*, London & New York: Wallflower Press.

Sutcliffe, Anthony (1993) *Paris An Architectural History*, New Haven and London: Yale University Press.

Tarr, Carrie (1998) 'L'Eternel Retour: a reflection of the occupation's crisis in French masculinity?', *SubStance 87: A Review of Theory and Literary Criticism*, Vol.27, No.3, pp. 55–72.

Tobin, Yann (1980) 'ich bin die fesche lola (lola montes)', *Positif*, No. 232/233, pp. 56–60.

Touati, Jean-Pierre (1988) 'Le celluloid et le staff: notes sur les studios et les décors dans le cinéma des années cinquante', in J-L Passek (ed.) *D'un cinéma l'autre: notes sur le cinéma français des années cinquante*, Paris: Centre Georges Pompidou, pp. 26–55.

Turquan, Gilberte (1953) 'Problème d'élégance: Les films en couleur', *Cinématographie française*, No. 1501, pp. 35–8.

Truffaut, François (1954) 'Une certaine tendance du cinéma français', *Cahiers du cinéma*, Vol. 6, No. 31, pp. 15–29.

Truffaut, François (1956) 'Lola au bûcher', *Cahiers du cinéma*, Vol. 10, No. 55, 28–30.

Truffaut, François (1975a) 'Sacha Guitry: Le Malicieux', in François Truffaut *Les Films de ma vie*, Paris: Flammarion, pp. 236–240.

Truffaut, François (1975b) 'Max Ophuls est mort', in Truffaut *Les Films de ma vie*, Paris: Flammarion, pp. 251–6.

Vignaux, Valérie (2000) *Jacques Becker, ou l'exécution de la liberté*, Liège, Editions du Céfal.

Vincendeau, Ginette (2005) *Stars and Stardom in French Cinema*, London and New York: Continuum.

Votolato, Gregory (2000) 'Léon Barsacq', in Tom Prendergast & Sara Prendergast *Writers and Production Artists*, 4th edition, London & New York: St James Press, pp. 66–7.

Warwick, Alexandra & Cavallaro, Dani (1998) *Fashioning the Frame: Boundaries, Dress and the Body*, Oxford: Berg.

Wilson, Elizabeth & de la Haye Amy (1999) 'Introduction' in Amy de la Haye & Elizabeth Wilson (eds.) *Defining Dress: Dress as object, meaning and identity*, Manchester: MUP Press, pp. 1–9.

Yamaguchi, Masao (1978) 'For an Archaeology of Lola Montes', in Paul Willemen (ed.) *Ophuls*, London, BFI, pp. 61–9.

Appendix

French Costume Drama of the 1950s

French Costume Drama of the 1950s*
[11 per cent of all output 109/972]*

1950

[In France: Top grossing French film *Nous irons à Paris* (6.6 m) 3rd after *Gone with the Wind* and *Cinderella*]

11/110 films

Film title	Director	Period	Stars	Audiences
Chéri	Billon (Pierre) Adapt of Colette	Belle Epoque	Jean Desailly	964,572
La Dame de chez Maxim	Aboulker (Marcel) Adapt of Feydeau farce	Belle Epoque	Arlette Poirier Saturnin Fabre	1,780,356
Le Dieu a besoin des hommes	Delannoy (Jean) Adapt of Henri Queffelec *Un recteur dans l'ile de Sein*	18c	Madeleine Robinson, Andrée Clément, Pierre Fresnay, Daniel Gélin	2,745,065
Maria Chapdelaine	Allégret (Marc) coprod Fr/GB Adapt Louis Hémon	Belle Epoque period but set in wilds of Canada	Michèle Morgan, Françoise Rosay	2,170,533
Minne l'ingénue libertine	Audrey (Jacqueline) Adapt Colette novel	Belle Epoque	Danièle Delorme/Frank Villard	1,776,482
Miquette et sa mère	Clouzot (H-G) Play adapt Robert de Flers & Gaston Arman de Caillavet	Belle Epoque	Daniélle Delorme Louis Jouvet	2,159,275
Nuit de noces	Jayet (René) Play adapt Henri Kéroul & A Barré	Belle Epoque 1 sketch	Martine Carol	1,012,157
La Ronde	Ophuls (Max) Play adapt Arthur Schnitzler	Belle Epoque	All star cast	1,509,923
Tire au flanc	Rivers (Fernand) Play adapt André Mouëzy-Eon	Belle Epoque military comedy		1,882,484
La Valse de Paris	Achard (Marcel)	Napoleon III 2nd Empire Biopic of Offenbach	Yvonne Printemps Pierre Fresnay	2,058,838
Véronique	Vernay (Robert) Operette adapt Albert Vanloo & Georges Duval	18c	Giselle Pascal Jean Desailly	1,927,942

* *All figures sourced from Simsi (2000); in bold: colour, scope productions; and co-productions with Italy.*

1951

[In France: Top grossing film *Samson and Delilah*, De Mille USA 7,116,327]

10/95 films

Title	Director	Period	Stars	Audiences
L'Auberge rouge	Autant-Lara (Claude)	1833	Fernandel	2,662,329
Barbe-bleue	Christian-Jaque Coprod Fr/Ger **Gevacolor**	Medieval	Pierre Brasseur Cécile Aubry	2,505,160
Caroline chérie	Pottier (Richard) adapt Cécil Saint-Laurent novel	1789	Martine Carole Yvonne de Bray Jane Marken	3,184,380 (9th)
Deburau	Guitry (Sacha) Based on his play	1839–46	Guitry	221,638
Dindon	Barma (Claude) adapt Feydeau farce	Belle Epoque	Lucienne Vatelin Jane Marken	
La Maison Bonnadieu	Rim (Carlo)	Belle Epoque	Danielle Darrieux, Françoise Arnoul, Bernard Blier	1,000,071
Le Mariage de mlle Beulemans	Cerf (André) Play adapt Franz Fonson & Fernand Wicheler	Belle Epoque	Farncine Vendel, Saturnin Fabre, Pierre Larquey	1,010,104
Monsieur Fabre	Diamant-Berger (Henri)	Napoleon III/2nd Empire/biopic entymologist	Fresnay	1,539,225
Olivia	Audrey (J) Adapt novel by Olivia	Belle Epoque	Edwige Feuillère, Simone Simon, Marie-Claire Olivia (as Olivia)	1,043,732
Les Petites Cardinal	Grangier (Gilles) Adapt novel of Ludovic Halévy by Françoise Giroud & Marc-Gilbert Sauvajon	Napoleon III 2nd Empire	Saturnin Fabre	813,990

1952

[In France: Top grossing film *Le Petit monde de don Camillo*, Duvivier, (Fr/It coprod) 12,790,676]

12/100 films

Title	Director	Period	Stars	Audiences
L'Agonie des aigles	Alden-Delos (Jean) **Gevacolor**	End of 1st Empire 1822 and into Restoration of monarchy	Roger Pigaut, Noël Roquevert	758,027
Les Belles de nuit	Clair (René)	1900=>1789 film à sketches	Gérard Philipe Mértine Carol	3,499,199
Buridan héros de la tour de Nesle	Couzinet (Emile)	Medieval		637,135
Casque d'or	Becker (Jacques)	Belle Epoque	Simone Signoret	1,917,248
Fanfan la tulipe	Christian-Jaque Dial Henri Jeanson	Louis XV 18c	Gérard Philipe	6,712,512 (3rd)
Il est minuit Dr Schweitzer	Haguet (André) <u>Play adapt</u> Gilbert Cesbron	1910–14 in the Gabon Belle Epoque	Pierre Fresnay Jeanne Moreau early vehicle	3,300,484
Jocelyn	De Casembroot (Jacques) <u>D'après</u> Lamartine	Revolution 18c about Lamartine	Jean Desailly, Jean Vilar	1,297,239
Le Nez de cuir	Allégret (Yves) <u>Adapt</u> Jean de la Varende novel	1814	Jean Marais	1,738,723
Le Plaisir	Ophuls (Maupassant <u>adapt</u>)	1880s	Gaby Morlay, Danielle Darrieux, Madeleine Renaud, Claude Dauphin, Jean Gabin	1,216,723
Procès au Vatican	Haguet (André)	Belle Epoque	France Descaut, Suzanne Flon Jean Debucourt	1,326,384
Trois femmes	Michel (André) (Maupassant adapt) *Mouche, Boitelle, l'Héritage*	Belle Epoque		535,041
Violettes impériales	Pottier (R) Fr/Sp coprod **Gevacolor** – it may have been but the copy I saw had no colour	Napoléon III 2nd Empire	Luis Mariano	8,125,766 (2nd top grossing)

1953

[In France: top grossing *The Greatest Show on Earth* de Mille USA 9.5m]

11/93 films

Title	Director	Period	Stars	Audiences
Les Amants de Tolède	Decoin (Henri) (based on novel *Le Coffre et le revenant*) Stendhal **FR/It coprod**	1825	Alida Valli Françoise Arnoul	1,158,231
Une Caprice de Caroline chérie	Devaivre (Jean) **Technicolor** Adapt novel Cécil Saint-Laurent	Bonaparte's Italian Campaign 18c	Martine Carole	2,836,858
Le Carrosse d'or	Renoir (Jean) **Coprod Fr/It Technicolor** Inspired by play of Prosper Mérimée	18c	Anna Magnani	780,205
Le Chemin de Damas	Glass (Max)	French Peplum Palestine St Paul's story	Line Noro Michel Simon	No figures
Les Crimes de l'amour(Mina de Vanghel & Le Rideau Cramoisi)	(Various) 1. Clavel, Barry 2.Astruc adapt 1.Stendhal; 2. d'Aurevilly	Restoration and late 19c film à sketches	1.OdileVersois/ Alain Cuny 2.Anouk Aimée/ Jean-Claude Pascal	No figures
La Dame aux camélias	Bernard (Raymond) **Fr/It coprod Gevacolor** Play adapt (Alexandre Dumas fils)	mid-19c	Micheline Presle Roland Alexandre Gino Cervi as Armand	2,611,365
Koenigsmark	Terac (Solange) supervised by Christian-Jaque adapt **Fr/It coprod**	Belle Epoque	Jean-Pierre Aumont Silvana Pampanini	2,119,107
Lucrèce Borgia	Christian-Jaque **Fr/It coprod Technicolor**	15c	Martine Carole	3,632,139
Madame de...	Ophuls (M) **Fr/It coprod** Adapt Louise de Vilmorin novel	Belle Epoque	Danielle Darrieux Charles Boyer	1,619,154
Le Marchand de Venise	Billon (Pierre) **Fr/It coprod** Play adapt (Shakespeare)	15–16c	Andrée Debar Michel Simon Rest of cast Italian	810,582
Les Trois Mousquetaires	Hunebelle (André) **Fr/It coprod Gevacolor** Adapt Dumas novel	17c	Yvonne Sanson Georges Marchal, Bourvil	5,354,739 (6th)

1954

[In France: Top grossing *Si Versailles m'était conté* Guitry 6,986.788]

19/77 films Big drop in production due possibly to fact that 30% of all films that year were in color and the need to accommodate 'scope meant more state money went to furbishing cinema theatres

Title	Director	Period	Stars	Audiences
Alibaba et les 40 voleurs	Becker (J) **Eastmancolor** <u>Lit adapt</u> *1001 Nights*	Vague eastern past	Fernandel	4,117,641
L'Aventurier de Séville	Vadja (Ladislav) **Fr/SP coprod** **Gevacolor**	A vague past End 18c	Mariano	2,487,427
La Belle Otéro	Pottier (R) **Fr/It coprod** **Eastmancolor**	Belle Epoque	Maria Félix Jacques Berthier	1,885,468
Cadet Rousselle	Hunebelle (A) **Eastmancolor**	Revolution/ pastiche of *Fanfan*	Dany Robin François Perier	3,995,795
C'est la vie parisienne	Rode (Alfred) **Gevacolor**	1900–50 story spans musichall period to jazz	Claudine Dupuis Philippe Lemaire, Saturnin Fabre	1,473,244
Chevalier de la nuit	Darène (Robert)	1884	Renée Saint-Cyr Jean-Claude Pascal	No figures
Les Destinées	Delannoy/Pagliero/ Christian-Jaque film à sketch **Fr/It coprod**	1.Joan of Arc, 2.Elizabeth I, 3.Lysistrata	1.Michèle Morgan 2.Claudette Colbert 3.Martine Carol/Raf Vallone	1,181,231
Les Lettres de mon moulin	Pagnol (Daudet <u>adapt</u>)	19c	Pierrette Bruno Rellys	2,399,645
Madame du Barry	Christian-Jaque **Fr/It coprod** **Eastmancolor**	18c	Martine Carole	2,378,009
Mam'zelle Nitouche	Allegret (Y) **Fr/It co prod** **Eastmancolour** <u>adapt</u>	1880s	Fernandel Pier Angeli	3,829,390
Par ordre du Tsar	Haguet (A) Fr/Ger **Gevacolor**	1840s based on Franz Liszt	Colette Marchand Jacques François	1,923,380

Raspoutine	Combret (Georges) **Fr/It coprod Eastmancolor**	Belle Epoque	Pierre Brasseur	2,216,785
La Reine Margot	Dréville (Jean) **Fr/It coprod Eastmancolor** Adapt Dumas novel	1572	Jeanne Moreau Françoise Rosay	2,600,759
Les Révoltés de Lomanach	Pottier (R) **Fr/It coprod Eastmancolor**	Chouans period (Revolution) 18c/19c	Dany Robin	1,830,168
Le Rouge et le Noir	Autant-Lara **Fr/It coprod Eastmancolor** Adapt Stendhal	1830s	Danielle Darrieux Gérard Philipe	4,342,365
Scènes de ménage	Berthomieu (André) Adapt Courteline	Belle Epoque	Sophie Desmarest François Périer, Bernard Blier	1,244,329
Les Secrets d'alcove	Jean Delannoy does Belle Epoque one **Fr/It coprod**	film à sketch 1 in Belle Epoque	Martine Carol Bertrand Blier	1,560,469
Si Versailles m'était conté	Guitry (film à sketches) **Eastmancolor**	Henri =>1914	Claudette Colbert, Gaby Morlay, Annie Cordy, Daniéle Delorme, Brigitte Bardot/Guitry, Georges Marchal, Jean Marais (etc)	6,986,788
Le Vicomte de Bragelonne	Cerchi (Fernando) **Fr/It coprod Eastmancolor** Adapt Dumas novel	Louis XIV/ Mazarin 17c	Georges Marchal	2,399,675

1955

[Top grossing French Film *Le Comte de Monte Cristo* Robert Vernay 7,780,642 (3rd overall); top grossing in France: *Beauty and the Tramp* Disney USA 11m]

13/91

Title	Director	Period	Stars	Audiences
L'Affaire des poisons	Decoin (H) **Fr/It coprod Eastmancolor**	Louis XIV 1676	Danielle Darrieux, Viviane Romance Paul Meurisse	1,507,420
La Castiglione	Combret (G) **Fr/It coprod Eastmancolor**	Napoleon III 2nd Empire	Yvonne de Carlo, Georges Marchal, Paul Meurisse	1,284,292
Le Comte de Monte-Cristo	Vernay (R) **Fr/It coprod Gevacolor** <u>Adapt</u> Dumas novel	1814-32	Jean Marais	7,780,642
Le Fil à la patte	Le Franc (Guy) <u>Play adapt</u> Feydeau (Noël-Noël did adapt)	Belle Epoque	Suzy Delair Noël-Noël	1,797,375
Le Fils de Caroline chérie	Devaivre (Jean) **Technicolor** <u>**Adapt**</u> Cécil Saint-Laurent novel	Napoleon I (1804)	Sophie Desmarets Brigitte Bardot Jean-Claude Pascal	1,667,829
French CanCan	Renoir (J) **Technicolor**	Belle Epoque	Françoise Arnoul Jean Gabin	3,963,928
Frou Frou	Genina (Augosto) **Fr/It coprod Eastmancolor/scope**	Belle Epoque	Dany Robin de Funès	2,300,666
Les Grandes manoeuvres	Clair (R) **Fr/It coprod Eastmancolor**	Belle Epoque	Michèle Morgan Gérard Philipe	5,301,504 (5th; Prix Louis Delluc)
Les Hussards	Joffé (Alex) <u>Play adapt</u> P-E Bréal	Bonaparte	Bourvil, Bernard Blier, De Funès	2,875,093
Lola Montès	Ophuls (M) Fr/Ger **Eastmancolor/scope** <u>Adapt</u> Cécil Saint-Laurent novel	19c 1850	Martine Carole/ Anton Walbrook, Peter Ustinov	1,323,062
Nana	Christian-Jaque **Fr/It coprod Eastmancolor** <u>Adapt</u> Zola novel	Napoleon III Second Empire	Martine Carole Charles Boyer	2,675,373
Napoléon	Guitry **Technicolor**	Napoleon I	Michèle Morgan, Danielle Darrieux, Dany Robin/Guitry	5,405,252 (4th)
La Tour de Nesle	Gance (A) <u>Adapt</u> Dumas père **Fr/It coprod Gevacolor**	Louis X period	Pierre Brasseur Silvana Pampanini	2,191,984

1956

[In France: Top grossing *Michel Strogoff* (Fr/It/Yug) C. Gallone 6.9m]

11/107 films

Title	Director	Period	Stars	Audiences
Les Aventures de Gil Blas de Santillane	Jolivet (René) Fr/Sp **Agfacolor** Adapt Lesage novel	18c	Georges Marchal	1,108,273
Les Aventures de Till L'Espiègle	Philipe (G) **Technicolor** Adapt Charles de Coster novel	17c (Flanders under Spain)	Gérard Philipe	2,304,114
C'est arrive à Aden	Boisrond (M) **Eastmancolor** Adapt Pierre Benoit novel	Belle Epoque	Dany Robin André Luguet	1,956,334
Don Juan	Berry (John) Fr/Sp **Technicolor** Adapt Maurice Clavel novel	Vague 18c	Fernandel as Sganarelle	3,442,194
Elena et les hommes	Renoir (J) **Fr/It coprod Eastmancolor**	Belle Epoque	Ingrid Bergman Jean Marais	2,116,337
Gervaise	Clément (CR) **Fr/It coprod** Adapt Zola Novel	19c 1850s	Maria Schell, Suzy Delair /François Périer etc	4,108,173
Marie Antoinette	Delannoy (J) **Fr/It coprod Technicolor**	18c	Michèle Morgan/ Richard Todd, Jacques Morel	2,280,704
Michel Strogoff	Gallone (Carmine) **Fr/It/Yug coprod Eastmancolor/scope** Adapt Jules Verne novel	Tsarist Russia 1880	Geneviève Page/Curd Jürgens	6,920,814
Milord L'Arsouille	Haguet (A) **Eastmancolor scope**	Paris 1847	Jean-Claude Pascal Simone Bach	1,632,851
Notre-Dame de Paris	Delannoy (J) **Fr/It Eastmancolor Scope** Adapt Hugo novel	Medieval	Gina Lollobrigida Anthony Quinn	5,693,719 (3rd ranking)

Si Paris nous était conté	Guitry film à sketch **Technicolor**	Lucrèce=>1950s	Michele Morgan, Danielle Darrieux, Françoise Arnoul, Renée Saint-Cyr/ Guitry, Robert Lamoureux, Jean Marais	2,813,682

1957

[In France Top grossing film *Bridge over the River Kwai*, David Lean 13.5m]

4/108

Title	*Director*	*Period*	*Stars*	*Audiences*
Les Aventures d'Arsène Lupin	Becker (J) **Fr/It coprod** **Technicolor** <u>Adapt</u> Maurice Leblanc novel	Belle Epoque	Robert Lamoureux	2,970,265
Bel-Ami made 1954 Released in France 3.4.57	Daquin (Louis) Fr/Austrian coprod **Agfacolor** <u>Adapt</u> Maupassant novel	1881–1887	Anne Vernon Jean Danet	612,525
Les Sorcières de Salem	Rouleau (Raymond) Fr/East Ger coprod <u>Adapt</u> Arthur Miller play	17c USA	Simone Signoret Yves Montand	1,686,749
Pot-Bouille	Duvivier (Julien) <u>Adapt</u> Zola novel	2nd Empire	Danielle Darrieux, Dany Carrel, Gérard Philipe	2,602,374

1958

[In France top grossing: *The Ten Commandments*, De Mille, 14.2m]

12/95

Title	Director	Period	Stars	Audiences
L'École des cocottes	Audrey (J) <u>Adapt</u> play by Paul Armont & Marcel Garbidon	Belle Epoque	Dany Robin Fernand Gravey	1,072,620
Le Bourgeois gentilhomme	Meyer (Jean) Film of the play	17c Molière	Jean Meyer, Louis Seigner	961,947
Christine	Huit (Pierre-Gaspard) **Fr/It coprod** **Eastmancolor** <u>Adapt</u> Schnitztler play *Libelei*	Belle Epoque	Alain Delon Romy Schneider Micheline Presle	2,848,858
Le Joueur	Autant-Lara **Fr/It coprod** **Eastmancolor** <u>adapt</u> Dostoievski novel		Françoise Rosay Gérard Philipe	937,475
La Bigorne, caporal de France	Darène (Robert) Eastmancolor **Dyaloscope**	18c	François Périer	1,165,131
La Tour prends garde	Lampin (Georges) **Fr/It/Yug coprod** **Eastmancolor** **dyaloscope**	18c	Jean Marais	2,311,061
Maxime	Verneuil (H) <u>Adapt</u> Henri Duvernois novel	Belle Epoque	Michèle Morgan Charles Boyer	1,978,792
Les Misérables	Le Chanois (JP) Fr/Ger coprod **Technicolor** **Technirama** <u>Adapt</u> Hugo novel	early 19c to 1830s Restoration-Louis Philippe	Danièle Delorme Gabin	9,966,274 (2nd ranking)
Sans famille	Michel (André) **Fr/It coprod** **Eastmancolor** <u>Adapt</u> Hector Malot novel	Belle Epoque	Simone Renant Pierre Brasseur	3,331,928

Sérénade au Texas	Pottier (R) **Eastmancolor**	Belle Epoque	Luis Mariano Bourvil	2,555,768
Si le roi savait ça	Canaille (Caro) **Fr/It coprod Eastmancolor** <u>Adapt </u>Ponson du Terrail novella	19c Napoleon I	Magali Noël Jean Danet	No figures
Tamango	Berry (J) **Fr/It coprod Technicolor** <u>Adapt </u>Prosper Mérimée novella	1820, black slave trade	Dorothy Dandridge, Curd Jürgens, Jean Servais, Roger Hanin, Alex Cressent	2,174,246
Une vie	Astruc (A) **Fr/It coprod Eastmancolor** <u>Adapt </u>Maupassant novel	1880	Maria Schell Christian Marquand	2,315,098

1959

[In France Top grossing *La Vache et le prisonnier*, Verneuil, 8.8m]

5/109

Title	Director	Period	Stars	Audiences
Messieurs les ronds de cuir	Diamant-Berger (H) <u>Adapt </u>Georges Courteline novel	Belle Epoque	Micheline Dax, Noël-Noël, Pierre Brasseur	1,141,278
La Belle et le tzigane	Dréville (J) **Eastmancolor Dyaloscope** Fr/Hungary co prod	Belle Epoque		767,376
La Jument verte	Autant-Lara **Eastmancolor Franscope**	1870 Napoleon III 2nd Empire		5,294,328
Les Naufrageurs	Brabant (Claude) **dyaloscope**	1852	Dany Carrel, Madeleine Solonge, Henri Vidal, Charles Vanel	554,664
Le Mariage de Figaro	Meyer (J) **Eastmancolor** Filmed version of Beaumarchais play	18c	Comédie française	No figures

Index

III. Costume dramas of the 1950s and
the historical periods referred to

IV. Film Titles

V. Film Personnel: directors, stars and other named actors, costume and set designers, directors of photography, scriptwriters

Costume designers

Costume design

Set Designers